Art | Basel | Miami Beach

The International Art Show
La Exposición Internacional de Arte

Art Basel Miami Beach | MCH Swiss Exhibition (Basel) Ltd. | CH-4005 Basel
Phone +41 58 200 20 20, Fax +41 58 206 31 32
miamibeach@artbasel.com, www.artbasel.com

Catalog | Produced with the generous support of UBS.

Publisher | Hatje Cantz Verlag
DE-73760 Ostfildern | Zeppelinstrasse 32
Phone +49 711 4405-0 | Fax +49 711 4405-220
www.hatjecantz.de
Editorial Board | Ursula Diehr (Art Basel Miami Beach)
Holger Steinemann (Hatje Cantz Verlag)
Design | Müller+Hess, Basel: Beat Müller, Wendelin Hess
Production | Christine Stäcker (Hatje Cantz Verlag)
Layout, Typesetting & Reproduction | Weyhing digital, Ostfildern
Print | appl druck GmbH & Co. KG, Wemding
Binding | Conzella Verlagsbuchbinderei, Urban Meister GmbH, Aschheim-Dornach near Munich
Distribution USA/North America | D.A.P./Distributed Art Publishers
US-New York, www.artbook.com

ISBN 978-3-7757-3388-5

Printed in Germany

CONTENTS

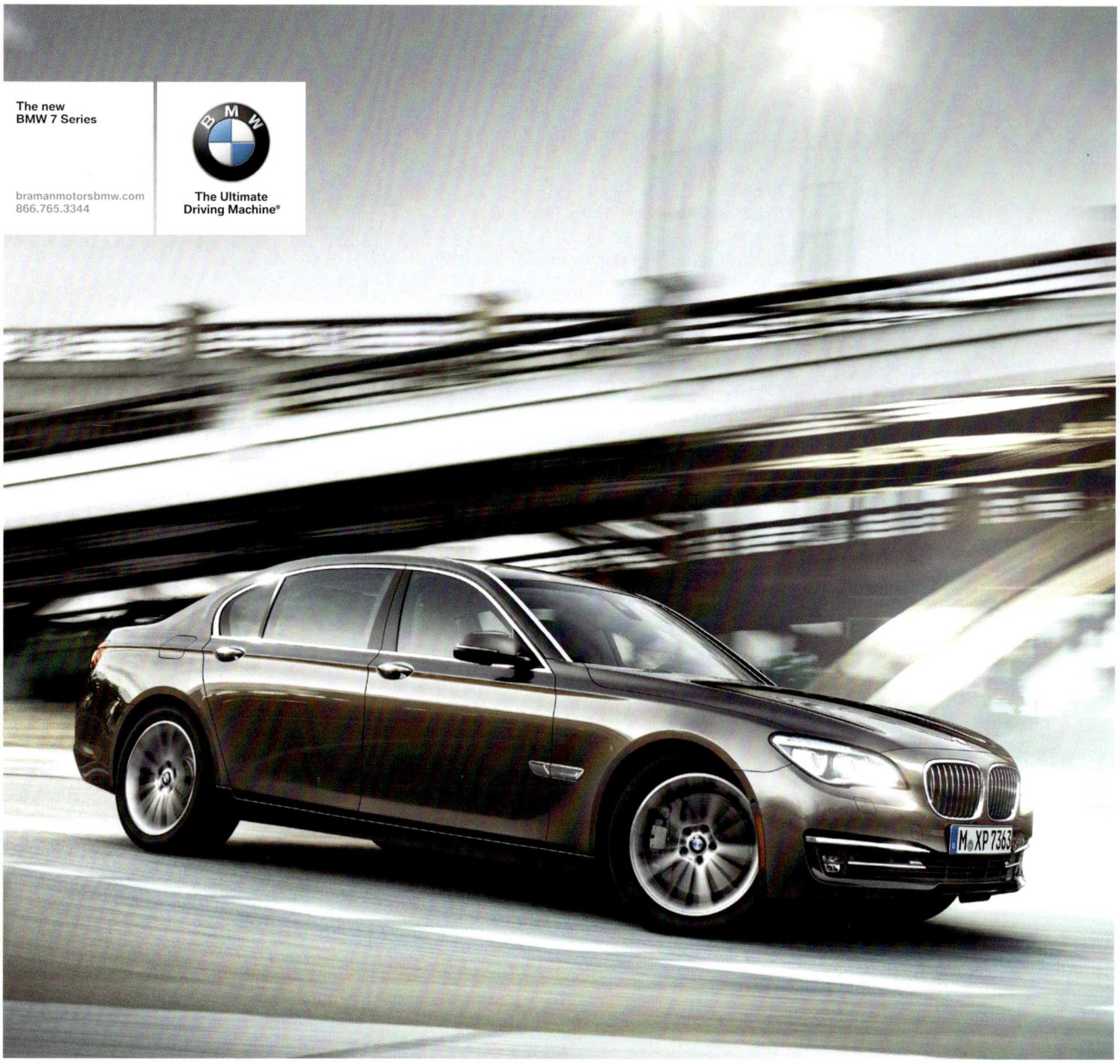

EDITORIALS, ORGANIZATION

WELCOME TO ART BASEL'S SECOND DECADE IN MIAMI BEACH

As Art Basel's Miami Beach show enters its second decade, this year's edition promises to be a celebration of the artists and the galleries playing a vital role in the art world today. Given the high quality and large quantity of galleries that applied to this year's edition, the selection committee worked particularly hard in making the choices that allow us to present an overview of the finest the international art world has to offer. And it is truly international – as the most prestigious art show of the Americas, it is natural that roughly 50 percent of the exhibiting galleries come from North and Latin America, but this American presence combines with a markedly strong list of European galleries and a steadily increasing number of galleries from Asia and Africa.

The art market evolves constantly and visitors will see these shifts reflected in the show. Alongside the remarkable roster of returning galleries, exciting new galleries will debut in all the sectors, including several specialized in the historical material that is growing ever rarer. The Art Kabinett sector within Art Galleries offers tightly focused exhibitions, curated especially for Miami Beach, showing historical projects as well as rising stars. With 16 solo projects by emerging artists, Art Positions showcases our youngest galleries. Art Nova juxtaposes recent works, presented by a variety of both young and well-established galleries.

The display of high-quality works extends beyond the halls, connecting Art Basel to the city of Miami Beach. For the second time, Art Public will transform Collins Park into an outdoor exhibition space, offering a vibrant platform for artists and making exceptional art accessible to all, free of charge. This project marks the continuation of our successful collaboration with the Bass Museum of Art, and is again curated by Christine Y. Kim of the Los Angeles County Museum of Art. Having drawn huge audiences last year, Art Video's outdoor screenings will feature recent video and film productions by some of today's most exciting artists. Playing on the New World Center's 7,000-square-foot projection wall, the program will be created in partnership with London's Artprojx. Additionally, This Brunner will again curate the Art Film night, offering art lovers an exceptional new film directly related to the visual arts. Finally, the ever-stimulating panels at Art Basel Conversations and Art Salon spotlight prominent art world figures exchanging and discussing new ideas, and providing the show's public with valuable insights into the current state and future evolutions of the art world.

Beyond Art Basel's programming, the relationship between Art Basel and South Florida's cultural institutions functions as a virtuous circle, with all the players benefiting from each other's efforts. We strongly encourage every visitor to discover the compelling exhibitions at the local museums and institutions, including the Bass Museum of Art, MOCA, Miami Art Museum, The Patricia & Phillip Frost Art Museum and the Wolfsonian-FIU. Equally engaged and adding strongly personal perspectives to the mix, the renowned private collections open to the public include Cisneros Fontanals Art Foundation, De la Cruz Collection Contemporary Art Space, The Margulies Collection, Rubell Family Collection and World Class Boxing.

The show also benefits enormously from the enthusiastic support of our Host Committee, our Junior Host Committee and the government officials from the City of Miami Beach, the City of Miami and Miami Dade County, whose efforts made this Swiss-born show into a Floridian phenomenon.

We are likewise grateful to our invaluable partners in the business world. Our main partner, UBS, has supported Art Basel since 1994, and partnered with the Miami Beach show from the very beginning. Our Associate Sponsors – Davidoff, NetJets and Absolut Art Bureau – demonstrate their commitment to the arts throughout the year, all over the world, and always bring a special dimension to the week.

Finally, we offer our deepest thanks to the Art Basel team, who have worked all year long in making Art Basel in Miami Beach an annual highlight for the art scene of the Americas.

And we hope that you will enjoy the show as much as our team enjoyed creating it,

Annette Schönholzer and Marc Spiegler
Directors, Art Basel

BIENVENIDOS A LA SEGUNDA DÉCADA DE ART BASEL EN MIAMI BEACH

Como la exposición de Art Basel Miami Beach entra en su segunda década, la edición de este año promete ser una celebración de los artistas y las galerías que desempeñan un papel fundamental en el mundo del arte de hoy. Dada la gran calidad y la enorme cantidad de galerías que postularon a la edición de este año, el comité de selección trabajó particularmente duro para efectuar las elecciones que nos permiten presentar una panorámica de lo mejor que el mundo internacional del arte tiene para ofrecer. Y es verdaderamente internacional; ya que se trata de la más prestigiosa exposición de arte de América, es natural que aproximadamente un 50% de las galerías expositoras provengan de América del Norte y América Latina, pero esta presencia americana se combina con una marcadamente sólida lista de galerías europeas y un continuamente creciente número de galerías de Asia y África.

El mercado del arte evoluciona constantemente y los visitantes verán estos cambios reflejados en la exposición. Junto a la destacada lista de galerías que vuelven a estar presentes, debutarán fascinantes galerías nuevas en todas las secciones, lo que incluye varias especializadas en el material histórico que se está tornando cada vez más excepcional. La sección Art Kabinett al interior de Art Galleries ofrece exhibiciones altamente focalizadas, curadas especialmente para Miami Beach y que exponen proyectos históricos y también estrellas emergentes. Con 16 proyectos individuales de artistas emergentes, Art Positions presenta a nostras galerías más jóvenes. Art Nova yuxtapone trabajos recientes presentados por una variedad de galerías, tanto jóvenes como consolidadas.

La presentación de trabajos de gran calidad se extiende más allá de los salones, conectando a Art Basel con la ciudad de Miami Beach. Por segunda vez, Art Public transformará Collins Park en un espacio de exhibición al aire libre que ofrece una vibrante plataforma para los artistas y que pone arte excepcional al alcance de todos en forma gratuita. Este proyecto marca la continuación de nuestra exitosa colaboración con el Bass Museum of Art y será curado nuevamente por Christine Y. Kim del Los Angeles County Museum of Art. Luego de atraer una enorme cantidad de visitantes el año pasado, las proyecciones al aire libre de Art Video presentarán producciones recientes de vídeo y cine de algunos de los artistas más fascinantes de la actualidad. El programa, que se reproduce sobre el muro de proyección de 650 metros cuadrados del New World Center, será creado en asociación con Artprojx de Londres. Además, This Brunner curará nuevamente la velada de Art Film, que ofrece a los amantes del arte una excepcional película nueva directamente relacionada con las artes visuales. Finalmente, las siempre estimulantes mesas redondas de Art Basel Conversations y Art Salon presentan a destacadas figuras del mundo del arte en un intercambio y debate de nuevas ideas y ofrecen al público de la exposición valiosas perspectivas sobre el estado actual y las evoluciones futuras del mundo del arte.

Más allá de la programación de Art Basel, la relación entre Art Basel y las instituciones culturales del sur de Florida funciona como un círculo virtuoso, donde todos los involucrados se benefician mutuamente de sus esfuerzos. Recomendamos con énfasis que cada visitante descubra las cautivadoras exhibiciones en los museos e instituciones locales, incluidos el Bass Museum of Art, el MOCA, el Miami Art Museum, The Patricia & Phillip Frost Art Museum y el Wolfsonian-FIU. Igualmente comprometidas e incorporando perspectivas marcadamente personales a la mezcla, las renombradas colecciones privadas abiertas al público incluyen Cisneros Fontanals Art Foundation, De la Cruz Collection Contemporary Art Space, The Margulies Collection, Rubell Family Collection y World Class Boxing.

La exposición también se beneficia enormemente del entusiasta apoyo de nuestro Host Committee (comité de recepción), de nuestro Junior Host Committee (comité auxiliar de recepción) y de los funcionarios gubernamentales de la Ciudad de Miami Beach, la Ciudad de Miami y el Condado de Miami Dade, cuyos esfuerzos transformaron esta exposición de origen suizo en un fenómeno floridiano.

Agradecemos igualmente a nuestros inestimables socios del mundo empresarial. Nuestro socio principal, UBS, ha brindado su apoyo a Art Basel desde 1994 y se asoció con la exposición de Miami Beach desde el primer momento. Nuestros patrocinadores asociados, Davidoff, NetJets y Absolut Art Bureau, demuestran su compromiso con las artes durante todo el año, en todo el mundo, y siempre aportan una dimensión especial a esta semana.

Finalmente, presentamos nuestros más profundos agradecimientos al equipo de Art Basel, que ha trabajado durante todo el año para hacer que Art Basel en Miami Beach sea un referente anual de la escena artística de América.

Y esperamos que disfrute de la exposición tanto como nuestro equipo ha disfrutado creándola,

Annette Schönholzer y Marc Spiegler
Directores, Art Basel

PARTNERS

Main Sponsor

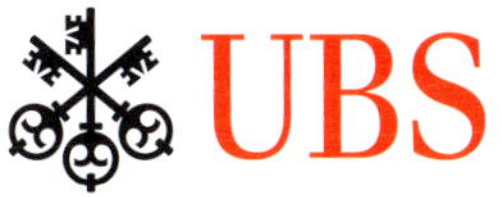

Associate Sponsors

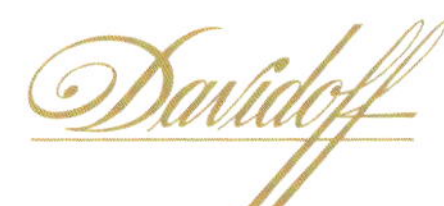

NETJETS

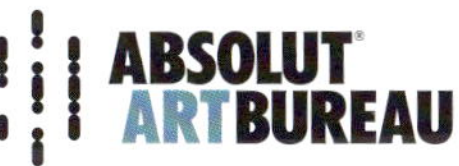

Lounge Hosts

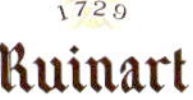

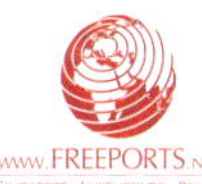

Official Partner
for Furniture and Interiors

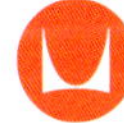
HermanMiller

Official Automotive Partner

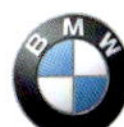

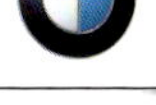

Official Carrier

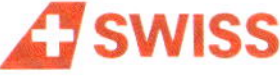

Official Partner

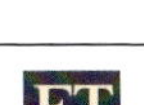

Official Media Partner

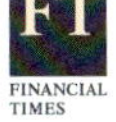

The Miami Herald

Official Supporter

MIAMIBEACH

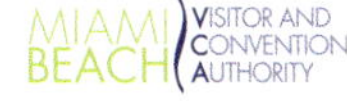

MESSAGE FROM MAIN SPONSOR

Celebrating an Important Partnership

Miami Beach has always been a city at the cutting edge – and the community's innovative and creative spirit is at the heart of Art Basel in Miami Beach. This year, more than 260 leading galleries from around the world will participate in the 11th edition of the show, and UBS is proud to be the Main Sponsor, as it has been from the beginning.

With Art Basel in Miami Beach now in its second decade, the event has blossomed into a sophisticated and forward thinking affair. Through unique exhibits and opportunities to learn from established and emerging artists, this show truly demonstrates the ability of the arts to educate and inspire.

Supporting the arts is a long-standing tradition at UBS, one that enables us to give back to the communities in which we live and work. On behalf of everyone at UBS, we look forward to celebrating the work of Art Basel in Miami Beach again this year and wish all visitors a rewarding and enjoyable experience.

Robert J. McCann
CEO, UBS Group Americas

MENSAJE DEL PATROCINADOR PRINCIPAL

Celebramos una gran asociación

Miami Beach siempre ha sido una ciudad que está a la vanguardia y el espíritu innovador y creativo de la comunidad es la esencia de Art Basel en Miami Beach. Este año, más de 260 importantes galerías de todo el mundo participarán en la 11.a edición de la exposición y UBS tiene el orgullo de ser el patrocinador principal, tal como ha occurido desde el inicio de esta.

Con Art Basel en Miami Beach en su segunda década, el evento se ha convertido en un acontecimiento sofisticado y con miras al futuro. A través de obras únicas y oportunidades para aprender de artistas consagrados y emergentes, esta exposición es una verdadera muestra de la capacidad que tiene el arte de educar e inspirar.

El apoyo a las artes es una tradición de larga data en UBS, que nos permite retribuir a las comunidades en las que vivimos y trabajamos. En nombre de todos en UBS, aguardamos con entusiasmo la oportunidad de celebrar la obra de Art Basel en Miami Beach otra vez este año y deseamos a todos los visitantes una experiencia placentera y gratificante.

Robert J. McCann
Director Ejecutivo de UBS Group, Américas

UBS & CONTEMPORARY ART

UBS has a rich history of actively supporting cultural and artistic endeavors across the world, with a focus on promotion, collection and educational activities in the world of contemporary art. A global partnership with the Solomon R. Guggenheim Foundation, long-standing commitments to the internationally renowned Art Basel and Art Basel in Miami Beach shows and our own UBS Art Collection offer a comprehensive and varied platform for UBS clients and art enthusiasts to participate in the art world, and testify to the passion for contemporary art which UBS shares with its clients.

Art sponsorship activities

UBS has an extensive art sponsorship portfolio, at the center of which are its partnerships with the prestigious Solomon R. Guggenheim Foundation launched in April 2012 and its long-term support for the premier international art shows Art Basel and Art Basel Miami Beach.

The Solomon R. Guggenheim Foundation and UBS collaborate on the Guggenheim UBS MAP Global Art Initiative. This ambitious five-year long initiative seeks to identify and support a network of art, artists and curators from South and Southeast Asia; Latin America; and the Middle East and North Africa, in a comprehensive program involving curatorial residencies, acquisitions for the Guggenheim's collection, international touring exhibitions, and far-reaching educational activities.

The UBS global art sponsorship activities are complemented by several regional platforms and partnerships. These include the Swiss Institute Contemporary Art in New York, the Nouveau Musée National de Monaco, Wolfsberg Arts Forums and the Fondation Beyeler in Switzerland and the Art Gallery of New South Wales in Sydney. UBS has also sponsored numerous exhibitions at leading museums around the world.

UBS Art Collection

UBS is itself an avid collector of contemporary art, boasting a significant collection of paintings, photographs, drawings, prints, video art and sculptures by talented artists from the 1960s onwards that is widely recognized as being one of the most important corporate contemporary art collections in the world. Not only do these works form an important part of UBS's corporate identity, they also contribute to a rewarding experience for clients and employees alike in UBS locations. To underline its support for the arts, UBS regularly makes individual loans of works from its collection to museums around the world, thereby also making its collection available for the enjoyment of the wider public. The collection is updated regularly to ensure that it maintains its strategic focus.

Community

As a firm, giving back is an important part of the culture as we believe that the lasting success of the firm is linked to the well-being of the communities where we live and work. In 2012, UBS partnered with Arts for Learning in Miami to support ArtWorks, a paid internship pilot program in the arts for high school students who live in the surrounding neighborhoods of Miami's Wynwood Arts District. ArtWorks is designed to engage students in the art-making process while providing meaningful employment as they develop an understanding and appreciation of the arts.

Through a strategic charitable grants program and volunteer initiatives, UBS strengthens long-standing relationships with nonprofit organizations globally. In the Americas, the firm partners with over 115 local nonprofits focusing on education and entrepreneurship programs including after-school initiatives, mentoring, and arts and culture. Additionally, our employees globally volunteer their time and talent in a wide array of nonprofits and contributed over 105,000 hours of service last year.

UBS Y EL ARTE CONTEMPORÁNEO

UBS tiene una amplia trayectoria apoyando iniciativas culturales y artísticas en todo el mundo, con énfasis en actividades de promoción, colección y educación en el ámbito del arte contemporáneo. Una asociación global con la Solomon R. Guggenheim Foundation, compromisos de larga data con las mundialmente famosas exposiciones de arte Art Basel y Art Basel en Miami Beach y nuestra propia Colección de Arte UBS proporcionan a los clientes de UBS y entusiastas del arte una plataforma integral y variada para participar en el mundo del arte y dan fe de la pasión por el arte contemporáneo que UBS comparte con sus clientes.

Actividades de patrocinio del arte

UBS cuenta con una amplia cartera de actividades de patrocinio del arte, centrada en sus asociaciones con la prestigiosa Solomon R. Guggenheim Foundation desde abril de 2012 y su apoyo permanente a las destacadas exposiciones de arte internacionales Art Basel y Art Basel Miami Beach.

La Solomon R. Guggenheim Foundation y UBS colaboran con la Guggenheim UBS MAP Global Art Initiative. Esta ambiciosa iniciativa de cinco años procura identificar y apoyar una red de arte, artistas y curadores del sur y sudeste de Asia, América Latina, el Medio Oriente y África del Norte, a través de un programa integral que incluye residencias curatoriales, adquisiciones para la colección del Guggenheim, exhibiciones itinerantes internacionales y actividades educativas de gran alcance.

Las actividades de patrocinio del arte globales de UBS se complementan con varias plataformas y asociaciones regionales, como por ejemplo el Swiss Institute Contemporary Art en Nueva York, el Nouveau Musée National de Mónaco, Wolfsberg Arts Forums y Fondation Beyeler en Suiza y la Art Gallery of New South Wales en Sídney. UBS también ha patrocinado numerosas exhibiciones en los principales museos de todo el mundo.

Colección de arte de UBS

UBS es un ávido coleccionista de arte contemporáneo y cuenta con una importante colección de pinturas, fotografías, dibujos, grabados, arte en video y esculturas de talentosos artistas de la década de 1960 en adelante, ampliamente reconocida como una de las colecciones de arte contemporáneo corporativas más importantes del mundo. Estas obras no solo son una parte importante de la identidad corporativa de UBS sino que además contribuyen a una experiencia gratificante para los clientes y empleados en las instalaciones de UBS. Para remarcar su apoyo a las artes, UBS presta periódicamente obras de su colección a museos de todo el mundo a fin de que el público general también pueda disfrutar de ella. La colección se actualiza periódicamente para garantizar que mantenga su enfoque estratégico.

Comunidad

Como empresa, poder retribuir a la comunidad es una parte importante de la cultura, ya que creemos que el éxito duradero de la empresa está ligado al bienestar de las comunidades en las que vivimos y trabajamos. En 2012, UBS se asoció con Arts for Learning en Miami para apoyar ArtWorks, un programa piloto de pasantías pagas en las artes dirigid a estudiantes secundarios de los vecindarios aledaños al distrito Wynwood Arts District de Miami. ArtWorks esta diseñado para compenetrar a los estudiantes en el proceso de creación del arte y, al mismo tiempo, ofrecerles un empleo significativo mientras desarrollan su entendimiento y apreciación de las artes.

A través de un programa estratégico de becas de caridad y de iniciativas de voluntariado, UBS fortalece sus relaciones de larga data con organizaciones sin fines de lucro en todo el mundo. En América, la empresa está asociada a más de 115 organizaciones sin fines de lucro locales en programas educativos y de emprendimientos que comprenden iniciativas extracurriculares, entrenamiento personal, arte y cultura. Además, nuestros empleados ofrecen voluntariamente su tiempo y su talento a un amplio rango de estas organizaciones en todo el mundo, y el año pasado, contribuyeron con más de 105.000 horas de servicio.

Until an empty space is transformed into a premier art show, Annette Schönholzer and Marc Spiegler will not rest.

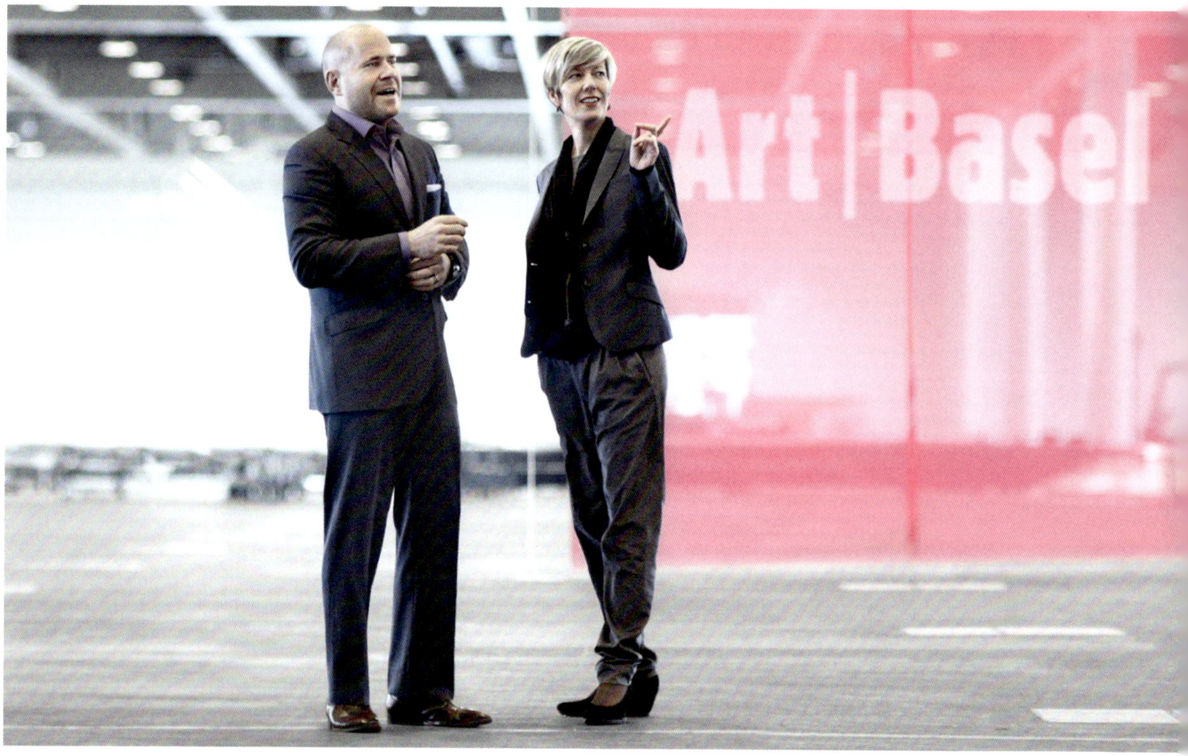

Art | Basel | Miami Beach

SHOW MANAGEMENT

Directors | **Annette Schönholzer**
Marc Spiegler
Director Asia | **Magnus Renfrew**
Head of General Management | **Andreas Bicker**
General Manager Miami Beach | **Maureen Bruckmayr**
Head of Gallery Relations | **Thomas Wüstenhagen**
Gallery & Project Manager | **Linda Briem**
François M. Croissant
Ursula Diehr
Dunja Gottweiss
Benjamin Grappin
Michael Müller
Eve Share Banghart
General Manager Hong Kong | **Andrew Strachan**
Head of Sponsorship | **Patrick Foret**
Sponsorship Manager | **Nadine Marti**
Sponsorship Manager Asia | **Dovenia Chow**
Associate Sponsorship Manager | **Gerda van den Bergh**
Head of Marketing & Communications | **Laura Blagho**
Marketing & Communications Manager Asia | **Jennifer Pratt**
Public Relations Manager | **Dorothee Dines**
Media Production Manager | **Kristi D'Arcy**
Urs Mangold
Event Manager | **Magdalena Dysli**
Associate Event Manager | **Claudio Vogt**
Event Production Manager | **Donnamarie Baptiste**
Head of VIP & Visitor Services | **Harry Guhl**
Visitor Services Manager | **Olivia Doppler**
Associate VIP Relations Manager | **Markus Mäder**
VIP Relations Manager | **Marina Mottin**
Sascha Nikitin, Switzerland
Deborah Ehrlich, Asia
Princess Alia Al-Senussi, Middle East
Stefanie Block Reed, South Florida, USA
Karen Boros, Germany
Mirta d'Argenzio, Italy
Sarah Hardin-White, East Coast, USA
Hélène Mairlot, Benelux
Mariana Munguia Matute, Mexico
Casilda Mora, Spain and Portugal
Iciar Sànchez-Mangas, Latin America
Ricardo Sardenberg, Brazil
Andreas Siegfried, United Kingdom
Lauren Taschen, West Coast, USA
Denise Vilgrain, France
Head of Operations & Logistics | **Sven Tresp**
Operations & Logistics Manager Hong Kong | **Trevor Hyland**
Associate Operations & Logistics Manager Hong Kong | **Suez Lui**
Coordinator Art Public | **Laurence Dalloz**
Directors Assistant | **Janett Schickler**
Director's Assistant Asia | **Jenny Or**
Gallery & Project Assistant | **Jonas Egli**
Dominik Honegger
Daniela Schimmel
Sponsorship Assistant | **Hanna Barber**
Marketing & Communications Assistant Asia | **Janice Ching**
Marketing & Communications Assistant | **Dominic Sutter**
VIP Relations Assistant | **Sarah Huber**
Verona Zeng
Operations & Logistics Assistant | **Nour El-Gourany**
Muriel Meidinger
Graphic Design | **Müller+Hess,** Basel
Architecture | **Tom Postma Design,** Amsterdam
Lighting Design | **Randy Taylor,** Dallas
Representation US | **FITZ & CO,** New York
Representation Florida | **Garber + Goodman, Inc.,** Miami

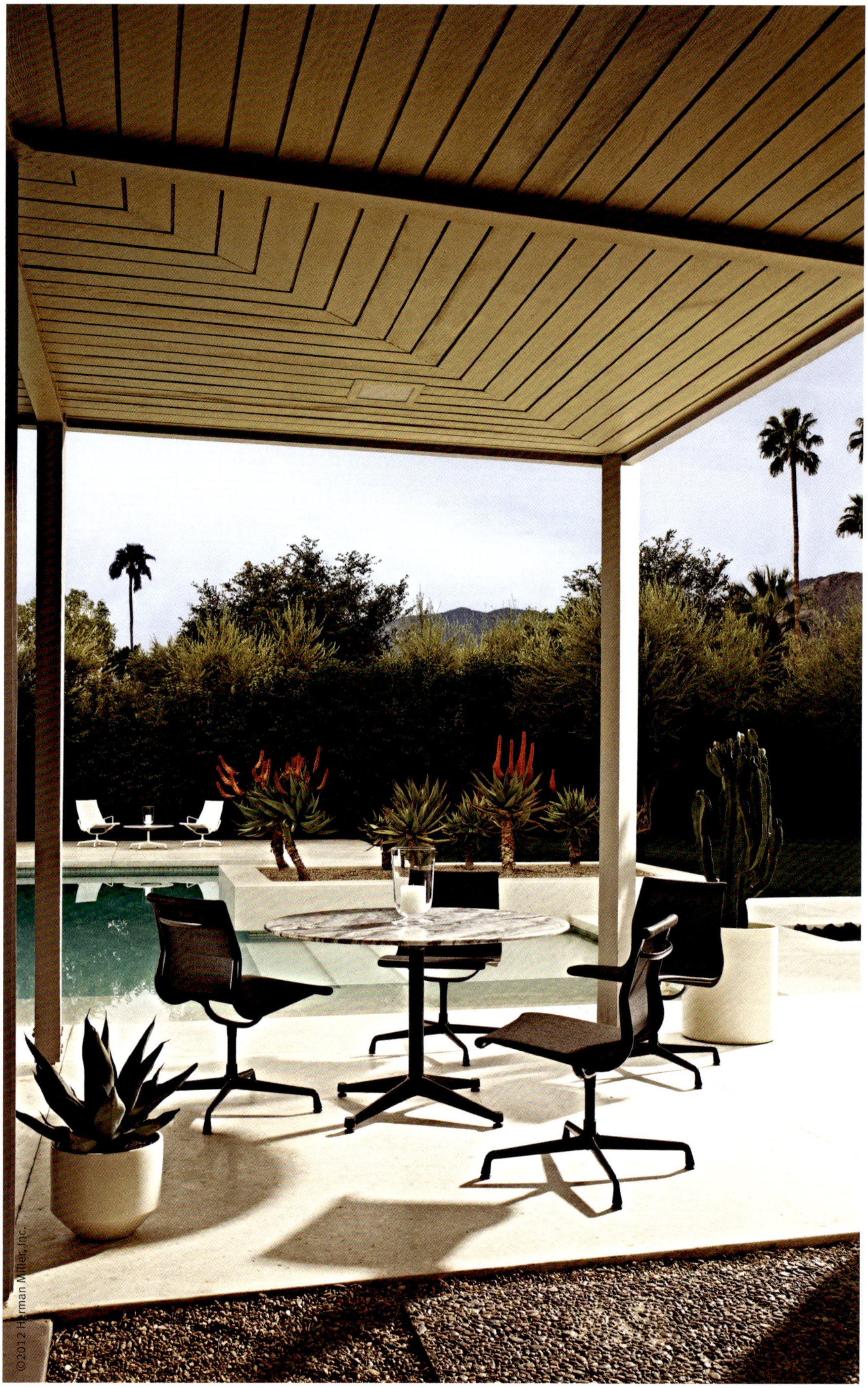

ART BASEL MIAMI BEACH SELECTION COMMITTEE

Marcío Botner A Gentil Carioca, Rio de Janeiro
Joanna Kamm Galerie Kamm, Berlin
Andrew Kreps Andrew Kreps Gallery, NewYork
Martin Klosterfelde Galerie Klosterfelde, Berlin
José Kuri kurimanzutto, Mexico City
Dr. Ursula Krinzinger Galerie Krinzinger, Vienna
Friedrich Petzel Friedrich Petzel Gallery, New York
Jeff Poe Blum & Poe, Los Angeles
Mathias Rastorfer Galerie Gmurzynska, Zurich
Mary Sabbatino Galerie Lelong, New York
Fredric Snitzer Fredric Snitzer Gallery, Miami
Luisa Strina Galeria Luisa Strina, São Paulo

CURATORS

Art Film | **This Brunner,** Zurich
Art Video | **David Gryn,** London
Art Public | **Christine Y. Kim,** Los Angeles
Art Salon, Art Basel Conversations | **Maike Cruse,** Berlin

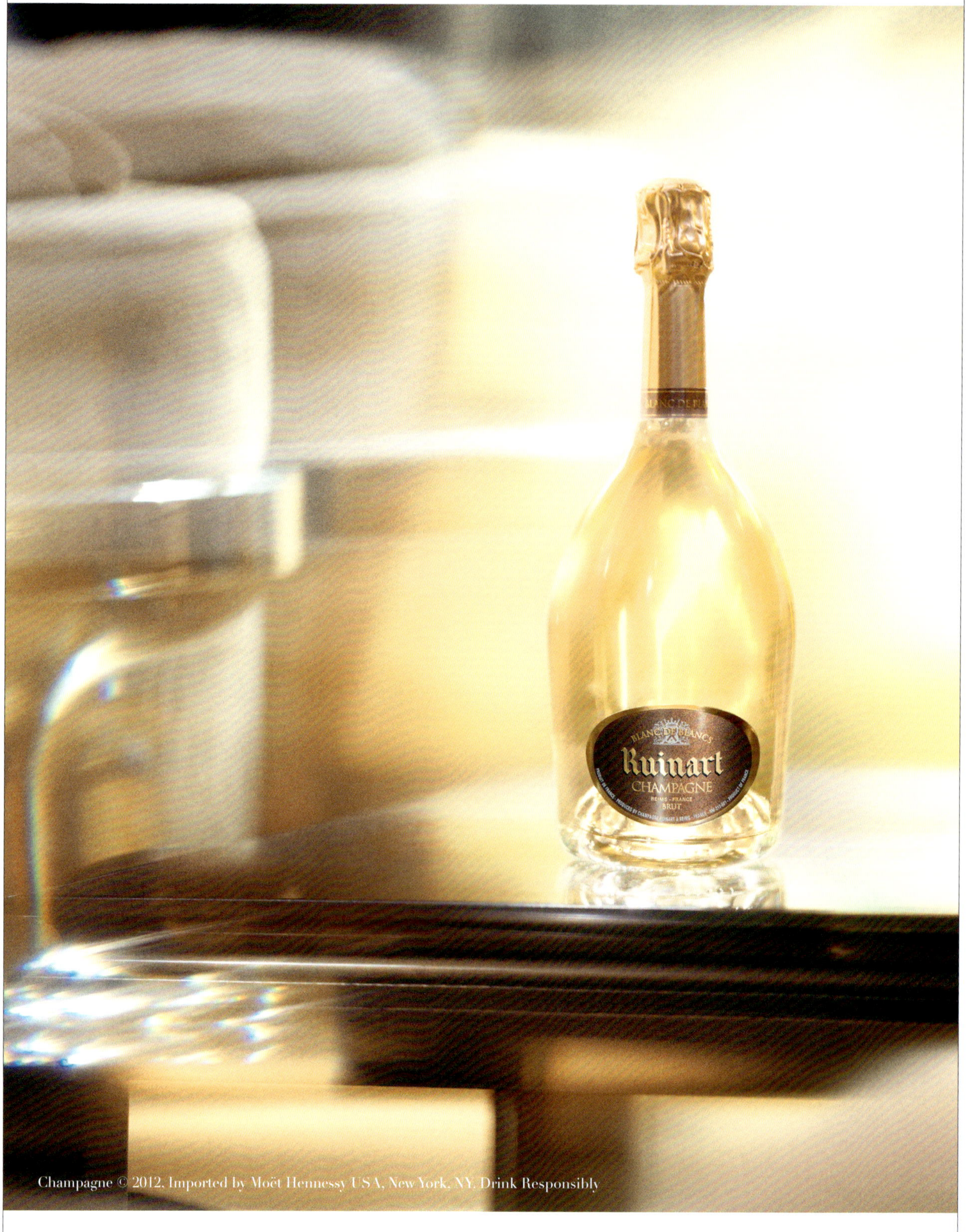

HOST COMMITTEE

Chairpersons **Norman & Irma Braman** | Honorary Chairperson **Matti Herrera Bower, Mayor City of Miami Beach**

A | **Shelly Acoca | Evelyn Aimis | Glenn Albin | Hope Alswang | Genaro Ambrosino D'Amico | Dale & Doug Anderson |
Sheldon T. Anderson | Toby Lerner Ansin | Mickey and Madeleine Arison** | B | **Bruno A. Barreiro, Commissioner,
Miami Dade County | Ted & Ruth Baum | Lang Baumgarten | Jose Bedia | Moises & Diana Berezdivin | Paul & Estelle Berg |
Larry & Mickey Beyer | Jason Binn | Wendy M. Blazier | George S. Bolge | Peter Boswell | Dr. Fredric S. Brandt |
Jonathan Breene | Gilbert & Catherine Brownstone | Kevin Bruk | Susan Brustman | Eli Butnaru** |
C | **Mario Cader-Frech & Robert Wennett | Emilio Calleja | Diane W. Camber | Amy Cappellazzo & Joanne Rosen |
Donald Carlin | Mickey Cartin | Ambassador Paul & Trudy Cejas | Ramon & Nercys Cernuda | Dr. Carl & Judith Chestler |
Jeremy and Tiffany Chestler | Bonnie Clearwater | Mark Coetzee | Diego Costa-Peuser | Charles Cowles** |
D | **Alberto & Maria de la Cruz | Carlos & Claudia de la Cruz, Jr. | Carlos & Rosa de la Cruz | Rosa de la Cruz Bonfiglio |
Martha de la Torre | Raul & Mily de Molina | Suzanne Delehanty | Ago Demirdjian & Tiqui Atencio| David Dermer |
Manny Diaz, Honorable | Victor Diaz | Miguel & Sylvia Dueñas | Brian A. Dursum** | E | **William & Janet Eaglstein |
Dr. Al & Kim Eiber | Mike Eidson | Sheila Elias | Gabriel A. Erem | Ricardo & Isabel Ernst | Jorge & Ursula Espirito Santo** |
F | **Alfonso Fanjul | Daphne Farago | Lori Ferrell | Milton & Sheila Fine | Neil & Dr. Kira Flanzraich | Aaron I. Fleischman |
Bud & Mimi Floback | Ella Fontanals Cisneros | Howard & Mary Frank | Dr. Phillip & Patricia Frost |
Richard & Rosemary Furman** | G | **Luis R. Garcia, Jr., Florida State Representative | Rafael & Jeannette Gelman |
Phillip & Judy George | Barbara Gillman | David A. Goldbaum | Jorge M. Gonzalez | Manuel E. Gonzalez |
Dr. Stanley & Pearl Goodman | Susan Gottlieb, Mayor of Aventura | Ambassador Steven & Dorothea Green |
Gerald & Rose Ellen Greene | Allen & Jill Greenwald | Saul Gross** | H | **J. Ira & Nicki Harris | Lydia Harrison | Cheryl Hartup |
Preston H. Haskell | Thomas Healy & Fred Hochberg | Ken & Karen Heithoff | Maggie Hernández | Larry & Deborah Hoffman |
Erika Hoffmann | Daniel & Antoinette Holtz | Jane B. Holzer | David Horvitz & Francie Bishop Good** |
I | **Alberto & Susana Ibarguen** | J | **Dr. Norman S. Jaffe** | K | **Monica Kalpakian | Neisen Kasdin | Jane & Gerald Katcher |
Robert Kay | Jay & Jean Kislak | Gary Knight | Arthur & Sara Jo Kobacker | Dr. Stephen & Dale Kulvin** | L | **David Landsberg |
Israel & Tania Lapciuc | Cathy Leff | Marcy Lefton | William & Shirley Lehman, Jr. | Herb & Marlene Levin |
Daniel & Mirella Levinas | Morris & Rhoda Levitt | Dr. Carl Lewis | Michael & Carmen Betancourt Lewis | Juan Lezcano |
Jerry Libbin, Commissioner, City of Miami Beach | Alan Lieberman | Nancy Liebman | Joan & Ronald Linclau |
George L. & Fraida Lindemann, Sr. | George Lindemann, Jr. | Dr. Urs Lindenmann, Consulate General of Switzerland |
Jerry M. Lindzon | David Lombardi | Juan P. Loumiet | Alfredo & Diana Lowenstein | Gloria Luria** | M | **David S. & Sondra Mack |
Gwen Margolis, Florida State Senator | Martin Z. Margulies | Maria Martinez-Cañas | Judi Matus | Laurans & Arlene
Mendelson | Peter Menendez | Sydell L. Miller | Steven & Solita Mishaan | Javier G. & Monica Mora | Marvin & Elayne Mordes |
Dahlia Morgan | Robert & Diane Moss | Dr. Arturo F. Mosquera** | O | **Mark & Nedra Oren | Christina Orr-Cahall** |
P | **Leslie Pantin, Jr. | Patricia Papper | Jorge M. & Darlene Perez | Aaron & Dorothy Podhurst | Ernesto & Cecilia Poma |
Irwin & Linda Potash** | R | **Carl & Toni Randolph | Evan J. Reed | Tomas Regalado, Mayor of Miami | Nathan & Carolee Reiber |
Dennis & Susan Richard | Terence Riley | Craig Robins | Marvin Ross Friedman | Donald & Mera Rubell |
Jason & Michelle Rubell | Jennifer Rubell | S. Jerome & Phyllis Rubin | Beth Rudin DeWoody | Isaac & Betty Rudman |
Michael Rush | Francien Ruwitch** | S | **Marvin & Ruth Sackner | Michael & Joan Salke | Gloria Scharlin |
Michael & Raquel Scheck | Rob & Terry Schechter | Barbara Schiff | Dennis & Debra Scholl | Ian Schrager |
Lee Brian Schrager | Jim & Karyn Schwade | Dr. Carl & Shirley Schwartz | Diane S. Sepler | Barbara Shack | Ruth Shack |
Jose Smith, City Attorney, City of Miami Beach | Fredric Snitzer | Frank & Ana Soler | Jack & Dani Sonnenblick |
Clarita Sredni | Celia Sredni de Birbragher | Elsie Sterling Howard | Rosa Sugrañes** | T | **Martin & Christine (Cricket) Taplin |
Jorge Tchinnosian | Michael Tilson Thomas | Ed Tobin, Commissioner, City of Miami Beach** | V | **Jose Valdes-Fauli |
Baroness Jeane von Oppenheim** | W | **Judy Weiser | Deede Weithorn, Commissioner, City of Miami Beach |
Jonah Wolfson, Commissioner, City of Miami Beach | Mitchell Wolfson, Jr. | Dr. William Wolgin** |
Y | **Richard & Janet Yulman**

JUNIOR HOST COMMITTEE

Co-Chairpersons | **Juan Carlos Arcila-Duque** | **Susanne Birbragher** | **Michelle & Jason Rubell**

A | **Glenn Albin | Alexis & Spencer Angel | Brian Antoni** | B | **André Balazs | Hernan Bas | Roberto Behar & Rosario Marquardt |
Nicholas Berggruen | Michael Block | Chip and Allison Weiss Brady | Michael Breene | Barry Brodsky | Juli Ann Brodsky |
Kevin Bruk | Michele Burger** | C | **Alejandra Canelos | Mariangela Capuzzo | Hernan Carraro | Pablo L. Cejas, Jr. |
Robert Chambers & Mette Tommerup | Alberto Chehebar | Jeremy & Tiffany Chestler | Alfredo & Silvia Cubiña |
Christina M. Cuervo** | D | **Jossie & Annelies Da Costa Gomez | Alberto & Maria de la Cruz | Carlos & Claudia de la Cruz, Jr. |
Rosa de la Cruz Bonfiglio | Gonzalo & Maria de la Pezuela | Meaghan Delmonico | Scott Deutsch | Silvia Dueñas Luna** |
E | **Gert & Ulla Elfering | Martin Elortegui & Flavia Lowenstein | Dr. Ernesto Erdmann | Ricardo Ernst & Isabel de la Cruz Ernst** |
F | **Maggie Fernandez | Andres Ferrandis & Dina Mitrani | Naomi Fisher | Andrew Frey | Aida Furmanski** | G | **Jorge A. Garcia |
Dr. Jeff Gelblum | Christina Getty Maercks | Joey Goldman | Thea Goldman | Jessica Goldman-Srebnick | René Gonzalez |
Alfonso Goyeneche & Munisha Underhill | Kimberly Green | Michele & Leticia Grendene | Giovanni Grimaldi** |
H | **Rex & Beryl Hamilton | Austin & Sarah Harrelson | Dr. Martin Hatebur | Cheryl Hartup | Jeanie Hernandez | Timothy Heuer |
Finn Hinke | Daniel & Toni Holtz | Max Holtzman & Heather Urban** | K | **Marina A. Kessler | Iran Issa Khan |
Michel & Erika Koopman | Steven Robert Kozlowski, Esq.** | L | **Pierre & Sarah Lacharlotte | Vincente Lago |
Steve & Rochelle Lanster | David & Alison Levin | Jonathan Lewis | Dennis Leyva & Clark Reynolds | George Lindemann, Jr. |
Lin Lougheed | Diego & Gisela Lowenstein** | M | **Tiffany Markofsky | David Martin | Richard Massey & Carolina Bilbao |
Paul Frank McCabe | Ambra Medda | Lorie Mertes | Kathryn & Dan Mikesell | Dawn & Stephen Miller | Natalia J. Miyar |
Javier G. & Monica Mora** | N | **Sam & Claire Nitze | Christina Nosti** | O | **Chad & Ilonna Oppenheim** | P | **Gonzalo Parodi |
Rina Paz | Vivian & Kenneth Pfeiffer | Eveline Pierre & Serge Rodríguez | Ernesto & Cecilia Poma | Elana Posner |
Jacquelynn Powers | Veronika Pozmentier | Tui Pranich | Andrew Preston & Tomas Maier** | R | **Evan & Stefanie Reed |
Jose Felix Remy & Sofia Lacayo Remy | Mia Romanik | Michael & Stephanie Rosen | Amy Rosenberg | Martin Rozenblum |
Francine & Leslie Rozencwaig | Jennifer Rubell** | S | **George Sanchez-Calderon | Veronica Scharf Garcia | Nicole Schechter |
Chana Budgazad Sheldon | David Simkins | Michael & Nicole Simkins | Alison Spear** | T | **Benedikt & Lauren Taschen |
Jeffrey H. Thrasher** | V | **Raul G. Valdés-Fauli** | W | **Walid & Susie Wahab | Jeffrey & Debi Wechsler |
Robert Wennett & Mario Cader-Frech | Alannah Weston | André L. Williams | Philip Michael Wolfson**

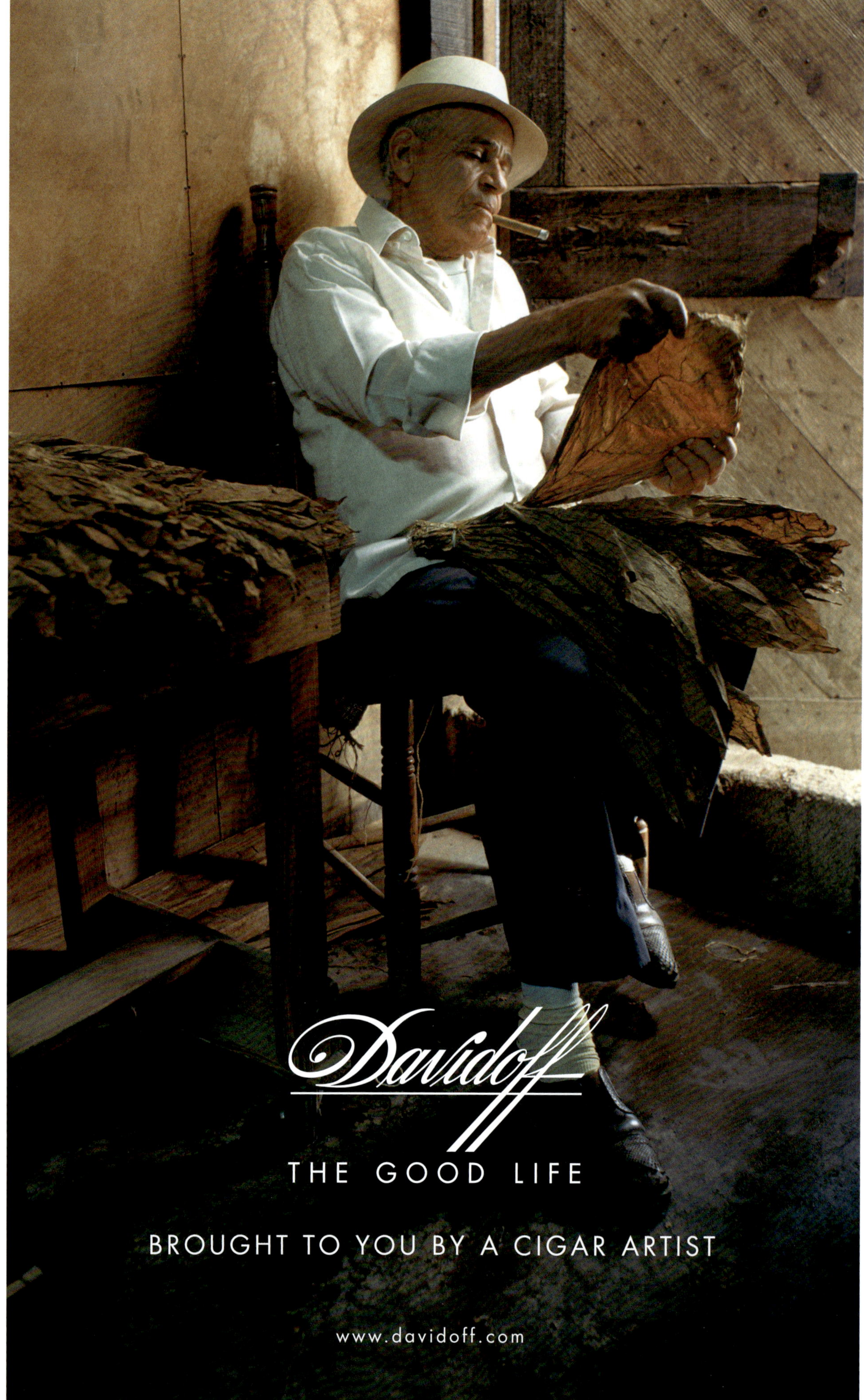
Davidoff
THE GOOD LIFE
BROUGHT TO YOU BY A CIGAR ARTIST
www.davidoff.com

GENERAL INFORMATION

GENERAL INFORMATION

Duration of the show | December 6-9, 2012

Locations | **Art Galleries, Art Nova, Art Positions, Art Kabinett, Art Magazines, Art Video, Art Basel Conversations, Art Salon, Art Collectors Lounge** | Miami Beach Convention Center

Art Public | Collins Park

Opening hours | Miami Beach Convention Center | Daily from 12 to 8pm, Sunday from 12 to 6pm
· Art Basel Conversations | Daily 10am
· Art Public | Day and night

Show Management Office | Miami Beach Convention Center, Entrance B
Information | Miami Beach Convention Center, Entrances B+D
VIP Desk | Miami Beach Convention Center, Entrance D
Coat Check | Miami Beach Convention Center, Entrances B+D

Admission Fees | Day ticket US $42
· Evening ticket (after 4pm) US $29
· Permanent pass US $90
· Reduced one-day ticket (seniors aged 62 and above, and groups of 10 and more) US $24
· School class one-day ticket (per person) US $10
· Children under 16 accompanied by their parents are admitted free of charge

ArtNexus Guided Tours | Daily official guided tours in English and Spanish
· Individuals US $20 (plus admission), private and group tours up to 10 people US $200 (plus admission), groups up to 10 students with 1 chaperone: US $100 (plus admission)
· Registration | ArtNexus Guided Tours counter in the Entrance of Hall D

Art Kids | Complimentary childcare – art experiences and games hosted by the Miami Beach Children's Museum, for children age 4 to 12 whose parents are visitors of Art Basel Miami Beach | Miami Beach Convention Center, Entrance D, 2nd level

Ombudsman | In case of complex issues – for example regarding the authenticity or state of preservation of a work of art – visitors and exhibiting galleries can contact the Ombudsman, who will help with the clarifications, give non-binding information and mediate in cases of complaints. Neither the Ombudsman nor MCH Swiss Exhibition (Basel) Ltd. can be held responsible for any information given. The Ombudsman can be contacted through the Show Management office.

Art Loss Register | We work with the Art Loss Reister (ALR), who compares all works of art shown in the Art Basel Miami Beach Catalog to its database with regard to legal status and provenance.

Private Jets | NetJets U.S., Phone +1 732 326 37 36
NetJets Europe, Phone +44 20 7361 96 00

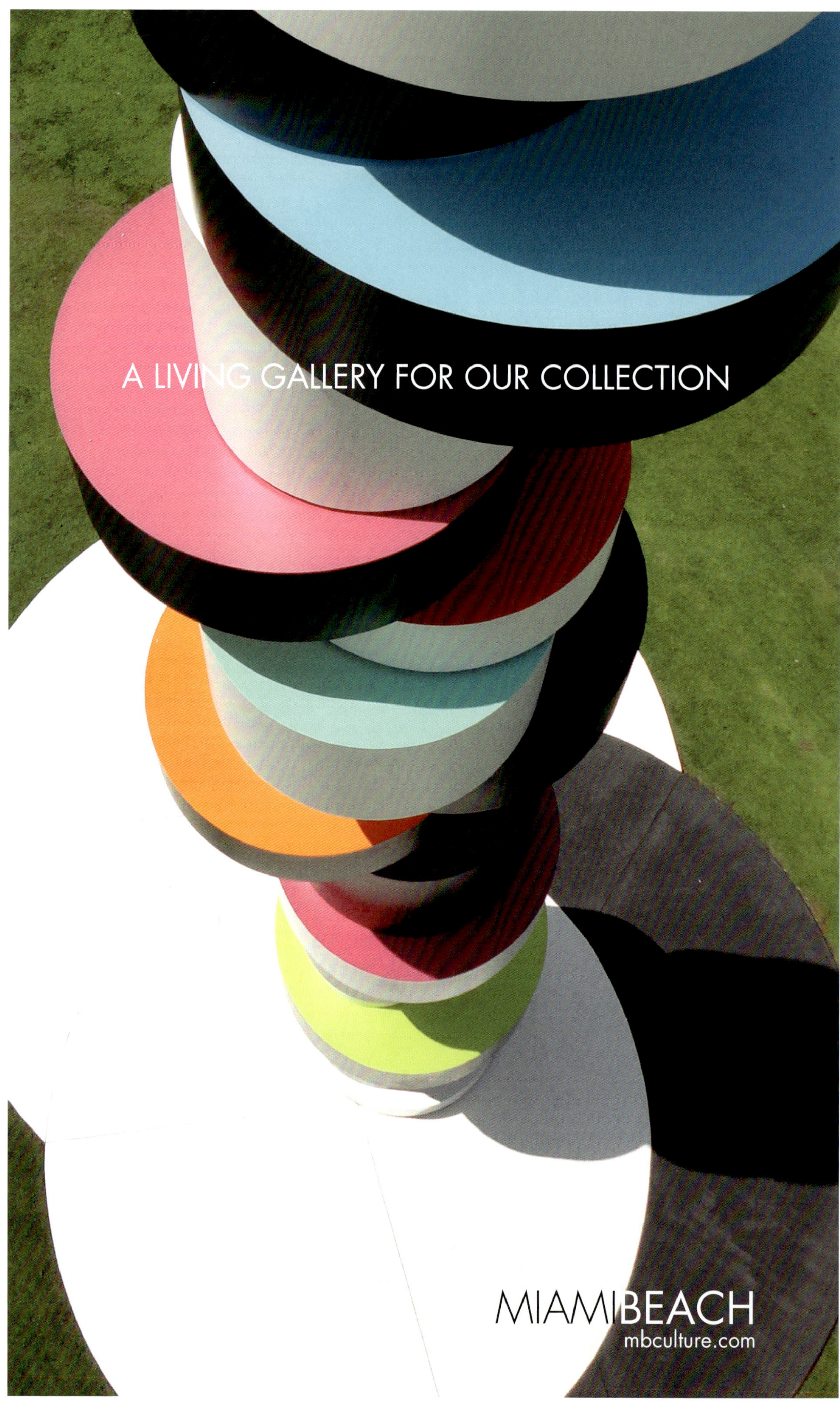
A LIVING GALLERY FOR OUR COLLECTION
MIAMIBEACH
mbculture.com

INFORMACIÓN GENERAL

Duración de la exposición | 6 al 9 de diciembre de 2012

Lugares | **Art Galleries, Art Nova, Art Positions, Art Kabinett, Art Magazines, Art Video, Art Basel Conversations, Art Salon, Art Collectors Lounge** | Miami Beach Convention Center

Art Public | Collins Park

Horario de funcionamiento | Miami Beach Convention Center | Diariamente desde el mediodía hasta las 8 p.m.; domingo desde el mediodía hasta las 6 p.m.
· Art Basel Conversations | Diariamente desde las 10 a.m.
· Art Public | Las 24 horas

Oficina de administración de la exposición | Miami Beach Convention Center, entrada B
Información | Miami Beach Convention Center, entradas B+D
Recepción de VIP | Miami Beach Convention Center: entrada D
Guardarropa | Miami Beach Convention Center, entradas B+D

Precios de entrada | Boleto para un día US $42
· Boleto vespertino (después de las 4 p.m.) US $29
· Pase permanente US $90
· Boleto rebajado para un día (adultos de 62 años y mayores, y grupos de 10 y más) US $24
· Boleto para grupo escolar para un día (por persona) US $10
· Los niños menores de 16 acompañados por sus padres no pagan entrada

ArtNexus Guided Tours | Recorridos oficiales guiados diariamente en inglés y en español.
· Por persona: US $20 (más el valor de la entrada). Privados y grupales (hasta 10 personas): US $200 (más el valor de la entrada). Grupos de hasta 10 estudiantes y 1 acompañante: US $100 (más el valor de la entrada).
· Inscripciones | Mostrador de Art Nexus Guided Tours en la entrada del salón D

Art Kids | Guardería gratuita, experiencias y juegos artísticos bajo la tutela del Miami Beach Children's Museum, para niños de 4 a 12 años de edad cuyos padres visitan Art Basel Miami Beach | Miami Beach Convention Center, entrada D, 2do nivel

Mediador | En caso de temas complejos (por ejemplo, con respecto a la autenticidad o estado de conservación de una obra de arte), los visitantes y las galerías expositoras pueden ponerse en contacto con el Ombudsman (Mediador), quien ayudará a clarificarlos, ofrecerá información no vinculante y mediará en casos de quejas. Ni el Mediador ni MCH Swiss Exhibition (Basel) Ltd. asumirán la responsabilidad de la información proporcionada. Es posible ponerse en contacto con el Mediador a través de la oficina de la administración de la exposición.

Art Loss Register | Funcionamos con el Art Loss Register (ALR), que compara todas las obras de arte que aparecen en el catálogo de Art Basel Miami Beach con una base de datos propia, en cuanto a su condición legal y su procedencia.

Aviones privados | NetJets EE. UU., Teléfono +1 732 326 37 36
NetJets Europa, Teléfono +44 20 7361 96 00

Art | Public

ART PUBLIC

This year's edition of Art Public marks my second year of collaboration with Art Basel in Miami Beach and the Bass Museum. The site-specific projects and outdoor works in sculpture, installation, video and performance will again span from the 1938 keystone façade of the Bass Museum in Miami Beach and reach across Collins Park. But while last year's concentration of critical and demonstrative gestures, evoked perhaps most memorably by Andrea Bowers' and Olga Koumoundouros' *Transformer Display of Community Information and Activation* (2011), Bruce Conner's *LOOKING FOR MUSHROOMS* (1959-1965), Kate Costello's *Untitled* (2011), Theaster Gates' *Stand-Ins for a Period of Wreckage* (2011) and Glenn Kaino's *Levitating the Fair* (2011), reflected ideas surrounding collective efforts and belief systems during an Occupy moment and spirit, this year's Art Public is more nuanced in its separation of parts as opposed to collaborative considerations of systems.

Art Public 2012 recalls in part Roland Barthes' position of 'Speech' (parole) in relation to 'Language' (langue). Taking on the notion of Speech as an essentially 'individual act of selection and actualization,' and as a 'combinative activity that corresponds to an individual act and not to a pure creation,' the selection of works reflect altered content within Language, its less malleable counterpart from which it is extracted but with which it exists in reciprocal comprehensiveness. In other words, each work takes cues and applies or implies meaning that derive from a common tongue but reorders and reintroduces curious utterances and phrases that connect to references outside of but inevitably intertwined with a specific lineage of modern and contemporary art.

In essence the speech acts represented by these disparate and variable works derive from, enable, converse with, and challenge systems or discourses such as modern art and architecture; urban myth and archive (both topiary and built); and the language of banners, flags and signage, among others. Many of these works are unexpected in scale, combination and delivery, but grounded in their connection to and the dialectics of language and speech, interdependent, where 'real linguistic praxis is situated,' according to Maurice Merleau-Ponty. Instead of the effort to 'weave more texture and openness into more conventional approaches to what is perceived as public art,' as I wrote about Art Public 2011, Art Public 2012 understands and underscores *langue* and takes on *parole* through the images, manipulations, forms and phrases.

Physically more concentrated on the site but dialectically more divergent, Art Public 2012 attempts to introduce elusive nuances and unexpected gestures to Miami Beach as part of Art Basel Miami Beach through over twenty works of art.

Christine Y. Kim
Associate Curator of Contemporary Art,
Los Angeles County Museum of Art,
and Co-founder, Los Angeles Nomadic
Division

ART PUBLIC

La edición de este año de Art Public marca mi segundo año de colaboración con Art Basel en Miami Beach y el Bass Museum. Los proyectos específicos para el lugar y los trabajos al aire libre de escultura, instalación, vídeo y performance se extenderán una vez más desde la fachada principal de 1938 del Bass Museum en Miami Beach y llegarán hasta Collins Park. Pero mientras la concentración del año pasado de gestos críticos y demostrativos, evocados quizás de manera más memorable por *Transformer Display of Community Information and Activation* (2011) de Andrea Bowers y Olga Koumoundouros, *LOOKING FOR MUSHROOMS* (1959-1965) de Bruce Conner, *Untitled* (2011) de Kate Costello, *Stand-Ins for a Period of Wreckage* (2011) de Theaster Gates y *Levitating the Fair* (2011) de Glenn Kaino, reflejó ideas en torno a los esfuerzos colectivos y los sistemas de creencias durante el momento y espíritu de un movimiento Occupy, la edición de Art Public de este año está más matizada por su separación de las partes en contraposición con las consideraciones colaborativas de los sistemas.

Art Public 2012 recupera en parte la posición de Roland Barthes del 'habla' (parole) en relación con la 'lengua' (langue). Adoptando la noción de habla básicamente como un 'acto individual de selección y realización' y como una 'actividad combinatoria que corresponde a un acto individual y no a una creación pura', la selección de trabajos refleja el contenido alterado al interior de la lengua, su contraparte menos maleable a partir de la cual se extrae este, pero junto a la cual existe este en recíproca amplitud. En otras palabras, cada trabajo se inspira en y aplica o implica un significado que deriva de un idioma común pero reordena y reintroduce expresiones y frases curiosas que se conectan con referencias que se encuentran fuera de un linaje específico del arte moderno y contemporáneo, pero inevitablemente entrelazadas con este.

Básicamente, los actos del habla representados por estos dispares y variables trabajos derivan de, posibilitan, dialogan con y desafían sistemas o discursos como el arte moderno y la arquitectura; el mito urbano y el archivo (tanto topiario como construido); y el lenguaje de pancartas, banderas y señalética, entre otros. Muchos de estos trabajos son inesperados en escala, combinación y entrega, pero fundamentados en su conexión con la dialéctica de lengua y habla, interdependiente, donde 'se sitúa la praxis lingüística real', según Maurice Merleau-Ponty. En lugar del esfuerzo de 'urdir más textura y apertura en enfoques más convencionales de lo que se percibe como arte público', como escribí acerca de Art Public 2011, Art Public 2012 comprende y subraya langue y adopta parole a través de las imágenes, manipulaciones, formas y frases.

Físicamente más concentrada en el lugar pero dialécticamente más divergente, la sección Art Public 2012 intenta introducir matices elusivos y gestos inesperados en Miami Beach a través de veinte trabajos de arte como parte de Art Basel en Miami Beach.

Christine Y. Kim
Curadora Asociada de Arte Contemporáneo, Los Angeles County Museum of Art, y Cofundadora, Los Angeles Nomadic Division

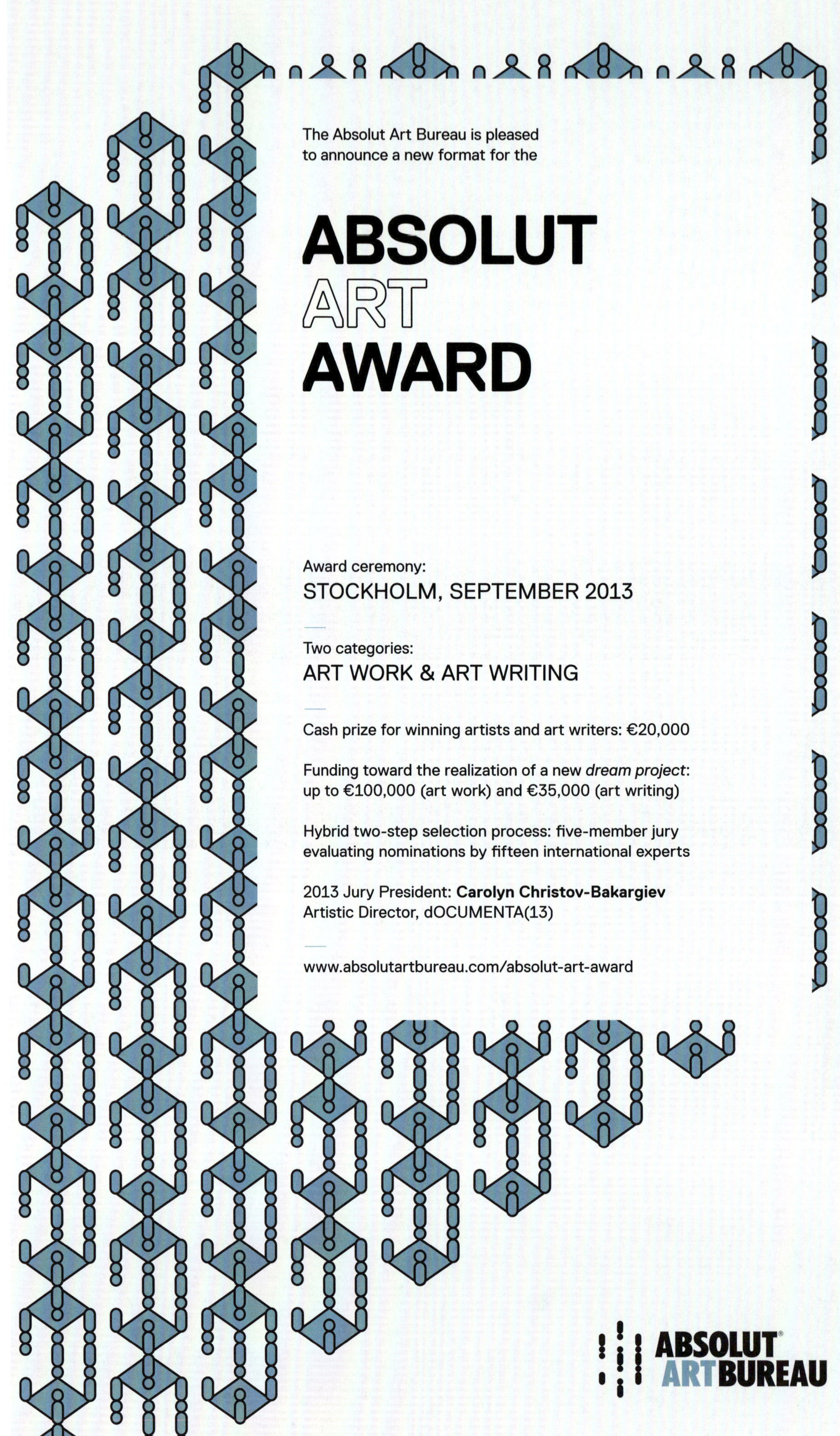
The Absolut Art Bureau is pleased
to announce a new format for the
ABSOLUT
ART
AWARD
Award ceremony:
STOCKHOLM, SEPTEMBER 2013
Two categories:
ART WORK & ART WRITING
Cash prize for winning artists and art writers: €20,000
Funding toward the realization of a new dream project:
up to €100,000 (art work) and €35,000 (art writing)
Hybrid two-step selection process: five-member jury
evaluating nominations by fifteen international experts
2013 Jury President: Carolyn Christov-Bakargiev
Artistic Director, dOCUMENTA(13)
www.absolutartbureau.com/absolut-art-award
ABSOLUT
ARTBUREAU

Art | Basel | Conversations
Art | Salon

ART BASEL CONVERSATIONS

Since its inauguration in 2002, Art Basel Conversations has offered the show's public a chance to see dynamic dialogs between prominent members of the international art-world, each offering their unique, first-hand perspective on producing, collecting, and exhibiting art.

In their inspiring and informative conversations, these cultural figures – all renowned artists, collectors, critics, curators, or museum directors – present their current and future projects, report on their personal experiences, reveal their professional challenges, and debate key issues facing the artworld today. Past participants of Art Basel Conversations have included Marina Abramovič, Ai Weiwei, John Baldessari, Klaus Biesenbach, Daniel Birnbaum, Iwona Blazwick, Christian Boltanski, Eli Broad, Chuck Close, Catherine David, Thomas Demand, Olafur Eliasson, Okwui Enwezor, Harald Falckenberg, Richard Flood, Yona Friedman, Massimiliano Gioni, Boris Groys, Zaha Hadid, Kathy Halbreich, Jens Hoffmann, Maja Hoffmann, Rem Koolhaas, Jeff Koons, Jannis Kounellis, Eugenio López, Roger Mandle, Paul McCarthy, Hans Ulrich Obrist, Gabriel Orozco, Otto Piene, Michelangelo Pistoletto, Anupam Poddar, Robert Rauschenberg, David Rockefeller, Patrizia Sandretto Re Rebaudengo, Uli Sigg, Robert Storr, Budi Tek, Adam Weinberg, and Lawrence Weiner.

Art Basel Conversations, curated by Maike Cruse, Berlin, takes place within the auditorium located in Hall D of Art Basel. Detailed programs for Art Basel Conversations and videos of recent panels can be found online at www.artbasel.com/conversations.

ART SALON

More informal than Art Basel Conversations but equally vibrant, the afternoon Art Salon program serves as an open space for short presentations such as artist talks, panels, lectures, and performances, with the range of speakers including artists, academics, curators, collectors, architects, art lawyers, critics, and many other cultural players. Recent participants at Art Basel in Basel and Miami Beach included Josh Baer, Nicolas Bourriaud, AA Bronson, Bonnie Clearwater, Patrick Charpenel, Jeffrey Deitch, Chris Dercon, Elmgreen and Dragset, Tracey Emin, Omer Fast, Cyprien Gaillard, Liam Gillick, RoseLee Goldberg, Douglas Gordon, Dan Graham, Konstantin Grcic, Mark Handforth, Gianni Jetzer, Joan Jonas, Emilia and Ilya Kabakov, Ulf Küster, Christine Macel, Chus Martinez, Cuauhtémoc Medina, Jonathan Monk, Mariko Mori, Adriano Pedrosa, Beatrix Ruf, Anri Sala, Jerry Saltz, Tomás Saraceno, Tino Sehgal, Nancy Spector, Philip Tinari, Theodora Vischer, Morgan Wong, Erwin Wurm, and Haegue Yang. The program offers a distinctly intimate experience, with ample time for the audience to ask questions.

Art Salon, curated by Maike Cruse, Berlin, takes place within the auditorium located in Hall D of Art Basel. Detailed programs for Art Salon and videos of recent panels can be found online at www.artbasel.com/salon.

ART BASEL CONVERSATIONS

Desde su inauguración en 2002, Art Basel Conversations ha ofrecido al público de la exposición una oportunidad para presenciar diálogos dinámicos entre destacados integrantes del mundo internacional del arte, donde cada uno ofrece su perspectiva única y de primera mano sobre lo que significa producir, coleccionar y exhibir arte.

En sus inspiradoras e informativas conversaciones, estas figuras culturales (todos renombrados artistas, coleccionistas, críticos, curadores o directores de museos) presentan sus proyectos actuales y futuros, informan sobre sus experiencias personales, revelan sus desafíos profesionales y debaten sobre cuestiones clave que el mundo del arte enfrenta hoy en día. Entre los participantes de las ediciones anteriores de Art Basel Conversations se incluyen: Marina Abramović, Ai Weiwei, John Baldessari, Klaus Biesenbach, Daniel Birnbaum, Iwona Blazwick, Christian Boltanski, Eli Broad, Chuck Close, Catherine David, Thomas Demand, Olafur Eliasson, Okwui Enwezor, Harald Falckenberg, Richard Flood, Yona Friedman, Massimiliano Gioni, Boris Groys, Zaha Hadid, Kathy Halbreich, Jens Hoffmann, Maja Hoffmann, Rem Koolhaas, Jeff Koons, Jannis Kounellis, Eugenio López, Roger Mandle, Paul McCarthy, Hans Ulrich Obrist, Gabriel Orozco, Otto Piene, Michelangelo Pistoletto, Anupam Poddar, Robert Rauschenberg, David Rockefeller, Patrizia Sandretto Re Rebaudengo, Uli Sigg, Robert Storr, Budi Tek, Adam Weinberg y Lawrence Weiner.

Art Basel Conversations, sección curada por Maike Cruse, Berlín, se lleva a cabo al interior del auditorio ubicado en el salón D de Art Basel. Los programas detallados de Art Basel Conversations y los vídeos de mesas redondas recientes, pueden encontrarse en línea en www.artbasel.com/conversations.

ART SALON

Más informal que Art Basel Conversations pero igualmente vibrante, el programa de la tarde de Art Salon sirve como un espacio abierto para presentaciones breves tales como charlas de artistas, mesas redondas, conferencias y performances, con una variedad de oradores que incluye a artistas, académicos, curadores, coleccionistas, arquitectos, abogados especializados en arte, críticos y muchos otros protagonistas de la cultura. Algunos de los participantes recientes en Art Basel en Basilea y Miami Beach fueron: Josh Baer, Nicolas Bourriaud, AA Bronson, Bonnie Clearwater, Patrick Charpenel, Jeffrey Deitch, Chris Dercon, Elmgreen and Dragset, Tracey Emin, Omer Fast, Cyprien Gaillard, Liam Gillick, RoseLee Goldberg, Douglas Gordon, Dan Graham, Konstantin Grcic, Mark Handforth, Gianni Jetzer, Joan Jonas, Emilia e Ilya Kabakov, Ulf Küster, Christine Macel, Chus Martínez, Cuauhtémoc Medina, Jonathan Monk, Mariko Mori, Adriano Pedrosa, Beatrix Ruf, Anri Sala, Jerry Saltz, Tomás Saraceno, Tino Sehgal, Nancy Spector, Philip Tinari, Theodora Vischer, Morgan Wong, Erwin Wurm y Haegue Yang. El programa brinda una experiencia inconfundiblemente íntima y tiempo de sobra para que los asistentes formulen sus preguntas.

Art Salon, sección curada por Maike Cruse, Berlín, se lleva a cabo al interior del auditorio ubicado en el salón D de Art Basel. Los programas detallados de Art Salon y los vídeos de mesas redondas recientes, pueden encontrarse en línea en www.artbasel.com/salon.

Art | Video

ART VIDEO

This year's edition of Art Video is the second year of the collaboration between Artprojx and Art Basel in selecting and showing works submitted by the show's galleries. The program will again be presented in two distinct locations: on the outside screening wall of the Frank Gehry-designed New World Center in SoundScape Park and within viewing pods inside the Miami Beach Convention Center.

It is challenging selecting film and videos from so many gallery submissions, but a delight in discovering work I do not know or even artists of whom I had never heard. Choosing is not just about deciding on what works I liked the 'best.' I have to find pieces that work being scaled up to 7,000 sq ft, films and videos that fit into a fixed time range and are suitable to play to a very varied audience and age range as this project is free and open to anyone to attend. In some ways the constraints help focus my decision-making.

Art Video was a great success last year. At times the art, its scale and sound, the audience and ambiance were simply mesmerising. I had for years resisted the potential of the outdoor screening, but it was a wonderfully pleasant and surprising discovery for me that the screening itself could be a social experience mixed with the focus and intensity of cinema. The size, projection and sound are so good that people can talk (quietly), move around, cars and traffic can drive past and still the films and videos stand out. Some films evoked a music-festival atmosphere. The audience was a great mix of galleries and collectors coming from the show and local Miami residents, artists and students, with some families and groups having picnics and all relishing the program.

Works by Dara Friedman, Rashaad Newsome, and Kota Ezawa tingled the hairs on my neck, not because of the art alone, but the chemistry of visuals, sound, music and audience engagement and the logic of the place they were shown. Dara's work *Dancer* was made in and around Miami and was a work she had always hoped to screen at this spot. Rashaad's work fusing *Carmina Burana* with hip hop in his poignant video called *Conductor,* and also Ezawa's *California Über Alles* – both made the audience feel like to be in the midst of a huge music-festival, with camera flashes going off and the audience cheering at the end of each piece.

In addition to the outdoor screenings, we used five wooden pods, which were prominently located on the show floor of the Miami Beach Convention Center. We screened a compilation of most of the shorter films from the outdoor screenings, we staggered each program so they were playing different films at the same time. These pods were constantly filled with collectors, visitors, curators and exhibitors viewing the films and videos for the duration of the show.

The collaboration with the New World Center and the City of Miami Beach proved to be excellent. We were also helped greatly by Picture This, from Bristol, who formatted the materials with technical perfection and precision.

With the amazing memories of last year's screenings still ringing in my head and all the great feedback and excitement it generated, I very much look forward to Art Video 2012.

David Gryn
Director Artprojx

ART VIDEO

La edición de este año de Art Video representa el segundo año de colaboración entre Artprojx y Art Basel para la selección y exhibición de trabajos presentados por las galerías de la exposición. Una vez más, el programa se presentará en dos lugares distintos: en el muro de proyección al aire libre del New World Centre diseñado por Frank Gehry en SoundScape Park y dentro de cápsulas de presentación al interior del Miami Beach Convention Centre.

Resulta desafiante seleccionar películas y vídeos a partir de tantas presentaciones de las galerías, pero es un placer descubrir trabajos que no conozco o incluso artistas de los que nunca había escuchado. Elegir no se trata únicamente sobre decidir qué trabajos fueron los que 'más' me gustaron. Debo encontrar obras que funcionen al ampliarse hasta 650 metros cuadrados; películas y vídeos compatibles con un intervalo fijo de tiempo y aptos para su reproducción ante un público y rango de edades muy diversos, ya que este proyecto es gratuito y está abierto para que cualquier persona asista. En cierta manera, las restricciones ayudan a orientar mi toma de decisiones.

Art Video tuvo un gran éxito el año pasado. Por momentos el arte, su escala y sonido, el público y el ambiente fueron sencillamente cautivantes. Durante años me había resistido a la posibilidad de la proyección al aire libre, pero resultó ser un descubrimiento maravillosamente placentero y sorprendente para mí que la proyección en sí pudiera ser una experiencia social combinada con el enfoque y la intensidad del cine. El tamaño, la proyección y el sonido son tan buenos que las personas pueden hablar (en voz baja) o desplazarse, y los automóviles y el tráfico pueden pasar a un lado y aun así las películas y los vídeos se distinguen. Algunas películas evocaban una atmósfera de festival musical. El público fue una gran mezcla de galerías y coleccionistas provenientes de la exposición; habitantes, artistas y estudiantes locales de Miami; y algunas familias y grupos haciendo picnic, todos ellos deleitándose con el programa.

Los trabajos de Dara Friedman, Rashaad Newsome y Kota Ezawa erizaron los cabellos de mi cuello, no debido al arte en sí, sino gracias a la química de los elementos visuales, el sonido, la música y la participación del público y a la lógica del lugar en el que se mostraron. El trabajo de Dara, *Dancer,* fue realizado en Miami y sus alrededores y se trataba de una obra que ella siempre había esperado proyectar en este lugar. Tanto el trabajo de Rashaad, que fusiona *Carmina Burana* con el hip hop en su incisivo vídeo llamado *Conductor,* como *California Über Alles* de Ezawa hicieron que el público se sintiera como si estuviera en medio de un enorme festival de música, con los disparos de los flashes de las cámaras y el público ovacionando al final de cada pieza.

Además de las proyecciones al aire libre, utilizamos cinco cápsulas de madera ubicadas de manera destacada en el área de la exposición del Miami Beach Convention Center. En ellos exhibimos una compilación de la mayor parte de las películas más cortas de las proyecciones al aire libre y alternamos cada programa de manera que se reprodujeran distintas películas al mismo tiempo. Estas cápsulas se llenaron constantemente con coleccionistas, visitantes, curadores y expositores que contemplaron las películas y los vídeos durante toda la exposición.

La colaboración con el New World Center y la Ciudad de Miami Beach resultó ser excelente. Además, recibimos mucha ayuda de Picture This, de Brístol, quienes formatearon los materiales con perfección y precisión técnica.

Con los sorprendentes recuerdos de las proyecciones del año pasado todavía resonando en mi cabeza y todos los comentarios y entusiasmo que estas generaron, espero con ansia la versión de Art Video 2012.

David Gryn
Director de Artprojx

Art | Galleries
Art | Nova
Art | Positions

303 GALLERY

303 Gallery
US-New York, NY 10011 | 547 West 21st Street
Phone +1 212 255 11 21 | Fax +1 212 255 55 63
info@303gallery.com | www.303gallery.com
Directors Lisa Spellman
Mari Spirito
Barbara Corti
Cristian Alexa

Artists at
Art Basel Miami Beach | **Doug Aitken**
Valentin Carron
Hans-Peter Feldmann
Ceal Floyer
Karel Funk
Maureen Gallace
Tim Gardner
Dominique Gonzalez-Foerster
Rodney Graham
Mary Heilmann
Jeppe Hein
Larry Johnson
Matt Johnson
Karen Kilimnik
Florian Maier-Aichen
Nick Mauss
Mike Nelson
Kristin Oppenheim
Eva Rothschild
Collier Schorr
Stephen Shore
Sue Williams
Jane & Louise Wilson

Gallery Information | Exhibitions 2012:
Matt Johnson, October 5-November 17, 2012
Marxism, curated by Jacob and Jens Hoffmann, June 29-August 3, 2012
Richard Prince 14 Paintings, May 18-June 22, 2012
Valentin Carron, *The dirty grey cube (you) turns around sadly and screams at us (he) 'ca-tarac-ta,'* April 6-May 12, 2012
Hans-Peter Feldmann, February 24-March 31, 2012

Matt Johnson
Sword and the Stone, 2012
Carved sandstone, stainless steel, and wood, 22 x 15 x 9 inches
Unique

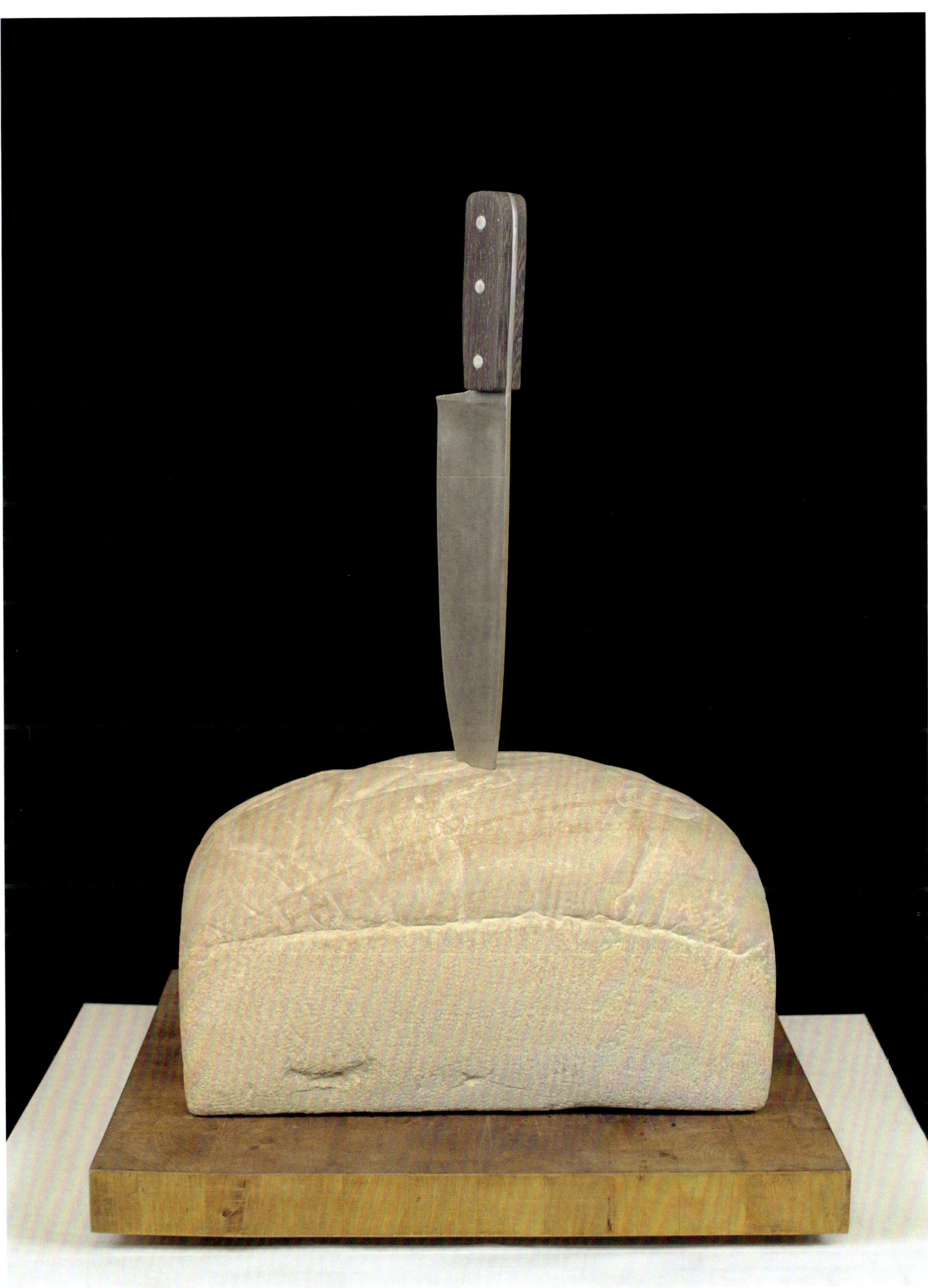

A GENTIL CARIOCA

Mobile +55 21 97 09 37 63

A Gentil Carioca
BR-Rio de Janeiro 20060-020 | Rua Gonçalves Lêdo, 17, sobrado, Centro
Phone +55 21 22 22 16 51 | Fax +55 21 22 22 16 51
correio@agentilcarioca.com.br | www.agentilcarioca.com.br
Directors Márcio Botner
Ernesto Neto
Laura Lima

Artists at
Art Basel Miami Beach | **Cabelo**
Maria Laet
Jarbas Lopes
Paulo Nenflidio
Maria Nepomuceno
Thiago Rocha Pitta

Further artists represented | Ricardo Basbaum
José Bento
Botner & Pedro
Carlos Contente
Lourival Cuquinha
Guga Ferraz
Fabiano Gonper
Laura Lima
Renata Lucas
Simone Michelin
João Modé
Bernardo Ramalho
Rodrigo Torres
Pedro Varela
Alexandre Vogler

Thiago Rocha Pitta
Monument to the Continental Drift, 2011
Cement on canvas on wood mast, dimensions variable

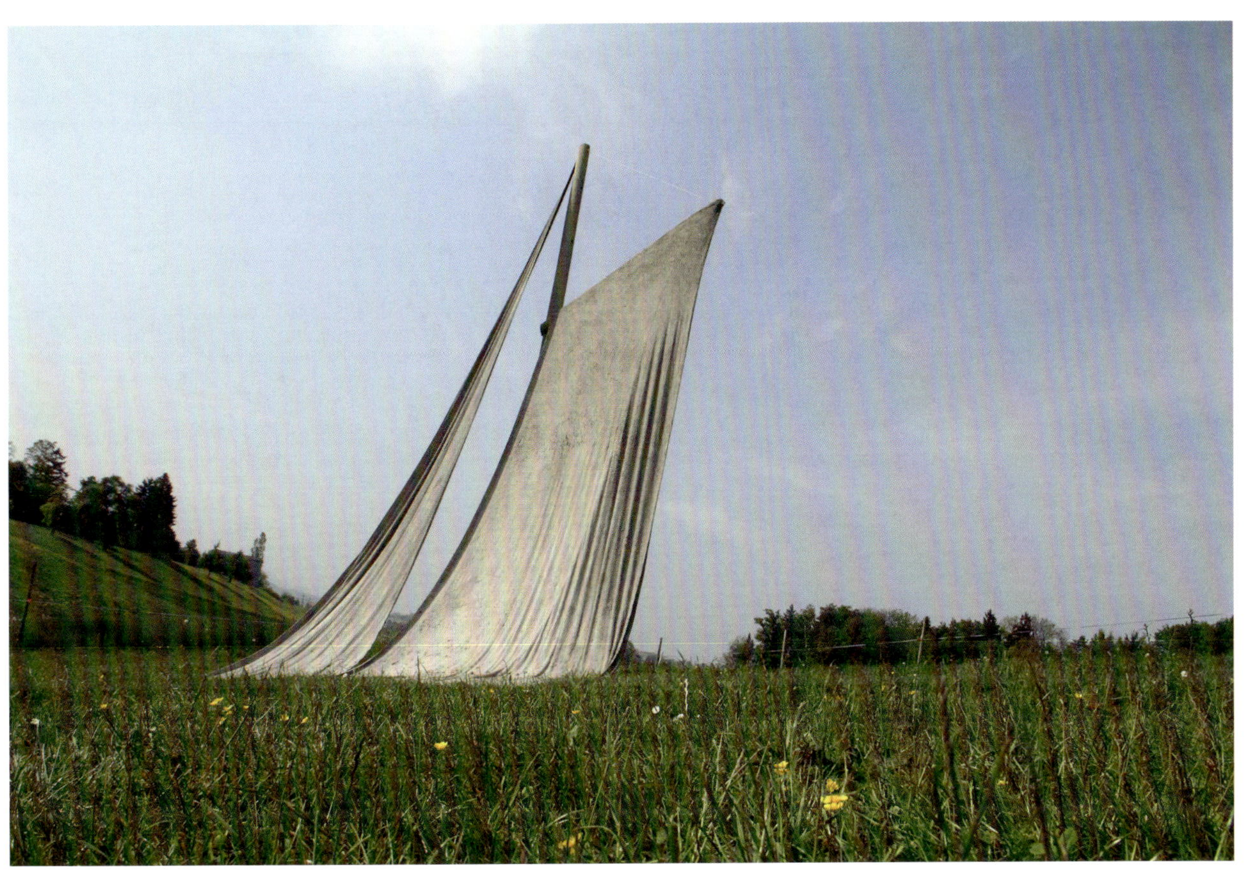

ABREU

Miguel Abreu Gallery
US-New York, NY 10002 | 36 Orchard Street
Phone +1 212 995 17 74 | Fax +1 646 688 23 02
post@miguelabreugallery.com | www.miguelabreugallery.com
Directors Miguel Abreu
Liz Stamplis
Andrea Neustein

Artists at
Art Basel Miami Beach | **Liz Deschenes**
Gareth James
Sam Lewitt
R. H. Quaytman
Blake Rayne
Pamela Rosenkranz

Gallery Information | Established in 2005 in New York City's Lower East Side, the gallery stages one-person and curated group exhibitions and organizes screenings of the films of Jean-Marie Straub and Danièle Huillet, as well as lectures by leading philosophers and critical theorists, such as Alain Badiou, Slavoj Žižek, François Laruelle, and Quentin Meillassoux.

In 2011, the gallery's publishing division, Sequence Press, was established as a collaborative enterprise with British publisher Urbanomic and, among other titles, released François Laruelle's *The Concept of Non-Photography,* Nick Land's *Fanged Noumena,* Quentin Meillassoux's *The Number and the Siren,* and *Spine* by R. H. Quaytman.

Further artists represented: Hans Bellmer
Scott Lyall
Eileen Quinlan
Raha Raissnia
Jimmy Raskin
Pieter Schoolwerth

Pamela Rosenkranz
Because They Try to Bore Holes in My Greatest and Most Beautiful Work, 2012
Inkjet print on photo paper, mounting glue, plexiglass, 80 x 56 inches

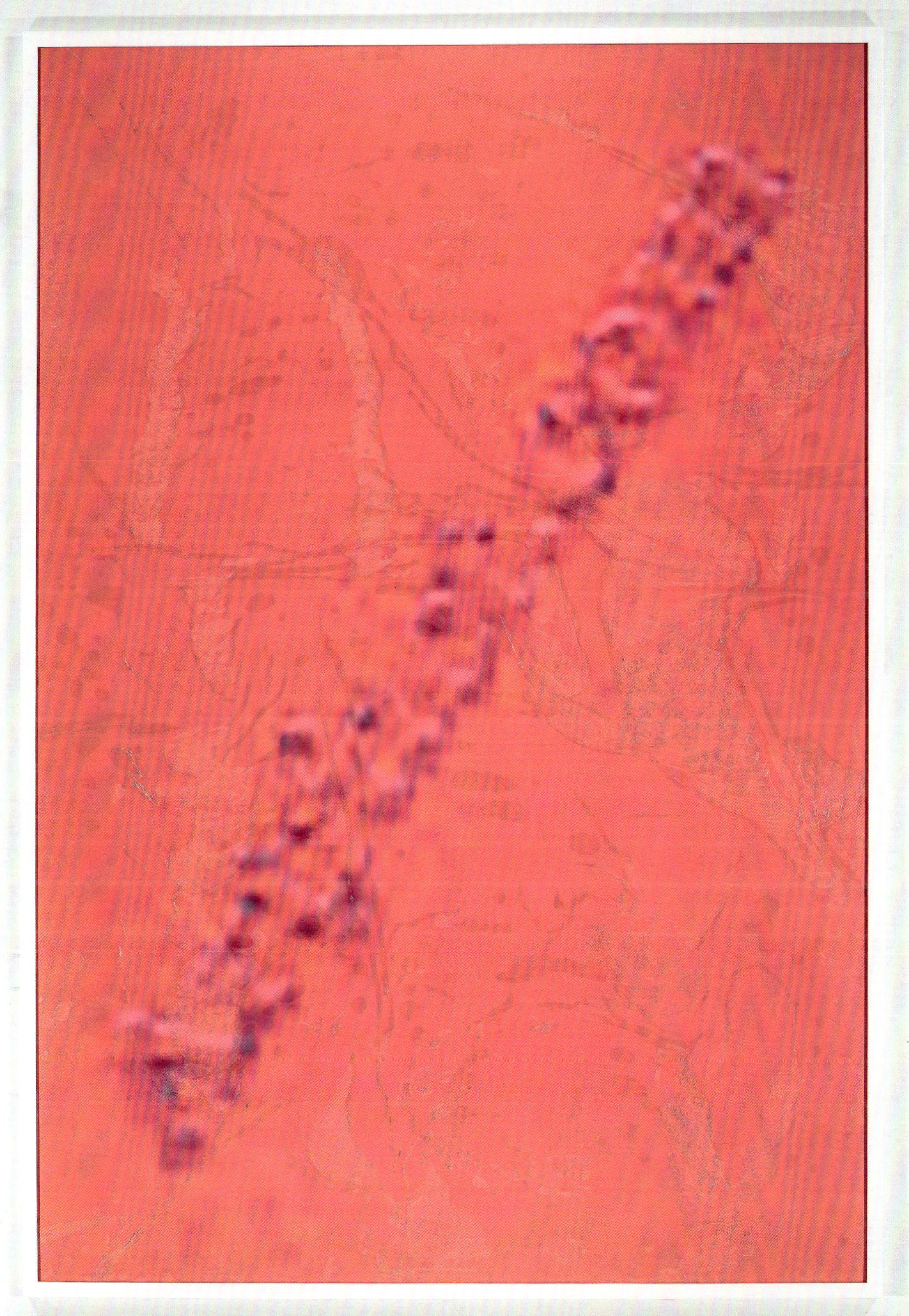

ACQUAVELLA

Acquavella Galleries, Inc.
US-New York, NY 10075 | 18 East 79th Street
Phone +1 212 7346300 | Fax +1 212 7949394
info@acquavellagalleries.com | www.acquavellagalleries.com
Directors William R. Acquavella
Esperanza Sobrino
Michael Findlay
Tsutomu Takashima
Eleanor Acquavella Dejoux
Nicholas Acquavella
Alexander Acquavella

Artists at
Art Basel Miami Beach | **Willem de Kooning**
Edgar Degas
Richard Diebenkorn
Jean Dubuffet
Lucian Freud
Jasper Johns
Fernand Léger
Roy Lichtenstein
Damian Loeb
René Magritte
Brice Marden
Henri Matisse
Joan Miró
Giorgio Morandi
Enoc Perez
Pablo Picasso
Jackson Pollock
Jean Paul Riopelle
James Rosenquist
Ed Ruscha
Wayne Thiebaud
Cy Twombly
Andy Warhol

Gallery Information | Acquavella Galleries was founded in 1921 by Nicholas Acquavella, father of the current owner, William Acquavella, who runs the gallery with his children Nicholas, Alexander, and Eleanor Acquavella. Acquavella Galleries specializes in Impressionist and twentieth-century works of art, including Post-Impressionist, Cubist, Surrealist, and post-war American art. The gallery is located just off Madison Avenue, at 18 East 79th Street in New York City, where it has been since the 1960s.

The gallery has done business with major museums in the United States, Europe, and Japan as well as private collectors throughout the world. The gallery has presented museum-quality exhibitions of Bonnard, Braque, Cézanne, Degas, Giacometti, Léger, Matisse, Melotti, Miró, Modigliani, Monet, Picasso, Pissarro, Rauschenberg, Renoir, and Sisley. Acquavella is the exclusive international agent for James Rosenquist, Damian Loeb, and Enoc Perez and the American agent for Wayne Thiebaud.

Brice Marden
Elements V, 1984
Oil on linen, 48x36 inches

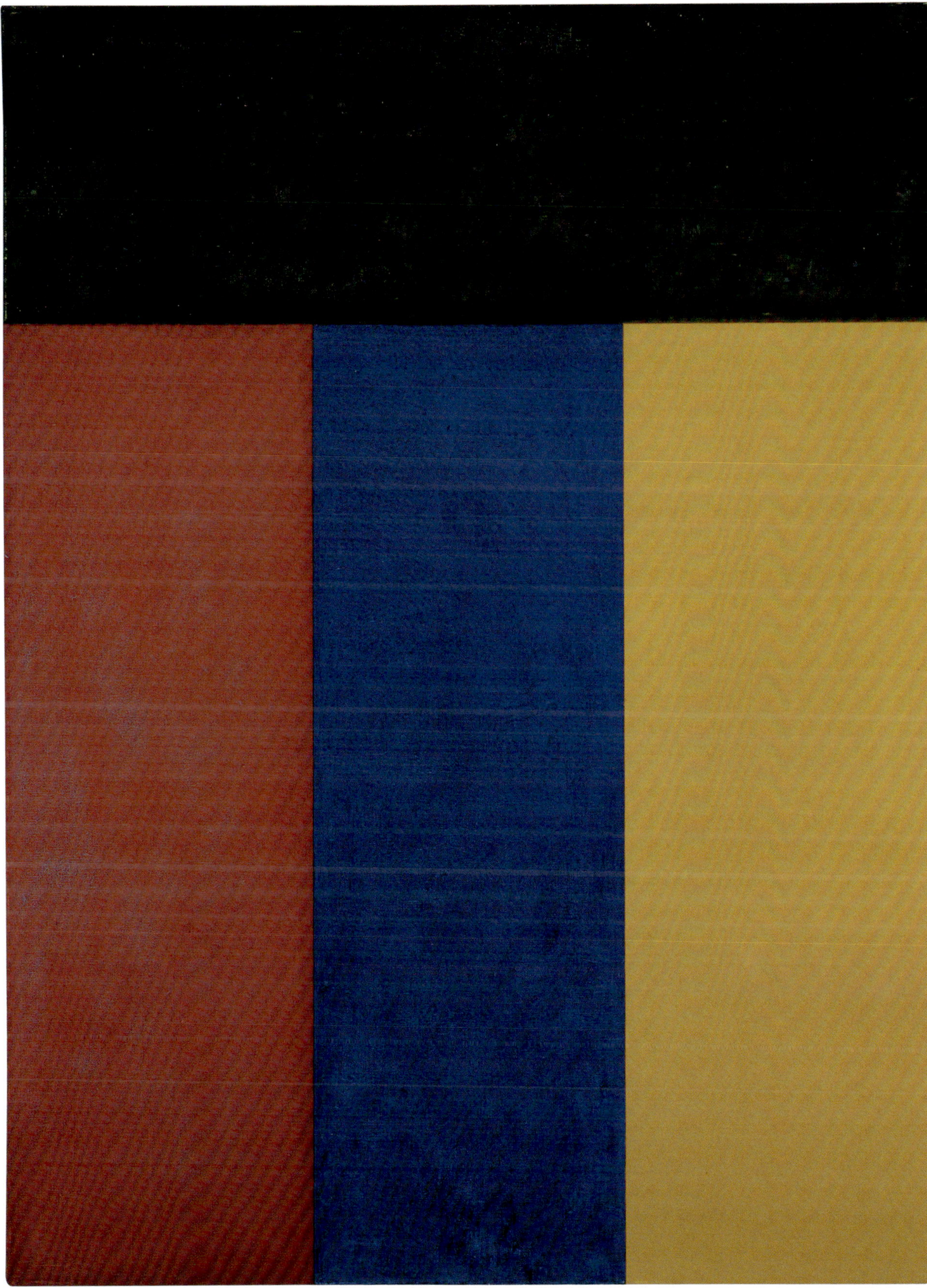

ALEXANDER AND BONIN

Alexander and Bonin
US-New York, NY 10011 | 132 Tenth Avenue
Phone +1 212 367 74 74 | Fax +1 212 367 73 37
gallery@alexanderandbonin.com | www.alexanderandbonin.com
Directors Carolyn Alexander
Ted Bonin

Artists at
Art Basel Miami Beach | **John Ahearn**
Matthew Benedict
Robert Bordo
Fernando Bryce
Michael Buthe
Willie Cole
Eugenio Dittborn
Willie Doherty
Victor Grippo
Mona Hatoum
Diango Hernández
Emily Jacir
Robert Kinmont
Stefan Kürten
Paul Etienne Lincoln
Jorge Macchi
Rita McBride
Ree Morton
Sylvia Plimack Mangold
Doris Salcedo
Paul Thek

Further artists represented | Peter Hujar
Sean Scully

Eugenio Dittborn
The 29th History of the Human Face (Sopap.)
Airmail Painting No. 168, 2007
Tincture, frottage, text, and photo silkscreen on 3 sections of duck fabric, 82½ x 82½ inches

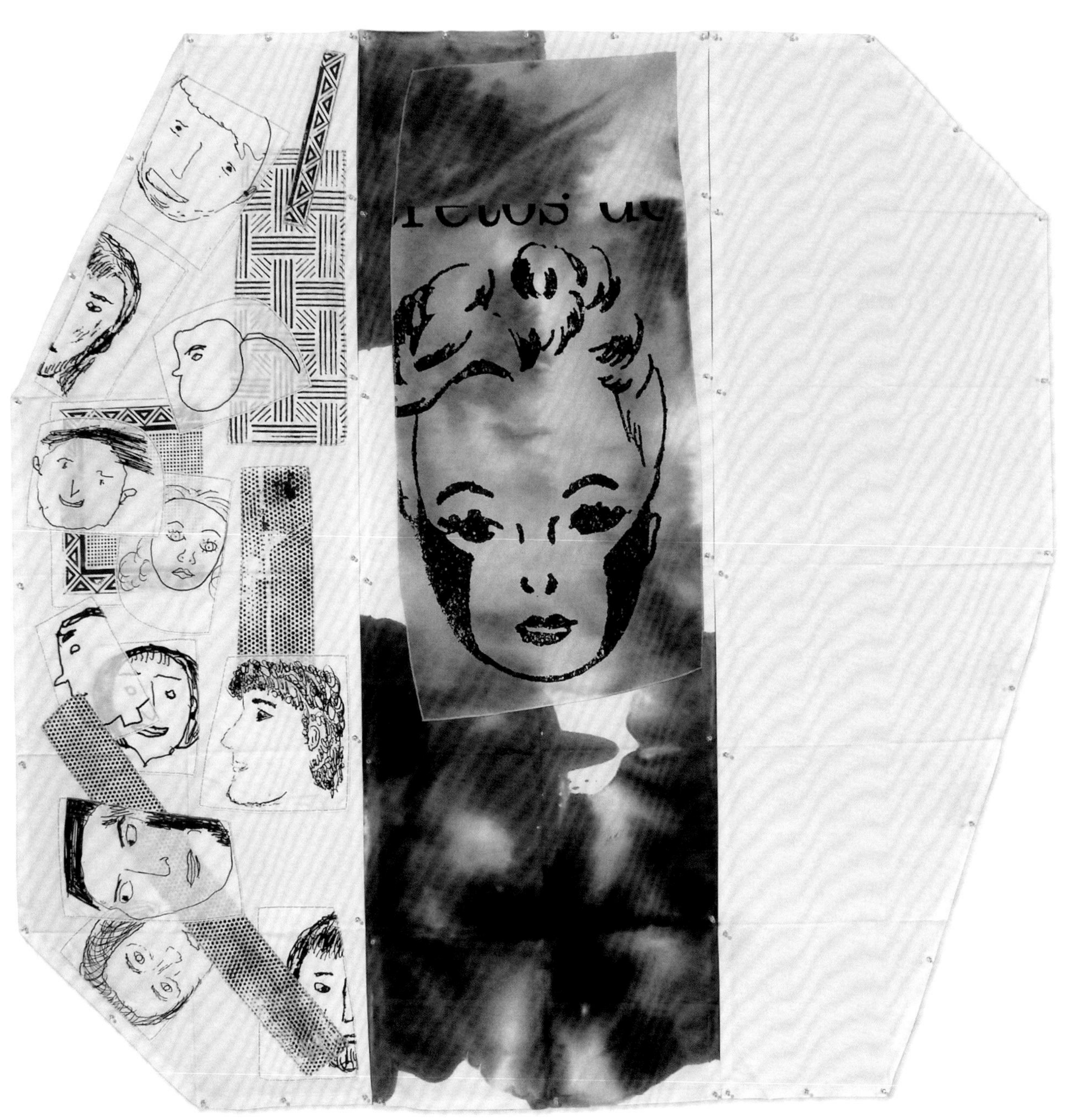

ALTMAN SIEGEL

Mobile +1 917 674 42 39

Altman Siegel
US-San Francisco, CA 94108 | 49 Geary Street
Phone +1 415 576 93 00 | Fax +1 415 373 44 71
info@altmansiegel.com | www.altmansiegel.com
Directors Claudia Altman-Siegel
Daelyn Short Farnham

One-Person Show | Artist Information

Matt Keegan

*1976, Manhasset, NY, United States
Lives and works in New York, NY, United States

Selected solo exhibitions:
2011 *Lengua,* Altman Siegel, San Francisco, CA
I Apple NY, D'Amelio Terras, New York, NY

Selected group exhibitions:
2012 *Found in Translation,* Deutsche Guggenheim, Berlin
2011 *Circulate,* FOAM, Amsterdam
Short Stories, SculptureCenter, Long Island City, NY
Exposure: Matt Keegan, Katie Paterson, Heather Rasmussen, Art Institute of Chicago, Chicago, IL
The Air We Breathe, curated by Apsara DiQunizio, San Francisco Museum of Modern Art, San Francisco, CA
The Anxiety of Photography, curated by Matthew Thompson, Aspen Art Museum, Aspen, CO
2010 *Image Transfer,* Henry Art Gallery, Seattle, WA
Contemplating the Void: Interventions in the Guggenheim Museum, Solomon R. Guggenheim Museum, New York, NY
2009 *Younger than Jesus,* New Museum, New York, NY
Reach of Realism, Museum of Contemporary Art, Miami, FL
2008 *Imaginary Thing,* curated by Peter Eleey, Aspen Art Museum, Aspen, CO

Gallery Information | Altman Siegel Gallery, founded in 2009, received the 2012 Alice Award for Best Emerging Private Gallery.

Further artists represented:
Nate Boyce
Shannon Ebner
Liam Everett
Fran Herndon
Chris Johanson
Shinpei Kusanagi
Devin Leonardi
Trevor Paglen
Will Rogan
Sara VanDerBeek
Emily Wardill
Garth Weiser

The foundation of Matt Keegan's interdisciplinary art practice is language, its day-to-day usage, and the complexities of interpretation. In 2010, Keegan started mining a single image archive originally assembled by his mother, who teaches English as a Second Language. This analog set comprises some 800 photo-based flash cards assembled from primarily commercial sources. Appropriating image selections to produce various works, Keegan explores the slippages between image and word, and the vast range of meanings embedded in even straightforward photographs.

Matt Keegan
Dead, 1990-2005
Laminated card, 12 x 9 inches

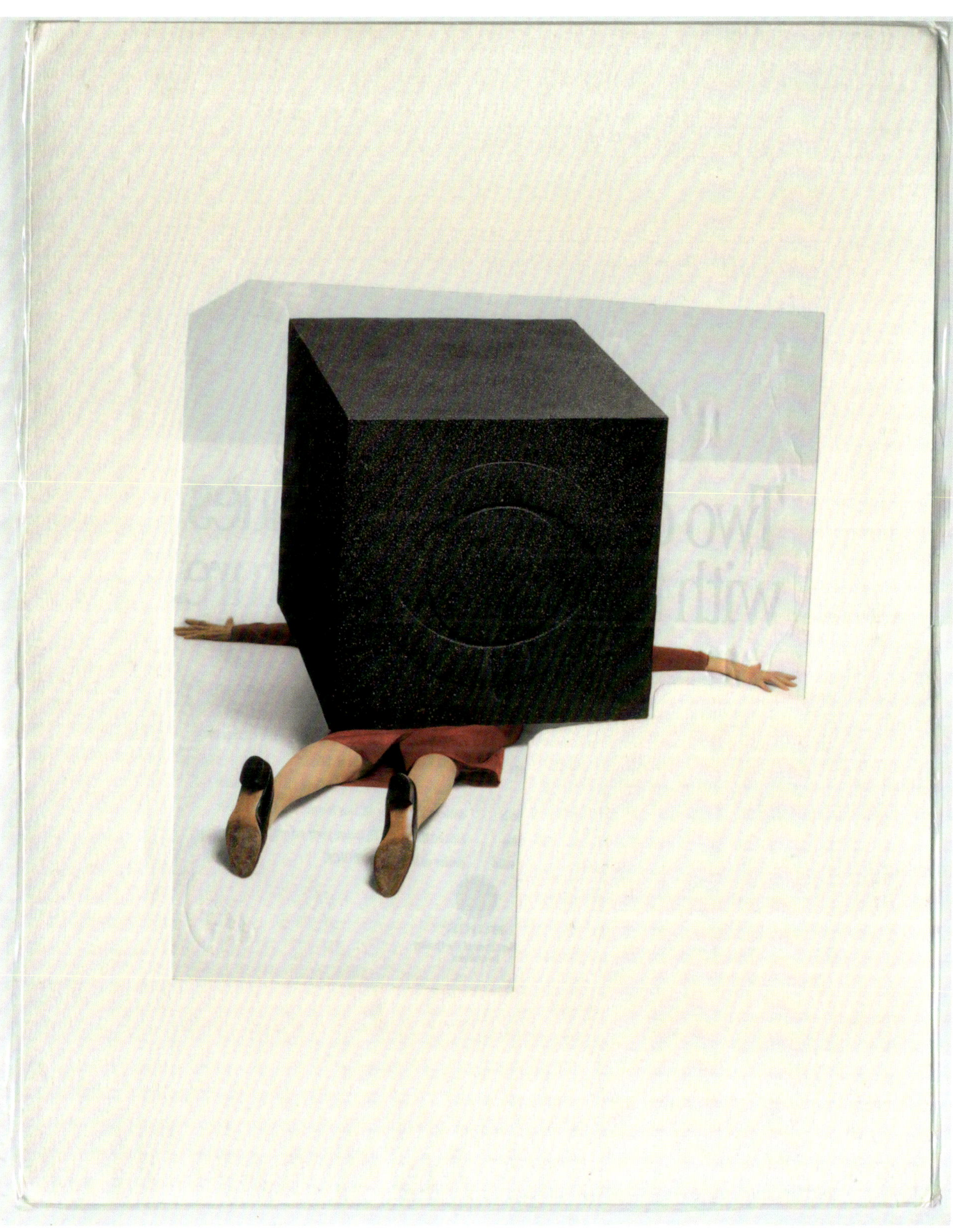

AMERINGER McENERY YOHE

Mobile +1 917 6589853

Ameringer/McEnery/Yohe
US-New York, NY 10011 | 525 West 22nd Street
Phone +1 212 4450051 | Fax +1 212 4450102
mm@amy-nyc.com | www.amy-nyc.com
Directors Will Ameringer
Miles McEnery
James Yohe

Artists at Art Basel Miami Beach | **Oliver Arms**
Thomas Burke
Rebecca Campbell
Suzanne Caporael
Rosana Castrillo Diaz
Gene Davis
Helen Frankenthaler
Iva Gueorguieva
Frederick Hammersley
Zach Harris
Al Held
Hans Hofmann
Wolf Kahn
Patrick Lee
Markus Linnenbrink
Morris Louis
George McNeil
John M. Miller
Robert Motherwell
Rod Penner
David Allan Peters
Judy Pfaff
Michael Reafsnyder
Tam Van Tran
Esteban Vicente
Patrick Wilson
Liat Yossifor

Patrick Lee
Deadly Friends (City of Angels),
2010
Graphite on paper, 36 x 24 inches

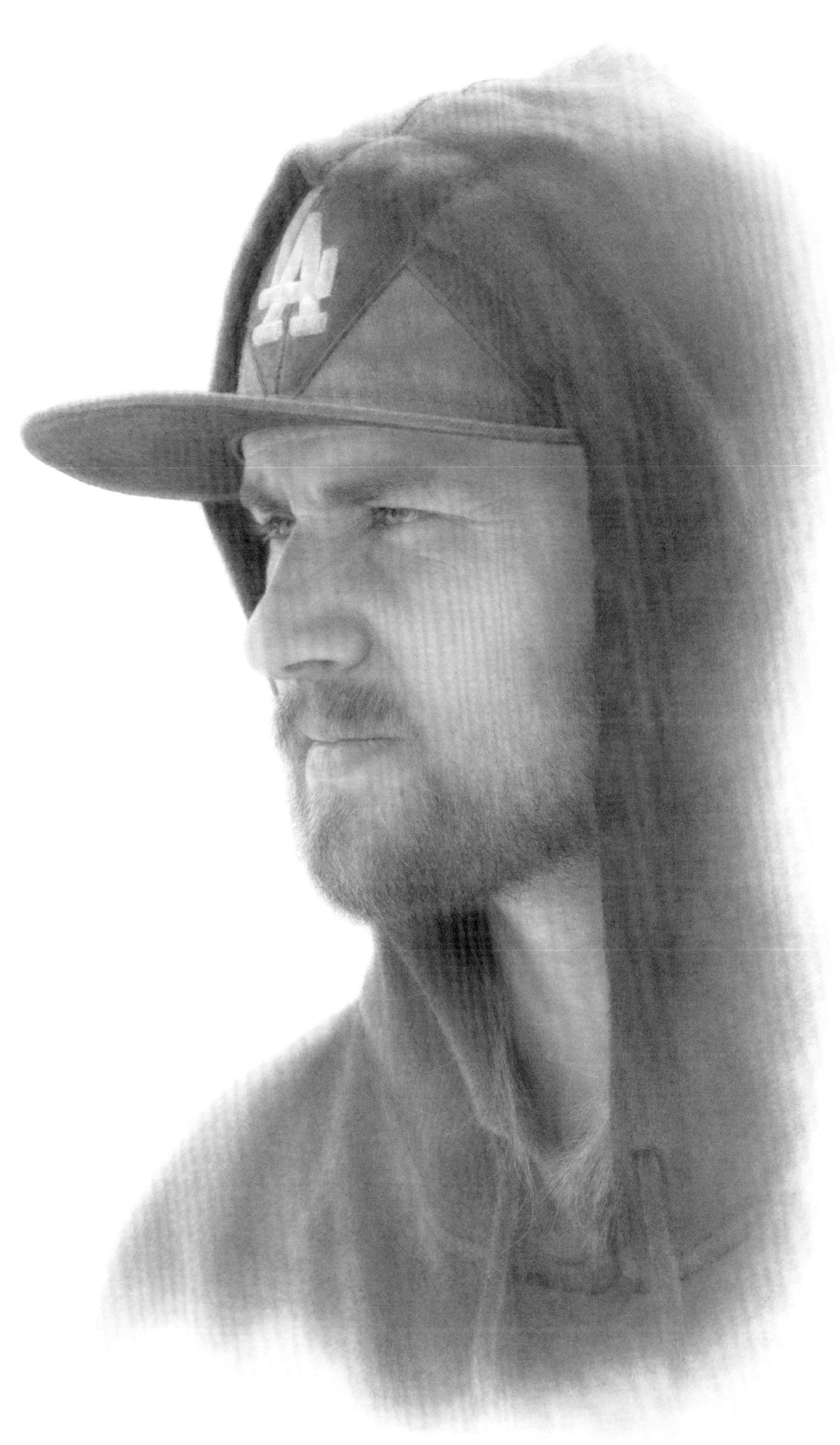
LA

ANDRÉHN-SCHIPTJENKO

Andréhn-Schiptjenko
SE-11330 Stockholm | Hudiksvallsgatan 8
Phone +46 8 6120075 | Fax +46 8 6120076
info@andrehn-schiptjenko.com | www.andrehn-schiptjenko.com
Directors Ciléne Andréhn
Marina Schiptjenko
Elin Hagström

Artists at
Art Basel Miami Beach | **Omid Delafrouz**
Brad Kahlhamer

Gallery Information | Further artists represented: Uta Barth
Tobias Bernstrup
Jacob Dahlgren
Maya Eizin Öijer
Carin Ellberg
Peter Hagdahl
Siobhán Hapaska
Katrine Helmersson
Martin Jacobson
Kristina Jansson
Lena Johansson
Anna Kleberg
Annika Larsson
Matts Leiderstam
Katarina Löfström
Tony Matelli
Marilyn Minter
Nandipha Mntambo
Julie Roberts
Mika Rottenberg
Xavier Veilhan
Annika von Hausswolff
Cajsa von Zeipel
Gunnel Wåhlstrand
Johan Zetterquist

Further information on illustration B:
Currently on exhibit at The Aldrich Contemporary Art Museum, Ridgefield, CT (July 15, 2012-February 24, 2013); to be exhibited at The Nelson-Atkins Museum of Art, Kansas City, MO, in March 2013

A | **Omid Delafrouz**
The Lonesome Skater, 2011
Digital color print, pencil drawing, 158 x 218 cm

B | **Brad Kahlhamer**
Bowery Nation, 1985-2012

A

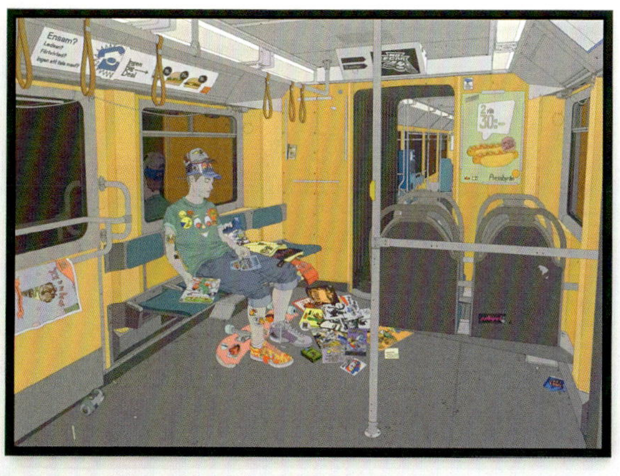

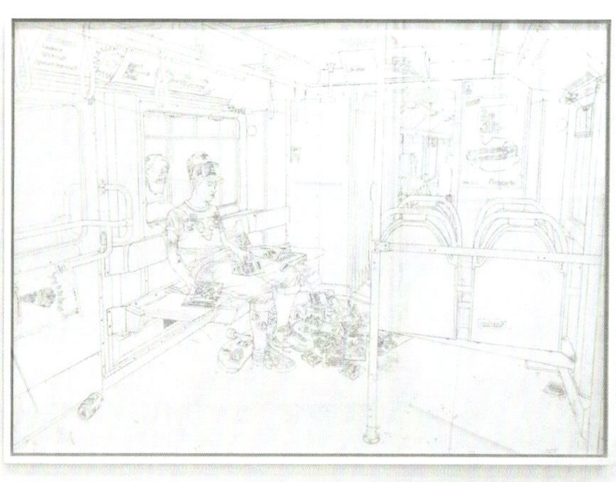

B

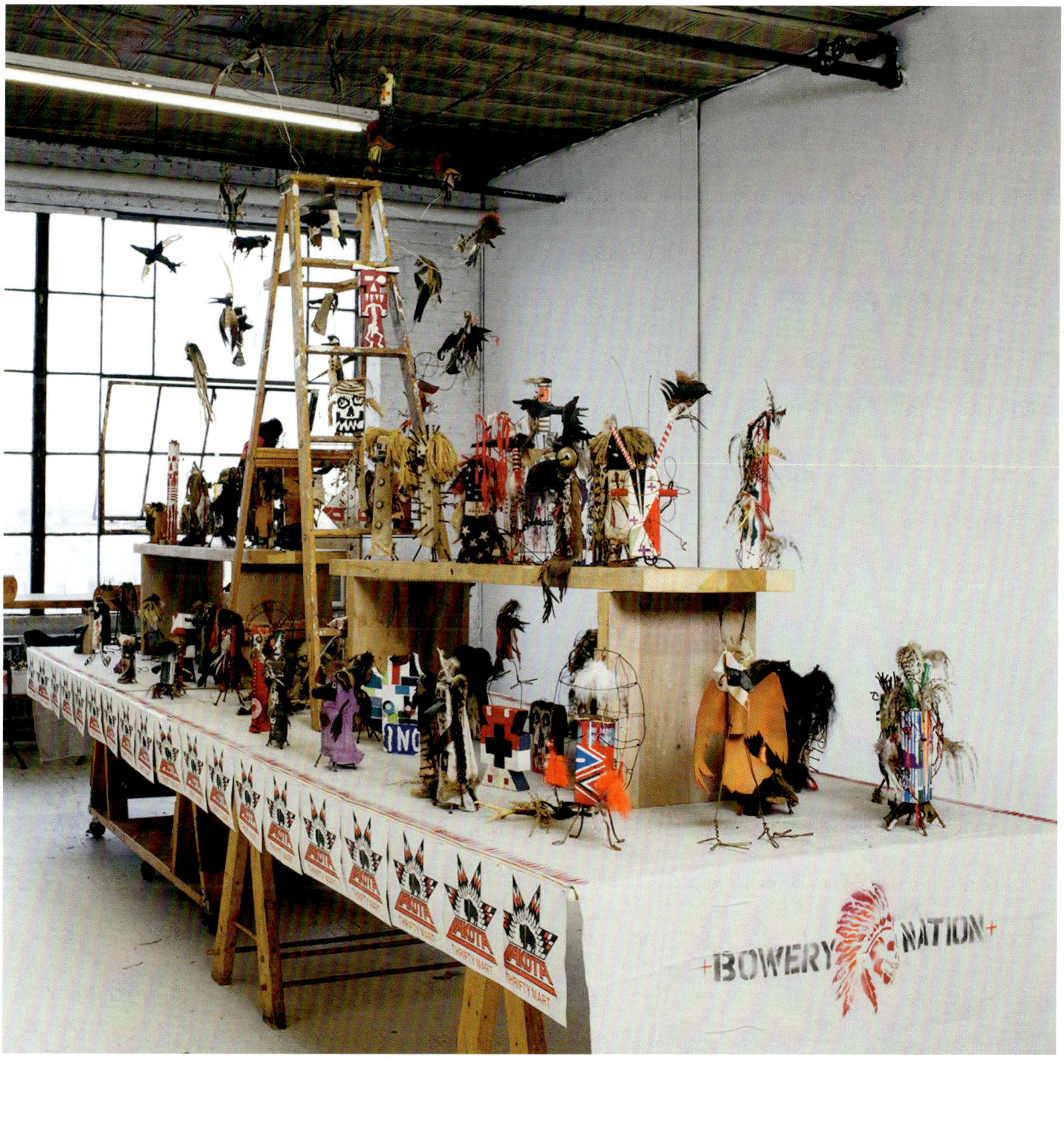

ARRATIA BEER

Arratia Beer
DE-10961 Berlin | Mehringdamm 55
Phone +49 30 23630805 | Fax +49 30 24781038
info@arratiabeer.com | www.arratiabeer.com
Directors Euridice Arratia
Elizabeth Beer

One-Person Show | Artist Information

Pablo Rasgado

*1984, Jalisco, Mexico
Lives and works in Mexico City, Mexico

Further artists represented | Patty Chang
Omer Fast
Fernanda Fragateiro
Jennie C. Jones
Matthew Metzger
Kateřina Šedá
Javier Téllez

Pablo Rasgado
Unfolded Architecture (Liquid Solid System No. 3), Walls from the Museo de Arte Moderno, Mexico, 2012
Drywall and vinyl paint on wood, 120 x 120 cm

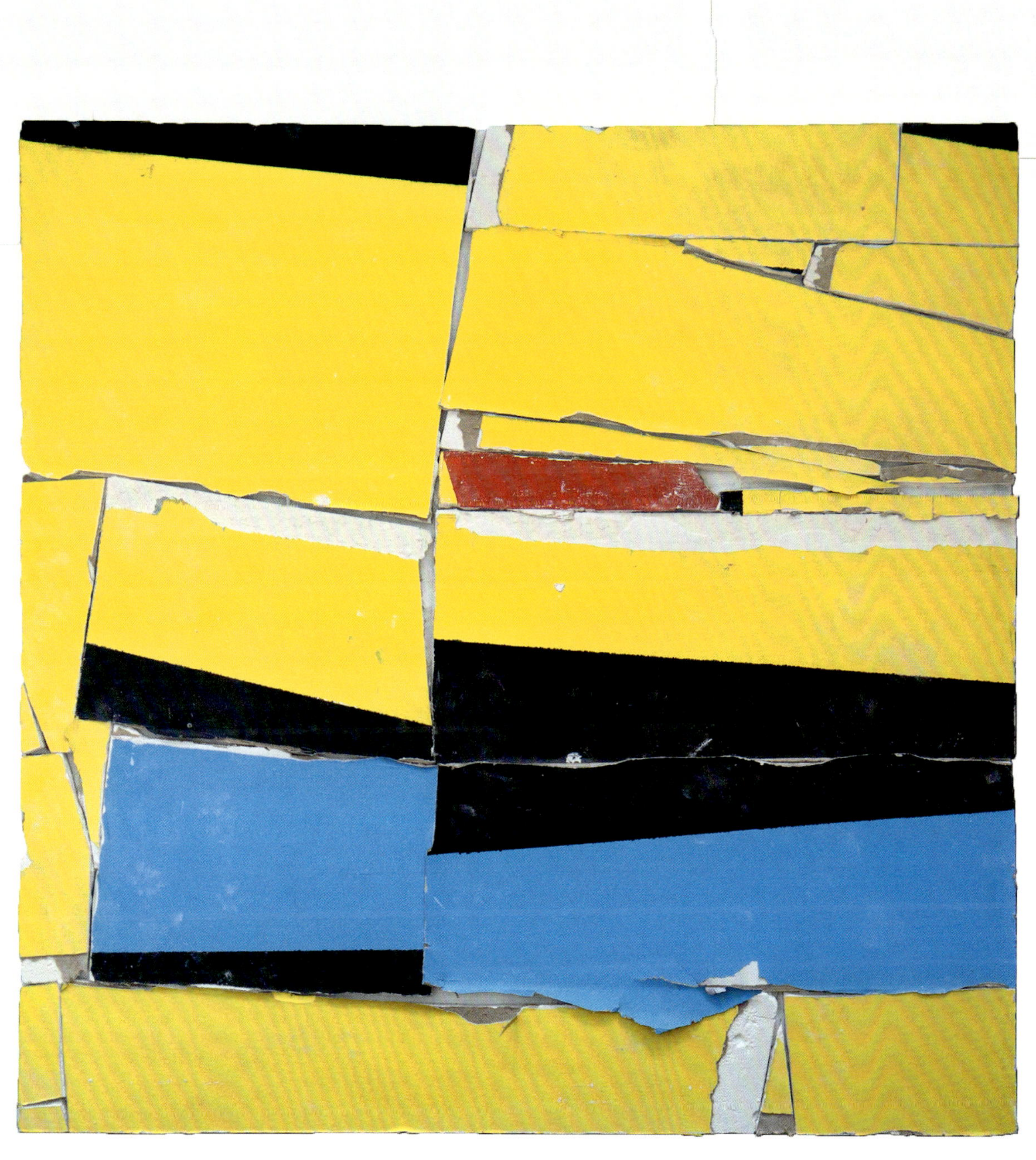

ART : CONCEPT

Mobile +33 614 486745

Art : Concept
FR-75003 Paris | 13, rue des Arquebusiers
Phone +33 153 609030 | Fax +33 153 609031
info@galerieartconcept.com | www.galerieartconcept.com
Director Olivier Antoine

Artists at
Art Basel Miami Beach | **Hubert Duprat**
Geert Goiris
Nathan Hylden
Jacob Kassay
Adam McEwen

Gallery Information | Exhibitions:
Andrew Lewis, December 1, 2012-January 5, 2013
Vidya Gastaldon, January 12-February 16, 2013
Jacob Kassay, opening February 23, 2013

Further artists represented: Martine Aballéa
Pierre-Olivier Arnaud
Julien Audebert
Francis Baudevin
Whitney Bedford
Jean-Luc Blanc
Michel Blazy
Jeremy Deller
Richard Fauguet
Vidya Gastaldon
Lothar Hempel
Andrew Lewis
Philippe Perrot
Pietro Roccasalva
Gedi Sibony
Roman Signer
Alexandre Singh
Ulla von Brandenburg

Further information on the illustration:
Duprat's intention isn't to surprise or to create 'out of the blue'; each one of his pieces is the result of a precise and tangible moment that pinpoints a significant experience meant to allow him to temporarily break with his previous schemes. He is at the crossing of two worlds: the world of free artistic expression and the world of rationally organized artifacts. Neither goldsmith nor sculptor, not an entomologist, definitely not an archeologist, not even an artist, he uses his knowledge to reach beyond a purely artistic sphere. His interest doesn't really lie in the transformation of something into something else that could be considered artwork, but rather in the creation of a metaphor between being and becoming, a 'know-how' and a possible 'how-to-know.'

Hubert Duprat always pays extra attention to the physical results of his pieces, both in the choice of materials and by the orientation that he chooses to give them. His works are not just works of art in their basic acceptance. Rather than merely judging this production on an aesthetic level, we try to reach out for it in a new field of knowledge. Beyond the sphere of functionality, these objects claim their simple 'Dasein,' or at least their ability to create links with other materials.

Hubert Duprat
Polystyrène & Galuchat, 2011/12
Polystyrene, wood, and sharkskin, dimensions variable
Detail

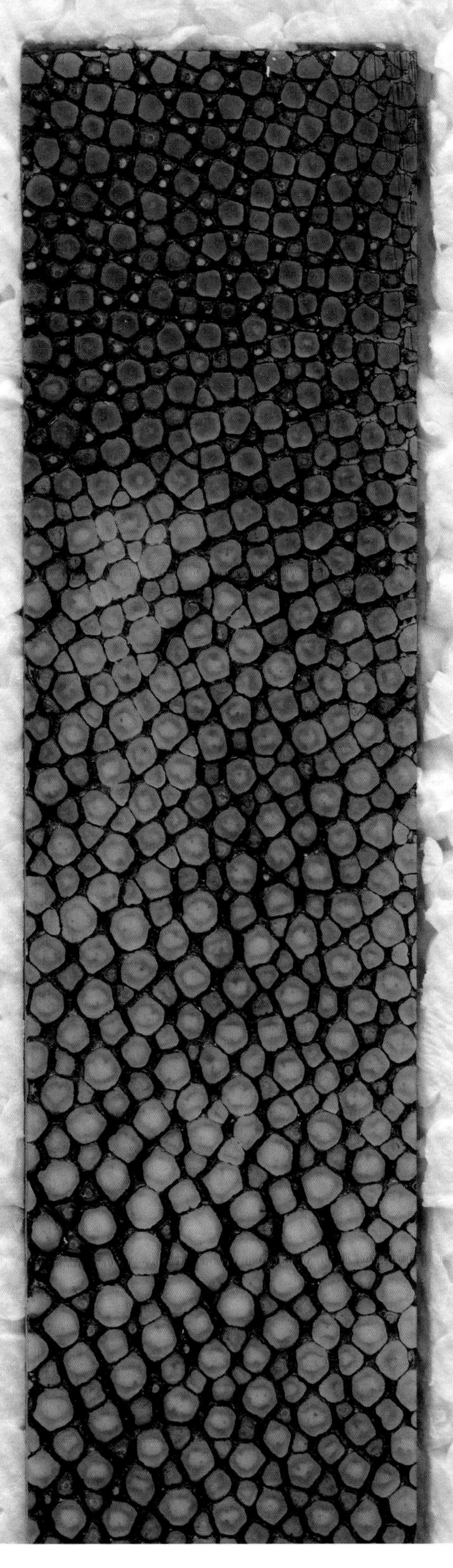

ARTIACO

Alfonso Artiaco
IT-80134 Naples | Piazzetta Nilo 7, Palazzo Principe Raimondo di Sangro
Phone +39 081 497 60 72 | Fax +39 081 19 36 01 64
info@alfonsoartiaco.com | www.alfonsoartiaco.com
Director Alfonso Artiaco

Artists represented | Darren Almond
Carl Andre
Giovanni Anselmo
Robert Barry
Botto & Bruno
Alan Charlton
Gilbert & George
Gioberto Noro
Laurent Grasso
Thomas Hirschhorn
Craigie Horsfield
Ann Veronica Janssens
Jannis Kounellis
Melissa Kretschmer
Wolfgang Laib
Sol LeWitt
Lello Lopez
Raffaele Luongo
Vera Lutter
Rita McBride
Gerhard Merz
Davide Minuti
Marco Neri
Albert Oehlen
Giulio Paolini
Giuseppe Penone
Perino & Vele
Anne & Patrick Poirier
Sergio Prego
Glen Rubsamen
Ulrich Rückriem
Anri Sala
Niele Toroni
David Tremlett
Lawrence Weiner

Thomas Hirschhorn
Collage-Truth n°4, 2012
Prints, tape, plastic foil,
31.5 x 39 cm

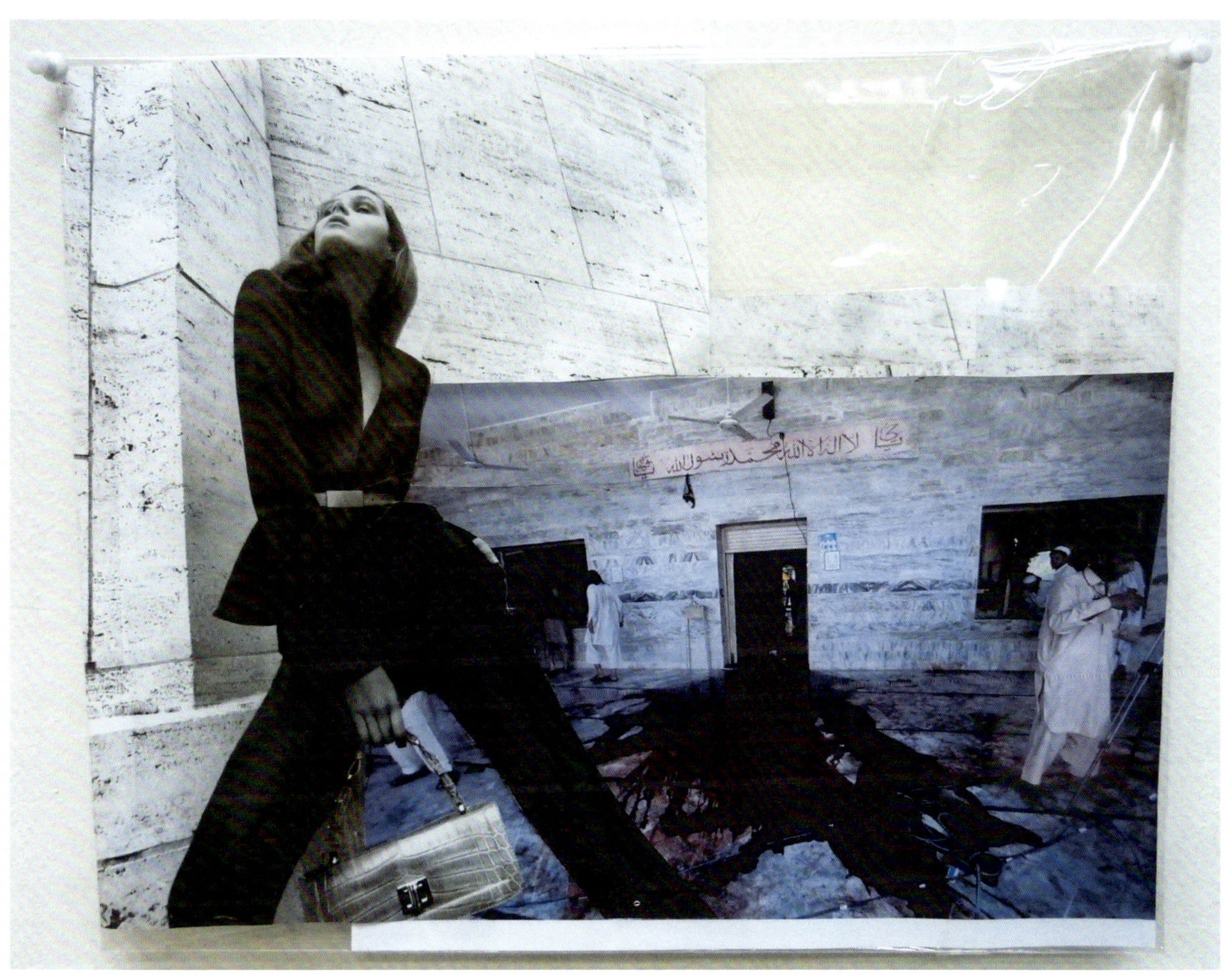
لا اله الا الله محمد رسول الله

BAUDACH

Mobile +49 174 9493944

Galerie Guido W. Baudach Wedding
DE-13347 Berlin | Oudenarder Strasse 16-20
Phone +49 30 28047727 | Fax +49 30 45024481
galerie@guidowbaudach.com | www.guidowbaudach.com
Directors Guido W. Baudach
Berit Homburg

Galerie Guido W. Baudach Charlottenburg
DE-10623 Berlin | Carmerstrasse 11
Phone +49 30 31998101 | Fax +49 30 31998103
galerie@guidowbaudach.com | www.guidowbaudach.com
Directors Guido W. Baudach
Sophie Prager

Artists at Art Basel Miami Beach | **André Butzer**
Björn Dahlem
Thilo Heinzmann
Thomas Helbig
Andy Hope 1930
Rashid Johnson
Jürgen Klauke
Erwin Kneihsl
Bjarne Melgaard
Aïda Ruilova
Markus Selg
Erik van Lieshout
Thomas Zipp

Björn Dahlem
Schleife (Epizyklus), 2012
Wood, steel, mineral lickstone,
lacquer, stain, 80 x 40 x 26 cm

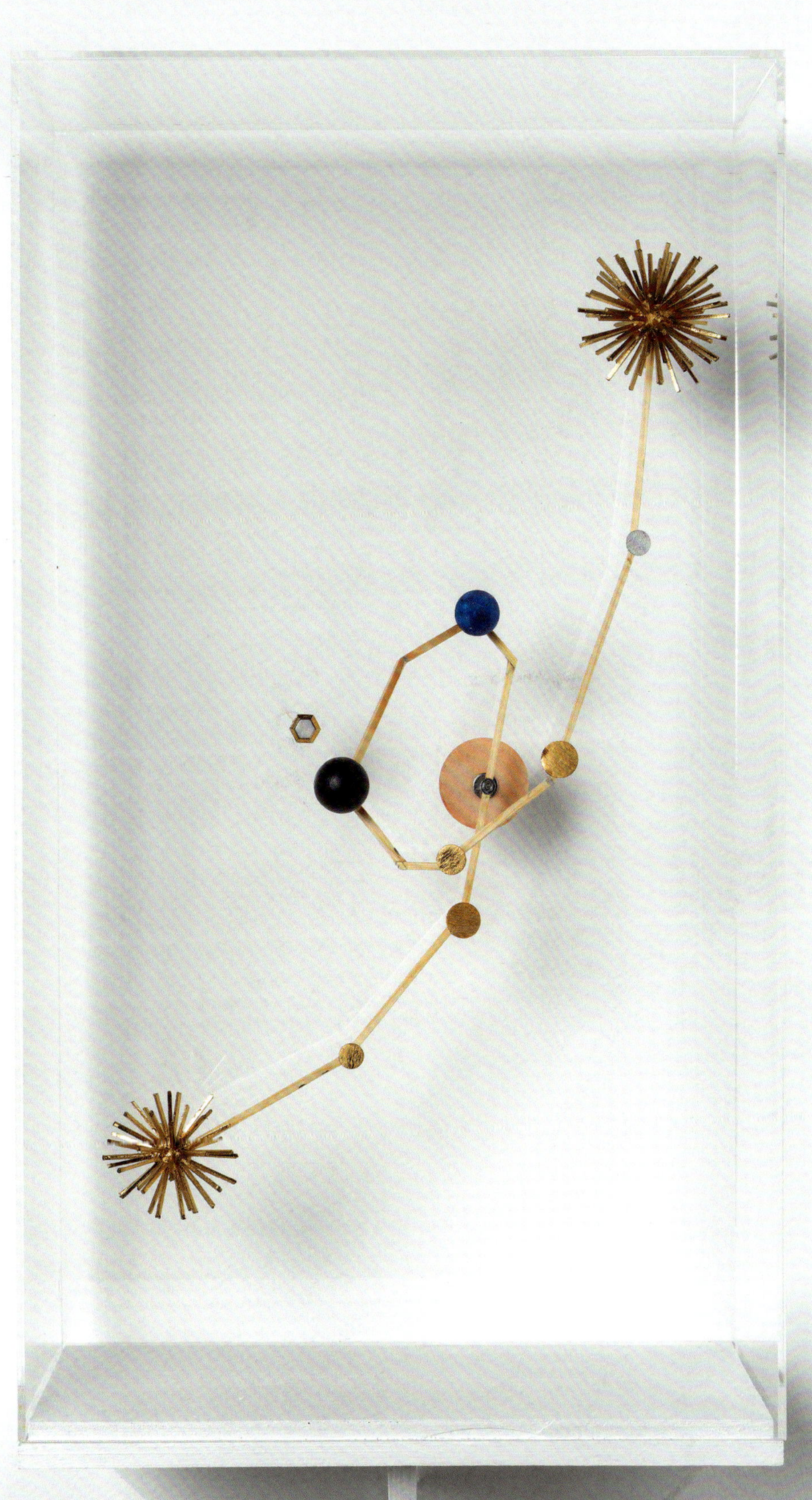

BENÍTEZ

Mobile +1 786 2539823

galería elba benítez
ES-28004 Madrid | C/ San Lorenzo 11
Phone +34 91 3080468 | Fax +34 91 3190169
info@elbabenitez.com | www.elbabenitez.com
Director Elba Benítez

Artists at
Art Basel Miami Beach | **Claudia Andujar**
Yaima Carrazana
Carlos Garaicoa
Mario García Torres
Vik Muniz
Ernesto Neto

Gallery Information | Further artists represented: Ignasi Aballí
Miriam Bäckström
Carlos Bunga
Cabello/Carceller
Juan Cruz
Gintaras Didžiapetris
El Último Grito
Fernanda Fragateiro
David Goldblatt
Cristina Iglesias
Francisco Ruiz de Infante
Francesc Torres

Collaborations with: Chantal Akerman
Lothar Baumgarten
Hreinn Fridfinnsson
Jorge Pardo
Alexander Sokurov

Claudia Andujar
Inauguração da 6a Bienal de São Paulo (Opening of the 6th Bienal de São Paulo), 1961
Silver gelatin print, 150 x 100 cm

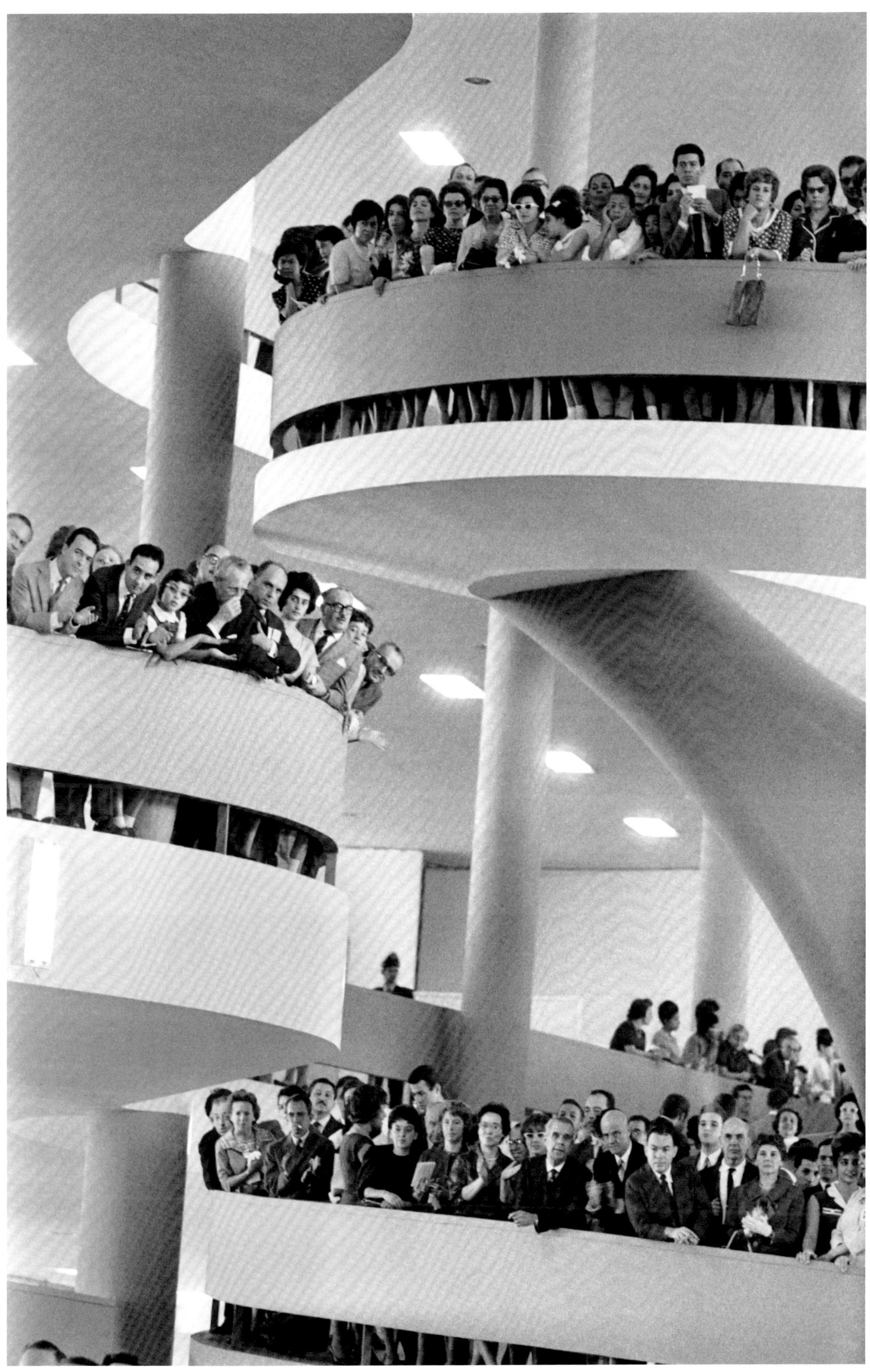

BENZACAR

Ruth Benzacar Galería de Arte
AR-C1005AAT Buenos Aires | Florida 1000
Phone +54 11 43138480 | Fax +54 11 43138480
info@ruthbenzacar.com | www.ruthbenzacar.com
Director Orly Benzacar

Artists at Art Basel Miami Beach | **Eduardo Basualdo**
Leo Chiachio & Daniel Giannone
Leandro Erlich
Carlos Herrera
Jorge Macchi
Mondongo
Liliana Porter

Gallery Information | Founded in 1965, Ruth Benzacar Galería de Arte has consistently been committed to contemporary art, focusing special attention on the work produced by Argentine artists.

Further artists represented: Flavia Da Rin
Marina De Caro
Leopoldo Estol
Max Gómez Canle
Carlos Huffmann
Luciana Lamothe
Marcos López
Fabián Marcaccio
Pablo Reinoso
Miguel Angel Ríos
Pablo Siquier
Adrián Villar Rojas

Eduardo Basualdo
Donde las aguas se juntan, 2012
Pencil on paper, 29 x 39 cm

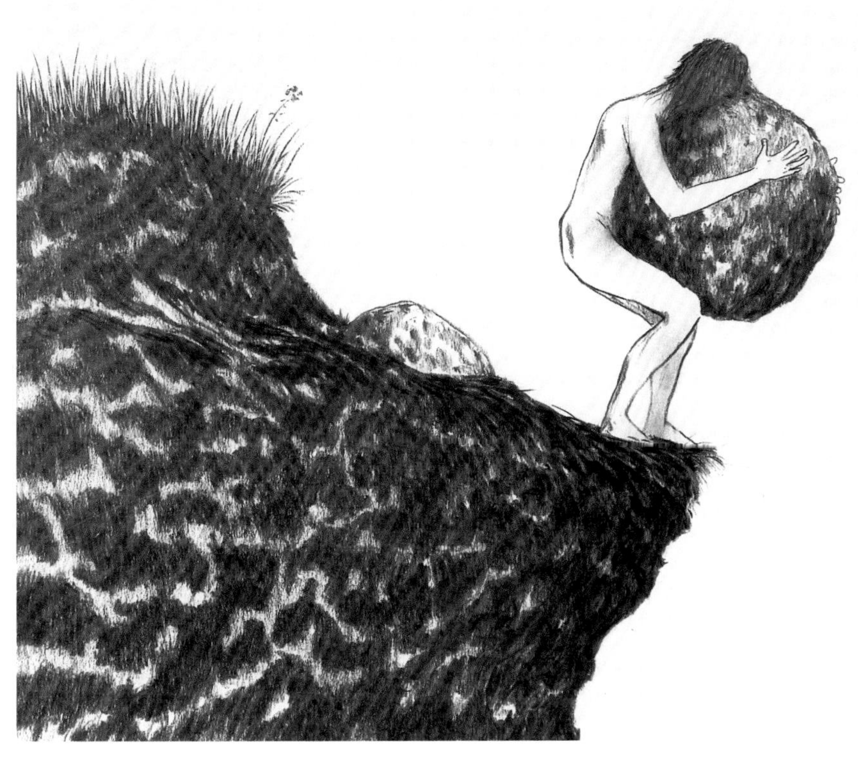

BERGGRUEN

Mobile +1 415 269 46 29

John Berggruen Gallery
US-San Francisco, CA 94108 | 228 Grant Avenue
Phone +1 415 781 46 29 | Fax +1 415 781 01 26
info@berggruen.com | www.berggruen.com
Directors John Berggruen
Gretchen Berggruen
Tatem Read

Artists at
Art Basel Miami Beach | **Josef Albers**
John Baldessari
Stephan Balkenhol
David Bates
Robert Bechtle
Christopher Brown
Alexander Calder
Willem de Kooning
Mark di Suvero
Richard Diebenkorn
Jim Dine
Iran do Espírito Santo
Helen Frankenthaler
Tom Friedman
Alexander Gorlizki
Isca Greenfield-Sanders
Stephen Hannock
Anish Kapoor
Yayoi Kusama
Enrique Martínez Celaya
Tom McKinley
Julie Mehretu
Beatriz Milhazes
Nathan Oliveira
Tom Otterness
David Park
Martin Puryear
Joel Shapiro
Kiki Smith
Wayne Thiebaud
William T. Wiley

Gallery Information | John Berggruen Gallery was founded in 1970 and has been a member of the Art Dealers Association of America since 1975.

John Baldessari
Pointing Hand, Desk, Lights, and Observers (Courtroom), 1995
Black-and-white and color photographs, acrylic, oil stick, pencil on paper,
100½ x 90¼ inches

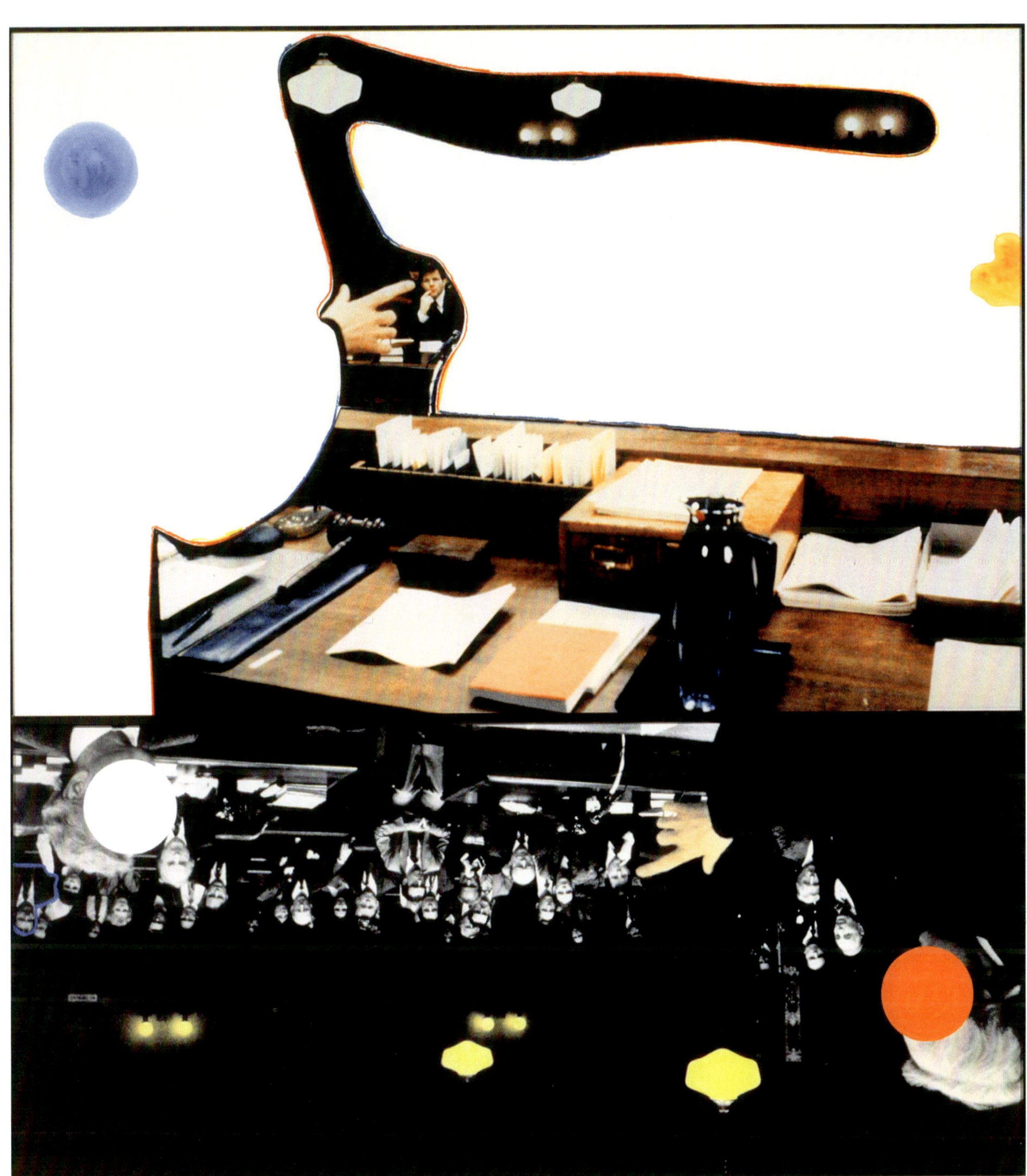

BERNIER/ELIADES

Mobile +30 69 44 30 48 28, +41 79 200 41 62

Gallery Bernier/Eliades
GR-11851 Athens | Eptachalkou 11
Phone +30 210 341 39 35 | +30 210 341 39 36 | Fax +30 210 341 39 38
bernier@bernier-eliades.gr | www.bernier-eliades.gr
Directors Jean Bernier
Marina Eliades

Artists at
Art Basel Miami Beach | **Pier Paolo Calzolari**
Wim Delvoye
Carroll Dunham
Lionel Estève
Gilbert & George
Hannah Greely
Cameron Jamie
Dionisis Kavallieratos
Jannis Kounellis
Justin Lieberman
Jonathan Meese
Marisa Merz
Tony Oursler

Gallery Information | The Bernier/Eliades Gallery was founded in Athens in 1977 and has since then continued working dynamically in the field of contemporary art in Greece.

After 21 years in its old space in Kolonaki, the commercial center of Athens, since January 1999 the gallery has been housed in a Neoclassical building in Thission, the historic center of Athens at the foot of the Acropolis.

Since the gallery went into operation, Jean Bernier and Marina Eliades have introduced the Greek public to numerous artistic currents, such as Arte Povera, Minimalism, Land and Conceptual Art, and the younger generation of American and European artists.

Further artists represented: Haluk Akakçe
Giovanni Anselmo
John Baldessari
Herbert Brandl
Stéphane Calais
Alan Charlton
Tony Cragg
Donald Judd
Moshekwa Langa
Richard Long
Mario Merz
Juan Muñoz
Nikos Navridis
Daniel Richter
Ry Rocklen
Susan Rothenberg
Ulrich Rückriem
Ed Ruscha
Charles Sandison
Thomas Schütte
Jim Shaw
Keith Sonnier
Christiana Soulou
Jeffrey Vallance
Marnie Weber
Sue Williams
Robert Wilson

Carroll Dunham
Late Trees #1, 2011
Mixed media on linen,
223.5 x 172.7 cm, framed:
230.5 x 179.8 cm

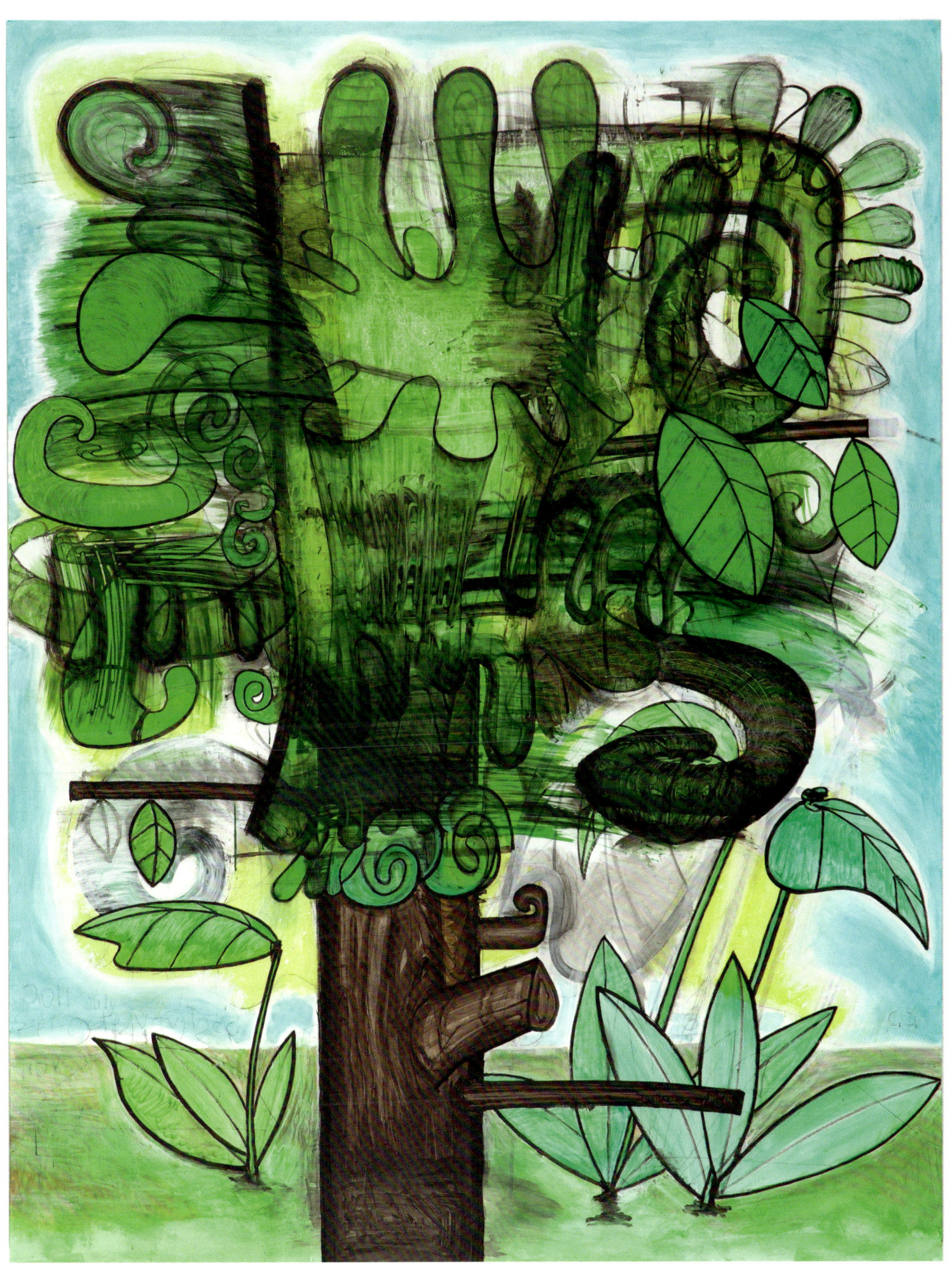

BOESKY

Marianne Boesky Gallery
US-New York, NY 10011 | 509 West 24th Street
Phone +1 212 680 98 89 | Fax +1 212 680 98 97
info@marianneboeskygallery.com | www.marianneboeskygallery.com
Directors Adrian Turner
Annie Rana
Serra Pradhan
Ricky Manne

Marianne Boesky Gallery
US-New York, NY 10065 | 118 East 64th Street
Phone +1 212 680 98 89 | Fax +1 212 680 98 97

Artists at
Art Basel Miami Beach | **Diana Al-Hadid**
Andisheh Avini
Pier Paolo Calzolari
Jay Heikes
Adam Helms
Donald Moffett
William O'Brien
Anthony Pearson
Kon Trubkovich
Hannah van Bart
Claudia Weiser

Further artists represented | Jesse Chapman
Sue De Beer
Svenja Deininger
Robert Elfgen
Rachel Feinstein
Barnaby Furnas
Melissa Gordon
Yuichi Higashionna
Jacco Olivier
Hans Op de Beeck
Salvatore Scarpitta
Mindy Shapero
John Waters

Kon Trubkovich
Put My Guns in the Ground, 2012
Oil on canvas, 72 x 60 inches

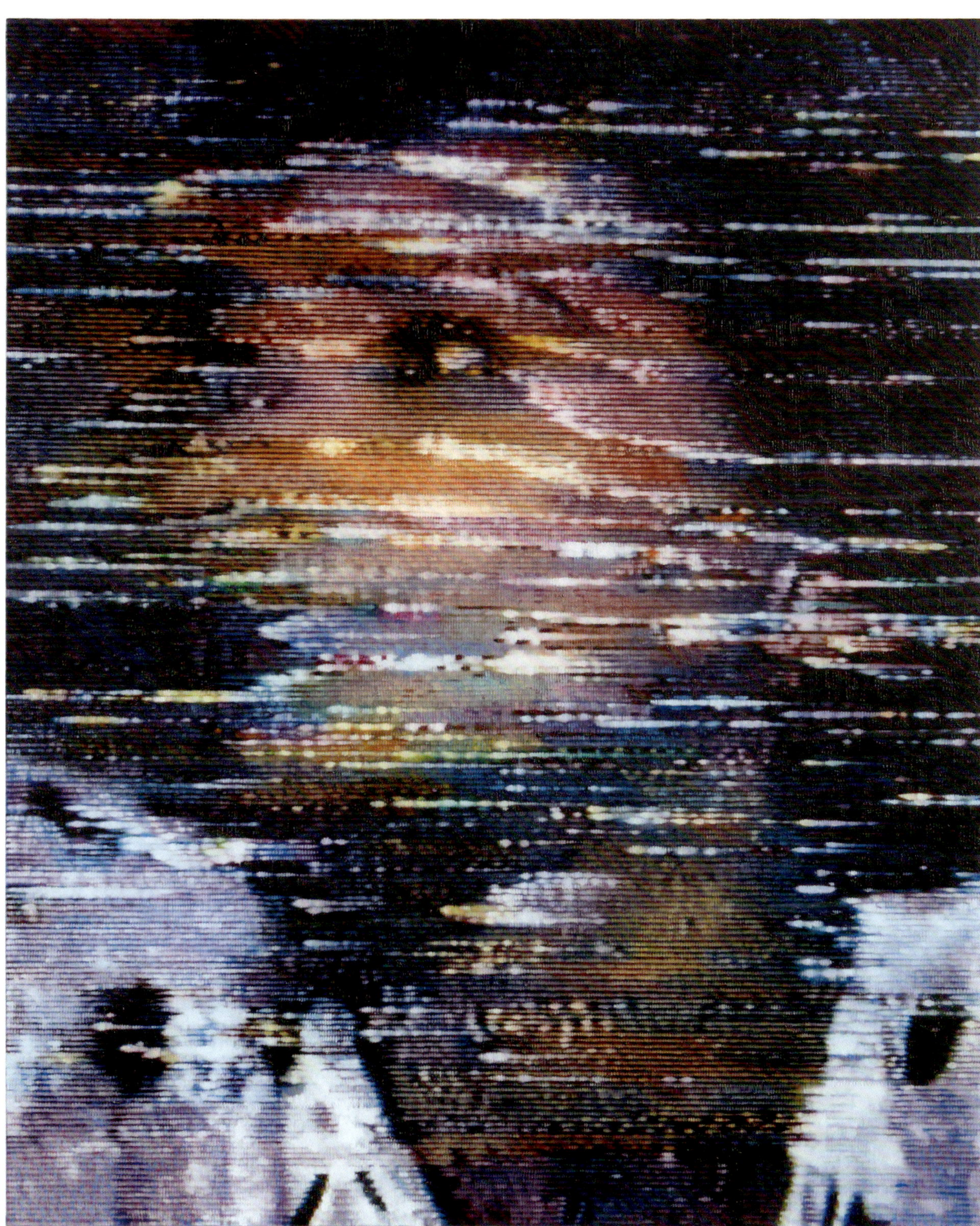

BONAKDAR

Tanya Bonakdar Gallery
US-New York, NY 10011 | 521 West 21st Street
Phone +1 212 414 41 44 | Fax +1 212 414 15 35
mail@tanyabonakdargallery.com | www.tanyabonakdargallery.com
Directors Tanya Bonakdar
Ethan Sklar
Claire Pauley
Renee Coppola

Artists at Art Basel Miami Beach | **Atelier Van Lieshout**
Uta Barth
Martin Boyce
Sandra Cinto
Phil Collins
Mat Collishaw
Mark Dion
Olafur Eliasson
Siobhán Hapaska
Sabine Hornig
Teresa Hubbard/Alexander Birchler
Ian Kiaer
Carla Klein
Liz Larner
Charles Long
Rita Lundqvist
Mark Manders
Jason Meadows
Ernesto Neto
Rivane Neuenschwander
Susan Philipsz
Peggy Preheim
Analia Saban
Tomas Saraceno
Thomas Scheibitz
Hannah Starkey
Haim Steinbach
Dirk Stewen
Jack Strange
Sarah Sze
Neal Tait
Jeffrey Vallance
Gillian Wearing
Nicole Wermers

A-C | **Tomas Saraceno**
Cloud City, 2012
Stainless steel and acrylic,
336 x 348 x 648 inches
Installation view, The Iris
and B. Gerald Cantor Roof
Garden, The Metropolitan
Museum of Art, New York,
NY, May 15-November 4,
2012

A

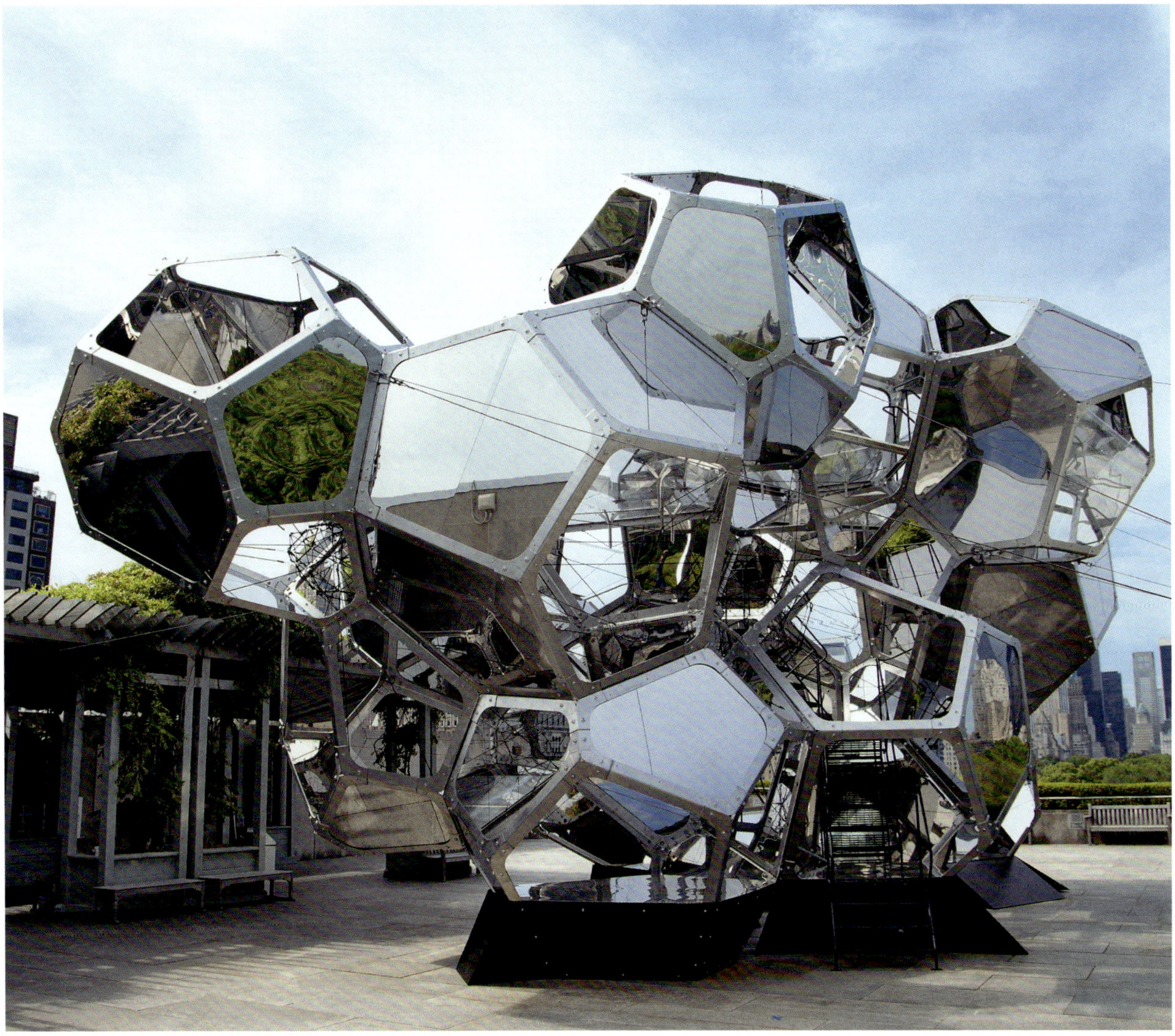

B

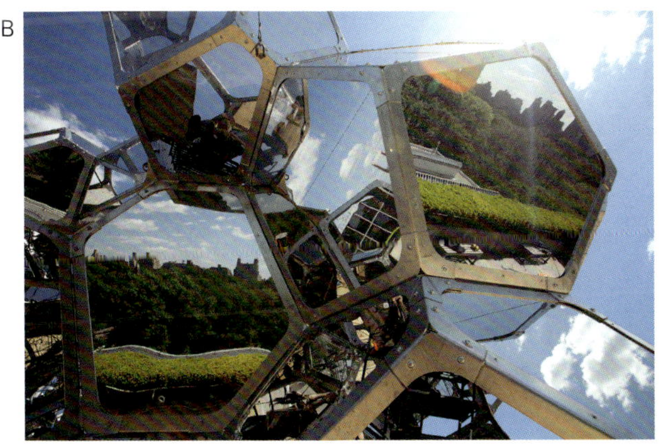

C

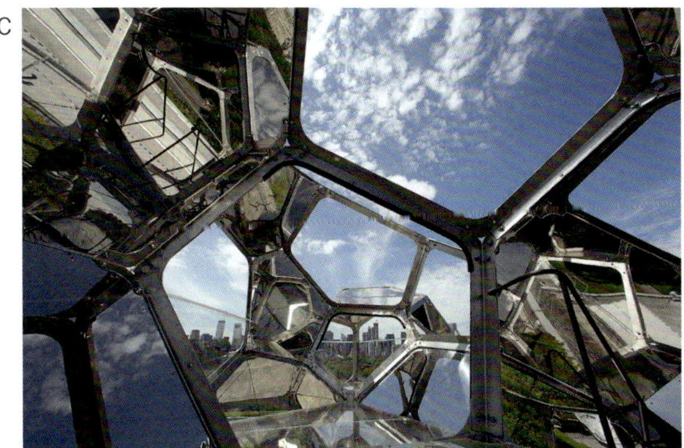

BOONE

Mobile +1 917 861 29 29

Mary Boone Gallery
US-New York, NY 10151 | 745 Fifth Avenue
Phone +1 212 752 29 29 | Fax +1 212 752 39 39
info@maryboonegallery.com | www.maryboonegallery.com
Directors Thomas Arnold
Jim Oliver

Mary Boone Gallery
US-New York, NY 10011 | 541 West 24th Street
Phone +1 212 752 29 29 | Fax +1 212 752 93 39
info@maryboonegallery.com | www.maryboonegallery.com
Director Ron Warren

Artists at Art Basel Miami Beach | **Ai Weiwei**
Joseph Beuys
Ross Bleckner
James Lee Byars
Nick Cave
Patty Chang
Francesco Clemente
Will Cotton
Eric Fischl
Chie Fueki
Luis Gispert
Peter Halley
Hilary Harkness
Jacob Hashimoto
Jim Isermann
Mel Kendrick
Barbara Kruger
Barry Le Va
Sherrie Levine
Liu Xiaodong
Andrew Masullo
Aleksandra Mir
Olivier Mosset
Ernst Wilhelm Nay
Marc Quinn
David Salle
Peter Saul
Keith Sonnier
Joe Zucker

Peter Saul
Peter Saul vs. Pop Art, 2012
Acrylic on canvas, 75 x 72 cm

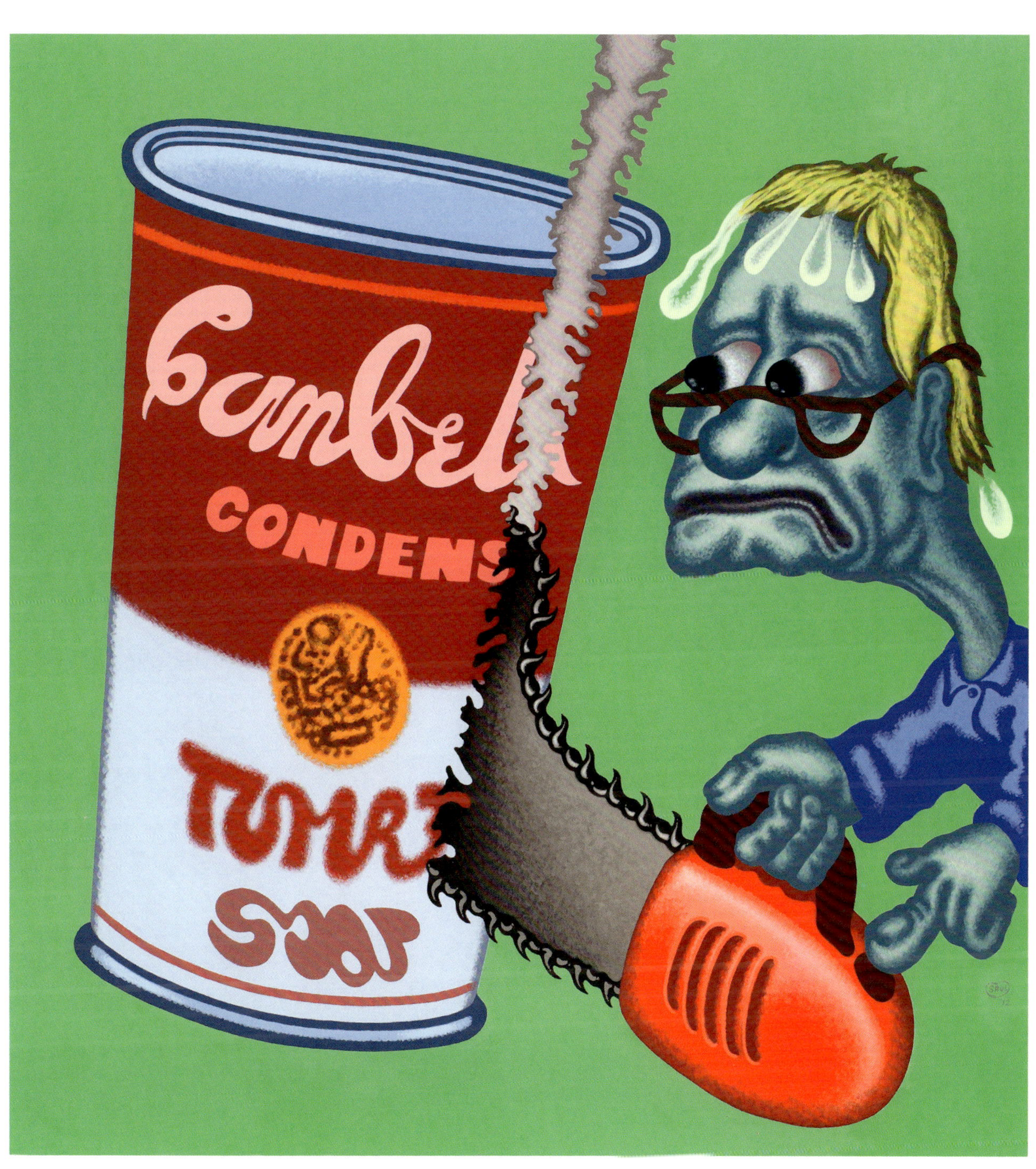
CONDENS

BORCH JENSEN

Mobile +45 27 58 46 76

Niels Borch Jensen Editions
DK-2300 Copenhagen | Prags Boulevard 49 E II
Phone +45 32 95 09 36
info@nielsborchjensen.dk | www.nielsborchjensen.dk
Directors Niels Borch Jensen
Lone Weigelt

Artists at
Art Basel Miami Beach | **Iñaki Bonillas**
Tacita Dean
Olafur Eliasson
Douglas Gordon
Keith Haring
Martin Kippenberger
Al Taylor
Danh Vo

Gallery Information | Since its foundation in 1979, the aim of Niels Borch Jensen Editions has been to publish print projects featuring the best contemporary artists – projects that stand as important and independent works by these artists. Our collaboration with the artists we publish usually continues over many years, and we are often able to provide well-rounded surveys of their work.

Further artists represented: William Anastasi
Lewis Baltz
Georg Baselitz
Thomas Demand
A K Dolven
Elmgreen & Dragset
Rodney Graham
Anton Henning
Carsten Höller
Clay Ketter
Per Kirkeby
Takehito Koganezawa
Bjarne Melgaard
Boris Mikhailov
Albert Oehlen
João Penalva
Tal R
Robin Rhode
Superflex
Rosemarie Trockel
Alan Uglow

Al Taylor
Mr., 1991
Gravure, 66 x 58 cm
From the set *Mr. and Mrs.*

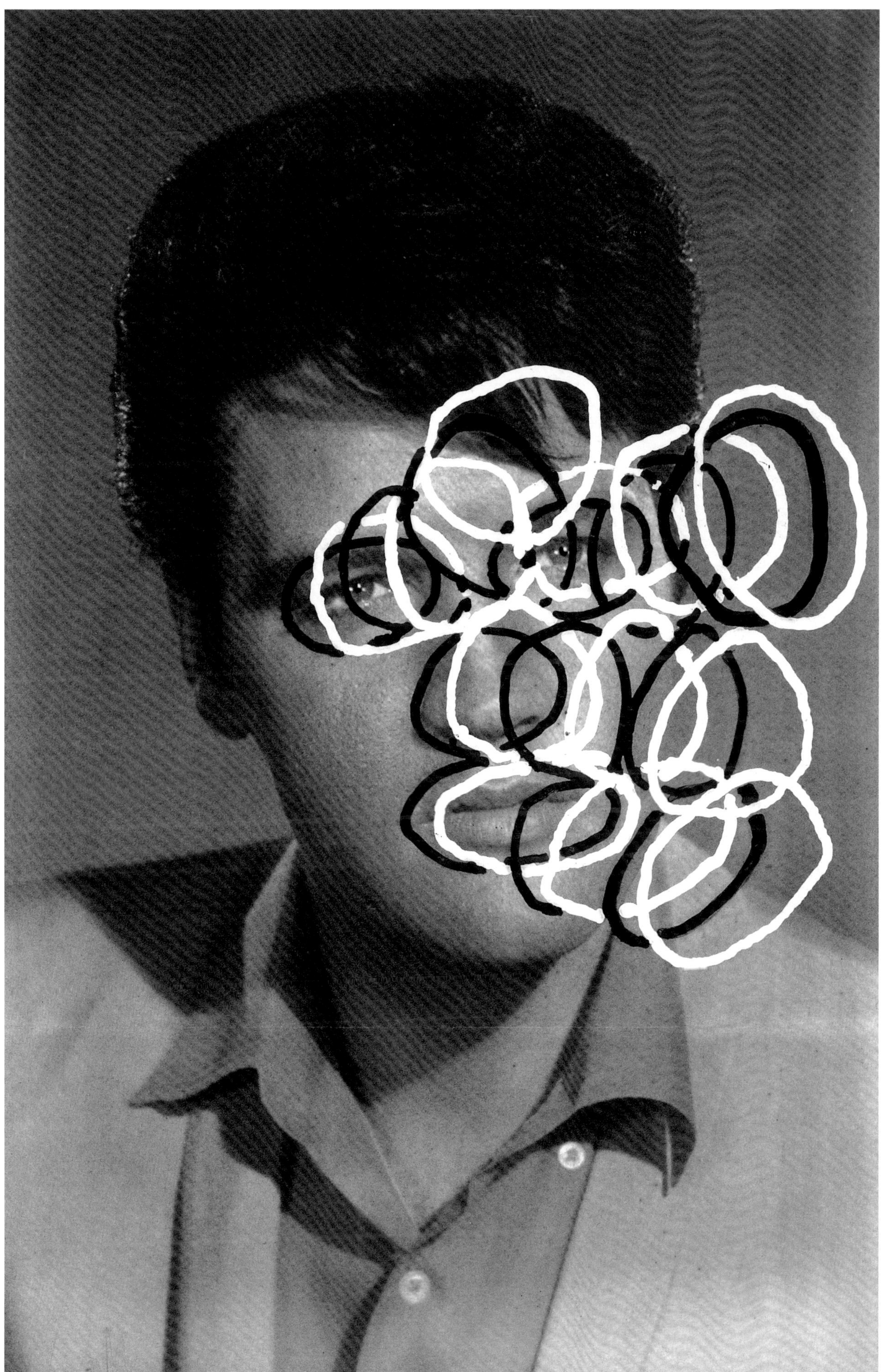

BORTOLAMI

Bortolami
US-New York, NY 10011 | 520 West 20th Street
Phone +1 212 727 20 50 | Fax +1 212 727 20 60
info@bortolamigallery.com | www.bortolamigallery.com
Directors Stefania Bortolami
Nicole Will
Christine Messineo
Charles Libeert

Artists at
Art Basel Miami Beach | **Richard Aldrich**
Tom Burr
Piero Golia
Anna Ostoya

Further artists represented | Avner Ben-Gal
Daniel Buren
Shane Campbell
Morgan Fisher
Michel François
Thilo Heinzmann
Patrick Hill
Piotr Janas
Barbara Kasten
Scott King
Jonathan Meese
Peter Peri
Ben Schumacher
Gary Webb
Eric Wesley
Aaron Young

Anna Ostoya
Invitations No 2, 2012
Acrylic, oil paint, archival print,
paper on art board gesso panel,
50 x 40 cm

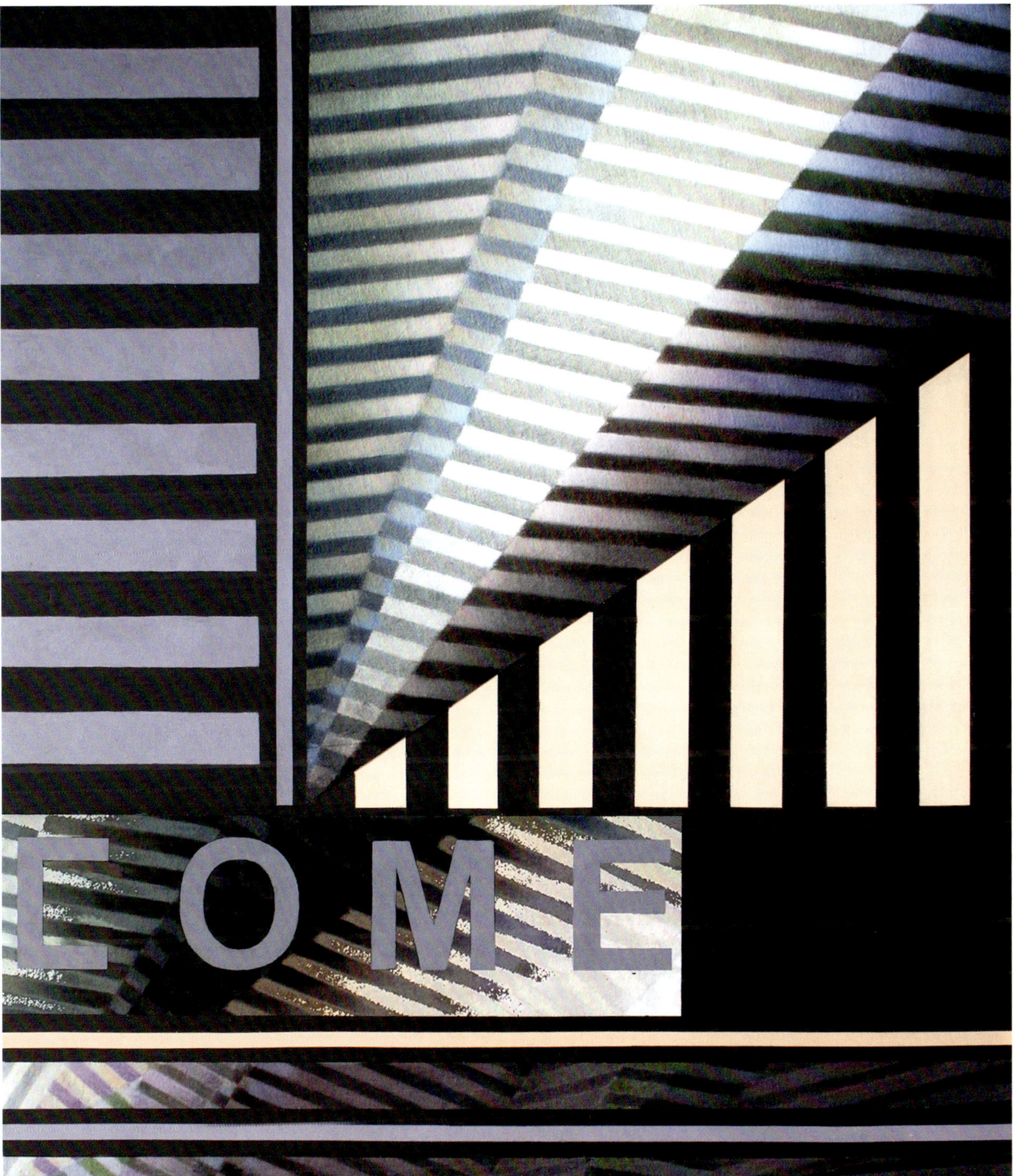
COME

BQ

Mobile +49 172 787 95 51

BQ
DE-10178 Berlin | Weydingerstrasse 10
Phone +49 30 23 45 73 16 | Fax +49 30 23 45 73 25
info@bqberlin.de | www.bqberlin.de
Directors Jörn Bötnagel
Yvonne Quirmbach

Artists at
Art Basel Miami Beach | **Dirk Bell**
Alexandra Bircken
Carina Brandes
Matti Braun
Owen Gump
Kriwet
Friedrich Kunath
Bojan Sarcevic

Further artists represented | Andrew Kerr
David Shrigley
Marcus Steinweg
Reinhard Voigt
Richard Wright

Carina Brandes
Untitled, 2012
Black-and-white photograph
on barite paper, 30.4 x 30 cm
Edition of 4

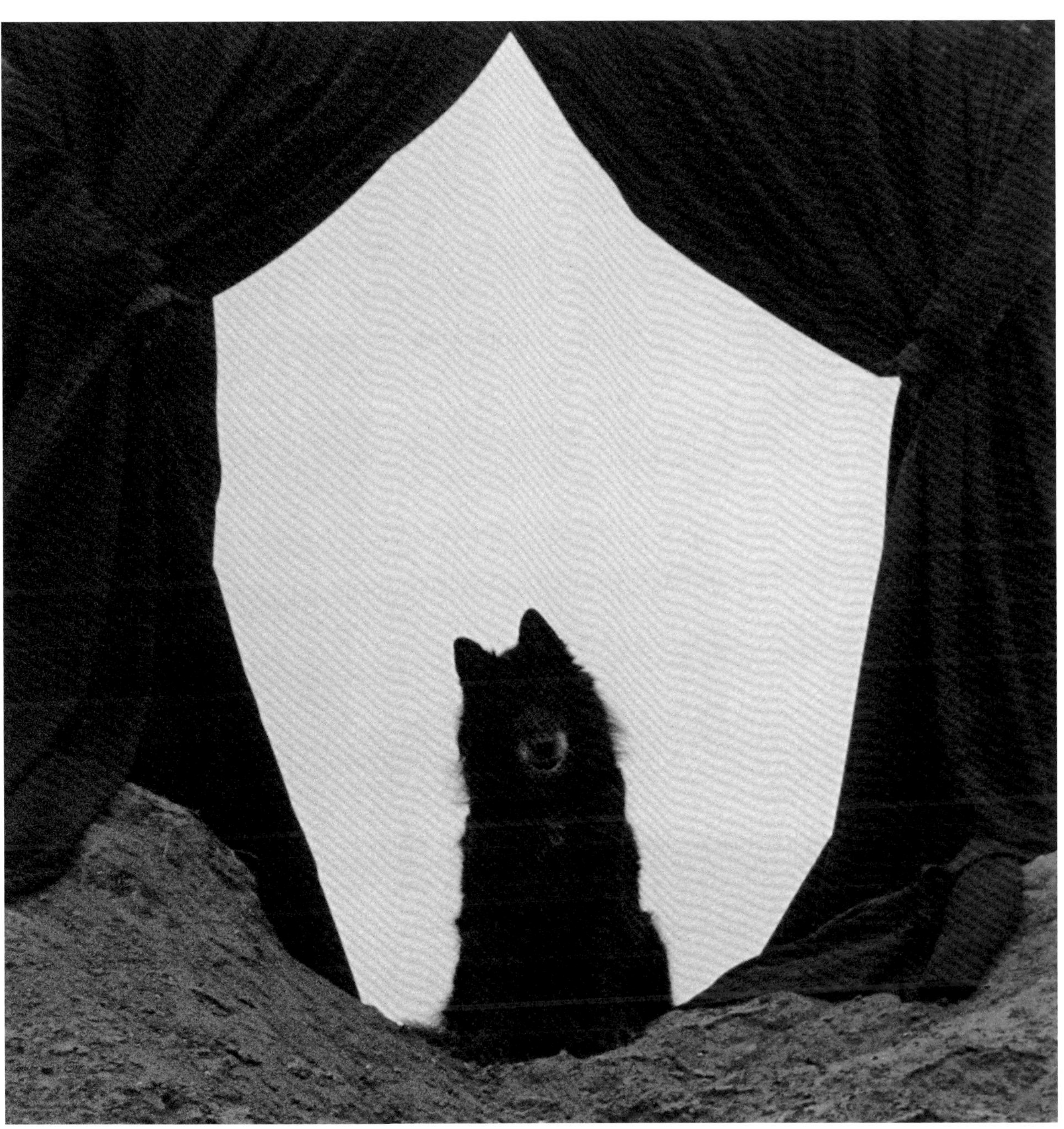

BRITO

Luciana Brito Galeria
BR-São Paulo 0454-7003 | Rua Gomes de Carvalho, 842
Phone +55 11 38420634 | Fax +55 11 38420635
info@lucianabritogaleria.com.br | www.lucianabritogaleria.com.br
Director Luciana Brito

Artists at
Art Basel Miami Beach | **Ricardo Basbaum**
Waldemar Cordeiro
Rochelle Costi
Geraldo de Barros
Pablo Lobato
Anthony McCall
Allan McCollum
Caio Reisewitz
Regina Silveira
Tiago Tebet
Delson Uchôa
Héctor Zamora
Raphaël Zarka

Further artists represented | Marina Abramovic
Lucas Bambozzi
Rafael Carneiro
Saint Clair Cemin
Fabiana de Barros/Michel Favre
Leandro Erlich
Paula Garcia
Alex Katz
João Luiz Musa
Mônica Nador
Fyodor Pavlov-Andreevich
Liliana Porter
Tobias Putrih
Eder Santos

Héctor Zamora
Orden y Progreso, 2012
Digital print on paper
Centro Abierto, Lima

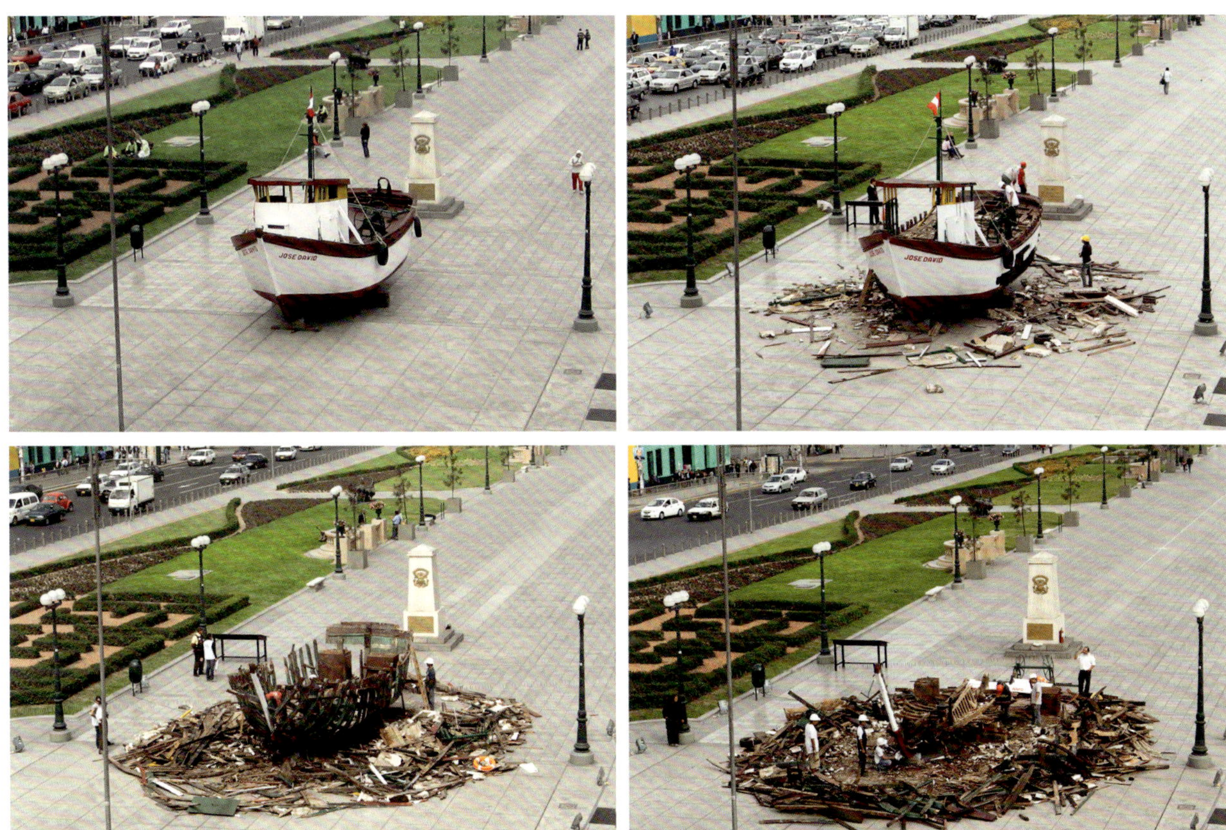
JOSE DAVID

BROWN

Gavin Brown's enterprise
US-New York, NY 10014 | 620 Greenwich Street
Phone +1 212 627 52 58 | Fax +1 212 627 52 61
gallery@gavinbrown.biz | www.gavinbrown.biz
Directors Gavin Brown
Corinna Durland
Lucy Chadwick

Artists at Art Basel Miami Beach | **Franz Ackermann**
Uri Aran
Thomas Bayrle
Dirk Bell
Jennifer Bornstein
Joe Bradley
Kerstin Brätsch
Martin Creed
Verne Dawson
Jeremy Deller
Peter Doig
Urs Fischer
Dara Friedman
Mark Handforth
Jonathan Horowitz
Alex Katz
Christopher Knowles
Udomsak Krisanamis
Ella Kruglyanska
Mark Leckey
Silke Otto-Knapp
Laura Owens
Oliver Payne
Elizabeth Peyton
Steven Pippin
Rob Pruitt
Nick Relph
Steven Shearer
Frances Stark
Katja Strunz
Sturtevant
Spencer Sweeney
Rirkrit Tiravanija

Laura Owens
Untitled, 2011
Oil, Flashe, and charcoal on linen,
73 x 51 inches

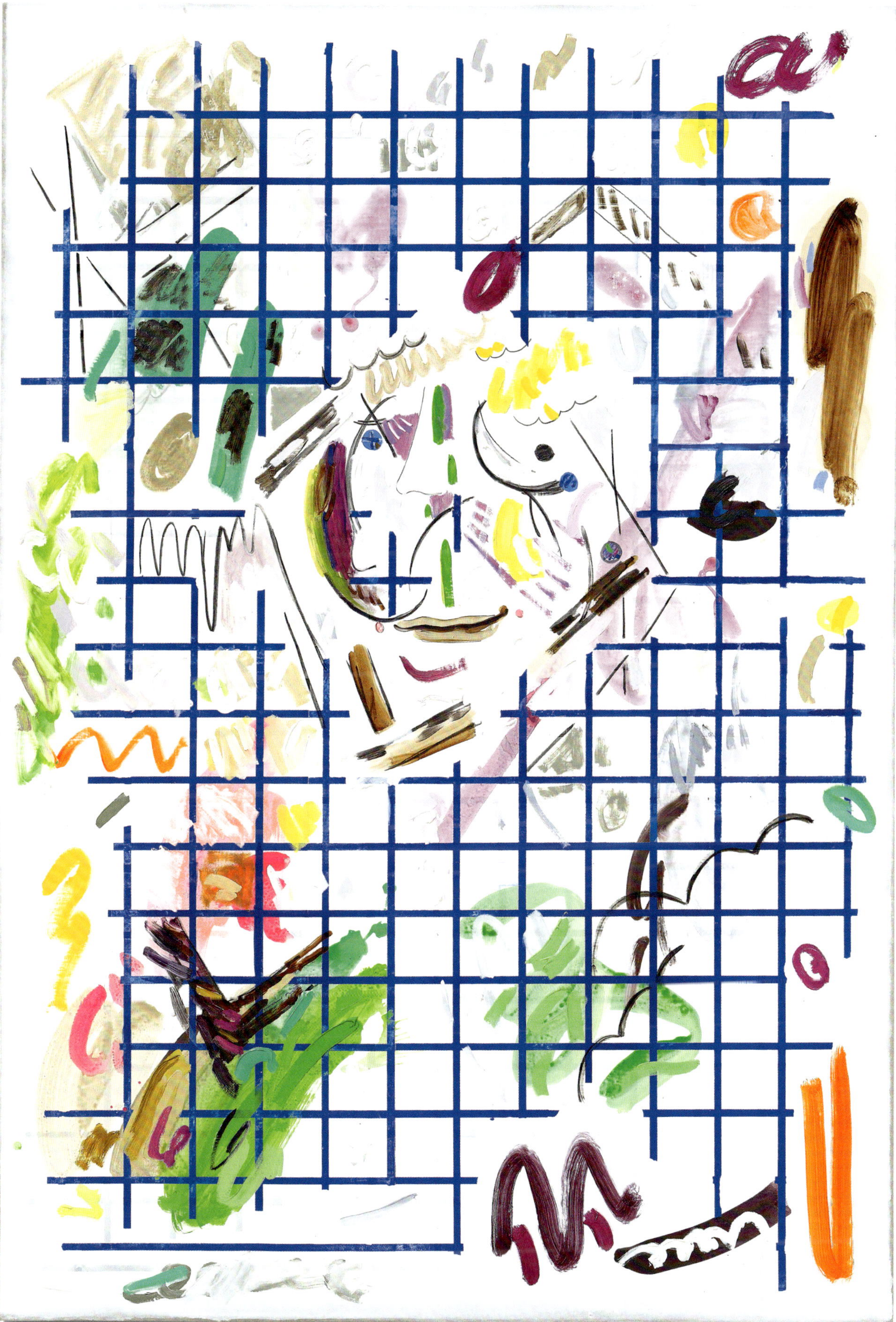

BUCHHOLZ

Mobile +49 170 4300153

Galerie Buchholz
DE-50667 Cologne | Neven-DuMont-Strasse 17
Phone +49 221 2574946 | Fax +49 221 253351
post@galeriebuchholz.de | www.galeriebuchholz.de
Directors Daniel Buchholz
Christopher Müller

Galerie Buchholz
DE-10719 Berlin | Fasanenstrasse 30
Phone +49 30 88624056 | Fax +49 30 88624057
post@galeriebuchholz.de | www.galeriebuchholz.de
Directors Daniel Buchholz
Christopher Müller

Artists at
Art Basel Miami Beach | **Tomma Abts**
Nairy Baghramian
Tony Conrad
Jeroen de Rijke/Willem de Rooij
Willem de Rooij
Simon Denny
Lukas Duwenhögger
Thomas Eggerer
Vincent Fecteau
Morgan Fisher
Isa Genzken
Jack Goldstein
Julian Göthe
Richard Hawkins
Jochen Klein
Jutta Koether
Michael Krebber
Mark Leckey
Sam Lewitt
Lucy McKenzie
Henrik Olesen
Paulina Olowska
Silke Otto-Knapp
Mathias Poledna
Florian Pumhösl
R.H. Quaytman
Frances Stark
Josef Strau
Stefan Thater
Cheyney Thompson
Wolfgang Tillmans
Danh Vo
Cosima von Bonin
Martin Wong
Katharina Wulff
Cerith Wyn Evans

Jack Goldstein
The Portrait of Père Tanguy, 1974
16mm, color, sound, 4min
Film stills

THE PORTRAIT OF PERE TANGUY

© 1974 JACK GOLDSTEIN

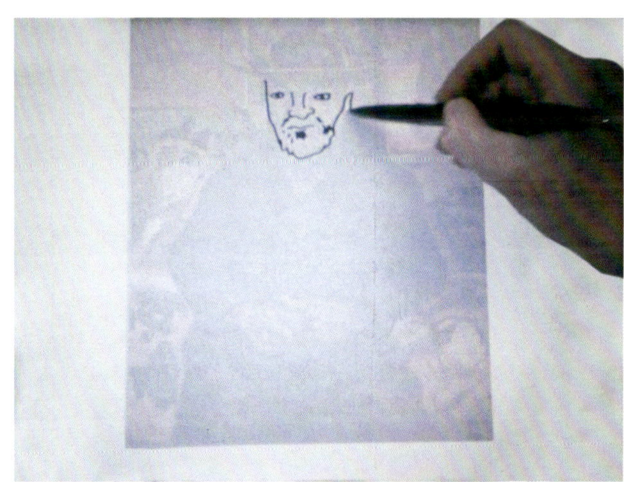

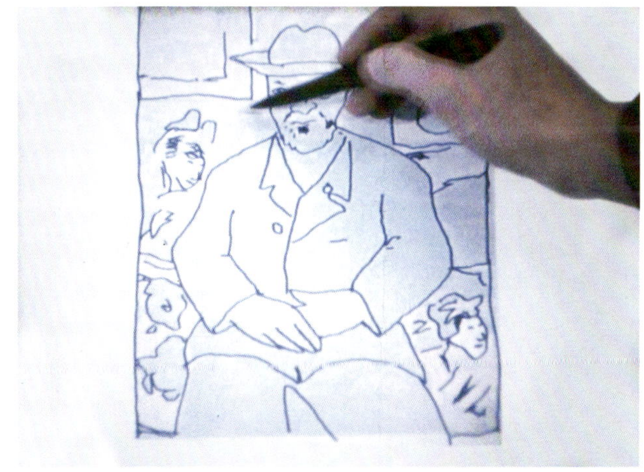

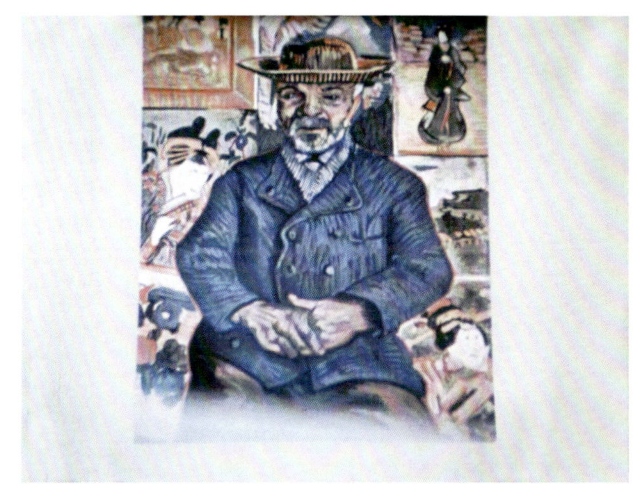

BUCHMANN

Buchmann Galerie
DE-10969 Berlin | Charlottenstrasse 13
Phone +49 30 25 89 99 29 | Fax +49 30 25 89 99 39
info@buchmanngalerie.com | www.buchmanngalerie.com
Director André Buchmann

Buchmann Galerie
CH-6927 Agra (Lugano) | Via Gamee
Phone +41 91 980 08 30 | Fax +41 91 980 08 32
buchmann.lugano@bluewin.ch | www.buchmanngalerie.com
Director Elena Buchmann

Artists at
Art Basel Miami Beach | **Lawrence Carroll**
Tony Cragg
Wolfgang Laib
Wilhelm Mundt
Bettina Pousttchi
Fiona Rae
Yutaka Takanashi
William Tucker
Clare Woods

Gallery Information | Buchmann Galerie Berlin:
More than meets the eye, group show,
November 2012-January 2013
Tatsuo Miyajima, January/February 2013
Lawrence Carroll, March/April 2013
Bettina Pousttchi, May/June 2013

Buchmann Box Berlin:
Wilhelm Mundt, *Aluminium/Aluminum,*
November 2012-January 2013
Tony Cragg, *Waldzimmer,* January/February 2013

Buchmann Galerie Agra/Lugano:
Emilio Vedova, *Small Sculptures,*
November/December 2012

Further artists represented: Anna & Bernhard Blume
Daniel Buren
John Chamberlain
Sean Dawson
Zaha Hadid
Mario Merz
Tatsuo Miyajima
Arnold Odermatt
Gerda Steiner &
Jörg Lenzlinger
Joel Sternfeld
Felice Varini
Lawrence Weiner

Clare Woods
Don't Hope, 2012
Oil on aluminum, 150 x 100 cm

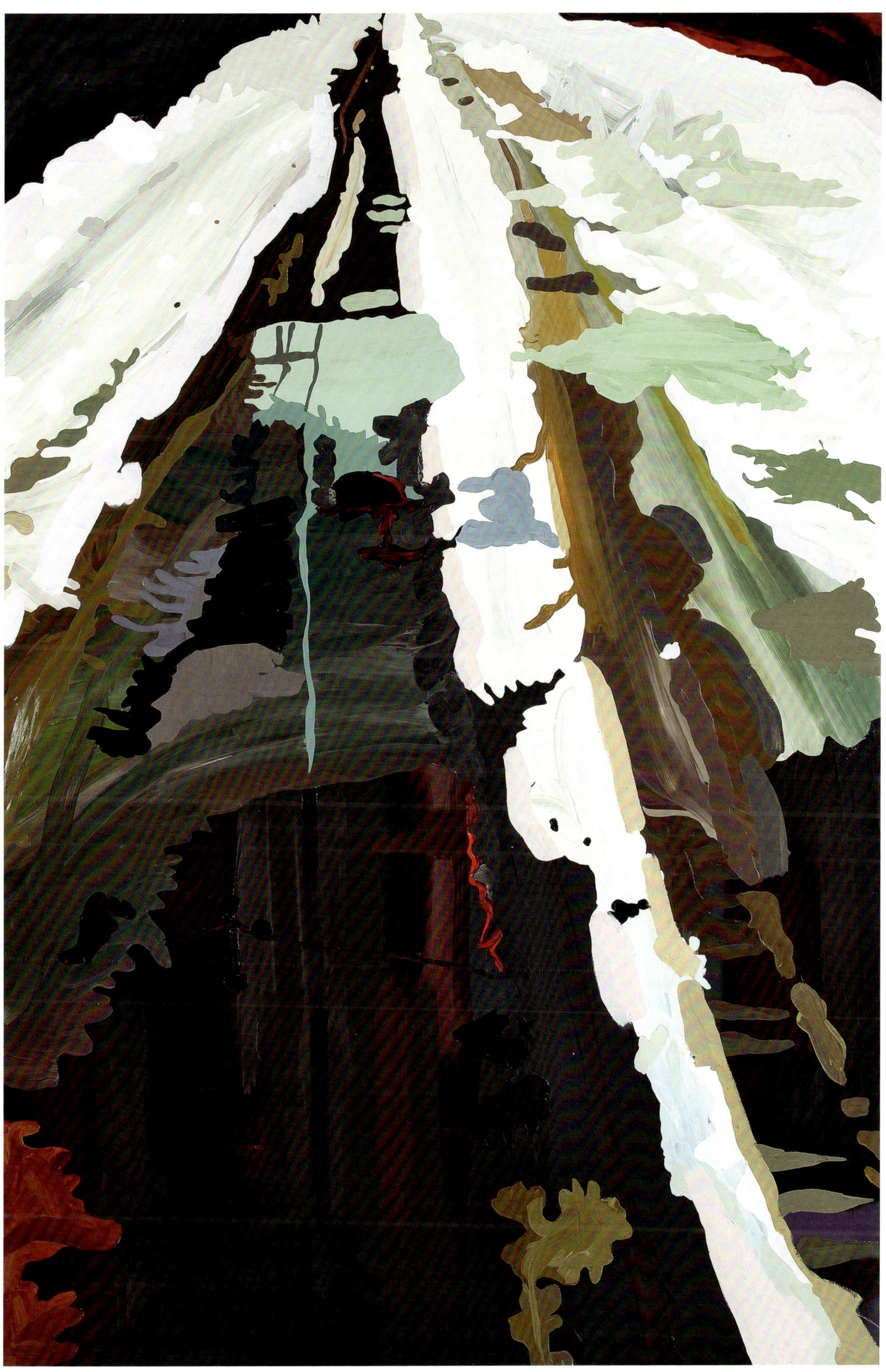

BUGADA & CARGNEL

Mobile +33 6 07 68 65 92

Bugada & Cargnel
FR-75019 Paris | 7-9, rue de l'Équerre
Phone +33 1 42 71 72 73 | Fax +33 1 42 71 72 00
contact@bugadacargnel.com | www.bugadacargnel.com
Directors Frédéric Bugada
Claudia Cargnel

Artists at Art Nova | Étienne Chambaud
Cyprien Gaillard
Julio Le Parc

Further artists represented | Wilfrid Almendra
Marc Bijl
Pierre Bismuth
Mat Collishaw
Nick Devereux
Piero Golia
Annika Larsson
Gianni Motti
Iris van Dongen
Nico Vascellari

For Art Nova at Art Basel Miami Beach, Gallery Bugada & Cargnel presents a coherent group of works which establishes a formal and conceptual dialogue between Julio Le Parc (*1928, Mendoza, Argentina; lives and works in Cachan, France), Étienne Chambaud (*1980, Mulhouse, France; lives and works in Paris, France), and Cyprien Gaillard (*1980, Paris, France; lives and works in Berlin, Germany, and New York, NY, United States). Ranging from Étienne Chambaud's collection of animal skins stretched over portrait format frames, to Cyprien Gaillard's landscapes, to Julio Le Parc's work systematically produced according to scientific principles, the works here play on the elaboration and alteration of a visual language, as well as on the idea of occulted vision, through the application of a systematic procedure. All the works function as palimpsests, with each of them guarding the traces of a former work while proposing a new composition, thus oscillating between inescapable repetition and continuous new horizons.

Julio Le Parc
Exhibition view, *The Eye of the Cyclops. Works from 1959 to 1971,* Galerie Bugada & Cargnel, Paris, September 10-November 5, 2011

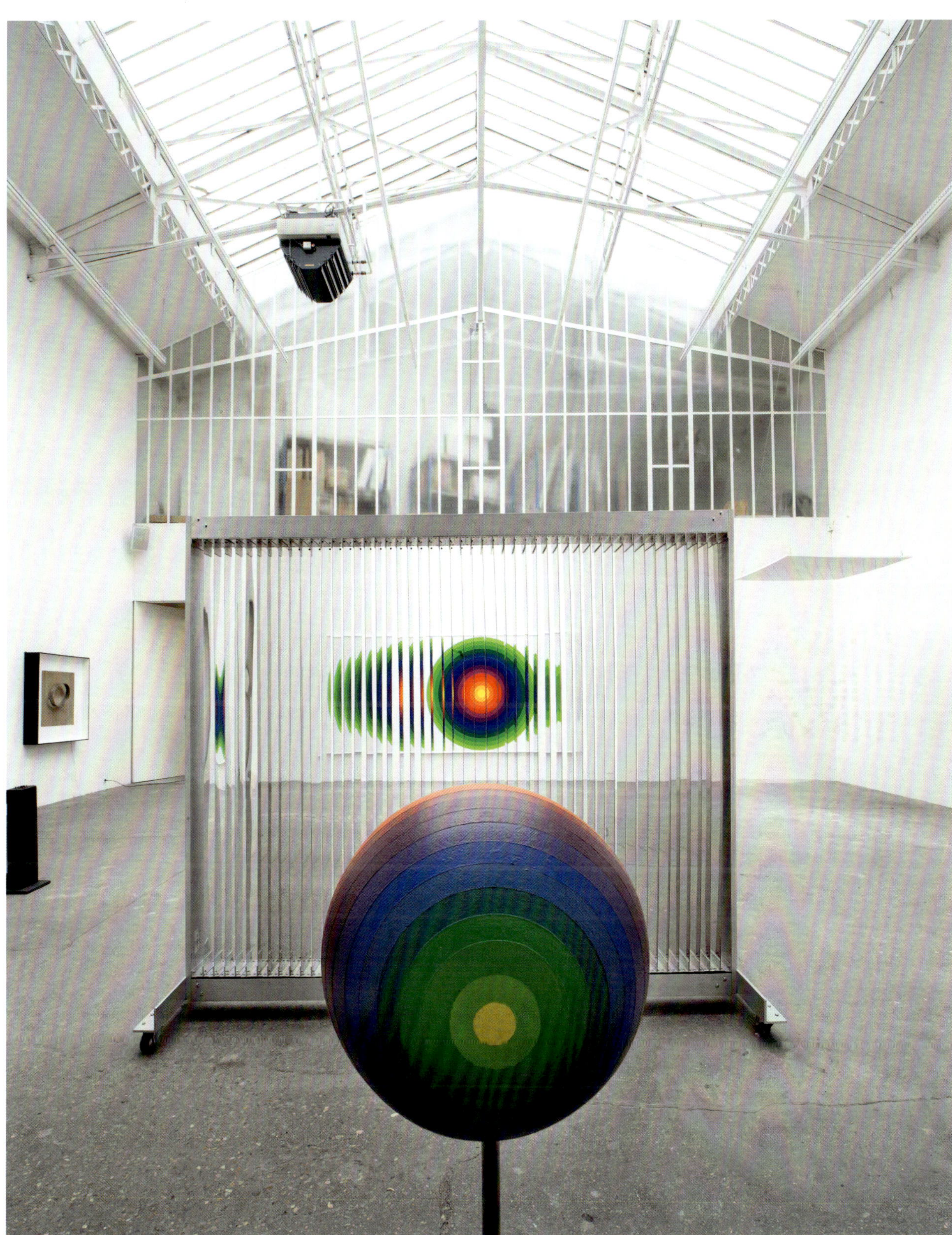

CAMPOLI PRESTI

Campoli Presti
GB-London E2 0EL | 223 Cambridge Heath Road
Phone +44 20 77 39 46 32
info@campolipresti.com | www.campolipresti.com
Directors Emanuela Campoli
Gil Presti
Cora Muennich

Campoli Presti
FR-75003 Paris | 6, rue de Braque
Phone +33 1 40 29 08 92
info@campolipresti.com | www.campolipresti.com
Directors Emanuela Campoli
Gil Presti

Artists at
Art Basel Miami Beach | **Liz Deschenes**
Jutta Koether
Scott Lyall
Olivier Mosset
Eileen Quinlan
Nora Schultz

Further artists represented | Roe Ethridge
Daniel Lefcourt
John Miller
Sean Paul
Pavel Pepperstein
Blake Rayne
Clément Rodzielski
Christoph Ruckhäberle
Reena Spaulings
Joanne Tatham & Tom O'Sullivan
Cheyney Thompson

Jutta Koether
Inkarnat gefunden festgestellt ausgeführt #2 (Diptych), 2009
Acrylic on canvas, 55 x 45 cm each

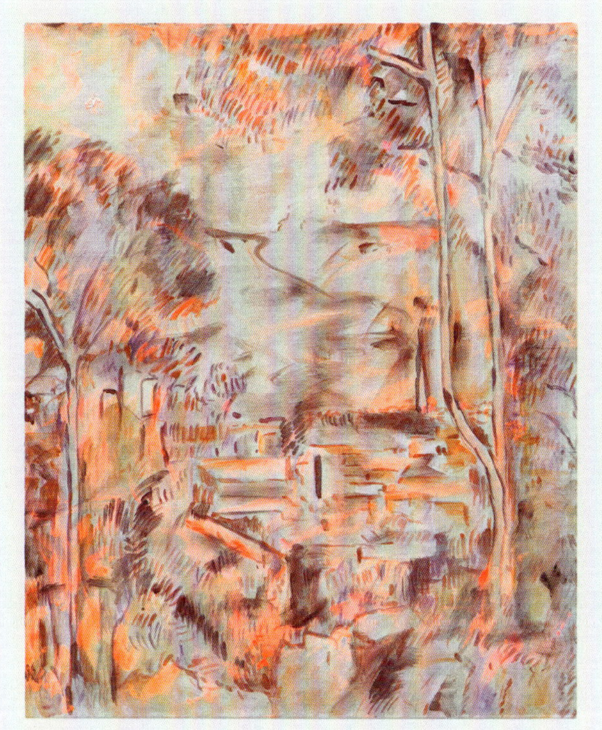

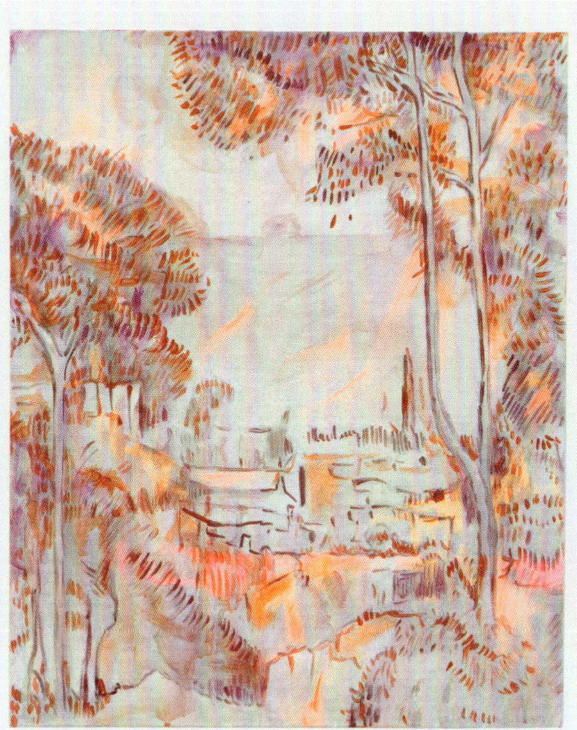

CARBERRY

Valerie Carberry Gallery
US-Chicago, IL 60611 | 875 N. Michigan Avenue, Suite 2510
Phone +1 312 397 99 90 | Fax +1 312 397 99 91
info@valeriecarberry.com | www.valeriecarberry.com
Directors Valerie Carberry
Susan Beagley

Artists at Art Basel Miami Beach | **Charles Biederman**
James Brooks
José de Rivera
Dorothy Dehner
Werner Drewes
Herbert Ferber
John Ferren
Carl Holty
Charles Howard
Paul Kelpe
Knud Merrild
Theodore Roszak
Judith Rothschild
Tony Smith
John Storrs
Jack Tworkov
Vaclav Vytlacil

Gallery Information | Valerie Carberry Gallery opened in 2002 with a focus on modern and contemporary American art. Areas of focus include abstract art of the 1930s and 1940s, modern sculpture, and the work of mid-career contemporary artists.

Gallery exhibitions are accompanied by scholarly publications written by leading art historians.

The gallery is a member of the Art Dealers Association of America.

Further artists represented: Judith Belzer
Susanna Coffey
Albert Gallatin
Sidney Gordin
Adolph Gottlieb
Grace Hartigan
Ellen Lanyon
Laura Letinsky
Jim Lutes
Louisa Matthíasdóttir
László Moholy-Nagy
Louise Nevelson
Charles Green Shaw
Evelyn Statsinger
Jean Xceron

Judith Rothschild
Pitt Street, 1950
Oil on canvas, 25 x 29 inches

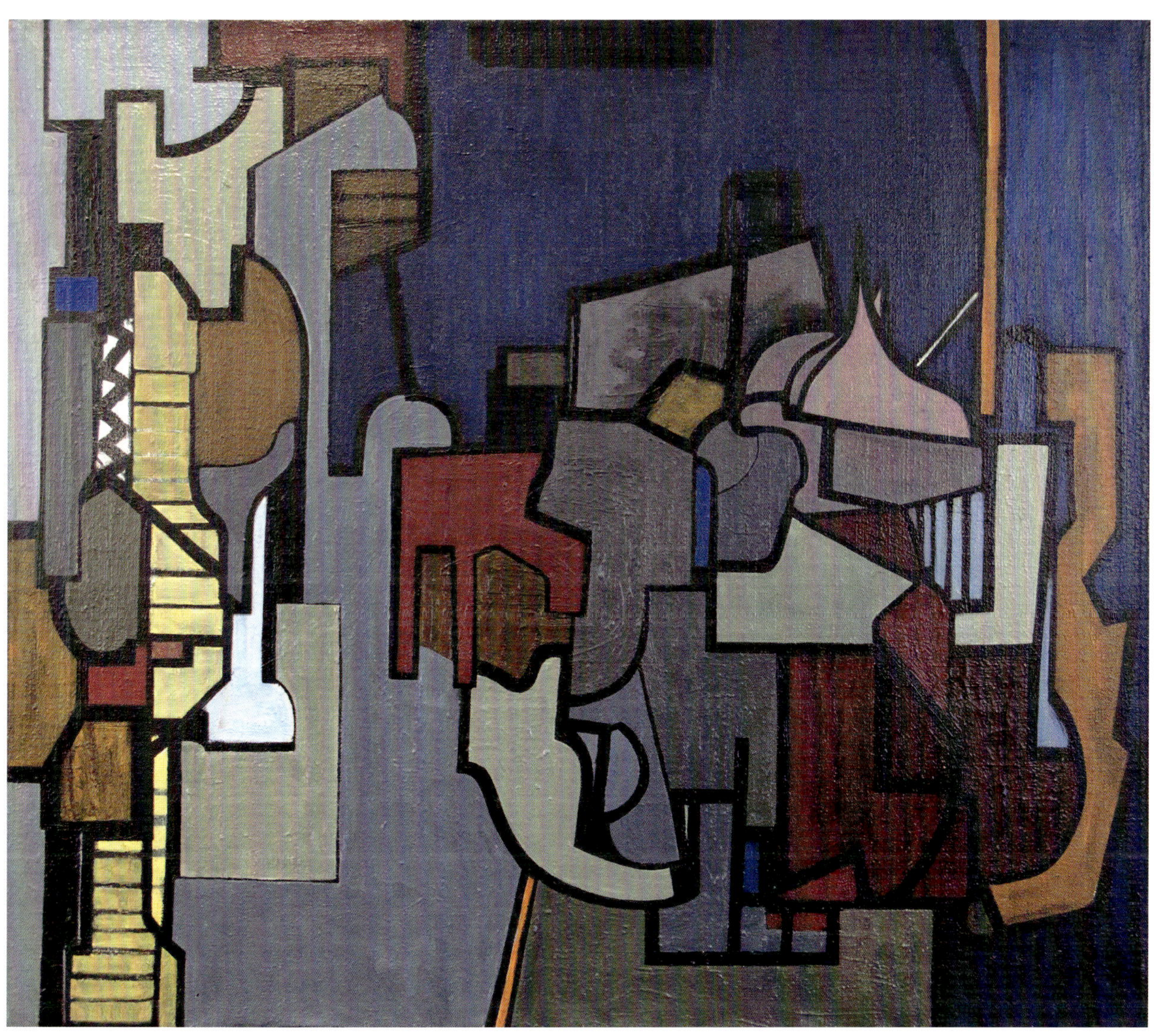

CARLIER GEBAUER

Mobile +49 160 90 98 56 89

carlier gebauer
DE-10969 Berlin | Markgrafenstrasse 67
Phone +49 30 24 00 86 30 | Fax +49 30 240 08 63 33
mail@carliergebauer.com | www.carliergebauer.com
Directors Marie-Blanche Carlier
Ulrich Gebauer

Artists at
Art Basel Miami Beach | **Rosa Barba**
Michel François
Asta Gröting
Tomasz Kowalski
Paul Pfeiffer

Further artists represented | Ernesto Caivano
Sebastian Diaz Morales
AK Dolven
Paul Graham
Dor Guez
Marcellvs L.
Marko Lehanka
Przemek Matecki
Julie Mehretu
Aernout Mik
Kirsi Mikkola
Jean-Luc Moulène
Jessica Rankin
Erik Schmidt
Thomas Schütte
Peter Stauss
Fred Tomaselli
Janaina Tschäpe
Mark Wallinger
Emily Wardill
Kailiang Yang

Kirsi Mikkola
Rebel: Rebel, 2012
Construction of painted paper,
320 x 280 cm

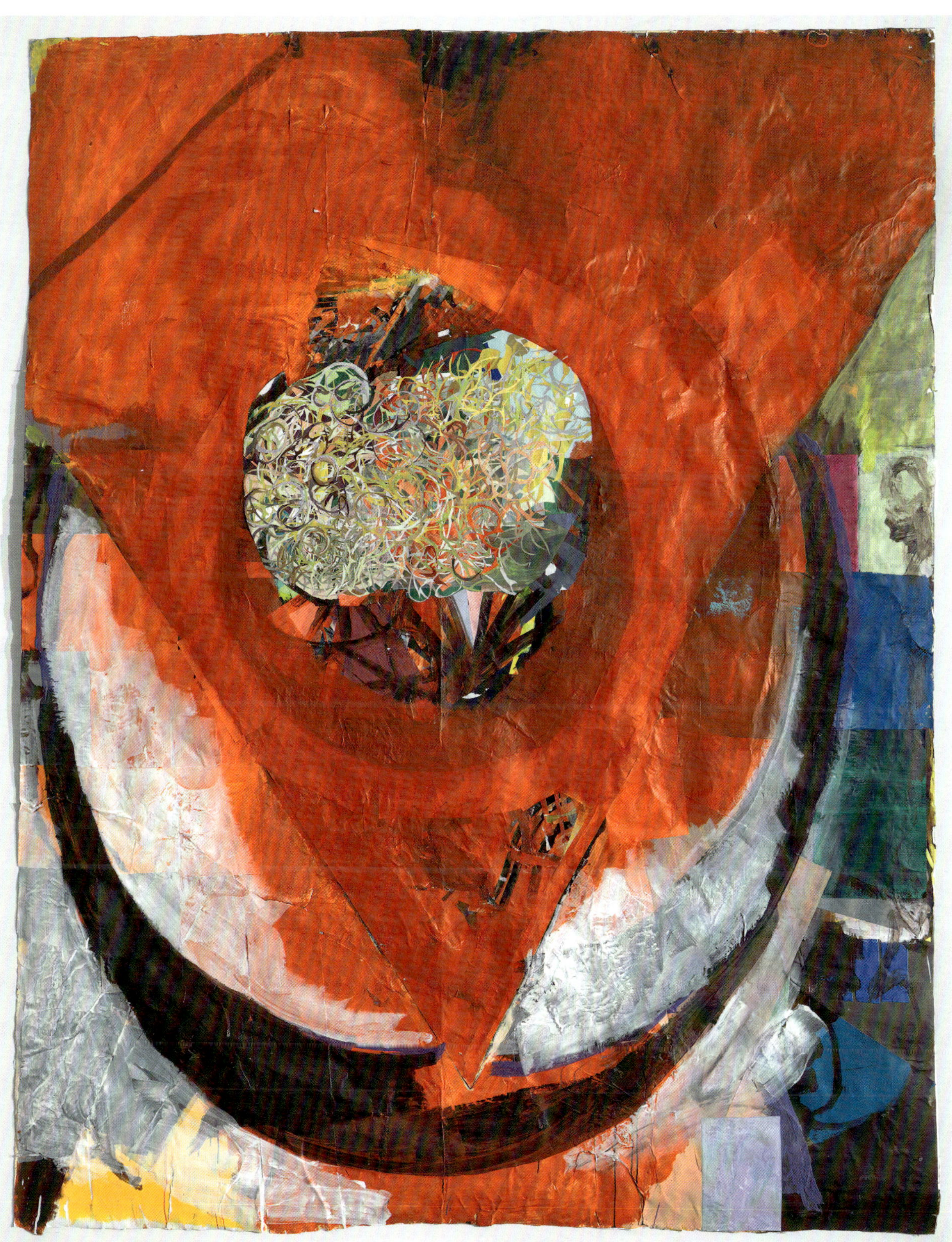

CASA TRIÂNGULO

Mobile +55 11 91 69 98 22

Casa Triângulo
BR-São Paulo 04531-090 | Rua Pais de Araujo 77
Phone +55 11 31 67 56 21 | Fax +55 11 31 68 16 40
info@casatriangulo.com | www.casatriangulo.com
Directors Ricardo Trevisan
Rodrigo Editore

Artists at Art Basel Miami Beach | **Daniel Acosta**
Albano Afonso
Assume Vivid Astro Focus
Eduardo Berliner
Tony Camargo
Flavio Cerqueira
Juliana Cerqueira Leite
Alex Cerveny
Sandra Cinto
Stephen Dean
Rogério Degaki
Valdirlei Dias Nunes
Yuri Firmeza
Max Gómez Canle
Vânia Mignone
Guillermo Mora
Nunca
Nazareth Pacheco
Mariana Palma
Reginaldo Pereira
Manuela Ribadeneira
Sergio Romagnolo
Camila Sposati
Pier Stockholm
Jack Strange
Joana Vasconcelos
Marcia Xavier

Mariana Palma
Untitled, 2012
Oil and acrylic on canvas,
200 x 120 cm

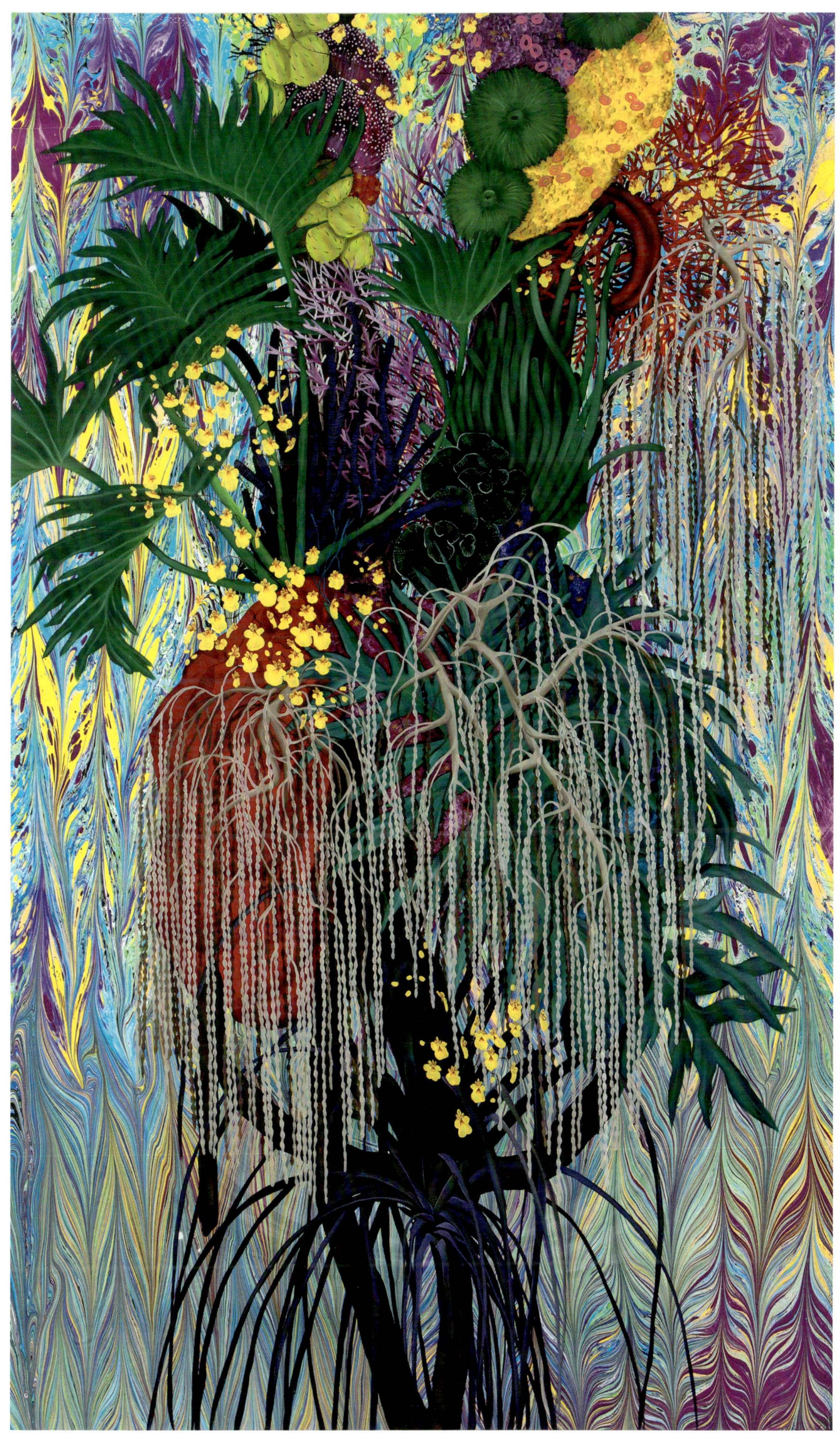

CHEIM & READ

Mobile +1 646 221 68 48

Cheim & Read
US-New York, NY 10001 | 547 West 25th Street
Phone +1 212 242 77 27 | Fax +1 212 242 77 37
gallery@cheimread.com | www.cheimread.com
Directors John Cheim
Howard Read
Mary Gail Parr
Adam Sheffer

Artists at Art Basel Miami Beach | **Ghada Amer**
Don Bachardy
Donald Baechler
Lynda Benglis
Louise Bourgeois
William Eggleston
Louise Fishman
Adam Fuss
Hans Hartung
Jenny Holzer
Bill Jensen
Chantal Joffe
Jannis Kounellis
Jonathan Lasker
McDermott & McGough
Barry McGee
Joan Mitchell
Paul Morrison
Jack Pierson
Tal R
Milton Resnick
John Sonsini
Pat Steir
Juan Uslé
Otto Zitko

Tal R
FLOVMAND, 2008
Gouache on paper,
12½ x 9⅜ inches

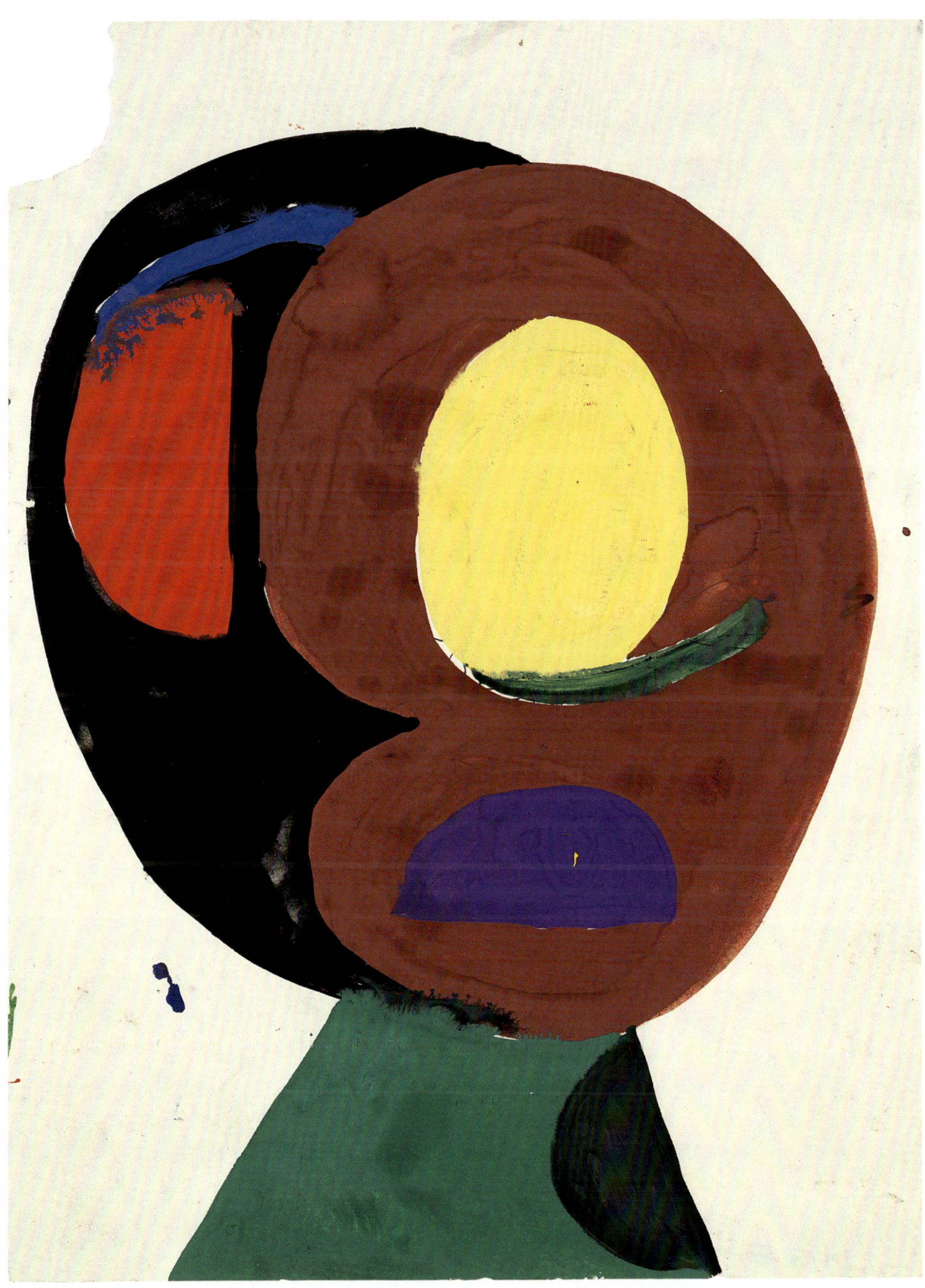

CHEMOULD

Mobile +91 982 005 02 91

Chemould Prescott Road
IN-400 001 Mumbai | G. Talwatkar Marg, Fort
Phone +91 22 22 00 02 11 | Fax +91 22 22 00 02 13
art@gallerychemould.com | www.gallerychemould.com
Director Shireen Gandhy

Artists at
Art Basel Miami Beach | **Shezad Dawood**
Atul Dodiya
Shilpa Gupta
Jitish Kallat
Rashid Rana
Reena Saini Kallat

Gallery Information | Founded by Kekoo and Khorshed Gandhy in Bombay in 1963, Gallery Chemould is one of India's oldest commercial art spaces, and has nurtured and represented many of the country's leading artists since then. Under the directorship of Shireen Gandhy since 1988, Gallery Chemould has expanded its roster of artists to represent those working in experimental and alternative mediums, and its exhibition program spans younger, mid-career, and senior artists. The gallery relocated in February 2007, as Chemould Prescott Road, to a modern, loft-like space equipped for large-scale exhibitions. The exhibitions have included experimental, cutting-edge installations by Atul Dodiya, Anant Joshi, Vivan Sundaram, L.N. Tallur, Wolfgang Laib, and Gigi Scaria; exhibitions of new media work by Rashid Rana, Jitish Kallat, Tushar Joag, Shezad Dawood, Shilpa Gupta, and Suhasini Kejriwal.

Chemould has collaborated with public institutions and galleries in Europe, Australia, and South Africa to present Indian art at major international venues. It has frequently lent artworks from its private collections for internationally curated shows, including the complete set of Atul Dodiya's *Antler Anthology* (2003/04) to *Documenta 12,* held in Kassel in 2007. In November 2009 Chemould collaborated in commissioning a work by Hema Upadhyay for a large exhibition, *Chalo! India: A New Era of Indian Art,* at the Mori Museum, Tokyo.

Further artists represented: Dhruvi Acharya
Anju Dodiya
Sheetal Gattani
Mehlli Gobhai
Archana Hande
N.S. Harsha
Tushar Joag
Anant Joshi
Surekha K
Suhasini Kejriwal
Bhupen Khakhar
Desmond Lazaro
Nalini Malani
Lavanya Mani
Pushpamala N.
Jagannath Panda
Gigi Scaria
Mithu Sen
Nilima Sheikh
Aditi Singh
Vivan Sundaram
L.N. Tallur
Hema Upadhyay

Jitish Kallat
Covering Letter, 2012
FogScreen projection,
dimensions variable

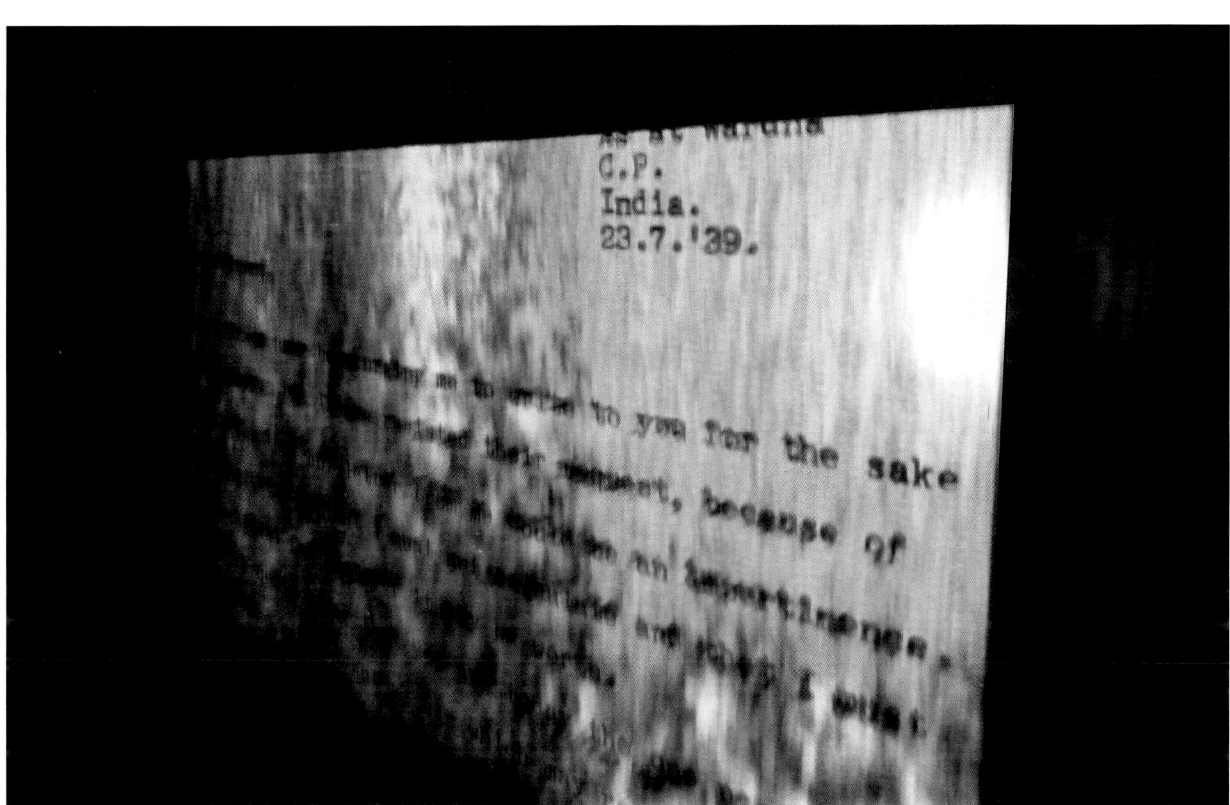

As at Wardha
C.P.
India.
23.7.'39.

... to you for the sake
... their request, because of
... an impertinence.

CHERRY AND MARTIN

Mobile +1 213 422 92 86

Cherry and Martin
US-Los Angeles, CA 90034 | 2712 S. La Cienega Blvd.
Phone +1 310 559 01 00 | Fax +1 310 559 01 20
info@cherryandmartin.com | www.cherryandmartin.com
Directors Mary Leigh Cherry
Philip Martin

Artists at Art Nova | Erik Frydenborg
T. Kelly Mason

Gallery Information | Since 2006, Cherry and Martin has exhibited innovative, experimental, and ambitious works in all media. In addition to its regular exhibition schedule, the gallery participates in art fairs in both the United States and abroad.

Recent publications by gallery artists include *Robert Heinecken: Object Matter* (2012), *Amanda Ross-Ho: TEENY TINY WOMAN* (2012), and *Matt Connors: Correspondences* (2011). Forthcoming solo exhibitions in 2013 include Bernard Piffaretti, Robert Overby, and T. Kelly Mason.

Further artists represented:
Brian Bress
Matt Connors
Holly Coulis
Mari Eastman
Robert Heinecken
Nathan Mabry
Florian Morlat
Amanda Ross-Ho
Noah Sheldon

T. Kelly Mason
Stars Stairs Potemkin Exorcism, 2012
Audio, audio playback equipment, speakers, fabric, lightboxes with cinema gels, MDF, plexiglass and T-8-32 lamps, speedrail, metal fittings, packing blankets, zip ties, 128 x 228 x 108 inches

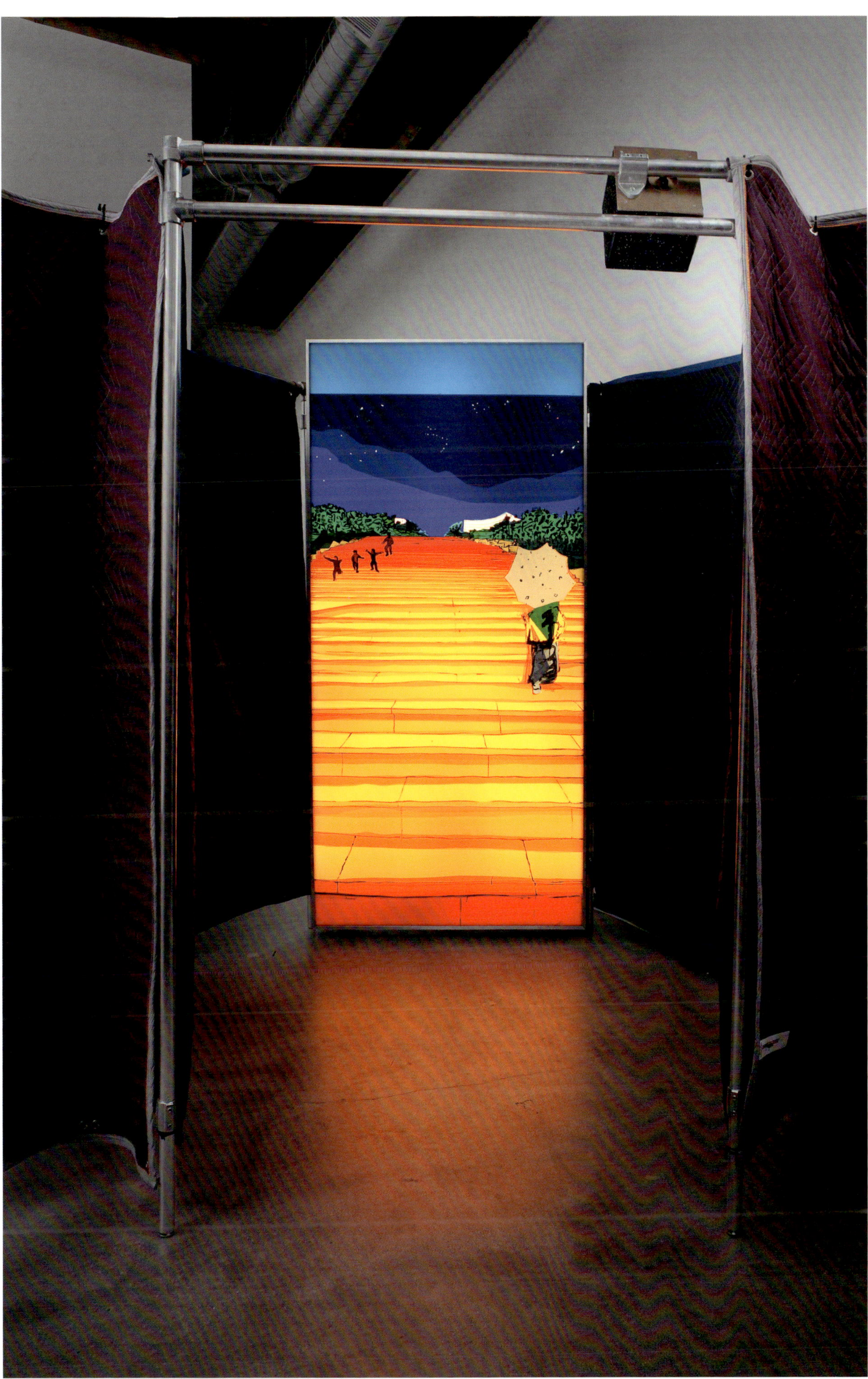

CHOUAKRI

Mobile +49 151 15 77 21 49

Mehdi Chouakri
DE-10115 Berlin | Invalidenstrasse 117, Entrance Schlegelstrasse 26
Phone +49 30 28 39 11 53 | Fax +49 30 28 39 11 54
galerie@mehdi-chouakri.com | www.mehdi-chouakri.com
Directors Mehdi Chouakri
Alexandra Alexopoulou

Artists at
Art Basel Miami Beach | **Saâdane Afif**
John M Armleder
Philippe Decrauzat
Hans-Peter Feldmann
Sylvie Fleury
Mathieu Mercier
Gerold Miller
Charlotte Posenenske
Gerwald Rockenschaub

Gallery Information | Current show at the gallery: Philippe Decrauzat

Further artists represented: Claude Closky
Isabell Heimerdinger
Peter Roehr
Gitte Schäfer
Vincent Szarek
Luca Trevisani

John M Armleder
Bingo, 2012
Acrylic on canvas,
280 x 170 x 5 cm

Blackjack Switch, 2012
Wall painting, dimensions variable

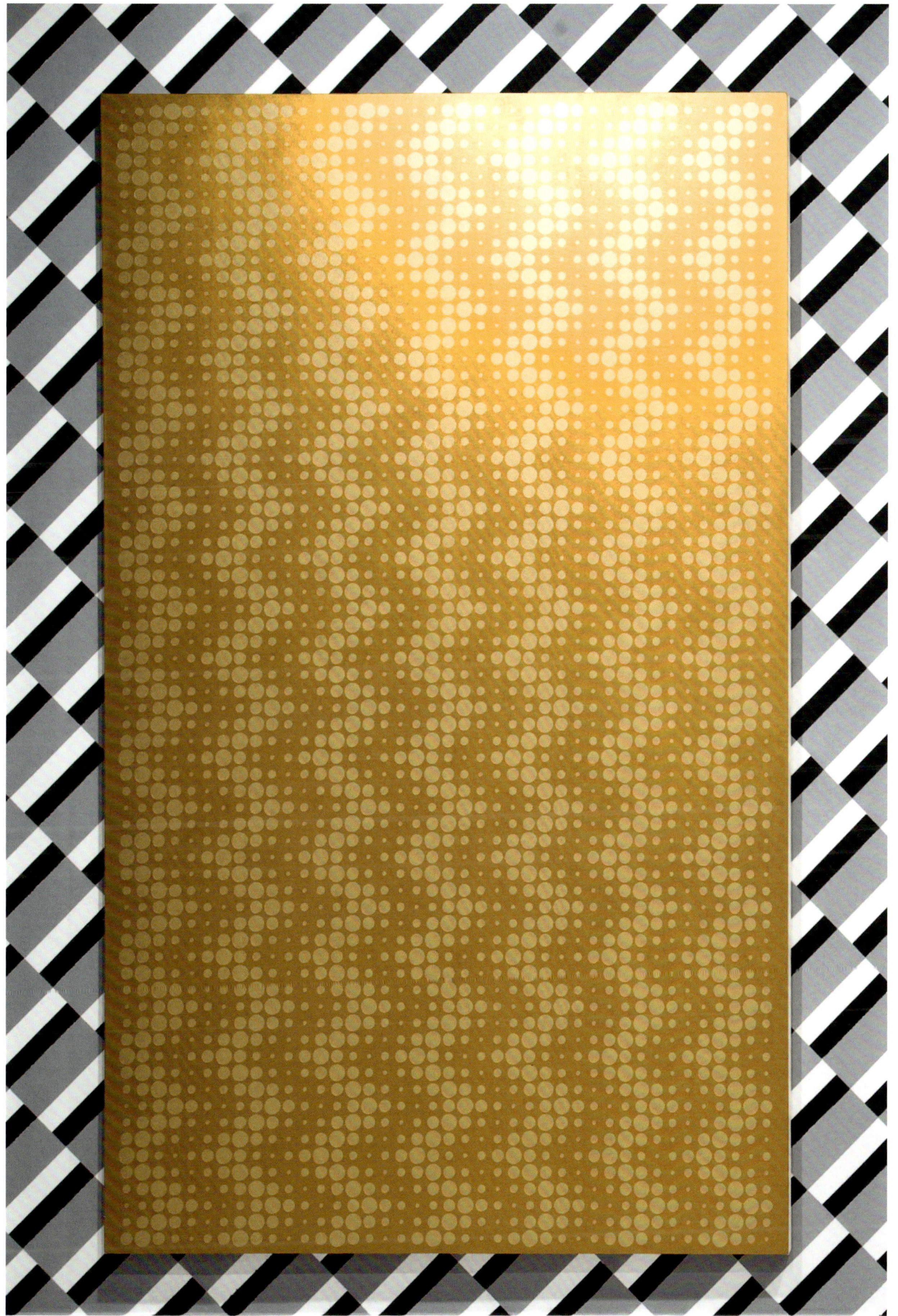

CINTRA + BOX4

Silvia Cintra + Box4
BR-Rio de Janeiro 22451-060 | Rua das Acacias, 104 – Gávea
Phone +55 21 25 21 04 26 | Fax +55 21 25 21 04 26
galeria@silviacintra.com.br | www.silviacintra.com.br
Directors Silvia Cintra
Juliana Cintra

Artists at Art Nova | Carlito Carvalhosa
Nelson Leirner
Rodrigo Matheus

Gallery Information | Exhibitions 2013:
Summer Show, curated by Luisa Duarte, February
Marcius Galan, April
SP-Arte, April
Iole de Freitas, May
Chiara Banfi, July
Carlito Carvalhosa, September
ArtRio Fair, September

Further artists represented:
Chiara Banfi
Débora Bolsoni
Cristina Canale
Leda Catunda
Amilcar de Castro
Iole de Freitas
Luiz Ernesto
Marcius Galan
Mariana Galender
Maria Klabin
Lucia Koch
Cinthia Marcelle
Pedro Motta
Henrique Oliveira
Laercio Redondo
Miguel Rio Branco
Daniel Senise
Paisagem Submersa
Ana Maria Tavares

Silvia Cintra + Box 4 have selected three important artists from different generations of the Brazilian art scene. This intergenerational dialogue reflects and emphasizes the gallery's profile.

At the project's core is Nelson Leirner, one of Brazil's most important, best-established living artists. Born in 1932, Leirner has created a markedly political oeuvre in which traces of humor and acid criticism walk together. During the 1970s and 1980s Leirner was a professor at the FAAP, where he taught and influenced a generation of artists. At Art Basel Miami Beach 2012 the artist is showing two *Abstract Figurativisms* and a new version of the series *The Grand Parade,* exhibited at the 48th Venice Biennale in 1999.

A representative of the 1980s generation, Carlito Carvalhosa works with painting, sculpture, and installations, engaging with a variety of means to explore these three aspects of art. Carvalhosa is at a special juncture in his career: His installation *Sum of Days* was shown in MoMA's atrium in 2011.

Rodrigo Matheus is a young intermedia artist whom the gallery Silvia Cintra + Box 4 is putting its faith in. The artist graduated from FAAP in São Paulo and is now studying for an arts doctorate at London's Royal Academy. For the present event, Matheus is producing a version of his series *Frames,* in which he makes reference to significant moments in art history.

A | **Nelson Leirner**
Abstract Figurativism, 2012
Cartoon stickers on wood, 150 x 200 x 3 cm

B | **Carlito Carvalhosa**
Untitled, 2011
Brushed aluminum sheet, 200 x 100 cm

C | **Rodrigo Matheus**
Landscape, 2011
Frames, glass, and steel wire, 65 x 112 cm

A

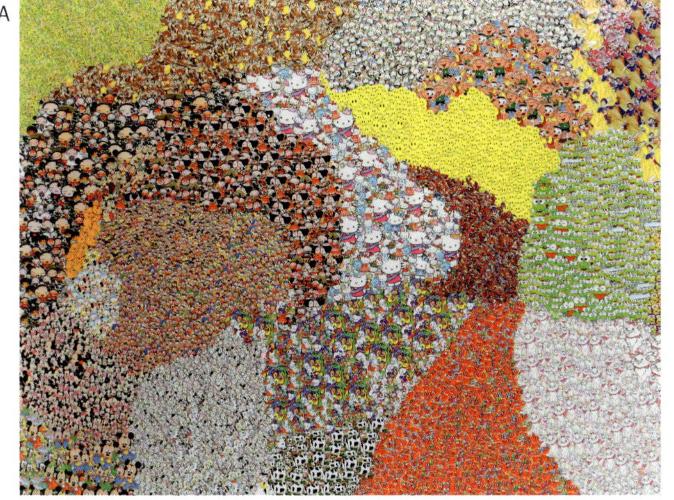

B

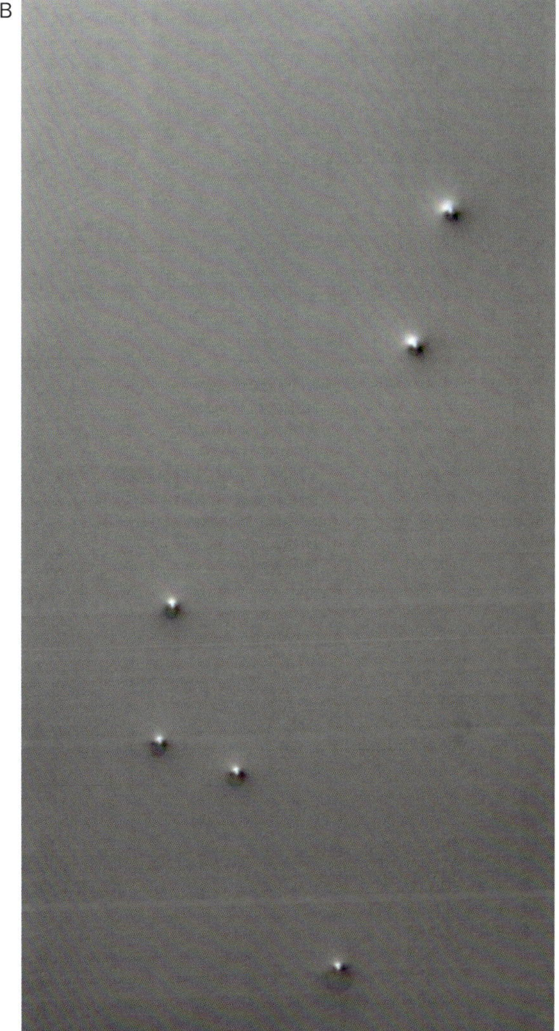

C

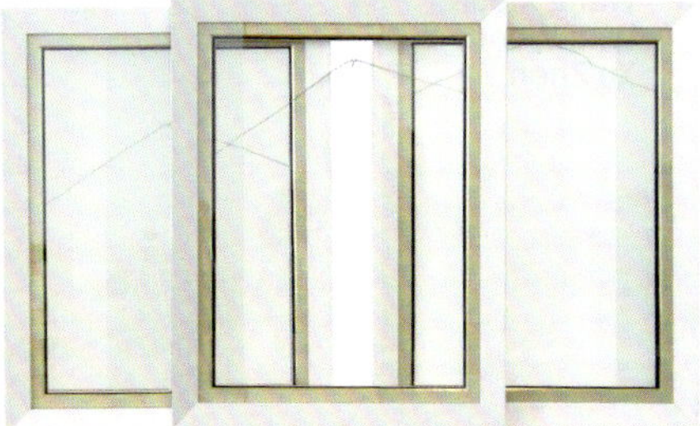

COLES

Sadie Coles HQ
GB-London W1K 2QZ | 69 South Audley Street
Phone +44 20 74938611 | Fax +44 20 74994878
info@sadiecoles.com | www.sadiecoles.com
Directors Sadie Coles
Pauline Daly

Sadie Coles
GB-London W1S 2HS | 4 New Burlington Place
Phone +44 20 74938611 | Fax +44 20 74994878
info@sadiecoles.com | www.sadiecoles.com
Directors Sadie Coles
Pauline Daly

Artists at Art Basel Miami Beach | **Carl Andre**
Matthew Barney
Dirk Bell
Avner Ben-Gal
Frank Benson
John Bock
Don Brown
Spartacus Chetwynd
Steven Claydon
John Currin
Sam Durant
Shannon Ebner
Angus Fairhurst
Urs Fischer
Florian Hecker
Georg Herold
Jonathan Horowitz
David Korty
Gabriel Kuri
Jim Lambie
Hilary Lloyd
Sarah Lucas
Helen Marten
Victoria Morton
JP Munro
Laura Owens
Simon Periton
Raymond Pettibon
Elizabeth Peyton
Richard Prince
Ugo Rondinone
Wilhelm Sasnal
Gregor Schneider
Daniel Sinsel
Andreas Slominski
Christiana Soulou
Rudolf Stingel
Nicola Tyson
Hellen van Meene
Paloma Varga Weisz
TJ Wilcox
Andrea Zittel

Jonathan Horowitz
Areca Palm, 2012
Interior wall paint on linen,
152.4 x 101.6 x 3.8 cm

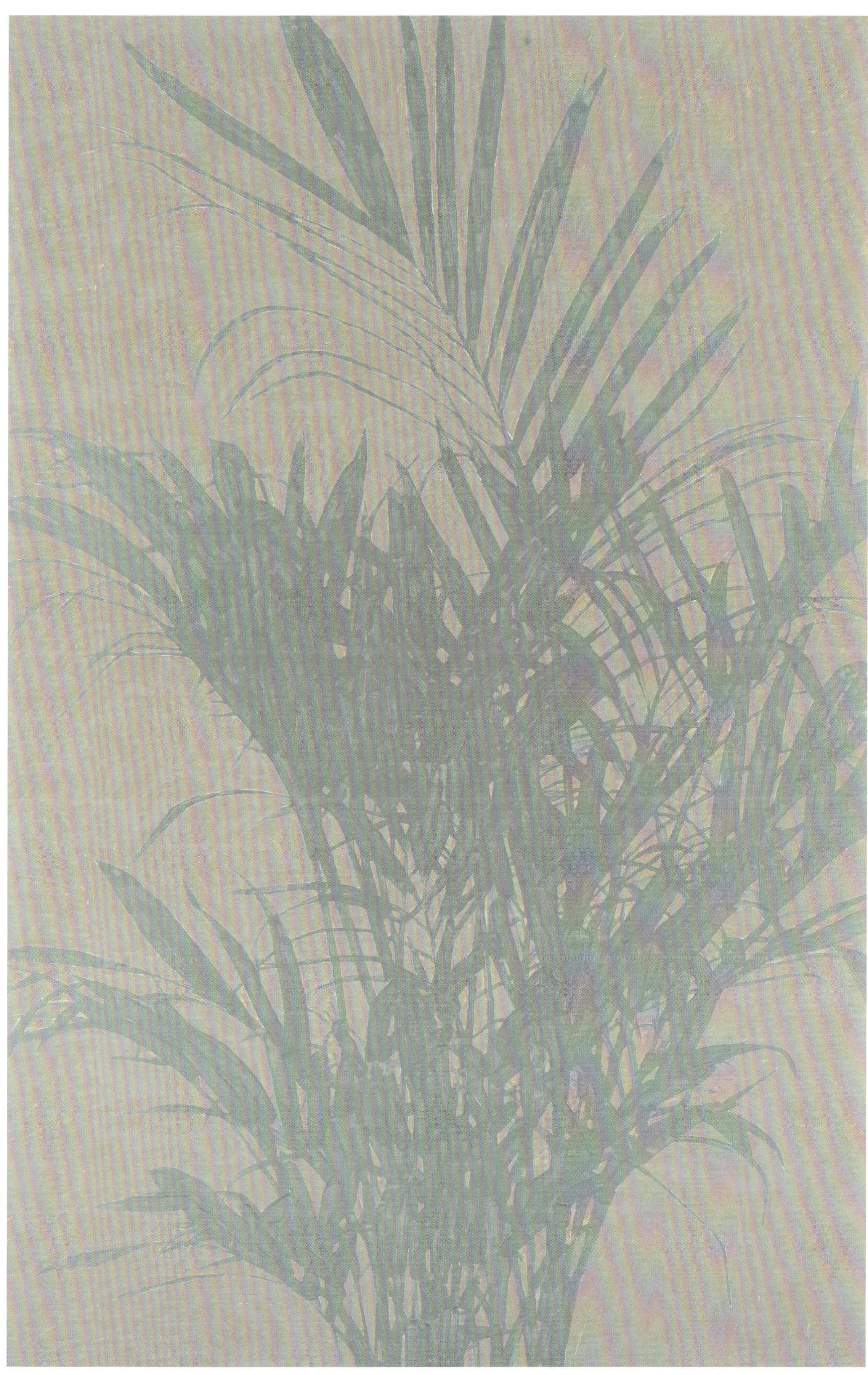

CONTEMPORARY FINE ARTS

Contemporary Fine Arts
DE-10117 Berlin | Am Kupfergraben 10
Phone +49 30 2887870 | Fax +49 30 28878726
gallery@cfa-berlin.de | www.cfa-berlin.com
Directors Bruno Brunnet
Nicole Hackert
Philipp Haverkampf

Artists at Art Basel Miami Beach | **Georg Baselitz**
Peter Böhnisch
Marc Brandenburg
Cecily Brown
Zhivago Duncan
Marcel Eichner
Max Frisinger
Georg Herold
Thomas Kiesewetter
Michael Kunze
Jonathan Meese
Chris Ofili
Raymond Pettibon
Tal R
Anselm Reyle
Daniel Richter
Julian Schnabel
Dana Schutz
Norbert Schwontkowski
Dash Snow
Katja Strunz
Gert & Uwe Tobias
Ralf Ziervogel

Gert & Uwe Tobias
Untitled, 2011
Mixed media on paper, 59 x 38 cm

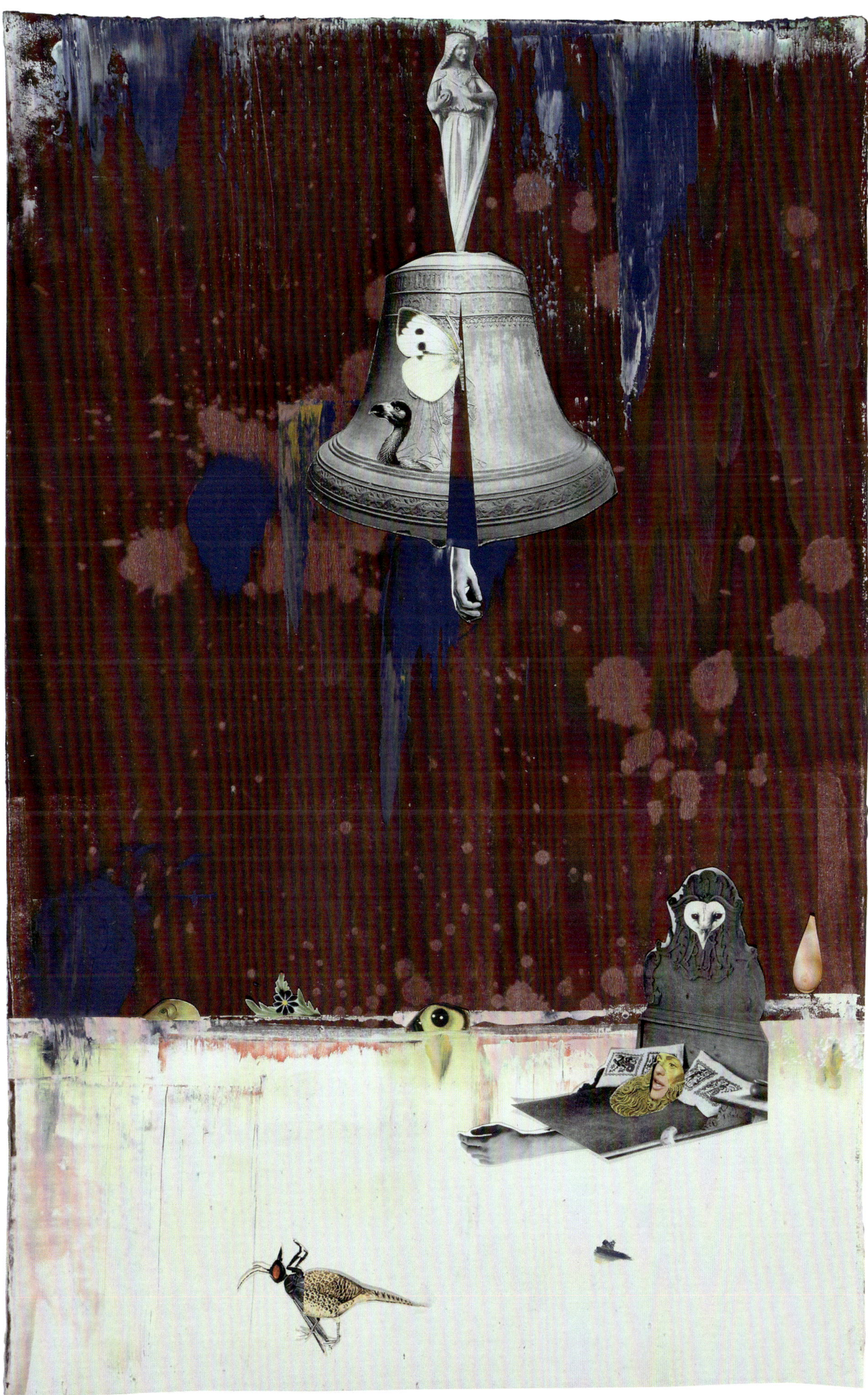

CONTINUA

Mobile +39 348 580 59 96, +39 348 580 59 97, +39 348 580 59 98

Galleria Continua
IT-53037 San Gimignano | Via del Castello, 11
Phone +39 05 77 94 31 34 | Fax +39 05 77 94 04 84
info@galleriacontinua.com | www.galleriacontinua.com
Directors Mario Cristiani
Lorenzo Fiaschi
Maurizio Rigillo

Galleria Continua/Beijing
CN-100015 Beijing | Dashanzi 798 #8503, 2 Jiuxianqiao Road
Phone +86 10 59 78 95 05 | Fax +86 10 59 78 97 74
beijing@galleriacontinua.com.cn

Galleria Continua/Le Moulin
FR-77169 Boissy-le-Châtel | 46, rue de la Ferté Gaucher
Phone +33 16 420 39 50
lemoulin@galleriacontinua.fr

Artists represented | Ai Weiwei
Kader Attia
Daniel Buren
Loris Cecchini
Chen Zhen
Nikhil Chopra
Berlinde De Bruyckere
Leandro Erlich
Meschac Gaba
Carlos Garaicoa
Kendell Geers
Antony Gormley
Gu Dexin
Shilpa Gupta
Subodh Gupta
Mona Hatoum
Ilya & Emilia Kabakov
Kan Xuan
Anish Kapoor
Kimsooja
Jorge Macchi
Sabrina Mezzaqui
Margherita Morgantin
Moataz Nasr
Hans Op de Beeck
Lucy + Jorge Orta
Giovanni Ozzola
Luca Pancrazzi
Bruno Peinado
Michelangelo Pistoletto
Arcangelo Sassolino
Manuela Sedmach
Serse
Nedko Solakov
Sun Yuan & Peng Yu
Pascale Marthine Tayou
Nari Ward
Sophie Whettnall
Sislej Xhafa
Yan Lei

Carlos Garaicoa
Fin de silencio/End of Silence,
2010
Installation: 7 tapestries, 2 Mini DVD videos transferred to DVD, site-specific dimensions, 15 min 45 sec, loop

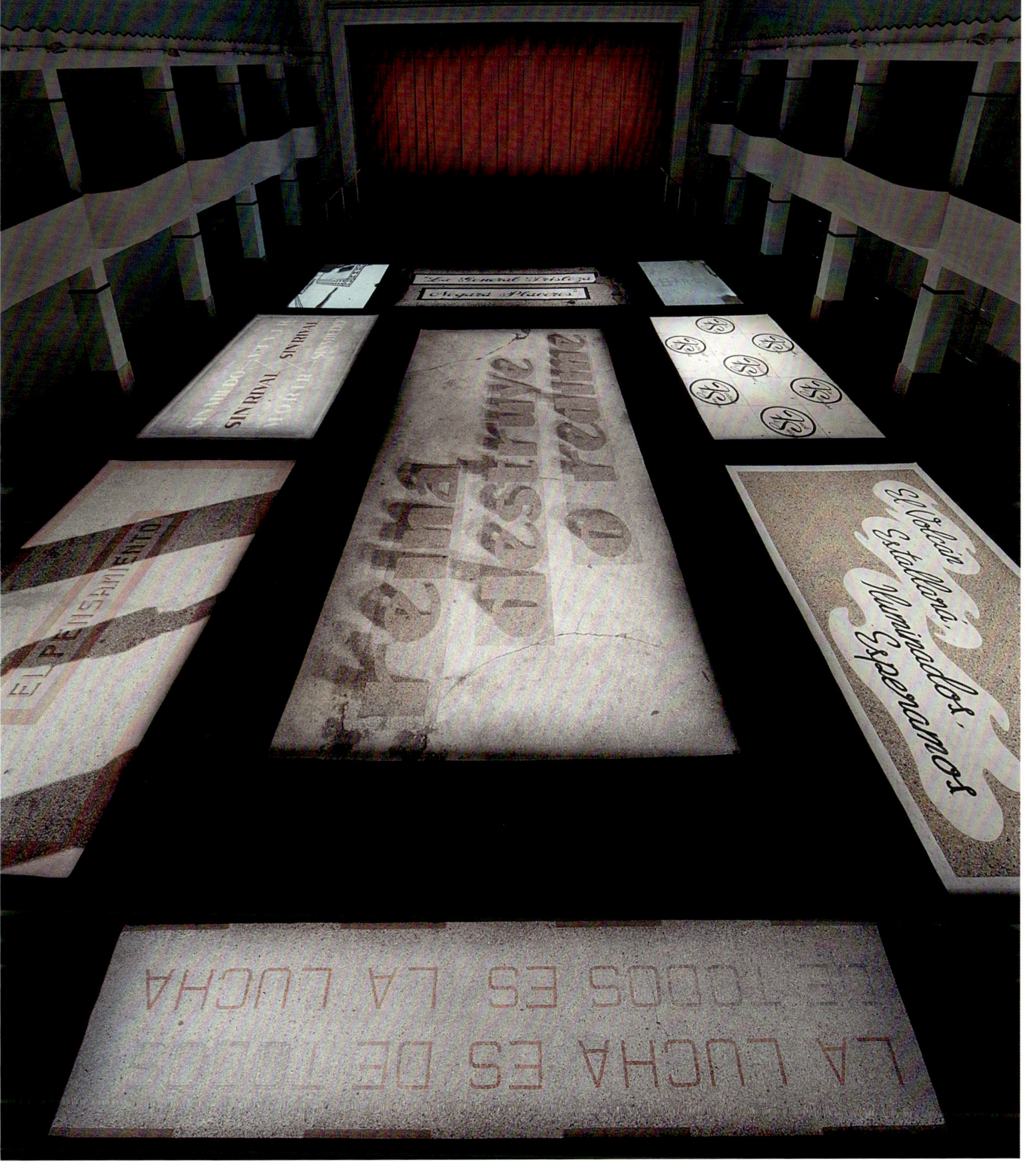

El Volcán
Estallará
Iluminados
Esperamos
EL PENSAMIENTO
SIN RIVAL
LA LUCHA ES DE TODOS
DE TODOS ES LA LUCHA

COOPER

Mobile +1 917 860 26 81

Paula Cooper Gallery
US-New York, NY 10011 | 534 West 21st Street
Phone +1 212 255 11 05 | Fax +1 212 255 51 56
info@paulacoopergallery.com | www.paulacoopergallery.com
Directors Paula Cooper
Steve Henry

Artists at
Art Basel Miami Beach | **Carl Andre**
Tauba Auerbach
Bruce Conner
Mark di Suvero
Sam Durant
Wayne Gonzales
Douglas Huebler
Julian Lethbridge
Sherrie Levine
Sol LeWitt
Christian Marclay
Justin Matherly
Paul Pfeiffer
Walid Raad
Rudolf Stingel
Kelley Walker
Dan Walsh
Meg Webster
Robert Wilson

Further artists represented | Céleste Boursier-Mougenot
Sophie Calle
Robert Grosvenor
Hans Haacke
Michael Hurson
Claes Oldenburg & Coosje van Bruggen
Jackie Winsor
Bing Wright
Carey Young

Kelley Walker
Untitled, 2011/12
Pantone and 4-color process silkscreen with acrylic ink on MDF, 166 panels: 16 x 16 inches, 29 panels: 24 x 24 inches, overall dimensions variable, pictured panel: 24 x 24 inches
Detail

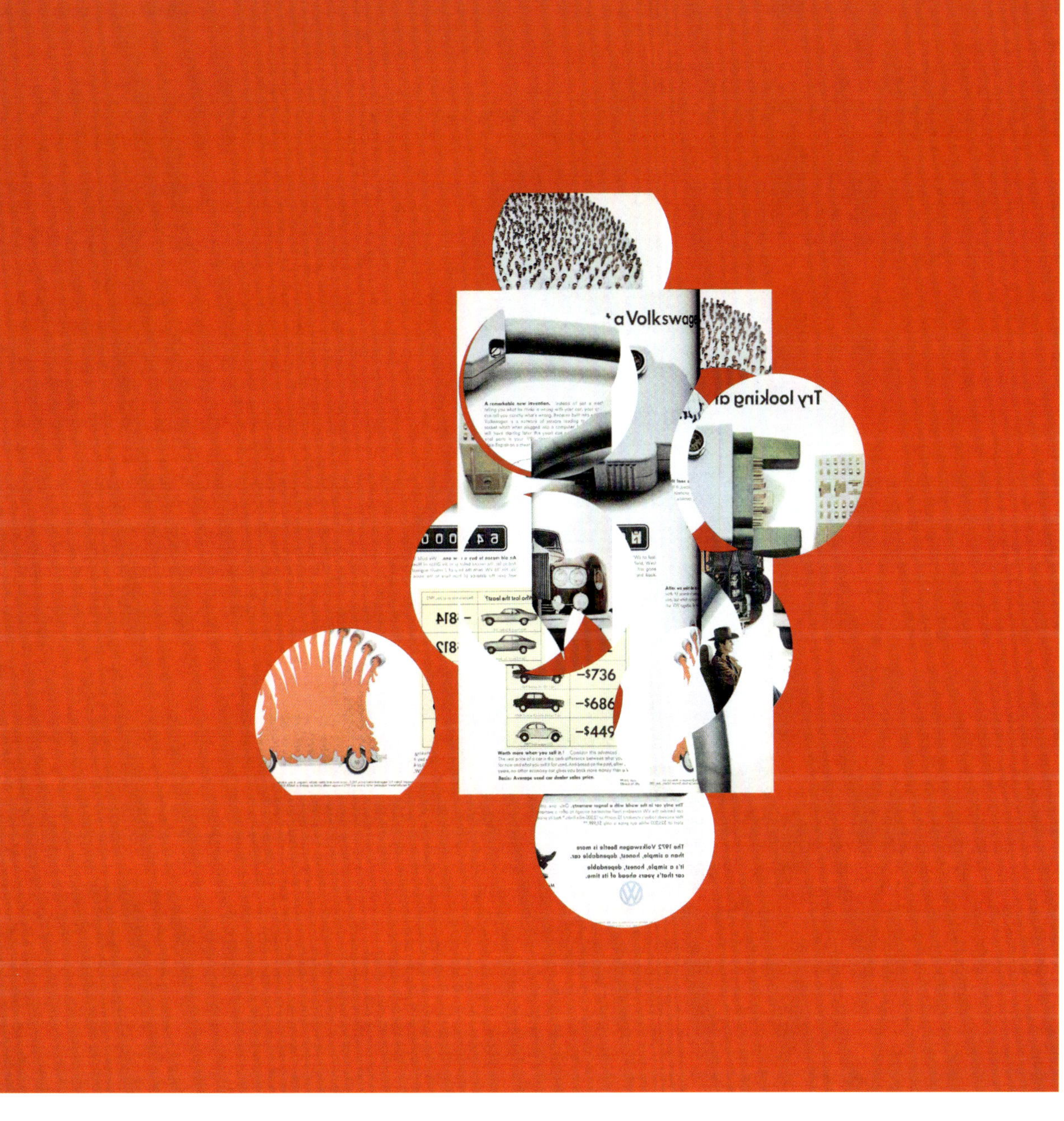

–$736
–$686
–$449
Basis: Average used car dealer sales price.
The only car in the world with a longer warranty.
The 1972 Volkswagen Beetle is more
than a simple, honest, dependable car.
It's a simple, honest, dependable
car that's years ahead of its time.

CORRIAS

Pilar Corrias
GB-London W1W 8EF | 54 Eastcastle Street
Phone +44 20 73237000 | Fax +44 20 73236400
sales@pilarcorrias.com | www.pilarcorrias.com
Director Pilar Corrias

Artists at Art Nova | Leigh Ledare
Julião Sarmento

Julião Sarmento (*1948, Lisbon, Portugal) and Leigh Ledare (*1976, Seattle, WA, United States) will present two bodies of work that examine desire and absence, the public and the private, the seen and the unseen. The two artists, who hail from different generations and different backgrounds, strive to deal with sexuality and images of women in different ways.

Portuguese artist Julião Sarmento draws upon themes of memory, sexuality, transgression, morality, and duality. Working across painting, collage, drawing, sculpture, and film, he deploys a concise vocabulary of images to explore ambiguity, incomplete narratives, and the nature of desire. Influenced heavily by writers who deal with sexual desire through symbols and fragments of the unconscious, such as Georges Bataille and Lacan, Sarmento's works examine taboo, the erotic impulse, and the relationship between death and eroticism.

For Art Nova Sarmento will create new monochromatic paintings that continue his explorations of the notions of absence, desire, and 'that which is seen and that which is not seen.'

These works will be accompanied by a rare series of 1970s Polaroids by Sarmento depicting the artist's intimate relationships with several women. The Polaroids, all of women, often naked and in erotic poses, reflect the ambiguous relationships of desire of both the artist and his subjects. Part of the Polaroid series will also be exhibited at Sarmento's solo exhibition at the Museu Serralves, Oporto, Portugal, which will run concurrently with Art Basel Miami Beach.

Leigh Ledare is an artist working with photography, archives, video, and text. Ledare's work questions the photographer's negotiations and the subject's relationship to agency, representation, self-presentation, and authorship.

For Art Nova Ledare will present works from his new, highly charged body of work *Untitled.* Commissioned by a well-known writer, the wife of a highly recognizable public figure with connections to the media and politics, and shot over seven consecutive days, it consists of a series of images of her in titillating, erotic poses, each image depicted against a silkscreened front page of the NY Times marking the respective date on which the photograph was taken. A contract between the model and the artist permits Ledare to use these images publicly under the strict proviso that they must not compromise the secrecy of her identity. A silk-screened cancellation printed over the face of each lithograph protects the subject's public profile from the actions of her own private exposure.

Gallery Information | Committed to the realization and presentation of ideas, Pilar Corrias Gallery seeks to reinstate the idea that the art object and its meaning exists before its market value. The gallery space is designed by the internationally acclaimed architect Rem Koolhass/The Office for Metropolitan Architecture. Since its inception the gallery has worked closely with its artists with the central aim of allowing their work to grow both in terms of curated gallery shows as well as production of new off-site projects. This ethos is as important to the younger artists as it is to the more established ones, and it is essential to the program that innovative new work is presented for each exhibition.

The gallery places great importance on dialogue with institutions. Pilar Corrias actively works to generate new possibilities of exhibition beyond the gallery itself, creating further potential for artistic exchange.

Further artists represented:
Charles Avery
Keren Cytter
Koo Jeong-A
Tala Madani
Elizabeth Neel
Philippe Parreno
Mary Ramsden
Tobias Rehberger
Mary Reid Kelley
Shahzia Sikander
Rirkrit Tiravanija
Tunga
Patrick Tuttofuoco
Ulla von Brandenburg

Julião Sarmento
Untitled, 1973
4 black-and-white photographs
mounted on PVC, 39.7 x 58.3 cm

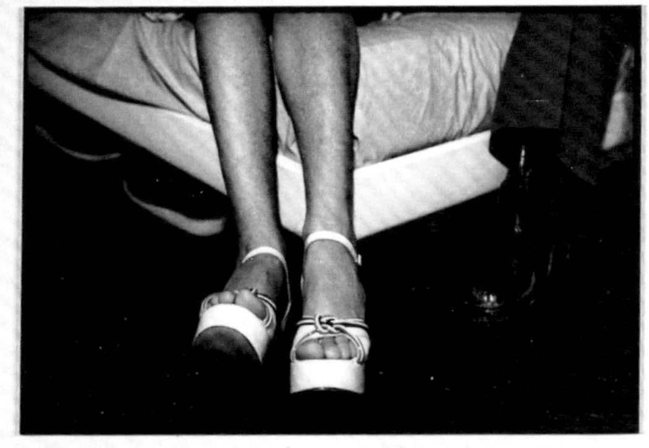
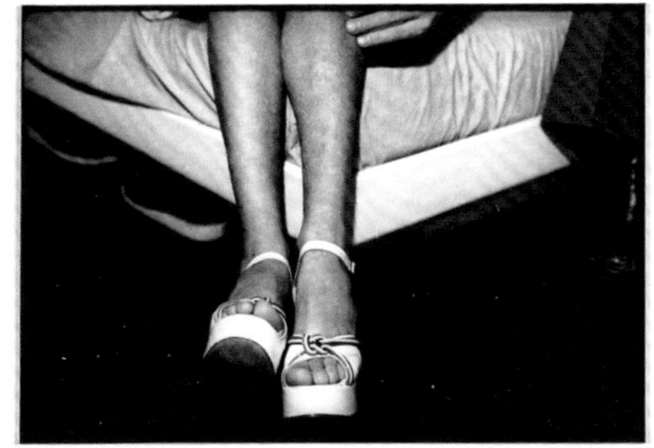
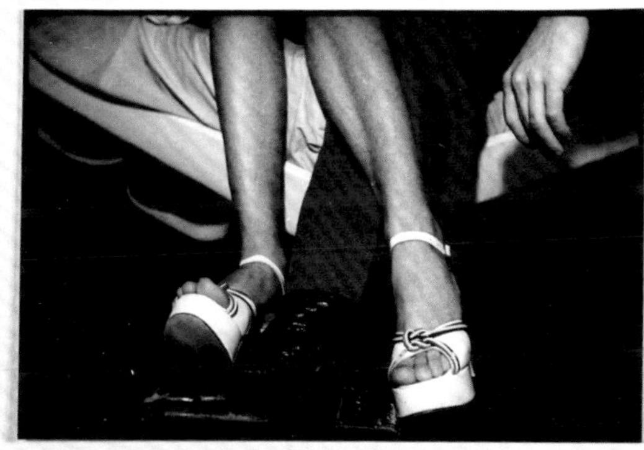
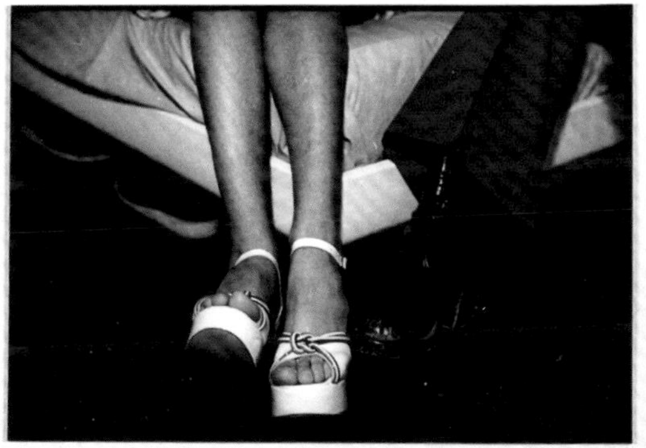

CRG

CRG Gallery
US-New York, NY 10011 | 548 West 22nd Street
Phone +1 212 229 27 66 | Fax +1 212 229 27 88
info@crggallery.com | www.crggallery.com
Directors Carla Chammas
Richard Desroche
Glenn McMillan

Artists at
Art Basel Miami Beach | **Tonico Lemos Auad**
Eva Berendes
Alexandre da Cunha
Pia Fries
Ori Gersht
Joana Hadjithomas/Khalil Joreige
Jumana Manna

Further artists represented | Steven Bindernagel
Colby Bird
Robert Buck
Russell Crotty
Tomory Dodge
Angela Dufresne
Lyle Ashton Harris
Butt Johnson
Tom LaDuke
Siobhan Liddell
Melissa McGill
Carmen McLeod
O Zhang
Sam Reveles
Steve Roden
Lisa Sanditz
Brian Tolle

Tonico Lemos Auad
Figa, 2012
Red brick, mortar,
188 x 66 x 38 cm
Edition of 3 + 1 AP

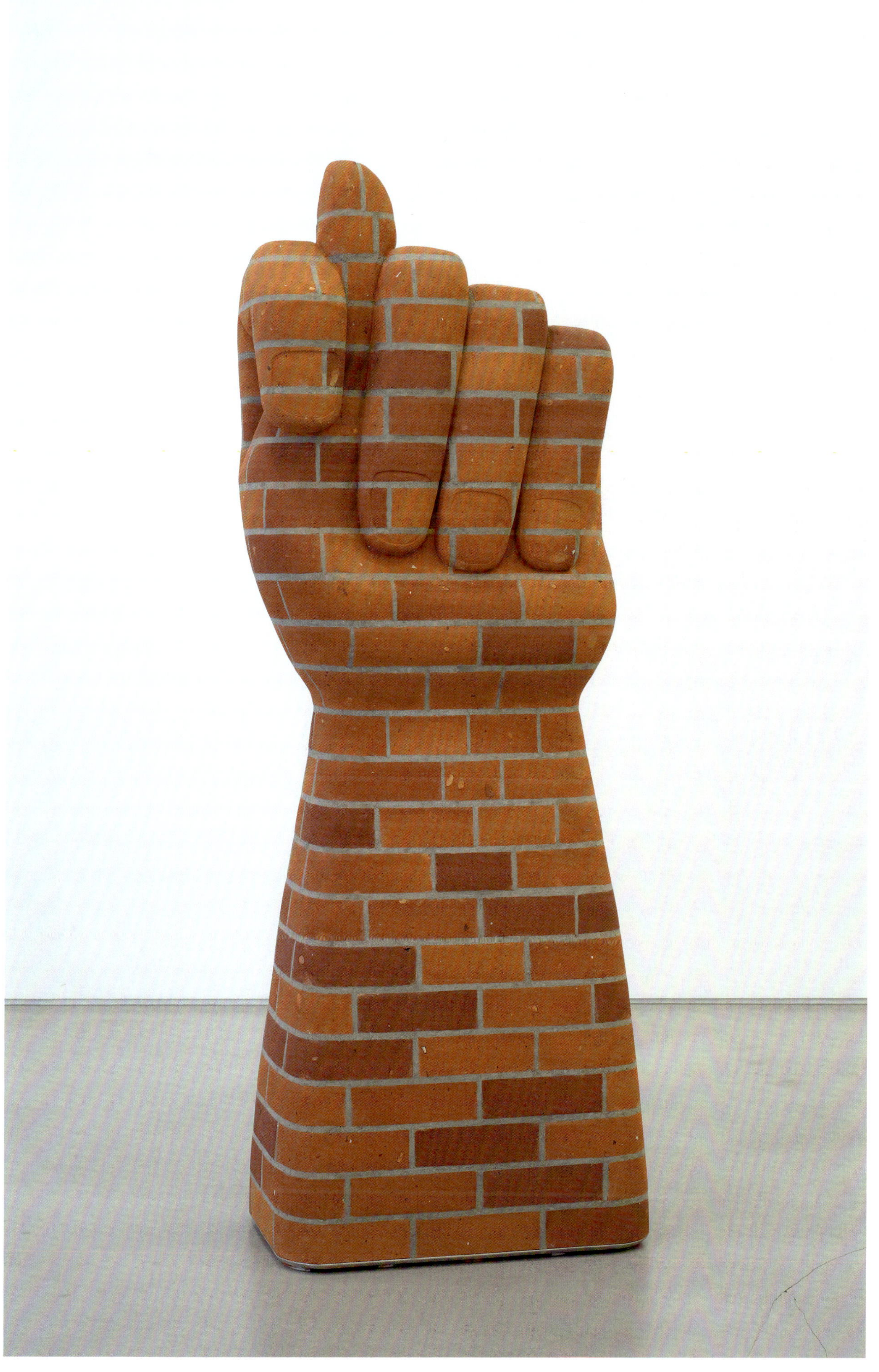

CROUSEL

Mobile +33 6 80 65 24 42, +33 6 79 89 39 38

Galerie Chantal Crousel
FR-75003 Paris | 10, rue Charlot
Phone +33 1 42 77 38 87 | Fax +33 1 42 77 59 00
galerie@crousel.com | www.crousel.com
Directors Chantal Crousel
Niklas Svennung

Le Douane – Galerie Chantal Crousel
FR-75011 Paris | 11F, rue Léon Jouhaux
Phone +33 1 42 01 64 97 | Fax +33 1 42 77 59 00
douane@crousel.com

Artists at
Art Basel Miami Beach | **Jennifer Allora & Guillermo Calzadilla**
Abraham Cruzvillegas
Claire Fontaine
Wade Guyton
Mona Hatoum
Thomas Hirschhorn
Jean-Luc Moulène
Gabriel Orozco
Clément Rodzielski
Anri Sala
Alain Séchas
José María Sicilia
Reena Spaulings
Wolfgang Tillmans
Rirkrit Tiravanija
Danh Vo
Haegue Yang
Heimo Zobernig

Gallery Information | Further artists represented: Fikret Atay
Willem de Rooij
Isa Genzken
Farbice Gygi
Hassan Khan
Michael Krebber
Moshe Ninio
Melik Ohanian
Sean Snyder
Wang Bing

Works by: Absalon
Marcel Broodthaears
Michael Buthe
Wolfgang Laib
Richard Long
Sigmar Polke
Andy Warhol

Rirkrit Tiravanija
Untitled 2012 (Comment Clichy s'est embrasé) (Raw), 2012
Silkscreen and acrylic on raw linen, 85 x 60 inches

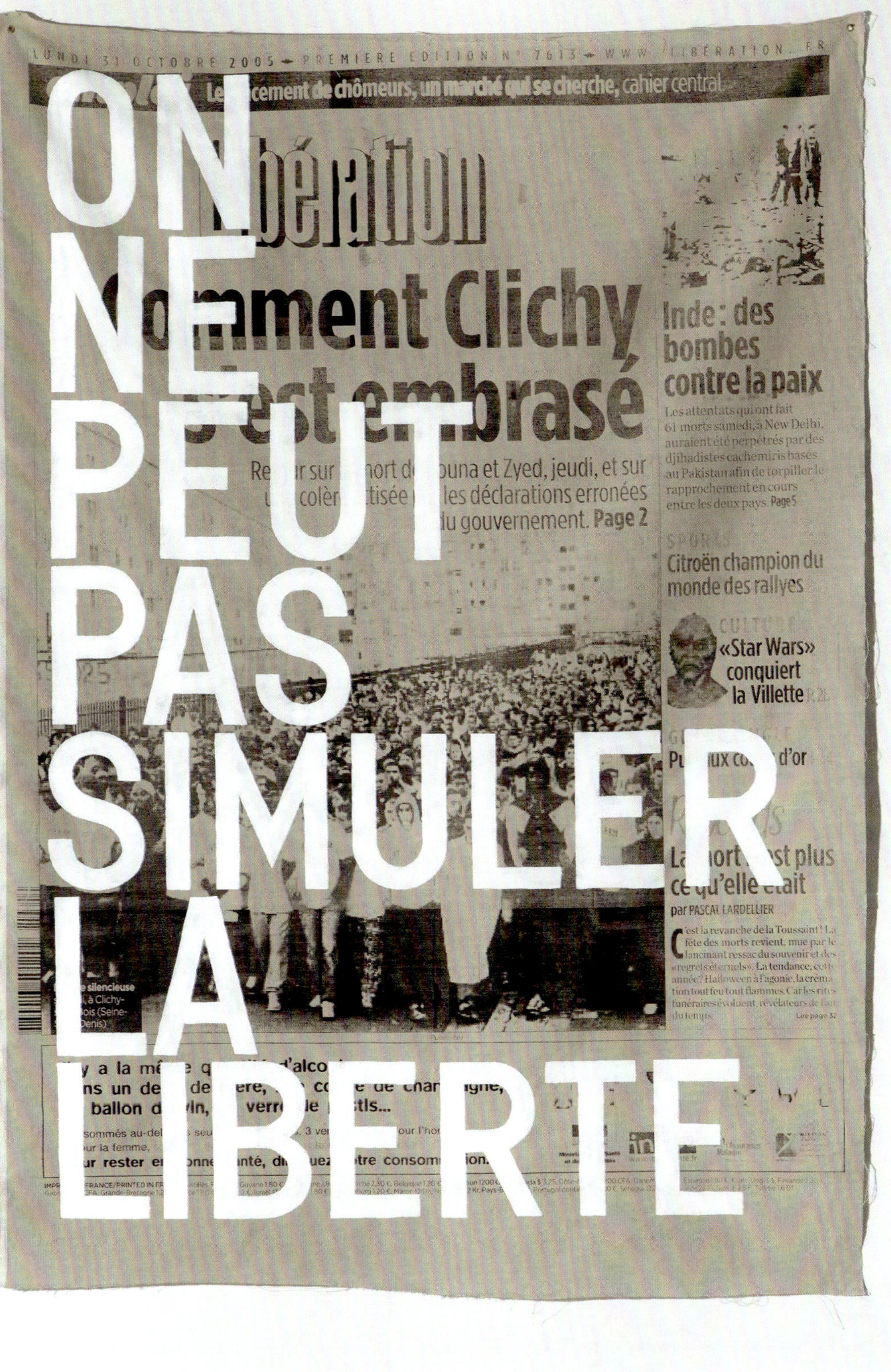
ON
NE
PEUT
PAS
SIMULER
LA
LIBERTE
LUNDI 31 OCTOBRE 2005 PREMIERE EDITION N° 7613 WWW.LIBERATION.FR
cement de chômeurs, un marché qui se cherche, cahier central
béation
omment Clichy
s'est embrasé
Retour sur la mort de Bouna et Zyed, jeudi, et sur une colère attisée par les déclarations erronées du gouvernement. Page 2
Inde : des bombes contre la paix
Les attentats qui ont fait 61 morts samedi, à New Delhi, auraient été perpétrés par des djihadistes cachemiris basés au Pakistan afin de torpiller le rapprochement en cours entre les deux pays. Page 5
Citroën champion du monde des rallyes
«Star Wars» conquiert la Villette
La mort n'est plus ce qu'elle était
par PASCAL LARDELLIER
C'est la revanche de la Toussaint! La fête des morts revient, mue par le lancinant ressac du souvenir et des «regrets éternels». La tendance, cette année? Halloween à l'agonie, la crémation tout feu tout flammes. Car les rites funéraires évoluent, révélateurs de l'air du temps.
Lire page 32

D'AMELIO

D'Amelio Gallery
US-New York, NY 10011 | 525 West 22nd Street
Phone +1 212 352 03 25 | Fax +1 212 352 03 20
info@dameliogallery.com | www.dameliogallery.com
Directors Christopher D'Amelio
Trina Gordon
Thalassa Balanis

Artists at
Art Basel Miami Beach | **Massimo Bartolini**
Tony Feher
Roland Flexner
Tamar Halpern
Henrik Olai Kaarstein
Zoe Leonard
Cady Noland
Heather Rowe

Gallery Information | Founded in 1996

Further artists represented: Polly Apfelbaum
Jedediah Caesar
Joanne Greenbaum
Daniel Hesidence
Karin Sander

Works by: Carl Andre
Dan Flavin
Christian Holstad
Donald Judd
Alex Katz
Yayoi Kusama
Robert Moskowitz
Steven Parrino
Cornelia Parker
Monique van Genderen

Heather Rowe
Cold Night, 2011
Black mirror, wood, wallpaper,
mirror, frames, 54 x 36 x 14 inches

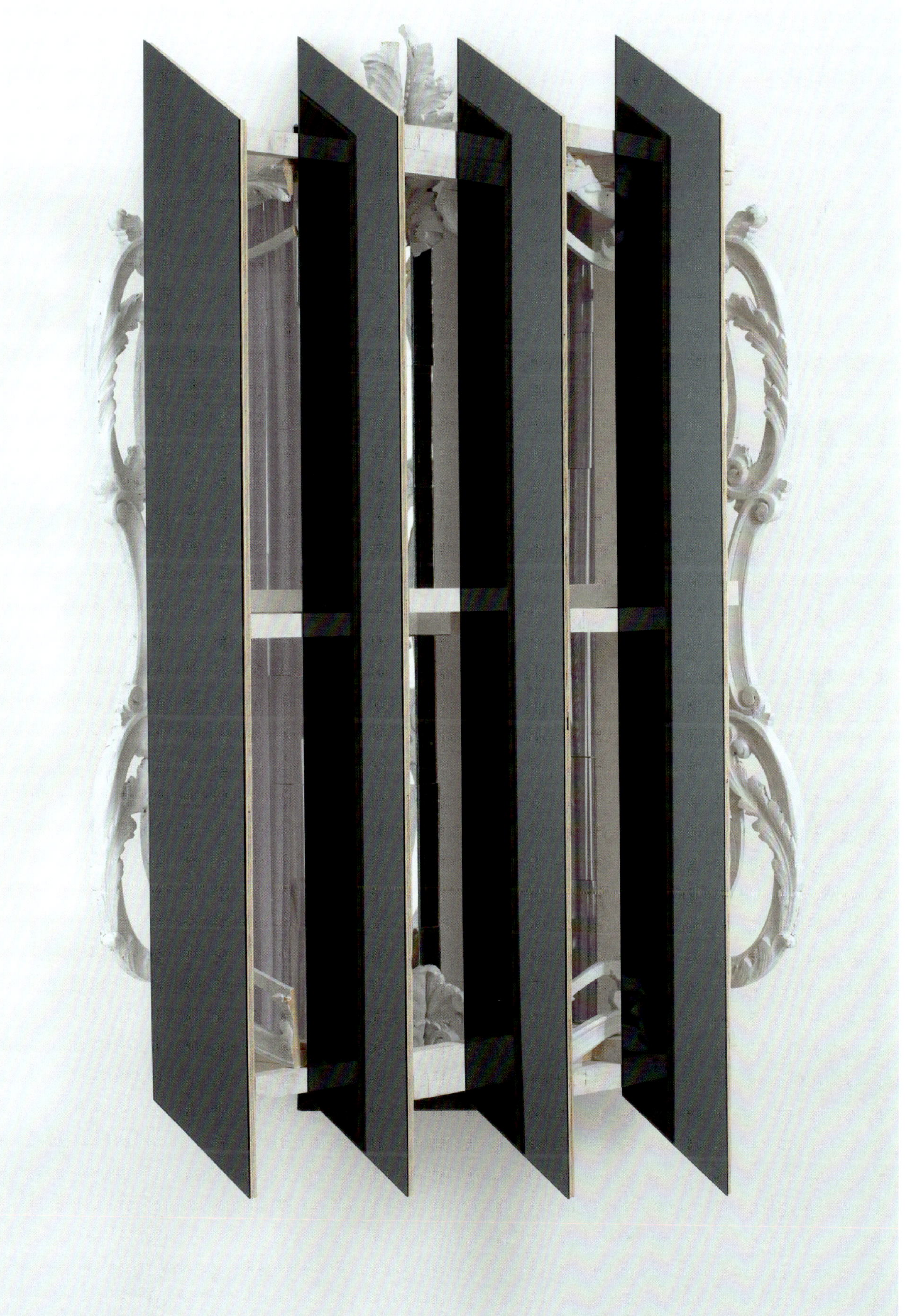

DAN

Mobile +55 11 991 86 06 82, +55 11 996 23 70 77

DAN Galeria
BR-São Paulo 01427-002 | Rua Estados Unidos, 1638
Phone +55 11 30 83 46 00 | Fax +55 11 30 85 74 29
flaviocohn@dangaleria.com.br | www.dangaleria.com.br
Directors Peter Cohn
Flavio Cohn
Ulisses Cohn

Artists at
Art Basel Miami Beach | **Josef Albers**
Ascânio M.M.M.
Hércules Barsotti
Max Bill
Sérgio Camargo
Lothar Charoux
Lygia Clark
Carlos Cruz-Diez
Bill Culbert
Geraldo de Barros
Willys de Castro
Norman Dilworth
Hermelindo Fiaminghi
Stephen Gilbert
Anthony Hill
Macaparana
Kenneth Martin
Mary Martin
Victor Pasmore
Luiz Sacilotto
Jesus Soto
Franz Weissmann
Alexandre Wollner

Further artists represented | Alejandro Corujeira
Christian Cravo
Dionísio del Santo
Adolfo Estrada
Sérgio Fingermann
Thomaz Ianelli
Linda Kohen
Cristiano Mascaro
Almir Mavignier
Laura Miranda
Yolanda Mohalyi
Bob Nugent
César Paternosto
José Spaniol
Eduardo Stupia
Amélia Toledo

Lygia Clark
Planos em Superfície Modulada,
1957
Cardboard collage, 21.6 x 20.7 cm

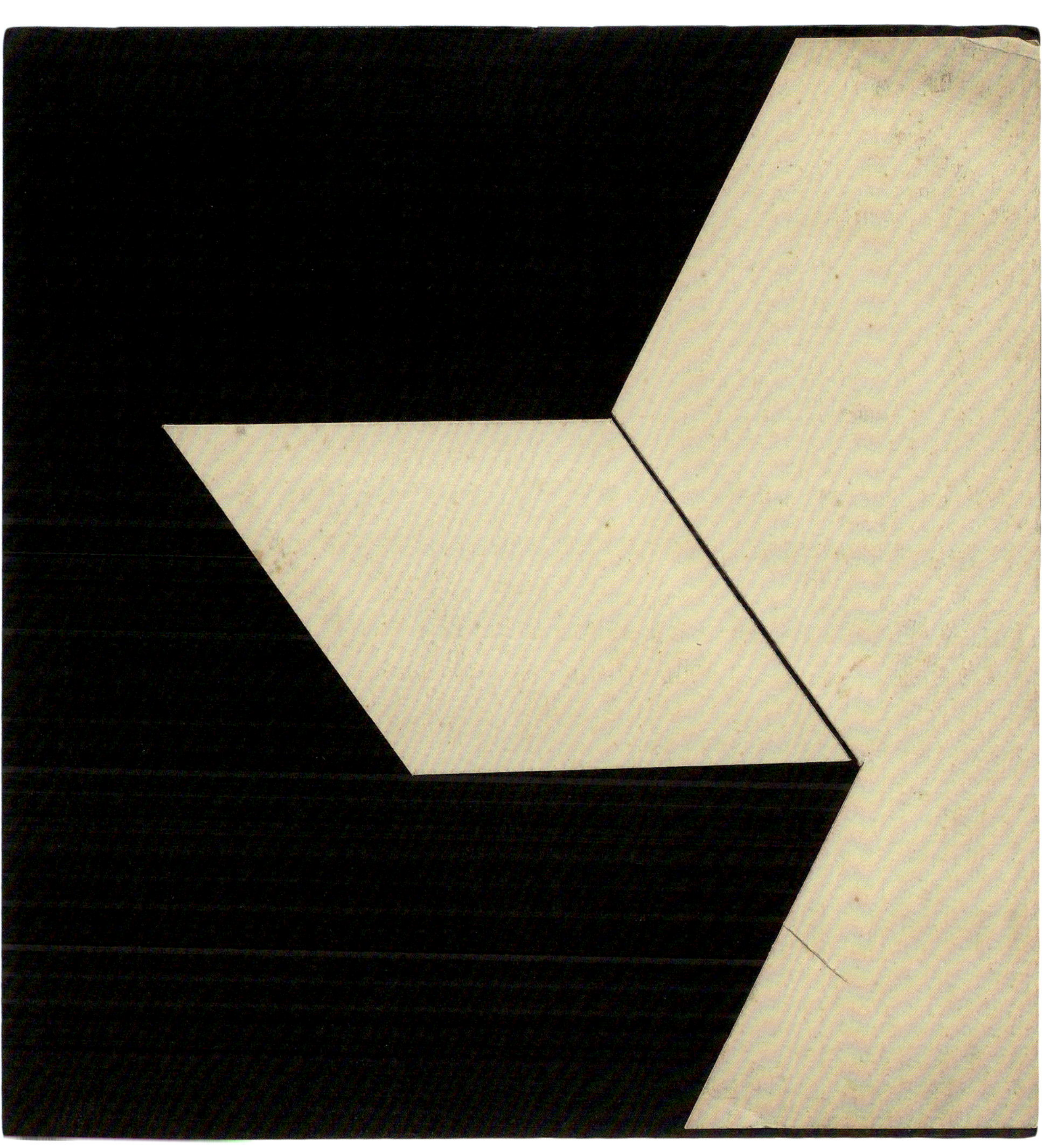

DANE

Thomas Dane Gallery
GB-London SW1Y 6BN | 3 & 11 Duke Street, St. James's
Phone +44 20 79252505 | Fax +44 20 79252506
info@thomasdane.com | www.thomasdane.com
Directors Thomas Dane
François Chantala
Martine d'Anglejan-Chatillon

Artists at
Art Basel Miami Beach | **Walead Beshty**
Abraham Cruzvillegas
Alexandre da Cunha
José Damasceno
Arturo Herrera
Luisa Lambri
Paul Pfeiffer
Lari Pittman
Kelley Walker

Further artists represented | Hurvin Anderson
Kutlug Ataman
Lynda Benglis
Michel François
Anya Gallaccio
John Gerrard
Michael Landy
Bob Law
Glenn Ligon
Steve McQueen
Tony Morgan
Jean-Luc Moulène
Jorge Queiroz
Caragh Thuring

Arturo Herrera
15 Stevens, 2012
Collage, 2 elements: mixed media on paper, 177.8 x 132 cm

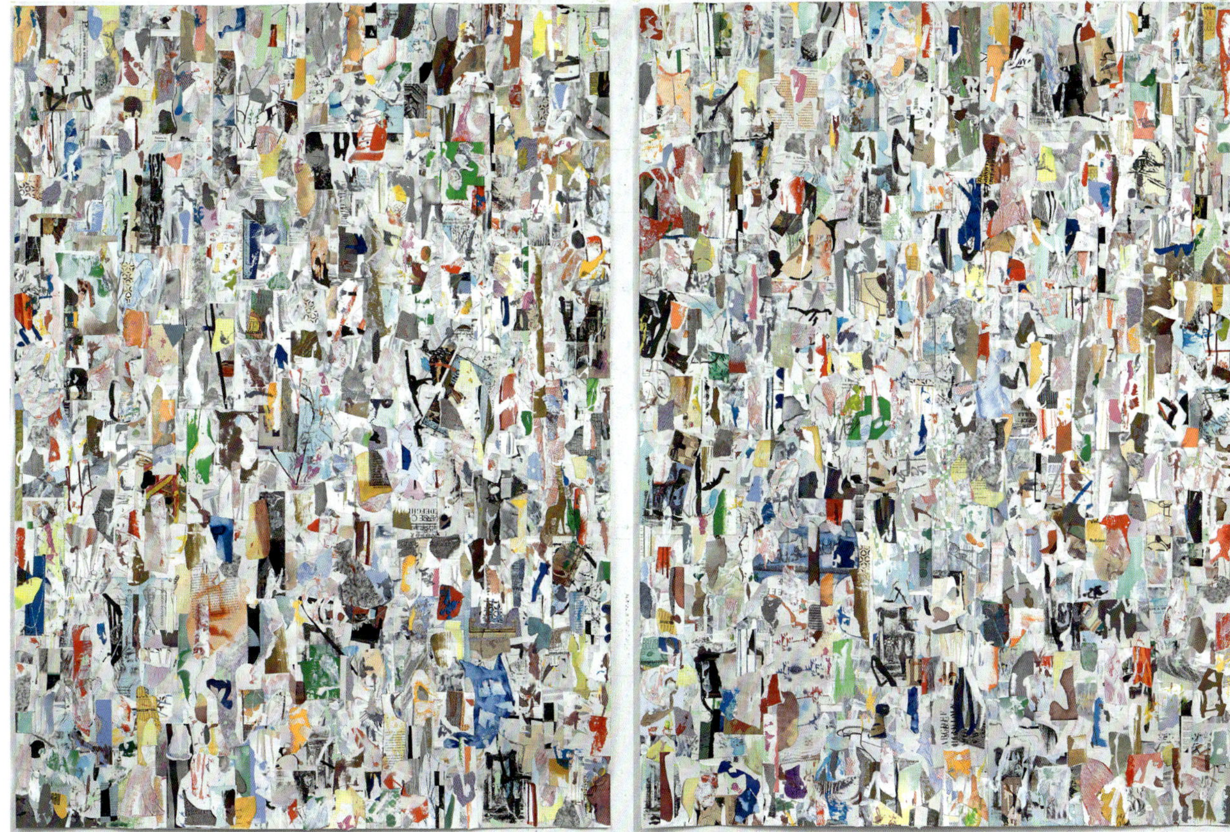

DAVIDSON

Maxwell Davidson Gallery
US-New York, NY 10019 | 724 Fifth Avenue
Phone +1 212 759 75 55 | Fax +1 212 759 58 24
info@davidsongallery.com | www.davidsongallery.com
Directors Maxwell Davidson, III
E. Mary C. Davidson
Maxwell Davidson, IV
Charles C. Davidson

Artists at
Art Basel Miami Beach | **Harry Bertoia**
Carlos Cruz-Diez
Pedro S. De Movellán
Kevin Osmond
Tim Prentice
George Rickey
Jesús Rafael Soto

Gallery Information | The Maxwell Davidson Gallery was founded in 1968 and has been a member of the Art Dealers Association of America since 1975. The gallery emphasizes Modern, postwar, and contemporary paintings, drawings, and sculpture with a concentration in Kinetic sculpture.

In addition to an expanding contemporary program, the gallery has mounted one-man exhibitions for Henri Matisse, Fernand Léger, Raoul Dufy, Roberto Matta, and Sam Francis. The gallery represents the Estates of Tom Wesselmann, George Segal, and Mary Ann Unger.
The gallery is also the preeminent dealer for the works of George Rickey, for whom the gallery has mounted 16 one-man exhibitions. The stable of contemporary artists that the gallery represents is international, with a concentration in young American and British artists who work in a wide variety of media.

Further artists represented: Christopher Brown
Ghost of a Dream
Neil Hamon
Sarah Hardesty
Kiel Johnson
Darren Lago
Ben Long
Sam Messenger
Megan Olson
Mel Rosas
George Segal
Mary Ann Unger
Tom Wesselmann
William T. Wiley

Carlos Cruz-Diez
Physichromie 1742, 2011
Aluminium and serigraph on plexiglass, 39 x 118 inches, 100 x 300 cm
Signed, titled, and dated verso
Unique

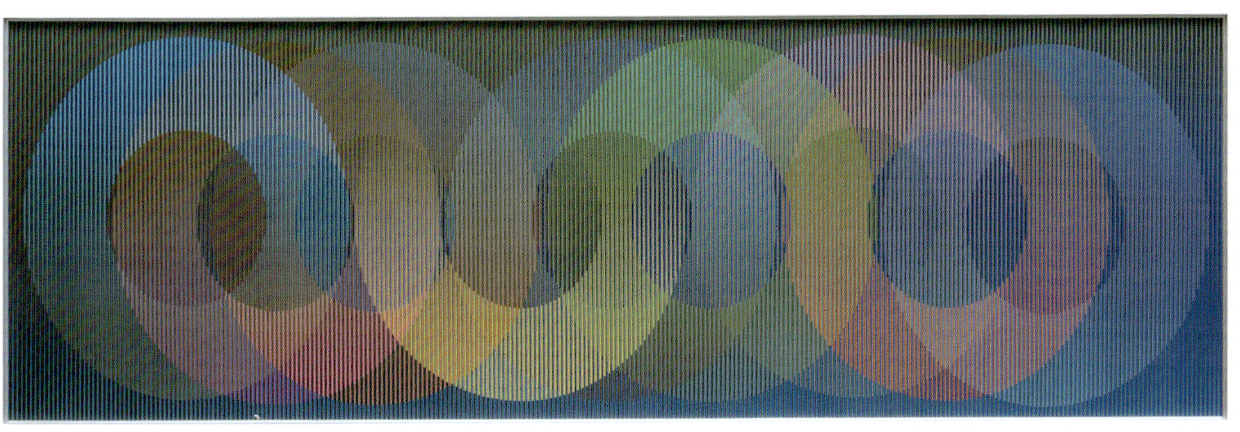

DE CARLO

Massimo De Carlo
IT-20134 Milan | Via Giovanni Ventura, 5
Phone +39 02 70003987 | Fax +39 02 7492135
info@massimodecarlo.it | www.massimodecarlo.it

Massimo De Carlo
GB-London W1K 2QH | 55 South Audley Street
Phone +44 20 72872005 | Fax +44 20 72872005

Artists at
Art Basel Miami Beach | **John M Armleder**
Massimo Bartolini
Alighiero Boetti
Steven Claydon
Dan Colen
Roberto Cuoghi
Christian Holstad
Rashid Johnson
Elad Lassry
Nate Lowman
Paola Pivi
Rob Pruitt
Rudolf Stingel
Piotr Uklanski
Kaari Upson

Gallery Information | Galleria Massimo De Carlo was founded in Milan in 1987. It opened in November in Via Panfilo Castaldi with an exhibition of Olivier Mosset. In 1992 it moved to a new space in Via Bocconi and in 1998 in Viale Corsica. In 2002 it moved to its present space in Via Ventura.

For over 15 years Galleria Massimo De Carlo has played an important role in introducing Italian artists to European and American audiences, and American and European artists to Italy, thereby helping to establish a vital dialogue amongst its artists and national and international institutions.

Galleria Massimo De Carlo works with diverse artists, all of whom work in different media. The gallery deals with a distinctive combination of painting, drawing, installation, sculpture, photography, and video.

The gallery's artists have all gained international recognition and have been shown in galleries, museums, and biennials in most of Europe and the United States. All the artists are represented in important private and public collections.

In 2009 Massimo De Carlo opened a new space in central London. As well as working with the historically represented artists, this new venue has, since its opening, focused on emerging American artists.

Further artists represented: Maurizio Cattelan
Spartacus Chetwynd
George Condo
Elmgreen & Dragset
Roland Flexner
Thomas Grünfeld
Carsten Höller
Sol LeWitt
Matthew Monahan
Olivier Mosset
Diego Perrone
Jim Shaw
Kelly Walker
Yan Pei-Ming
Andrea Zittel

Alighiero Boetti
Mimetico, 1966
Camouflage on plywood,
21 x 29.5 cm

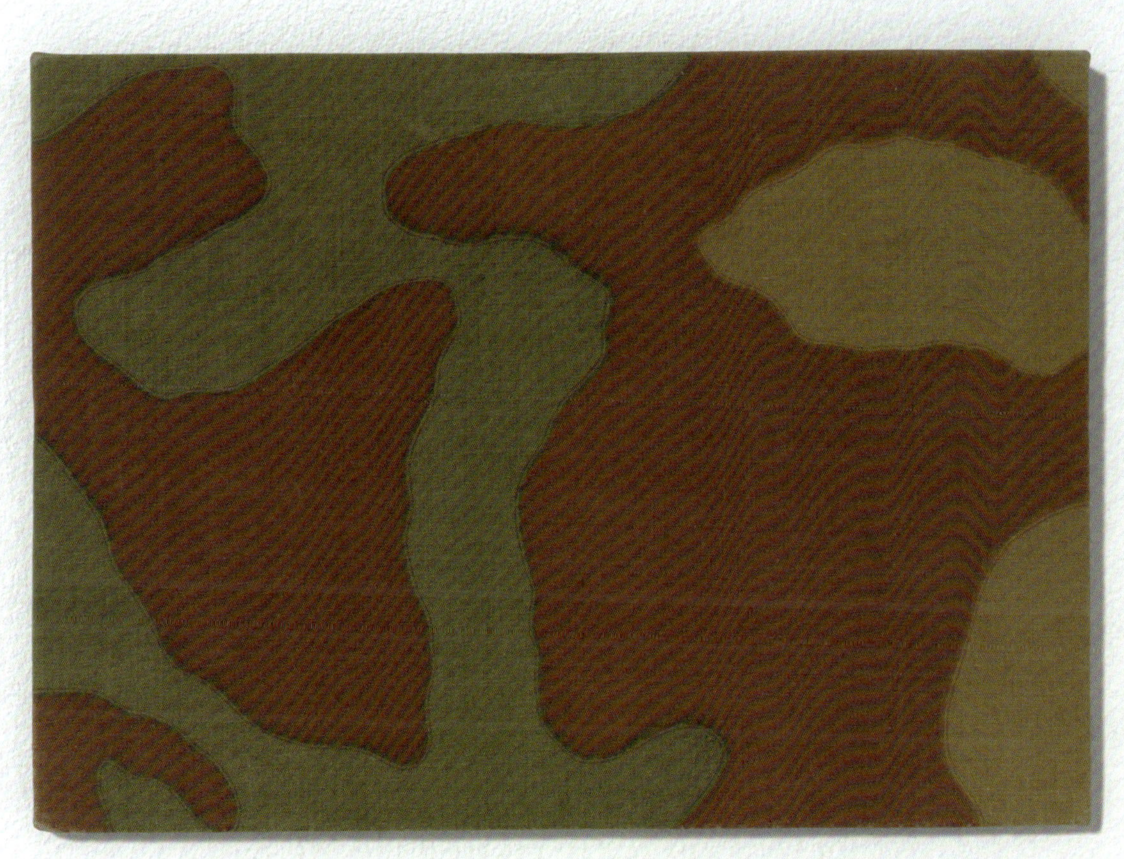

DE OSMA

Mobile +34 609 00 28 80

Galería Guillermo de Osma
ES-28001 Madrid | Claudio Coello 4 – 1º izda
Phone +34 91 435 59 36 | Fax +34 91 431 31 75
info@guillermodeosma.com | www.guillermodeosma.com
Director Guillermo de Osma

Artists at
Art Basel Miami Beach | **Josef Albers**
José Alemany
Willi Baumeister
Georges Braque
Alexander Calder
Eduardo Chillida
Carlos Cruz-Díez
Óscar Domínguez
Eugenio Granell
Sarah Grilo
José Gurvich
Alfredo Hlito
Hannah Höch
Esteban Lisa
Man Ray
Roberto Matta
Joan Miró
László Moholy-Nagy
César Paternosto
Pablo Picasso
Franz Roh
Mira Schendel
Kurt Schwitters
Richard Serra
Luis Tomasello
Joaquín Torres-García

Further artists represented | Washington Barcala
Dis Berlin
Maruja Mallo
Francisco Sobrino

Carlos Cruz-Díez
C.A. 109/Couleur Additive, 1974
Acrylic on canvas mounted on board, 80 x 80 cm

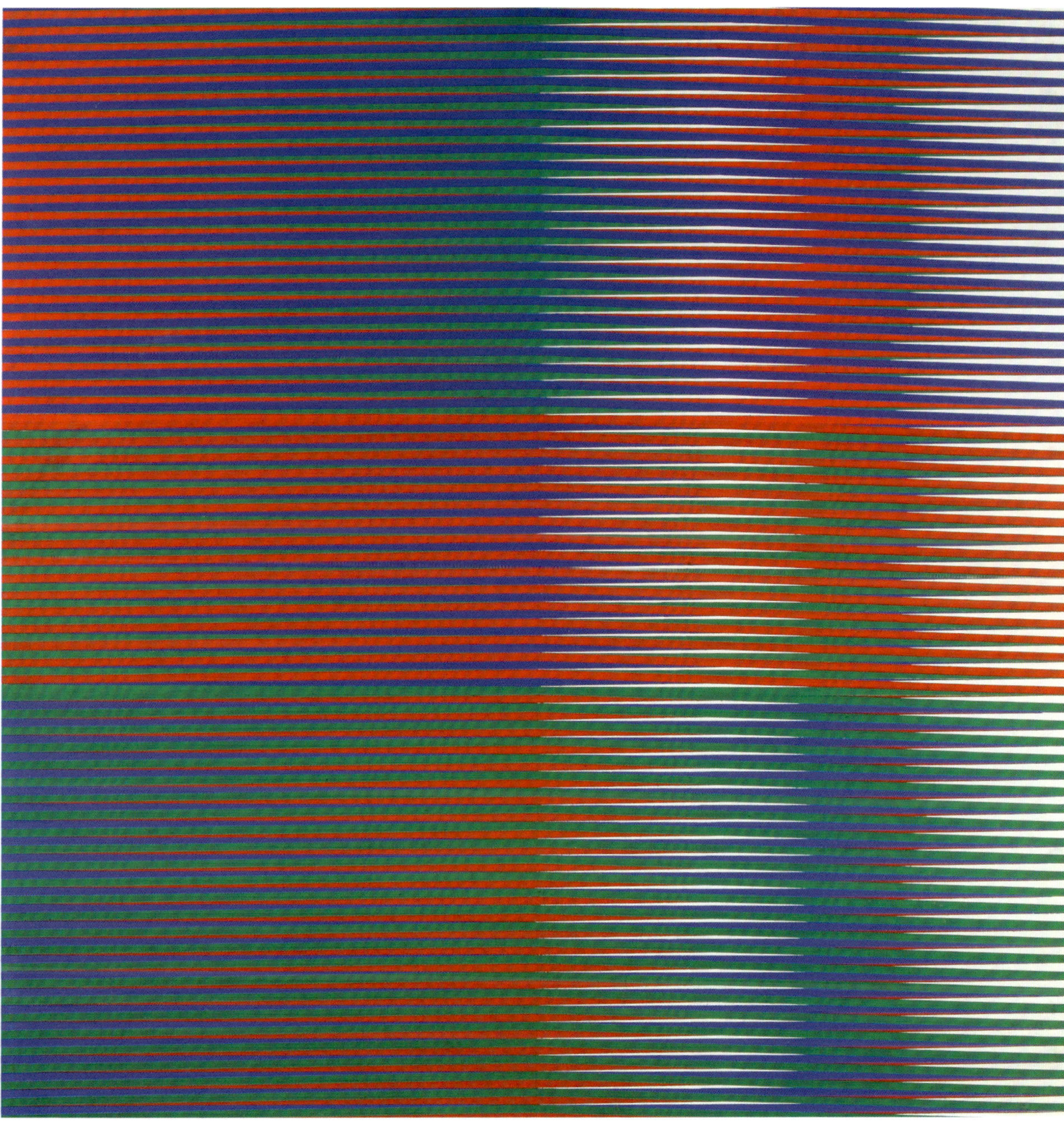

EIGEN + ART

Galerie Eigen + Art Berlin
DE-10117 Berlin | Auguststrasse 26
Phone +49 30 280 66 05 | Fax +49 30 280 66 16
berlin@eigen-art.com | www.eigen-art.com
Directors Gerd Harry Lybke
Kerstin Wahala

Galerie Eigen + Art Leipzig
DE-04179 Leipzig | Spinnereistrasse 7/Hall 5
Phone +49 341 960 78 86 | Fax +49 341 225 42 14
leipzig@eigen-art.com | www.eigen-art.com

Eigen + Art Lab
DE- 10117 Berlin | Auguststrasse 11-13
Phone +49 30 246 28 40 | Fax +49 30 24 62 84 20
lab@eigen-art.com | www.eigen-art.com

Artists at Art Basel Miami Beach | **Marc Desgrandchamps**
Martin Eder
Tim Eitel
Uwe Kowski
Ryan Mosley
Neo Rauch
David Schnell
Matthias Weischer

Gallery Information | Exhibitions Eigen + Art Leipzig 2012/13:
Uwe Kowski, April 28-August 25, 2012
David Schnell, September 15-December 15, 2012

Exhibitions Eigen + Art Lab 2012/13:
Marc Desgrandchamps, September 6-October 27, 2012
Lada Nakonechna, November 15, 2012-January 12, 2013

Further artists represented: Akos Birkas
Birgit Brenner
Nina Fischer/Maroan El Sani
Stella Hamberg
Jörg Herold
Christine Hill
Maix Mayer
Carsten Nicolai
Olaf Nicolai
Ricarda Roggan
Yehudit Sasportas
Annelies Strba

Neo Rauch
Nest, 2012
Oil on canvas, 300 x 250 cm

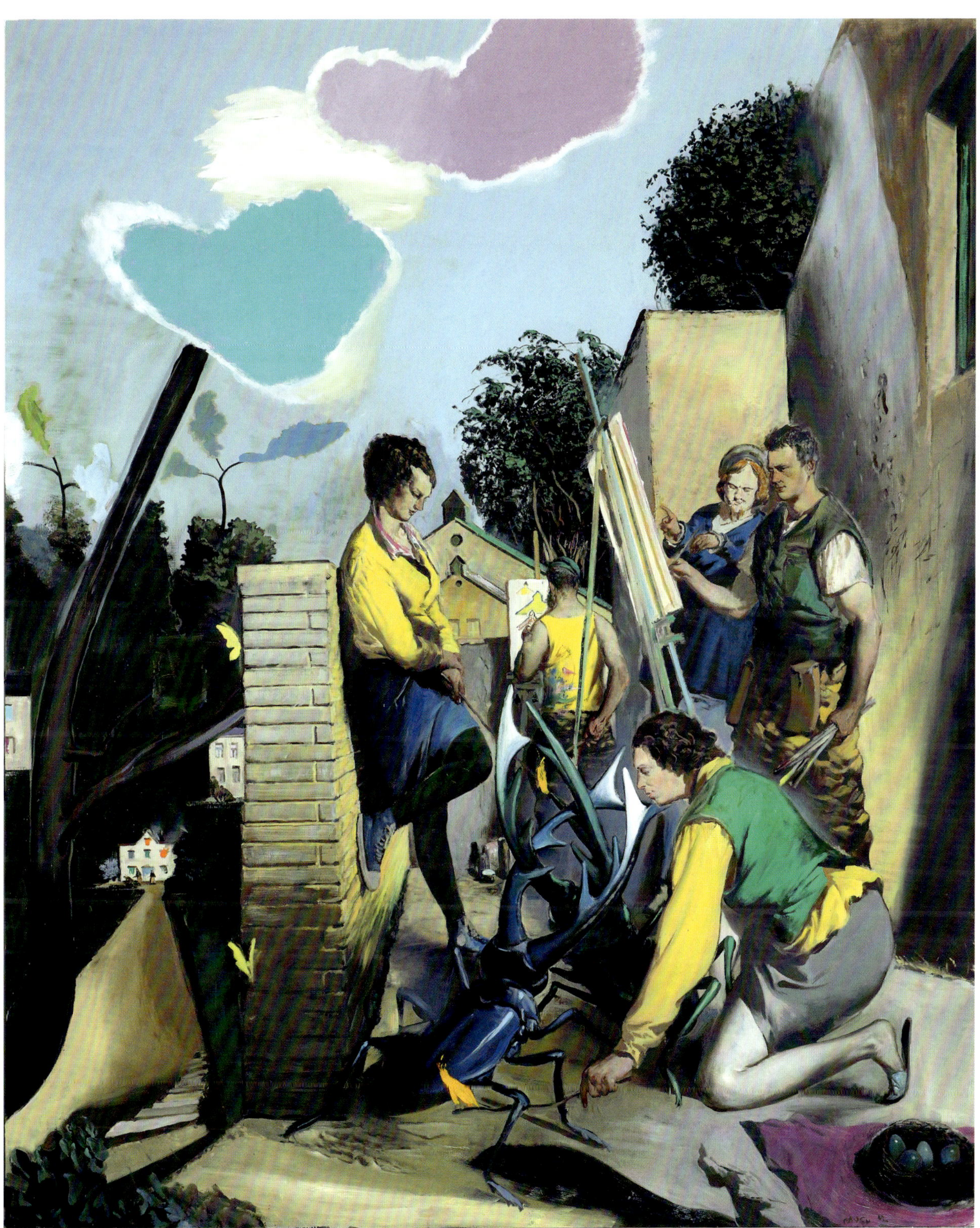

ELBAZ

Mobile +33 6 03 33 85 85

Galerie Frank Elbaz
FR-75003 Paris | 66, rue de Turenne
Phone +33 1 48 87 50 04
info@galeriefrankelbaz.com | www.galeriefrankelbaz.com
Director Frank Elbaz

Artists at Art Nova | Davide Balula
Gyan Panchal

Gallery Information | Galerie Frank Elbaz opened in September 2002 in the district of Le Marais in Paris.

The gallery is committed to working with French and international artists, representing emerging as well as mid-career artists.

Over the years the gallery has also focused on rediscovering older artists such as the Californian Beat Generation artist Wallace Berman.

Further artists represented:
Jesus Alberto Benitez
Wallace Berman
Julije Knifer
Justine Kurland
Rainier Lericolais
Mangelos
Ari Marcopoulos
Kaz Oshiro
Bernard Piffaretti
Meredyth Sparks
Blair Thurman
Josip Vanista

'In the place of geometrical forms and exact proportions, Davide Balula pursues the traces of reality in his material paintings. Standing between protophysics and abstract expressionism, the artist sets up a topography of chance, in which artistic intent combines with the world's fortuitousness.' (Béatrice Gross, excerpt from the press release 'A Compass in the Eye,' Galerie Frank Elbaz, Paris, 2010)

'I'm making sculpture as a way of asking the material if it still bears the traces of its own story. What kind of link is there between a synthetic fabric and a natural pigment? What can I construct out of their abstract relationship? I see sculpture as an unresolved question. By confronting the material with its origin and its making, I reflect on our relationship with the mute materials that compose today's environment.' (Gyan Panchal)

Davide Balula
Burnt Painting/Imprint of the Burnt Painting, 2012
Charred wood, dust of charred wood on canvas, each element 210 x 150 cm

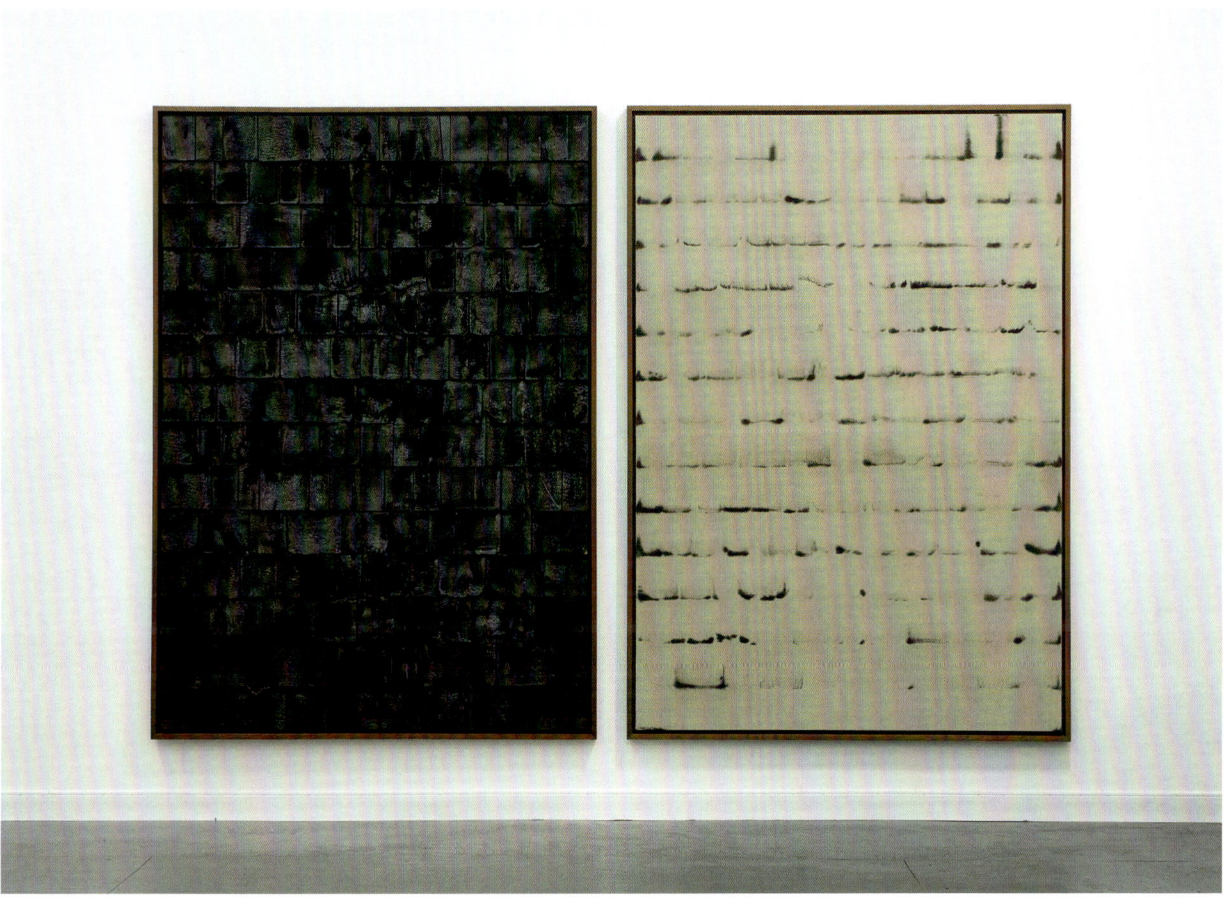

ELEVEN RIVINGTON

Eleven Rivington
US-New York, NY 10002 | 11 Rivington Street
Phone +1 212 982 19 30 | Fax +1 212 982 19 36
office@elevenrivington.com | www.elevenrivington.com
Directors Augusto Arbizo
Elizabeth Raizes Sadeghi
Todd von Ammon

Artists at Art Nova | Hilary Berseth
Michael DeLucia
Katrín Sigurdardóttir

Further artists represented | Chris Caccamise
Tm Davy
Caetano de Almeida
Matt Ducklo
Jeronimo Elespe
Volker Hueller
Cameron Martin
Miko & Thayer
Ishmael Randall Weeks
Jackie Saccoccio
Adam Shecter
Valeska Soares
Kevin Zucker

The gallery presents new work by Hilary Berseth (*1979, United States), Michael DeLucia (*1976, United States), and Katrín Sigurdardóttir (*1967, Iceland).

Katrín Sigurdardóttir
Boiseries (Hôtel de Crillon), 2010
Mixed media, dimensions variable

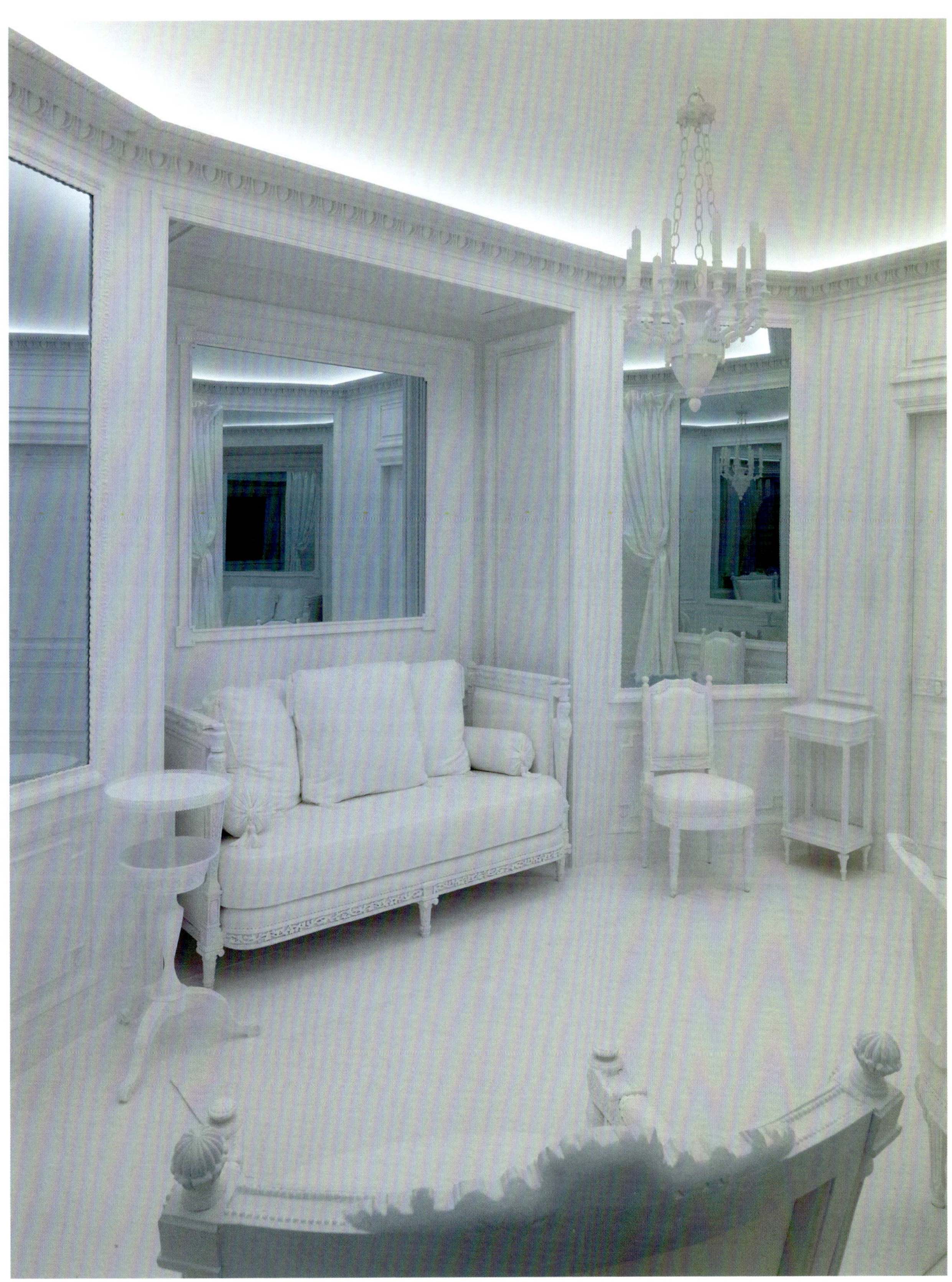

FARIA

Mobile +1 917 378 55 85

Henrique Faria Fine Art
US-New York, NY 10065 | 35 East 67th Street, 4th Floor
Phone +1 212 517 46 09 | Fax +1 212 517 76 29
info@henriquefaria.com | www.henriquefaria.com
Director Aimé Iglesias Lukin

Artists at
Art Basel Miami Beach | **Álvaro Barrios**
Luis F. Benedit
Jaime Davidovich
Mirtha Dermisache
Eugenio Espinoza
Anna Bella Geiger
Carlos Ginzburg
Leandro Katz
Marta Minujín
Claudio Perna
Alejandro Puente
Osvaldo Romberg
Pedro Terán
Yeni & Nan
Horacio Zabala

Gallery Information | Henrique Faria opened as an art cabinet on Madison Avenue, New York, in 2001, specializing in Latin American geometric abstract artists such as modern masters Jesús Soto, Raúl Lozza, Gego, Mathias Goeritz, María Freire, and Alejandro Otero as well as contemporary mid-career artists such as Luis Roldán, Jose Bechara, Eugenio Espinoza, and José Gabriel Fernández.

In 2007, the gallery decided to venture into the much lesser known world of conceptual practices from Latin America, including artists Juan Downey, Claudio Perna, Nicolás García Uriburu, Diego Barboza, Marta Minujín, Clemente Padín, Guillermo Deisler, and Horacio Zabala.

In 2009, we opened a new gallery with an exhibition by Argentine artist, poet, and filmmaker Leandro Katz. The next year, we doubled the size of the gallery, which allowed us to continue exhibiting historical Latin American works from the 50s, 60s, and 70s in addition to a program of exhibitions by contemporary artists such as Emilio Chapela, Alessandro Balteo Yazbeck, Javier Téllez, and Alexander Apóstol.

Since we opened the gallery, the demand for Latin American works has increased exponentially. Our client base has expanded from mainly Latin American collectors to international institutions, foundations, and museums.

Further artists represented: Alessandro Balteo Yazbeck
Emilio Chapela
Eduardo Costa
Guillermo Deisler
José Gabriel Fernández
Michael Gitlin
Luis Roldán

Pedro Terán
A | *Develamiento*, 1972-2011
Gelatin silver print,
19¾ x 34¼ inches
Edition of 3 + 1 AP

B | *Identity Card,* 1972-2011
Gelatin silver print,
19⅝ x 13¾ inches
Edition of 3 + 1 AP

A

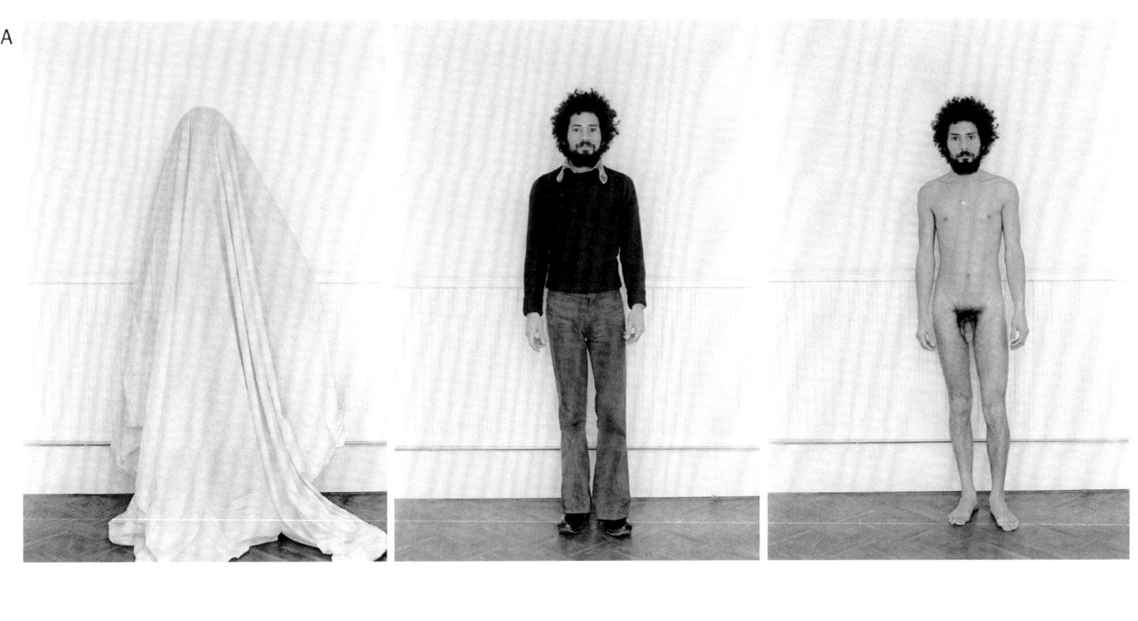

B

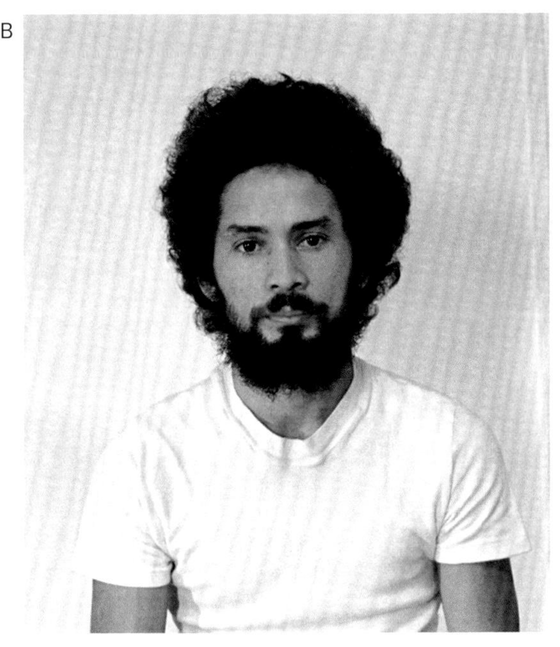

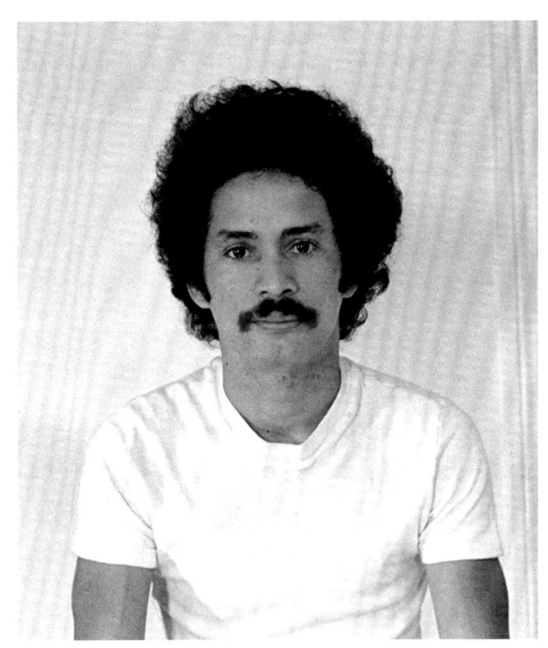

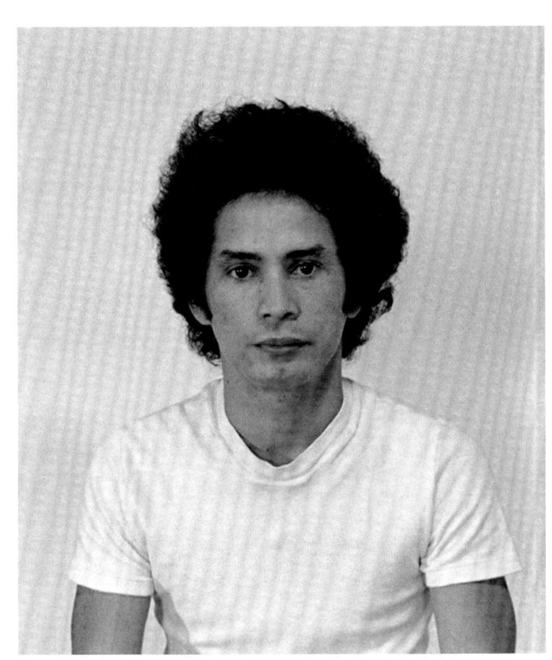

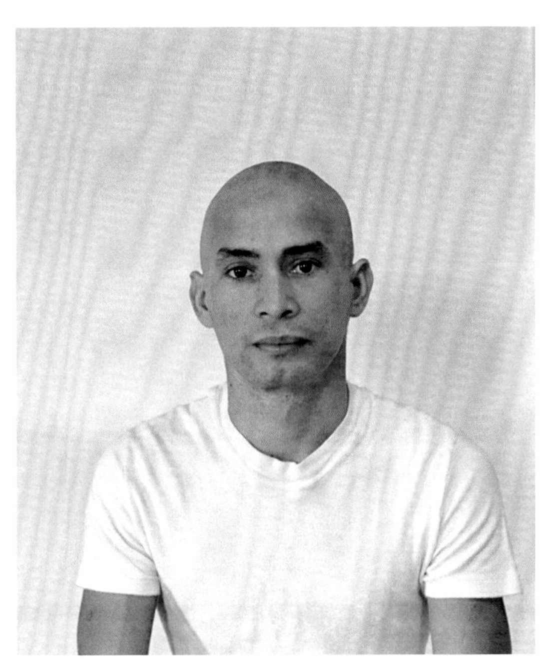

FISCHER

Mobile +49 177 356 18 26, +49 171 473 02 72

Konrad Fischer Galerie
DE-40233 Düsseldorf | Platanenstrasse 7
Phone +49 211 68 59 08 | Fax +49 211 68 97 80
office@konradfischergalerie.de | www.konradfischergalerie.de
Director Dorothee Fischer

Konrad Fischer Galerie
DE-10969 Berlin | Lindenstrasse 35
Phone +49 30 50 59 68 20 | Fax +49 30 50 59 68 21
berlin-office@konradfischergalerie.de | www.konradfischergalerie.de
Directors Dorothee Fischer
Daniel Marzona

Artists at
Art Basel Miami Beach | **Carl Andre**
Giovanni Anselmo
Bernd & Hilla Becher
Guy Ben-Ner
Stanley Brouwn
Matthew Buckingham
Peter Buggenhout
Daniel Buren
Nina Canell
Alan Charlton
Hanne Darboven
Jan Dibbets
Cristina Iglesias
Zon Ito
Stephen Kaltenbach
On Kawara
Harald Klingelhöller
Jannis Kounellis
Melissa Kretschmer
Wolfgang Laib
Jim Lambie
Sol LeWitt
Richard Long
Robert Mangold
Rita McBride
Mario Merz
Bruce Nauman
Maria Nordman
Giuseppe Penone
Manfred Pernice
Magnus Plessen
Wolfgang Plöger
Charlotte Posenenske
Thomas Ruff
Robert Ryman
Gregor Schneider
Thomas Schütte
Juergen Staack
Yuji Takeoka
Tatjana Valsang
Paloma Varga Weisz
Johannes Wald
Lawrence Weiner
Petra Wunderlich
Jerry Zeniuk

Gallery Information | Exhibitions in 2012/13: Stephen Antonakos
Stanley Brouwn
Peter Buggenhout
Alan Charlton
Tony Cragg
Max Neuhaus
Manfred Pernice
Thomas Ruff
Juergen Staack
Sol LeWitt

Jan Dibbets
Tollebeek Winter, 1998
Color photograph on wall,
66 x 138 cm

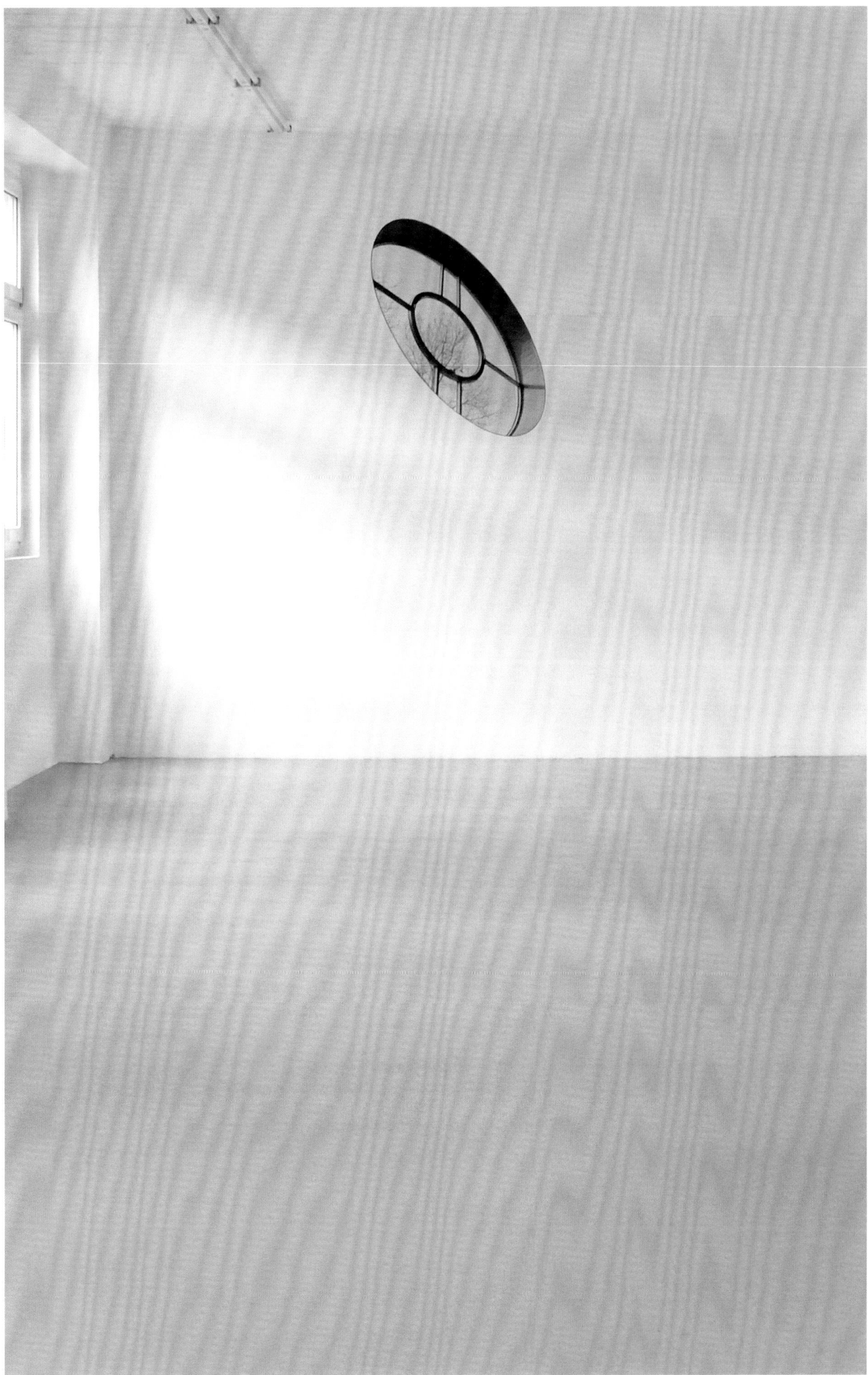

FITZROY

Fitzroy Gallery
US-New York, NY 10002 | 195 Chrystie Street
Phone +1 212 3438670 | Fax +1 212 3438671
info@fitzroygallery.com | www.fitzroygallery.com
Director Maureen Sarro

One-Person Show | Artist Information

Colby Bird

*1978, Austin, TX, United States
Lives and works in New York, NY, United States

Selected solo exhibitions:
2012 *Double Acting Hinge,* Fitzroy Gallery, New York, NY
2011 *Dust Breeds Contempt,* Lora Reynolds Gallery, Austin, TX
2010 *Knoll Sofa,* Real Fine Arts, Brooklyn, NY
2009 *Cold End,* Okay Mountain, Austin, TX
Colby Bird, CRG Gallery, New York, NY
2001 *1994,* The Space at Alice, Providence, RI

Selected group exhibitions:
2011 *The Anxiety of Photography,* Arthouse at the Jones Center, Austin, TX
The Anxiety of Photography, Aspen Art Museum, Aspen, CO
Cover Version LP, BAM, New York, NY
2010 *Inaugural Exhibition,* CRG Gallery, New York, NY
Contemporary Prints, CRG Gallery, New York, NY
Big Apple, Clifton Benevento Gallery, New York, NY
Ends and Means, RVF Museum, California State University, San Bernadino, CA
2009 *QVNOXW//,* 86 Forsyth, New York, NY
Guilty Feet, performance at 179 Canal, New York, NY
Gruppenausstellung, organized by Max Hans Daniel, at AutoCenter, Berlin
Contemporary Culture, Lora Reynolds Gallery, Austin, TX
Single Vision, presented by ApartmentShow, New York, NY
FAX, The Drawing Center, New York, NY

Further artists represented | Drew Conrad
Sean Dack
Michelle Elzay
Simone Forti
Todd Norsten
Paul Pascarella
Gibb Slife
Kianja Strobert
Georgi Tushev
Robert Žungu

This is an exploration of creative versus professional labor in the field of art. Colby Bird presents seven color photographs, shot by an anonymous professional photographer in the early 1980s, in their original form, with no intervention by the artist. On the adjacent wall, Bird installs seven trompe-l'oeil photographs of the original photographs framed and displayed at the same scale. The subject matter of the professional photographs is largely flora/fauna and landscape imagery – two areas germane to the amateur and professional photographer but largely taboo for a contemporary artist.

The re-photographing of the images provides mediation from this creative faux-pas and couches the images in a conceptual and formal visual language. The insouciance of the 'creative' gesture of framing and hanging prefabricated material is mediated by the 'professional' gesture of re-photography (copy work) and framing.

Colby Bird
White Button Down Shirt (Kodak Star 110), 2012
Pigment print on cotton paper, 7 x 5 inches

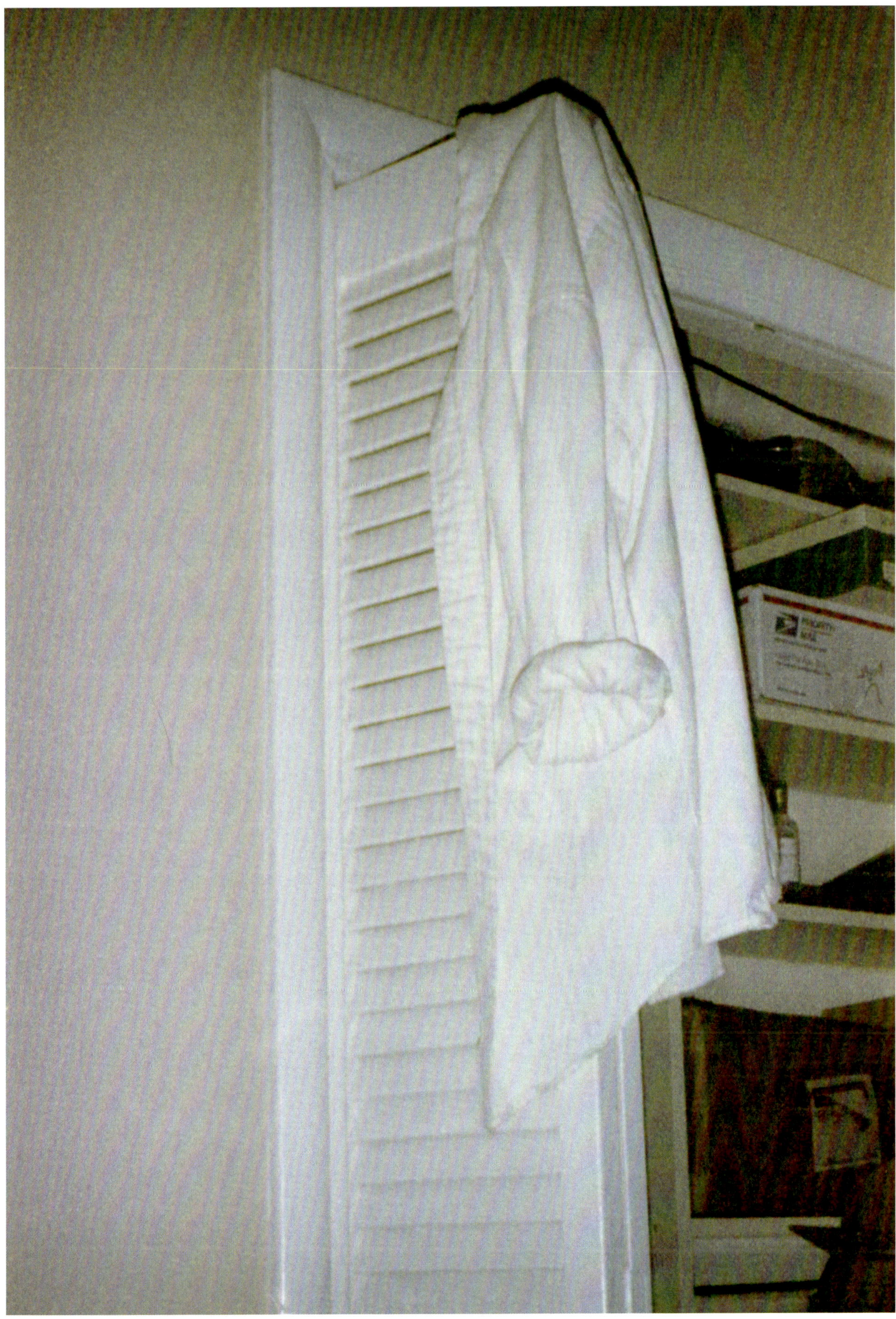

FONTI

Mobile +39 348 821 05 13

Fonti
IT-80132 Naples | Via Chiaia 229
Phone +39 081 41 14 09 | Fax +39 081 41 14 09
info@galleriafonti.it | www.galleriafonti.it
Director Giangi Fonti

One-Person Show | Artist Information

Christian Flamm

*1974, Stuttgart, Germany
Lives and works in London, United Kingdom

Selected solo exhibitions:
2012 Galerie Karin Guenther, Hamburg
2009 *A une condition,* Dépendance, Brussels
2008 *Per un motivo o per un altro,* Fonti, Naples
2006 *Pictures the Problem Orchestra,* André Schlechtriem Gallery, New York, NY
2005 *Realism of the Heart,* Alison Jacques Gallery, London
Der Mond in den Antennen, Galerie Neu, Berlin
2004 *La legge da me non scritta,* Fonti, Naples
Für immer Mensch, Locus Amoenus, Canossa
2002 *Take Care of Yourselves,* asprey jacques, London
Urlaub vom ich, Galerie Neu, Berlin
Meine Sorgen will ich haben!, Ascan Crone, Hamburg
2001 *Phasen von Schweigen,* Galerie Nomadenoase, Hamburg
2000 *Wir müssen miteinander reden,* Galerie Neu, Berlin
1999 *Umsonst ist das Leben,* Frankfurter Kunstverein, Frankfurt am Main
1998 *Der Apfel fällt nicht weit vom Stamm,* Künstlerhaus, Stuttgart

Selected group exhibitions:
2011 *No Neutral Ground,* German Embassy, London
2010 *NOVEL,* Dépendance, Brussels
2009 *After Twilight,* Kölnischer Kunstverein, Cologne
2007 *re-dis-play,* Kunstverein Heidelberg, Heidelberg
2006 *Optik Schröder – Werke der Sammlung Schröder,* Kunstverein Braunschweig, Braunschweig
2005 *The Addiction,* Gagosian Gallery, New York, NY
2004 *The Future as a Silver Lining,* migros museum für gegenwartskunst, Zurich
Happy Days Are Here Again, David Zwirner Gallery, New York, NY

Gallery Information | Galleria Fonti was established in 2004.

Further artists represented:
Michel Auder
Marc Camille Chaimowicz
Marieta Chirulescu
Peter Coffin
Nicola Gobbetto
Piero Golia
Delia Gonzalez
Delia Gonzalez & Gavin Russom
Kiluanji Kia Henda
Daniel Knorr
Fabian Marti
Birgit Megerle
Seb Patane
Manfred Pernice
Giulia Piscitelli
Gavin Russom
Lorenzo Scotto di Luzio
Eric Wesley

Christian Flamm's research reveals the false mechanism of images and ideas imposed by mainstream media. His point of view is from a critical distance, a sort of veto on acceptance or rejection. It is a different understanding of history. Flamm's work is an act of reflection; it shows contradictions, making moral or political judgments.

An Alphabet is an installation project whose main element is an alphabet especially created by the artist.

The whole arrangement is built around a piece on the floor that spells the words 'Make Of That What You Wish.' The abstract quality of the alphabet keeps the meaning from becoming immediately obvious. To enable interested viewers to decipher it easily, the full alphabet is displayed on the wall right behind the piece.

There is also a series of five drawings in which the artist recalls the alphabet created by William Nicholson in the 1890s.

Christian Flamm
An Alphabet, 2012
Screenprint, gouache on paper,
118.9 x 84.1 x 5 cm

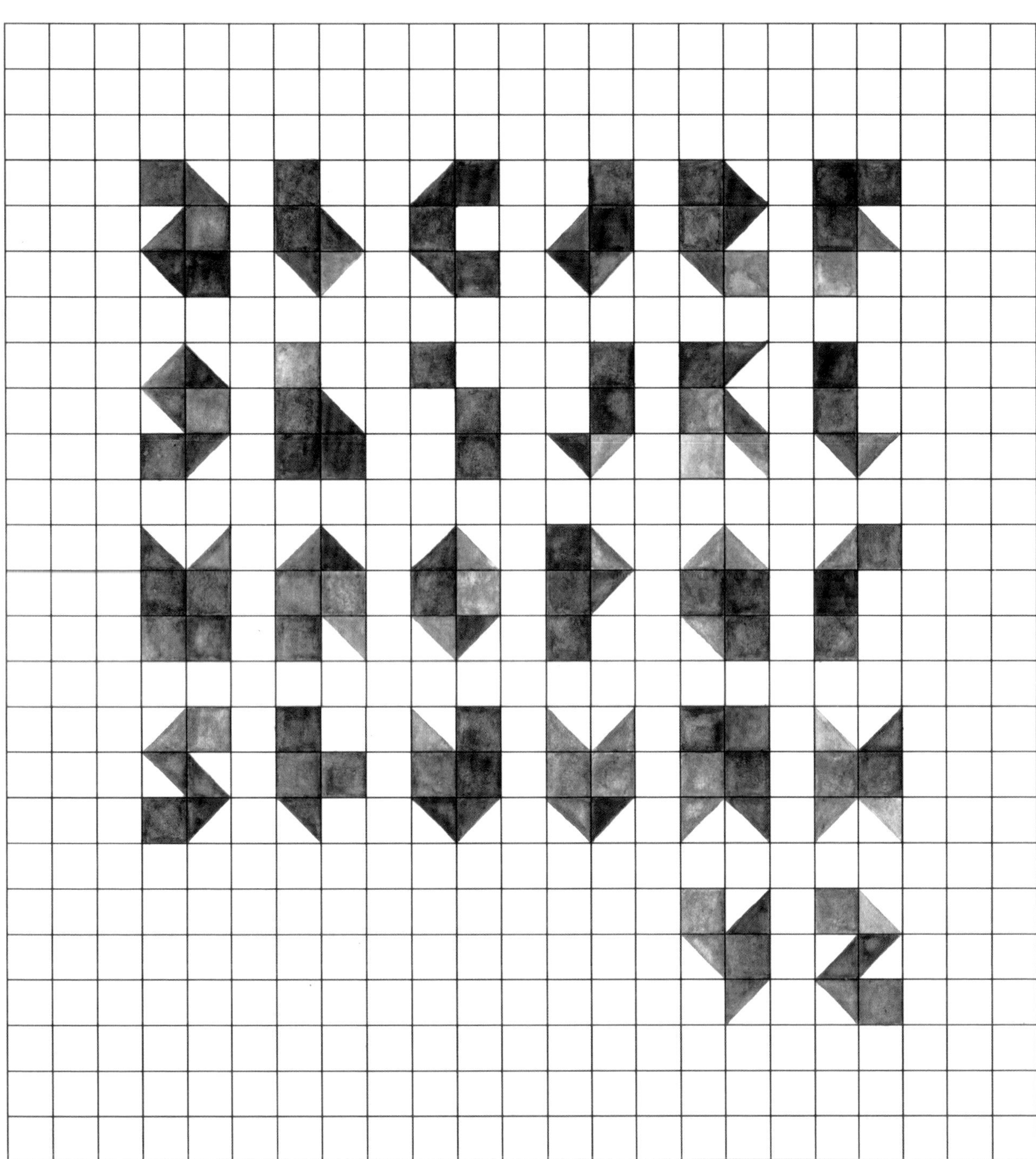

FORTES VILAÇA

Galeria Fortes Vilaça
BR-São Paulo 05416-001 | Rua Fradique Coutinho, 1500
Phone +55 11 30327066 | Fax +55 11 30970384
galeria@fortesvilaca.com.br | www.fortesvilaca.com.br
Directors Márcia Fortes
Alessandra Ragazzo d'Aloia
Alexandre Gabriel

Galpão Fortes Vilaça
BR-São Paulo 01138-000 | Rua James Holland, 71
Phone +55 11 33923942 | Fax +55 11 33925969

Artists at Art Basel Miami Beach | **Franz Ackermann**
Efrain Almeida
Armando Andrade Tudela
Barrão
Carlos Bevilacqua
Tiago Carneiro da Cunha
Leda Catunda
José Damasceno
Iran do Espírito Santo
Simon Evans
Tamar Guimarães
João Maria Gusmão & Pedro Paiva
Marine Hugonnier
Sergej Jensen
Lucia Laguna
Jac Leirner
Los Carpinteros
Rodrigo Matheus
Beatriz Milhazes
Gerben Mulder
Ernesto Neto
Rivane Neuenschwander
Damián Ortega
osgemeos
Sara Ramo
Nuno Ramos
Mauro Restiffe
Marina Rheingantz
Michael Sailstorfer
Julião Sarmento
Valeska Soares
Janaina Tschäpe
Adriana Varejão
Erika Verzutti
Cerith Wyn Evans
Luiz Zerbini

Lucia Laguna
Paisagem Nº 58, 2012
Acrylic and oil on canvas,
160 x 160 cm

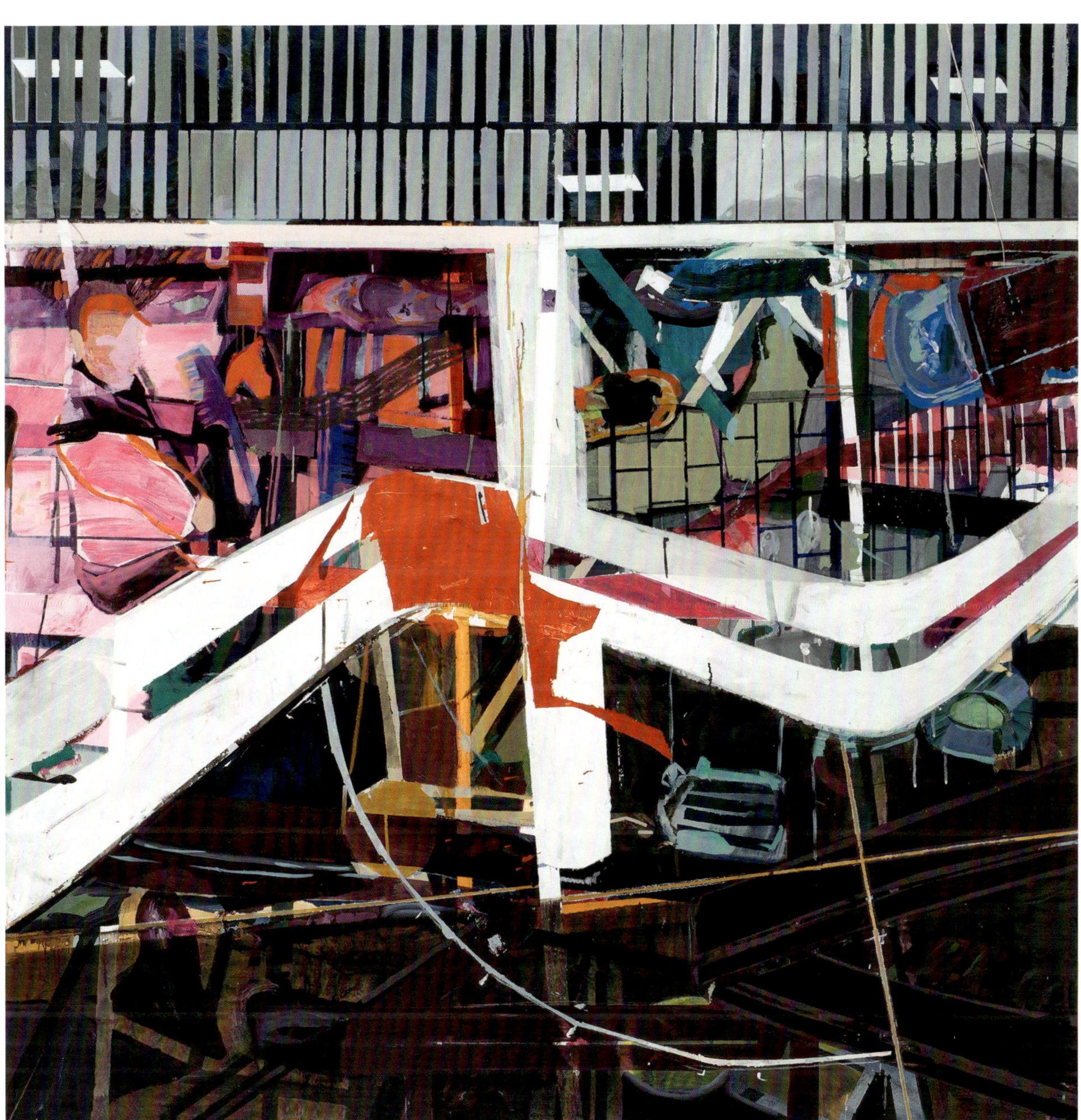

FREEMAN

Peter Freeman, Inc.
US-New York, NY 10013 | 140 Grand Street
Phone +1 212 966 51 54 | Fax +1 212 966 53 49
info@peterfreemaninc.com | www.peterfreemaninc.com
Directors Peter C. Freeman
Susie Rodriguez Guzman

Artists at
Art Basel Miami Beach | **David Adamo**
Silvia Bächli
Mel Bochner
Marcel Broodthaers
Pedro Cabrita Reis
Alexander Calder
James Castle
James Ensor
Alex Hay
Michael Heizer
Donald Judd
Ellsworth Kelly
Mangelos
Ralph Eugene Meatyard
Helen Mirra
Catherine Murphy
Bruce Nauman
Claes Oldenburg
Sigmar Polke
Charlotte Posenenske
Robert Rauschenberg
Gerhard Richter
Jan Schoonhoven
Thomas Schütte
Richard Serra
Frank Stella
Richard Tuttle
Franz Erhard Walther
Richard Wentworth

Gallery Information | Founded in 1990, Peter Freeman, Inc. specializes in important 20th-century and contemporary paintings, drawings, and sculpture with a particular focus on Pop and Minimal works.

Catherine Murphy
Snowflakes, 2011
Oil on canvas, 52 x 52 inches

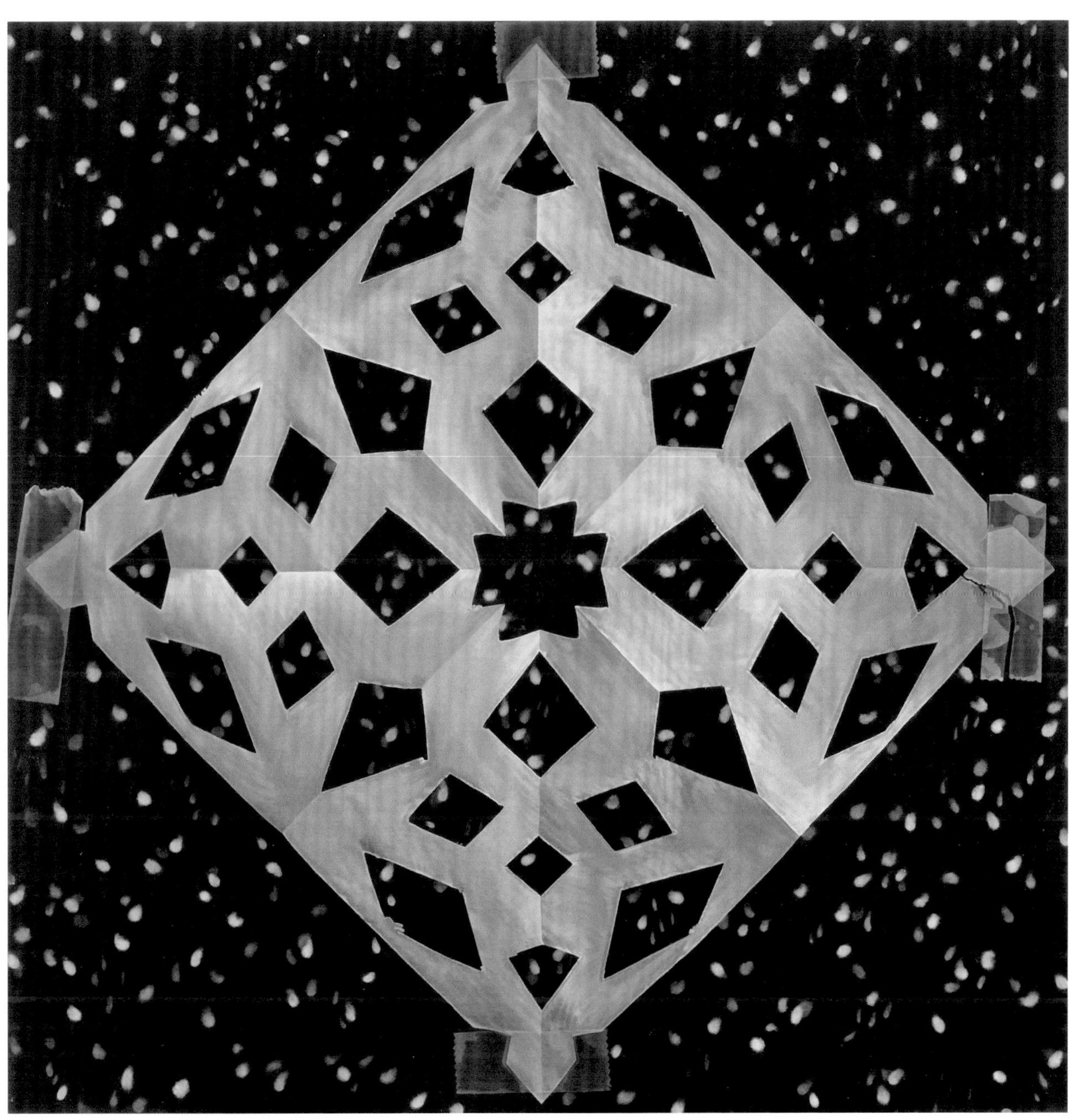

FRIEDMAN

Stephen Friedman Gallery
GB-London W1S 3AN | 25-28 Old Burlington Street
Phone +44 20 74 94 14 34 | Fax +44 20 74 94 14 31
info@stephenfriedman.com | www.stephenfriedman.com
Directors Stephen Friedman
David Hubbard
Ticiana Correa

Stephen Friedman Gallery
GB-London W1S 3AQ | 11 Old Burlington Street
Phone +44 20 74 94 14 34 | Fax +44 20 74 94 14 31

Artists at
Art Basel Miami Beach | **Mamma Andersson**
Stephan Balkenhol
Claire Barclay
Huma Bhabha
Robert Buck
Andreas Eriksson
Tom Friedman
Kendell Geers
Wayne Gonzales
Daniel Guzmán
Thomas Hirschhorn
Jim Hodges
Li Tianbing
Paul McDevitt
Beatriz Milhazes
Yoshitomo Nara
Rivane Neuenschwander
Thomas Nozkowski
Catherine Opie
Cornelius Quabeck
Ged Quinn
Jennifer Rubell
Lucas Samaras
Mira Schendel
Yinka Shonibare, MBE
David Shrigley
Anne Truitt

Gallery Information | International contemporary art

Ged Quinn
Bunker Archeology, 2012
Oil on canvas, 50 x 61 x 5 cm

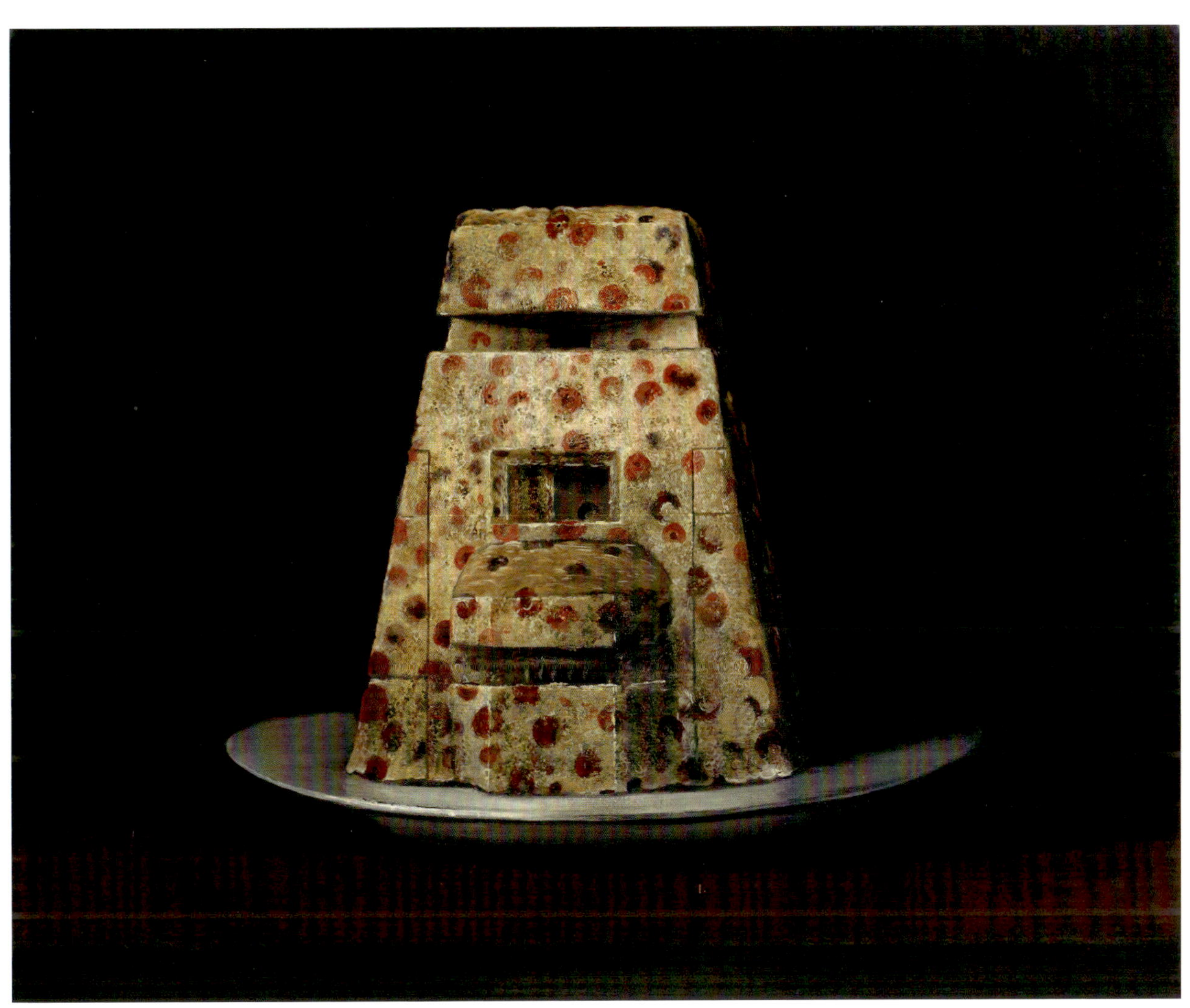

GAGOSIAN

Gagosian Gallery
US-New York, NY 10075 | 980 Madison Avenue
Phone +1 212 744 23 13 | Fax +1 212 710 38 25
newyork@gagosian.com

Gagosian Gallery
US-New York, NY 10011 | 555 West 24th Street
Phone +1 212 741 11 11 | Fax +1 212 741 96 11
newyork@gagosian.com

Gagosian Gallery
US-New York, NY 10011 | 522 West 21st Street
Phone +1 212 741 17 17 | Fax +1 212 741 00 06
newyork@gagosian.com

Gagosian Gallery
US-Beverly Hills, CA 90210 | 456 North Camden Drive
Phone +1 310 271 94 00 | Fax +1 310 271 94 20
losangeles@gagosian.com

Gagosian Gallery
GB-London WC1X 9JD | 6-24 Britannia Street
Phone +44 20 78 41 99 60 | Fax +44 20 78 41 99 61
london@gagosian.com

Gagosian Gallery
GB-London W1K 3DE | 17-19 Davies Street
Phone +44 20 74 93 30 20 | Fax +44 20 74 93 30 25
london@gagosian.com

Gagosian Gallery
FR-75008 Paris | 4 rue de Ponthieu
Phone +33 1 75 00 05 92 | Fax +33 1 70 24 87 10
paris@gagosian.com

Gagosian Gallery
IT-00187 Rome | via Francesco Crispi 16
Phone +39 06 42 08 64 98 | Fax +39 06 42 01 47 65
roma@gagosian.com

Gagosian Gallery
GR-10671 Athens | 3 Merlin Street
Phone +30 210 364 02 15 | Fax +30 210 364 02 04
athens@gagosian.com

Gagosian Gallery
CH-1204 Geneva | 19 Place de Longemalle
Phone +41 22 319 36 19 | Fax +41 22 319 36 10
geneva@gagosian.com

Gagosian Gallery
CN-999077 Central Hong Kong | 7/F Pedder Building, 12 Pedder Street
Phone +852 21 51 05 55 | Fax +852 21 51 08 53
hongkong@gagosian.com

A+B | **Cy Twombly**
The Last Paintings
Installation view, Gagosian Gallery, 456 North Camden Drive, Beverly Hills, CA, April 27-June 9, 2012, travelling to New York Fall of 2012

A

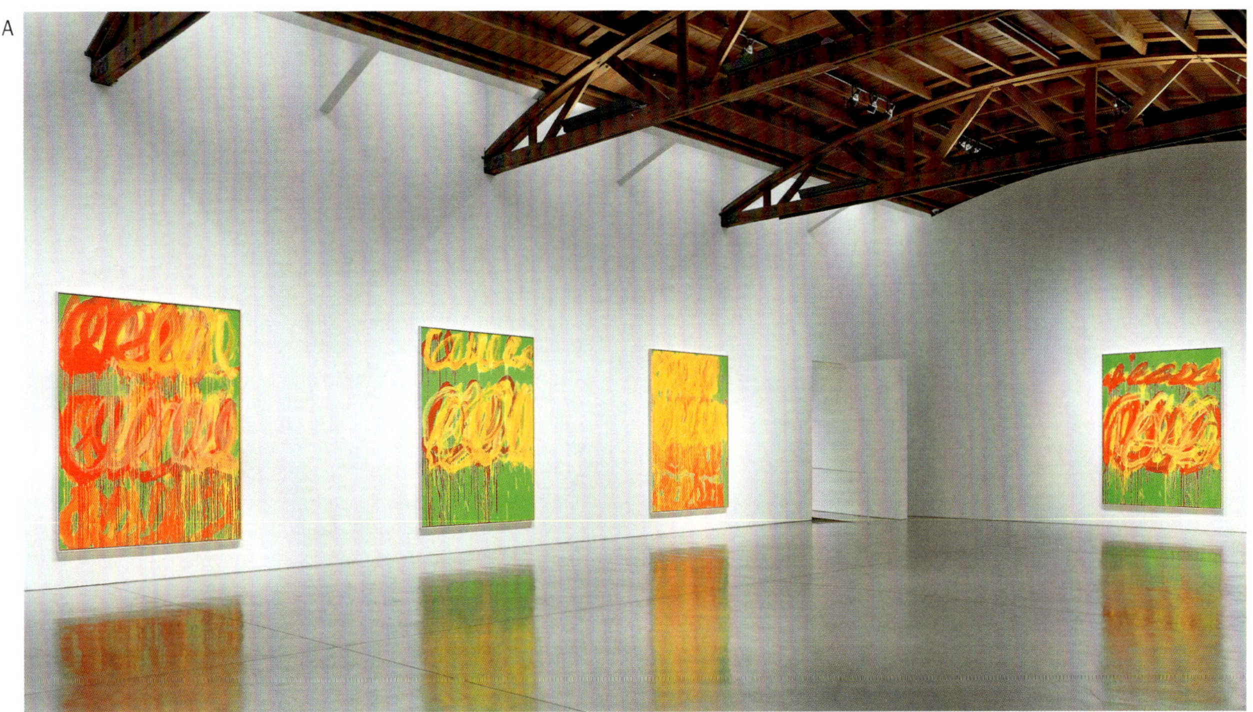

B

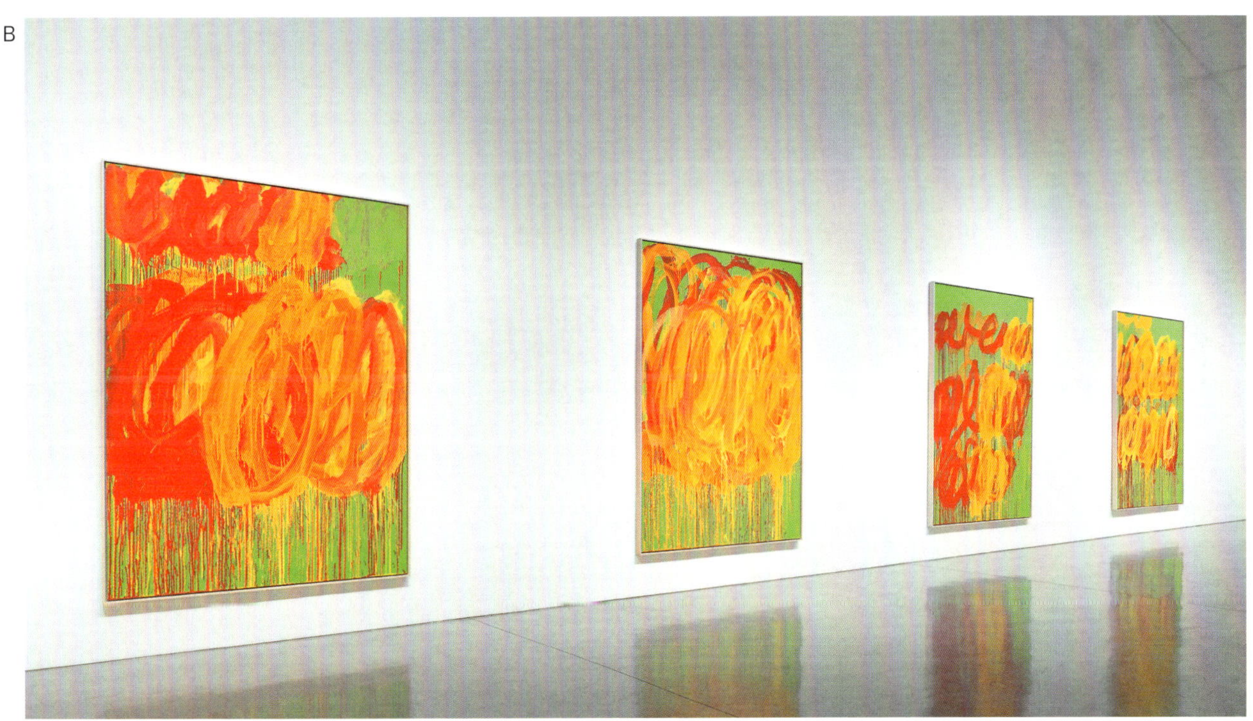

GALERIE 1900 - 2000

Mobile +33 6 09 05 00 61

Galerie 1900-2000
FR-75006 Paris | 8, rue Bonaparte
Phone +33 1 43 25 84 20 | Fax +33 1 46 34 74 52
info@galerie1900-2000.com | www.galerie1900-2000.com
Directors Marcel Fleiss
David Fleiss

Artists at
Art Basel Miami Beach | **Hans Bellmer**
Jean Dubuffet
Marcel Duchamp
Tetsumi Kudo
Wifredo Lam
Man Ray
Roberto Matta
Pierre Molinier
Francis Picabia
Edda Renouf
Miguel Rio Branco
Ed Ruscha
Robert Whitman

Gallery Information | In 1972 Marcel Fleiss, encouraged by his friend Man Ray, opened the Galerie des Quatre Mouvements with an exhibition of forty of the artist's rayographs.

Then, from 1981, at the Galerie 1900-2000, Marcel Fleiss organized more than 200 exhibitions devoted to major artists or rediscoveries, and published more than 150 catalogs, some of which are considered sources of rare and important primary documentation.

Since 1991, his son David has, among other things, developed the photographic department.

Currently, Marcel and David Fleiss devote themselves primarily to Surrealism (paintings, drawings, and photographs), while continuing to champion the art of the 20th century and the emerging art of the 21st century.

Further artists represented: Ben
Gaston Bertin
Aube Elléouët
Xavier Escriba
Philippe Jusforgues
Jean-Jacques Lebel
Frédéric Léglise
Jackson Mac Low
Joan Rabascall

Man Ray
Suzy Solidor, 1929
Solarized vintage silver print, 28 x 18.6 cm
Titled and dated on the back, stamped on the back: 'Man Ray, 31 bis rue campagne première, Paris'

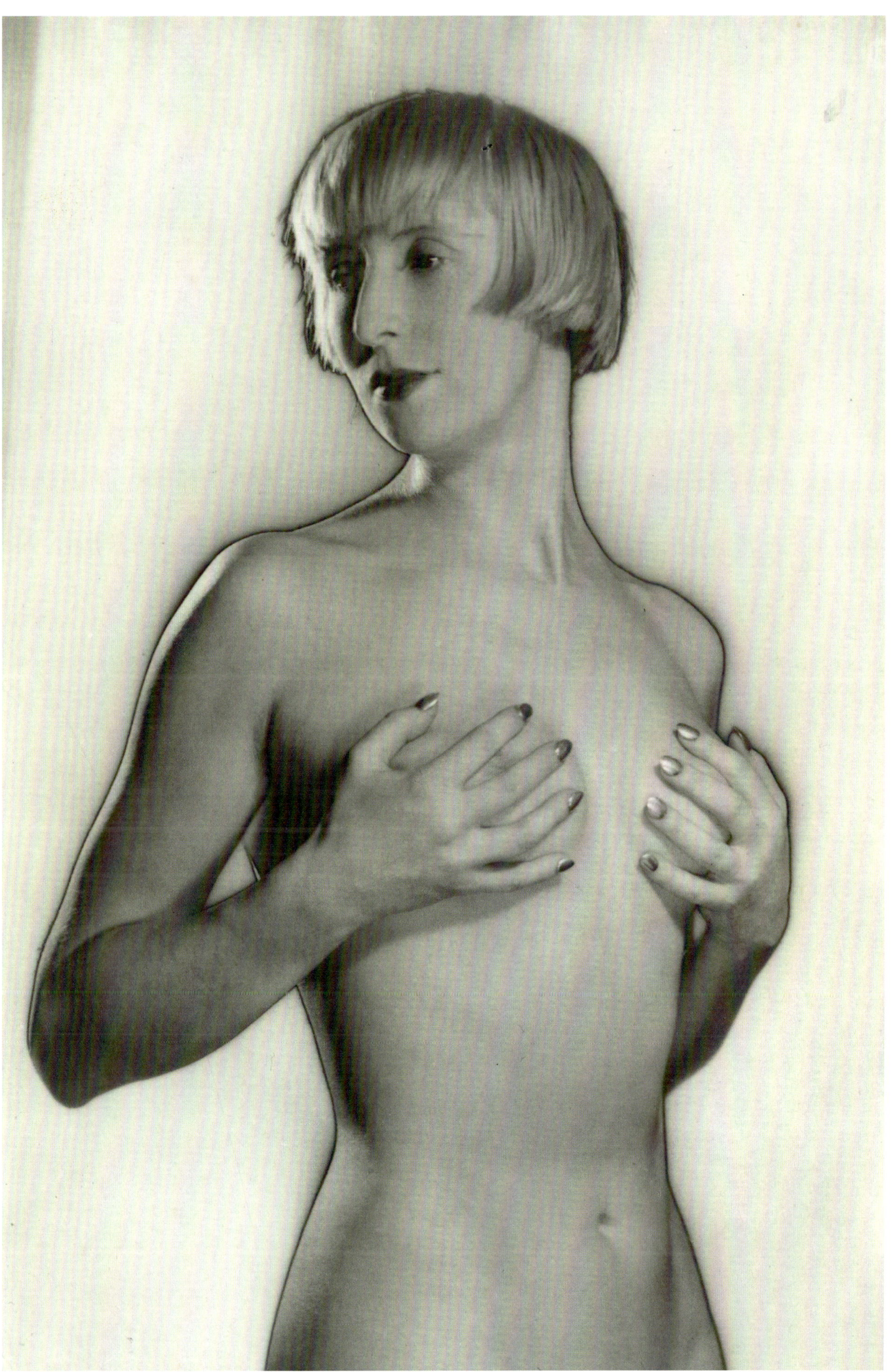

GAUDEL DE STAMPA

Mobile +33 6 19 55 53 69

Gaudel de Stampa
FR-75011 Paris | 3, rue de Vaucouleurs
Phone +33 1 40 21 37 38 | Fax +33 1 40 21 37 38
rany@gaudeldestampa.com | www.gaudeldestampa.com
Director Denis Gaudel

Artists at Art Nova | Dove Allouche
Jonathan Binet
Jessica Warboys

Further artists represented | Hildegarde Duane & David Lamelas
Ida Ekblad
Emil Michael Klein
Lina Viste Grønli

Jessica Warboys
Sea Painting, Les Orpelliers, Serignan Plage, 2012
Pigment, canvas, 210 x 600 cm

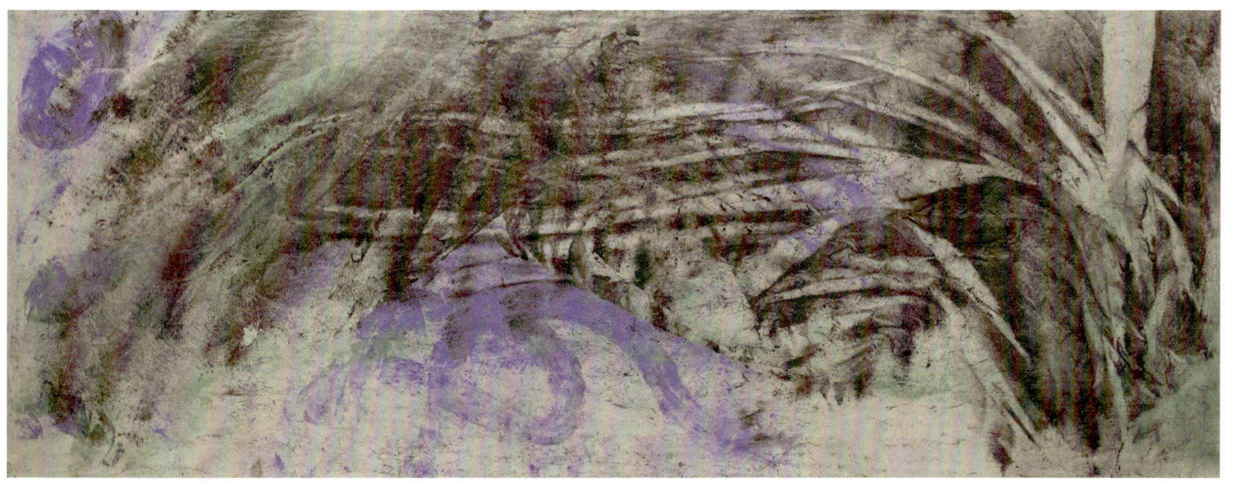

GEMINI

Gemini G.E.L. LLC
US-Los Angeles, CA 90069 | 8365 Melrose Avenue
Phone +1 323 651 05 13 | Fax +1 323 651 44 18
editions@geminigel.com | www.geminigel.com
Directors Sidney B. Felsen
Stanley Grinstein

Artists at Art Basel Miami Beach | **Josef Albers**
Richard Artschwager
John Baldessari
Jonathan Borofsky
Cecily Brown
Chris Burden
Daniel Buren
Sophie Calle
Vija Celmins
John Chamberlain
Richard Diebenkorn
Sam Francis
Frank Gehry
Robert Gober
Philip Guston
Ann Hamilton
David Hammons
David Hockney
Jasper Johns
Ellsworth Kelly
Edward & Nancy Kienholz
Roy Lichtenstein
Brice Marden
Julie Mehretu
Malcolm Morley
Elizaberth Murray
Bruce Nauman
Isamu Noguchi
Claes Oldenburg
Darryl Pottorf
Ken Price
Robert Rauschenberg
James Rosenquist
Susan Rothenberg
Ed Ruscha
Richard Serra
Joel Shapiro
Frank Stella
Richard Tuttle
Franz West

Gallery Information | Founded in 1966, Gemini G.E.L. is an artists workshop and publisher of original limited editions. Gemini has collaborated with more than 67 highly accomplished artists in lithography, etching, screenprinting, woodcut, and a variety of sculptural materials. Artists who work at Gemini draw or carve directly onto the printing elements. The edition is hand-printed by Gemini's master printers, and each print is signed and numbered by the artist as well as embossed with the Gemini 'chop.'

In 1981, the National Gallery of Art, Washington, D.C., established the Gemini G.E.L. Archive, which functions as a study center for scholars and collectors, and contains a complete history of the workshop. Included in the archive is one example from each of the more than 2,300 editions published. Three major exhibitions with works from the archive have been organized and exhibited by the National Gallery in the past 29 years.

Detailed information on the history of the workshop and the artworks in the Gemini Archive is available in the digital Catalogue Raisonné, on view at the National Gallery's website: www.nga.gov/gemini.

John Baldessari
Tomato Soup, 2012
Multi-color screenprint,
38 x 24¼ inches
Edition of 50

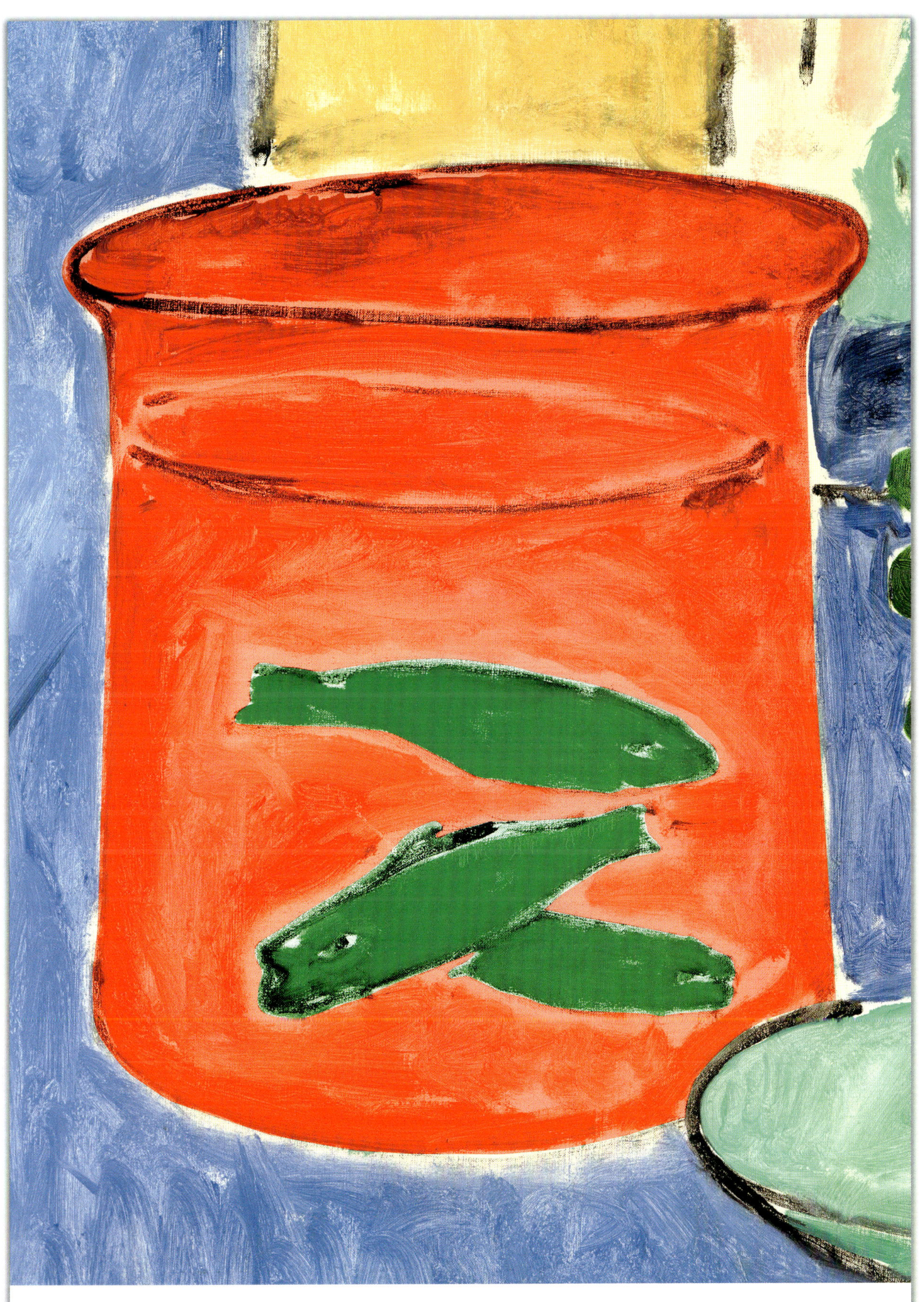

TOMATO
SOUP

GLADSTONE

Gladstone Gallery
US-New York, NY 10011 | 515 West 24th Street
Phone +1 212 206 93 00 | Fax +1 212 206 93 01
info@gladstonegallery.com | www.gladstonegallery.com
Directors Maxime Falkenstein
Molly Epstein
Simone Battisti

Gladstone Gallery
US-New York, NY 10011 | 530 West 21st Street
Phone +1 212 206 76 06 | Fax +1 212 206 76 05
info@gladstonegallery.com | www.gladstonegallery.com
Director Angela Brazda

Gladstone Gallery
BE-1000 Brussels | 12 Rue du Grand Cerf
Phone +32 2 513 35 31 | Fax +32 2 513 34 97
brussels@gladstonegallery.com | www.gladstonegallery.com
Director Gael Diercxsens

Artists at
Art Basel Miami Beach | **Allora & Calzadilla**
Kai Althoff
Miroslaw Balka
Matthew Barney
Robert Bechtle
Alighiero e Boetti
Jan Dibbets
Carroll Dunham
Cecilia Edefalk
Cyprien Gaillard
Keith Haring
Gary Hill
Thomas Hirschhorn
Jim Hodges
Huang Yong Ping
Cameron Jamie
Anish Kapoor
Sharon Lockhart
Andrew Lord
Sarah Lucas
Victor Man
Mario Merz
Marisa Merz
Dave Muller
Wangechi Mutu
Jean-Luc Mylayne
Shirin Neshat
Damián Ortega
Walter Pichler
Lari Pittman
Magnus Plessen
R. H. Quaytman
Ugo Rondinone
Jack Smith Archive
Rosemarie Trockel
Paloma Varga Weisz
Andro Wekua

Gallery Information | Works by: Roe Ethridge
Dan Flavin
Lucio Fontana
Gilbert & George
Donald Judd
Mike Kelley
Martin Kippenberger
Sol LeWitt
Fausto Melotti
Anna Parkina
Raymond Pettibon
Elizabeth Peyton
Sigmar Polke
Richard Prince
Gerhard Richter
Dieter Roth
Robert Ryman
Gedi Sibony
Banks Violette

Anish Kapoor
Untitled, 2012
Weathering steel,
568 x 779 x 803 cm

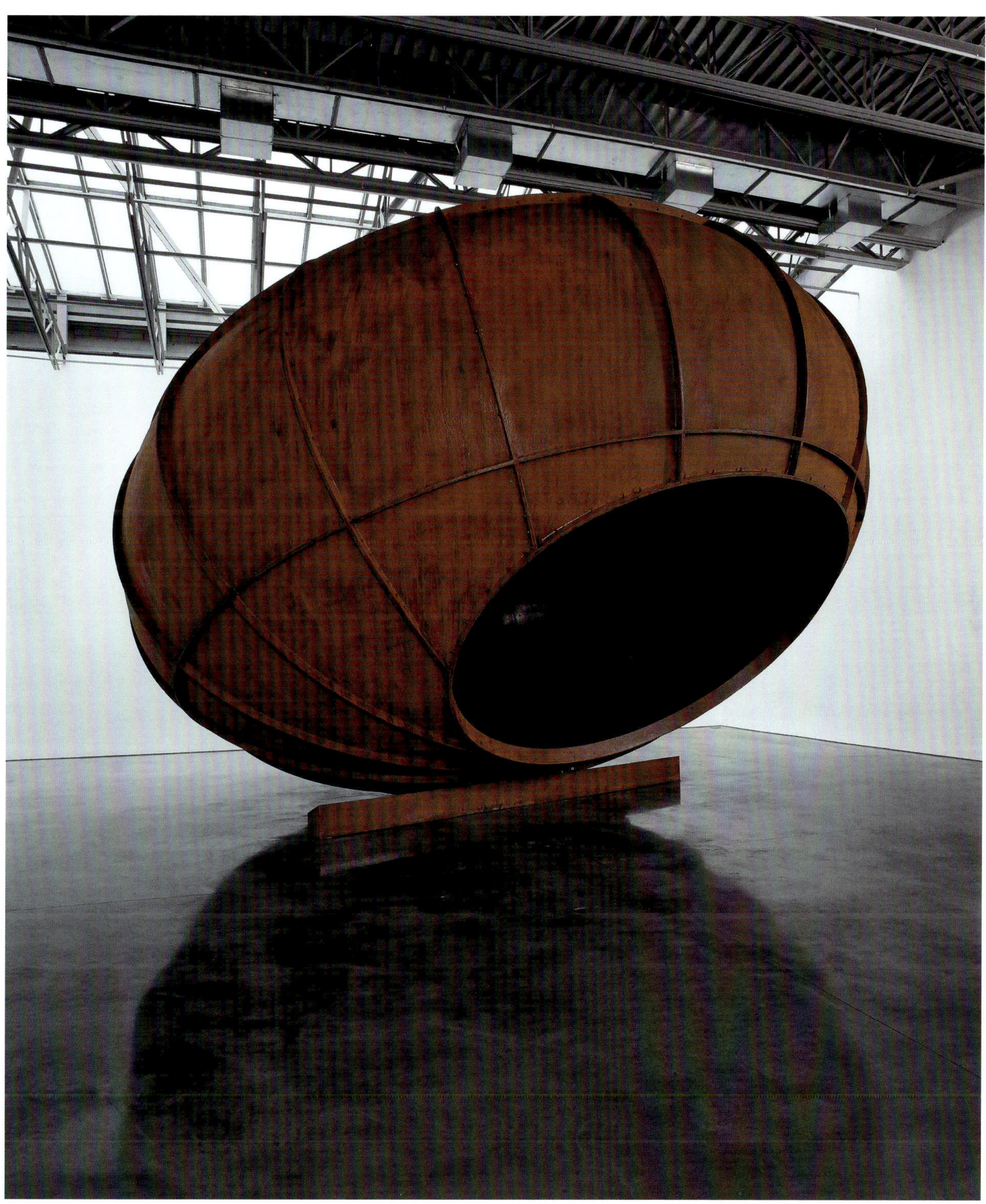

GMURZYNSKA

Galerie Gmurzynska
CH-6300 Zug | Unter Altstadt 20
Phone +41 41 710 25 02 | Fax +41 41 710 26 75
galerie@gmurzynska.com | www.gmurzynska.com
Directors Krystyna Gmurzynska
Mathias Rastorfer

Galerie Gmurzynska
CH-8001 Zurich | Paradeplatz 2
Phone +41 44 226 70 70 | Fax +41 44 226 70 90

Galerie Gmurzynska
CH-7500 St. Moritz | Via Serlas 22
Phone +41 81 833 36 51 | Fax +41 81 833 36 58

Artists at
Art Basel Miami Beach | **Fernando Botero**
Alexander Calder
Scott Campbell
Marc Chagall
Ronnie Cutrone
Robert Delaunay
Sonia Delaunay
Lyonel Feininger
Lucio Fontana
Robert Indiana
Yves Klein
Robert Klippel
Karl Lagerfeld
Wifredo Lam
Mikhail Larionov
Henri Laurens
Fernand Léger
Jani Leinonen
El Lissitzky
Kazimir Malevich
Joan Miró
Louise Nevelson
Marco Perego
Pablo Picasso
Liubov Popova
Mel Ramos
Alexander Rodchenko
Karl-Peter Röhl
Kurt Schwitters
David Smith
Chaim Soutine
Sylvester Stallone
Varvara Stepanova
Nikolai Suetin
Joaquín Torres-Garcia
Theo van Doesburg
Georges Vantongerloo
Tom Wesselmann
Pat York

Gallery Information | Art of the 20th century, Classical Modern, Eastern European avant-garde of the 1920s and 1930s

Wifredo Lam
Table dans le jardin, 1943/44
Oil on paper mounted on canvas,
148 x 95 cm

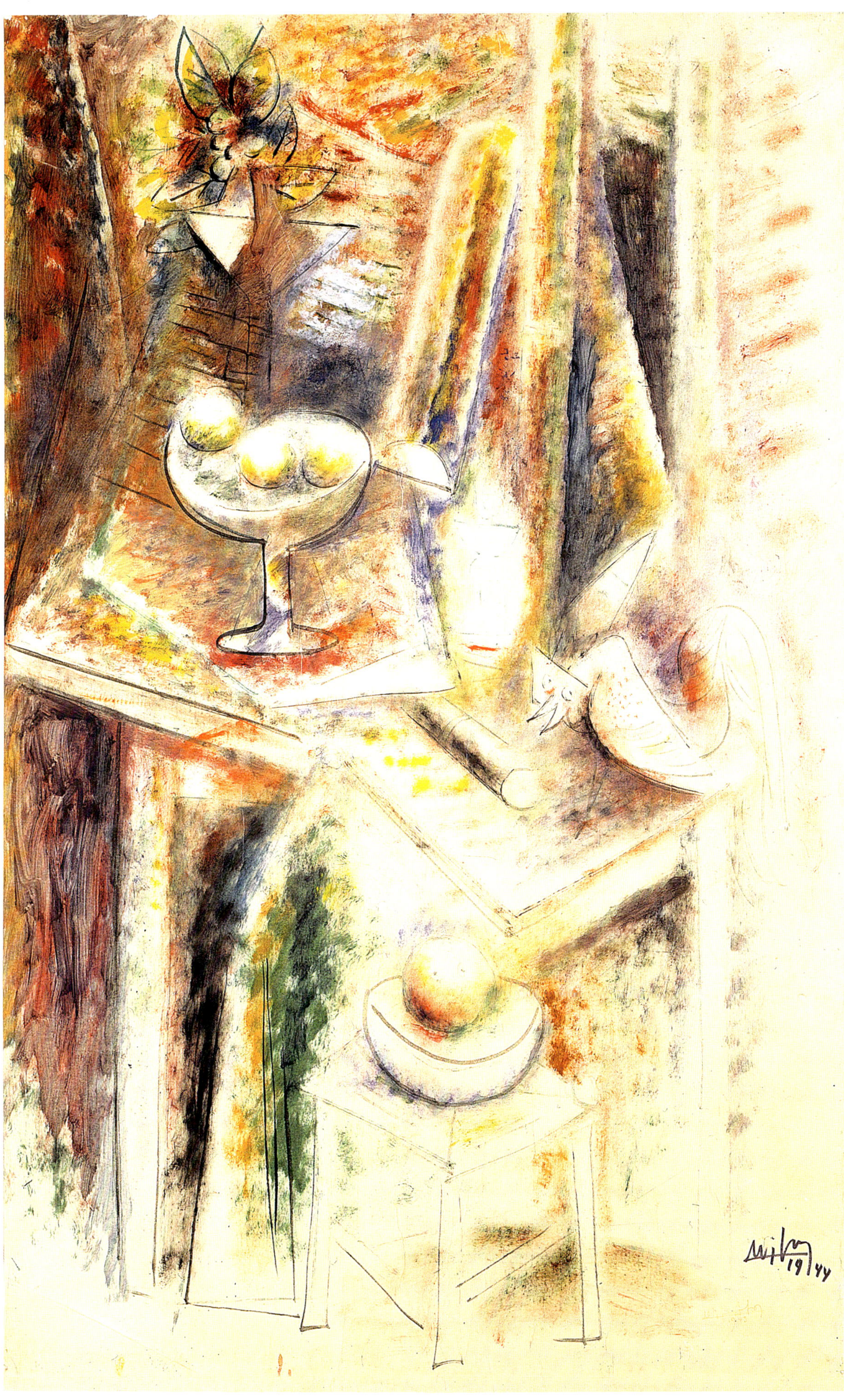

GONZÁLEZ

Mobile +34 699 496875

Galería Elvira González
ES-28004 Madrid | General Castaños, 3
Phone +34 91 3195900 | Fax +34 91 3196124
info@galeriaelviragonzalez.com | www.galeriaelviragonzalez.com
Directors Elvira Mignoni
Fernando Mignoni
Isabel Mignoni

Artists at
Art Basel Miami Beach | **Uta Barth**
Waltercio Caldas
Alexander Calder
Elena del Rivero
Dan Flavin
Adolph Gottlieb
Robert Irwin
Donald Judd
Robert Mangold
Robert Mapplethorpe
Lee Ufan
Esteban Vicente

Further artists represented | Juan Asensio
Olafur Eliasson
Lucio Fontana
Julio González
Fausto Melotti
Michelangelo Pistoletto
Adolfo Schlosser
Jesús Rafael Soto
Antoni Tàpies
Dan Walsh

Uta Barth
Deep Blue Day (Untitled 12.10), 2012
Color photograph,
37⅝ x 40⅜ inches,
95.6 x 102.5 cm

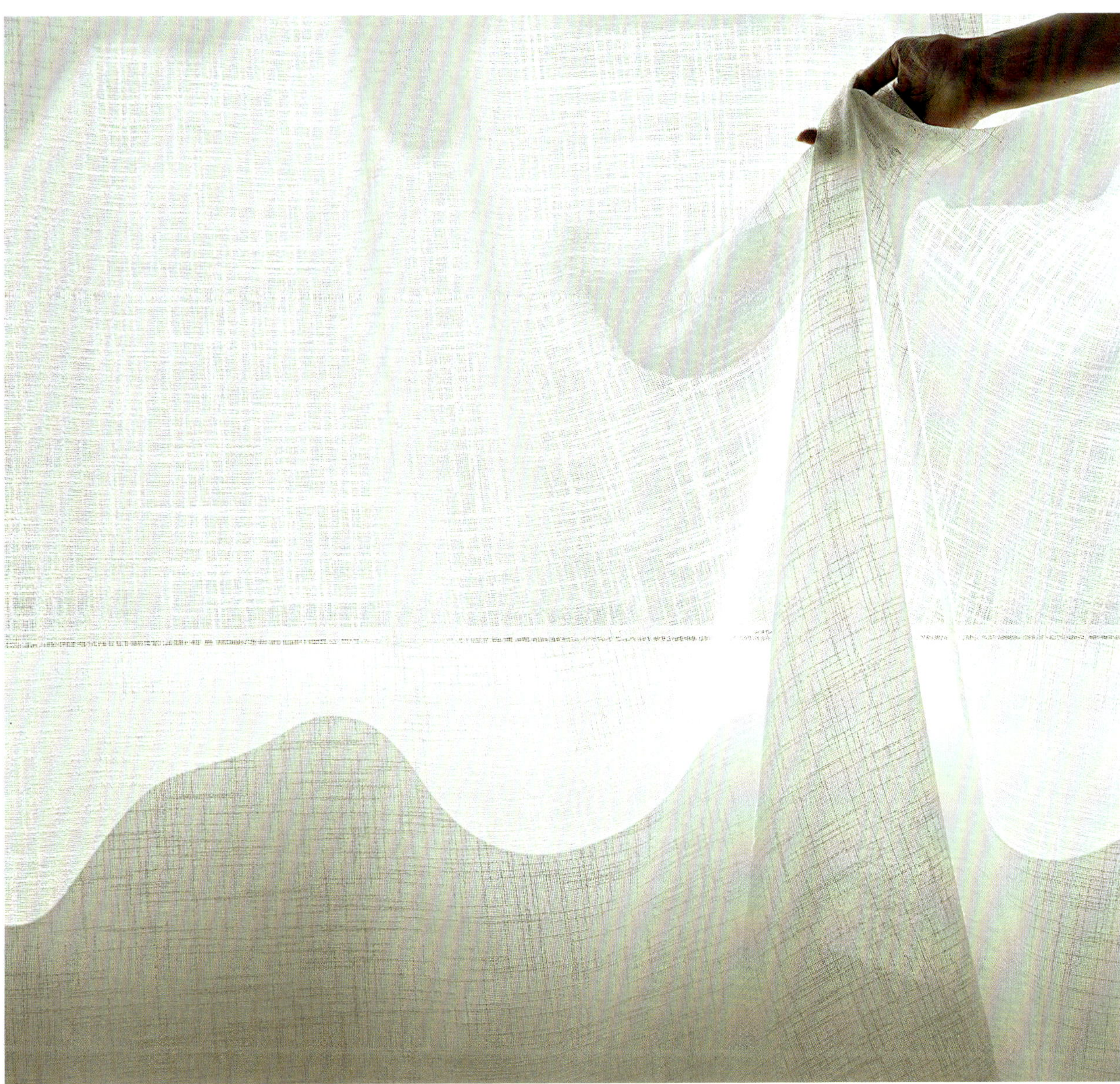

MARIAN GOODMAN

Marian Goodman Gallery
US-New York, NY 10019 | 24 West 57th Street
Phone +1 212 977 71 60 | Fax +1 212 581 51 87
goodman@mariangoodman.com | www.mariangoodman.com
Directors Andrew Richards
Rose Lord
Leslie Nolen
Lissa McClure
Karina Daskalov
Alice Kim

Galerie Marian Goodman
FR-75003 Paris | 79, rue du Temple
Phone +33 1 48 04 70 52 | Fax +33 1 40 27 81 37
parisgallery@mariangoodman.com | www.mariangoodman.com
Directors Andrew Leslie Heyward
Johanna Wiström

Artists at Art Basel Miami Beach | **Eija-Liisa Ahtila**
Chantal Akerman
Giovanni Anselmo
John Baldessari
Lothar Baumgarten
Dara Birnbaum
Christian Boltanski
Marcel Broodthaers
Maurizio Cattelan
James Coleman
Tony Cragg
Richard Deacon
Tacita Dean
Rineke Dijkstra
David Goldblatt
Dan Graham
Pierre Huyghe
Cristina Iglesias
Amar Kanwar
William Kentridge
Steve McQueen
Julie Mehretu
Annette Messager
Juan Muñoz
Maria Nordman
Gabriel Orozco
Giulio Paolini
Giuseppe Penone
Gerhard Richter
Anri Sala
Matt Saunders
Tino Sehgal
Thomas Struth
Niele Toroni
Danh Vo
Jeff Wall
Lawrence Weiner
Francesca Woodman
Yang Fudong

Eija-Liisa Ahtila
The Annunciation (Detail), 2010
3-channel projected HD
installation with 5.1 channel
audio, 32 min 10 sec
Edition of 5

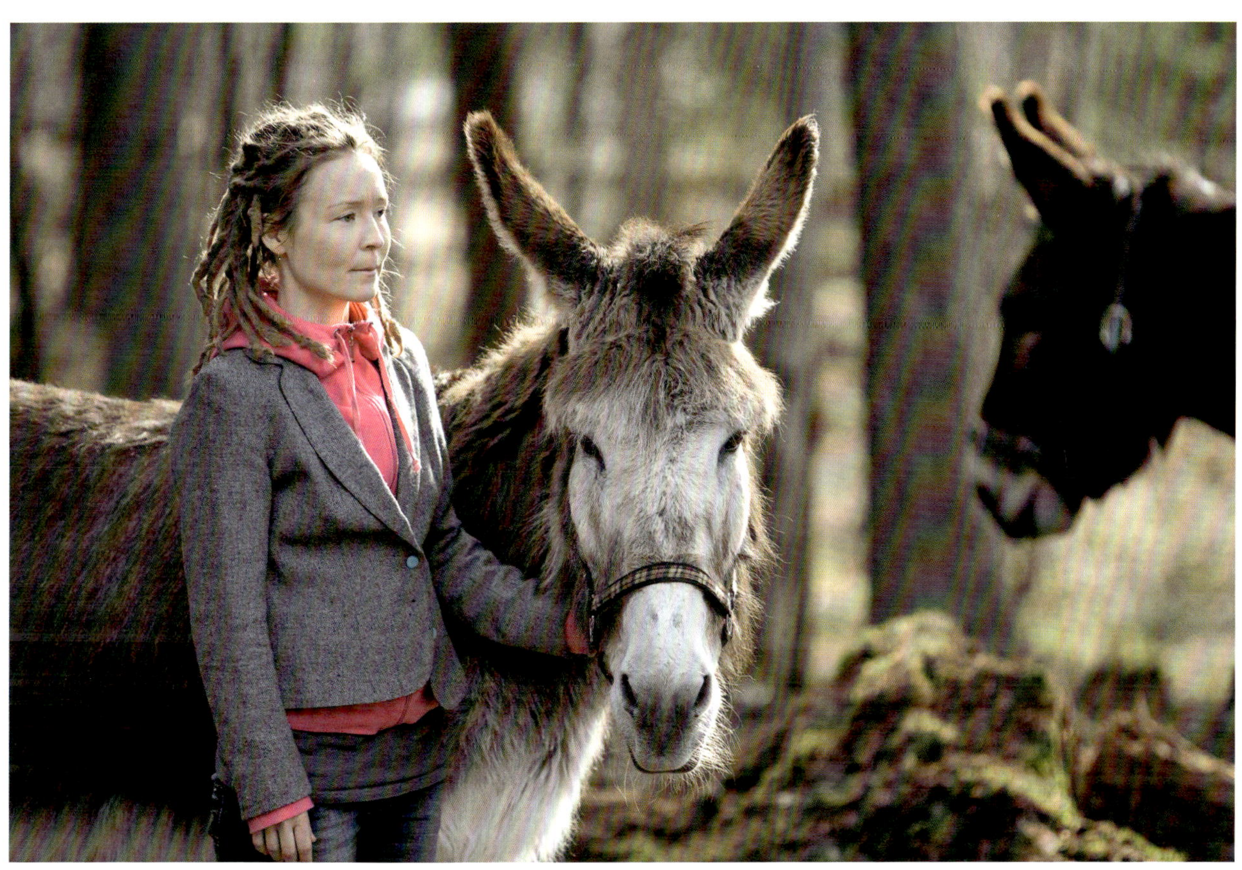

GOODMAN GALLERY

Goodman Gallery
ZA-2193 Johannesburg | 163 Jan Smuts Ave, Parkwood
Phone +27 11 788 11 13 | Fax +27 11 788 98 87
jhb@goodman-gallery.com | www.goodman-gallery.com
Director Liza Essers

Goodman Gallery
ZA-7925 Woodstock, Cape Town | 3rd Floor, Fairweather House, 176 Sir Lowry Road
Phone +27 21 462 75 73 | Fax +27 21 462 75 79
cpt@goodman-gallery.com | www.goodman-gallery.com
Director Liza Essers

Artists at
Art Basel Miami Beach | **Candice Breitz**
Carla Busuttil
Kudzanai Chiurai
Kendell Geers
David Goldblatt
William Kentridge
Moshekwa Langa
Mikhael Subotzky
Hank Willis Thomas
Nelisiwe Xaba & Mocke van Veuren

Further artists represented | Ghada Amer
Kader Attia
Jodi Bieber
Willem Boshoff
Lisa Brice
Adam Broomberg & Oliver Chanarin
Hasan & Husain Essop
Mounir Fatmi
Claire Gavronsky
David Koloane
Kagiso Pat Mautloa
Thomas Mulcaire
Brett Murray
Sam Nhlengethwa
Walter Oltmann
Stefanus Rademeyer
Rosenclaire
Rose Shakinovsky
Gavin Turk
Clive van den Berg
Hentie van der Merwe
Minnette Vári
Nontsikelelo Veleko
Diane Victor
Jeremy Wafer
Sue Williamson

Moshekwa Langa
Somebody Is Always Willing to Tell, 2011
Mixed media on paper,
140 x 100 cm

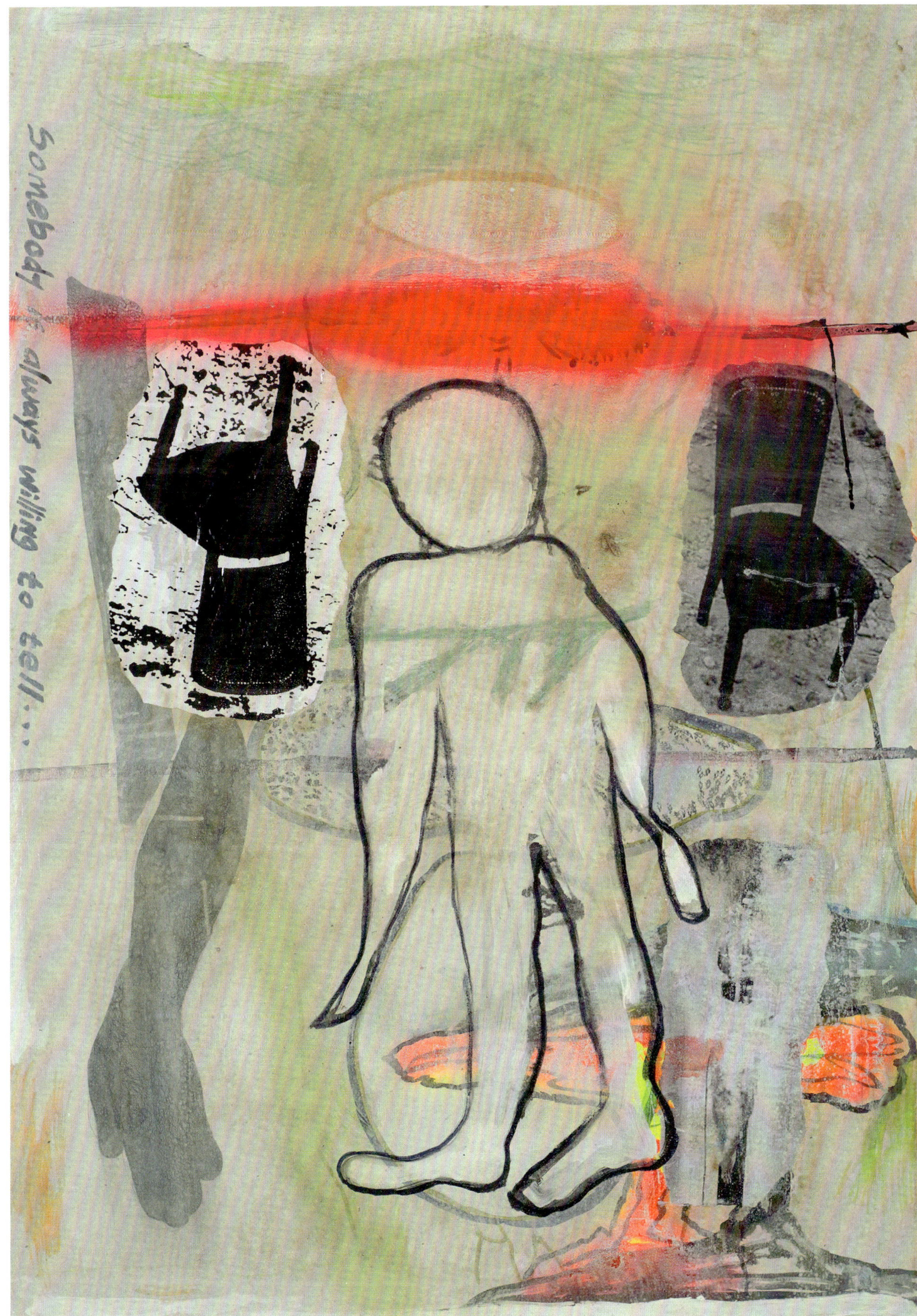
Somebody always willing to tell...

GRAÇA BRANDÃO

Mobile +351 919 86 44 69

Galeria Graça Brandão
PT-1200-079 Lisbon | Rua dos Caetanos, 26A
Phone +351 213 46 91 83 | Fax +351 213 46 91 85
galgblx@mail.telepac.pt | www.galeriagracabrandao.com
Director José Mário Brandão

Artists at
Art Basel Miami Beach | **Fernanda Gomes**
João Maria Gusmão & Pedro Paiva
Lygia Pape
Nuno Sousa Vieira

Gallery Information | Galeria Graça Brandão opened in 2002, first in Oporto and then in Lisbon, giving continuity to the work of its director, José Mário Brandão, who since 1996 has devoted himself to promoting contemporary art, focusing on that of Portugal and Brazil.

For this year's edition of Art Basel Miami Beach, Galeria Graça Brandão is committed to presenting a selection of artworks that represent what is most exciting and captivating in Portuguese and Brazilian contemporary art. Its choice mirrors recent developments in the field and highlights current exhibitions, like that of Lygia Pape at the Museo Nacional Centro de Arte Reina Sofía (Madrid) and at the Serpentine Gallery (London), João Maria Gusmão & Pedro Paiva's at IMO Copenhagen, or Nuno Sousa Vieira's exhibition at Pavilhão Branco, Museu da Cidade (Lisbon) and Galeria Raquel Arnaud in São Paulo.

Further artists represented: Albano Afonso
Orla Barry
Mauro Cerqueira
Carla Filipe
João Maria Galrão
António Leal
Nelson Leirner
Albuquerque Mendes
Gonçalo Pena
Nuno Ramalho
Glen Rubsamen
Sam Samore
Daniel Senise
João Tabarra
Pedro Tudela
Ana Vieira

João Maria Gusmão & Pedro Paiva
Newton's Monkey, Darwin's Apple, 2012
Chromogenic color print,
120 x 160 cm

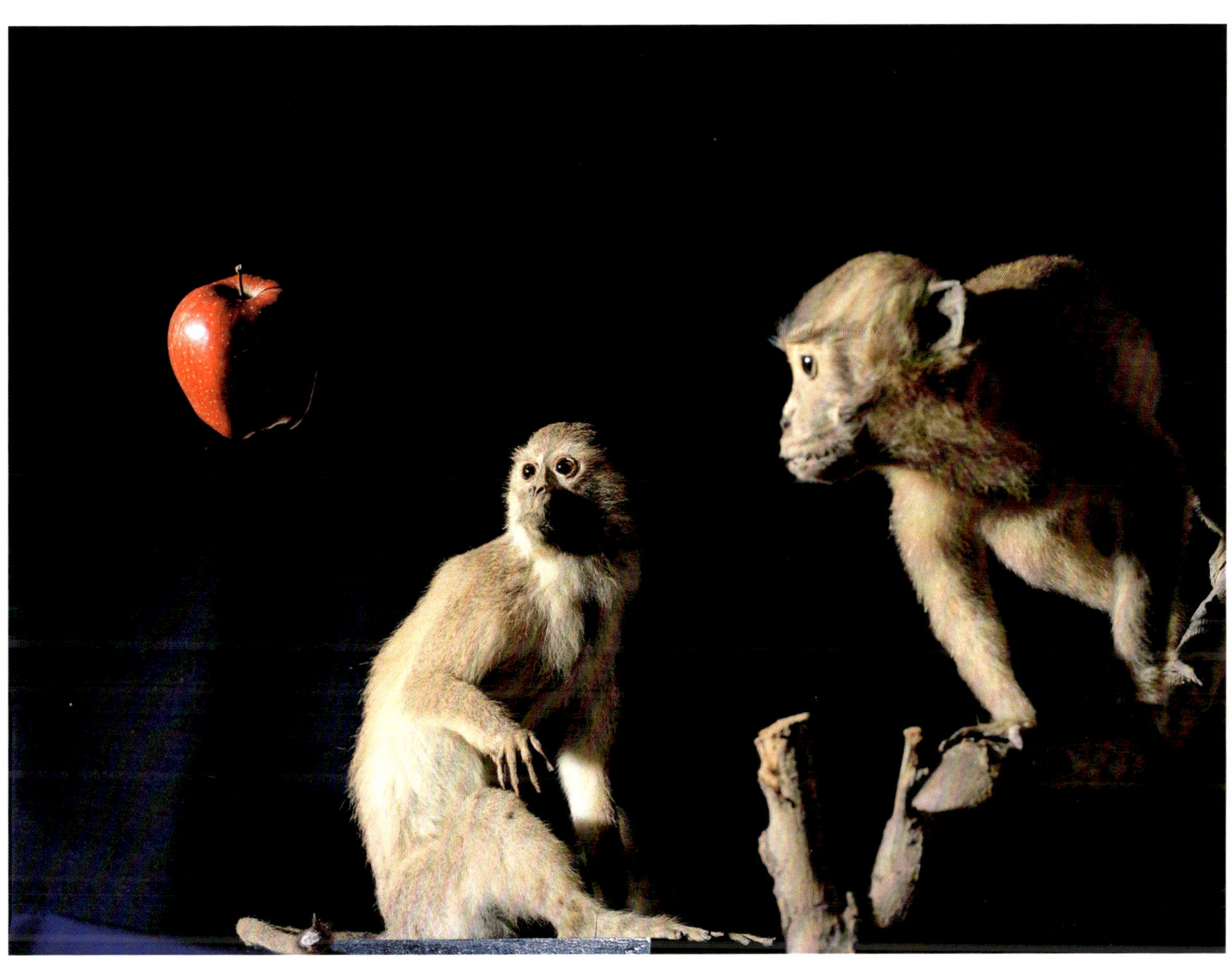

GRÄSSLIN

Mobile +49 172 6150653

Galerie Bärbel Grässlin
DE-60313 Frankfurt am Main | Schäfergasse 46 B
Phone +49 69 29924670 | Fax +49 69 29924 6729
mail@galerie-graesslin.de | www.galerie-graesslin.de
Directors Bärbel Grässlin
Klaus Webelholz

Artists at
Art Basel Miami Beach | **Günther Förg**
Georg Herold
Martin Kippenberger
Imi Knoebel
Franz West
Heimo Zobernig

Further artists represented | Michael Beutler
Herbert Brandl
Werner Büttner
Helmut Dorner
Hubert Kiecol
Meuser
Reinhard Mucha
Stefan Müller
Christa Näher
Manuel Ocampo
Albert Oehlen
Markus Oehlen
Tobias Rehberger
Thomas Werner

Günther Förg
Untitled, 2007
Acrylic, oil on canvas,
175 x 225 cm

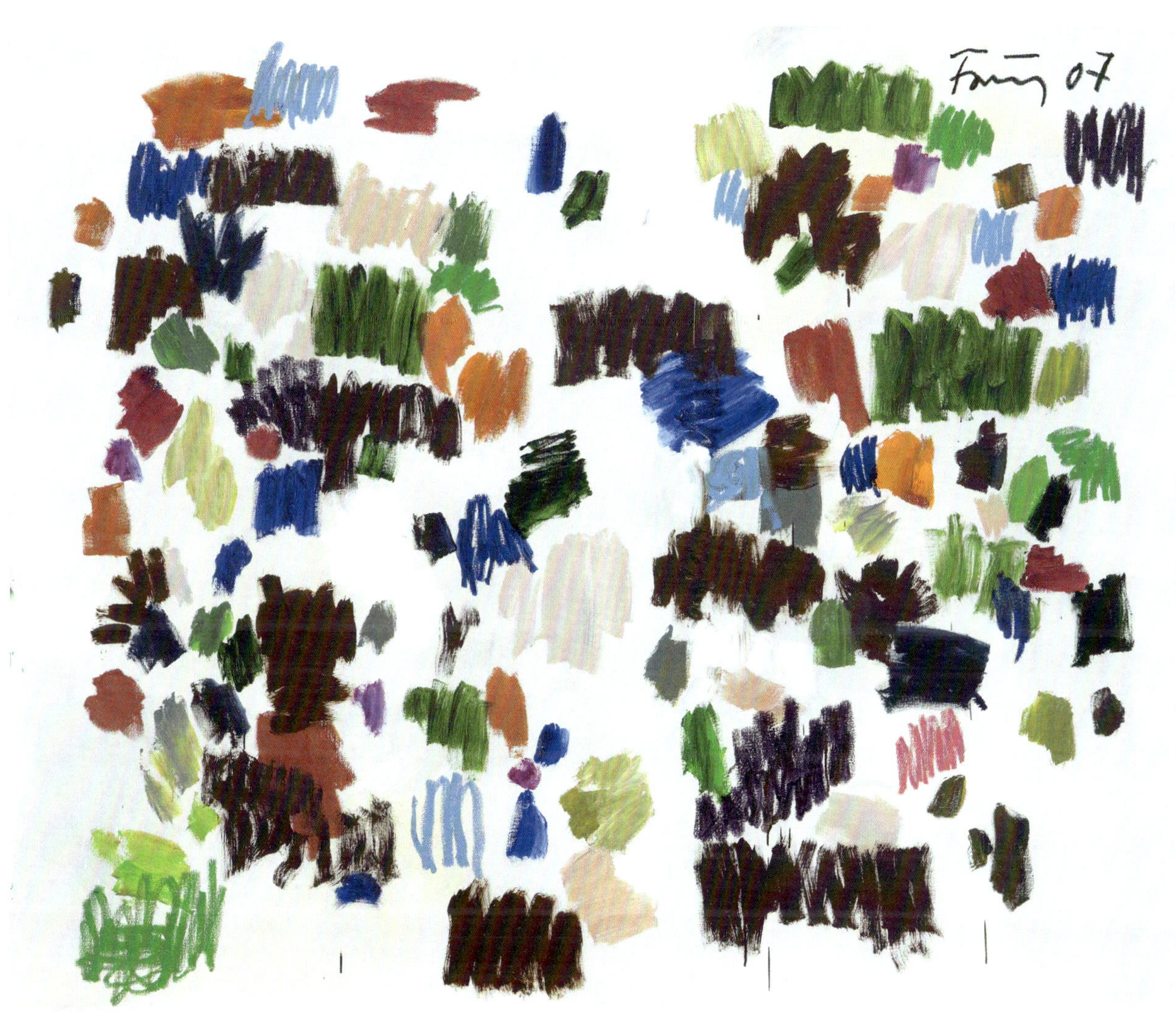

ALEXANDER GRAY

Mobile +1 646 642 26 36

Alexander Gray Associates
US-New York, NY 10001 | 508 West 26th Street, #215
Phone +1 212 399 26 36 | Fax +1 212 399 26 84
info@alexandergray.com | www.alexandergray.com
Directors Alexander Gray
David Cabrera

Artists at
Art Basel Miami Beach | **Coco Fusco**
Lorraine O'Grady
Dawit L. Petros
Joan Semmel
Regina Silveira
Hugh Steers
Jack Whitten

Gallery Information | Alexander Gray Associates, a contemporary art gallery, opened in 2006, establishing a profile for high-quality exhibitions focused on mid-career artists who emerged in the 1960s, 1970s, 1980s, and 1990s. These diverse artists are notable for their spheres of influence that cross generations, disciplines, and political perspectives.

Further artists represented: Luis Camnitzer
Melvin Edwards
Jeremy Gilbert-Rolfe
Paul Ramírez Jonas
Hassan Sharif

Lorraine O'Grady
The Fir-Palm, 1991/2012
Silver gelatin print (photo-montage), 50 x 40 inches

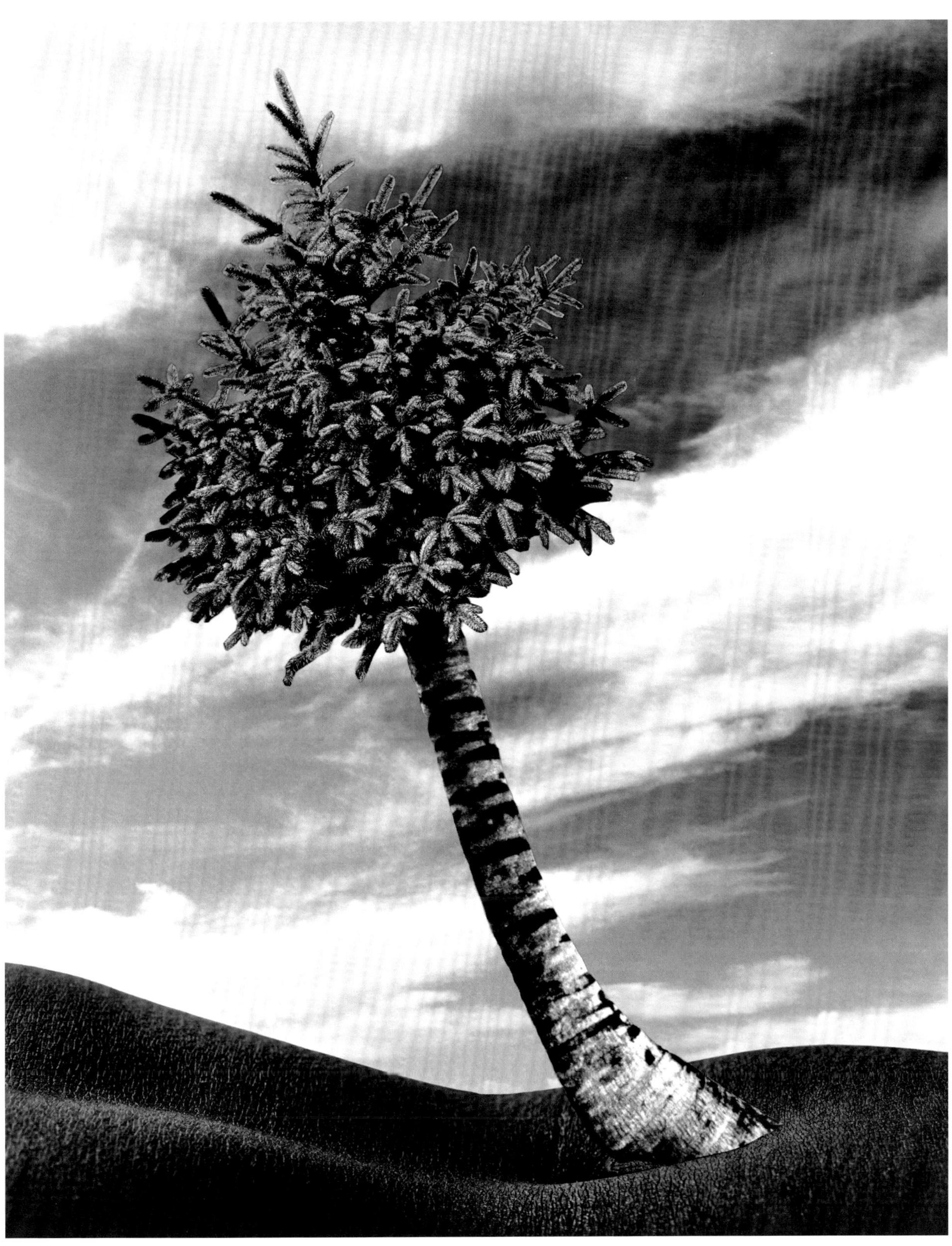

RICHARD GRAY

Richard Gray Gallery
US-Chicago, IL 60611 | 875 North Michigan Avenue, Suite 2503
Phone +1 312 642 88 77 | Fax +1 312 642 84 88
info@richardgraygallery.com | www.richardgraygallery.com
Directors Richard Gray
Paul Gray

Richard Gray Gallery
US-New York, NY 10075 | 1018 Madison Avenue, 4th Floor
Phone +1 212 472 87 87 | Fax +1 212 472 25 52
info@richardgraygallery.com | www.richardgraygallery.com
Director Andrew Fabricant

Artists at
Art Basel Miami Beach | **Magdalena Abakanowicz**
Josef Albers
Francis Bacon
Georg Baselitz
Alexander Calder
Joseph Cornell
Willem de Kooning
Richard Diebenkorn
Jim Dine
Jean Dubuffet
Sam Francis
Alberto Giacometti
Ewan Gibbs
Philip Guston
David Hockney
Hans Hofmann
Jasper Johns
Rashid Johnson
Alex Katz
Franz Kline
Fernand Léger
Roy Lichtenstein
Brice Marden
Henri Matisse
Joan Miró
Joan Mitchell
Henry Moore
Robert Motherwell
Pablo Picasso
Jaume Plensa
Jackson Pollock
Richard Prince
Robert Rauschenberg
Mark Rothko
Ed Ruscha
Frank Stella
Marc Swanson
Jan Tichy
Cy Twombly
Andy Warhol
Christopher Wool

Gallery Information | Founded in 1963. Specializing in contemporary art and European and American modern master paintings, drawings, and sculpture.

Member:
Art Dealers Association of America, ADAA
Confédération Internationale des Négociants en Œuvres d'Art, CINOA

Frank Stella
Mrs. Rabbit's Rainbow III, 1974
Acrylic on canvas, 69 x 69 inches

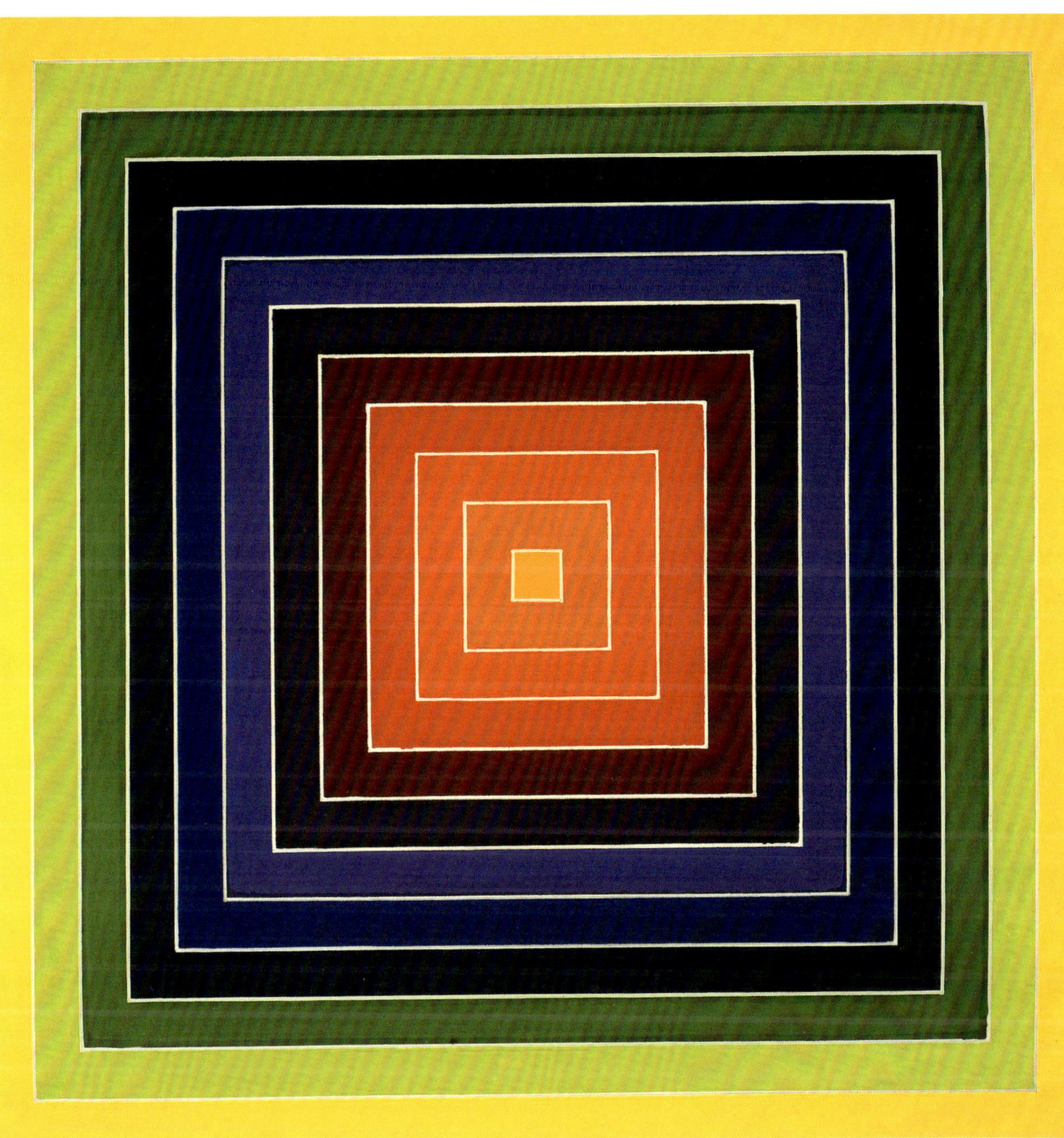

HOWARD GREENBERG

Howard Greenberg Gallery
US-New York, NY 10022 | 41 East 57th Street, Suite 1406
Phone +1 212 334 00 10 | Fax +1 212 941 74 79
info@howardgreenberg.com | www.howardgreenberg.com
Directors Karen Marks
Nancy Lieberman
Susan Sherrick

Artists at Art Basel Miami Beach | **Edward Burtynsky**
Bruce Davidson
David Goldblatt
Kenro Izu
William Klein
Saul Leiter
Joel Meyerowitz
Edward Steichen

Gallery Information | Howard Greenberg Gallery, founded in 1981, has been a fundamental force in establishing the market for classic photography. The gallery's holdings include many of the most important artists in the medium. The following list reflects both photographers with primary representation at the gallery as well as those regularly held in inventory: Berenice Abbott
Henri Cartier-Bresson
Roy DeCarava
Walker Evans
Allen Ginsberg
Eikoh Hosoe
Kenro Izu
André Kertész
Jacque Henri Lartigue
Leon Levinstein
George Platt Lynes
Man Ray
Charles Marville
Arnold Newman
Gordon Parks
Josef Sudek
Alfred Stieglitz
Weegee
Edward Weston
Minor White
Garry Winogrand

Joel Meyerowitz
Bay/Sky, 1977
Archival pigment print,
24 x 20 inches

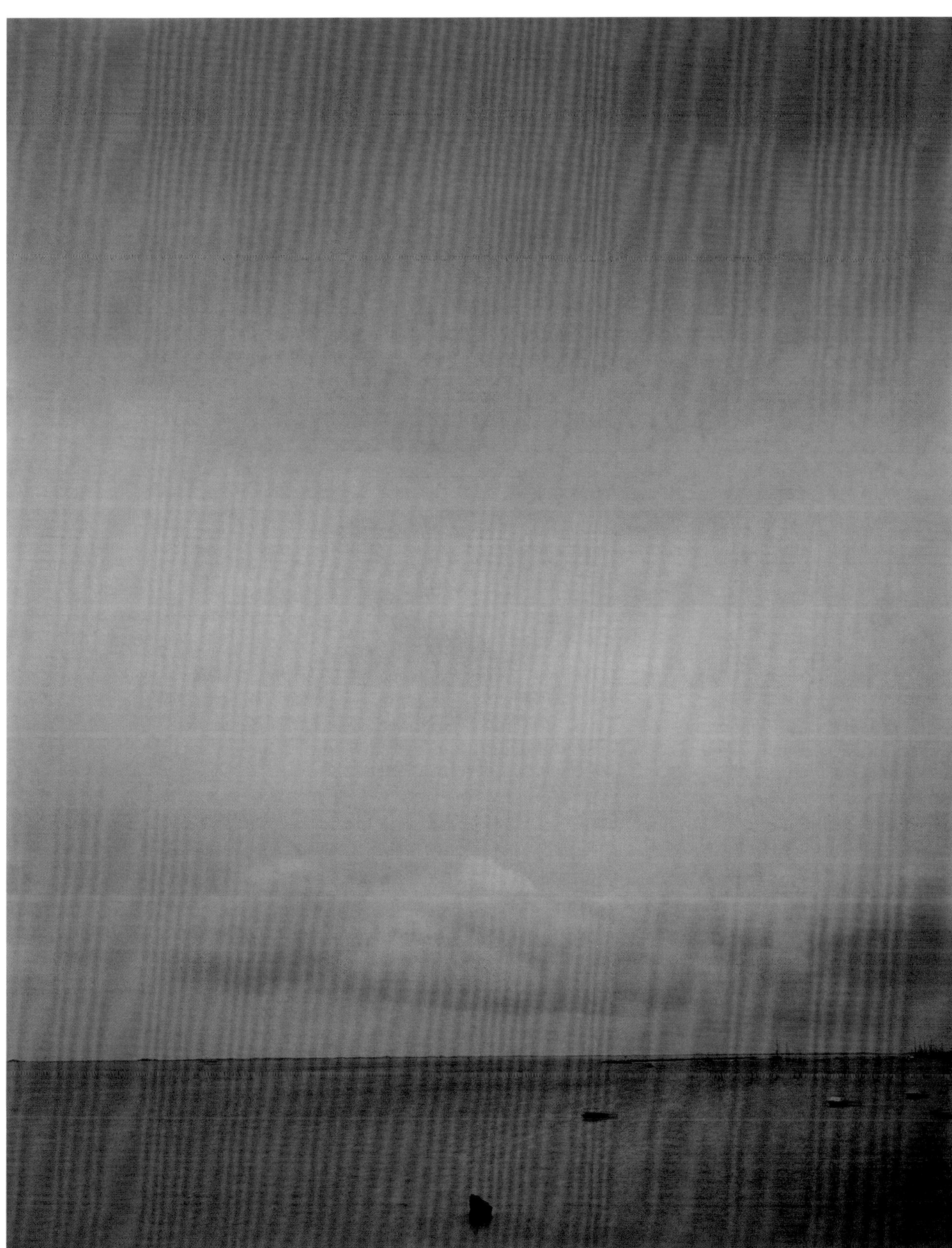

GREENBERG VAN DOREN

Greenberg Van Doren Gallery
US-New York, NY 10019 | 730 Fifth Avenue
Phone +1 212 445 04 44 | Fax +1 212 445 04 42
info@gvdgallery.com | www.gvdgallery.com
Directors Dorsey Waxter
Elizabeth Raizes Sadeghi

Artists at Art Basel Miami Beach | **James Brooks**
Anthony Caro
John Chamberlain
Richard Diebenkorn
Dorothea Rockburne

Gallery Information | Greenberg Van Doren Gallery specializes in modern and contemporary masters, mid-career artists, and emerging artists. The diversity of artists handled by the gallery creates a broad-based exhibition program, which rotates bimonthly. In addition to artwork on exhibit, the gallery maintains an inventory of select secondary-market works of art. Greenberg Van Doren is a member of the Art Dealers Association of America.

Further artists represented: Emi Avora
Jessica Craig-Martin
Tim Davis
Sharon Ellis
Katsura Funakoshi
Alexander Gorlizki
Julia Kunin
Eva Lundsager
Cameron Martin
Kanishka Raja
Alan Shields
Katrin Sigurdardottir
Alexis Smith
Valeska Soares
Sung
Kevin Zucker

Richard Diebenkorn
Untitled, 1949
Oil on canvas, 121.3 x 83.2 cm

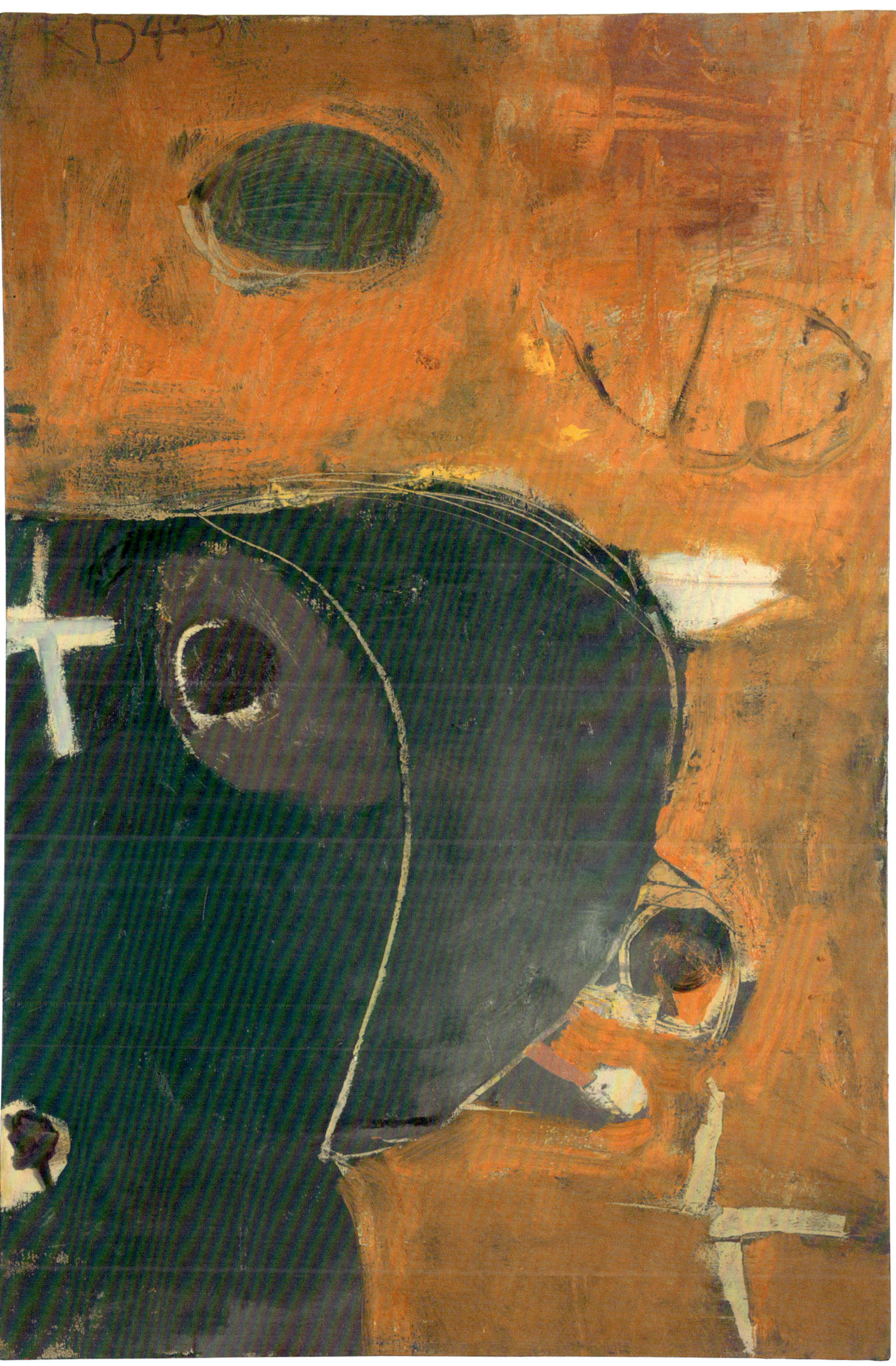

GREENE NAFTALI

Greene Naftali Gallery
US-New York, NY 10001 | 508 West 26th Street
Phone +1 212 4637770 | Fax +1 212 4630890
info@greenenaftaligallery.com | www.greenenaftaligallery.com
Directors Carol Greene
Alexandra Tuttle
Vera Alemani
Jeffrey Rowledge

Artists at Art Basel Miami Beach | **Trisha Baga**
Julie Becker
Bernadette Corporation
Paul Chan
Tony Conrad
Guy de Cointet
Jim Drain
Ida Ekblad
Harun Farocki
Günther Förg
Michael Fullerton
Gelitin
Lucy Gunning
Guyton\Walker
Rachel Harrison
Richard Hawkins
Jacqueline Humphries
John Knight
Joachim Koester
Michael Krebber
William Leavitt
Helen Marten
Michaela Meise
Daniel Pflumm
Daniela Rossell
Allen Ruppersberg
Paul Sharits
Gedi Sibony
Michael Smith
Josef Strau
Daan van Golden
Sophie von Hellermann
Katharina Wulff
Haegue Yang

Günther Förg
Untitled, 2008
Acrylic and oil on canvas,
114⅛ x 157½ inches,
289.9 x 400.1 cm
Installation view, Greene Naftali,
2012

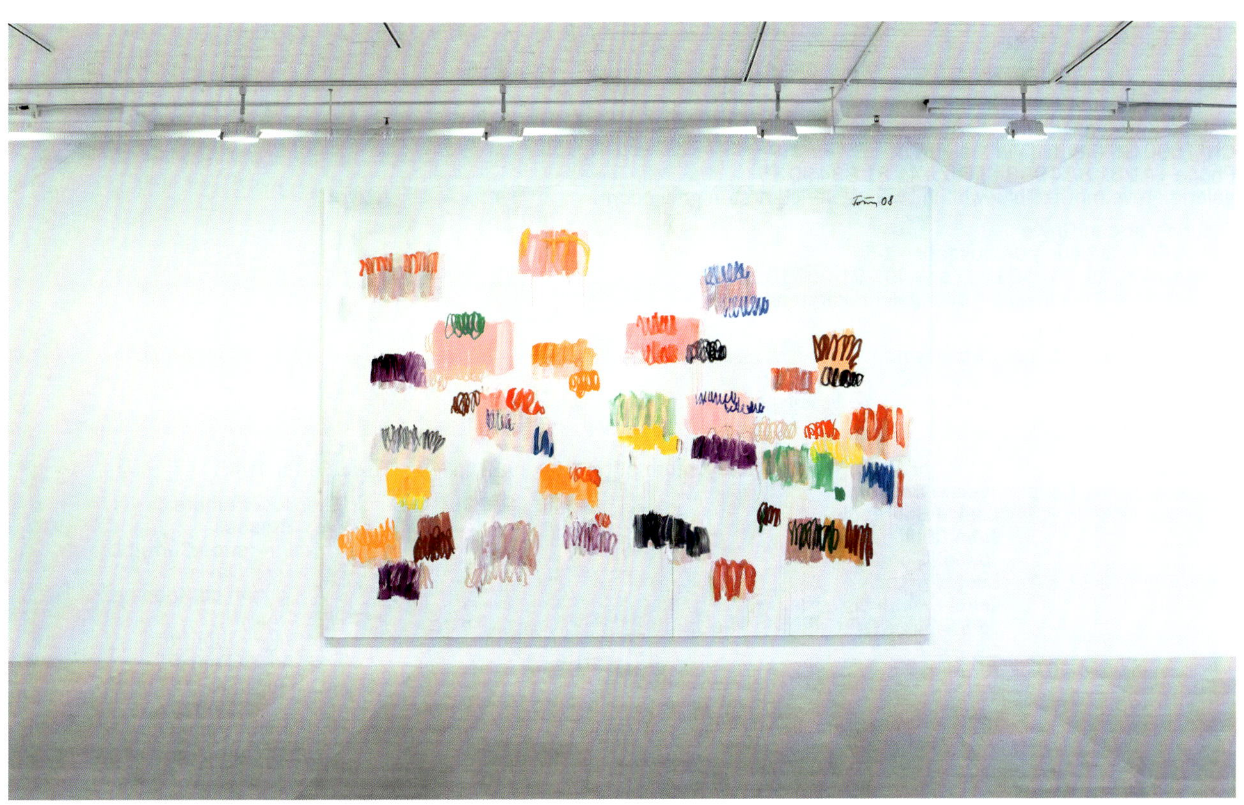

GUERRA

Mobile +351 91 8436069

Cristina Guerra Contemporary Art
PT-1350-291 Lisbon | Rua de Santo António à Estrela, 33
Phone +351 21 3959559 | Fax +351 21 3959567
galeria@cristinaguerra.com | www.cristinaguerra.com
Director Cristina Guerra

Artists at
Art Basel Miami Beach | **Christian Andersson**
Juan Araujo
Michael Biberstein
Angela Bulloch
Filipa César
Tatjana Doll
Sabine Hornig
José Loureiro
João Louro
Edgar Martins
Matt Mullican
João Onofre
Rosângela Rennó
Julião Sarmento
Rui Toscano
Lawrence Weiner
Erwin Wurm
Yonamine

Gallery Information | Exhibitions in 2012: João Paulo Feliciano
Yonamine
Edgar Martins
Group show, *A man is walking down the street. At a certain moment, he tries to recall something, but the recollection escapes him. Automatically, he slows down,* curated by Luiza Teixeira de Freitas and Thom O'Nions
João Onofre
Michael Biberstein

Further artists represented: John Baldessari
Luís Paulo Costa
João Paulo Feliciano
Daniel Malhão
Jonathan Monk

Rosângela Rennó
A | *Assault on Power,* 1992
15 black-and-white prints on RC paper, plexiglass, screws, green fluorescent lamps, and vinyl lettering on the wall, 320 x 25 x 25 cm
Exhibition view, *Rosângela Rennó – Strange Fruits,* Fotomuseum Winterthur, 2012

B | *Two Lessons of Fantastic Realism (magic lanterns detail),* 1991
3 encapsulated resin-coated black-and-white photographic prints with 9 portraits each and 2 magic lanterns with photographic negatives, each lantern: 220 x 20 x 20 cm, each photo: 101 x 63 cm
Exhibition view, *Rosângela Rennó – Strange Fruits,* Fotomuseum Winterthur, 2012

A

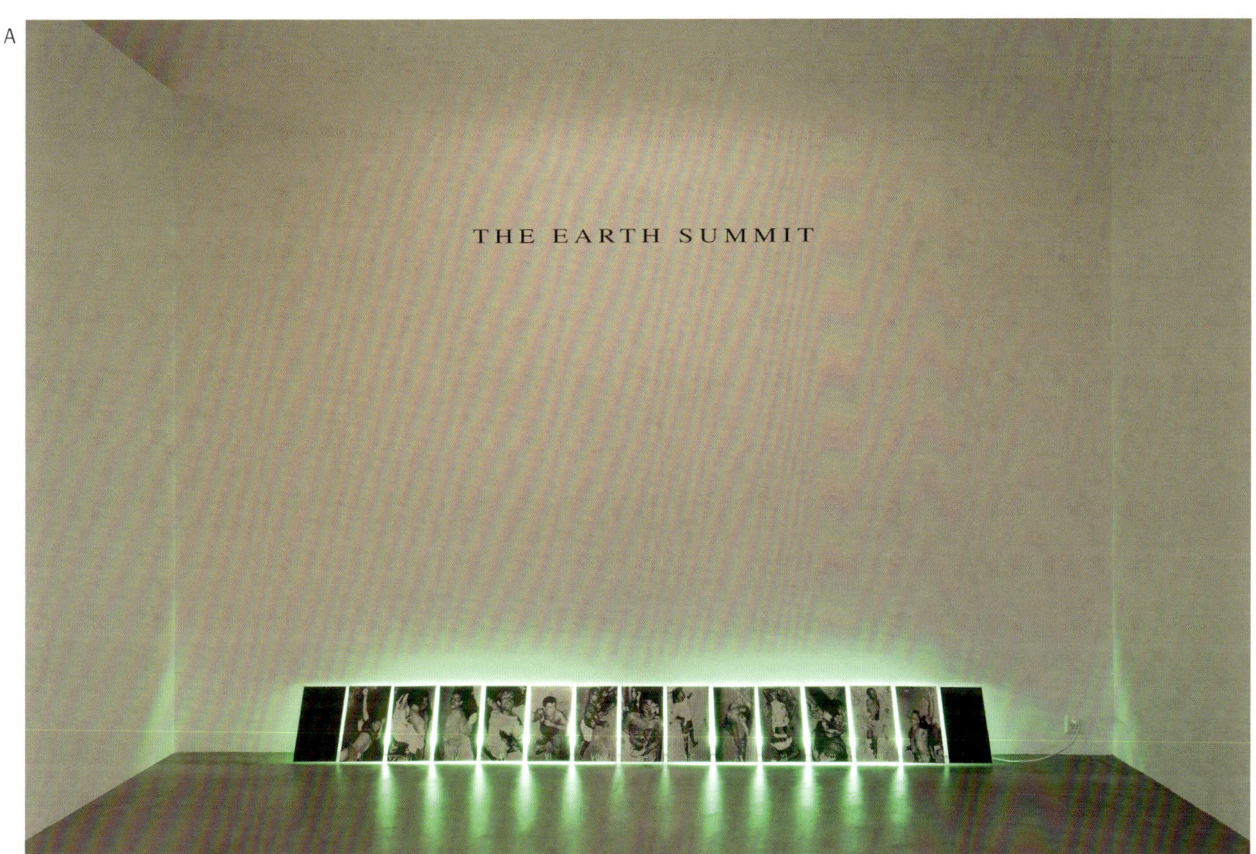

B

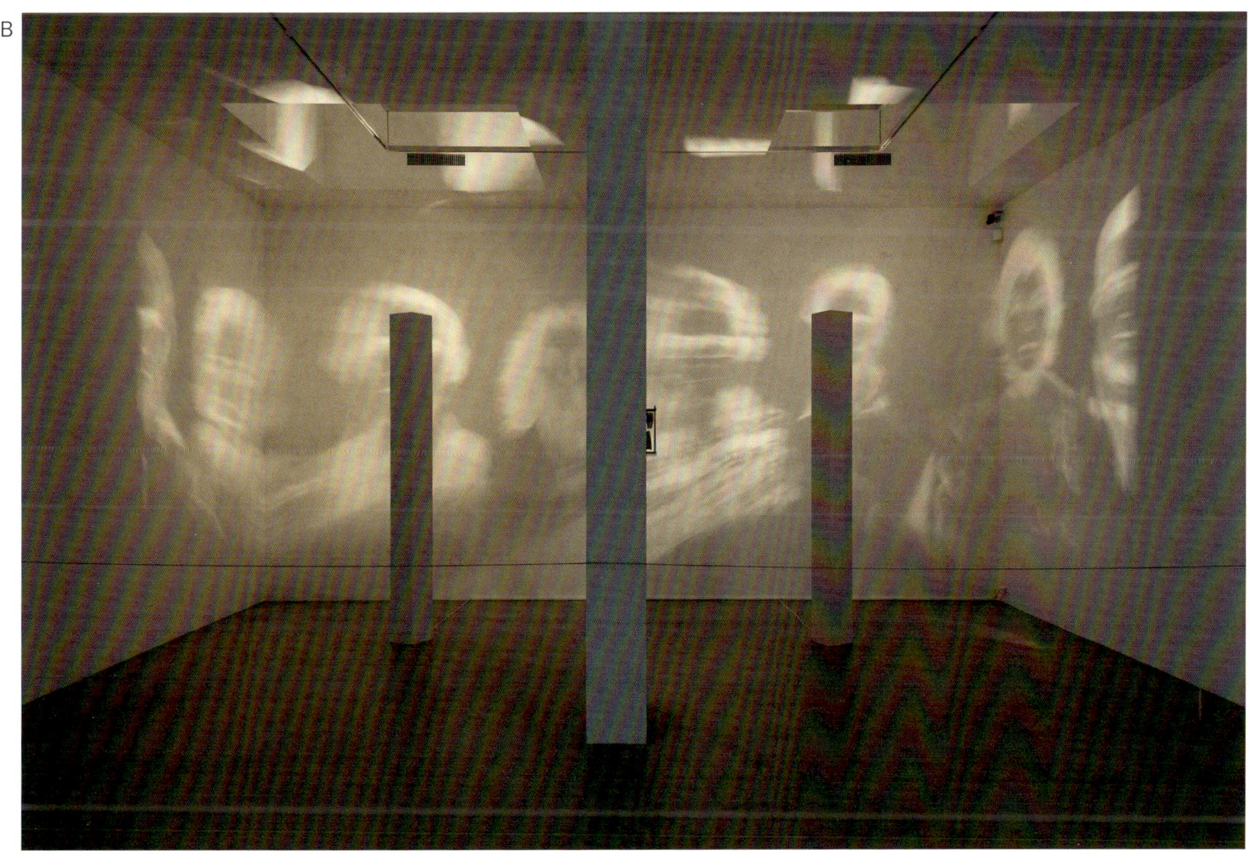

GUPTA

Kavi Gupta Chicago/Berlin
US-Chicago, IL 60607 | 835 W Washington Blvd
Phone +1 312 432 07 08 | Fax +1 312 432 07 09
info@kavigupta.com | www.kavigupta.com
Directors Kavi Gupta
Julia Fischbach

Kavi Gupta Chicago/Berlin
DE-10785 Berlin | Kluckstrasse 31
Phone +49 30 54 46 50 10
marc@kavigupta.com | www.kavigupta.com
Director Marc LeBlanc

Artists at Art Nova | Theaster Gates
Angel Otero

Gallery Information | Kavi Gupta gallery was established in 2002 with a focus on presenting exhibitions by international emerging and mid-career artists in all media. Since its inception, the gallery program has been supplemented by curated projects at art fairs and off-site locations.

The original Chicago venue comprises two main spaces and an adjacent project room. An additional 7,000-square-foot free-standing gallery for museum-scale works and ambitious projects was created in 2012. After establishing itself as one of the preeminent galleries in Chicago, Kavi Gupta opened a second location in Berlin's Schöneberg district in 2008.

Currently represented artists demonstrate a strong exhibition record including museum solo shows and biennials. The gallery has been recognized for discovering and fostering new talent while placing works into important collections. Kavi Gupta was the recipient of the U.S. Art Critics Association award for Best Show in a Commercial Gallery Nationally for Theaster Gates, *An Epitaph for Civil Rights and Other Domesticated Structures,* 2011.

Further artists represented:
Johanna Billing
Antonia Gurkovska
James Krone
Curtis Mann
Ari Marcopoulos
Scott Reeder
Clare E. Rojas
Melanie Schiff
Claire Sherman
Tony Tasset
Scott Treleaven

Theaster Gates (*1973) repurposes collections of knowledge that are physically embodied in outmoded forms into new objects and situations that reclaim the cultural value of discarded materials and spent labor. This process extends to transforming foreclosed buildings in blighted neighborhoods around the United States by financing improvements and social enterprise through collaborations with architects, researchers, and performers. Recently, Gates created an exchange for *dOCUMENTA (13)* between two disused residences (6901 S. Dorchester, Chicago, and the Huguenot House, Kassel), which were linked through a series of performances, structural interventions, and the establishment of a studio practice in Kassel with his Chicago workforce. Gates is also a founder and principal member of the musical ensemble the Black Monks of Mississippi.

Angel Otero (*1981) is a painter and sculptor whose work has been influenced by memories based in photographs and family memorabilia combined with the gestures of 20th-century painting. But the artist's unique process serves as a form of narrative in itself. Otero has developed a 'deformation' approach by first painting across glass and then, once it is dry, flaying the dried paint and reconstructing the composition across large canvasses, representative of how the artist perceives the process of reconfiguring both personal and historical narratives. Recent works in sculpture feature hand-manipulated fences that have evolved from practical barriers offering psychological comfort into objects imbued with aesthetic value. Otero's work is always negotiating between the individual and art history.

A | **Theaster Gates**
12 Ballads for Huguenot House, 2012
Installation view, *dOCUMENTA (13),* Kassel, 2012

B | **Angel Otero**
Untitled, 2012
Oil paint and oil paint skins collaged on canvas, 89 x 112 x 3½ inches

A

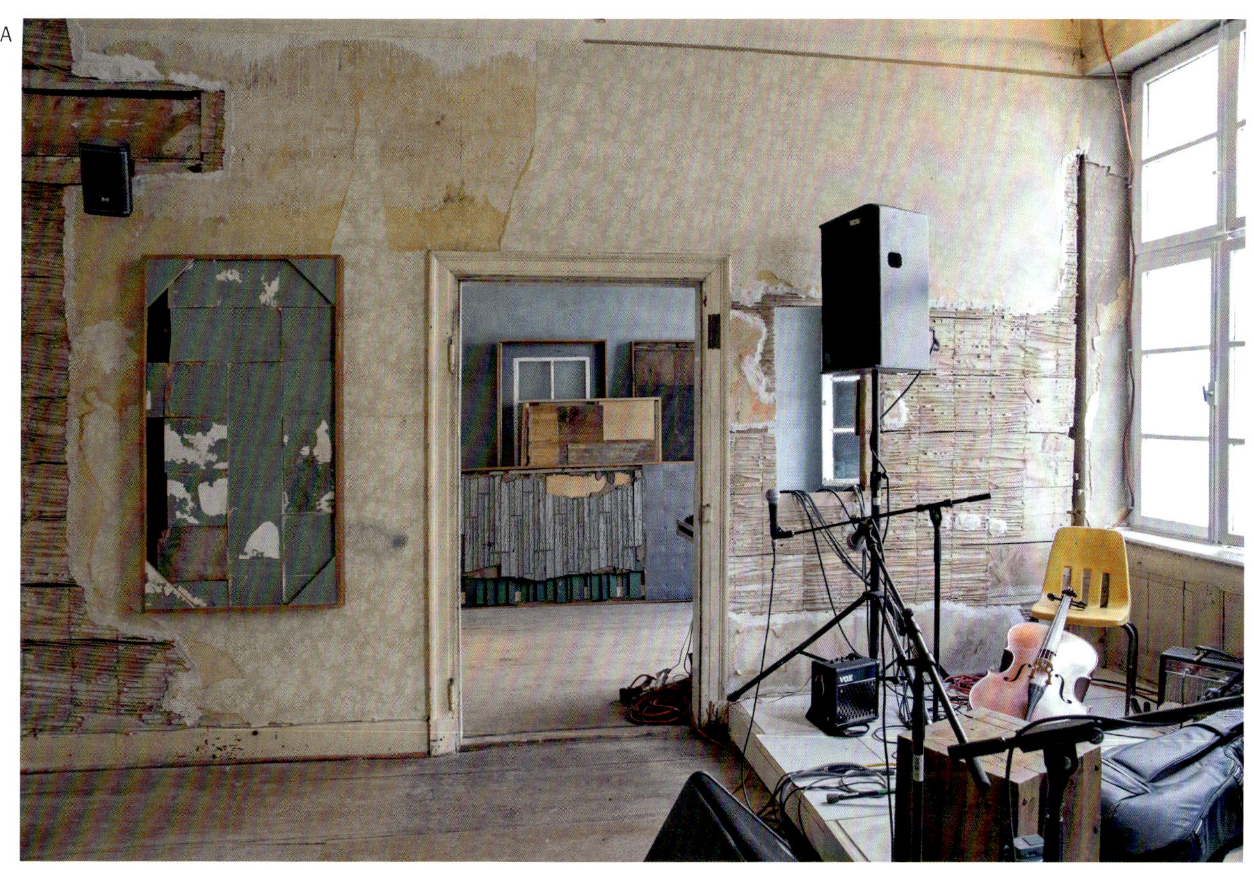

B

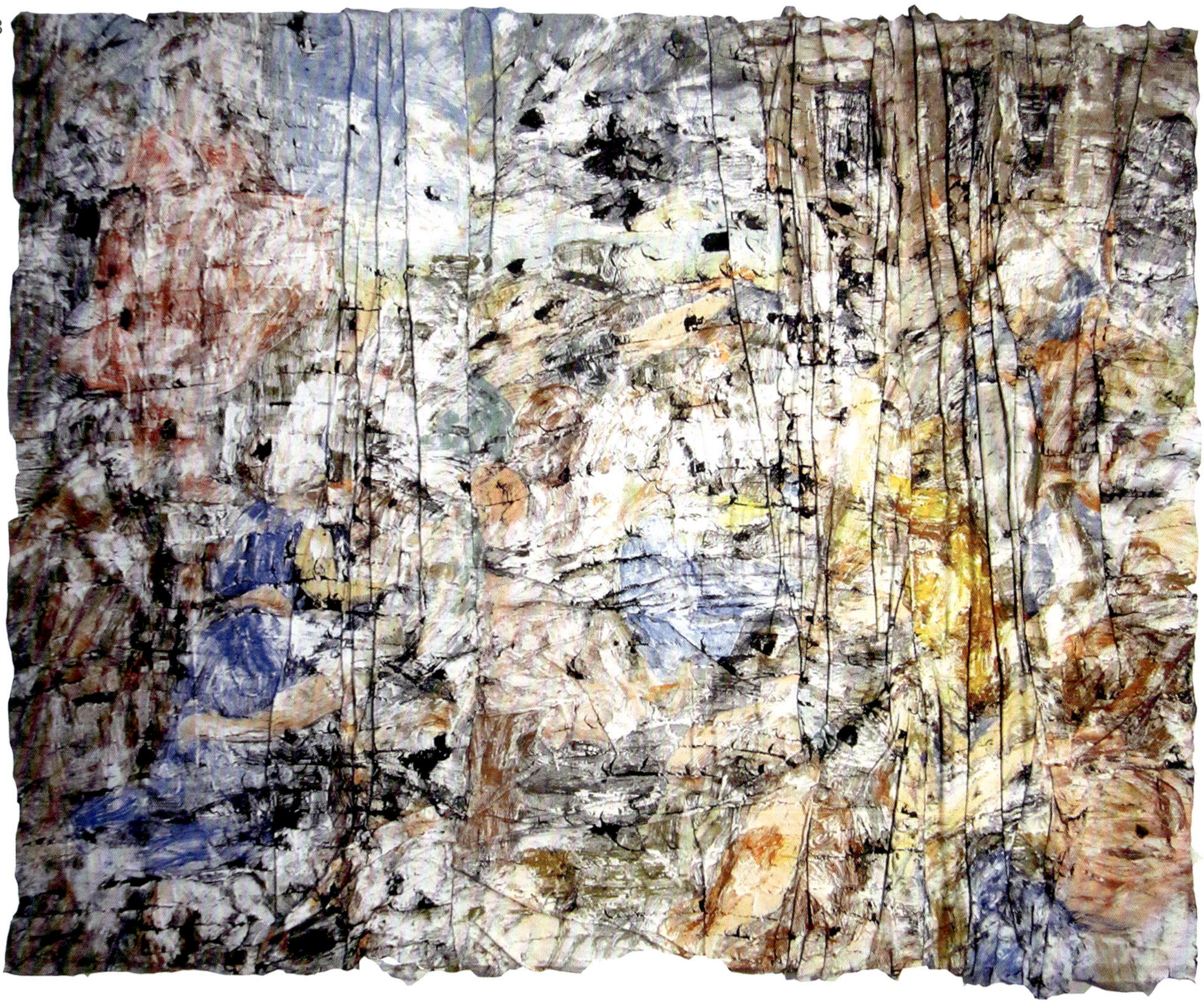

HAAS

Galerie Michael Haas
DE-10629 Berlin | Niebuhrstrasse 5
Phone +49 30 88 92 91 0 | Fax +49 30 88 92 91 10
contact@galeriemichaelhaas.de | www.galeriemichaelhaas.de
Director Michael Haas

Artists at
Art Basel Miami Beach | **Valerio Adami**
Peter Blake
Otto Dix
Jean Dubuffet
Max Ernst
Marianna Gartner
Franz Gertsch
George Grosz
Howard Hodgkin
John Isaacs
Howard Kanowitz
Konrad Klapheck
Paul Klee
Gary Kuehn
René Magritte
Maryan
Roberto Matta
Charles Matton
Joan Miró
Kenton Nelson
David Nicholson
Philip Pearlstein
Francis Picabia
Pablo Picasso
Anton Räderscheidt
Dimitris Tzamouranis
Bernar Venet
Andy Warhol
René Wirths

Further artists represented | Nicole Bianchet
Abraham David Christian
Kerstin Grimm
Julius Grünewald
Leiko Ikemura
Richard Jordan
Gustav Kluge
Dirk Lange
Stefan Mannel
Diana Rattray
Pia Stadtbäumer

René Magritte
La belle lurette (Ages Ago), 1965
Oil on canvas, 33 x 41 cm

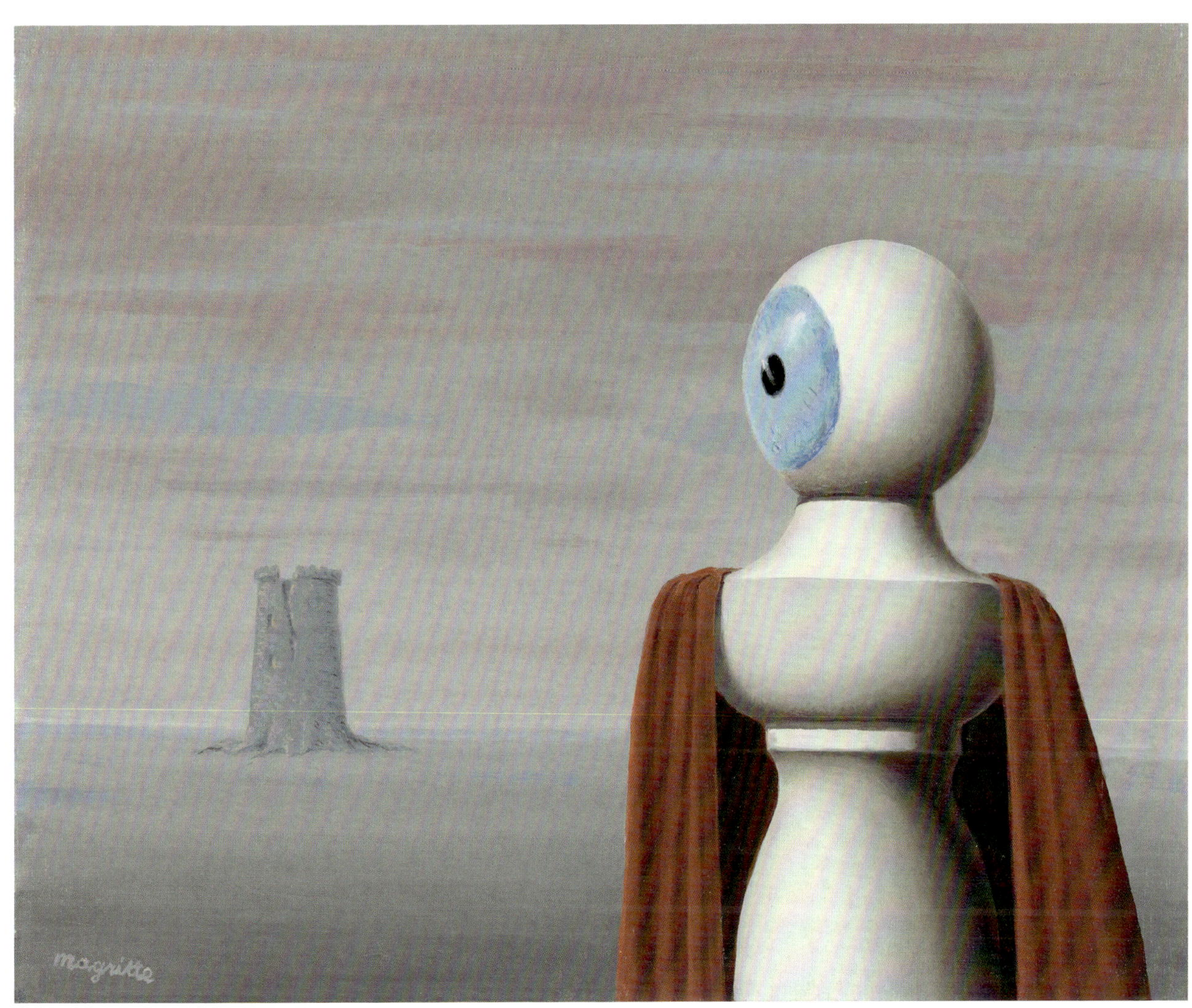
magritte

HAMMER

Hammer Galleries
US-New York, NY 10022 | 475 Park Avenue
Phone +1 212 644 44 00 | Fax +1 212 644 44 07
info@hammergalleries.com | www.hammergalleries.com
Directors Howard Shaw
Iris Krenzis Cohen

Artists at
Art Basel Miami Beach | **Alexander Calder**
Fernand Léger
Joan Miró

Gallery Information | Founded in 1928 by industrialist and philanthropist Dr. Armand Hammer, Hammer Galleries today specializes in Impressionist, Modern, and Post-War masters.

Hammer Galleries quickly rose to prominence when, in the early 1930s, it exhibited the world-famous Russian Imperial Easter Eggs by celebrated court jeweler Karl Fabergé. After beginning with a primary focus on Russian icons, Imperial porcelains, and rare art objects, in the 1960s Hammer Galleries shifted its focus to 19th- and 20th-century European and American masters. In 1980, Hammer moved into a turn-of-the-century townhouse on 57th Street, its home for the next thirty years.

In 2010, Hammer Galleries moved to new premises at 475 Park Avenue. Hammer's change in location was accompanied by an expansion of its focus. Hammer continues to concentrate on Impressionist and Modern masters, while now also handling important works by Post-War masters. Recent exhibitions have included *Modern Masters: Paris and Beyond* and *On Paper: Works by Impressionist, Modern and Post-War Masters.* For our debut at Art Basel Miami Beach, we are presenting selections from our current exhibition entitled *Objects in Space: Works by Calder, Leger & Miró.*

Howard Shaw, who began his career at Hammer Galleries in 1981, is the current President and Director.

Further artists represented: Pierre Bonnard
Mary Cassatt
Marc Chagall
Chen Yifei
Salvador Dalí
Henri de Toulouse-Lautrec
Maurice de Vlaminck
Edgar Degas
Paul Delvaux
Raoul Dufy
Sam Francis
Wassily Kandinsky
René Magritte
Édouard Manet
Henri Matisse
Amedeo Modigliani
Henry Moore
Claude Monet
Berthe Morisot
Pablo Picasso
Camille Pissarro
Pierre-Auguste Renoir
Alfred Sisley
Chaim Soutine
Yves Tanguy
Kees van Dongen
Andy Warhol
Tom Wesselmann

Alexander Calder
Red, Blue and Black Cascade,
1974
Painted sheet metal and steel wire, 38 x 52 inches

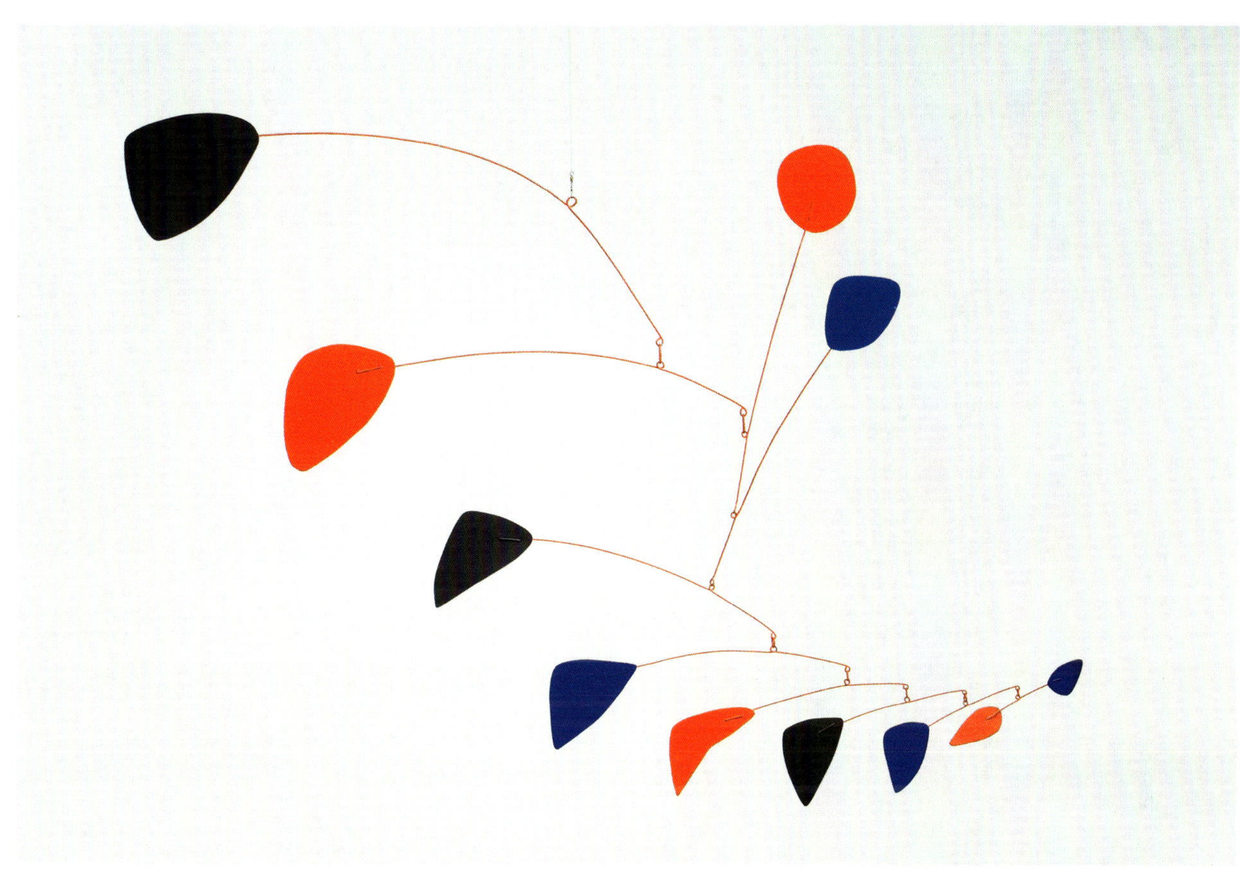

HARRIS LIEBERMAN

Harris Lieberman
US-New York, NY 10001 | 508 West 26th Street
Phone +1 212 206 12 90
gallery@harrislieberman.com | www.harrislieberman.com
Directors Jessie Washburne-Harris
Michael Lieberman

Artists at
Art Basel Miami Beach | **Armin Boehm**
Matthias Dornfeld
Stef Driesen
Daniel Guzmán
Karl Haendel
Julian Hoeber
Evan Holloway
Alicja Kwade
Ohad Meromi
Rebecca Morris
Lisa Oppenheim
Zak Prekop
Bernd Ribbeck
Matt Saunders
Tommy White
Thomas Zipp

Bernd Ribbeck
Untitled, 2012
Acrylics and pigmented marker
on MDF, 70 x 40 cm

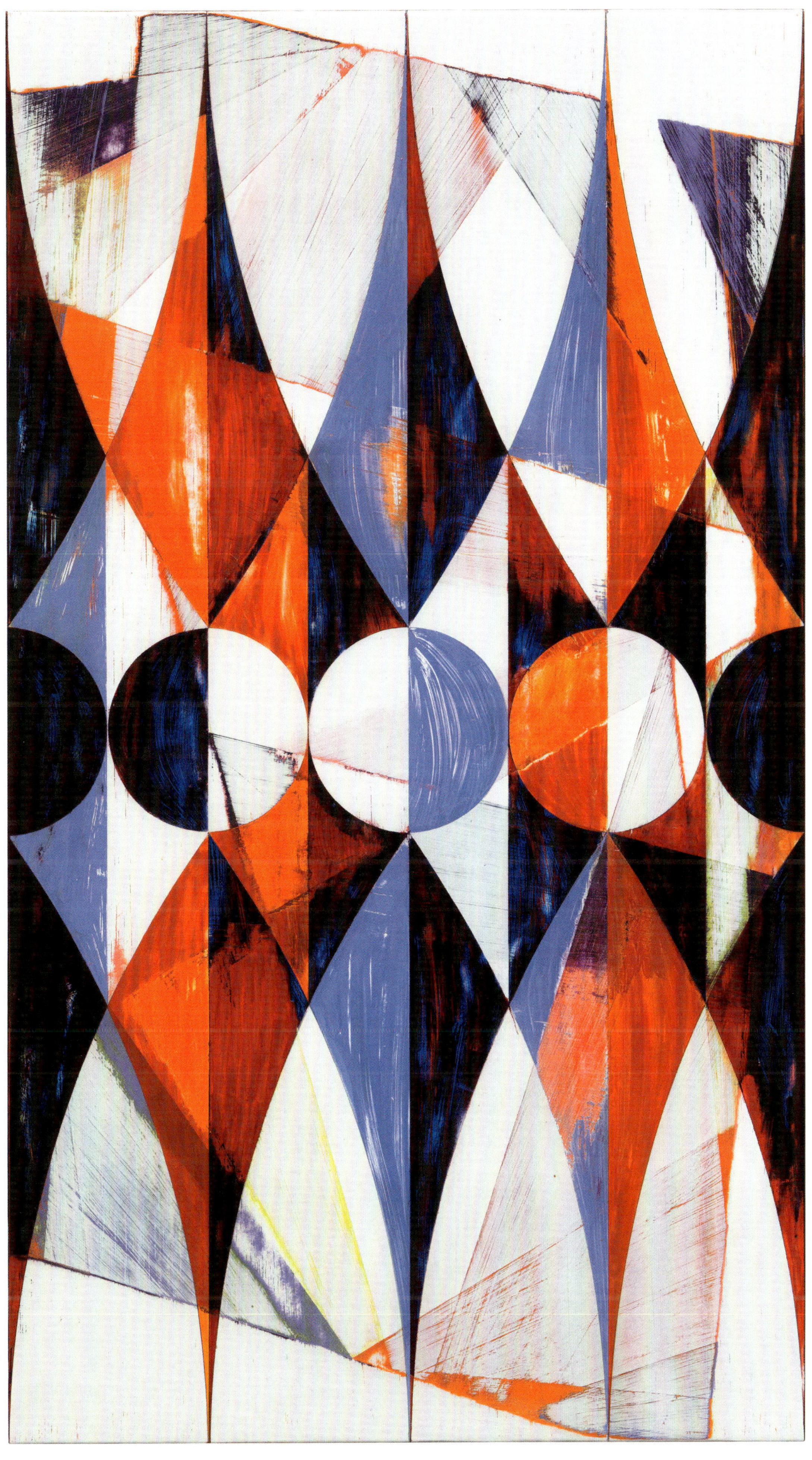

HAUSER & WIRTH

Hauser & Wirth
CH-8005 Zurich | Limmatstrasse 270
Phone +41 44 446 80 50 | Fax +41 44 446 80 55
zurich@hauserwirth.com | www.hauserwirth.com

Hauser & Wirth
GB-London W1J 9DY | 196A Piccadilly
Phone +44 20 7287 2300 | Fax +44 20 7287 6600
london@hauserwirth.com | www.hauserwirth.com

Hauser & Wirth
GB-London W1S 2ET | 23 Savile Row
Phone +44 20 7287 2300 | Fax +44 20 7787 6600
london@hauserwirth.com | www.hauserwirth.com

Hauser & Wirth
US-New York, NY 10021 | 32 East 69th Street
Phone +1 212 794 49 70 | Fax +1 212 794 49 71
newyork@hauserwirth.com | www.hauserwirth.com

Artists at Art Basel Miami Beach | **Rita Ackermann**
Ida Applebroog
Phyllida Barlow
Louise Bourgeois
Christoph Büchel
David Claerbout
Martin Creed
Berlinde De Bruyckere
Martin Eder
Ellen Gallagher
Isa Genzken
Dan Graham
Rodney Graham
Subodh Gupta
Mary Heilmann
Eva Hesse
Andy Hope 1930
Roni Horn
Thomas Houseago
Matthew Day Jackson
Richard Jackson
Rashid Johnson
Josephsohn
Allan Kaprow
Rachel Khedoori
Bharti Kher
Guillermo Kuitca
Maria Lassnig
Lee Lozano
Paul McCarthy
Joan Mitchell
Henry Moore
Ron Mueck
Caro Niederer
Christopher Orr
Djordje Ozbolt
Michael Raedecker
Jason Rhoades
Pipilotti Rist
Dieter Roth
Anri Sala
Wilhelm Sasnal
Cristoph Schlingensief
Roman Signer
Anj Smith
Monika Sosnowska
Diana Thater
André Thomkins
Ian Wallace
Zhang Enli
David Zink Yi
Jakub Julian Ziolkowski

Rita Ackermann
Fire by Days Blues V, 2012
Oil and spray paint on canvas,
105 x 73 inches, 266.7 x 185.4 cm

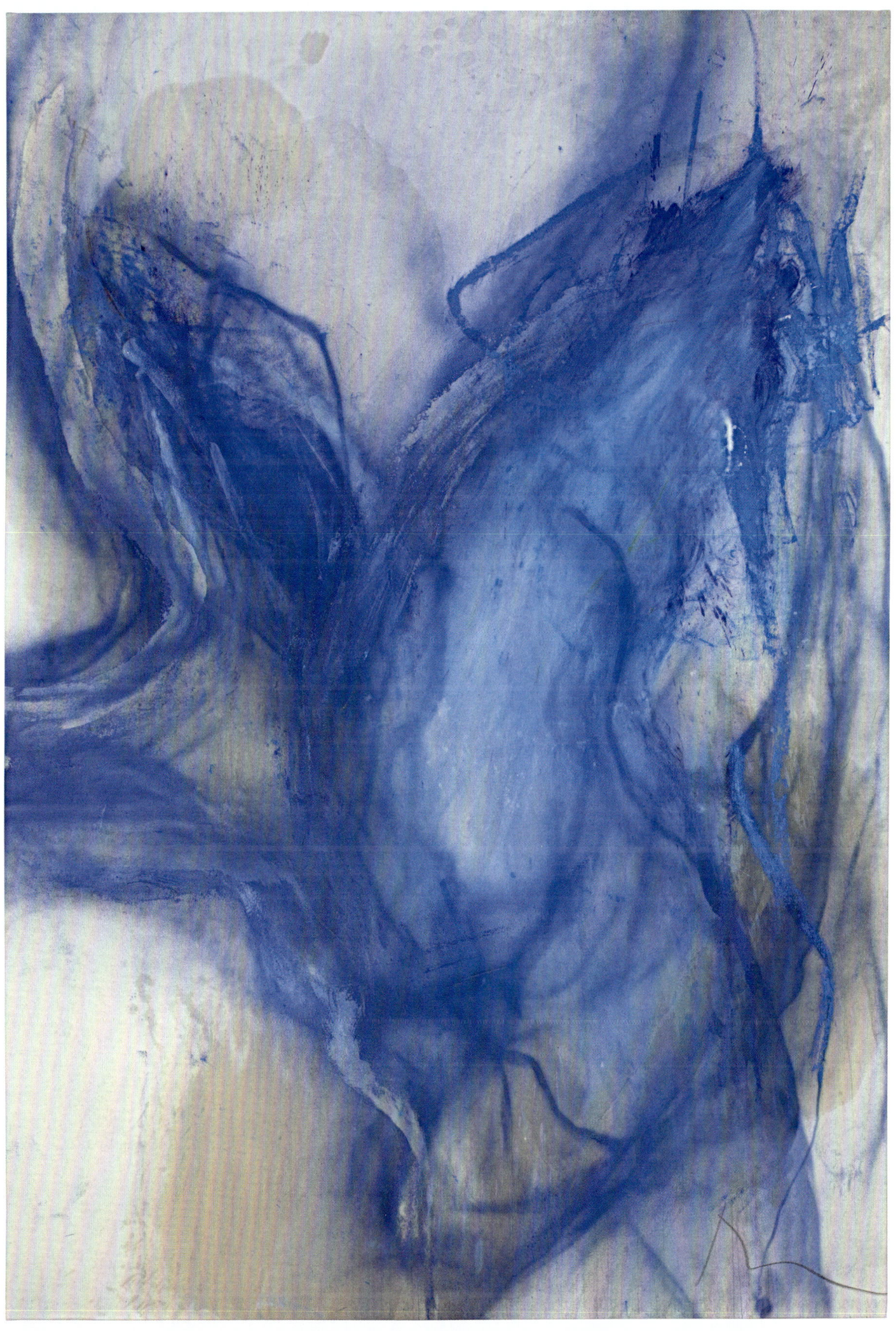

HERALD ST

Herald St
GB-London E2 6JT | 2 Herald Street
Phone +44 20 71682566 | Fax +44 20 76130009
mail@heraldst.com | www.heraldst.com
Directors Nicky Verber
Ash L'Ange

Artists at
Art Basel Miami Beach | **Markus Amm**
Josh Brand
Pablo Bronstein
Matt Connors
Cary Kwok
Djordje Ozbolt
Amalia Pica
Nicole Wermers

Further artists represented | Alexandra Bircken
Peter Coffin
Matthew Darbyshire
Michael Dean
Ida Ekblad
Annette Kelm
Scott King
Christina Mackie
Oliver Payne
Nick Relph
Tony Swain
Donald Urquhart
Klaus Weber

Matt Connors
Soul Error (Colby Version), 2012
Acrylic and pencil on canvas,
200 x 157 cm

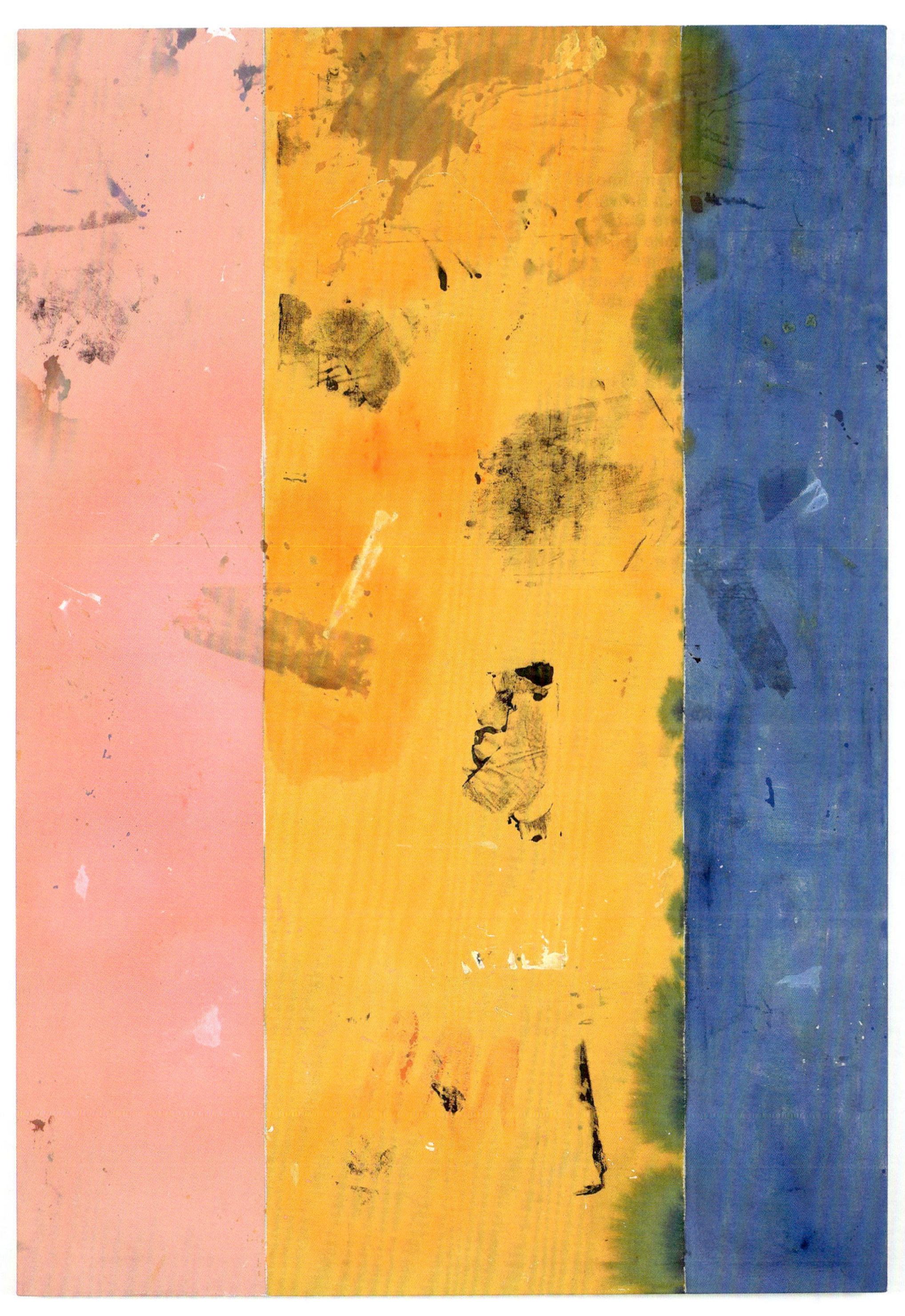

HIRSCHL & ADLER

Hirschl & Adler Modern
US-New York, NY 10019 | 730 Fifth Avenue
Phone +1 212 535 88 10 | Fax +1 212 772 72 37
modern@hirschlandadler.com | www.hirschlandadler.com
Directors Shelley Farmer
Stuart P. Feld

Artists at Art Basel Miami Beach | **Milton Avery**
Thomas Hart Benton
Oscar Bluemner
Charles Burchfield
Stuart Davis
Charles Demuth
Preston Dickinson
Arthur Dove
Albert Gallatin
Marsden Hartley
Edward Hopper
Raymond Jonson
Gaston Lachaise
Blanche Lazzell
Edmund Lewandowski
Paul Manship
John Marin
Elie Nadelman
Georgia O'Keeffe
Agnes Pelton
Niles Spencer
Joseph Stella
Warren Wheelock

Gallery Information | Founded 1981, specializing in American and European Modernism, 20th-century masters, contemporary paintings, works on paper, and sculpture.

Further artists represented: Arthur Wesley Dow
David Ligare
Richard Lonsdale-Hands
John Moore
Fairfield Porter
Stone Roberts
Bill Traylor
Marc Trujillo
Elizabeth Turk
Stanley Twardowicz

Agnes Pelton
Sand Storm, 1932
Oil on canvas, 30¼ x 22 inches

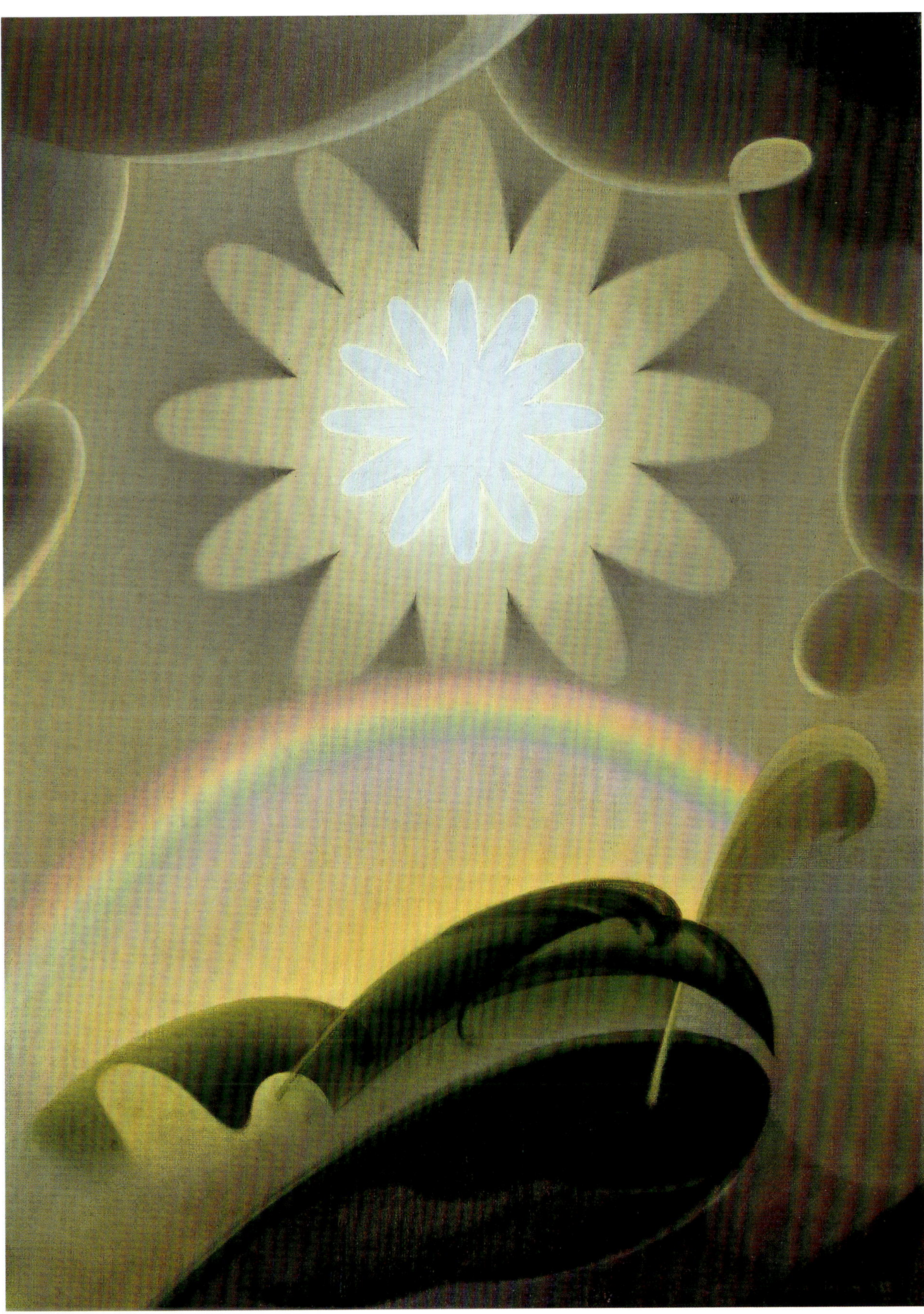

HOFFMAN

Mobile +1 312 961 16 66

Rhona Hoffman Gallery
US-Chicago, IL 60607 | 118 North Peoria Street
Phone +1 312 455 19 90 | Fax +1 312 455 17 27
rhoffman@rhoffmangallery.com | www.rhoffmangallery.com
Directors Rhona Hoffman
Charlotte Marra
Sibylle Friche

Artists at
Art Basel Miami Beach | **Carla Accardi**
Vito Acconci
Huma Bhabha
Mel Bochner
André Butzer
Todd Chilton
Spencer Finch
Julia Fish
Luis Gispert
Jacob Hashimoto
Susan Hefuna
Robert Heinecken
Sol LeWitt
Carmen McLeod
Robert Overby
Karthik Pandian
Richard Rezac
Fred Sandback
Mickalene Thomas
Siebren Versteeg
Kehinde Wiley

Gallery Information | Specializes in contemporary art by well-established and emerging artists working in all media. Established 1983.

Further artists represented: Hamish Fulton
Chris Garofalo
Leon Golub
Jenny Holzer
Judy Ledgerwood
Robert Ryman
Nancy Spero
Richard Tuttle
Anne Wilson

Carla Accardi
Svelarlo al vento, 2012
Gouache on canvas, 120 x 160 cm

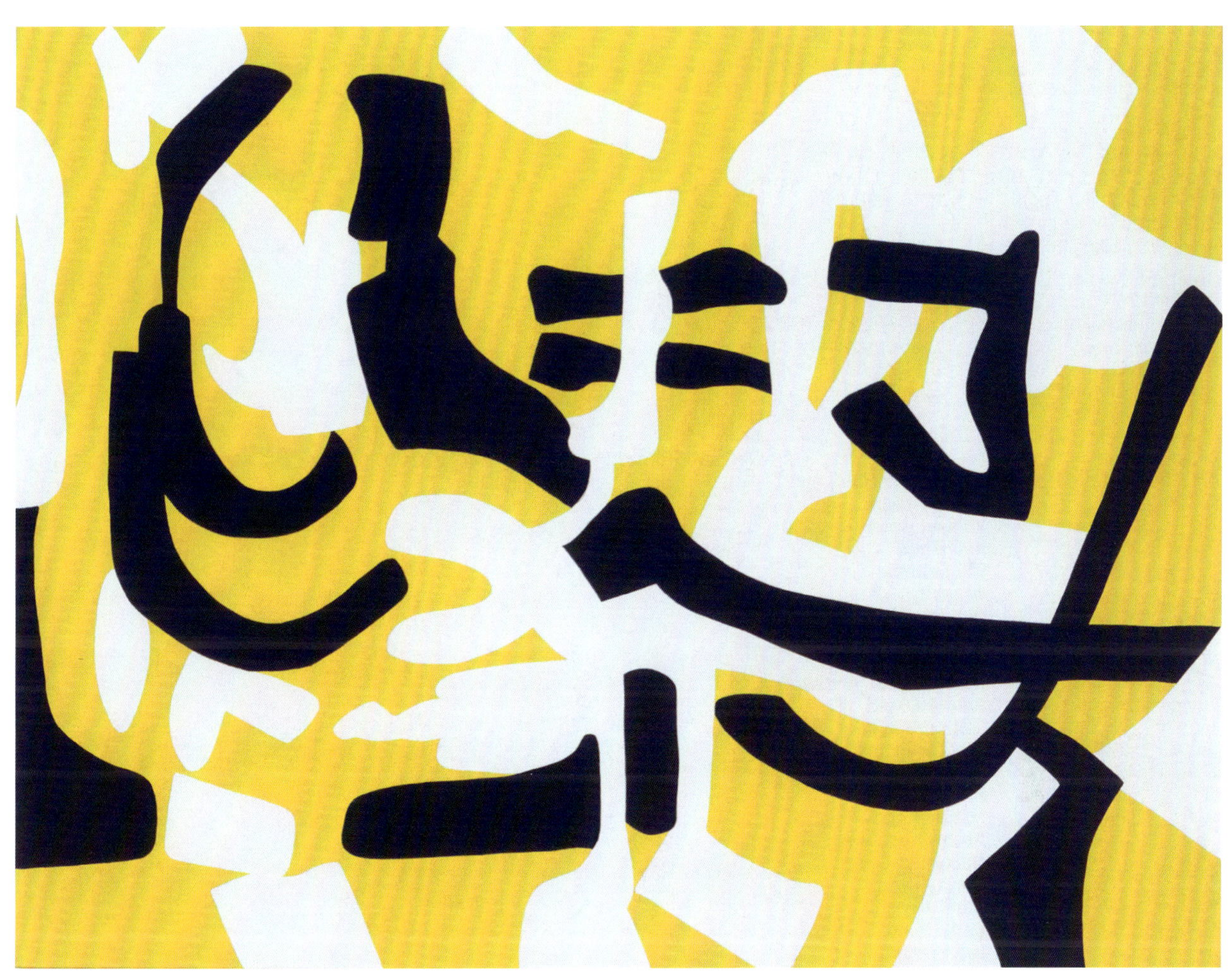

HOUK

Mobile +1 917 528 08 95

Edwynn Houk Gallery
US-New York, NY 10151 | 745 Fifth Avenue
Phone +1 212 750 70 70 | Fax +1 212 688 48 48
info@houkgallery.com | www.houkgallery.com
Directors Edwynn Houk
Julie Castellano

Galerie Edwynn Houk
CH-8002 Zurich | Stockerstrasse 33
Phone +41 44 202 69 25 | Fax +41 44 202 82 51
zuerich@houkgallery.com | www.houkgallery.com
Directors Daniel Blochwitz
Diana Poole

Artists at
Art Basel Miami Beach | **Gail Albert Halaban**
Diane Arbus
Valérie Belin
Ilse Bing
Bill Brandt
Brassaï
Manuel Álvarez Bravo
Sebastiaan Bremer
Harry Callahan
Henri Cartier-Bresson
Elliott Erwitt
Lalla Essaydi
Walker Evans
Sissi Farassat
Robert Frank
Nadav Kander
André Kertész
Dorothea Lange
Danny Lyon
Man Ray
Sally Mann
David Michalek
Tina Modotti
László Moholy-Nagy
Vik Muniz
Robert Polidori
Herb Ritts
August Sander
Hannes Schmid
Stephen Shore
Alfred Stieglitz
Paul Strand
Edward Weston

Gallery Information | Specializing in 20th-century and contemporary photography

Man Ray
Untitled (Dora Maar), 1936
Vintage silver print, 7.4 x 5.5 cm

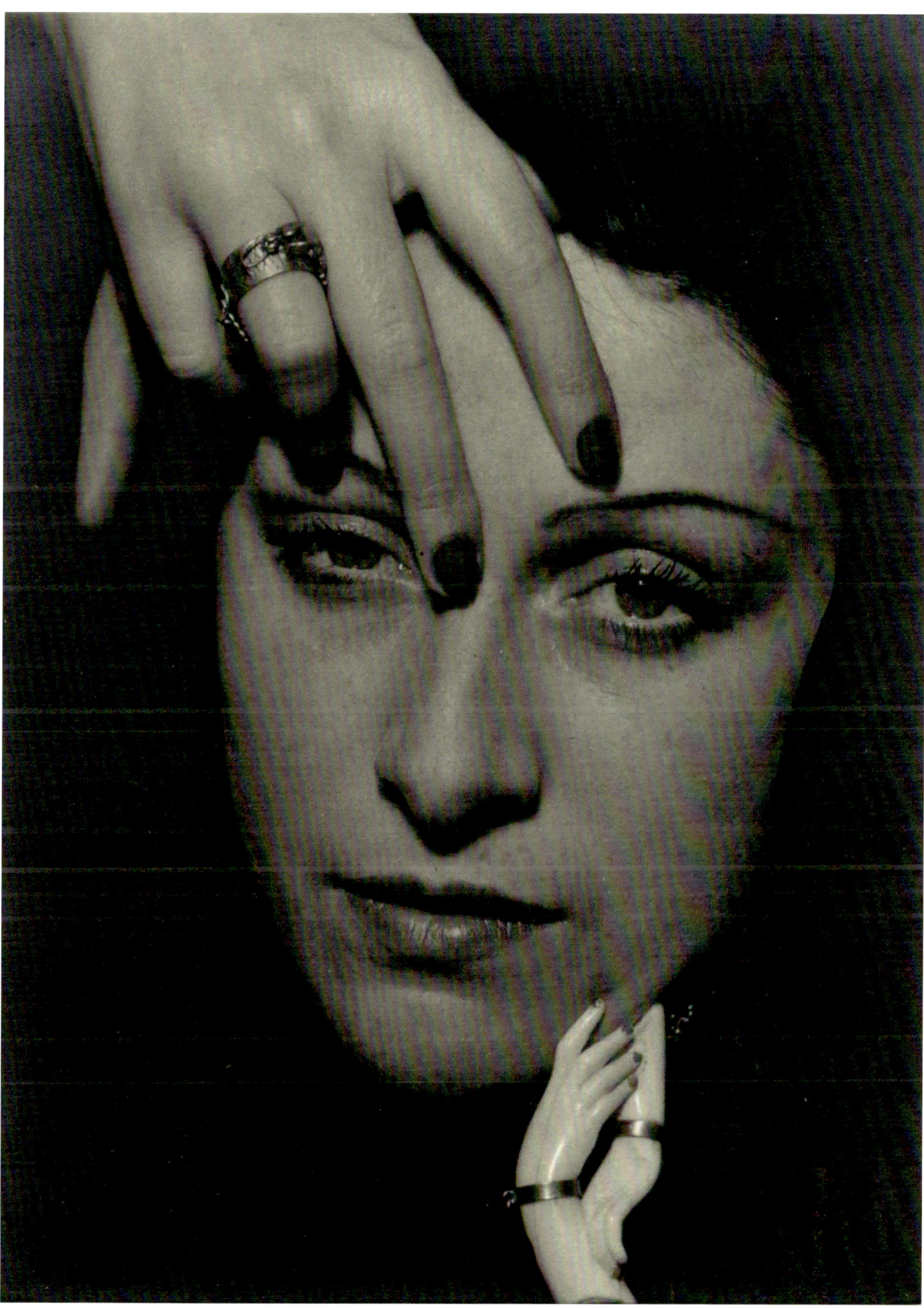

HUFKENS

Xavier Hufkens
BE-1050 Brussels | Rue Saint-Georges 6-8
Phone +32 2 639 67 30 | Fax +32 2 639 67 38
info@xavierhufkens.com | www.xavierhufkens.com
Director Xavier Hufkens

Artists at
Art Basel Miami Beach | **Harold Ancart**
Richard Artschwager
Daniel Buren
Michel François
Adam Fuss
Evan Holloway
Roni Horn
Thomas Houseago
Jacob Kassay
Robert Mapplethorpe
Malcolm Morley
Jack Pierson
Tim Rollins and K.O.S.
Sterling Ruby

Further artists represented | Saâdane Afif
Philip Allen
David Altmejd
Louise Bourgeois
Cris Brodahl
Jean-Marc Bustamante
John Chamberlain
George Condo
Thierry De Cordier
Willem de Kooning
William Eggleston
Antony Gormley
Pierre Huyghe
Bertrand Lavier
José Lerma
David Noonan
Hans Op de Beeck
Alessandro Pessoli
Michelangelo Pistoletto
Ken Price
Robert Ryman
Padraig Timoney
Lesley Vance
Jan Vercruysse
Erwin Wurm

Adam Fuss
Medusa, 2010
Unique gelatin silver print
photogram, 240 x 144 cm
From the series *Home and the World*
Edition of 9 + 2 AP

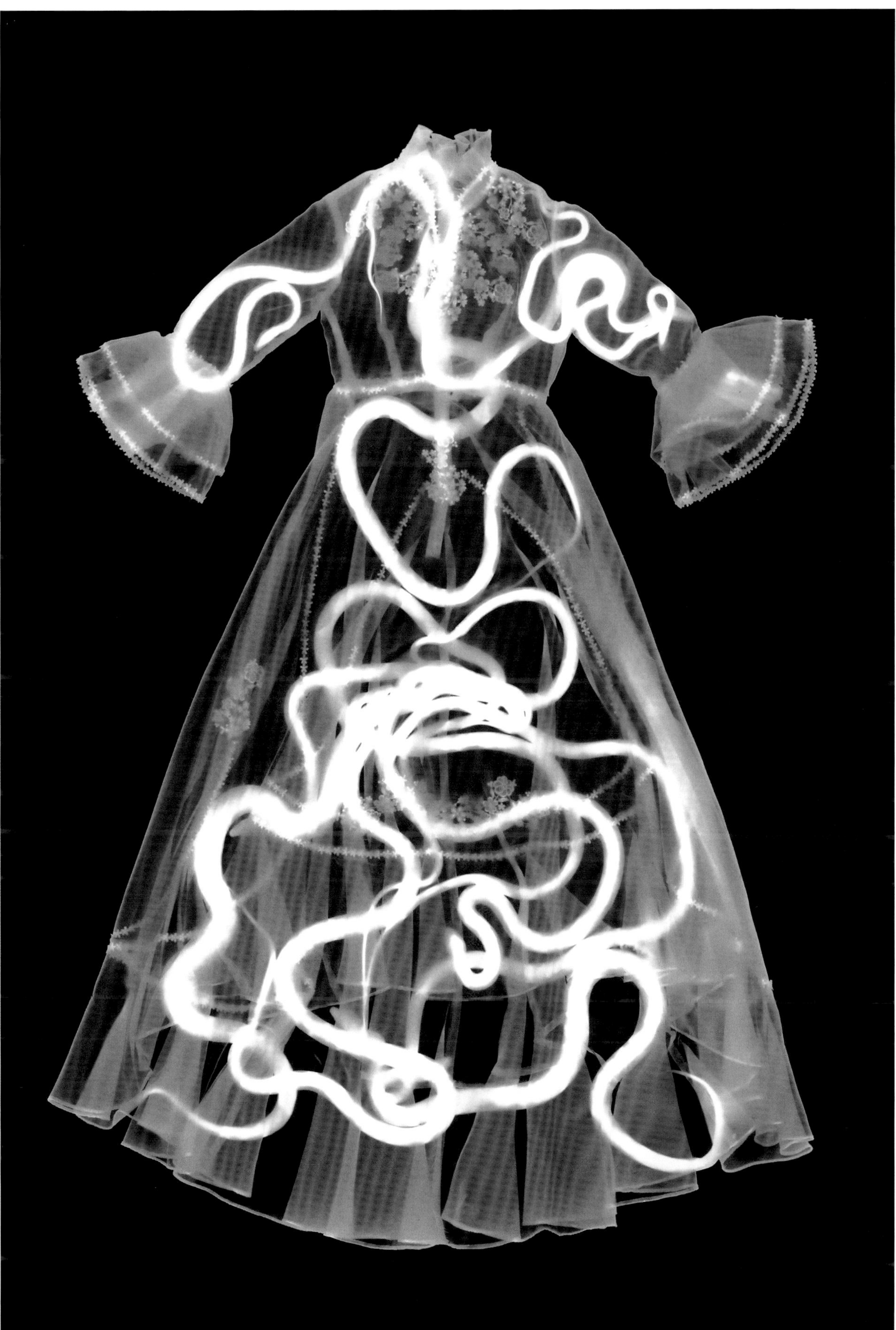

i8

Mobile +354 659 36 66, +354 695 83 88

i8 Gallery
IS-101 Reykjavik | Tryggvagata 16
Phone +354 551 36 66 | Fax +354 578 36 67
info@i8.is | www.i8.is
Directors Borkur Arnarson
Audur Jorundsdottir

Artists at Art Nova | Janice Kerbel
Egill Saebjornsson

Further artists represented | Birgir Andresson
Olafur Eliasson
Hreinn Fridfinnsson
Kristjan Gudmundsson
Sigurdur Gudmundsson
Elin Hansdottir
Roni Horn
Ragnar Kjartansson
Eggert Petursson
Finnbogi Petursson
Ragna Robertsdottir
Karin Sander
Hrafnkell Sigurdsson
Ignacio Uriarte
Ivar Valgardsson
Thor Vigfusson
Lawrence Weiner

Egill Sæbjörnsson's installations combine elements of sculpture, animation, and sound in a playful and inventive way. Sæbjörnsson's latest work uses video-game aesthetics where communication between computer-animated image projections and sculptural objects create self-generative pieces that investigate the power of the art object as a species. The works that also double as instruments relate to the artist's continued research into the potential of music and his investigation and development of the 'pseudo instrument.'

Janice Kerbel is known for rigorous 'studies' that are at once realizable and imaginary. The question of visibility is a common factor in her work – trying to find form for things that otherwise cannot be seen. Kerbel strives to understand existing languages and structures and what happens to them when they are looked at in isolation from their expected use. Her research into what narrative might look like has attracted her to forms such as scripts, letters, theater, and animation – manifested in such disparate projects as a detailed master plan to rob a bank and a play written for theatrical lights.

Egill Saebjornsson
La Linea, 2012
Mixed media, dimensions variable

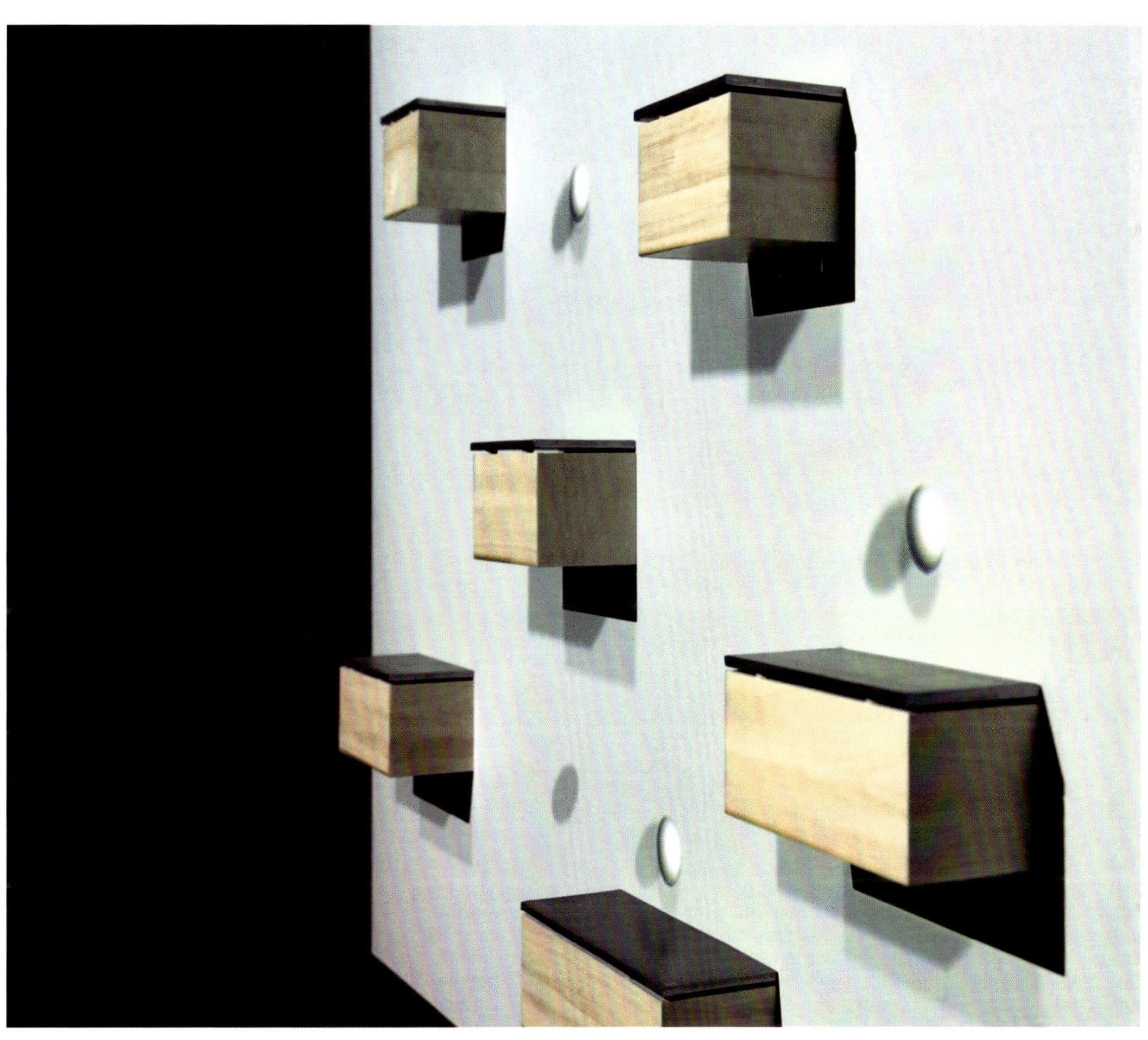

JACOBSON

Bernard Jacobson Gallery
GB-London W1S 3NX | 6 Cork Street
Phone +44 20 7343431 | Fax +44 20 7343277
mail@jacobsongallery.com | www.jacobsongallery.com
Director Bernard Jacobson

Bernard Jacobson Gallery
US-New York, NY 10021 | 17 East 71st Street
Phone +1 212 8791100 | Fax +44 20 7343277
mail@jacobsongallery.com
Director Bernard Jacobson

Artists at
Art Basel Miami Beach | **Larry Bell**
Bram Bogart
Sam Francis
Helen Frankenthaler
Pia Fries
Shirley Kaneda
Bruce McLean
Robert Motherwell
Pierre Soulages
Frank Stella
William Tillyer
Marc Vaux
Tom Wesselmann

Gallery Information | Founded in 1969, the Bernard Jacobson Gallery deals in modern and contemporary British and international art.

The London gallery has two main exhibition spaces and a graphics department all within 6 Cork Street.

In March 2011 Bernard Jacobson Gallery opened a new space in New York at 17 East 71st Street.

Robert Motherwell
Open No. 18: In Ultramarine with White Line, 1968
Acrylic on canvas,
289.6 x 175.3 cm

JACQUES

Mobile +44 791 719 49 38

Alison Jacques Gallery
GB-London W1T 3LN | 16-18 Berners Street
Phone +44 20 76 31 47 20 | Fax +44 20 76 31 47 50
info@alisonjacquesgallery.com | www.alisonjacquesgallery.com
Directors Alison Jacques
Roger Tatley

Artists at Art Basel Miami Beach | **Haluk Akakçe**
Michael Bauer
Lygia Clark
Tomory Dodge
Dan Fischer
Saul Fletcher
Matt Johnson
Ian Kiaer
Klara Kristalova
Graham Little
Robert Mapplethorpe
Ryan McGinley
Ana Mendieta
Paul Morrison
Ryan Mosley
Hélio Oiticica
Alessandro Raho
Bernd Ribbeck
Dorothea Tanning
Michael van Ofen
Mathew Weir
Hannah Wilke
Catherine Yass
Thomas Zipp

Saul Fletcher
Untitled #257 (Clock), 2012
C-print, unframed: 19.8 x 16.2 cm,
7¾ x 6⅜ inches, framed:
56.8 x 47.1 cm, 22⅜ x 18½ inches

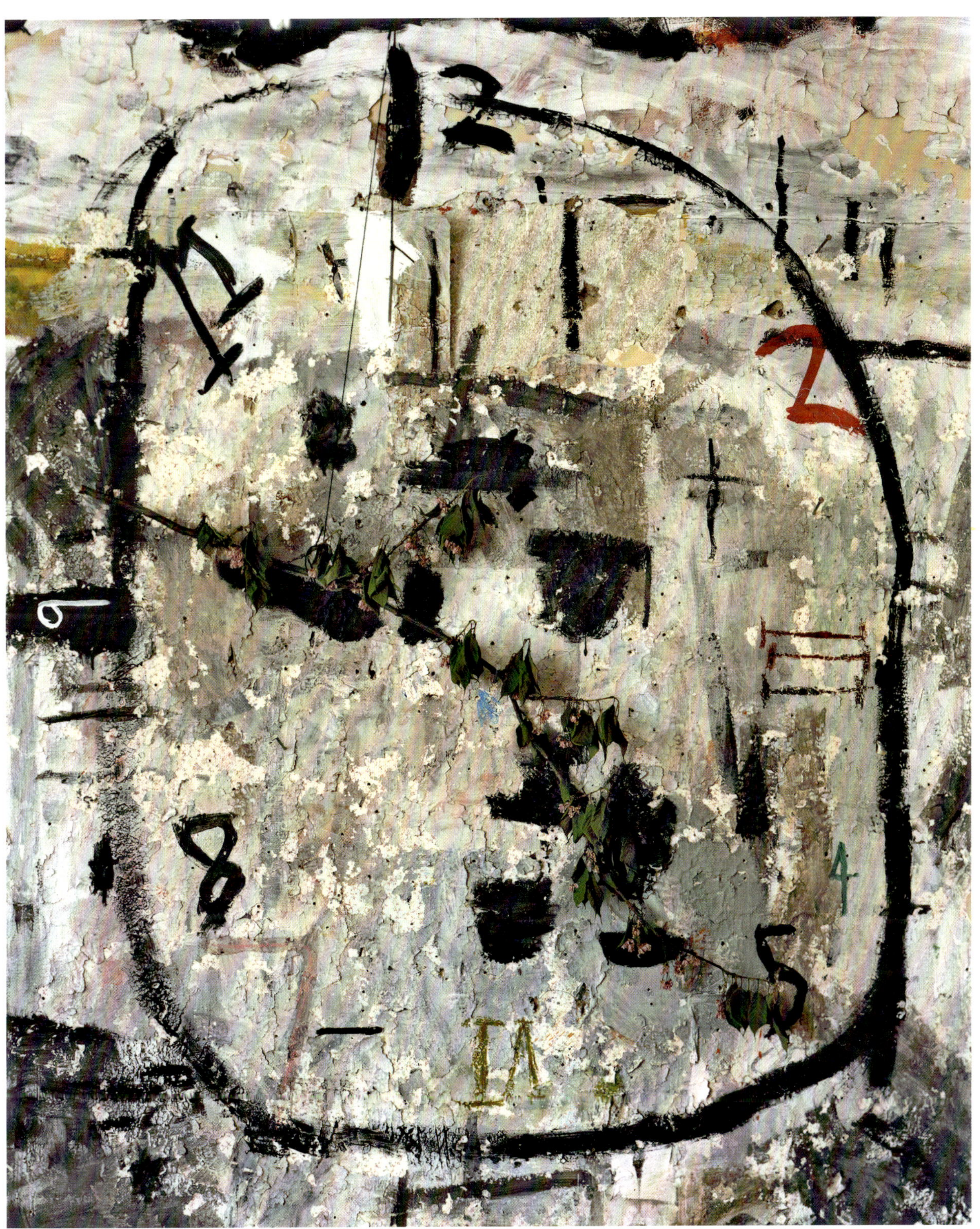

JANDA

Mobile +43 664 2335429

Galerie Martin Janda
AT-1010 Vienna | Eschenbachgasse 11
Phone +43 1 5857371 | Fax +43 1 5857372
galerie@martinjanda.at | www.martinjanda.at
Directors Martin Janda
Elisabeth Konrath

Artists at Art Basel Miami Beach | **Martin Arnold**
Alessandro Balteo Yazbeck
Benjamin Butler
Adriana Czernin
Raoul De Keyser
Svenja Deininger
Milena Dragicevic
Werner Feiersinger
Giuseppe Gabellone
Christine & Irene Hohenbüchler
Christian Hutzinger
Jakob Kolding
Július Koller
Jan Merta
Roman Ondák
Peter Pommerer
Allen Ruppersberg
Joe Scanlan
Ene-Liis Semper
Gabriel Sierra
Roman Signer
Adrien Tirtiaux
Johannes Vogl
Maja Vukoje
Corinne Wasmuht
Donelle Woolford
Sharon Ya'ari
Jun Yang
Jakub Julian Ziolkowski

Svenja Deininger
Untitled, 2012
Oil on canvas, 50 x 50 cm

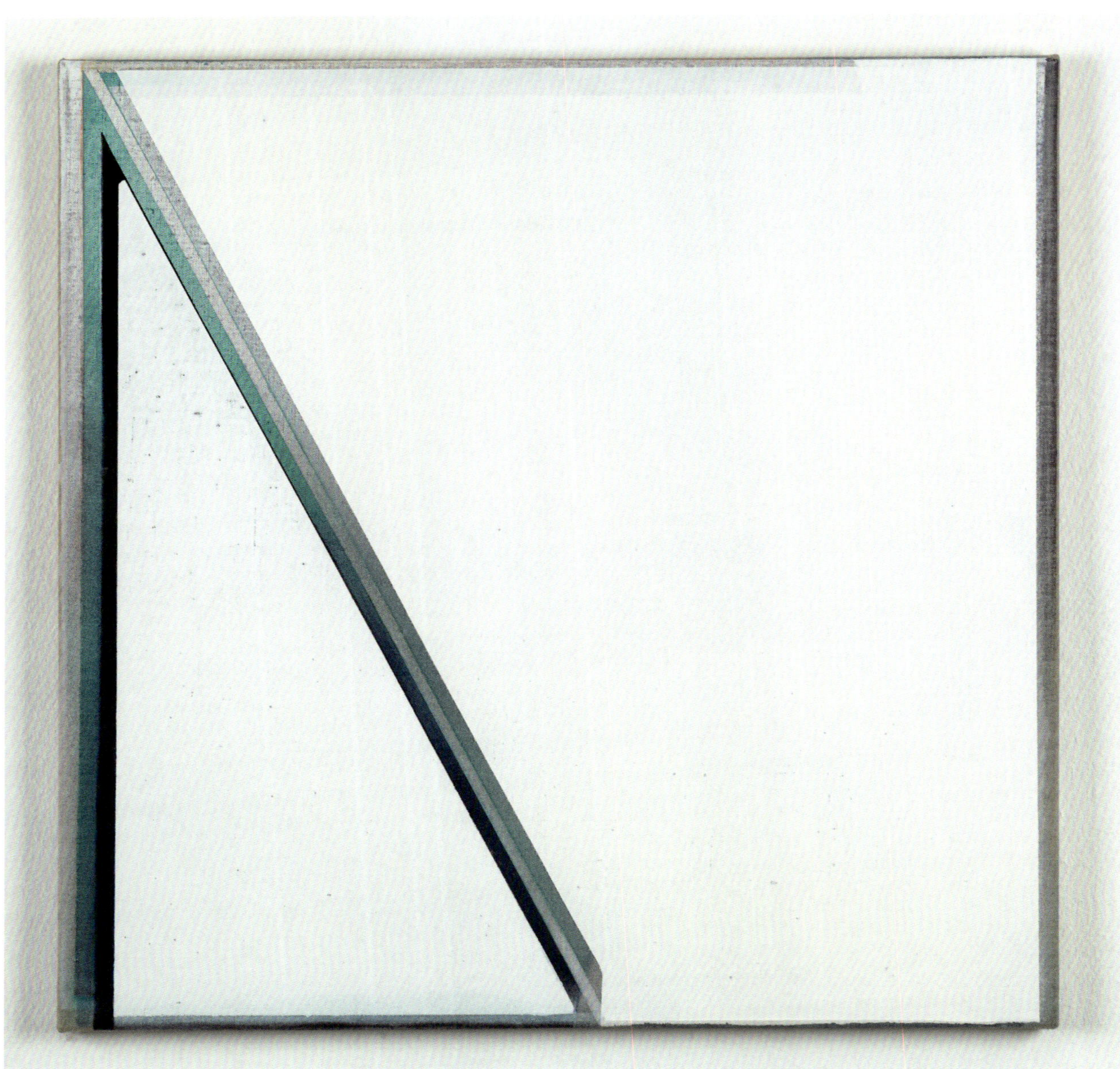

MICHAEL JANSSEN

Galerie Michael Janssen
DE-10969 Berlin | Rudi-Dutschke-Strasse 26
Phone +49 30 25927250 | Fax +49 30 25927 2518
berlin@galeriemichaeljanssen.de | www.galeriemichaeljanssen.de
Directors Dane Reinacher
Nina Borgmann

Artists at Art Nova | Anne Chu
Meg Cranston
Rose Wylie

Gallery Information | In addition to its longtime collaboration with artists such as Thomas Grünfeld and Peter Zimmermann, the gallery also constantly strives to introduce young artists such as Emil Holmer, Mario Ybarra Jr., and Joris van de Moortel in Germany for the first time, but has also focused on older artists such as Lynda Benglis, Gianfranco Baruchello, and Lili Dujourie.

Further artists represented:
Julieta Aranda
Gianfranco Baruchello
Lynda Benglis
Nicole Cherubini
Lili Dujourie
Martin Fletcher – Systems House
Thomas Grünfeld
Emil Holmer
Christof Mascher
Trine Lise Nedreaas
Tim Roda
Julika Rudelius
Christoph Steinmeyer
Shaan Syed
Joris van de Moortel
Monique van Genderen
Mario Ybarra Jr.
Peter Zimmermann

Anne Chu's (*1959, New York, NY) sculptures are often defined by unconventional material transpositions, like aluminum cast from carved foam. These processes produce figures so degenerated that the figurative and the abstract become fused, an approach amplified by Chu's use of applied color. Her figures appropriate archetypal images from Tang Dynasty tomb sculptures, European mythological characters, or mass-produced figurines.

Meg Cranston's (*1960, Baldwin, NY) work includes sculptures, performance, drawings, photographs, installations, and books and has been shown internationally since 1990, including at the Venice Biennale in 1993. Cranston's longstanding interests in anthropology and cultural history have always shaped her approach to making art in both material and conceptual ways.

Rose Wylie's (*1934, Kent, United Kingdom) large-scale paintings and drawings depict simple motifs – animals, cartoonlike figures, insects, skulls, and flowers – and follow a faux-naïf strain in English art history.

Meg Cranston
Myth of Symmetry, 2006
Collage on paper, 14 x 11 inches, 35.5 x 28 cm

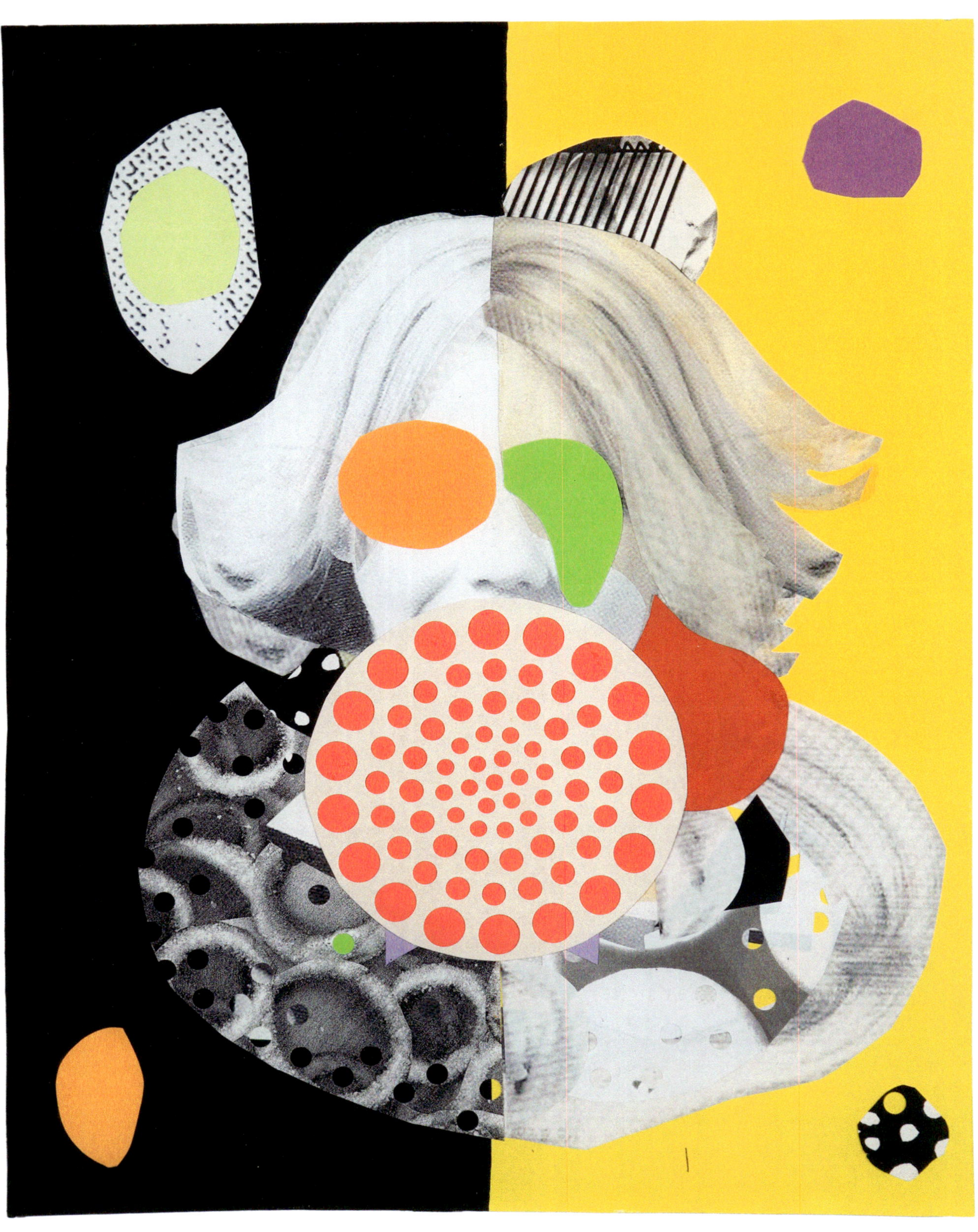

RODOLPHE JANSSEN

Mobile +32 475 47 14 02

Galerie Rodolphe Janssen
BE-1050 Brussels | Rue de Livourne 35 Livornostraat
Phone +32 2 538 08 18 | Fax +32 2 538 56 60
info@galerierodolphejanssen.com | www.galerierodolphejanssen.com
Director Rodolphe Janssen

Artists at
Art Basel Miami Beach | **Wim Delvoye**
Jürgen Drescher
Kendell Geers
Sean Landers
Justin Lieberman
Chris Martin
Adam McEwen
Sam Moyer
David Ratcliff
Sam Samore
Betty Tompkins
Banks Violette

Gallery Information | Exhibitions 2012/13:
Jürgen Drescher, September/October 2012
Sean Landers, November/December 2012
Sam Moyer, January/February 2013
Farhad Moshiri, March/April 2013
Sam Samore, May/June 2013
Kendell Geers, September/October 2013

Further artists represented: Walead Beshty
Mitch Epstein
Thomas Lerooy
Esko Männikkö
Jean-Luc Moerman
Farhad Moshiri
Mrzyk & Moriceau
Torbjørn Rødland
Lisa Sanditz
Stephen Shore
Gert & Uwe Tobias

Wim Delvoye
Daphnis & Chloë (Clockwise),
2009
Patinated bronze, 165 x Ø 85 cm
Edition 1 of 1

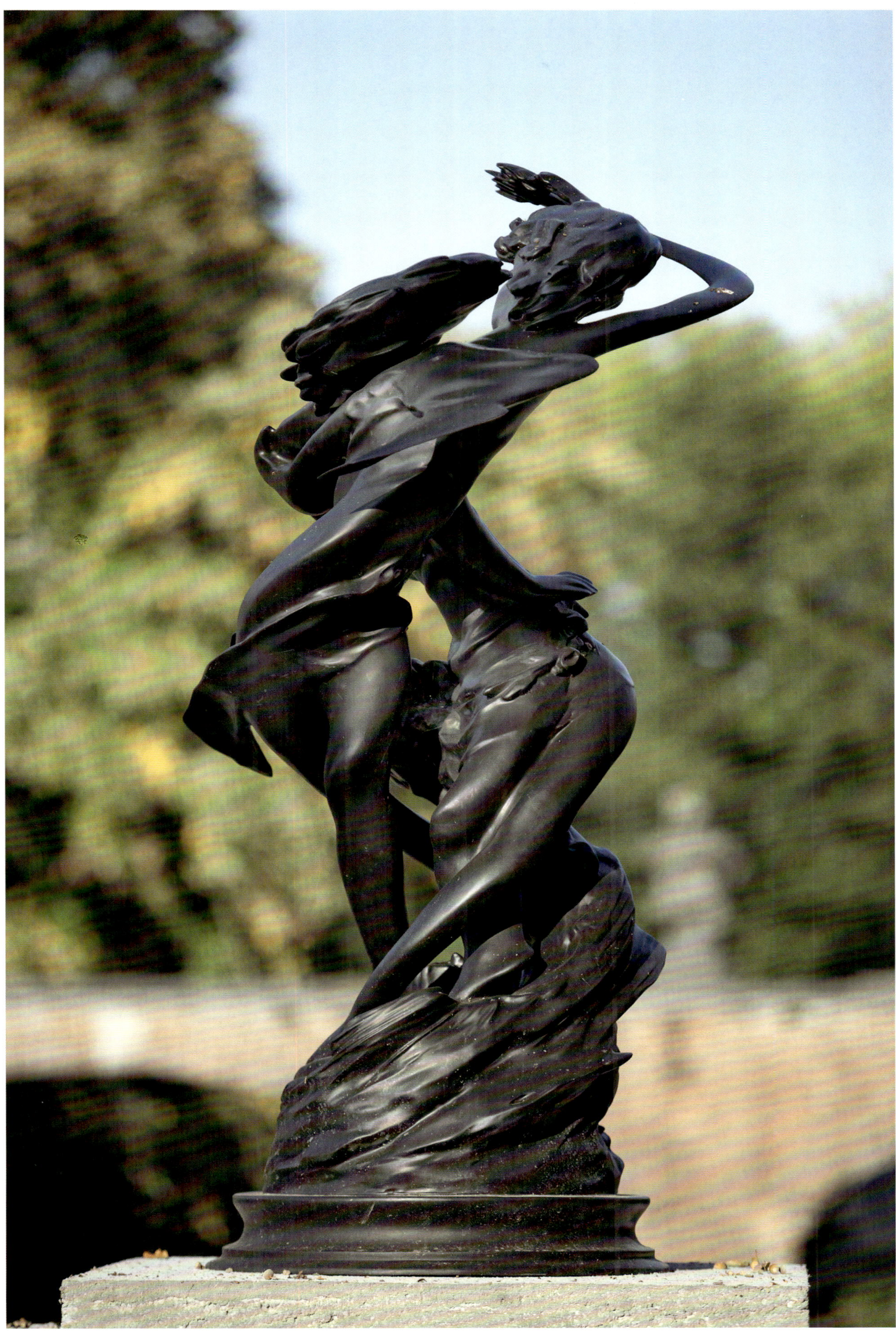

JUDA

Annely Juda Fine Art
GB-London W1S 1AW | 23 Dering Street
Phone +44 20 76 29 75 78 | Fax +44 20 74 91 21 39
ajfa@annelyjudafineart.co.uk | www.annelyjudafineart.co.uk
Director David Juda

Artists at
Art Basel Miami Beach | **Roger Ackling**
Anthony Caro
Christo
Katsura Funakoshi
Naum Gabo
Nigel Hall
David Hockney
Sigrid Holmwood
Tadashi Kawamata
Leon Kossoff
Kazimir Malevich
François Morellet
David Nash
Kazuo Shiraga
Yuko Shiraishi

Gallery Information | Current exhibition:
Sigrid Holmwood and Duan Jianyu,
October 9-December 21, 2012

Further artists represented: Alan Charlton
Prunella Clough
Duan Jianyu
Gloria Friedmann
Philipp Goldbach
Werner Haypeter
Darren Lago
Edwina Leapman
Catherine Lee
Kenneth & Mary Martin
László Moholy-Nagy
Sarah Oppenheimer
Alan Reynolds
Yoshishige Saito
Suzanne Treister
Georges Vantongerloo
Friedrich Vordemberge-Gildewart
Graham Williams

Katsura Funakoshi
The Tale of the Deep Forest, 2011
Painted camphor wood and
marble, 146 x 46 x 91 cm

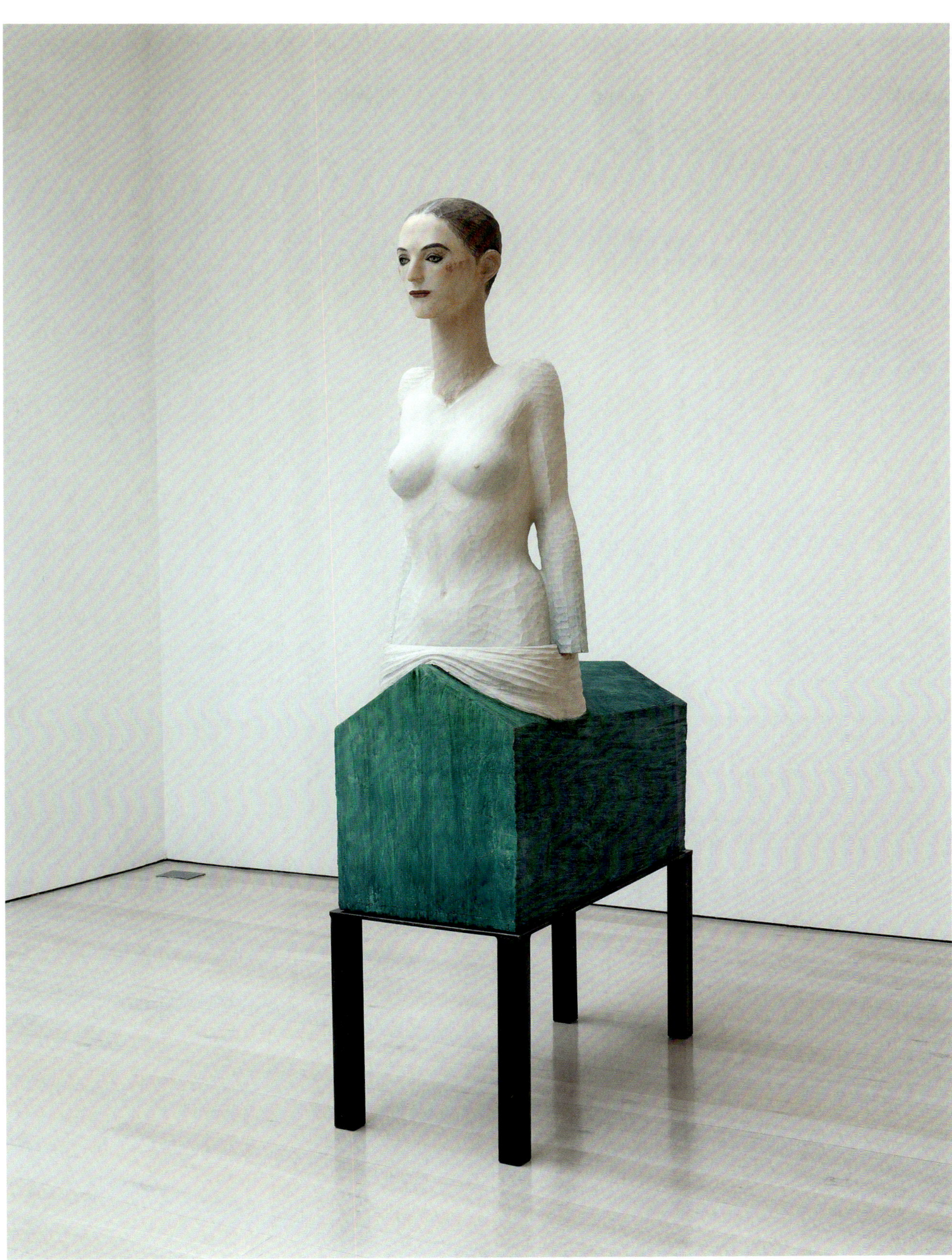

KAMM

Mobile +49 175 5900655

Galerie Kamm
DE-10178 Berlin | Rosa-Luxemburg-Strasse 45
Phone +49 30 28386464 | Fax +49 30 28386464
info@galeriekamm.de | www.galeriekamm.de
Director Joanna Kamm

Artists at Art Nova | Kate Davis
Charlie Hammond
Kathrin Sonntag

Further artists represented | Agnieszka Brzezanska
Michele Di Menna
Amy Granat
Katharina Jahnke
Annette Kisling
Lorna Macintyre
Christoph Meier
Simon Dybbroe Møller
Pavel Pepperstein
Bernd Ribbeck
Annette Ruenzler
Albrecht Schäfer
Claudia Wieser

The works of Kate Davis, Charlie Hammond, and Kathrin Sonntag focus in a subjective way on situations of a historical, political, and everyday nature. All three artists reshape reality in their own intensely personal way, bringing to our attention issues that otherwise remain at the fringes of our perception.

Kathrin Sonntag's photographic view of the inconspicuous in everyday life ushers the viewer into a miraculous world of similarities. Objects are duplicated, twisted, and deconstructed from unusual perspectives to reveal new visions of the everyday.

Working from a contemporary perspective, Kate Davis 'revisits' art historical works. She has worked across a range of media to both imagine a past that could have happened differently and delineate alternative ways to move forward.

Charlie Hammond is interested in the struggle for political ideas in combination with pictorial invention. Very particular motifs, such as the sweating armpit, become a structural tool for his paintings as well as loaded signifiers for work. The loss of control over the initial idea – and the often-resulting collapse of an ambitious social commentary in visual form – defines Hammond's work.

Whilst the themes that are dealt with are universal, the artistic execution of each work renders them intimate. None of the artists produce work in large format, which requires the viewer to take a closer look, allowing them to become an active participant who engages their own personal subjectivity.

Charlie Hammond
Negative Sweaty Space, 2012
Oil and charcoal on canvas,
61 x 36 cm

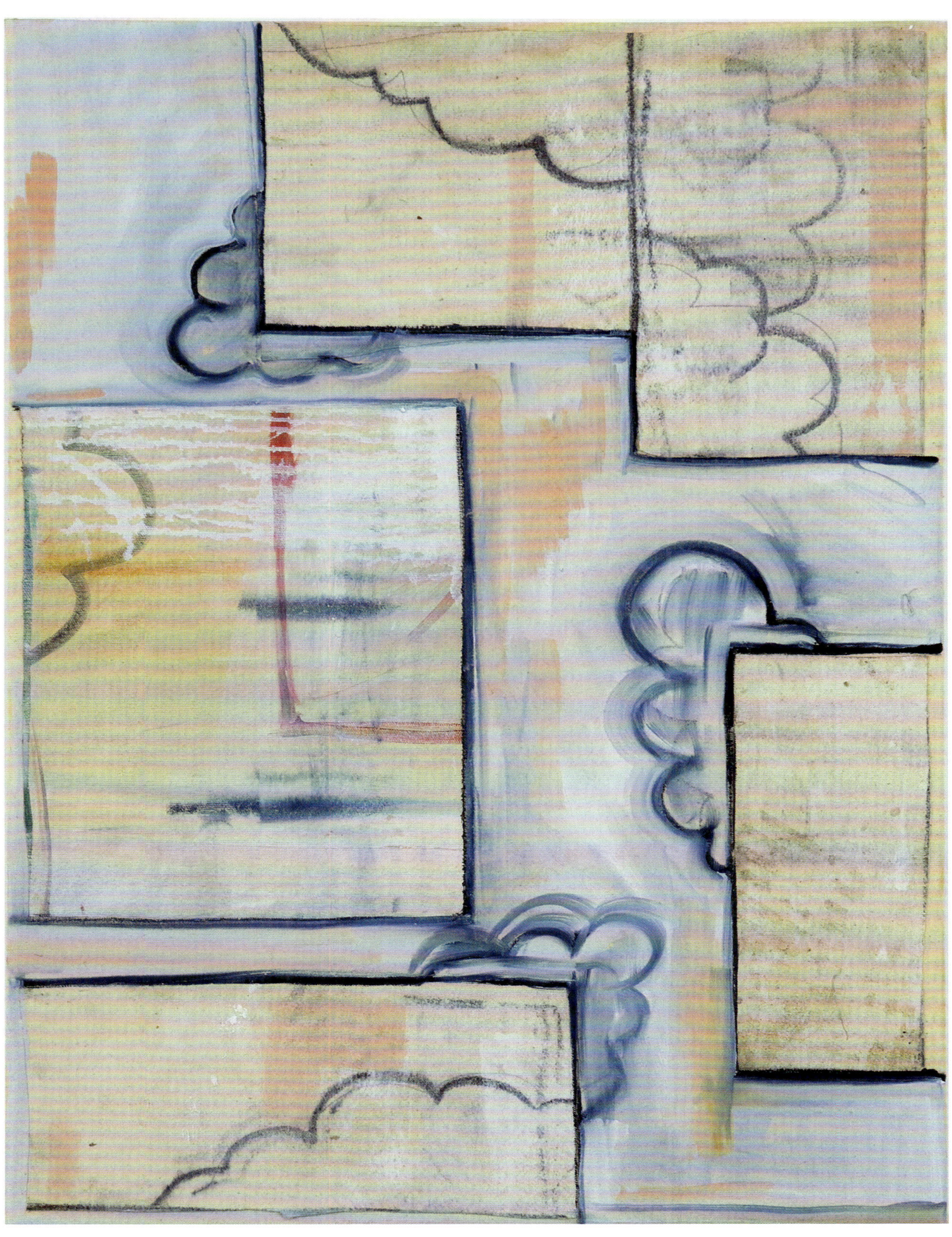

KAPLAN

Mobile +1 917 602 67 02

Casey Kaplan
US-New York, NY 10011 | 525 West 21st Street
Phone +1 212 645 73 35 | Fax +1 212 645 78 35
info@caseykaplangallery.com | www.caseykaplangallery.com
Directors Casey Kaplan
Loring Randolph
Alice Conconi

Artists at
Art Basel Miami Beach | **Henning Bohl**
Matthew Brannon
Jeff Burton
Nathan Carter
Jason Dodge
Trisha Donnelly
Geoffrey Farmer
Liam Gillick
Giorgio Griffa
Brian Jungen
Jonathan Monk
Marlo Pascual
Diego Perrone
Pietro Roccasalva
Julia Schmidt
Simon Starling
David Thorpe
Annika von Hausswolff
Gabriel Vormstein
Garth Weiser
Johannes Wohnseifer

Gallery Information | The gallery was founded in March 1995.

Giorgio Griffa
Policromo, 1976
Acrylic on canvas, 147 x 137 cm

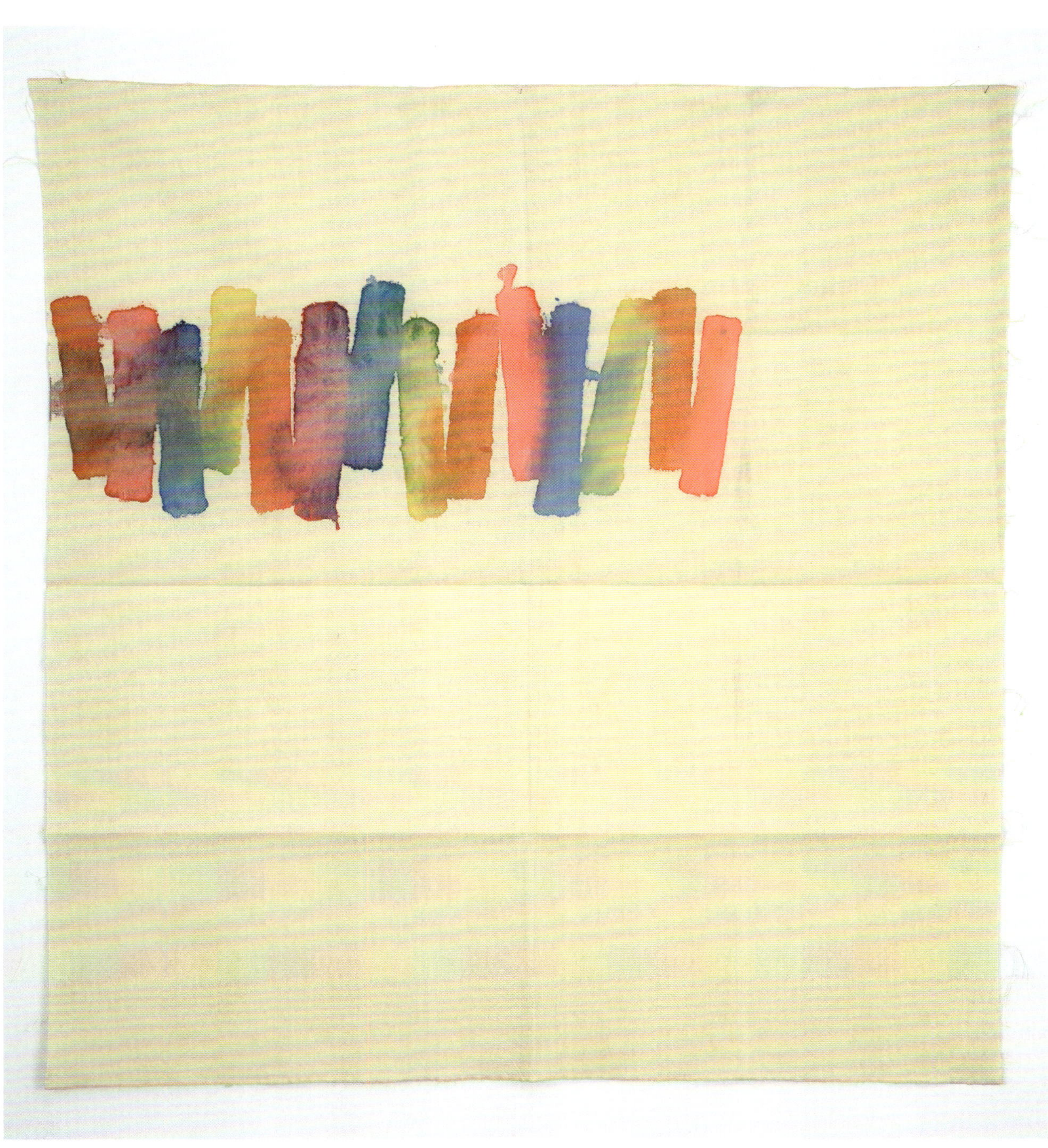

KARMA INTERNATIONAL

Mobile +41 79 457 76 59

Karma International
CH-8037 Zurich | Hönggerstrasse 40
Phone +41 435 35 85 91
info@karmainternational.org | www.karmainternational.org
Directors Karolina Dankow
Marina Leuenberger

Artists at Art Nova | Agnieszka Brzezanska
Tobias Madison

Further artists represented | Kim Seob Boninsegni
Ida Ekblad
David Hominal
Thomas Julier
Carissa Rodriguez
Pamela Rosenkranz
Emanuel Rossetti
Thomas Sauter
Martin Soto Climent

Tobias Madison
Untitled, 2012
Epson DuraBrite print mounted on acrylic glass, aluminum frame, 39 x 30 x 2.5 cm

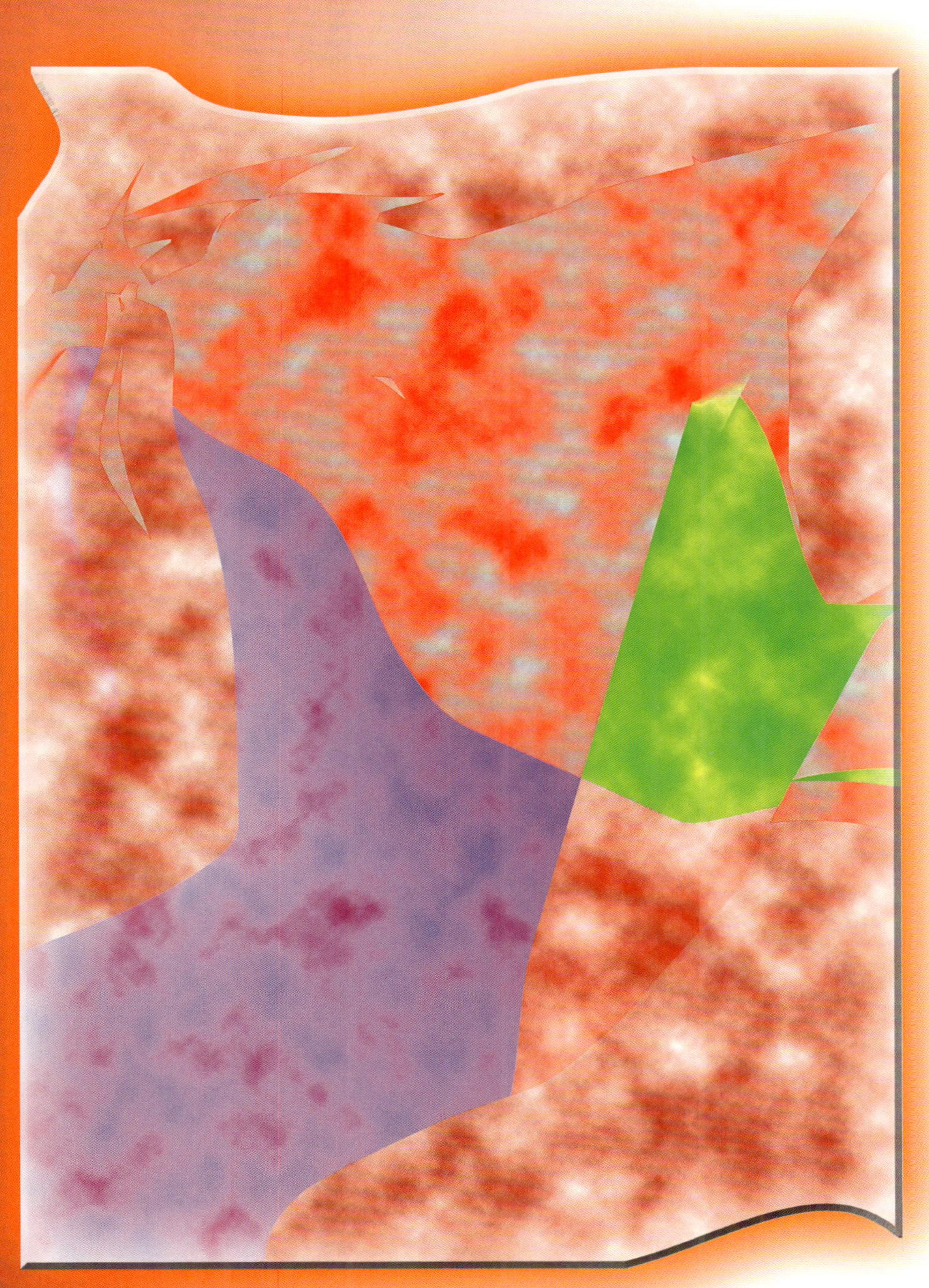

KASMIN

Paul Kasmin Gallery
US-New York, NY 10001 | 293 Tenth Avenue
Phone +1 212 5634474 | Fax +1 212 5634494
info@paulkasmingallery.com | www.paulkasmingallery.com
Directors Paul Kasmin
Clara Ha
Hayden Dunbar
Nick Olney
Bethanie Brady

Paul Kasmin Gallery
US-New York, NY 10001 | 515 West 27th Street
Phone +1 212 5634474 | Fax +1 212 5634494
info@paulkasmingallery.com | www.paulkasmingallery.com

Artists at
Art Basel Miami Beach | **Arman**
Mattia Bonetti
Saint Clair Cemin
William N. Copley
Ian Davenport
Barry Flanagan
Caio Fonseca
Walton Ford
Simon Hantai
Nir Hod
Robert Indiana
Deborah Kass
David LaChapelle
Claude & François-Xavier Lalanne
Morris Louis
Nyoman Masriadi
Santi Moix
James Nares
Iván Navarro
Erik Parker
Elliott Puckette
Nancy Rubins
Mark Ryden
Will Ryman
Makoto Saito
Kenny Scharf
Tseng Kwong Chi
Bernar Venet
Andy Warhol

Makoto Saito
Face to Face (Felini), 2011/12
Acrylic and oil ink on canvas with supported canvas, 214 x 158 cm

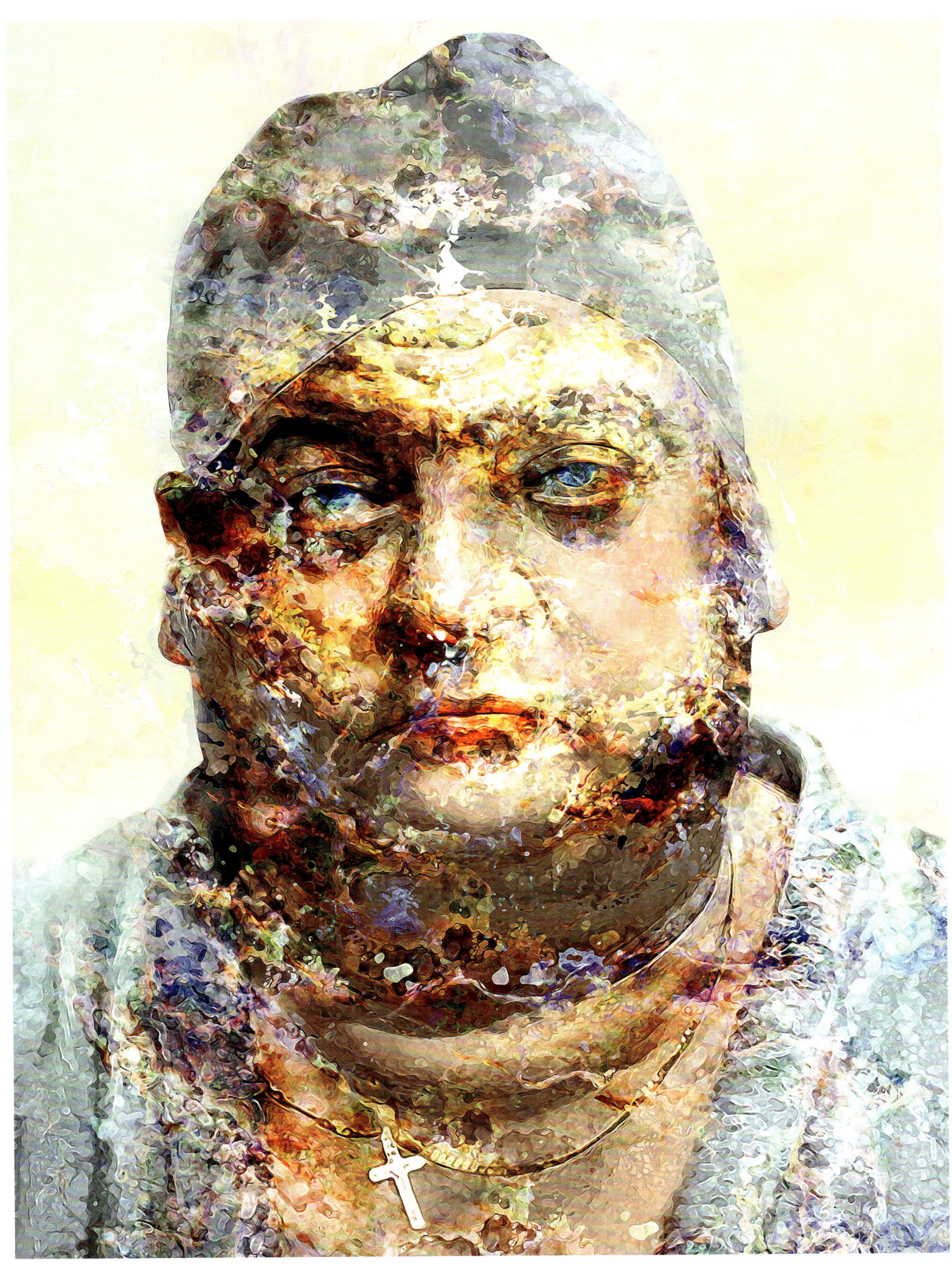

KAUFMANN REPETTO

Mobile +39 327 208 28 44

kaufmann repetto
IT-20121 Milan | Via di Porta Tenaglia 7
Phone +39 02 72 09 43 31 | Fax +39 02 72 09 68 73
info@kaufmannrepetto.com | www.kaufmannrepetto.com
Directors Francesca Kaufmann
Chiara Repetto

Artists represented | Candice Breitz
Pierpaolo Campanini
Gianni Caravaggio
Maggie Cardelùs
Talia Chetrit
Thea Djordjadze
Shannon Ebner
Latifa Echakhch
Edi Hila
Judith Hopf
Carlo Mollino
Yoshua Okón
Adrian Paci
Eva Rothschild
Aïda Ruilova
Matt Sheridan Smith
Billy Sullivan
Lily van der Stokker
Pae White
Thomas Zipp

Judith Hopf
Palmenbaum, 1999-2012
Site-specific installation: wire, jute, paper, dimensions variable
Installation view, *A Sudden Walk,* kaufmann repetto, Milan, 2012

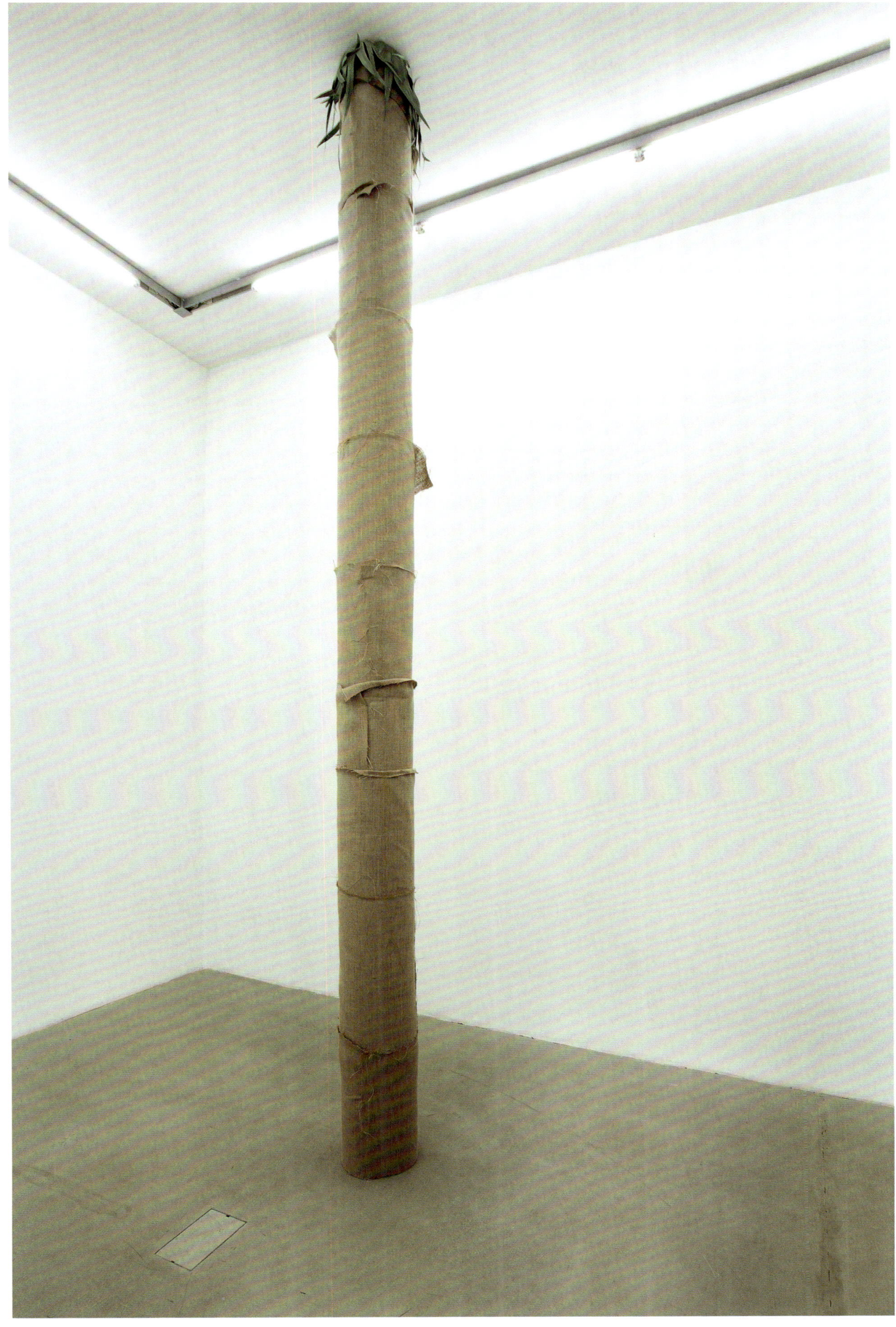

KELLY

Sean Kelly Gallery
US-New York, NY 10018 | 475 Tenth Ave
Phone +1 212 239 11 81 | Fax +1 212 239 24 67
info@skny.com | www.skny.com
Directors Cécile Panzieri
Maureen Bray
Janine Cirincione
Lauren Kelly

Artists at Art Basel Miami Beach | **Marina Abramovic**
James Casebere
Iran do Espírito Santo
Leandro Erlich
Antony Gormley
Laurent Grasso
Johan Grimonprez
Rebecca Horn
Tehching Hsieh
Callum Innes
Idris Khan
Terence Koh
Joseph Kosuth
Wolfgang Laib
Peter Liversidge
Los Carpinteros
Nathan Mabry
Robert Mapplethorpe
Anthony McCall
Julião Sarmento
Alec Soth
Frank Thiel
Kehinde Wiley

Laurent Grasso
Studies into the Past, 2012
Animal adhesive, resin, boiled oil, and pigments on wood panel, 123 x 85 cm

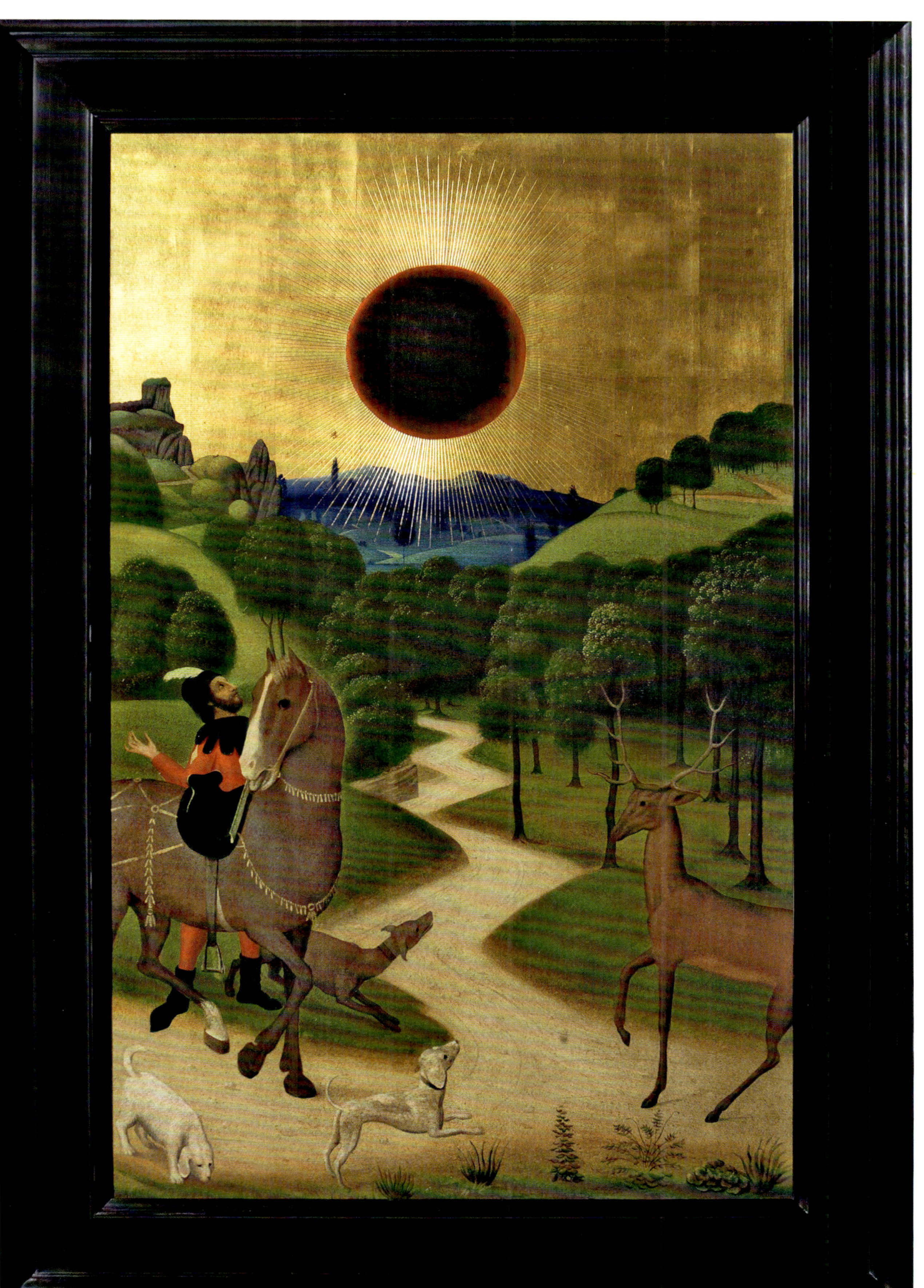

KERN

Anton Kern Gallery
US-New York, NY 10011 | 532 West 20th Street
Phone +1 212 367 96 63 | Fax +1 212 367 81 35
info@antonkerngallery.com | www.antonkerngallery.com
Director Christoph Gerozissis

Artists at Art Basel Miami Beach | **Nobuyoshi Araki**
Ellen Berkenblit
John Bock
Brian Calvin
Anne Collier
Saul Fletcher
Mark Grotjahn
Bendix Harms
Eberhard Havekost
Lothar Hempel
Richard Hughes
Sergej Jensen
Sarah Jones
Edward Krasinski
Shio Kusaka
Jim Lambie
Marepe
Dan McCarthy
Enrique Metinides
Matthew Monahan
Marcel Odenbach
Manfred Pernice
Alessandro Pessoli
Wilhelm Sasnal
Lara Schnitger
David Shrigley
Andy Warhol
Jonas Wood

Jim Lambie
Vortex 'Love Song,' 2012
MDF, full gloss paint, and hand-blown glass (Loredano Rosin sculpture, Murano, Italy, ca. 1980),
vortex: 12 x 12 x 16½ inches,
installation: 46¼ x 10 x 17¾ inches

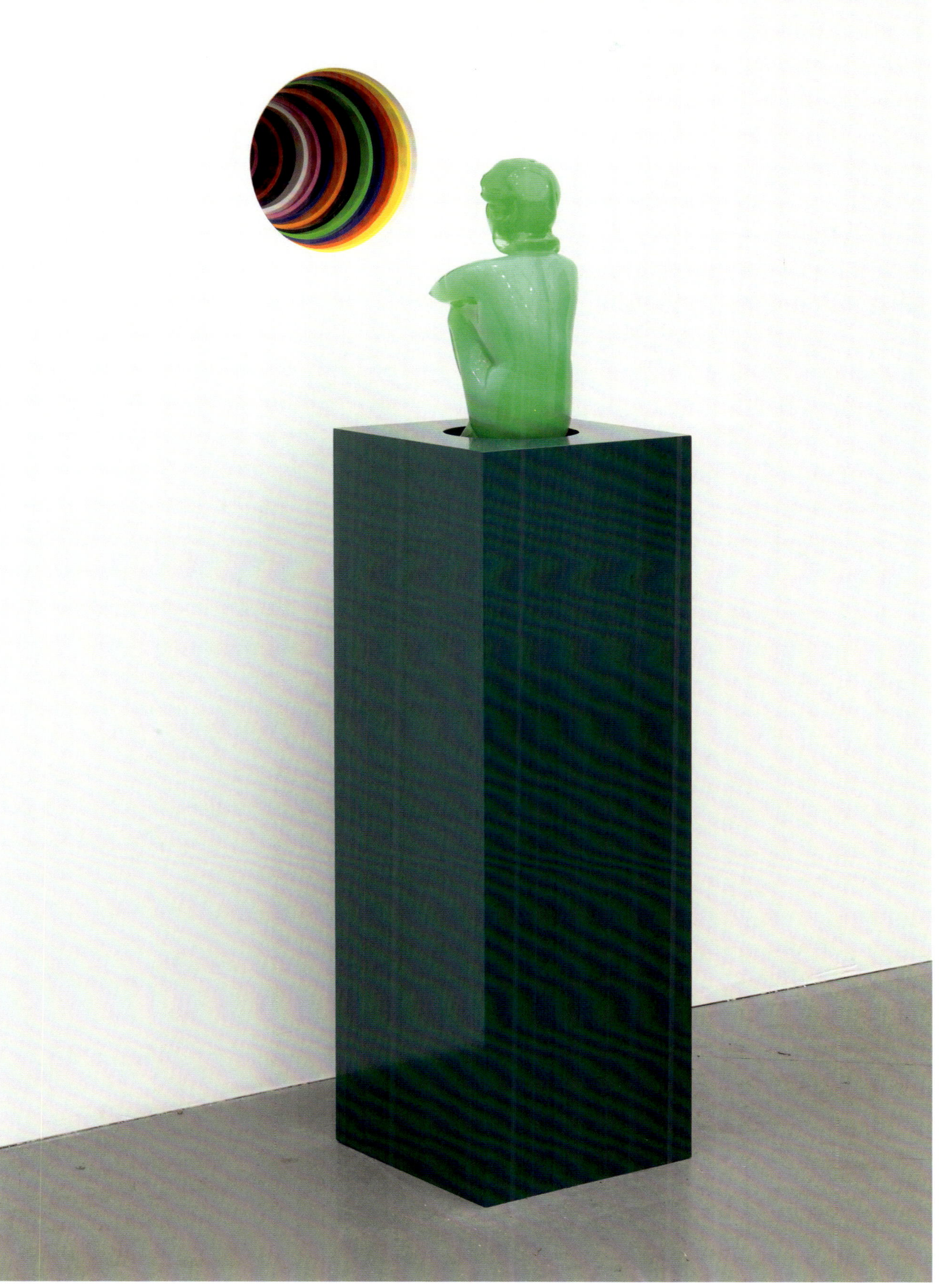

KEWENIG

Mobile +49 171 444 84 67

Kewenig Galerie
DE-10178 Berlin | Brüderstrasse 10
info@kewenig.com | www.kewenig.com
Director Michael O. Kewenig

Galería Kewenig
ES-07012 Palma de Mallorca | Oratorio de Sant Feliu C/ Sant Feliu s/n
Phone +34 971 71 61 34 | Fax +34 971 71 45 14
info@kewenig.com | www.kewenig.com
Director Jule Kewenig

Artists at Art Basel Miami Beach |
Christian Boltanski
Marcel Broodthaers
Hanne Darboven
Bert de Beul
Ilya & Emilia Kabakov
Imi Knoebel
Jannis Kounellis
Bertrand Lavier
Mario Merz
Pavel Pepperstein
Viktor Pivovarov
Gerhard Richter
Miroslav Tichy
James Turrell
Sandra Vásquez de la Horra
Marcelo Viquez

Gallery Information | The Kewenig Galerie was founded in 1986 as the Jule Kewenig Galerie, based in Haus Bitz in Frechen near Cologne. The gallery is now located in a historic building in the center of Berlin. In 2004, a second gallery was opened in a 13th-century chapel in Palma de Mallorca. The primary focus of the Kewenig Galerie is international contemporary art since the 1960s, whereby the artistic dialogue between various generations and cultures plays a substantial role.

The works of artists such as Marcel Broodthaers, Imi Knoebel, Bertrand Lavier, and Niele Toroni deal conceptually with art and the mechanisms of the artworld. On the other hand, artists such as Christian Boltanski and Hanne Darboven address the issue of history and the passing of time. Ilya and Emilia Kabakov, Viktor Pivovarov, and Pavel Pepperstein, each in their own way, reflect on the content of art within the context of failed political utopias. Arte Povera artists Giovanni Anselmo, Pier Paolo Calzolari, Mario Merz, and Jannis Kounellis play a substantial role.

Further representatives of the gallery are the Korean artist Kimsooja, who follows traces of migration through performance art, video, and photography, and the Chilean graphic artist Sandra Vásquez de la Horra, who deals with the human dramas surrounding religion, fear, and death. In his genre-crossing works, Marcelo Viquez questions the contradictions of society from the point of view of an 'inmigrant-outsider.'

Further artists represented:
Giovanni Anselmo
Ivan Bazak
Frédéric Bruly Bouabré
James Lee Byars
Ian Hamilton Finlay
Seydou Keïta
Bernd Koberling
Hendrik Krawen
A.R. Penck
Giuseppe Penone
Niele Toroni

Jannis Kounellis
Senza titolo, 2011
Steel, sailcloth, 205 x 185 x 8 cm

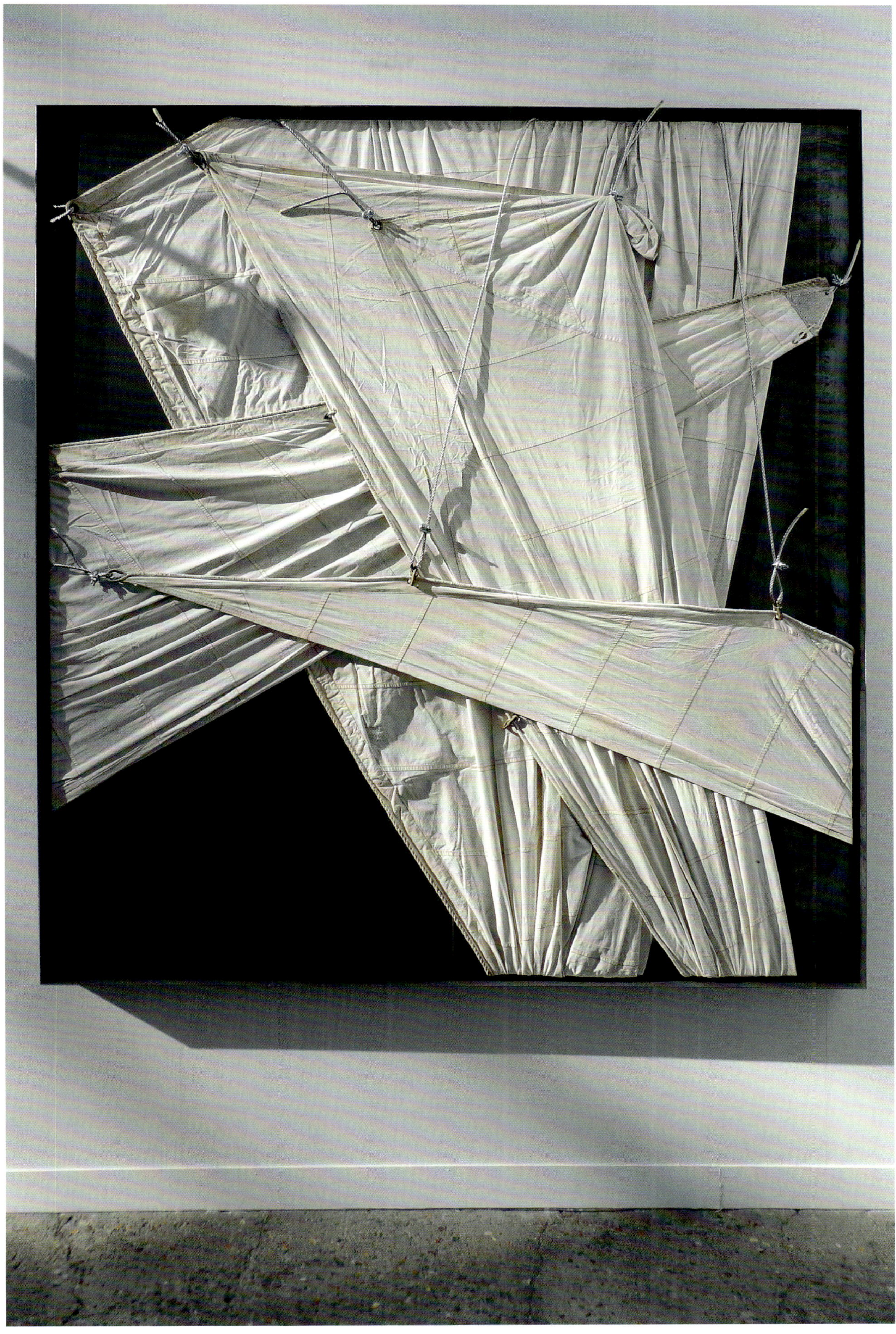

KICKEN

Mobile +49 172 880 12 34

Kicken Berlin
DE-10115 Berlin | Linienstrasse 161A
Phone +49 30 28 87 78 82 | Fax +49 30 28 87 78 83
kicken@kicken-gallery.com | www.kicken-gallery.com
Directors Annette Kicken
Rudolf Kicken
Petra Helck
Ina Schmidt-Runke

Artists at
Art Basel Miami Beach | **Dieter Appelt**
Bauhaus
Bernd & Hilla Becher
Erwin Blumenfeld
Joachim Brohm
Götz Diergarten
František Drtikol
Charles Fréger
Lee Friedlander
Jaromír Funke
Jitka Hanzlová
André Kertész
Rudolf Koppitz
Helmar Lerski
Man Ray
Werner Mantz
László Moholy-Nagy
Helmut Newton
Helga Paris
Albert Renger-Patzsch
Alexander Rodchenko
August Sander
Hans-Christian Schink
Alfred Seiland
Otto Steinert
Christer Strömholm
Josef Sudek
Ed van der Elsken

Gallery Information | Kicken Berlin has specialized in 19th- and 20th-century and contemporary photography since 1974. Since its foundation the gallery has explored the relationship between photography and the other arts in over 220 exhibitions. It maintains a large collection of high-quality master prints from 1900 to 1950.

Further artists represented: Sibylle Bergemann
Karl Blossfeldt
Anna & Bernhard Blume
Rudolf Bonvie
Constantin Brancusi
Arno Fischer
fotoform
Ernst Fuhrmann
F.C. Gundlach
Heinz Hajek-Halke
Peter Keetman
Heinrich Kühn
Arnold Newman
Richard Pare
Heinrich Riebesehl
Jaroslav Rössler
Wilhelm Schürmann
Stephen Shore
Anton Josef Trcka
Umbo (Otto Umbehr)
Dr. Paul Wolff

Bernd & Hilla Becher
From the series *Mineheads*,
ca. 1970s-early 1980s
Gelatin silver prints,
17 x 12.5 cm each

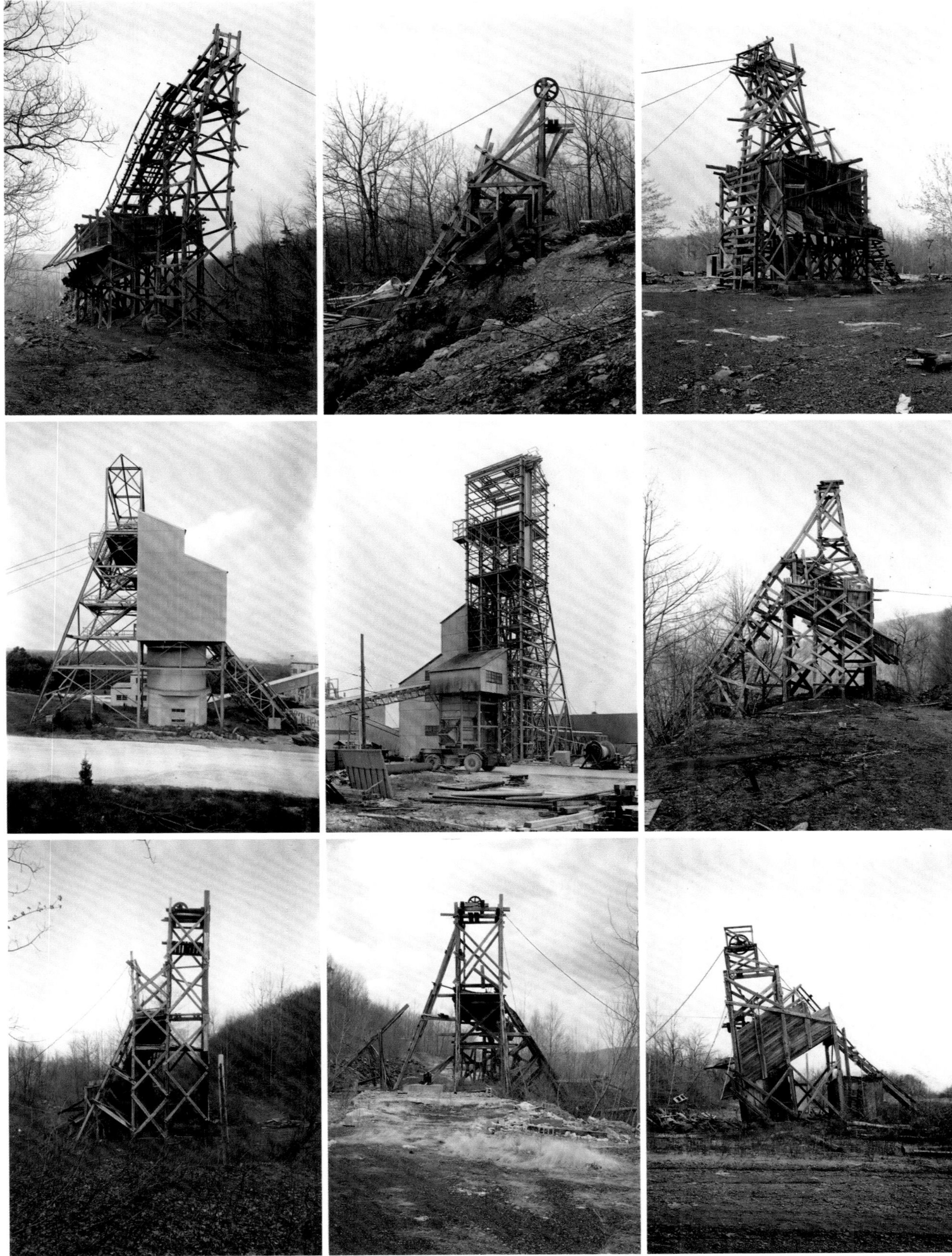

KILCHMANN

Mobile +1 646 785 26 06

Galerie Peter Kilchmann
CH-8005 Zurich | Zahnradstrasse 21
Phone +41 44 278 10 10 | Fax +41 44 278 10 11
info@peterkilchmann.com | www.peterkilchmann.com
Directors Peter Kilchmann
Annemarie Reichen

Artists at
Art Basel Miami Beach | **Francis Alÿs**
Michael Bauer
Raffi Kalenderian
Los Carpinteros
Jorge Macchi
Teresa Margolles
Adrian Paci
Melanie Smith
Javier Téllez
Tercerunquinto

Further artists represented | Hernan Bas
Armin Boehm
Willie Doherty
Valérie Favre
Bruno Jakob
Zilla Leutenegger
Fabian Marti
Bernd Ribbeck
Erika Verzutti
Arthur Żmijewski

Jorge Macchi
Illumination/Iluminación, 2012
7 flashlights, cement,
290 x 215 x 220 cm

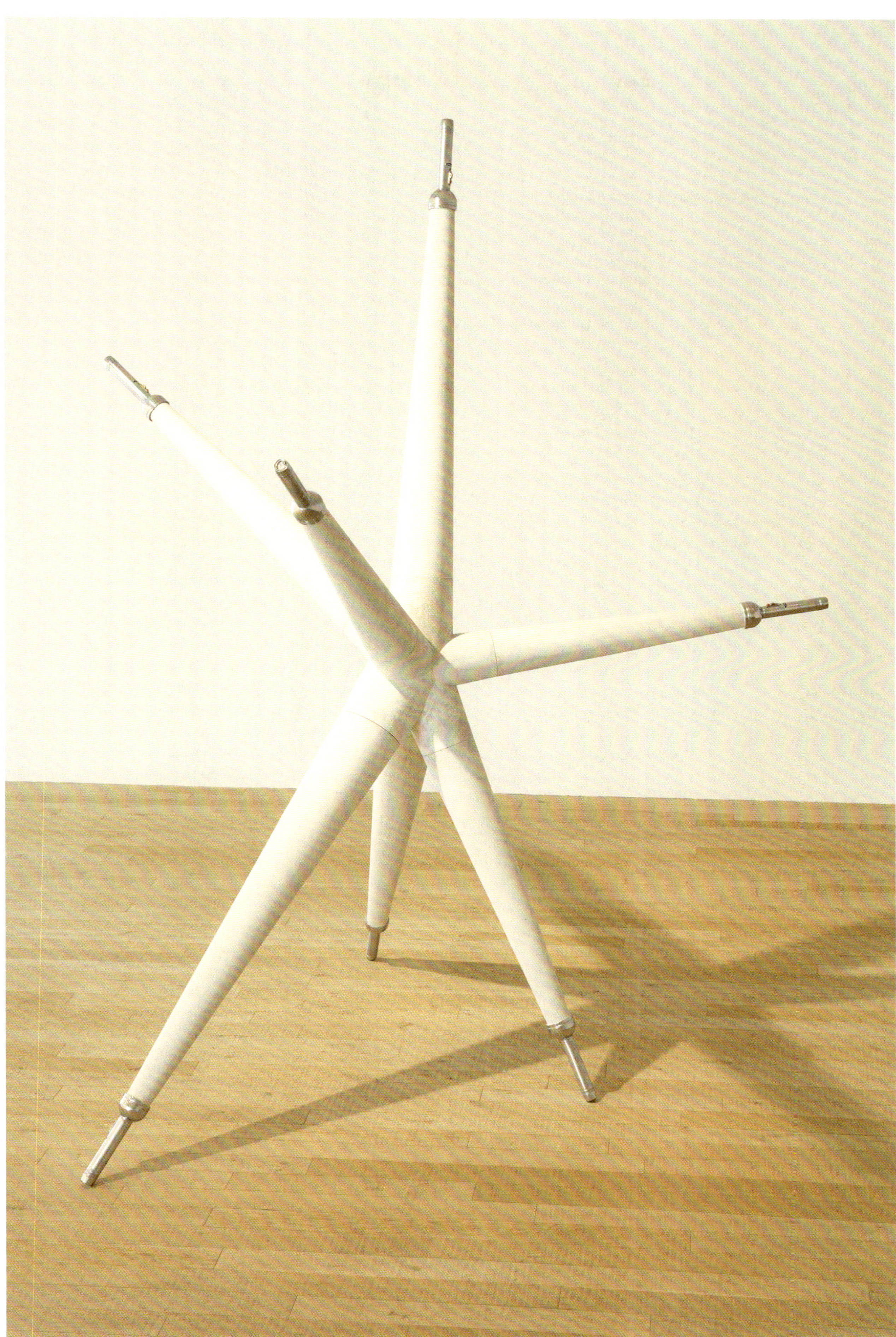

KLOSTERFELDE

Mobile +49 163 2835305

Klosterfelde
DE-10785 Berlin | Potsdamer Strasse 93
Phone +49 30 2835305 | Fax +49 30 2835306
office@klosterfelde.de | www.klosterfelde.de
Director Lena Kiessler

Artists at Art Basel Miami Beach | **Nader Ahriman**
Matthew Antezzo
John Bock
Tobias Buche
Hanne Darboven
Jürgen Drescher
Lara Favaretto
Christian Jankowski
Edward Krasinski
Ulrike Kuschel
Armin Linke
Jonas Lipps
Matt Mullican
Lisa Oppenheim
Dan Peterman
Steven Pippin
Kay Rosen
Michael Snow
Vibeke Tandberg
Jorinde Voigt

Christian Jankowski
Monument to the Bourgeois Working Class, 2012
Cardboard, wood, PVC plastic, paint, polyurethane foam, and resin, 360 x 390 x 300 cm
Installation view, Sala de Arte Público Siqueiros (SAPS), Mexico City

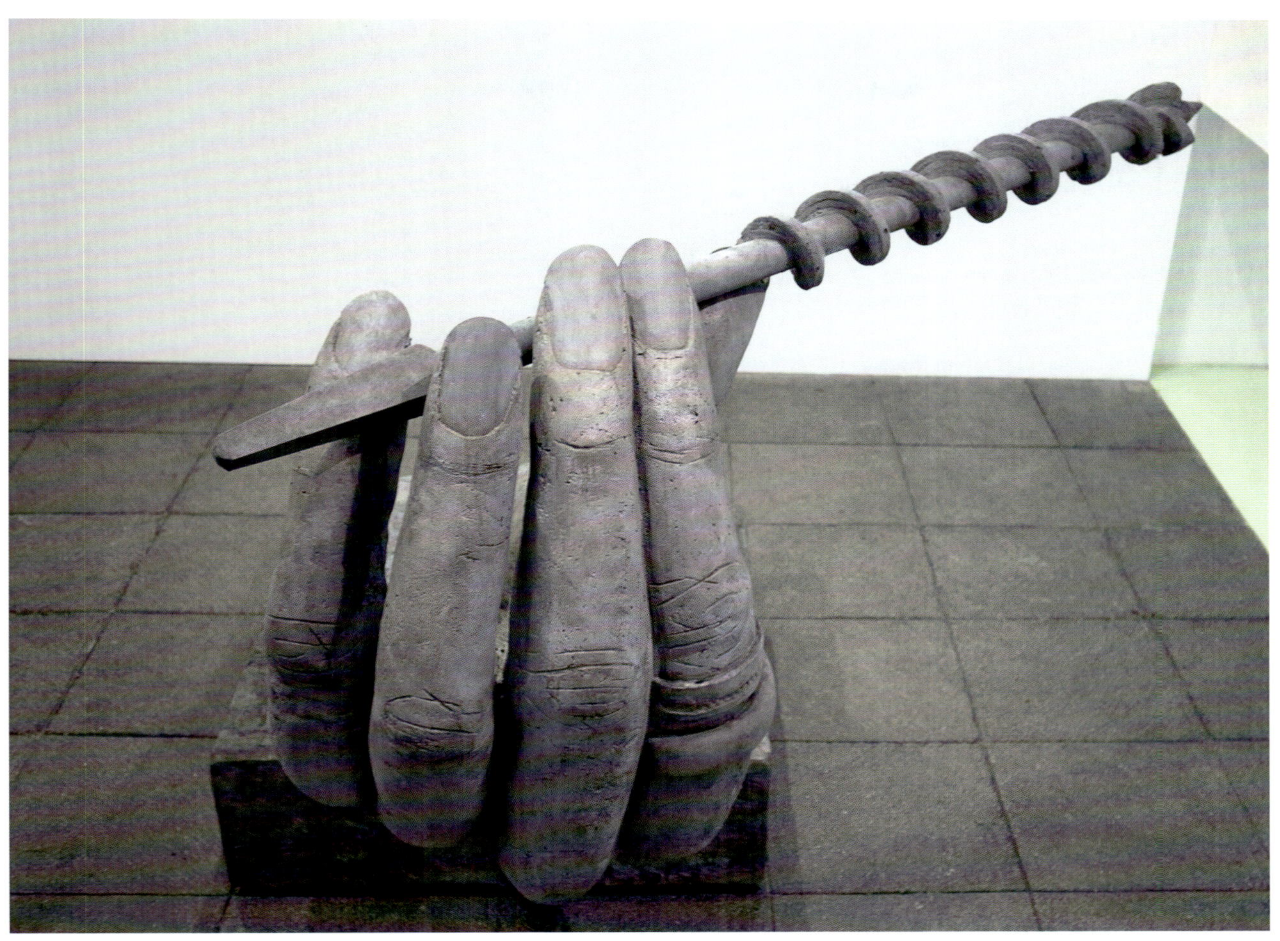

KNUST

Sabine Knust
DE-80539 Munich | Ludwigstrasse 7
Phone +49 89 29 16 07 03 | Fax +49 89 29 16 07 73
mail@sabineknust.com | www.sabineknust.com
Directors Sabine Knust
Matthias Kunz

Artists at
Art Basel Miami Beach | **Georg Baselitz**
Eberhard Havekost
Per Kirkeby
Jonathan Lasker
Jonathan Meese
Katharina Sieverding
Gert & Uwe Tobias
Franz West

Further artists represented | John M Armleder
John Baldessari
Peter Doig
Liam Gillick
Thomas Hirschhorn
Olaf Holzapfel
Andy Hope 1930
Alex Katz
Imi Knoebel
Michael Landy
Markus Lüpertz
Paul Morrison
Olaf Nicolai
Jorge Pardo
Jack Pierson
Richard Prince
Tal R
Arnulf Rainer
Anselm Reyle
Daniel Richter
Christopher Wool

Gert & Uwe Tobias
Untitled, 2012
Lithograph, 42.5 x 37 cm

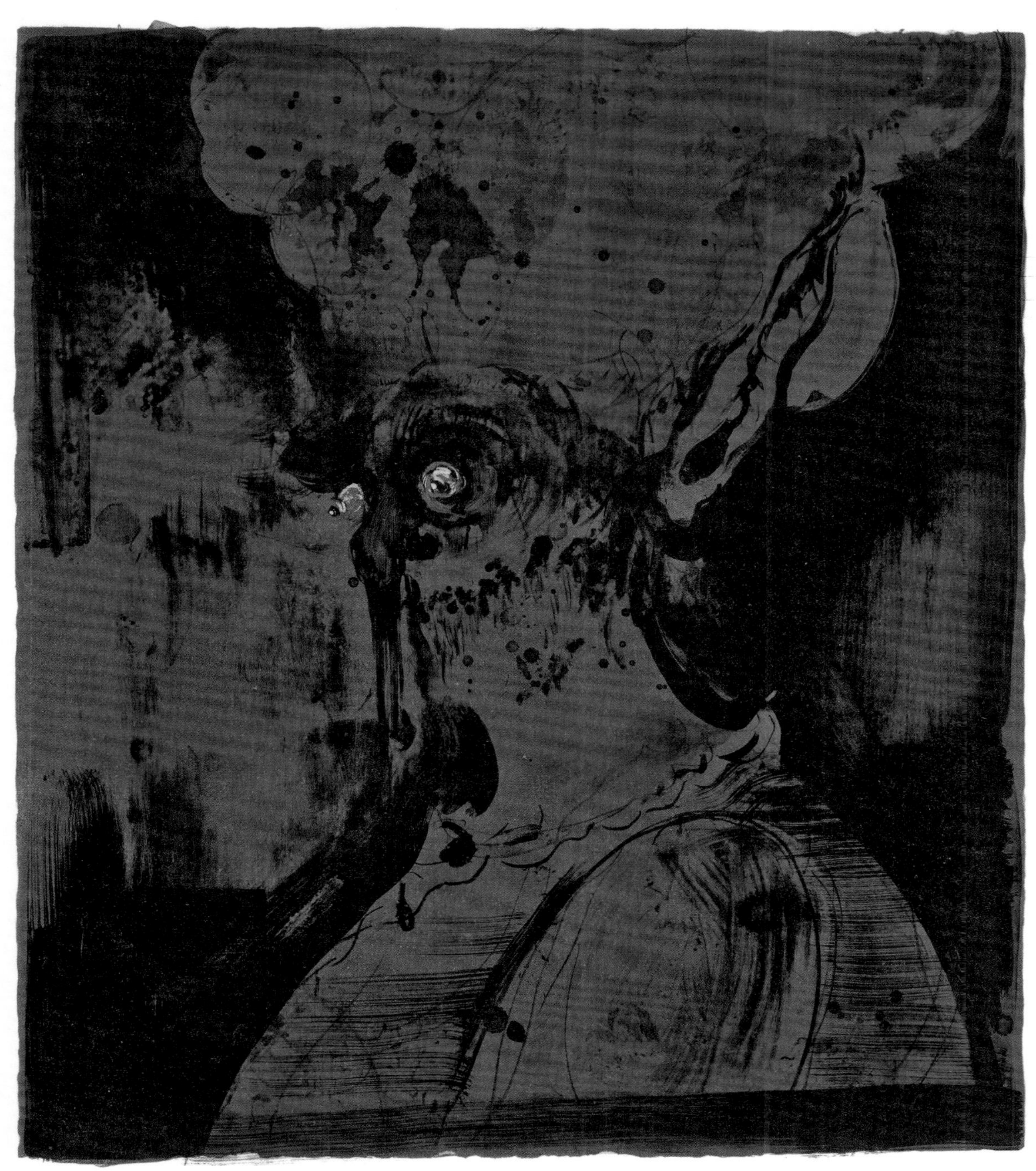

KOHN

Michael Kohn Gallery
US-Los Angeles, CA 90048 | 8071 Beverly Blvd
Phone +1 323 658 80 88 | Fax +1 323 658 80 68
samantha@kohngallery.com | www.kohngallery.com
Director Samantha Glaser

Artists at
Art Basel Miami Beach | **Wallace Berman**
Bruce Conner
Camille Rose Garcia
Joe Goode
Ryan McGinness
James Nares
Mark Ryden
Simmons & Burke

Gallery Information | For the past 26 years the Michael Kohn Gallery has mounted museum-quality exhibitions in Los Angeles, including the work of Andy Warhol (during his lifetime), Richard Tuttle, Peter Halley, Keith Haring, Dan Flavin, Mark Tansey, Jay DeFeo, Lorna Simpson, Kenny Scharf, Christopher Wool, and Diane Arbus, among many other notable and talented artists. Michael Kohn Gallery also represents the Estates of Wallace Berman, Charles Brittin, and Bruce Conner, important California-based artists whose work, from the 1950s through their lifetime, paralleled and often led to notable developments in late 20th-century art.

Always with an eye towards the future, the Michael Kohn Gallery will continue to mount bold exhibitions and nurture younger talent, blending historically important works of art with emerging talent of the 21st century.

Further artists represented: Charles Brittin
Will Cotton
Stephen Hannock
John Hawke
Allyson Hollingsworth
Dennis Hollingsworth
Mark Innerst
Guy Limone
Rosa Loy
Joan Nelson
Christine Nguyen
Darren Waterston
Cristof Yvoré

Bruce Conner
De Detroit UXA, 1978
Unique black-and-white photograph

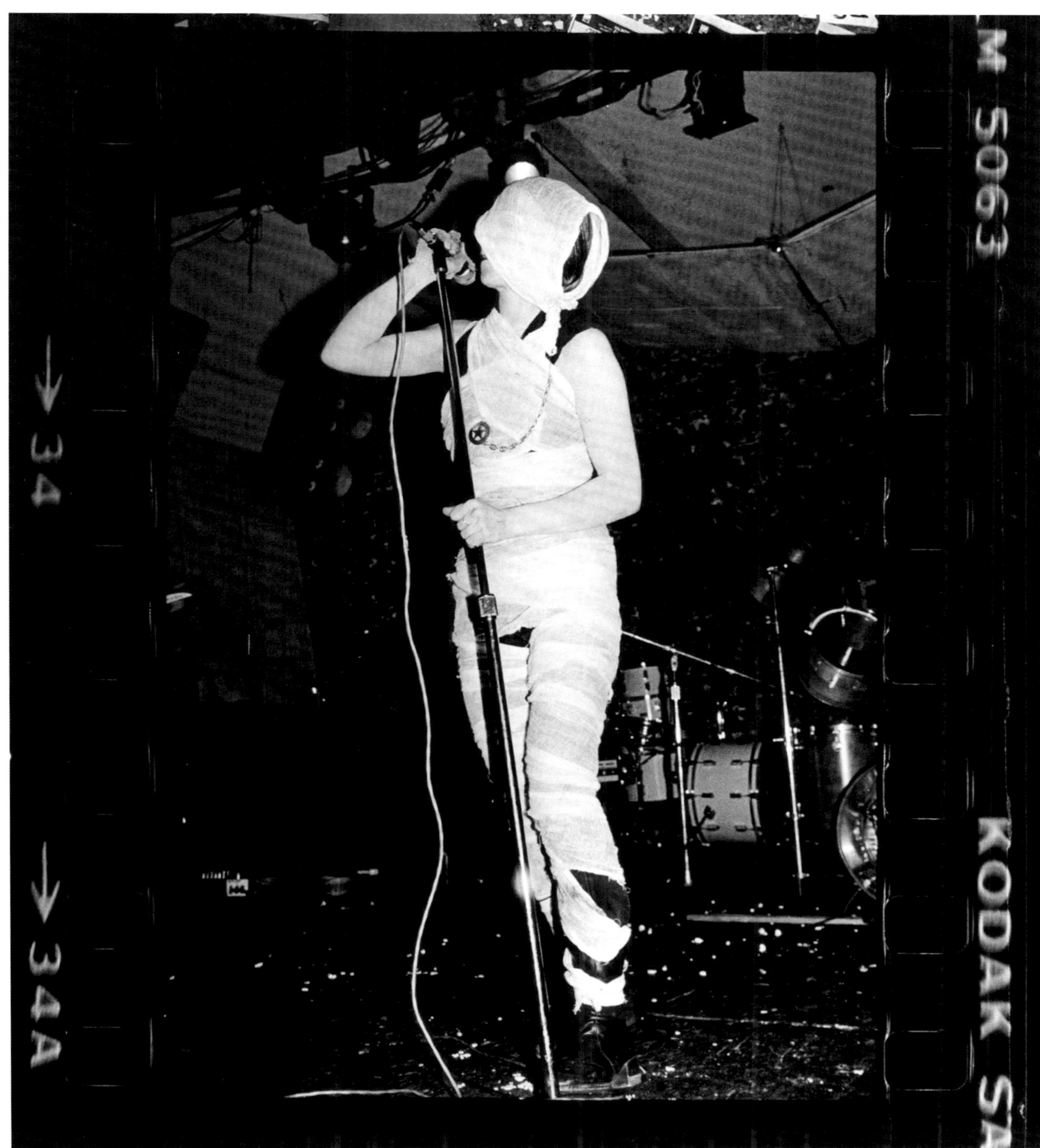
34
34A
5063
KODAK

KÖNIG

Johann König
DE-10963 Berlin | Dessauer Strasse 6-7
Phone +49 30 26103080 | Fax +49 30 26103 0811
info@johannkoenig.de | www.johannkoenig.de
Directors Johann König
Erika Weiss

Artists at Art Basel Miami Beach | **Henning Bohl**
Katharina Grosse
Jeppe Hein
Nathan Hylden
Annette Kelm
Alicja Kwade
Lisa Lapinski
Helen Marten
Michael Sailstorfer
Tatiana Trouvé
Johannes Wohnseifer
David Zink Yi

Further artists represented | Micol Assaël
Tue Greenfort
Manfred Kuttner
Michaela Meise
Natascha Sadr Haghighian
Corinne Wasmuht
Jordan Wolfson

Katharina Grosse
They Had Taken Things Along To Eat Together, 2012
Installation view, Johann König, Berlin, 2012

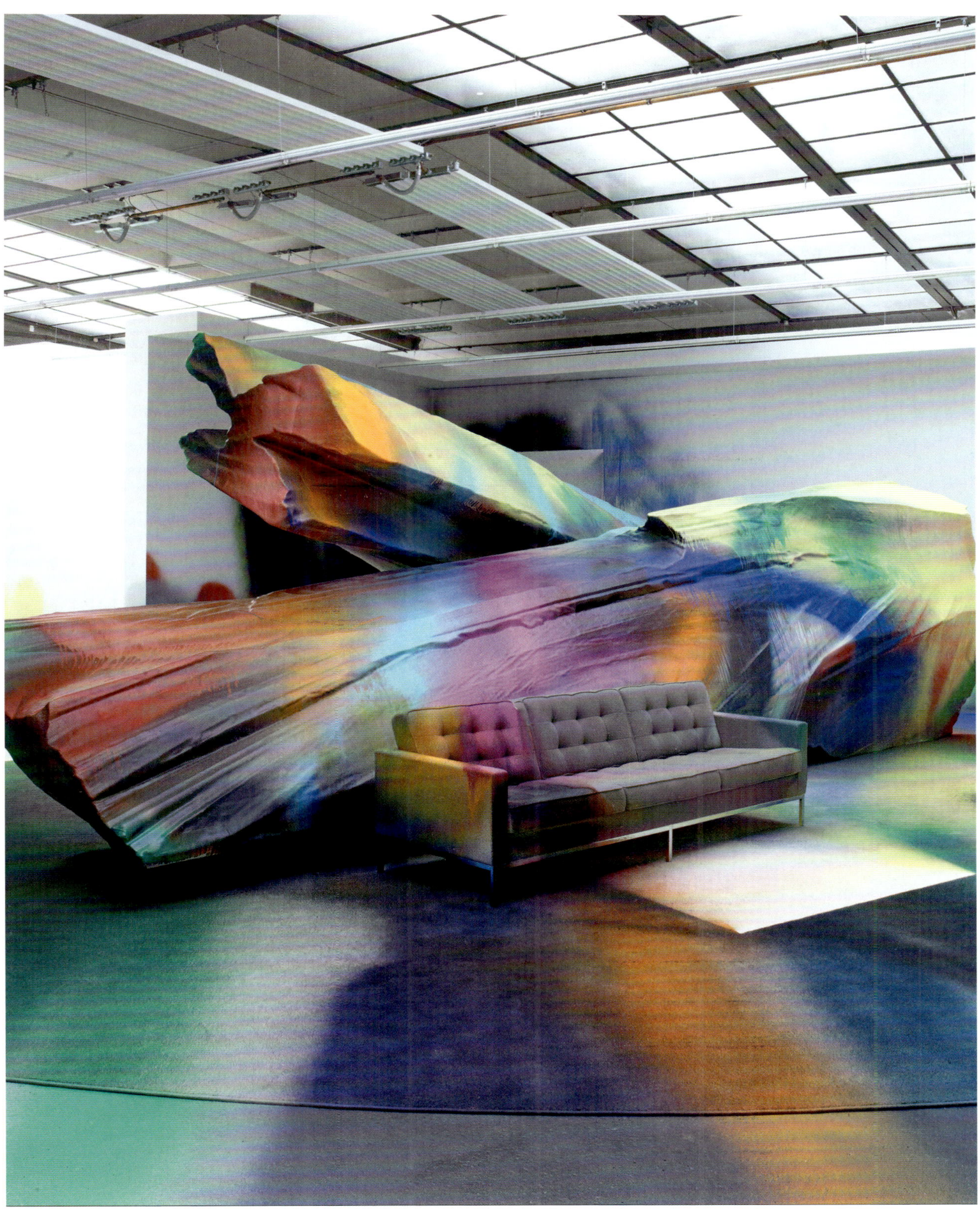

KORDANSKY

Mobile +1 917 859 77 47

David Kordansky Gallery
US-Los Angeles, CA 90016 | 3143 S. La Cienega Blvd., Unit A
Phone +1 310 558 30 30 | Fax +1 310 558 30 60
info@davidkordanskygallery.com | www.davidkordanskygallery.com
Directors Mike Homer
Stuart Krimko

Artists at Art Basel Miami Beach | **Kathryn Andrews**
Valentin Carron
Aaron Curry
Mai-Thu Perret

Gallery Information | Since its inception in 2003, David Kordansky Gallery has exhibited some of the most pioneering and critically acclaimed artists working in Los Angeles, the greater United States, and abroad. Broadly speaking, the gallery's geographical and generational perspective foregrounds conceptual rigor and formal experimentation as intersecting modes of inquiry.

The program represents a visually diverse array of practices in all media, and has evolved from an early focus on emerging artists to a concentration on numerous generational lineages. It is designed both to showcase individual artists and to draw attention to the dialogues, both implicit and explicit, between them.

While maintaining a focus on the development of contemporary art in its home city, the gallery has worked to document the dynamic cross-pollination of ideas that takes place between Los Angeles and other global centers.

David Kordansky Gallery operates two spaces in the Culver City district, allowing for an ambitious program of solo, group, and historical exhibitions.

Further artists represented: Markus Amm
Amy Bessone
Matthew Brannon
Steven Claydon
Heather Cook
Will Fowler
Sam Gilliam
Patrick Hill
Richard Jackson
Larry Johnson
Rashid Johnson
William E. Jones
Elad Lassry
Thomas Lawson
Alan Michael
Ruby Neri
David Noonan
Anthony Pearson
Jon Pestoni
Pietro Roccasalva
Lesley Vance
John Wesley
Jonas Wood

Valentin Carron
Archaïque archaïque mate, 2011
Cast bronze, black lacquer,
diameter 9.3 cm
Unique

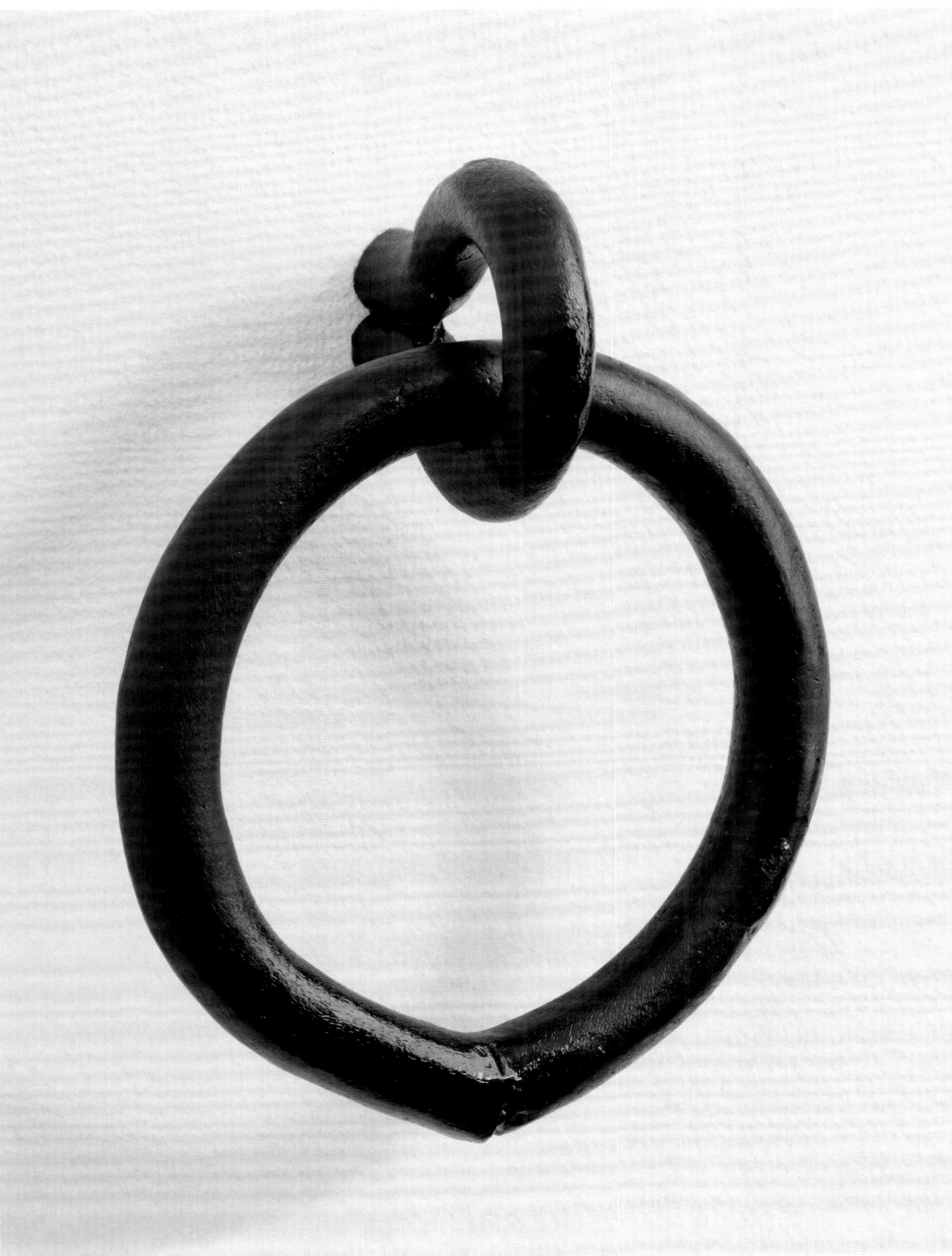

KOYAMA

Tomio Koyama Gallery Tokyo
JP-Tokyo 135-0024 | 1-3-2-7F Kiyosumi, Koto-ku
Phone +81 3 36424090 | Fax +81 3 36424091
info@tomiokoyamagallery.com | www.tomiokoyamagallery.com
Directors Tomio Koyama
Yuko Nagase

Tomio Koyama Gallery Kyoto
JP-Kyoto 600-8325 | 483 Nishigawa-cho, Shimogyo-ku
Phone +81 75 3539992 | Fax +81 75 3539993
kyoto@tomiokoyamagallery.com | www.tomiokoyamagallery.com

Tomio Koyama Gallery Singapore
SG-109444 Singapore | 47 Malan Road, #01-26 Gillman Barracks
singapore@tomiokoyamagallery.com | www.tomiokoyamagallery.com
Director Daisuke Watanabe

Artists at
Art Basel Miami Beach | **Inka Essenhigh**
Daisuke Fukunaga
Aya Ito
Hideaki Kawashima
Masahiko Kuwahara
Toru Kuwakubo
Yoshitomo Nara
Diego Singh
Hiroshi Sugito

Further artists represented | Franz Ackermann
Masako Ando
Ryota Aoki
Naomi Ashida
Stephan Balkenhol
Benjamin Butler
Varda Caivano
Jeremy Dickinson
Tom Friedman
Atsushi Fukui
Nobuhiro Fukui
Nana Funo
Gelitin
Rieko Hidaka
Satoshi Hirose
Tamami Hitsuda
Dennis Hollingsworth
Yuka Kashihara
Mika Kato
Naoki Koide
Makiko Kudo
Takuro Kuwata
Lee Youngbin
Yoshino Masui
Ryan McGinley
Shintaro Miyake
Satoko Nachi
Tomoko Nagai
Ernest Neto
Mika Ninagawa
Tam Ochiai
Satoshi Ohno
Yoko Ono
Rieko Otake
Jonathan Pylypchuck
Tal R
David Ratcliff
Mark Ryden
Tom Sachs
Makoto Saito
Midori Sato
Adam Silverman
Laurie Simmons
Yuko Someya
Kishio Suga
Vibeke Tandberg
Jason Teraoka
Gert & Uwe Tobias
Kumie Tsuda
Naoyuki Tsuji
Mamoru Tsukada
Richard Tuttle
Wang Yahui
Yutaka Watanabe
Terry Winters
Erwin Wurm
Keisuke Yamamoto

Masahiko Kuwahara
Quiet End of Summer, 2008
Acrylic on canvas,
145.5 x 145.5 cm

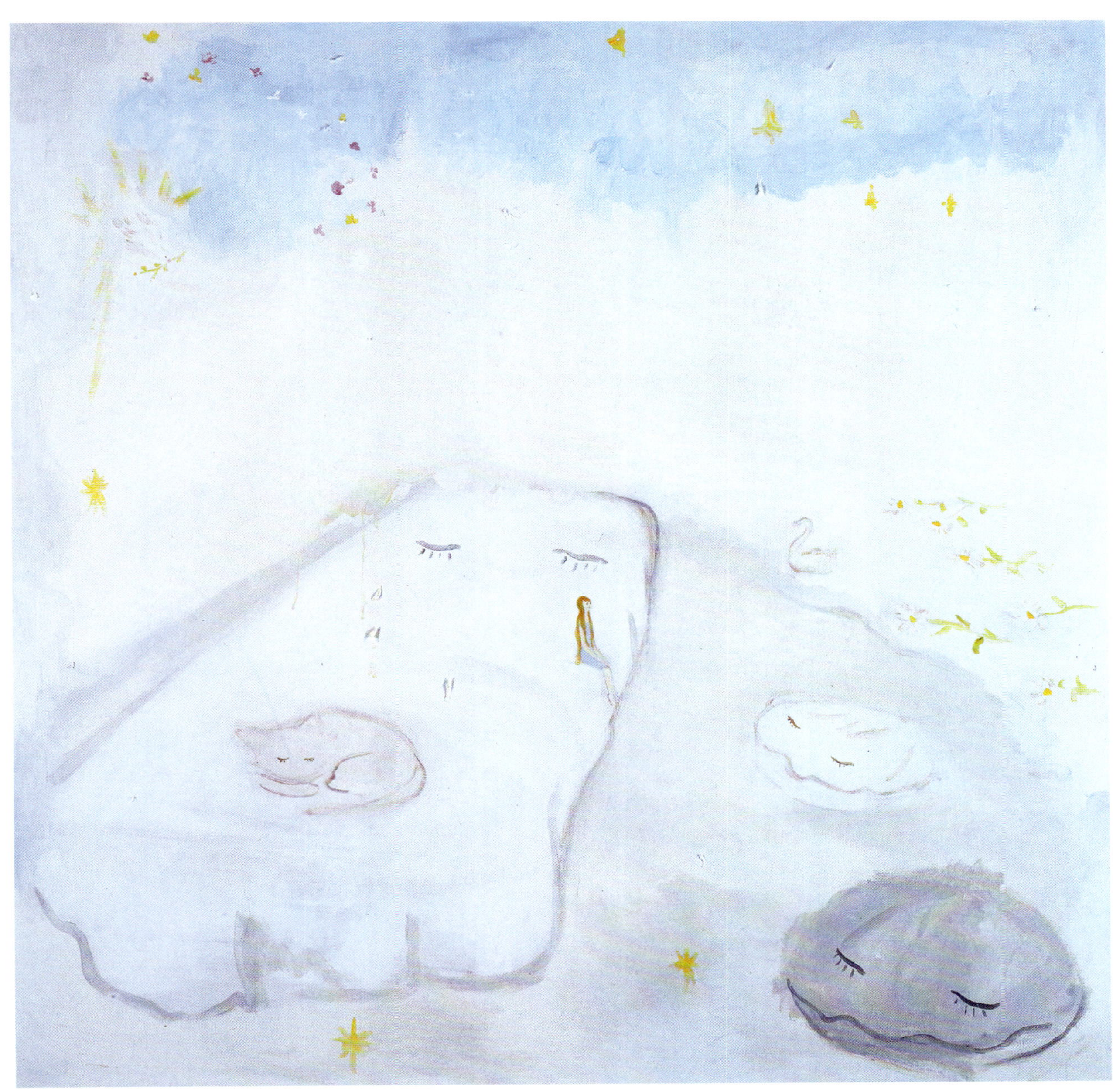

KREPS

Mobile +1 917 660 06 01

Andrew Kreps Gallery
US-New York, NY 10011 | 525 West 22nd Street
Phone +1 212 741 88 49 | Fax +1 212 741 81 63
contact@andrewkreps.com | www.andrewkreps.com
Directors Andrew Kreps
Liz Mulholland
Timo Kappeller

Artists at Art Basel Miami Beach | **Ricci Albenda**
Darren Bader
Martin Barré
Frank Benson
Andrea Bowers
Marc Camille Chaimowicz
Roe Ethridge
Uwe Henneken
Christian Holstad
Jamie Isenstein
Annette Kelm
Goshka Macuga
Ján Mančuška
Robert Melee
Robert Overby
Peter Piller
Ruth Root
Cheyney Thompson
Hayley Tompkins
Padraig Timoney
Klaus Weber

Andrea Bowers
Tree Sits – Canopy Camping, Earth First! Direct Action Manual with Dream Platform, 2011
Recycled wood, rope, carabiners, miscellaneous equipment and supplies, 108 x 60 x 5 cm

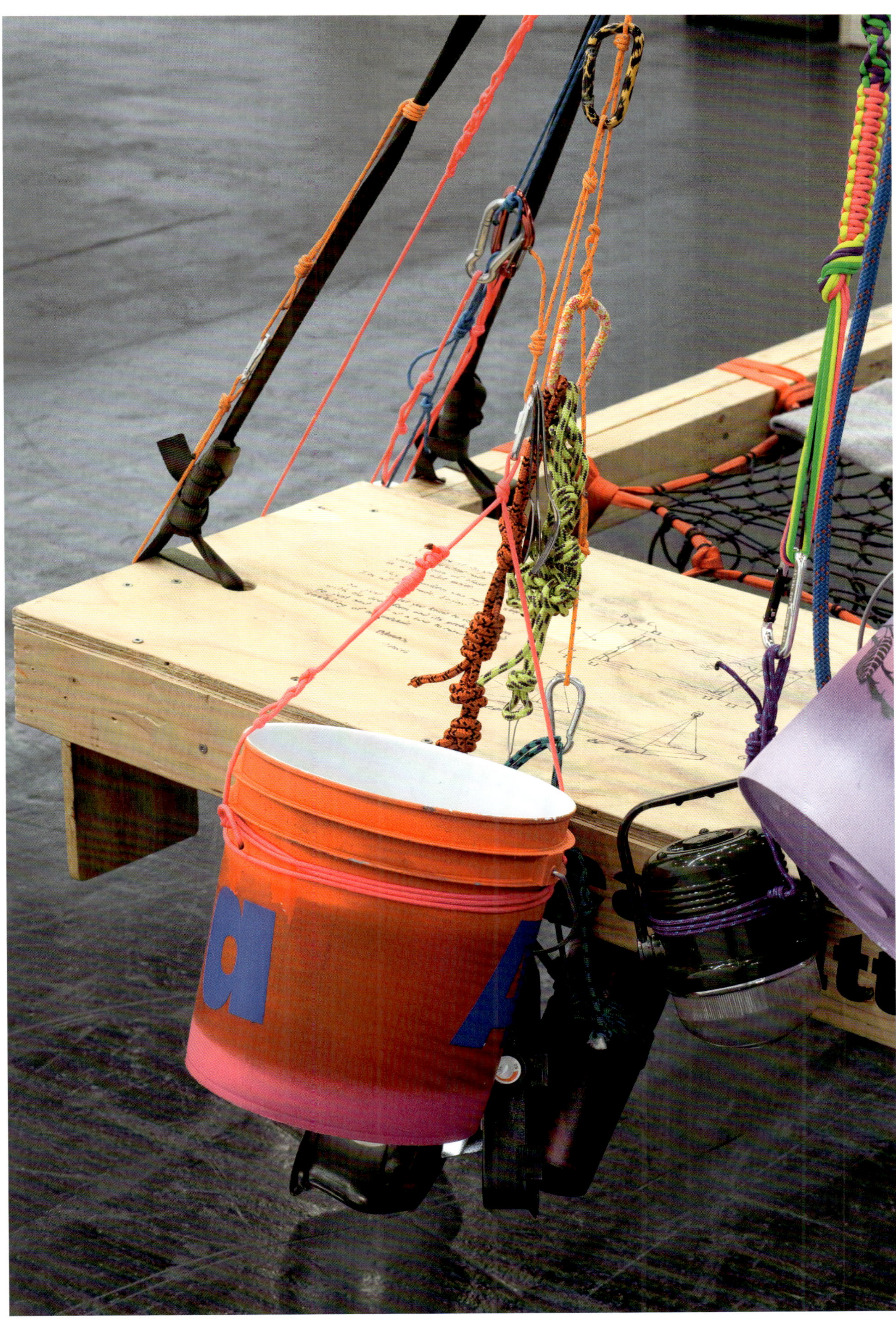

KRINZINGER

Mobile +43 676 324 83 79

Galerie Krinzinger
AT-1010 Vienna | Seilerstätte 16
Phone +43 1 513 30 06 | Fax +43 1 513 30 06 33
galeriekrinzinger@chello.at | www.galerie-krinzinger.at
Directors Ursula Krinzinger
Thomas Krinzinger

Artists at
Art Basel Miami Beach | **Marina Abramovic**
Nader Ahriman
Atelier Van Lieshout
Kader Attia
Gottfried Bechtold
Günter Brus
Chris Burden
Angela de la Cruz
Dubossarsky & Vinogradov
Abdulnasser Gharem
Sakshi Gupta
Jonathan Hernández
Secundino Hernández
Zenita Komad
Valerie Koshlyakov
Angelika Krinzinger
Oleg Kulik
Ahmed Mater
Jonathan Meese
Bjarne Melgaard
Shintaro Miyake
Otto Muehl
Hermann Nitsch
Hans Op de Beeck
Meret Oppenheim
Werner Reiterer
Eva Schlegel
Erik Schmidt
Rudolf Schwarzkogler
Mithu Sen
Sudarshan Shetty
Eliezer Sonnenschein
Frank Thiel
Gavin Turk
Erik van Lieshout
Jannis Varelas
Martin Walde
Mark Wallinger
Zhang Ding
Thomas Zipp

Gallery Information | Galerie Krinzinger was founded in 1971. Since then at least 300 exhibitions of national and international artists, solo shows, group shows, and thematic shows have been organized.

The main trajectory of the gallery program results on the one hand from international performance art and body-related art (Chris Burden, Paul McCarthy, Mike Kelley, Nancy Rubins) based originally on Viennese Actionism (Rudolf Schwarzkogler, Günter Brus, Hermann Nitsch, Otto Muehl). Besides that the gallery has been working with young national and international artists for 30 years and is now presenting the following younger artists: Atelier Van Lieshout, Dubossarsky & Vinogradov, Erik van Lieshout, Jonathan Meese, Bjarne Melgaard, Shintaro Miyake, Eva Schlegel, Frank Thiel, Gavin Turk, Keith Tyson, Martin Walde, and Erwin Wurm.

Apart from the gallery program, Dr. Ursula Krinzinger also organizes and curates important exhibitions in various spaces outside the gallery.

Since May 2002 the gallery has also run a large new space – Krinzinger Projekte – in addition to the main gallery, to present young and exciting artists in curated thematic, group, and solo shows. Galerie Krinzinger has continuously participated in the most important art fairs for more than 25 years.

Hans Op de Beeck
Small Constructions
Exhibition view, Galerie Krinzinger,
Vienna, 2012

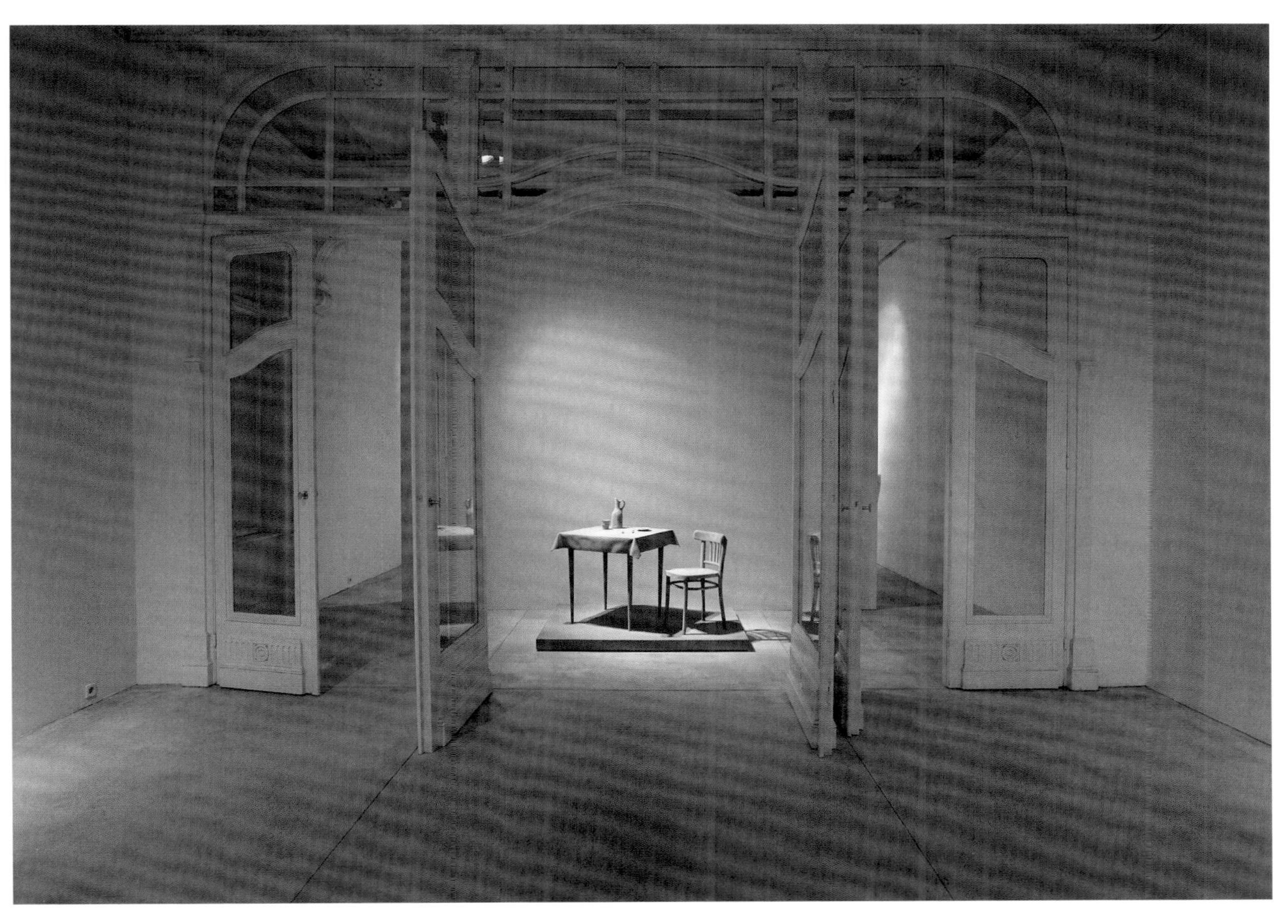

KUKJE

Mobile +1 917 376 24 81

Kukje Gallery
KR-110-200 Seoul | 54 Samcheong-ro Jongno-gu
Phone +82 2 735 84 49 | Fax +82 2 733 48 79
kukje@kukjegallery.com | www.kukjegallery.com
Directors Hyun-Sook Lee
Charles Kim
Suzie Kim

Tina Kim Gallery
US-New York, NY 10001 | 545 West 25th Street
Phone +1 212 716 11 00 | Fax +1 212 716 12 50
info@tinakimgallery.com | www.tinakimgallery.com
Director Tina Kim

Artists at
Art Basel Miami Beach | **Gada Amer**
Gada Amer & Reza Farkhondeh
Louise Bourgeois
Cecily Brown
Alexander Calder
Duck Hyun Cho
Jae-Eun Choi
Gimhongsok
Damien Hirst
Candida Höfer
Jenny Holzer
Roni Horn
Kyung Jeon
Michael Joo
Yeondoo Jung
Eemyun Kang
Anish Kapoor
Kimsooja
Joan Mitchell
Hein-Kuhn Oh
Julian Opie
Jean-Michel Othoniel
Anselm Reyle
Kibong Rhee
Lee Ufan
Bill Viola
Haegue Yang

Gallery Information | Kukje, which means 'international,' is an apt name for the Korean gallery that has most shaped and directed the domestic art market since opening in 1982. Through its work with important collectors, museums, and the world's leading galleries, Kukje has introduced and supported both established and emerging artists, and mounted world-class exhibitions including Louise Bourgeois, Anselm Kiefer, Bill Viola, Joan Mitchell, and Eva Hesse.

Kukje Gallery also plays an important role in promoting Korean artists. The gallery has an unmatched reputation for introducing artists like Lee Ufan, Kibong Rhee, and Haegue Yang to domestic and international audiences through its exhibition program and participation in art fairs worldwide.

In 2003, Kukje's New York affiliate, Tina Kim Gallery, opened in Manhattan, specializing in modern and post-war art. In Fall 2007, the gallery moved to its new home on West 25th Street in Chelsea, where it continues to focus on the work of mid-20th-century masters while developing an exhibition program devoted to international contemporary art and design.

Further artists represented: Joseph Beuys
Anthony Caro
Hyun Roh Choong
Eva Hesse
Seung-Hye Hong
Anselm Kiefer
Hye Rim Lee
Sungsic Moon
David Nash
Jack Pierson
Kiki Smith
Frank Stella
Jeff Wall

Gimhongsok
Love, 2012
Stainless steel,
292 x 300 x 123.5 cm

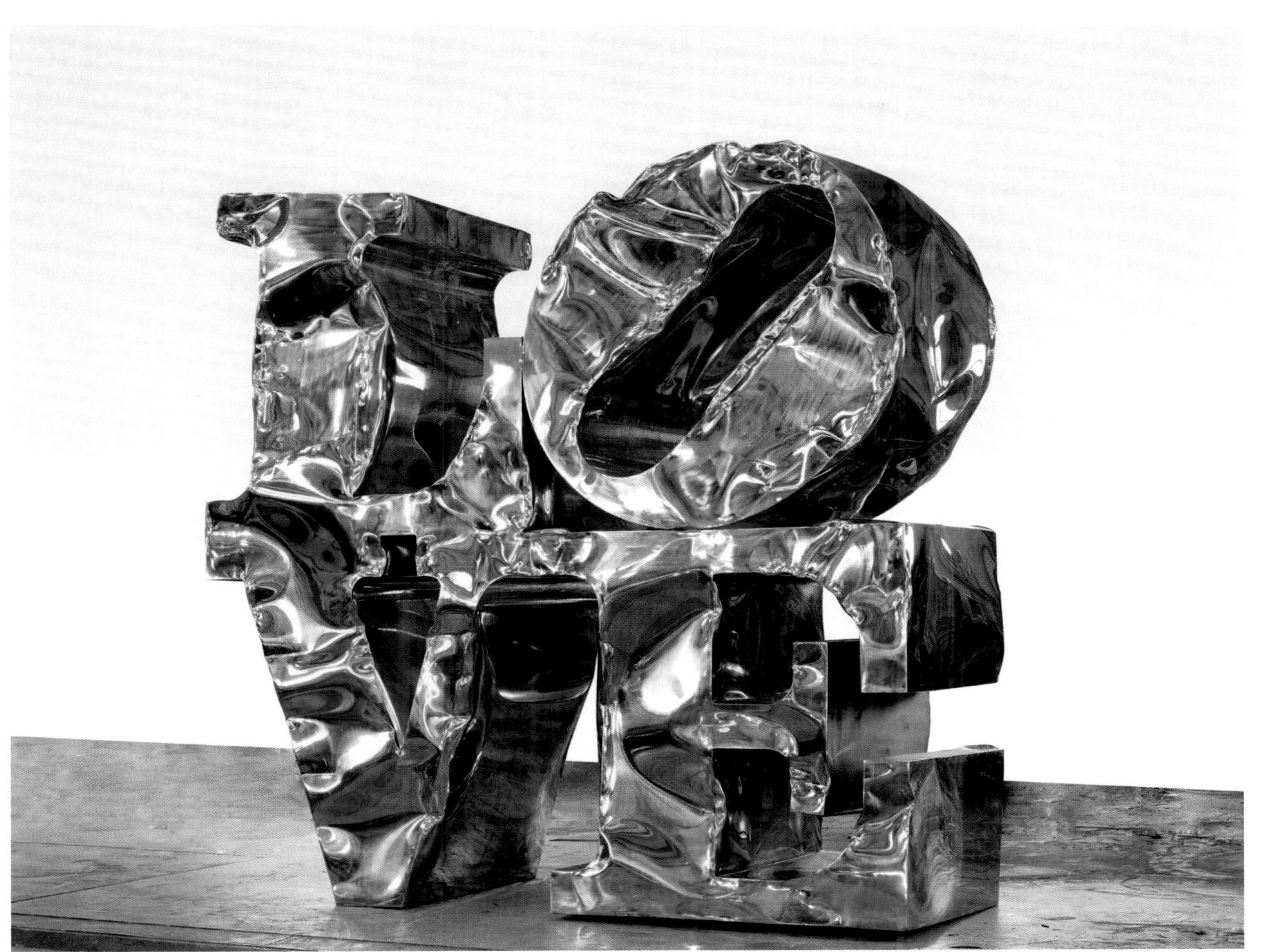

KURIMANZUTTO

Mobile +52 1 55 34 33 33 44

kurimanzutto
MX-11850 Mexico City | Gob. Rafael Rebollar 94, Colonia San Miguel Chapultepec
Phone +52 55 52 86 30 59 | Fax +52 55 52 56 24 08
daniela@kurimanzutto.com | www.kurimanzutto.com
Directors Mónica Manzutto
José Kuri

Artists at
Art Basel Miami Beach | **Eduardo Abaroa**
Jennifer Allora & Guillermo Calzadilla
Carlos Amorales
Miguel Calderón
Abraham Cruzvillegas
Minerva Cuevas
Jimmie Durham
Daniel Guzmán
Jonathan Hernández
Gabriel Kuri
Dr. Lakra
Roman Ondák
Gabriel Orozco
Damián Ortega
Fernando Ortega
Anri Sala
Gabriel Sierra
Monika Sosnowska
Sofía Táboas
Rirkrit Tiravanija
Adrián Villar Rojas
Apichatpong Weerasethakul

Gabriel Sierra
Hang It All, madrastra naturaleza series, 2003
Metal and fresh fruits,
38 x 51 x 18 cm

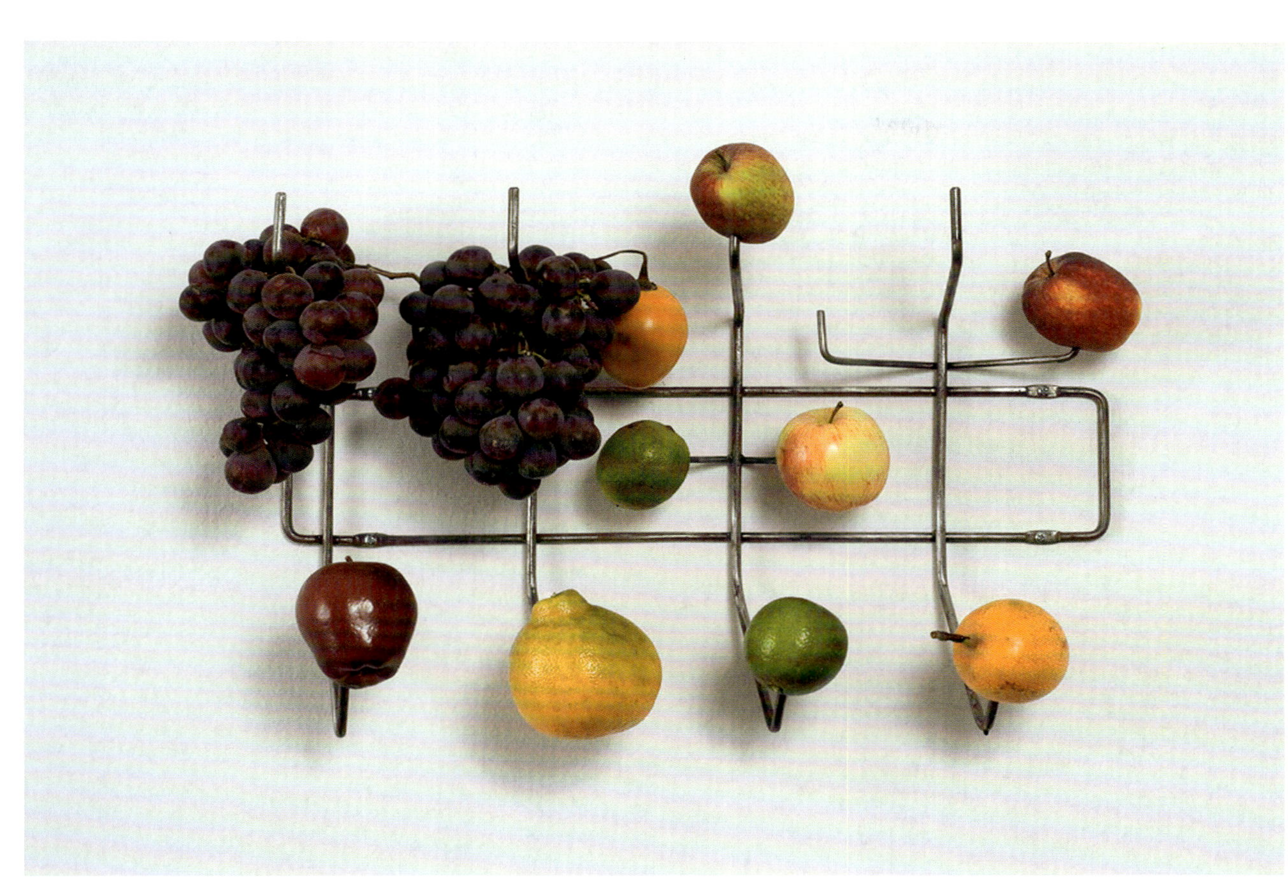

L&M

L&M Arts
US-New York, NY 10075 | 45 East 78th Street
Phone +1 212 861 00 20 | Fax +1 212 861 78 58
info@lmgallery.com | www.lmgallery.com
Directors Dominique Lévy
Robert Mnuchin

L&M Arts LA
US-Los Angeles, CA 90291 | 660 Venice Blvd.
Phone +1 310 821 64 00 | Fax +1 310 821 64 42

Artists at
Art Basel Miami Beach | **John Baldessari**
Alexander Calder
John Chamberlain
Joseph Cornell
Willem de Kooning
Lucio Fontana
Sam Francis
Alberto Giacometti
David Hammons
Damien Hirst
Thomas Houseago
Donald Judd
Yves Klein
Franz Kline
Barbara Kruger
Sol LeWitt
Roy Lichtenstein
Liza Lou
Agnes Martin
Paul McCarthy
Pablo Picasso
Michelangelo Pistoletto
Gerhard Richter
Mark Rothko
Robert Ryman
Cy Twombly
Andy Warhol
Tom Wesselmann

Gallery Information | L&M Arts specializes in postwar American art and European modern masters.

L&M Arts represents Yves Klein in North America and the Estate of Joseph Cornell.

Past exhibitions include:
Picasso's Dora Maar/de Kooning's Women
Women of Warhol: Marilyn, Liz & Jackie
Naked Since 1950
Picasso: The Classical Period
Jeff Koons: Highlights of 25 Years
Yves Klein: A Career Survey
Tom Wesselmann: The 60's
Andy Warhol: Mao
Hammons
Willem de Kooning: 1981-1986
Complexity of the Simple
Liza Lou
John Chamberlain: The Early Years
Sam Francis: 1953-1959
Tanguy/Calder: Between Surrealism and Abstraction
Damien Hirst: The Medicine Cabinets
Thomas Houseago: All Together Now
Günther Uecker: The Early Years
Andy Warhol Colored Campbell's Soup Cans
Barbara Kruger
Robin Rhode: Imaginary Exhibition
Frank Stella: Black, Aluminum, Copper Paintings
Alexander Calder
Jean-Michel Othoniel

A+B | **Barbara Kruger**
Money Makes Money (Room Wrap), 2011
Digital print on vinyl, dimensions variable
Unique

A

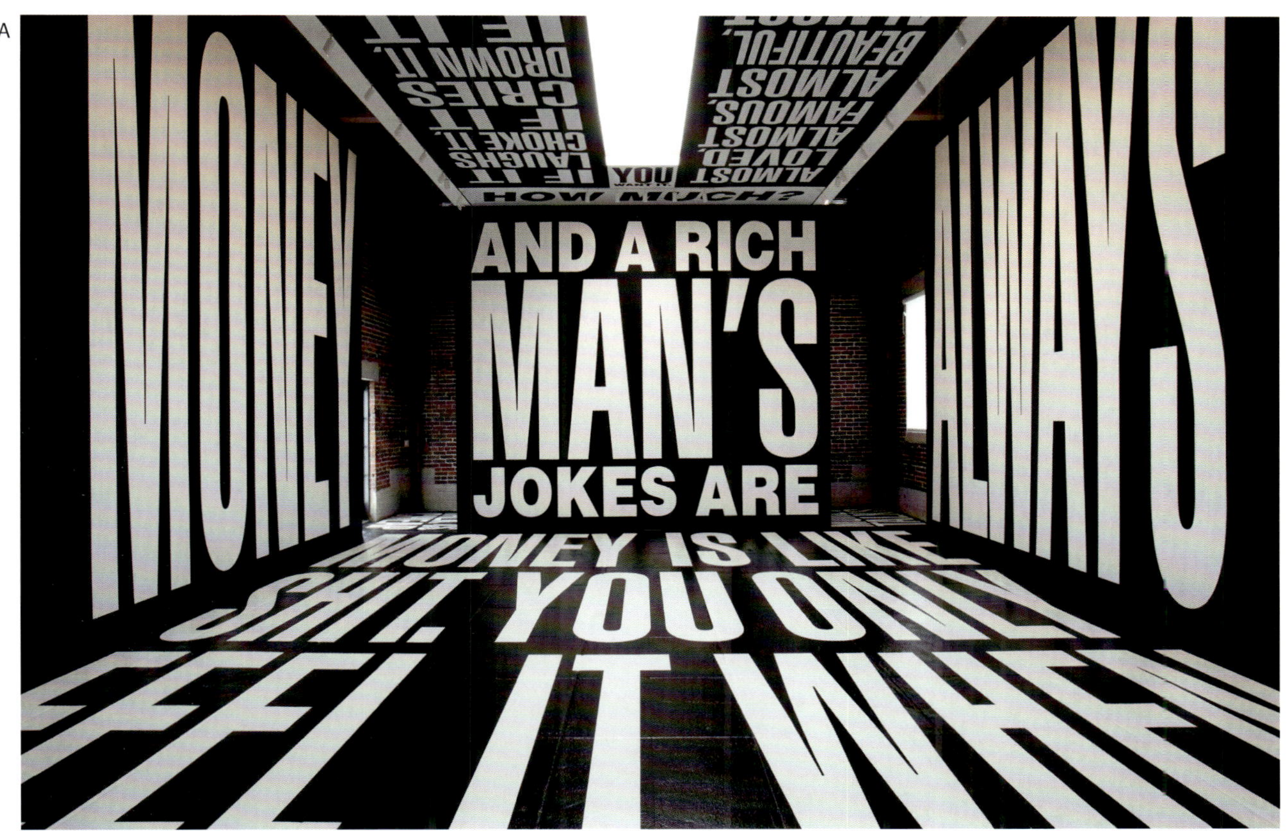

MONEY
IF IT LAUGHS CHOKE IT, IF IT CRIES DROWN IT,
ALMOST LOVED, ALMOST FAMOUS, ALMOST BEAUTIFUL,
YOU
HOW MUCH?
AND A RICH MAN'S JOKES ARE
ALWAYS
MONEY IS LIKE
SHIT. YOU ONLY
FEEL IT WHEN

B

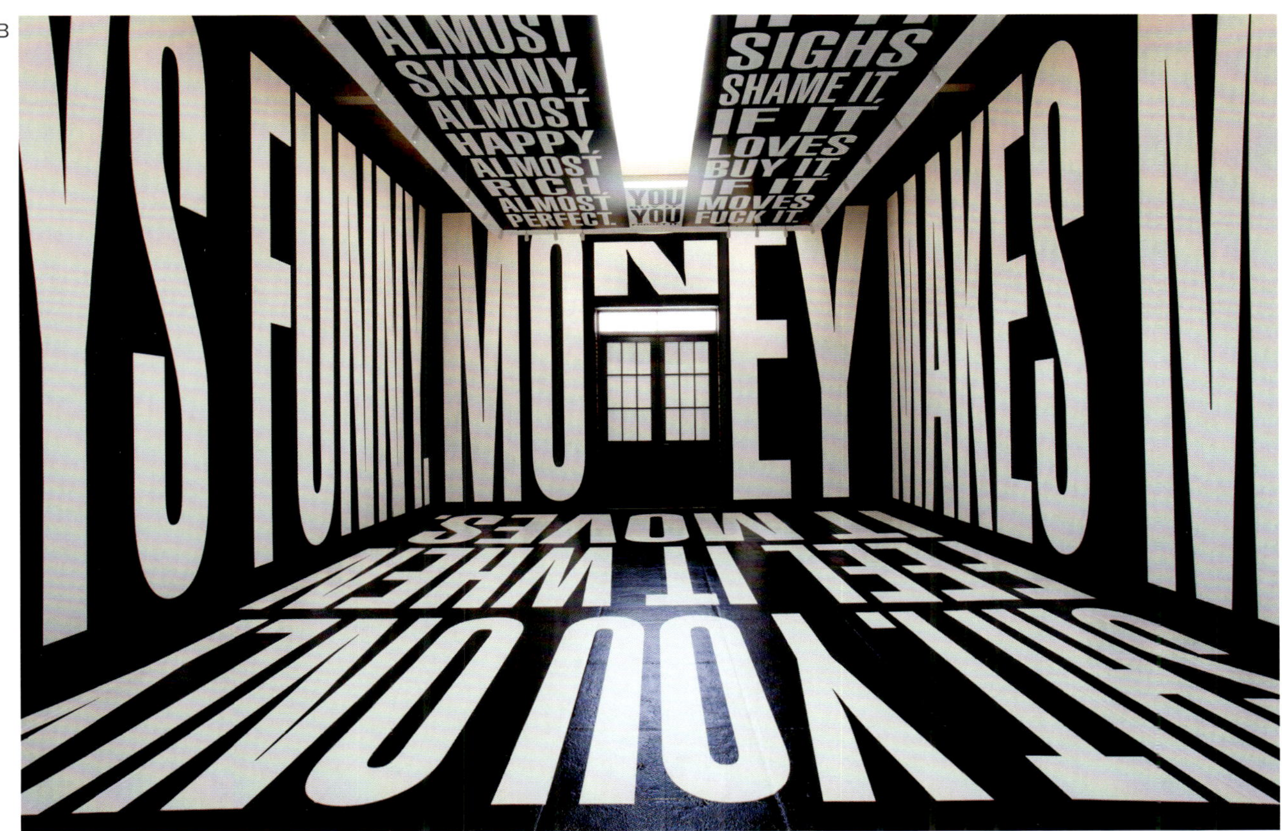

ALMOST SKINNY, ALMOST HAPPY, ALMOST RICH, ALMOST PERFECT.
YOU
YOU
SIGHS SHAME IT, IF IT LOVES BUY IT, IF IT MOVES FUCK IT.
FUNNY. MONEY MAKES
FEEL IT WHEN IT MOVES.

LA CENTRAL

Mobile +57 313 791 95 19

La Central
CO-Bogotá | Cra. 12a #77a-72
Phone +57 1 757 44 10 | Fax +57 1 757 44 10
info@lacentral.com.co | www.lacentral.com.co
Directors Beatriz Lopez
Katy Hernandez

One-Person Show | Artist Information

Felipe Arturo

*1979, Bogotá, Colombia
Lives and works in Bogotá, Colombia

Gallery Information | The work of La Central focuses on the production and dissemination of projects with a special interest in those who, committed to social, political, and cultural themes, present an original relationship with their environment.

Using a hybrid and multidisciplinary model, La Central approaches the processes of contemporary culture by proposing a special way of adapting to the circumstances and connect with the meanings, senses and relationships found in art. Our goal is to propose an original approach and attitude to the circumstances and characteristics of our time.

Further artists represented:
Otto Berchem
Pia Camil
Carolina Caycedo
Nicolas Consuegra
Juan David Laserna
Matthieu Laurette
Miltos Manetas
Mateo Rivano
Ana Roldan
Manuela Viera Gallo

Felipe Arturo is an architect and artist born in Bogotá in 1979. His practice takes elements from a variety of fields centering on urbanism, architecture, the history of the city, and art in relation to politics, history, geography, and economics. His works and projects are mainly sculptures, installations, and videos based on concepts like structure, sequence, and matter. Arturo's work is deeply influenced by the traces of history present in vernacular architectures and constructional techniques as well as by the consequences of processes of colonization and de-colonization in contemporary culture.

Ten Letters is a project of three works dealing with concrete as a mark of colonization and modernity and the way this mark has not only a material presence but also a representation in language and literature. These works have a conceptual origin in Japanese and Latin American concrete poetry, as exemplified by the Brazilian Noingandres group. In these movements the hidden poetic as an artistic operation is replaced by the meaning itself, in other words the signifier and the signified are condensed in a single entity.

Ten Letters is a clear example of this logic since 'ten letters' mean ten letters but at the same time are ten letters. A group of ten letters cast in concrete is the first work of the project.

The second work of the project is a series of three different sentences following the logic of a Haiku: the river follows gravity-colonization follows the river-colonization follows gravity. The letters of this poem are made in wooden cases containing sand and cement, where these two materials give shape to each other without mixing.

Finally, the third work of the project is a conversion to waveforms in concrete of the sentence 'primero estaba el mar,' which gives its name to Colombian writer Tomas Gonzales' first novel. In this work each wave represents a syllable of the sentence that follows. The variation of the waves changes the order of the words, creating different sentences and the idea of the repetition and variation of the sea.

Felipe Arturo
Primero estaba el mar, 2012
Concrete casting,
72 x 576 x 144 cm

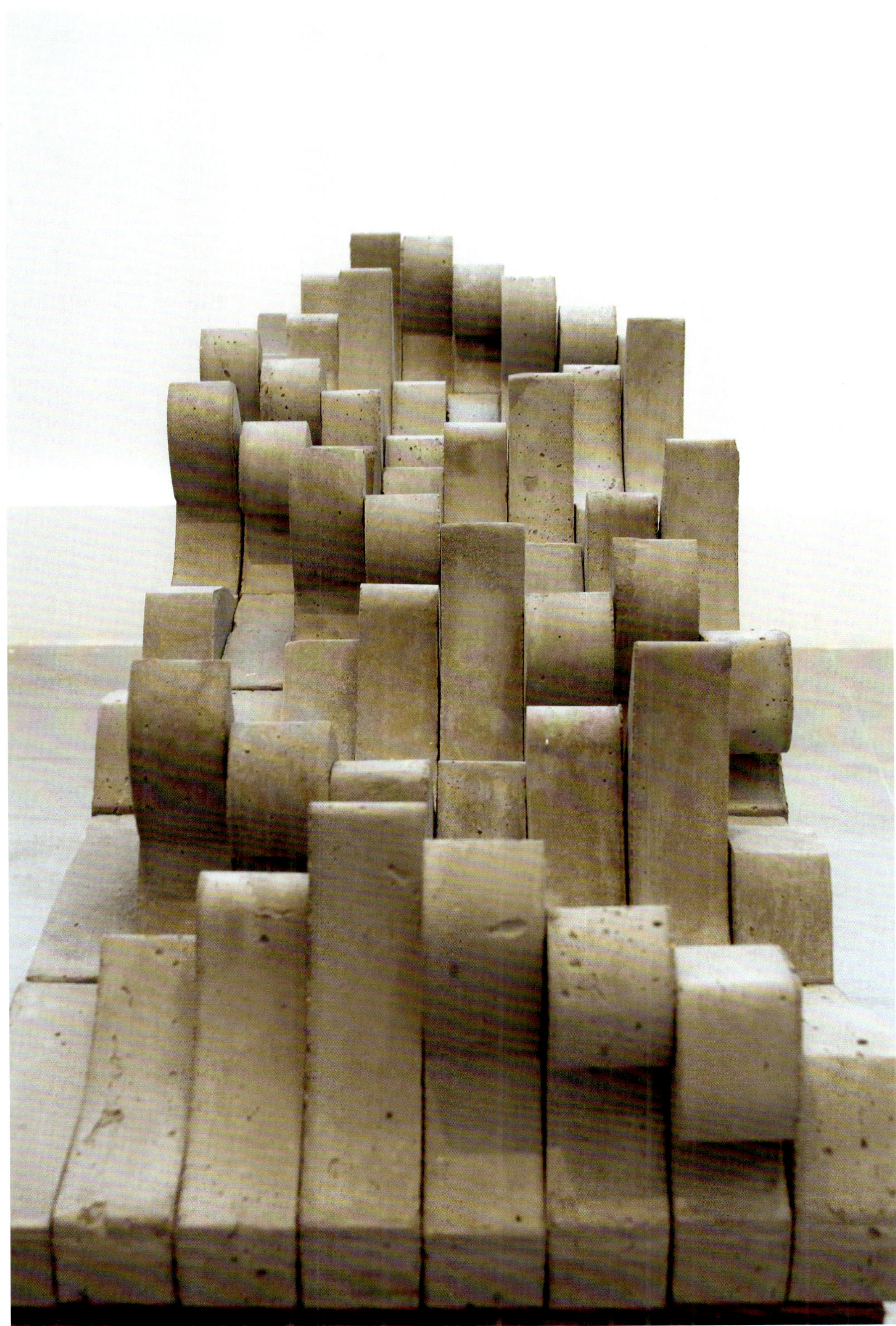

LABOR

Mobile +52 1 55 14 74 51 96

Labor
MX-11540 Mexico City | Francisco Ramírez 5
Phone +52 55 63 04 87 55 | Fax +52 55 63 04 87 55
info@labor.org.mx | www.labor.org.mx
Director Pamela Echeverría

One-Person Show | Artist Information

Irene Kopelman

*1974, Córdoba, Argentina
Lives and works in Amsterdam, Netherlands

Further artists represented | Erick Beltrán
Etienne Chambaud
Santiago Cucullu
Terence Gower
Nicholas Mangan
Teresa Margolles
Raphael Montañez Ortiz
Pedro Reyes
Jorge Satorre
Pablo Vargas Lugo
Antonio Vega Macotela
Héctor Zamora

Irene Kopelman reads her practice within the notion of models. She uses the term 'models' as an instance of materialization between the thinking process and the word. Kopelman is inspired by this concept, which is used by most of the disciplines of knowledge. Many areas of studies generate models with the aim of granting access to, and subsequently organizing, the world (for instance, models of the planets in astronomy, chemical models to represent atoms, archeological models to represent lost civilizations, and even abstract, though not formal, models as found in mathematics or economics).

Kopelman hopes to demonstrate that it is impossible to enclose the complexity of things in tightly compartmentalized categories: During the 19th century, a scientific project needed to force things into categories in order to visualize the rules to which they responded and organize the world in a logical system. This was a fundamental process to schematize how we look at things and simplify it to the extreme, thereby overlooking any singularities.

The artist seeks to explore the link between two sources: direct contact with the landscape and mediated contact with it via museum collections. She searches for a way to bring together these elements, working towards the generation of a narrative that will emerge when all these components coexist. This dynamic of difference and repetition is the central axis of her work.

Irene Kopelman
La morfología del paisaje determina sus vistas (The Morphology of the Landscape Determines Its Views), 2011
Fired clay, 4 x 220 x 280 cm
Detail

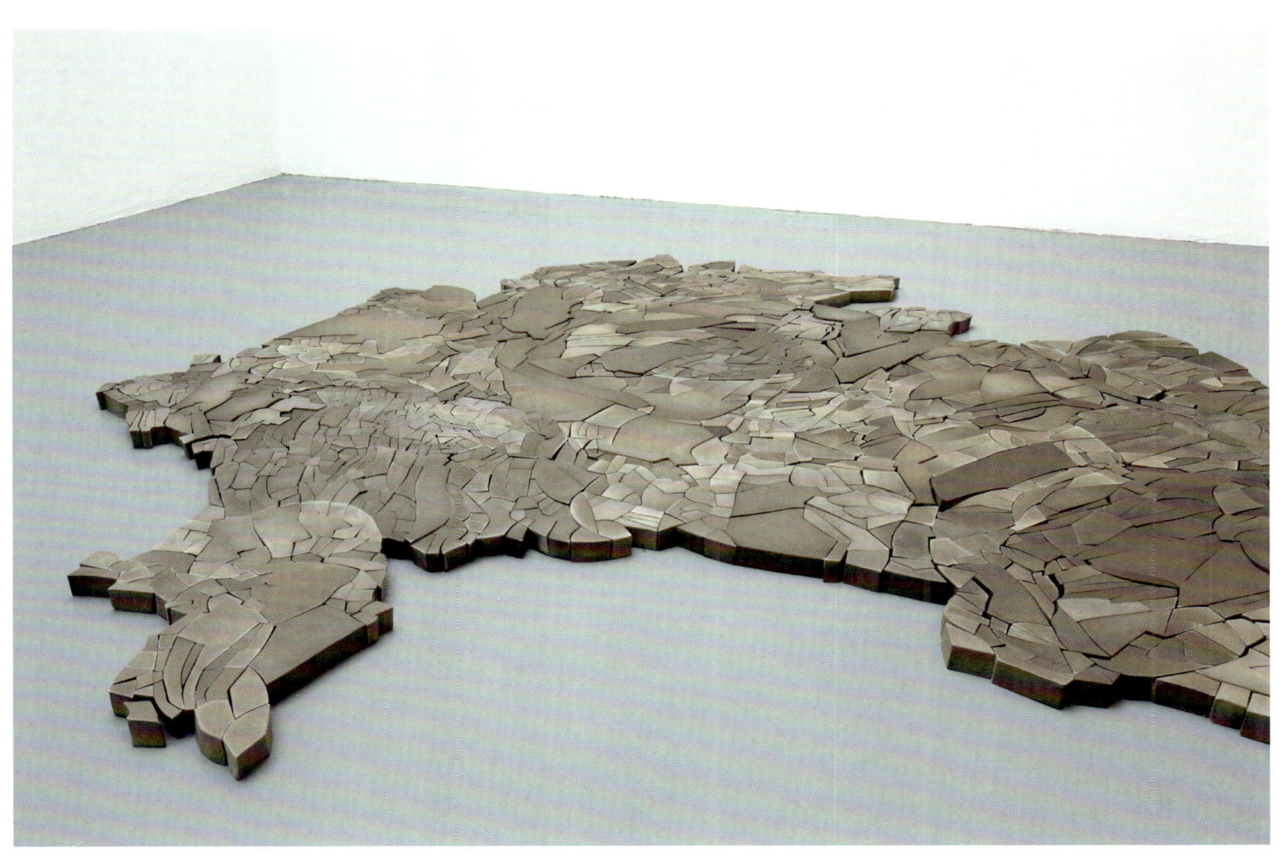

LAMBERT

Yvon Lambert
FR-75003 Paris | 108, rue Vieille-du-Temple
Phone +33 1 42 71 09 33 | Fax +33 1 42 71 87 47
paris@yvon-lambert.com | www.yvon-lambert.com
Directors Yvon Lambert
Olivier Bélot
Nicolas Nahab
Mélanie Meffrer-Rondeau
Eléonore Lambertie
Luisa Lagos

Artists at Art Basel Miami Beach | **Douglas Gordon**
Loris Gréaud
Jenny Holzer
Markus Schinwald
Francesco Vezzoli

Gallery Information | Yvon Lambert opened Galerie Yvon Lambert in Paris in 1967.

The Collection Lambert in Avignon opened in 2000 and presents more than 350 works from Yvon Lambert's personal collection.

Further artists represented: Carlos Amorales
Carl Andre
Robert Barry
Stefan Brüggemann
Mircea Cantor
David Claerbout
Jason Dodge
Gardar Eide Einarsson
Spencer Finch
Vincent Ganivet
Anna Gaskell
Kendell Geers
Nan Goldin
Shilpa Gupta
Karl Haendel
Candida Höfer
Koo Jeong-A
Joan Jonas
On Kawara
Zilvinas Kempinas
Idris Khan
Anselm Kiefer
Barbara Kruger
Bertrand Lavier
Louise Lawler
Sol LeWitt
Jill Magid
Jonathan Monk
Roman Opalka
Giulio Paolini
Diogo Pimentão
Charles Sandison
Ariel Schlesinger
Andres Serrano
David Shrigley
Shinique Smith
Mario Testino
Niele Toroni
Salla Tykkä
Nick van Woert
Ian Wallace
Lawrence Weiner
Cerith Wyn Evans

Markus Schinwald
Untitled (Legs) #24, 2011
Wood, 350 x 350 x 200 cm

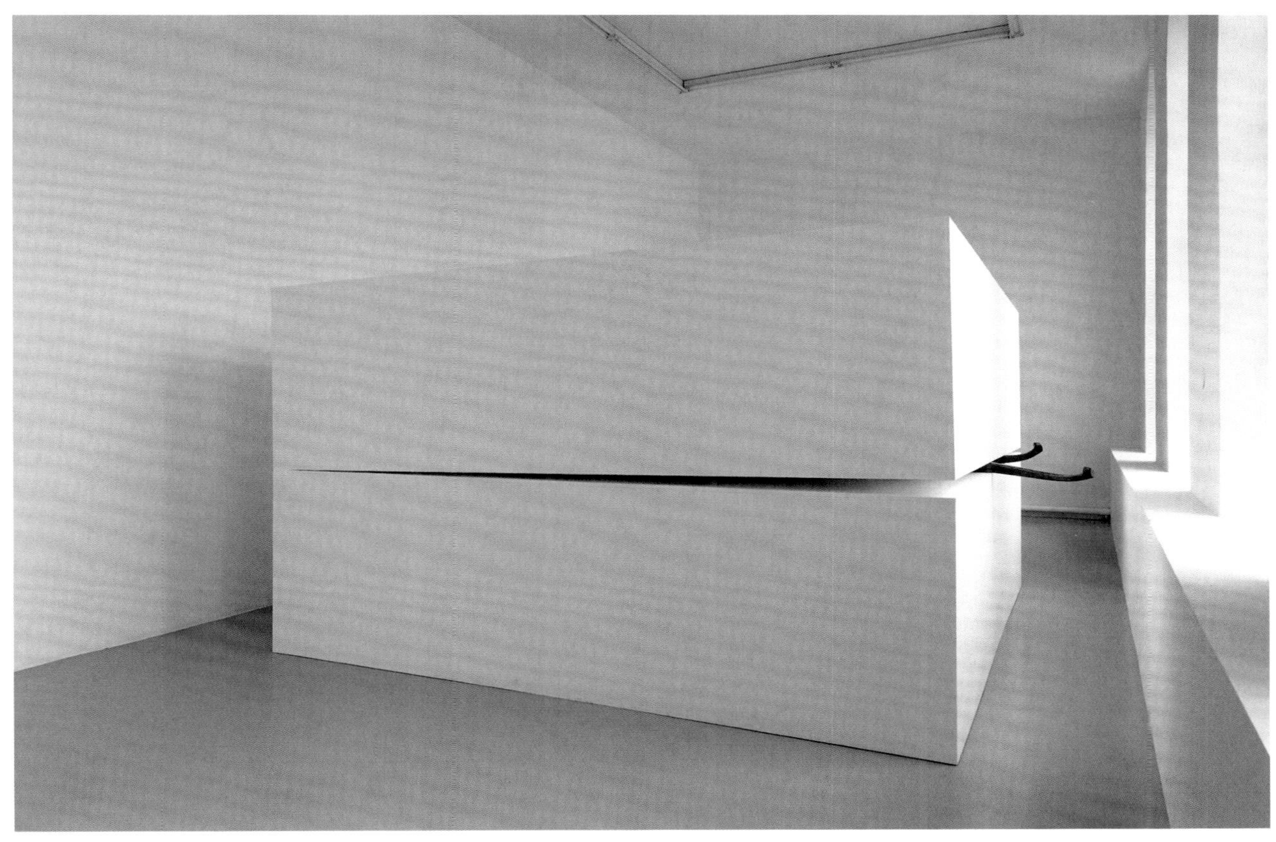

LANDAU

Mobile +1 514 865 32 63, +41 79 777 47 89

Landau Fine Art, Inc.
CA-Montreal H3G 1K4 | 1456 Sherbrooke Street West, #200
Phone +1 514 849 33 11 | Fax +1 514 289 94 48
landau@landaufineart.ca | www.landaufineart.ca
Directors Robert Landau
Alice Landau

Artists at
Art Basel Miami Beach |
Josef Albers
Alexander Archipenko
Jean Arp
Heinrich Campendonk
Lynn Chadwick
Marc Chagall
Kwang-Young Chun
Giorgio de Chirico
Edgar Degas
Jean Dubuffet
Max Ernst
Lyonel Feininger
Alberto Giacometti
Juan Gris
Wassily Kandinsky
Christoph Kiefhaber
Paul Klee
Henri Laurens
Le Corbusier
Fernand Léger
Jacques Lipchitz
René Magritte
Marino Marini
Henri Matisse
Joan Miró
Amedeo Modigliani
Henry Moore
Pablo Picasso
Georges Rouault
Georges Valmier
Kees van Dongen
Alexej von Jawlensky

Gallery Information | Landau Fine Art is a family-run gallery that is unique in Canada, since it is the only venue in the country where museum-quality works by international masters can be found. Robert and Alice Landau travel extensively not only to exhibit their latest acquisitions at the Basel, Miami, Paris, and Maastricht art fairs but also to search out important works from private estates.

It is hardly surprising that so many dealers and collectors from around the globe make regular visits to Montreal (only 50 minutes by air from New York) for a private view in a gallery where works by Picasso, Miró, Léger, Moore, Chagall, Giacometti, Jawlensky, Dubuffet, etc., abound and where many living artists are exclusively represented.

Pablo Picasso
Femme assise, 1953
Oil on canvas, 46 x 38 cm

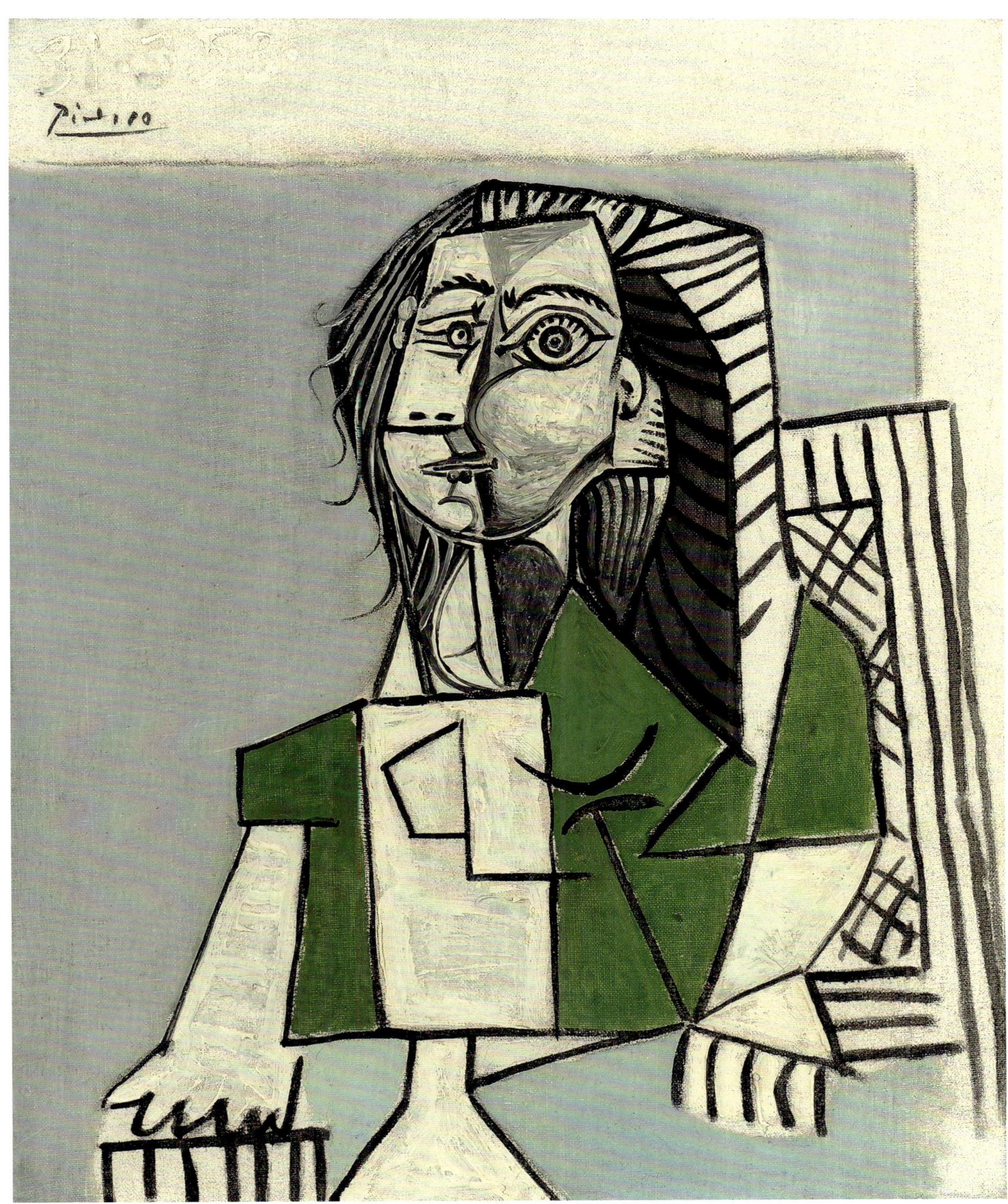

LEE

Mobile +44 78 54 21 56 92

Simon Lee Gallery
GB-London W1J 8DT | 12 Berkeley Street
Phone +44 20 74 91 01 00 | Fax +44 20 74 91 02 00
info@simonleegallery.com | www.simonleegallery.com
Directors Lindsay Ramsay
Claudia Milic
Katharine Burton

Simon Lee Gallery
CN-Hong Kong | 304, 3/F The Pedder Building, 12 Pedder Street, Central
Phone +852 28 01 62 52 | Fax +852 28 01 68 58

Artists at Art Basel Miami Beach | **John M Armleder**
Mel Bochner
Alighiero e Boetti
Angela Bulloch
Merlin Carpenter
Larry Clark
James Coleman
George Condo
Matias Faldbakken
Hans-Peter Feldmann
Bernard Frize
Alex Hubbard
Donald Judd
Sherrie Levine
Paulina Olowska
Claudio Parmiggiani
João Penalva
Michelangelo Pistoletto
Josephine Pryde
Jim Shaw
Gary Simmons
Robert Therrien
Marnie Weber
Christopher Wool
Toby Ziegler
Heimo Zobernig

João Penalva
Looking up in Osaka K Minamisemba 1 cho-me,
2005/06
Archival pigment print on Innova Smooth Cotton High White 315 gsm paper, dry-mounted on Alu Reynobond, acrylic glass, oak frame, 202.7 x 152.7 cm

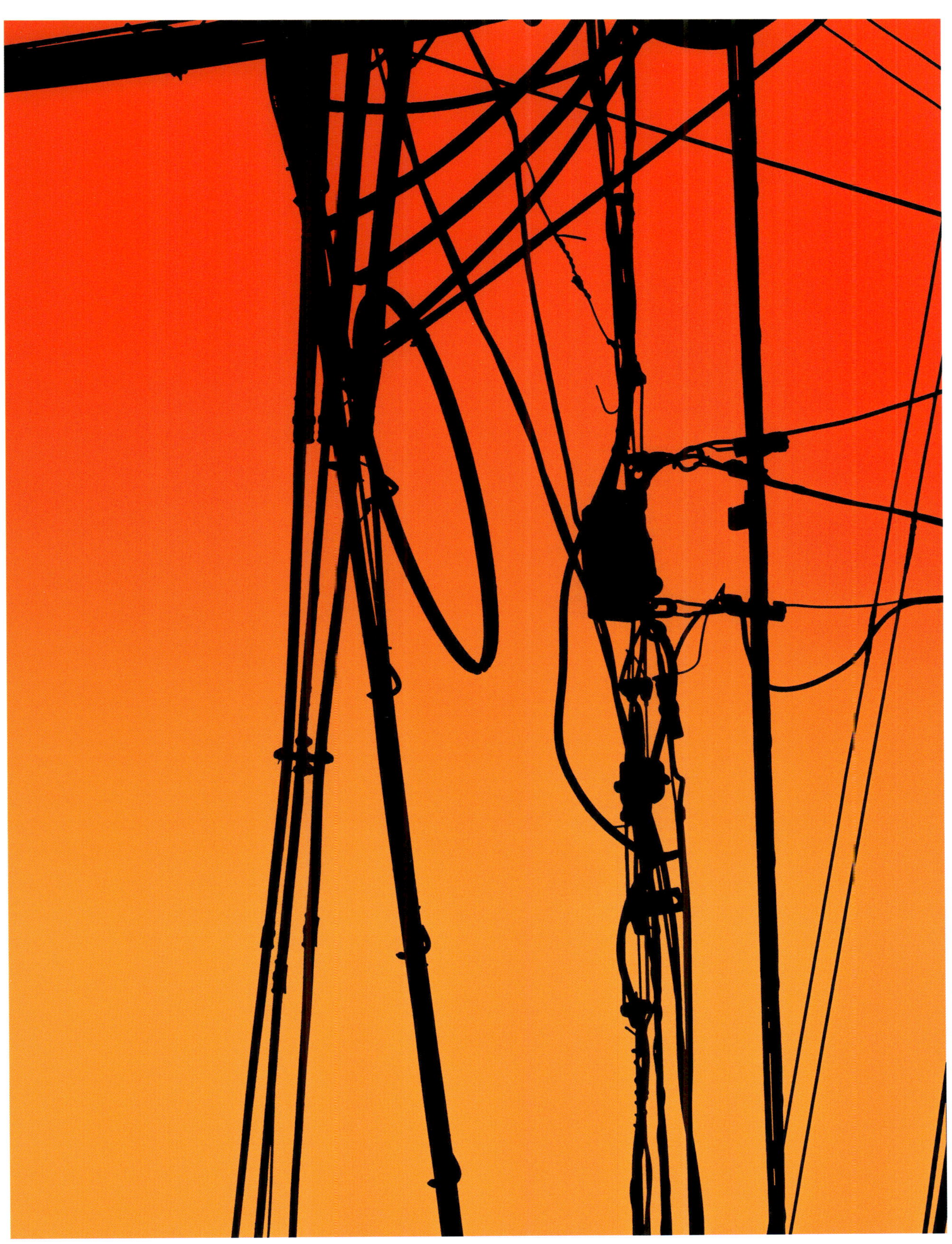

LEHMANN MAUPIN

Lehmann Maupin
US-New York, NY 10001 | 540 West 26th Street
Phone +1 212 255 29 23 | Fax +1 212 255 29 24
info@lehmannmaupin.com | www.lehmannmaupin.com
Directors Rachel Lehmann
David Maupin
Carla Camacho
Katelijne De Backer
Courtney Plummer
Stephanie Smith

Lehmann Maupin
US-New York, NY 10002 | 201 Chrystie Street
Phone +1 212 254 00 54 | Fax +1 212 254 00 55
info@lehmannmaupin.com | www.lehmannmaupin.com
Directors Rachel Lehmann
David Maupin
Carla Camacho
Katelijne De Backer
Courtney Plummer
Stephanie Smith

Artists at Art Basel Miami Beach | **Stefano Arienti**
Hernan Bas
Ashley Bickerton
Ross Bleckner
Billy Childish
Mary Corse
Tracey Emin
Teresita Fernández
Anya Gallaccio
Gilbert & George
Shirazeh Houshiary
Klara Kristalova
Lee Bul
Liu Wei
Mr.
Jun Nguyen-Hatsushiba
Angel Otero
Tony Oursler
Robin Rhode
Tim Rollins and K.O.S.
Rei Sato
Jennifer Steinkamp
Do Ho Suh
Juergen Teller
Mickalene Thomas
Adriana Varejão
Suling Wang
Nari Ward
Erwin Wurm
Mario Ybarra, Jr.

Robin Rhode
A | *School of Fish*, 2012
Photography, 9 parts,
15⅝ x 23⅜ inches each

B | *School of Fish,* 2012
Photography, 9 parts,
15⅝ x 23⅜ inches
Detail

A

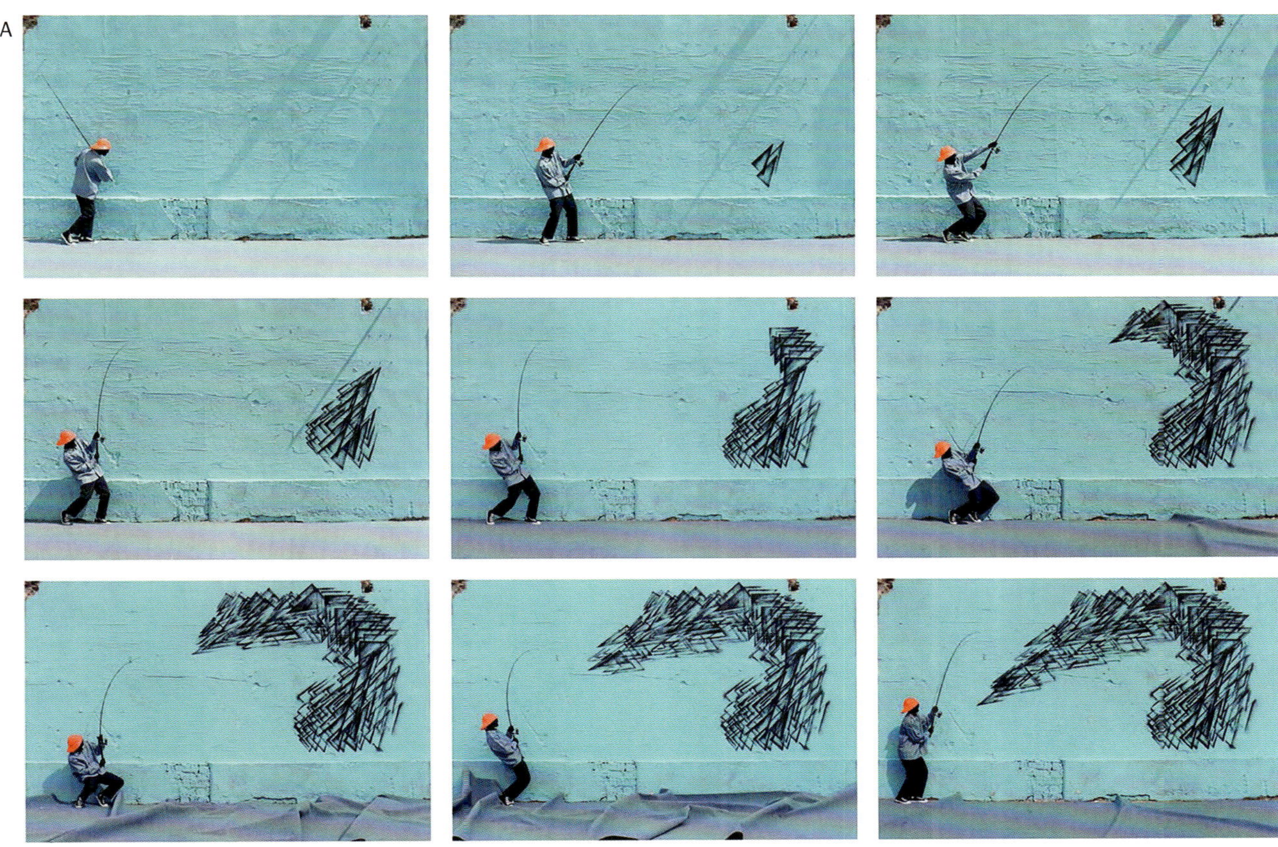

B

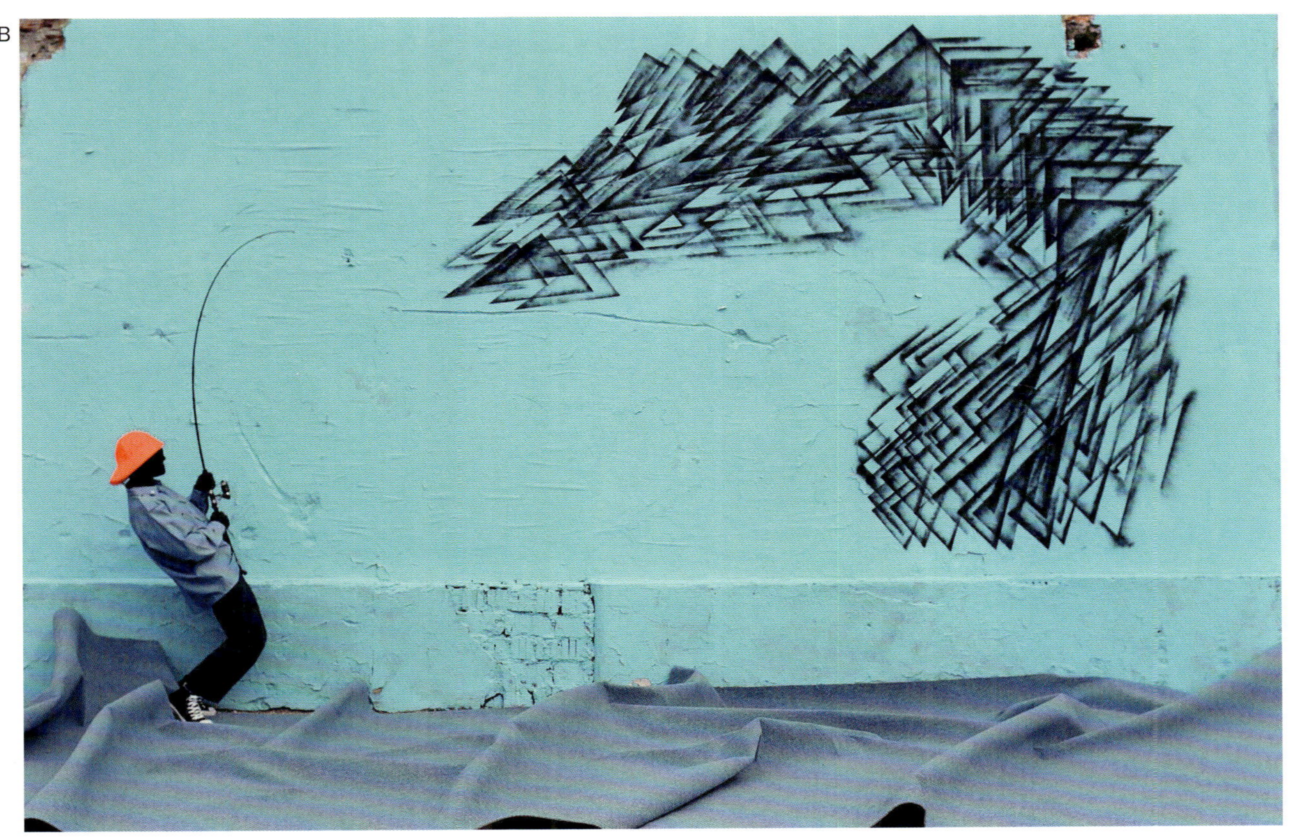

LELONG

Mobile +33 603 85 40 68, +1 917 470 83 86

Galerie Lelong
FR-75008 Paris | 13, rue de Téhéran
Phone +33 1 45 63 13 19 | Fax +33 1 42 89 34 33
info@galerie-lelong.com | www.galerie-lelong.com
Directors Daniel Lelong
Jean Frémon
Patrice Cotensin

Galerie Lelong
US-New York, NY 10001 | 528 West 26th Street
Phone +1 212 315 04 70 | Fax +1 212 262 06 24
art@galerielelong.com | www.galerielelong.com
Directors Mary Sabbatino
Lindsay Danckwerth
Dan Burns

Artists at
Art Basel Miami Beach | **Petah Coyne**
Angelo Filomeno
Günther Förg
Alfredo Jaar
Jannis Kounellis
Cildo Meireles
Ana Mendieta
Hélio Oiticica
Emilio Perez
Jaume Plensa
Kate Shepherd
Kiki Smith
Nancy Spero

Further artists represented | Eduardo Chillida
Jan Dibbets
Barry Flanagan
Andy Goldsworthy
Jane Hammond
David Hockney
Rebecca Horn
Konrad Klapheck
Rosemary Laing
Catherine Lee
Lin Tianmiao
Nalini Malani
Joan Miró
Robert Motherwell
David Nash
Arnulf Rainer
Sean Scully
Antoni Tàpies
Barthélémy Toguo
Juan Uslé
Ursula von Rydingsvard
Krzysztof Wodiczko
Catherine Yass

Jannis Kounellis
The Museum of Cycladic Art,
Nicholas and Dolly Goulandris
Foundation, Athens,
April-September 2012

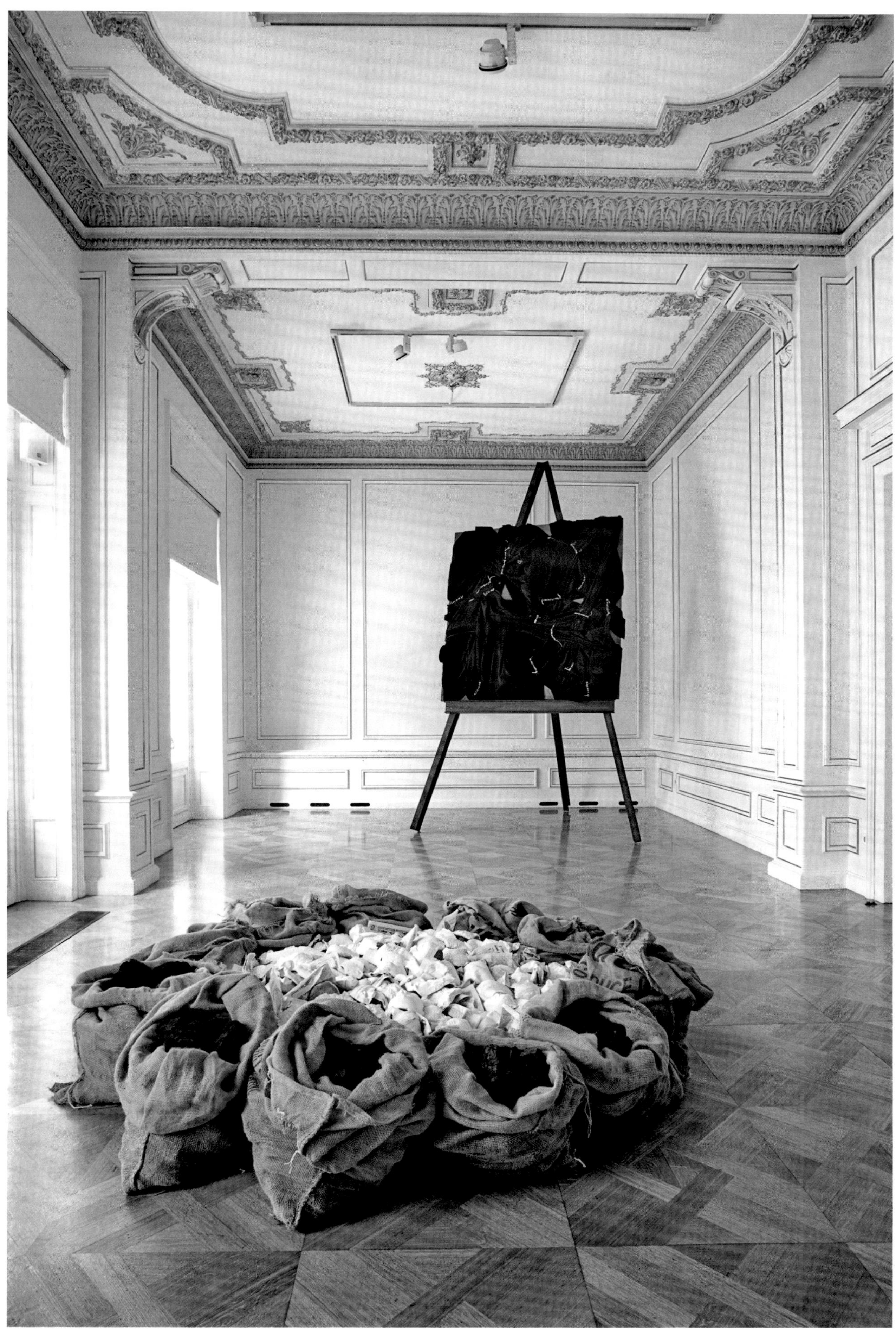

LEME

Galeria Leme
BR-São Paulo 05501-000 | Avenida Valdemar Ferreira, 130
Phone +55 11 38148184 | Fax +55 11 30938182
eduardo@galerialeme.com | www.galerialeme.com
Director Eduardo Leme

Artists at Art Nova | Gabriel Acevedo Velarde
Zilvinas Kempinas
Jessica Mein

Further artists represented | Paulo Almeida
AVPD (Aslak Vibæk & Peter Døssing)
David Batchelor
Luiz Braga
Sebastiaan Bremer
Felipe Cama
Marcia de Moraes
Ana Elisa Egreja
Richard Galpin
Sandra Gamarra
Neil Hamon
Henry Krokatsis
Mariana Manhães
Milton Marques
José Carlos Martinat
Mariana Mauricio
Flavia Metzler
Marcelo Moscheta
Patrícia Osses
Rosana Palazyan
Nina Pandolfo
Mauro Piva
Elaine Tedesco
Frank Thiel
João Pedro Vale
Gustavo Von Ha

Berlin-based Peruvian artist Gabriel Acevedo Velarde's work reflects on instances in which one's experience of objects and situations results in the materialization of boundaries. His latest projects include objects that refer to the relation between institutions and individuals, like that of a state with a citizen. Using the formal appeal of almost unnamed objects, like the concave metal piece that is used to slide money across a bank counter, Acevedo points at the recognition of our own complicity as the starting point for any political critique.

New York-based Lithuanian artist Zilvinas Kempinas presents a selection of his ongoing series of resin-cast wall pieces. Defying traditional categories of drawing, painting, or sculpture, these pieces boast intricate patterns derived from a simple, repetitive procedure. Created using either magnetic tape or polyester fibers, these complex renderings allude both to the dense symbolism of the round form (already addressed in some of his well-known kinetic works) and to the surprising potential of modular-based processes.

Living between New York and Dubai, Brazilian artist Jessica Mein presents a new, wall-sized installation, taking one step further her continuous series on discarded billboard advertisement sheets. By painstakingly punching out holes and reglueing the resulting discs, or else by cutting and pasting parts of the sheets, Mein creates new patterns and enigmatic images that preserve the appealing iconography of advertisement, while at the same time contaminating it with a subtle, not fully graspable menace of dissolution.

Zilvinas Kempinas
Nashira, 2011
MDF, nails, cotton thread, and resin, diameter 180 cm

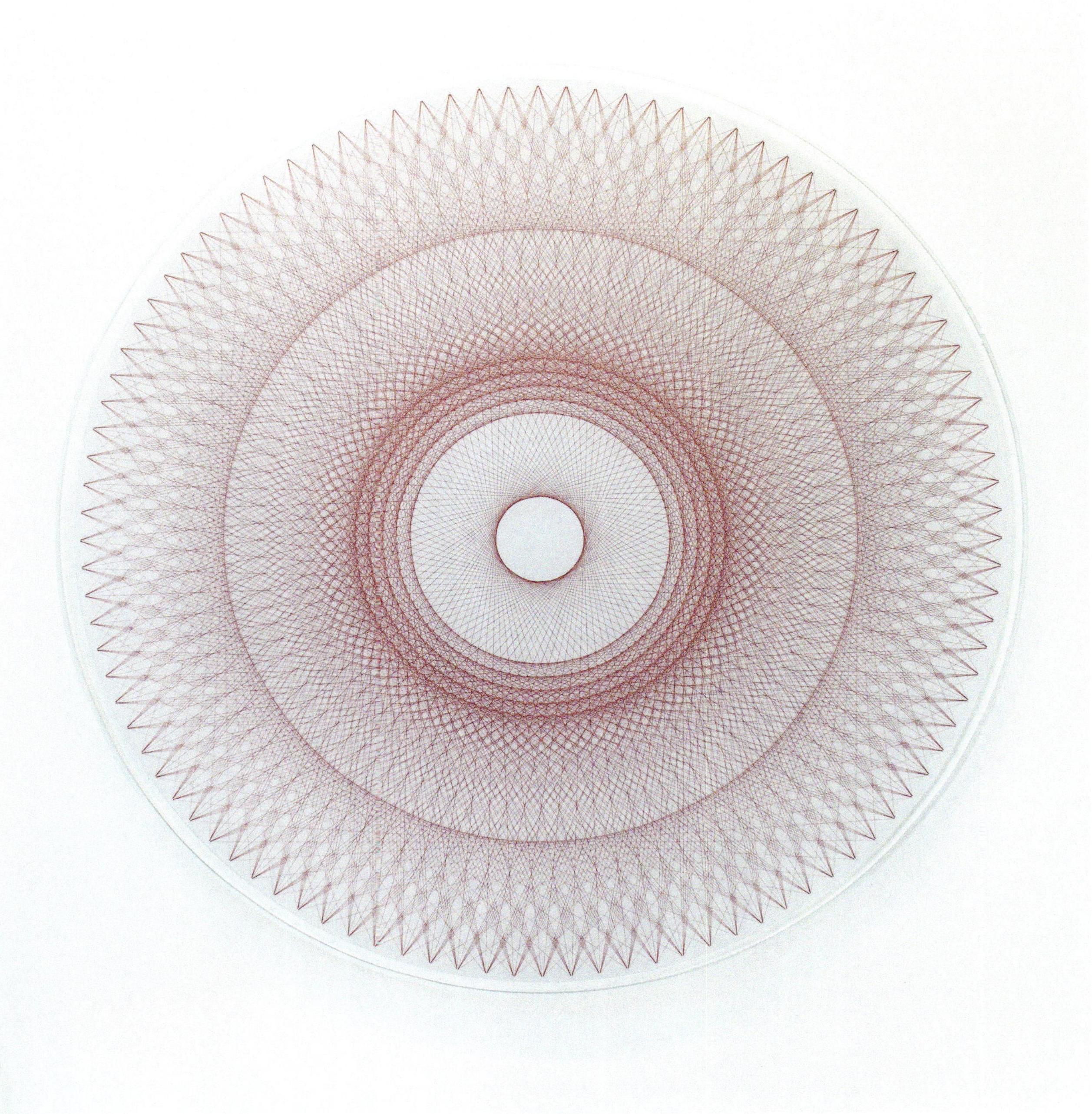

LIPRANDI

Mobile +54 911 66 66 33 86

Ignacio Liprandi Arte Contemporáneo
AR-1085 Buenos Aires | Av. de Mayo 1480 – 3º izquierdo
Phone +54 11 4381 06 79
info@ignacioliprandi.com | www.ignacioliprandi.com
Director Ignacio Liprandi

Artists at Art Nova | Pablo Accinelli
Mathieu Mercier
Jorge Pedro Núñez

Gallery Information | Ignacio Liprandi Contemporary Art is a space dedicated to the exhibition and diffusion of international contemporary art. Founded by Ignacio Liprandi in May 2009, it is characterized by a curatorial premise that articulates a program of exhibitions, participation in international fairs, and the development of a network of curators, galleries, and institutions to allow the insertion of its artists in the international circuit.

Further artists represented:
Fabián Bercic
Adriana Bustos
Alejandro Cesarco
Tomás Espina
Claudia Fontes
Ana Gallardo
Magdalena Jitrik
David Lamelas
Mauricio Lupini
Eduardo Navarro
Vijai Patchineelam
Cristina Piffer
José Alejandro Restrepo
Leandro Tartaglia

Contemporary Possibilities of Collage

Pablo Accinelli's (*1983, Buenos Aires, Argentina) collages are made of cut-out pictures of crowds from newspapers and magazines. The work can be thought of as a collective file of us all, while at the same time referring to the relationship we establish internally when we skim newspapers and magazines, and continuously watch the news without making it 'real.' The various shapes are arranged randomly in several sheets, forming different maps and fluid interactions.

Jorge Pedro Núñez's (*1976, Caracas, Venezuela) *In Advance to Broken Arms* (title after one of Duchamp's first ready-mades) are also collages: in this case from old football magazines that the artist scans and enlarges up to a 1:1 scale. Playing with the colors and designs of different shirts, Núñez creates a sort of geometric abstraction based on the human body.

Mathieu Mercier (*1970, France) associates objects of everyday use with depictions of measuring tools, encyclopedia illustrations, and pictograms intended to convey directions or instructions. All these representations are printed on white Corian pedestals. These combinations of the concrete and the abstract, the body and the geometric, bring to mind the potential of collage to yield, through addition, a third image in the mind of the viewer.

A | **Mathieu Mercier**
Untitled (Candle/J.Itten Chromatic Circle), 2012
Candle, sublimation on Corian pedestal, 117.5 x Ø 35 cm

B | **Pablo Accinelli**
Collages: Archive, 2012
Newspaper and magazine cut-outs on paper, 32 x 41 cm

C | **Jorge Pedro Núñez**
In Advance to Broken Arms, 2012
Photographic collage on paper, 120 x 150 cm

A

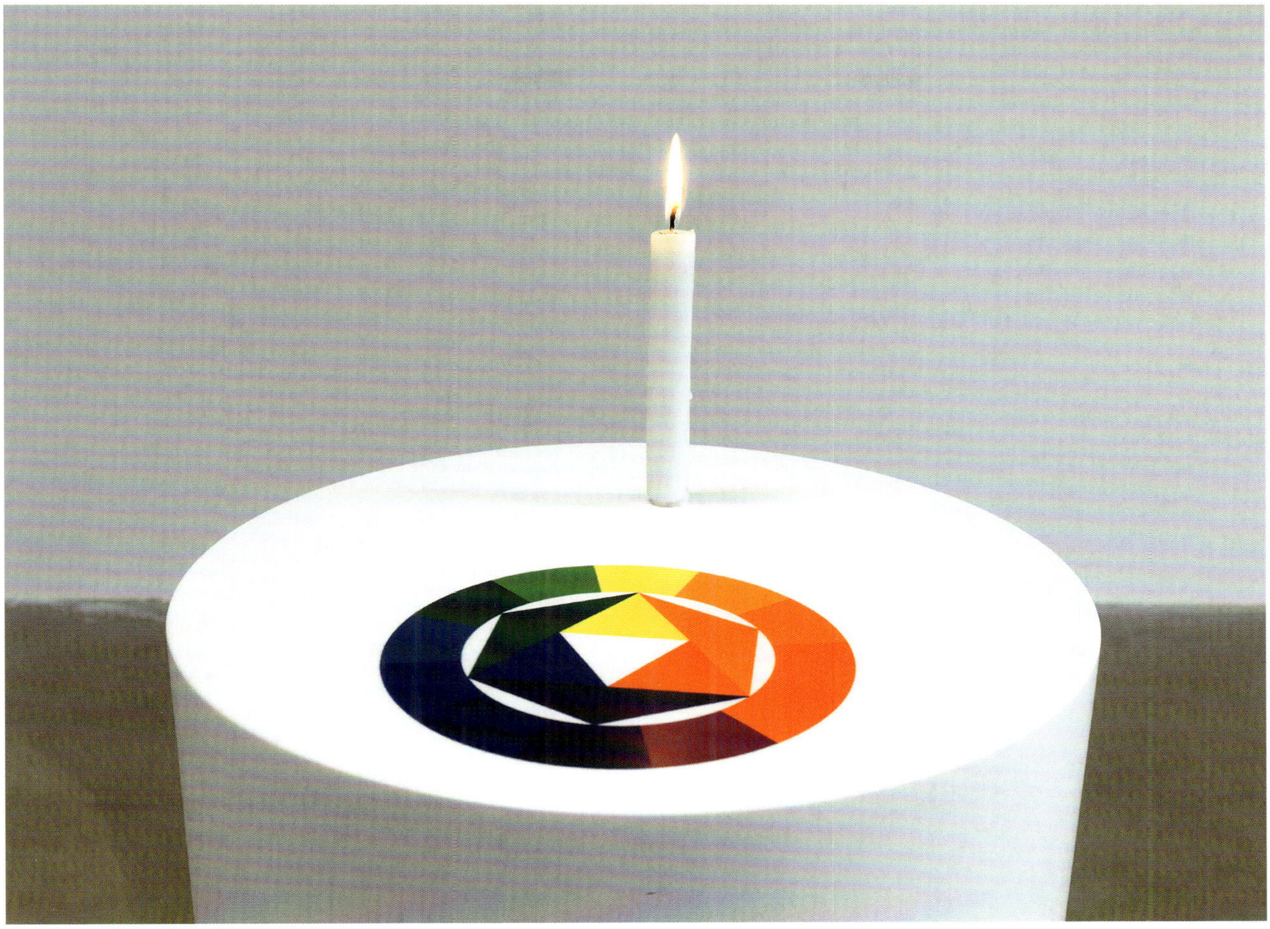

B

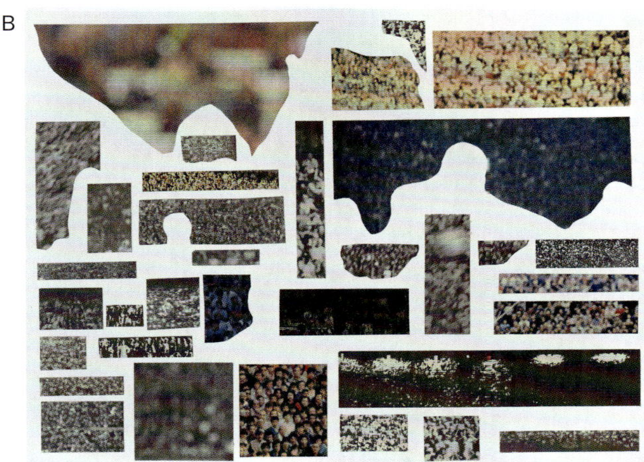

C

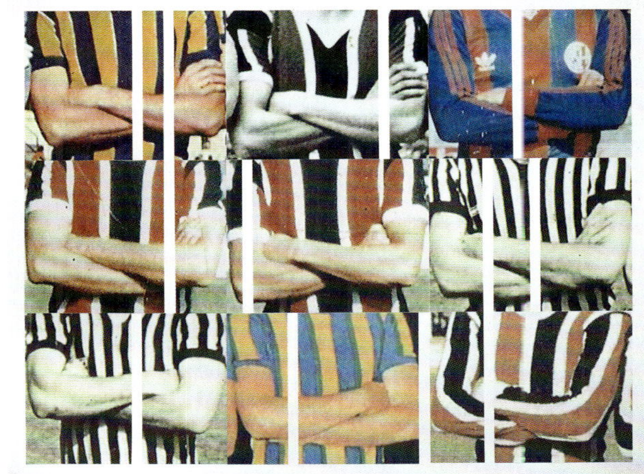

LISSON

Lisson Gallery
GB-London NW1 5DA | 29&52-54 Bell Street
Phone +44 20 77 24 27 39 | Fax +44 20 77 24 71 24
contact@lissongallery.com | www.lissongallery.com
Directors Nicholas Logsdail
Alex Logsdail
Greg Hilty
Joanna Thornberry

Lisson Gallery
IT-20123 Milan | Via Zenale, 3
Phone +39 02 89 05 06 08
milan@lissongallery.com | www.lissongallery.com
Director Annette Hofmann

Lisson Gallery
US-New York, NY 10002 | 241 Eldridge Street
Phone +1 212 505 64 31
contact@lissongallery.com | www.lissongallery.com
Directors Jeannie Freilich
Blair Brooks

Artists at
Art Basel Miami Beach | **Marina Abramović**
Ai Weiwei
Allora & Calzadilla
Cory Arcangel
Art & Language
Daniel Buren
Gerard Byrne
James Casebere
Tony Cragg
Angela de la Cruz
Richard Deacon
Spencer Finch
Ceal Floyer
Ryan Gander
Dan Graham
Rodney Graham
Carmen Herrera
Shirazeh Houshiary
Christian Jankowski
Peter Joseph
Anish Kapoor
John Latham
Tim Lee
Sol LeWitt
Liu Xiaodong
Robert Mangold
Jason Martin
Haroon Mirza
Tatsuo Miyajima
Jonathan Monk
Julian Opie
Tony Oursler
Giulio Paolini
Florian Pumhösl
Rashid Rana
Santiago Sierra
Sean Snyder
Lee Ufan
Lawrence Weiner
Richard Wentworth

Gallery Information | Established in 1967 by owner Nicholas Logsdail, Lisson Gallery has maintained its international perspective and position as one of the world's most innovative galleries.

Over the past forty-five years Lisson Gallery has identified and supported successive generations of the most significant and intellectually cutting-edge artists with radical and distinctive approaches to the artistic possibilities of their times. This includes the pioneers of Minimal Conceptualism: Sol LeWitt, Dan Graham, and Lawrence Weiner; The New British Sculptors such as Tony Cragg, Richard Deacon, and Anish Kapoor; and newer generations that include Liu Xiaodong and Ai Weiwei.

Lisson Gallery artists take prominence at the world's most important exhibitions; six Lisson Gallery artists, including Marina Abramović, Ceal Floyer, Ryan Gander, and Gerard Byrne, were included in *dOCUMENTA (13)*. Allora & Calzadilla presented the American Pavilion at the 54th Venice Biennale, where Haroon Mirza was awarded the Silver Lion for most promising young artist.

Carmen Herrera
Black and White, 2012
Acrylic on canvas, 36 x 36 inches

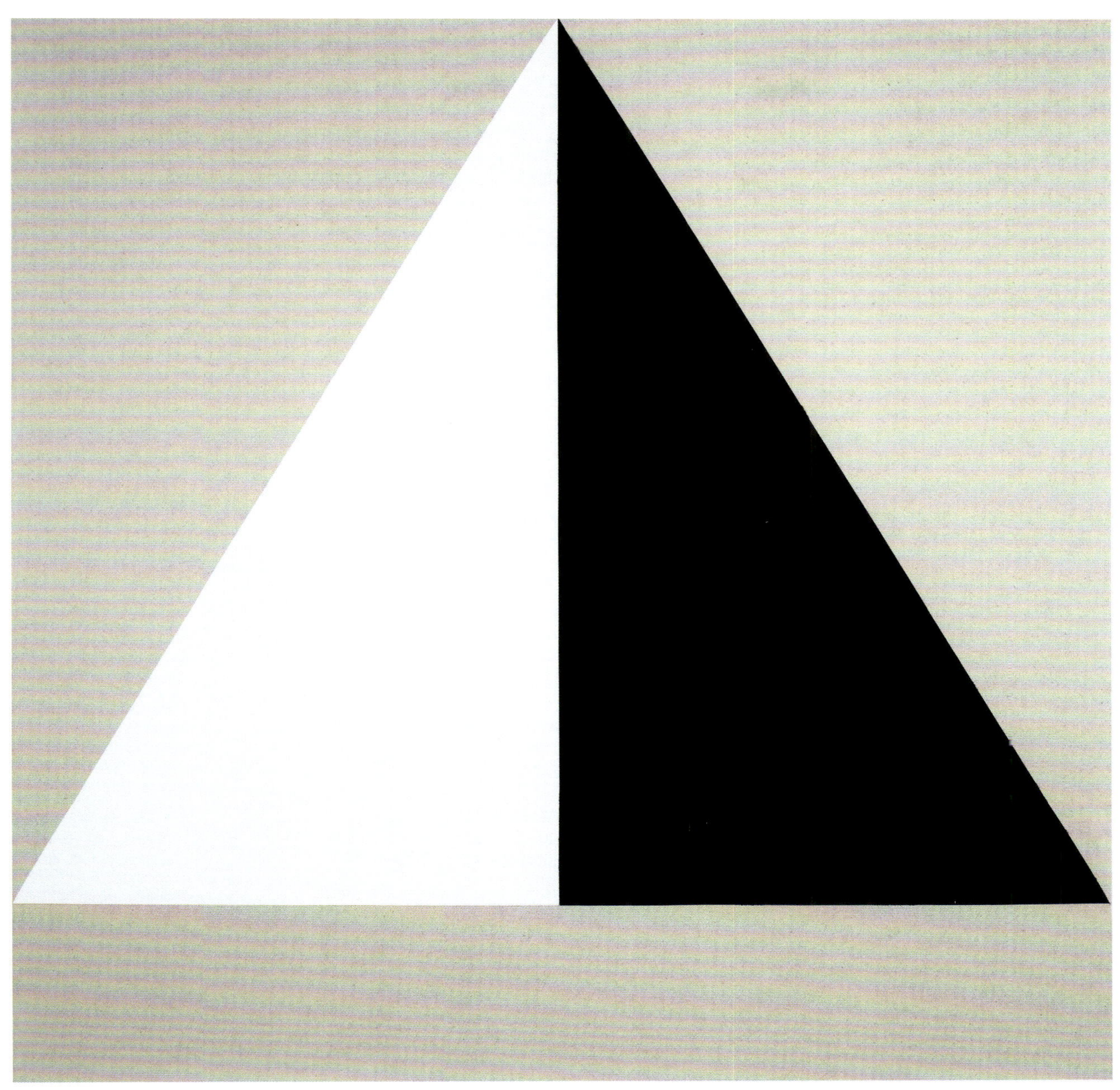

LOMBARD FREID

Lombard Freid Gallery
US-New York, NY 10011 | 518 West 19th Street
Phone +1 212 967 80 40 | Fax +1 212 967 06 69
info@lombardfreid.com | www.lombardfreid.com
Directors Jane Lombard
Lea Freid
Lisa Carlson

Artists at Art Nova | Lee Kit
Kemang Wa Lehulere
Nina Yuen

Further artists represented | Haig Aivazian
Cao Fei
Motoyuki Daifu
Mounir Fatmi
William Earl Kofmehl III
Ulrich Lamsfuss
Lee Mingwei
Eko Nugroho
Dan Perjovschi
Ana Prvacki
Michael Rakowitz
Mona Vatamanu & Florin Tudor

Lombard Freid Gallery features new work by three rising artists Kemang Wa Lehulere (Capetown, South Africa), Lee Kit (Hong Kong), and Nina Yuen (Hawaii, US) in *Confessions.* An intimate and deeply personal exploration of identity, daily ritual, and revelation brings together these artists of diverse cultural and geographic backgrounds. 'Confessions' provides a common ground to share their unique relationships with history, objects, and people in their lives by utilizing performance, video, and drawing. Having the affects of time as an overarching theme, their stories have emerged from many outward changes, be it political, economical or social, but always focusing on the personal. Their inwardness and earnestness evoke this slightly gloomy but highly immersive atmosphere embracing the visitors.

Kemang Wa Lehulere (*1984, Capetown, South Africa) addresses his cultural inheritance and its relationship to the ongoing historical amnesia that continues to pervade aspects of daily life in South Africa. Wa Lehulere, now in his late 20s, experienced apartheid and his work acts as witness to a close past haunted with unexplainable acts of brutality. With a background in theater, writing, and performance, his innate storytelling abilities are powerfully employed in his street-raw, darkly comic-like wall murals, and ink drawings. Reminiscent of storyboards, they are concurrently witty and threatening. The result is unnerving, offering just enough information to perplex the viewer, yet presenting no resolution.

Similarly, Nina Yuen (*1981, Hawaii) mines past histories of anonymous and known characters and creates poetic narrative short films. Enchanting and hauntingly beautiful, Yuen's work is addictive to watch and listen to, engaging the viewer in a diaristic series of events and original voice. Obsessions with false personal memories, stirring family disagreements, and anonymous stories culled from local newspapers pervade her work. In her most recent short films, she reexamines themes of memory and teen confession by featuring high school students grappling with universally complex themes of childhood, rites of passage, and loss. Yuen's *The School* (2012) inadvertently teaches students about death, not by a lesson plan, but by descriptions of experiences of lives going terribly wrong. Like Wa Lehulere's revisiting the past, *The School* beautifully unfolds into a moment when the students turn to the teacher with a question that the teacher cannot answer.

Growing up in Hong Kong during the time when the territory returned to Chinese rule, Lee Kit (*1978, Hong Kong) articulates questions of meaning and identity through a love affair with western consumer products. Conceptually Lee's work is about imbuing meaningless everyday things, activities, and obsessions with desire and incorporating them into daily life. His home is his studio, which is in constant change as his works travel to exhibitions. The repetitive practice in creating hand-painted patterned tablecloths to be used for picnics or dinners with friends, painting of lyrics from Sonic Youth, Velvet Underground, and Carpenters songs onto pillowcases and sheets transform these utilitarian household items into confessional artifacts of Hong Kong life.

Lee's installation features a glimpse into his personal life and also creates a cozy personal space not only for himself but also Yuen and Wa Lehulere where intimate stories are shared with the viewer.

A | **Kemang Wa Lehulere**
Remembering the Future of a Hole as a Verb 1, 2010
Chalk on black acrylic paint, nails, plastic string, soil, afro-combs, red velvet pillows, video, dimensions variable
Installation/performance at Kwazulu Natal Society of Arts, Durban

B | **Lee Kit**
Johnson's (Johnson's), 2011
Acrylic, emulsion paint, and inkjet ink on cardboard, 44½ x 33⅞ inches, 113 x 86 cm

C | **Nina Yuen**
Heather Who?, 2011
Single-channel video, 4 min
Still

A

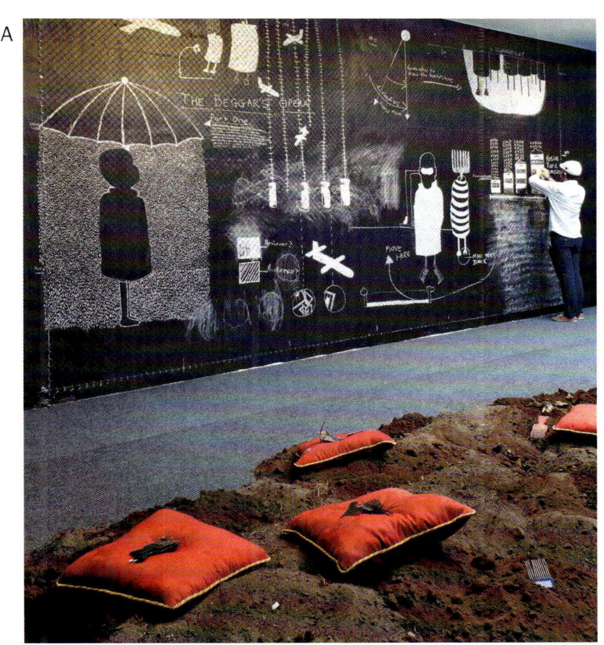

B

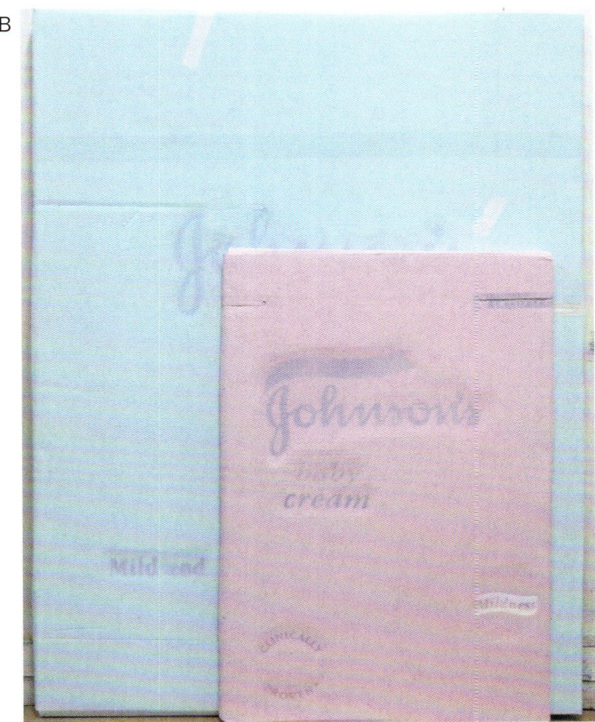

C

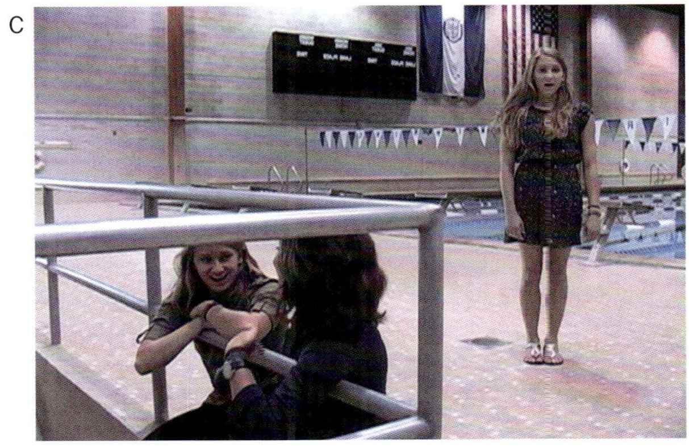

LONG MARCH

Long March Space
CN-100015 Beijing | 4 Jiuxianqiao Road, Chaoyang District
Phone +86 10 59 78 97 68 | Fax +86 10 59 78 97 64
lm@longmarchspace.com | www.longmarchspace.com
Directors Lu Jie
David Tung
Li Danqing

Artists at Art Basel Miami Beach | **Liu Wei**
MadeIn Company
Wu Shanzhuan
Wu Shanzhuan & Inga Svala Thorsdottir
Yang Shaobin
Zhan Wang
Zhang Hui

Gallery Information | Founded by Lu Jie in the 798 Art District of Beijing in 2002, Long March Space plays a vital role in pursuing new avenues of production, discourse, and promotion of contemporary art in China. Working to advance the careers of 18 artists across three generations, the gallery looks to establish a portfolio of the most progressive artists working in contemporary China today.

Long March Space has produced over 80 exhibitions and projects in its ten-year history. The gallery tirelessly revolutionizes the ways in which art is perceived and presented, offering one of the most comprehensive resource platforms for the local arts community in China.

Long March Space represents artists who are considered to be at the forefront of contemporary art, working in diverse mediums from painting, sculpture, installation, and video to performance.

As one of the first China-based galleries participating in prominent international art fairs, Long March Space shows actively both locally and internationally, including at Art Basel, Art Basel Miami Beach, Art Hong Kong, and Frieze Art Fair London and New York.

Further artists represented: Chen Chieh-Jen
Guo Fengyi
Hu Xiangqian
Li Tianbing
Ran Huang
Wang Jianwei
Wang Sishun
Xu Zhen
Yu Hong
Zhou Xiaohu
Zhu Yu

Zhang Hui
Neon, 2012
Acrylic on canvas, 190 x 259 cm

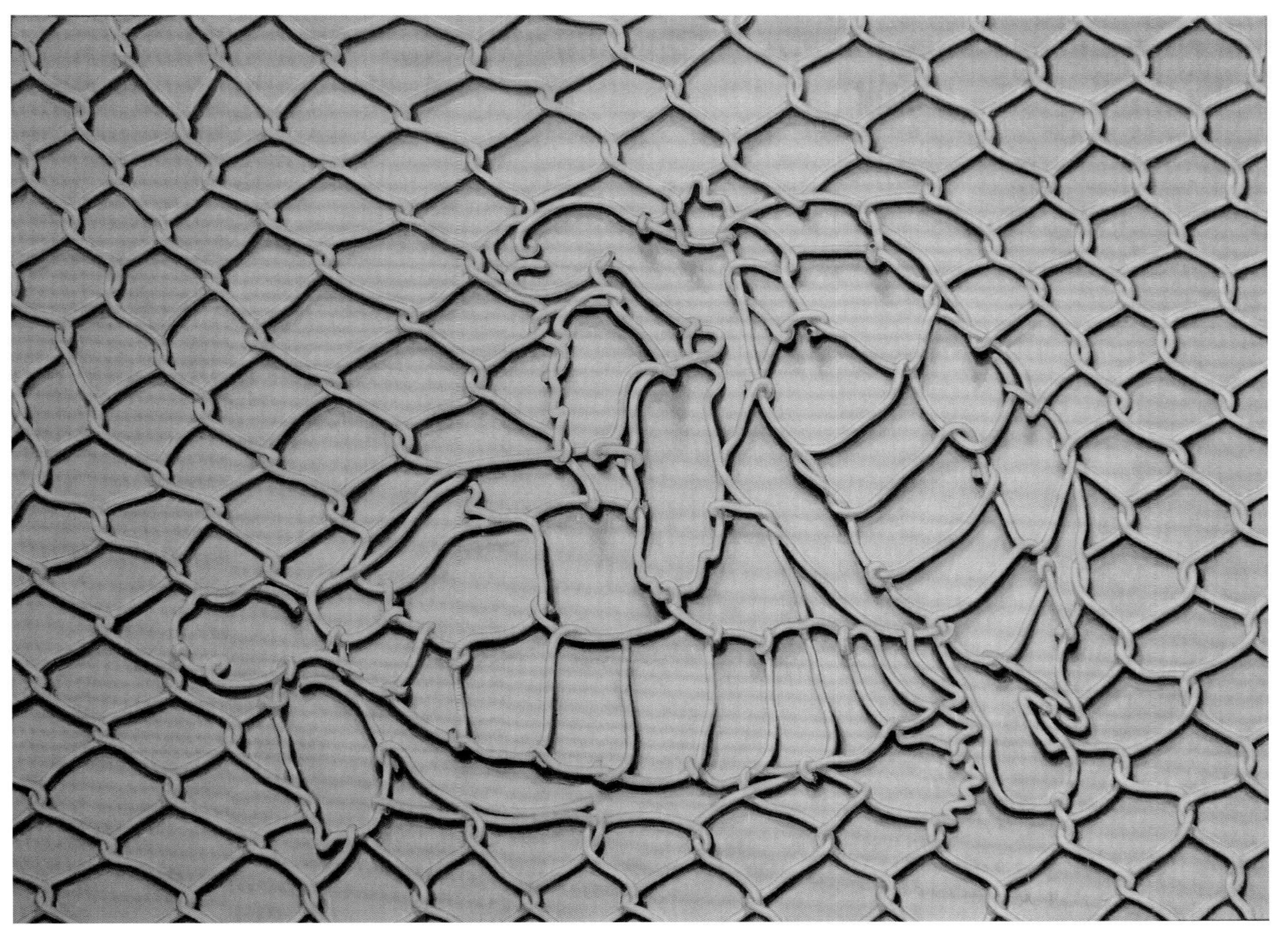

LUHRING AUGUSTINE

Luhring Augustine
US-New York, NY 10011 | 531 West 24th Street
Phone +1 212 206 91 00 | Fax +1 212 206 90 55
info@luhringaugustine.com | www.luhringaugustine.com
Directors Natalia Sacasa
Vanessa Critchell
Kristen Becker
Lisa Varghese
Lauren Wittels

Artists at
Art Basel Miami Beach | **Janine Antoni**
Charles Atlas
Janet Cardiff & George Bures Miller
Larry Clark
William Daniels
Tom Friedman
Zarina Hashmi
Johannes Kahrs
Ragnar Kjartansson
Luisa Lambri
Elad Lassry
Glenn Ligon
Yasumasa Morimura
Daido Moriyama
Reinhard Mucha
David Musgrave
Michelangelo Pistoletto
Pipilotti Rist
Josh Smith
Joel Sternfeld
Tunga
Guido van der Werve
Rachel Whiteread
Steve Wolfe
Christopher Wool

Gallery Information | The gallery was founded in 1985 by co-owners Lawrence R. Luhring and Roland J. Augustine. Its principal focus is the representation of an international group of contemporary artists whose diverse practices include painting, drawing, sculpture, video, and photography.

Each artist of the gallery has exhibited widely in museum and gallery contexts and has been regularly included in international exhibitions such as the Venice Biennale, The Carnegie International, and *Documenta.* The exhibition program is best characterized by its adherence to a rigorous curatorial model that has incorporated critical monographic exhibitions such as *Marcel Duchamp* (1987), *Gerhard Richter* (1995), *Donald Judd* (1999), and *Martin Kippenberger* (2005), which have served as historical antecedents for the contemporary program of the gallery.

Since its founding, the gallery has also specialized in the resale of select works of art from the 20th century by artists such as Pablo Picasso, Jackson Pollock, Andy Warhol, Gerhard Richter, and Sigmar Polke. As a member of the Art Dealers Association of America (ADAA) the gallery subscribes to the highest standard of connoisseurship, scholarship, and ethical practice, and offers an effective and confidential alternative for the resale of important works of art from and on behalf of private individuals and institutions.

Joel Sternfeld
New York City (#1), 1976,
print: 2011
Pigment print, 13 x 17¼ x 1½ inches
Edition of 5 + 2 AP

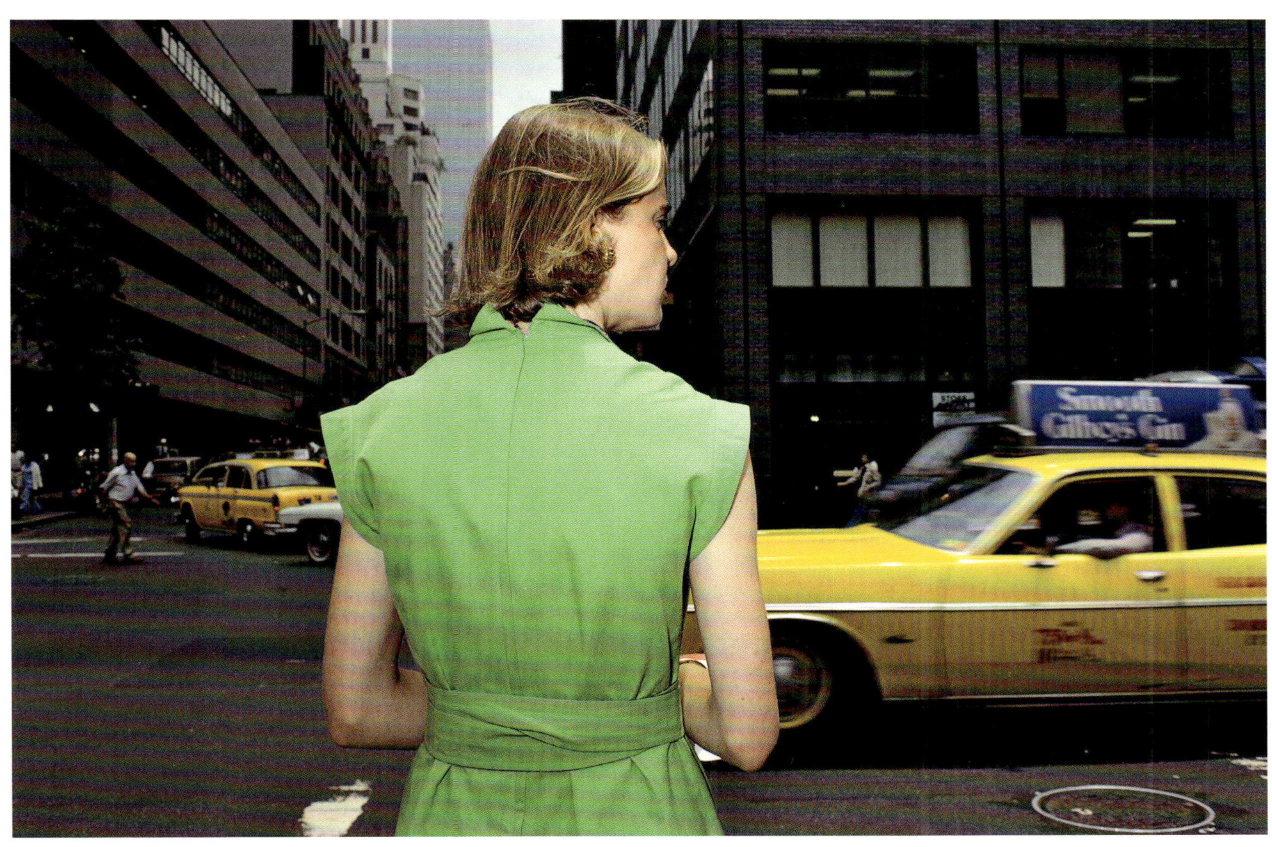
Smooth
Gilbey's Gin

MAGAZZINO

Mobile +39 335 4338 74, +39 339 766 62 40

Magazzino
IT-00186 Rome | Via dei Prefetti 17
Phone +39 06 687 59 51 | Fax +39 06 68 13 56 35
info@magazzinoartemoderna.com | www.magazzinoartemoderna.com
Directors Mauro Nicoletti
Gabriele Gaspari
Tanya Tikhnenko

Artists at
Art Basel Miami Beach | **Massimo Bartolini**
Elisabetta Benassi
Antonio Biasiucci
Pedro Cabrita Reis
Mircea Cantor
Jonas Dahlberg
Jan Fabre
Alberto Garutti
Gianluca Malgeri
Domenico Mangano
Aleksandra Mir
Jeannette Montgomery Barron
Jorge Peris
Alessandro Piangiamore
Daniele Puppi
Serge Spitzer
Ouattara Watts

Gallery Information | Further information on the illustration:

In this work, Mircea Cantor uses an iconic part of the city of Rome, the basilica of St Peter's, reduced to its essential structure, a wooden frame made with traditional Romanian artisanal techniques, to which, however, is added an extraneous element, an instrument that moves marionettes. The double reference multiplies the potential meanings and creates tension between them: spirituality and falseness; the eternal and the ephemeral; great art and theatrical illusion. The emblem of Catholic tradition thus transforms itself into a device in order to compromise the traditional – and authoritarian – idea of a monument and at the same time to rediscover the unseen potential of a 'form' perhaps worn out from overuse. Thus lowering what is normally on high, the artist reminds us that history needs to be continually reinvented.

Mircea Cantor
Anima, 2012
Wood, rope, 770 x 750 x 1000 cm
Exhibition view, *Sic Transit Gloria Mundi,* MACRO Museum of Contemporary Art, Rome

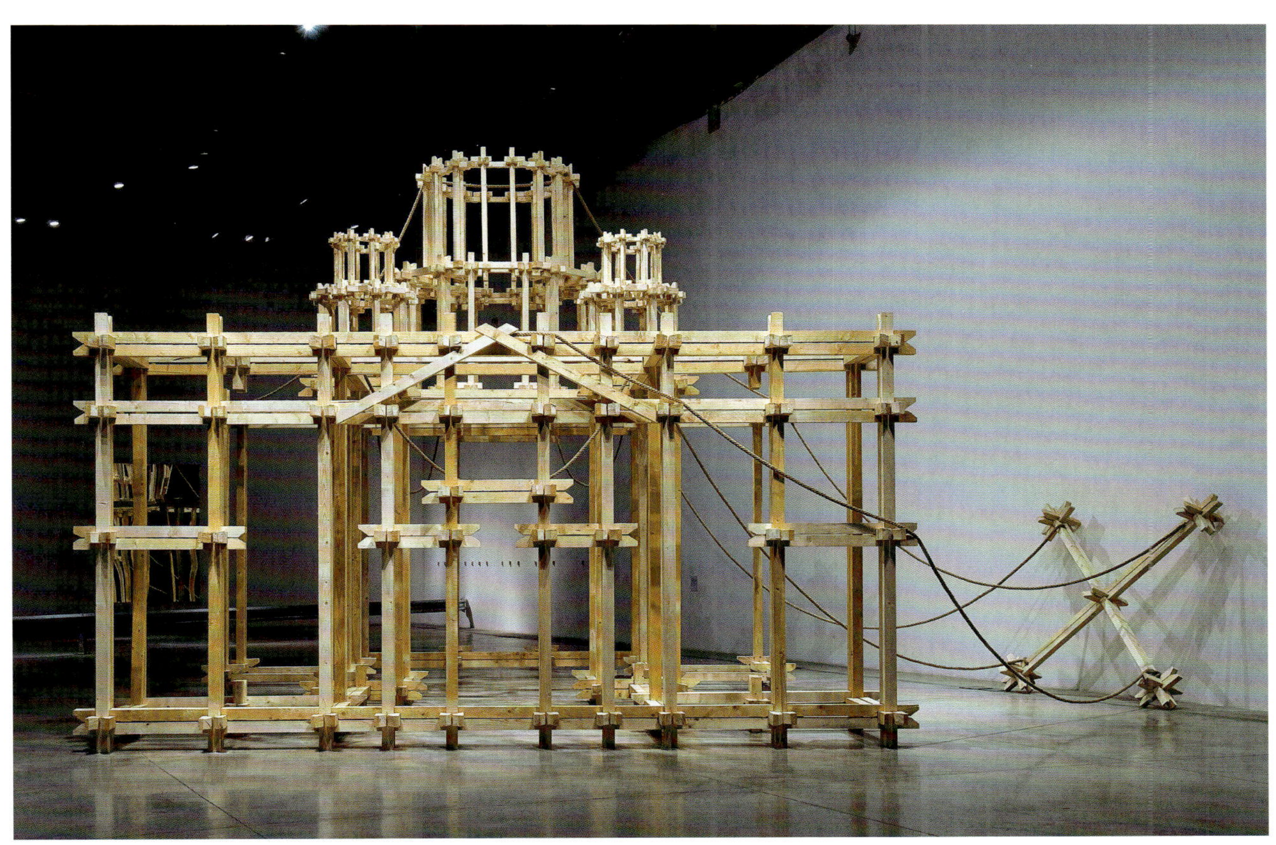

MAI 36

Mobile +41 76 322 50 24

Mai 36 Galerie
CH-8001 Zurich | Rämistrasse 37
Phone +41 44 261 68 80 | Fax +41 44 261 68 81
mail@mai36.com | www.mai36.com
Director Victor Gisler

Artists at
Art Basel Miami Beach | **Franz Ackermann**
John Baldessari
Stephan Balkenhol
Raúl Cordero
Jürgen Drescher
Flavio Garciandía
Matt Mullican
Michel Pérez El Pollo
Thomas Ruff
Paul Thek

Further artists represented | Ian Anüll
Matthew Benedict
Troy Brauntuch
Pedro Cabrita Reis
Ernst Caramelle
Koenraad Dedobbeleer
Roe Ethridge
Pia Fries
General Idea
Luigi Ghirri
Jitka Hanzlová
Robert Mapplethorpe
Rita McBride
Harald F. Müller
Manfred Pernice
Magnus Plessen
Glen Rubsamen
Christoph Rütimann
Stefan Thiel
Daan van Golden
Lawrence Weiner
Rémy Zaugg
Matthias Zinn

Thomas Ruff
ma.r.s.01_III, 2011
C-print, Diasec Face,
255 x 185 cm
Edition of 3 + 1 AP

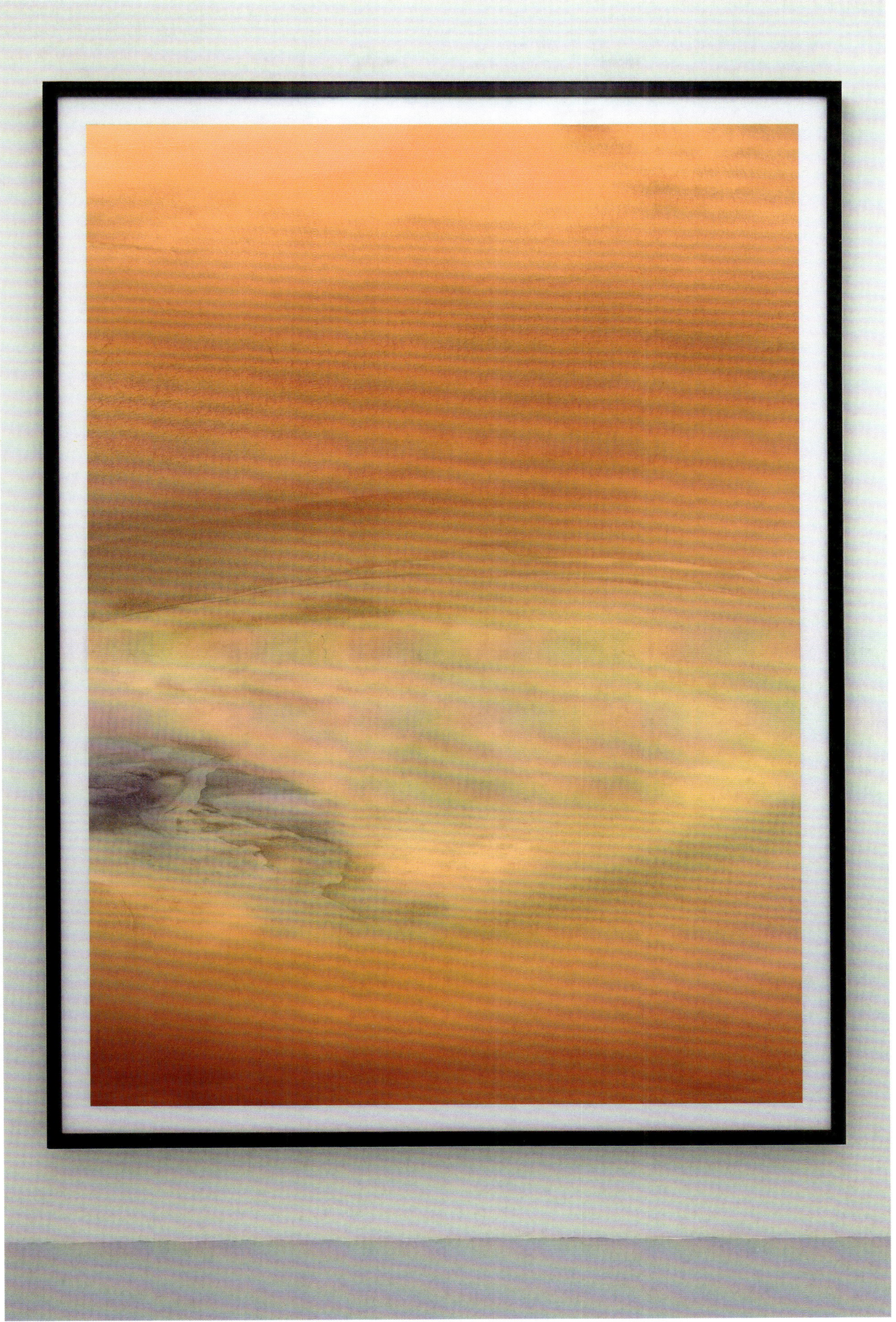

MAISTERRAVALBUENA

Mobile +34 66 441 42 96

Maisterravalbuena
ES-28012 Madrid | Doctor Fourquet 6
Phone +34 91 173 30 34
galeria@maisterravalbuena.com | www.maisterravalbuena.com
Directors Pedro Maisterra
Belén Valbuena

Artists at Art Nova | A Kassen
Karmelo Bermejo
Néstor Sanmiguel Diest

Further artists represented | Antonio Ballester Moreno
Ana Cardoso
Regina De Miguel
Kate Gilmore
Claire Harvey
Maria Loboda
Erlea Maneros Zabala
Hiraki Sawa
Kateřina Šedá
Cristián Silva

A Kassen's uncanny actions are not always perceptible at first sight, but their work ultimately takes on the form of performative installations and sculptures that succeed in altering the viewer's perception, with an added dose of humor. Testing the boundaries between what is considered art and what is not, they often draw upon references to 1960s conceptual art in their critical reflections on the absurdity of situations that arise in specific contexts, both artistic and mundane.

Karmelo Bermejo's work is concentrated in finding the ways that put in evidence certain economies of value – commercial value or prestige – of the visible/invisible structures of contemporary art and their private or public funding. Bermejo has set in motion a mechanism that ultimately underlines the superstructure of the raw consumer economy to the extent that it generates the paradox of it folding into itself and financing the celebration of its own destruction. The logic of his actions and works refers to a critical waste: the manipulation of the luxury economy that exists around every work of art.

Néstor Sanmiguel Diest is one of those artists associated with slowness. Allied perhaps with the *différend* of Lyotard, he seems to identify with that tradition that drives artists to exhibit their growth as a perhaps unique way of doing things. Time and its use are one of the main elements in the construction of his work. Paintings, sculptures, actions, installations, solo pieces, and group works all reveal his creative position, which has always been critical.

A Kassen
Door#2, 2012
Glass, wood, metal,
116 x 90 x 35 cm

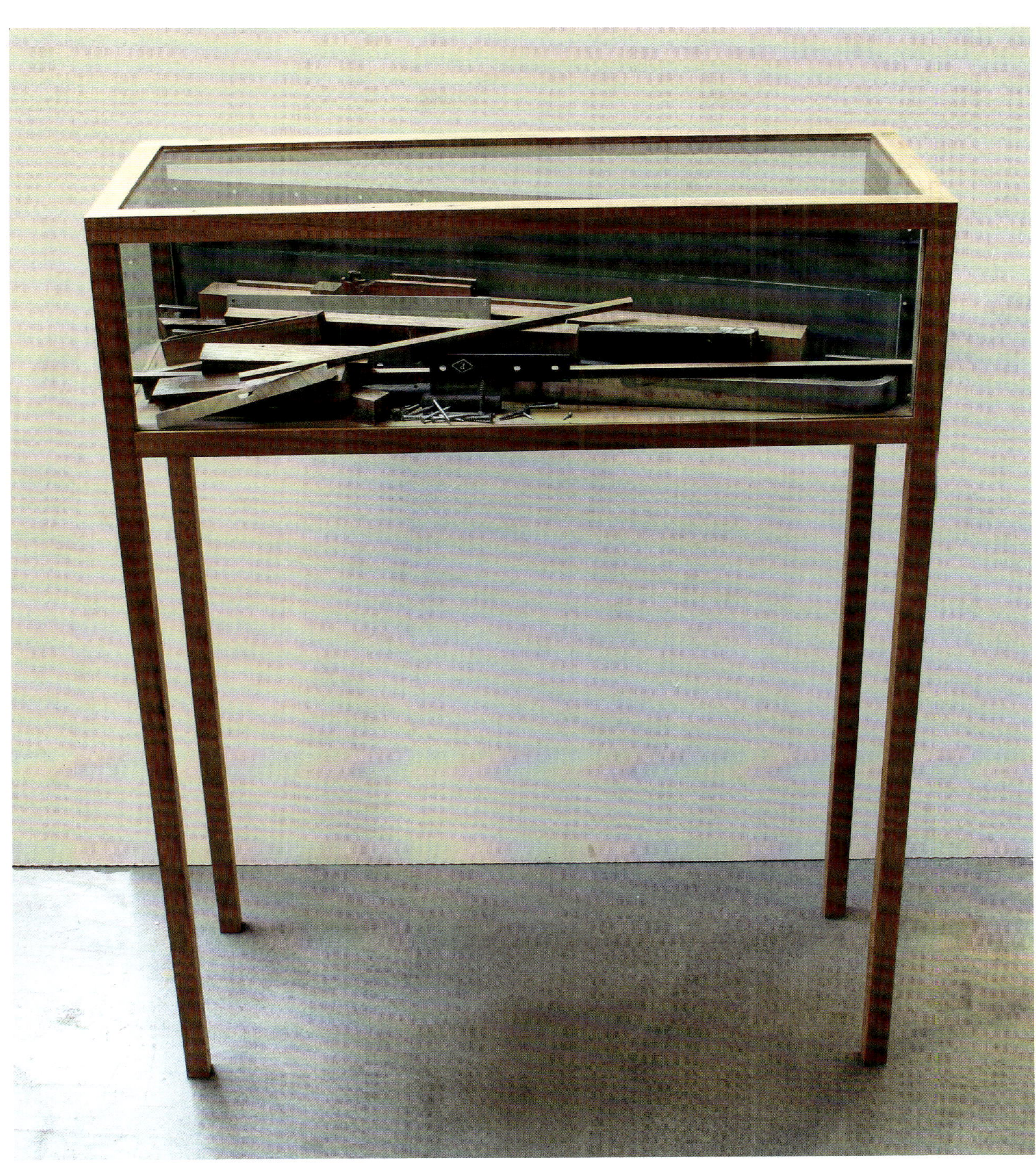

MARA LA RUCHE

Mobile +54 911 44 35 11 63

Galería Jorge Mara – La Ruche
AR-C1018ADC Buenos Aires | Paraná 1133
Phone +54 11 48 13 05 52 | Fax +54 11 48 13 39 09
info@jorgemaralaruche.com.ar | www.jorgemaralaruche.com.ar
Directors Jorge Mara
Nelly Corral

Artists at
Art Basel Miami Beach | **Horacio Coppola**
Sarah Grilo
Alfredo Hlito
Macaparana
Amalia Nieto
Ana Sacerdote
Grete Stern
Eduardo Stupía

Gallery Information | The Jorge Mara – La Ruche gallery, which was inaugurated in late 2001, is a new space continuing the tradition of the Jorge Mara gallery renowned in Buenos Aires in the 1980s and in Madrid from 1990 to 1998.

Exhibits in Spain in the 1990s included: *Millares sobre papel; Feito año 1960; Guerrero en Nueva York; Henri Michaux; Mark Tobey; Ben Nicholson; Rafael Barradas; Estrada; Washington Barcala;* and *Zoran Music,* among others; and in Argentina in the 1980s: *Alfredo Guttero; Aizenberg y el surrealismo;* and *La Nueva Figuración: De la Vega, Maccio, Deira, Noe,* among others.

The following artists have exhibited in the new Jorge Mara – La Ruche space: Kirin, Fidel Sclavo, Carlos Arnaiz, Eduardo Stupía, Estrada, César Paternosto, Fernando Maza, Alfredo Hlito, Sarah Grilo, José Antonio Fernández-Muro, Amalia Nieto, Henri Michaux, León Ferrari, etc. All have exhibited abroad and are represented by us. We also represent the work of two outstanding photographers: Grete Stern and Horacio Coppola.

We have also mounted joint exhibitions with the Museo de Arte Latinoamericano de Buenos Aires (MALBA), the Instituto Moreira Salles in Brazil, the Fundación Telefónica in Spain, the Círculo de Bellas Artes in Madrid, and the Instituto Valenciano de Arte Moderno (IVAM), Valencia, Spain.

Further artists represented: Carmelo Arden-Quin
Carlos Arnaiz
Adolfo Estrada
José Antonio Fernández-Muro
León Ferrari
Kirin
Juan Lecuona
Fidel Sclavo

Ana Sacerdote
Untitled, 1966
Oil on canvas, 80 x 76 cm

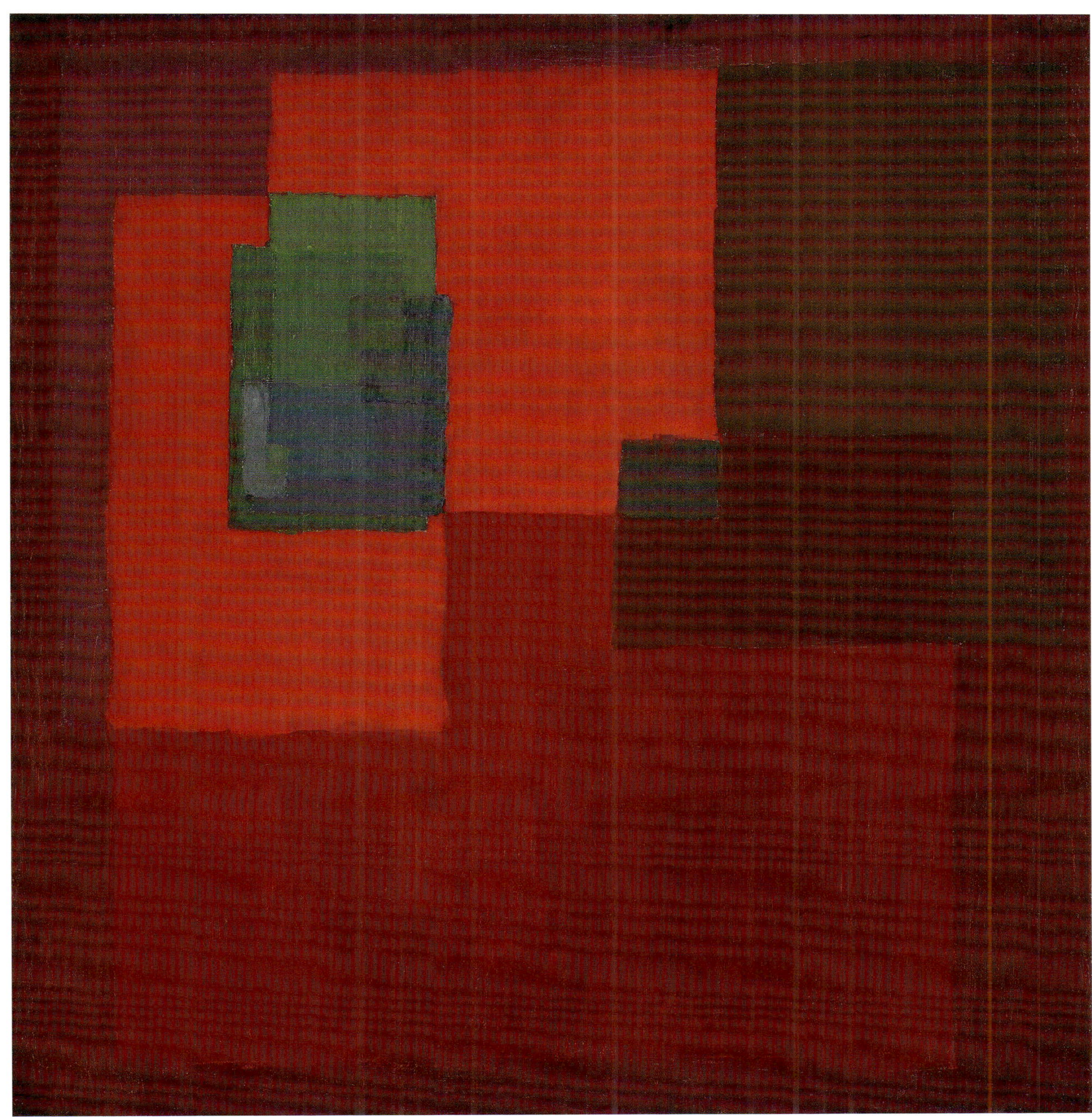

MARKS

Matthew Marks Gallery
US-New York, NY 10011 | 502, 522 and 526 West 22nd Street
Phone +1 212 2430200 | Fax +1 212 2430047
info@matthewmarks.com | www.matthewmarks.com
Directors Jeffrey Peabody
Stephanie Dorsey
Jacqueline Tran

Matthew Marks Gallery
US-Los Angeles, CA 90046 | 1062 North Orange Grove
Phone +1 323 6541830 | Fax +1 212 2430047
Directors Adrian Rosenfeld
Victoria Cuthbert Quinn

Artists at
Art Basel Miami Beach | **Robert Adams**
Darren Almond
Nayland Blake
Peter Cain
Thomas Demand
Vincent Fecteau
Peter Fischli/David Weiss
Lucian Freud
Katharina Fritsch
Luigi Ghirri
Robert Gober
Nan Goldin
Martin Honert
Peter Hujar
Gary Hume
Jasper Johns
Ellsworth Kelly
Brice Marden
Ken Price
Charles Ray
Paul Sietsema
Tony Smith
Anne Truitt
Rebecca Warren
Terry Winters

Gallery Information | Exhibitions 2012:

New York: Terry Winters, February-April
Anne Truitt, February-April
Brice Marden, April-June
Gary Hume, May/June
Thomas Demand, May-July
Tony Smith, September/October
Robert Adams, September-November
Charles Ray, November/December

Los Angeles: Ellsworth Kelly, January-April
Charles Ray, April-June
Darren Almond, Katharina Fritsch, Martin Honert, Gary Hume, Paul Sietsema, Rebecca Warren, Terry Winters, July/August
Ken Price, September/October
Jasper Johns, November/December

Exhibitions 2013:

New York: Darren Almond, February-April
Nayland Blake, February-April
Luigi Ghirri, February-April
Ellsworth Kelly, May/June

Los Angeles: Robert Gober, January-April
Nan Goldin, April-June

Katharina Fritsch
Heiligenfigur (St. Michael)/
Figure of a Saint (St. Michael),
2009-2012
Polyester, paint,
66½ x 26 x 22 inches,
169 x 66 x 57 cm

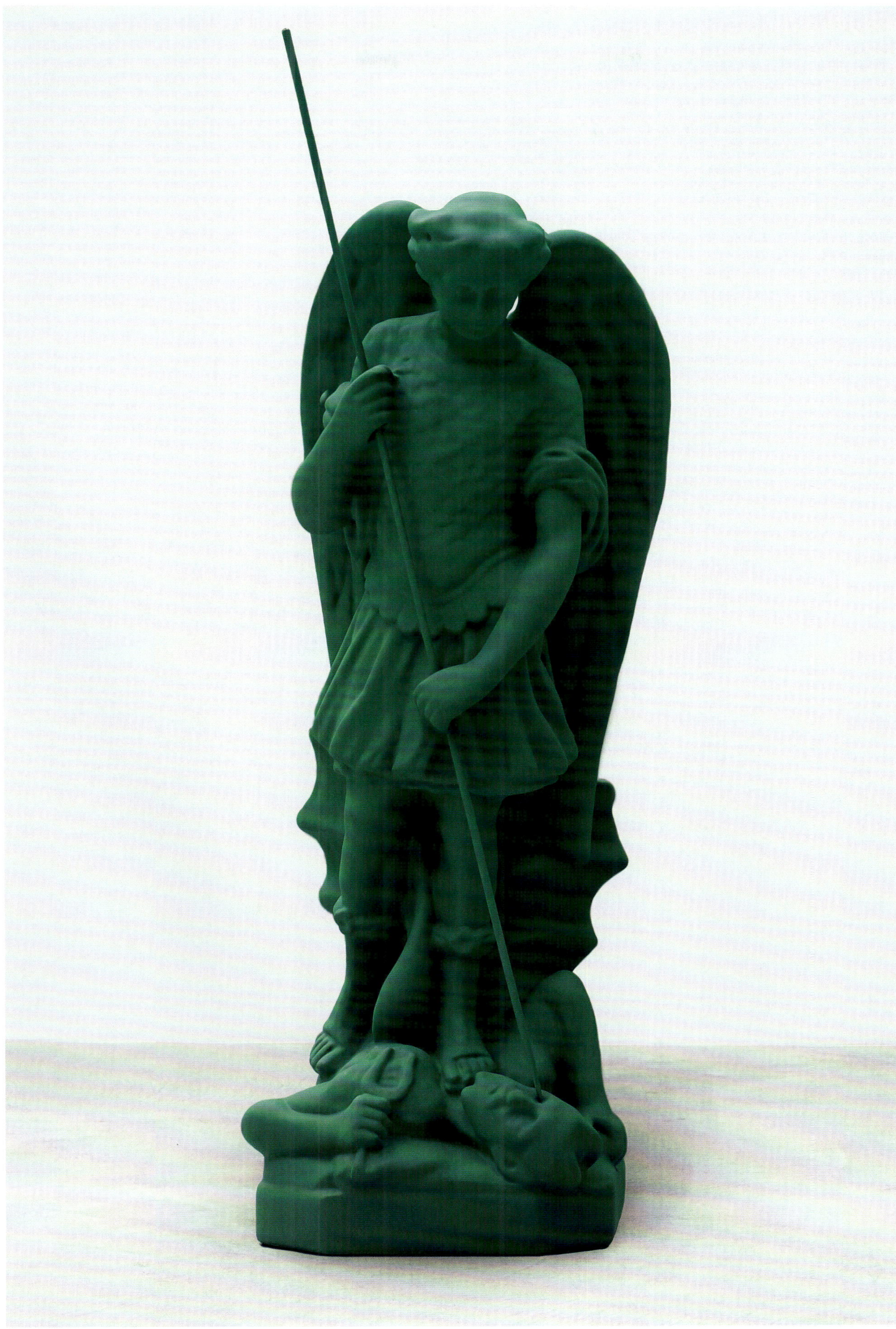

MARLBOROUGH

Marlborough Gallery, Inc.
US-New York, NY 10019 | 40 West 57th Street
Phone +1 212 541 49 00 | Fax +1 212 541 49 48
mny@marlboroughgallery.com | www.marlboroughgallery.com

Marlborough Chelsea
US-New York, NY 10001 | 545 West 25th Street
Phone +1 212 463 86 34 | Fax +1 212 463 96 58
chelsea@marlboroughgallery.com | www.marlboroughchelsea.com

Marlborough Fine Art (London) Ltd
GB-London W1S 4BY | 6 Albemarle Street
Phone +44 20 76 29 51 61 | Fax +44 20 76 29 63 38
mfa@marlboroughfineart.com | www.marlboroughfineart.com

Galería Marlborough S.A.
ES-28010 Madrid | Orfila 5
Phone +34 91 319 14 14 | Fax +34 91 308 43 45
info@galeriamarlborough.com | www.galeriamarlborough.com

Marlborough Monaco
MC-98000 Monte Carlo | 4 Quai Antoine 1er
Phone +377 97 70 25 50 | Fax +377 97 70 25 59
art@marlborough-monaco.com | www.marlborough-monaco.com

Galería Marlborough
ES-08007 Barcelona | Valencia 284
Phone +34 93 467 44 54 | Fax +34 93 467 44 51
infobarcelona@galeriamarlborough.com

Galería A.M.S. Marlborough
CL-76300000 Vitacura, Santiago | Avenida Nueva Costnera 3723
Phone +56 2 799 31 80 | Fax +56 2 799 31 81

Artists at
Art Basel Miami Beach | **Magdalena Abakanowicz**
Frank Auerbach
Francis Bacon
Claudio Bravo
Chu Teh-Chun
Vincent Desiderio
Richard Estes
Juan Genovés
Red Grooms
Stephen Hannock
Jacques Lipchitz
Robert Motherwell
Tom Otterness
Arnaldo Pomodoro
Paula Rego
George Rickey
Manolo Valdés

Gallery Information | Marlborough Gallery was established in London in 1946 and now includes locations in New York, Madrid, Monaco, and Barcelona. In addition to handling important works of art by Impressionists, Post-Impressionists, and modern masters, Marlborough represents more than fifty contemporary artists internationally.

Richard Estes
Broadway and 68th St., 2012
Oil on canvas, 96.5 x 152.4 cm

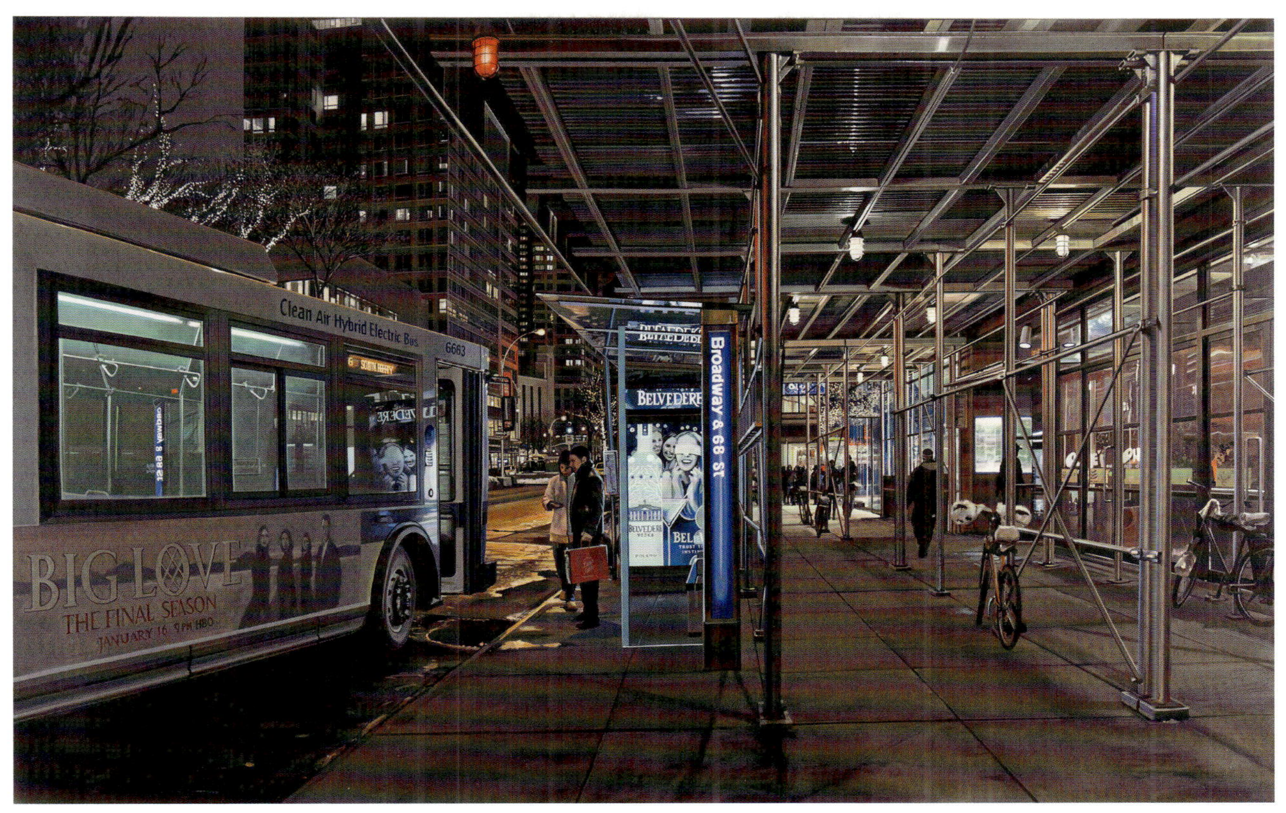
Clean Air Hybrid Electric Bus
6663
BIG LOVE
THE FINAL SEASON
JANUARY 16 9PM HBO
BELVEDERE
Broadway & 68 St

MARSIAJ

Mobile +55 21 81 81 43 69

Galeria Laura Marsiaj
BR-Rio de Janeiro 22410-010 | Rua Teixeira de Melo, 31 C
Phone +55 21 25 13 20 74 | Fax +55 21 25 13 20 74
contato@lauramarsiaj.com.br | www.lauramarsiaj.com.br
Director Laura Marsiaj

One-Person Show | Artist Information

Paulo Vivacqua

*1971, Vitoria, Brazil
Lives and works in Rio de Janeiro, Brazil

Residencies and Awards:
2008 Arte e Patrimônio Prize, Palacio Gustavo Capanema, Rio de Janeiro
2006 Open Studio Project, Cairo
Projéteis Funarte Prize, Rio de Janeiro
2001 Ministry of Culture scholarship Bolsa Virtuose, at apexart, New York, NY

Paulo Vivacqua's body of work tends to create a narrative for the viewers of his anti-forms. The idea is not for it to be a spectacle, nor exactly to work with silence or delicacy. It makes noise not because it establishes some connection between sound and form, but because it refers to daily life, to the perverse state of the world. A sense of mystery hovers over the scene.

Both we viewers and the work itself seem to reflect upon the exercise of functionality, even though we are not sure where to go from there.

The sound that issues from the work is a mantra that does not define space, time, or permanence. We live in an economy of the attention span. The rationale of capital constantly introduces new products and rapid obsolescence, manipulating our attention and inattention. New technologies assail us with information and images. The city is increasingly overwhelmed with stimuli. We are faced with new regimes for disciplining, controlling, and classifying our attention. Along with this thinking, Vivacqua's work/trajectory raises another issue: How can we live in a world where what we once understood as citizenship and civility are pushed close to their limits, their exhaustion? His works continually renew a debate that touches on the concept of destruction or 'setting adrift.' Contexts and circumstances involving these two ideas are brought to light and construct a web of meanings that prompts questions about the idea of a breakdown in contemporary times.

Gallery Information | Directed by Laura Marsiaj, the gallery was inaugurated in Rio de Janeiro in April 2000. It established itself as a space for the dissemination of contemporary art and artists at a time when the city's principal galleries were closing their doors.

Believing in Rio de Janeiro's potential, the gallery has been focusing on the interchange and introduction of new names in national and international circuits.

Committed to the institutional strengthening of art and the market, it validates local work and promotes exchange with artists from other regions of the country.

A second exhibition space, called ANEXO, was inaugurated in 2005 to house exhibitions by guest artists and to promote work of an experimental nature.

The gallery represents artists who work with a wide variety of media including photography, painting, installations, sculpture, video, and site-specific works, among others.

Further artists represented:
Waléria Américo
Arnaldo Antunes
Fábio Baroli
Barrão
Fernanda Chieco
Eduardo Climachauska
Lenora de Barros
Renata de Bonis
Hildebrando de Castro
Alan Fontes
Kilian Glasner
Thiago Honório
Eduardo Kac
Clemens Krauss
Gabriela Machado
Fábio Magalhães
Carolina Martinez
Edgar Martins
Amanda Melo
Carlos Mélo
Ana Miguel
Daniel Murgel
Alexandre Mury
Isaque Pinheiro
Monica Rizzolli
Elder Rocha
Cristián Silva-Avária
Bruno Vilela
Marcus Vinicius
Márcia Xavier
Rafael Zavagli

Paulo Vivacqua
Desert, 2012
Installation, dimensions variable

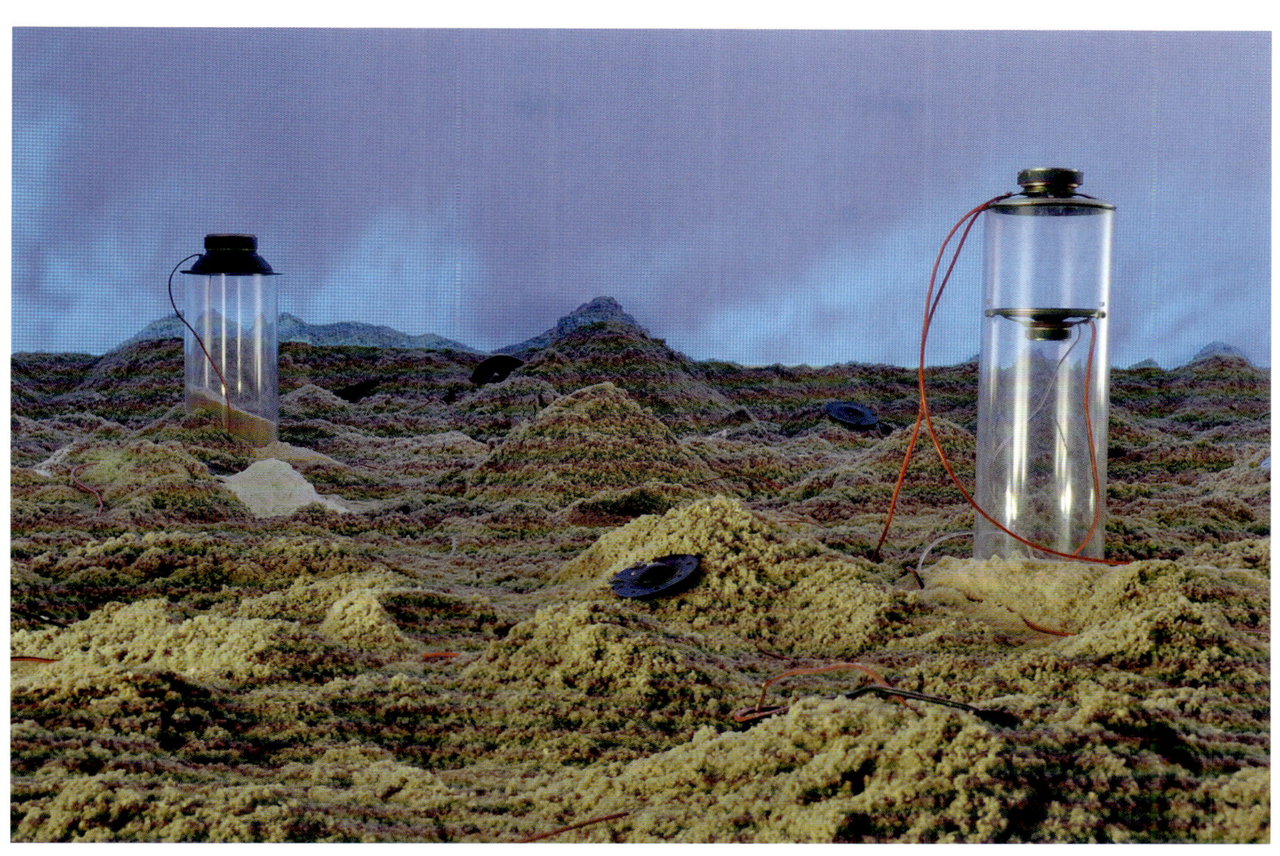

MARTIN

Mary-Anne Martin/Fine Art
US-New York, NY 10021 | 23 East 73rd Street
Phone +1 212 288 22 13 | Fax +1 212 861 76 56
mail@mamfa.com | www.mamfa.com
Directors Mary-Anne Martin
Sofia Lacayo

Artists at Art Basel Miami Beach | **Mary Bauermeister**
Claudio Bravo
Leonora Carrington
Alfredo Castañeda
Elena Climent
Miguel Covarrubias
Isabel De Obaldía
Gunther Gerszo
Mathias Goeritz
Maria Izquierdo
Frida Kahlo
Wifredo Lam
Roberto Matta
Carlos Mérida
Beatriz Milhazes
José Clemente Orozco
Alice Rahon
Diego Rivera
David Alfaro Siqueiros
Rufino Tamayo
Francisco Toledo
Joaquín Torres-García
Alejandro Xul Solar

Gallery Information | Founded in 1982, Mary-Anne Martin/Fine Art is devoted to the field of Latin American art and is well known for its extensive inventory of works by classic masters such as Gerzso, Kahlo, Lam, Matta, Orozco, Rivera, Siqueiros, Tamayo, Toledo, and Torres-García. In addition to mounting historical and thematic exhibitions, the gallery also represents the artist Isabel De Obaldía and the Estate of Gunther Gerzso.

Member: Art Dealers Association of America

Isabel De Obaldía
Cocodrilo Tallado (Carved Crocodile), 2010
Sand-cast glass engraved with hand saw, 51 x 8½ x 3½ inches

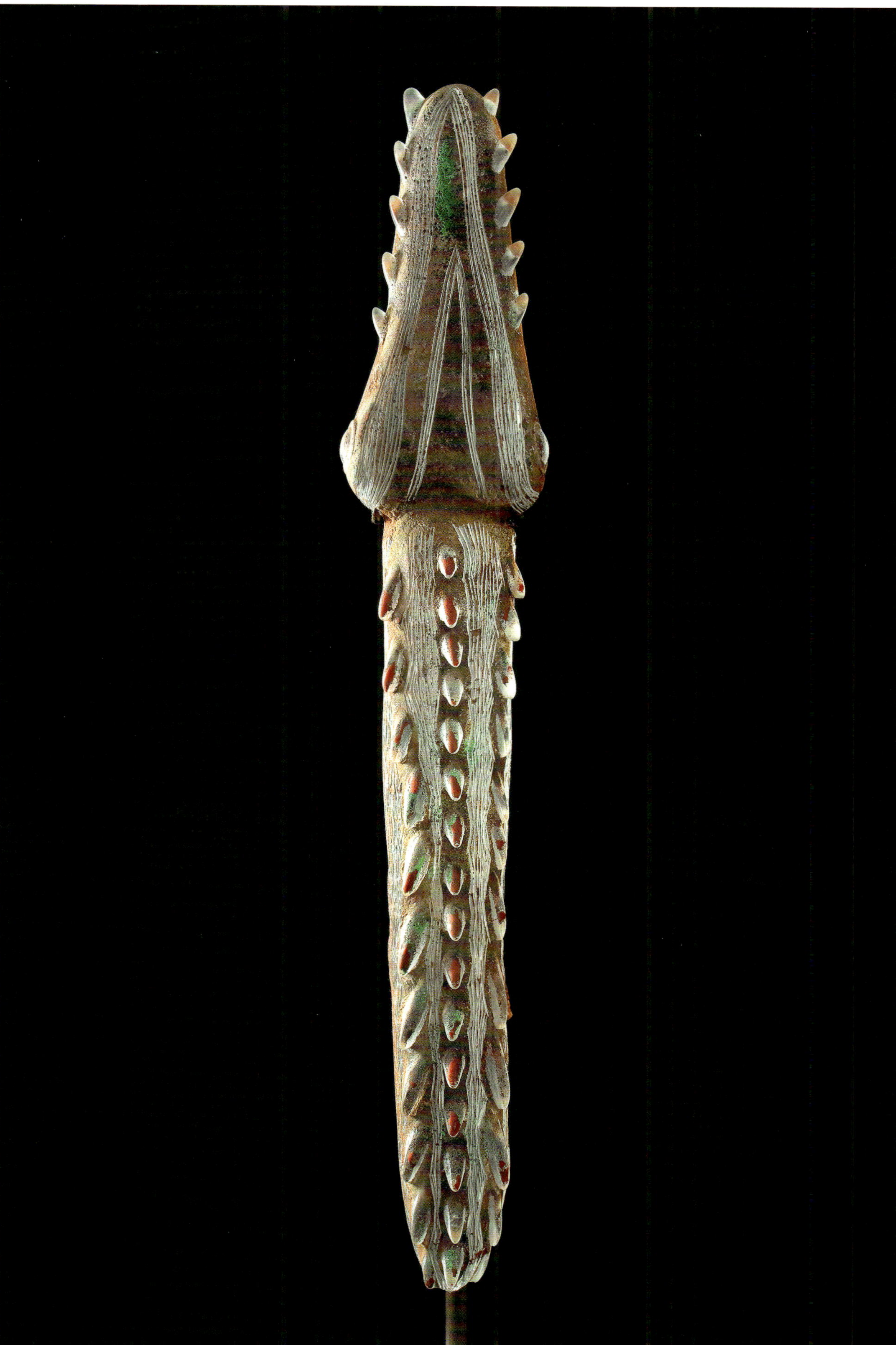

MATHES

Mobile +1 646 623 04 45

Barbara Mathes Gallery
US-New York, NY 10075 | 22 East 80th Street
Phone +1 212 570 41 90 | Fax +1 212 570 41 91
art@barbaramathesgallery.com | www.barbaramathesgallery.com
Directors Barbara Mathes
Jill Bishins

Artists at
Art Basel Miami Beach | **Larry Bell**
Agostino Bonalumi
Alexander Calder
Enrico Castellani
John Chamberlain
Dadamaino
Craig Kauffman
Anselm Kiefer
Yayoi Kusama
Sol LeWitt
Brice Marden
Fausto Melotti
Joan Mitchell
Ad Reinhardt
Gerhard Richter
Ed Ruscha
Lucas Samaras
Paolo Scheggi
Frank Stella
Joseph Stella
Andy Warhol

Gallery Information | Barbara Mathes Gallery was founded in 1978 and specializes in paintings, sculpture, and works on paper by American and European modern and contemporary masters.

The gallery presents both contemporary and historical exhibitions. Our program focuses on unexplored relationships between artists, a re-examination of unrecognized work by major figures, and the introduction of contemporary artists whose work is unfamiliar to collectors in the United States.

Further artists represented: Louise Bourgeois
Joseph Cornell
Lucio Fontana
Damien Hirst
Jasper Johns
Robert Mangold
Sigmar Polke
Martin Puryear
Fred Sandback
David Smith

Yayoi Kusama
Increment in the Spring, 1986
Mixed media,
39½ x 23⅝ x 11⅞ inches,
100 x 60 x 30 cm
Signed, titled, and dated on the bottom

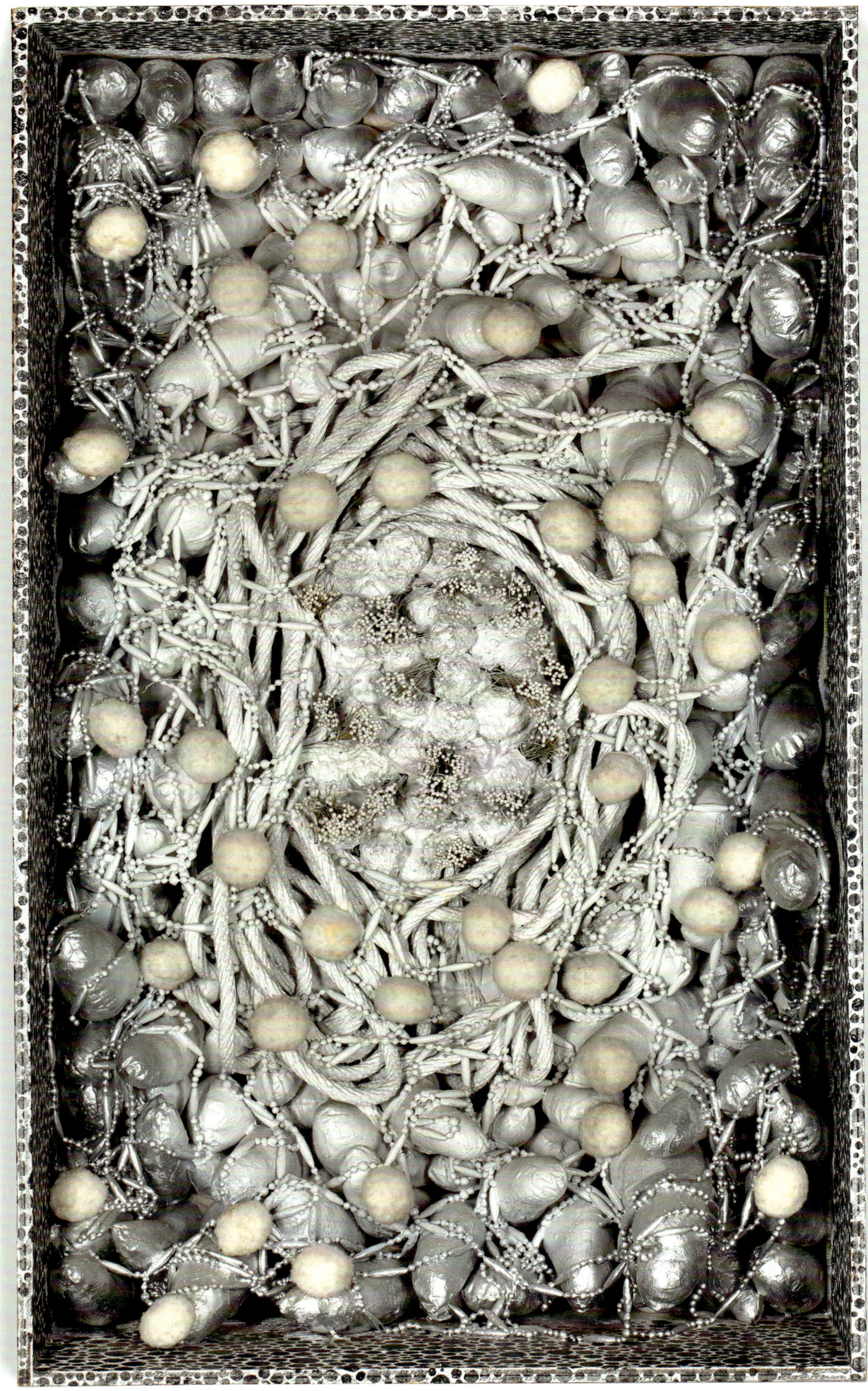

MAYER

Galerie Hans Mayer
DE-40213 Düsseldorf | Grabbeplatz 2
Phone +49 211 13 21 35 | Fax +49 211 13 29 48
galerie@galeriemayer.de | www.galeriehansmayer.de
Director Hans Mayer

Artists at
Art Basel Miami Beach | **Bill Beckley**
Anthony Caro
Keith Haring
Dennis Hopper
Jürgen Klauke
Peter Lindbergh
Robert Longo
Markus Oehlen
Tony Oursler
C.O. Paeffgen
Nam June Paik
Robert Rauschenberg
Kenny Scharf
Andy Warhol
Tom Wesselmann
Ben Willikens

Gallery Information | Galerie Hans Mayer was established in 1965 in Esslingen. Thanks to exhibitions on Op Art, Contemporary Constructivism, and Kinetic Art, the gallery became very well known in the 1960s. Since 1970 Hans Mayer has been based in Düsseldorf.

In the 1970s, 1980s, and 1990s the gallery program grew continuously. In 1969 Hans Mayer was the first to show Andy Warhol in Düsseldorf. In 1989 Nam June Paik joined the gallery. The gallery then added American artists such as Frank Stella, Ellsworth Kelly, Sol LeWitt, Robert Rauschenberg, Roy Lichtenstein, and Tom Wesselmann, and representatives of a younger generation, including Keith Haring, Jean Michel Basquiat, Kenny Scharf, Robert Longo, Bill Beckley, and Tony Oursler, to its program. European painting is represented by C.O. Paeffgen and Markus Oehlen.

Apart from putting on gallery exhibitions, Hans Mayer deals in European and American art after 1945.
The gallery is also specialized in large outdoor sculptures.

Tony Oursler
Determinist Dilemma, 2012
2 projectors, speakers, media players, 417 x 127 x 104 cm

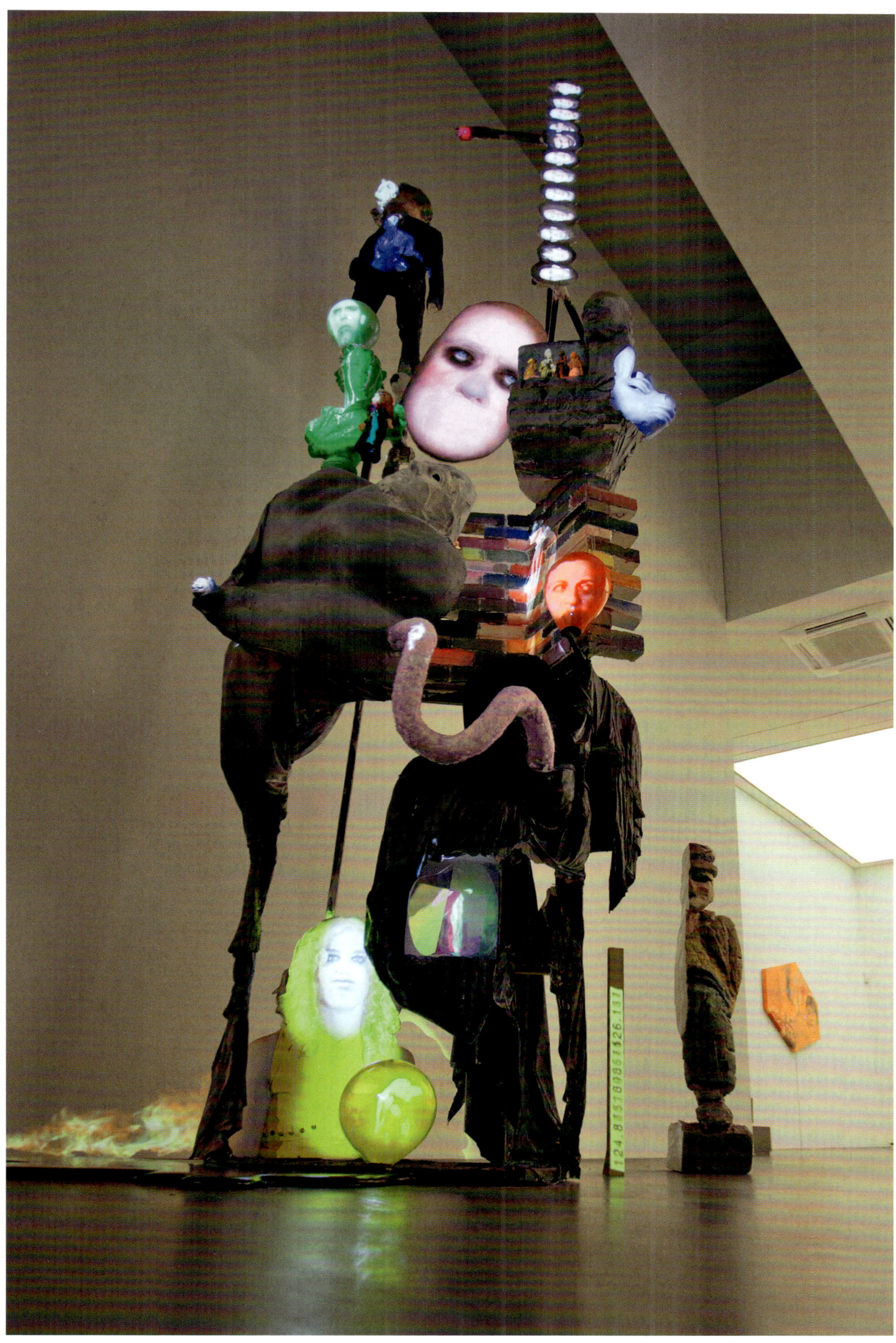

McCAFFREY

McCaffrey Fine Art
US-New York, NY 10065 | 23 East 67th Street
Phone +1 212 988 22 00 | Fax +1 212 988 22 50
info@mccaffreyfineart.com | www.mccaffreyfineart.com
Director Lisa Panzera

Artist at
Art Basel Miami Beach | **Jiro Takamatsu**

Gallery Information | McCaffrey Fine Art represents postwar and contemporary artists from the US, the UK, and Germany, with a particular focus on Japan. We regularly publish museum-quality monographs to accompany exhibitions and have collaborated with leading scholars and museum curators, including David Anfam, Martha Buskirk, Magdalena Dabrowski, Reiko Tomii, and David Raskin.

Further artists represented: Jack Early
Koji Enokura
Noriyuki Haraguchi
Sadamasa Motonaga
Saburo Murakami
Tomoharu Murakami
Hitoshi Nomura
Sigmar Polke
Gary Rough
William Scott
Kazuo Shiraga
Andy Warhol

Jiro Takamatsu
Shadow, 1969-1997
Acrylic on canvas,
74¼ x 89½ inches,
181.8 x 227.3 cm

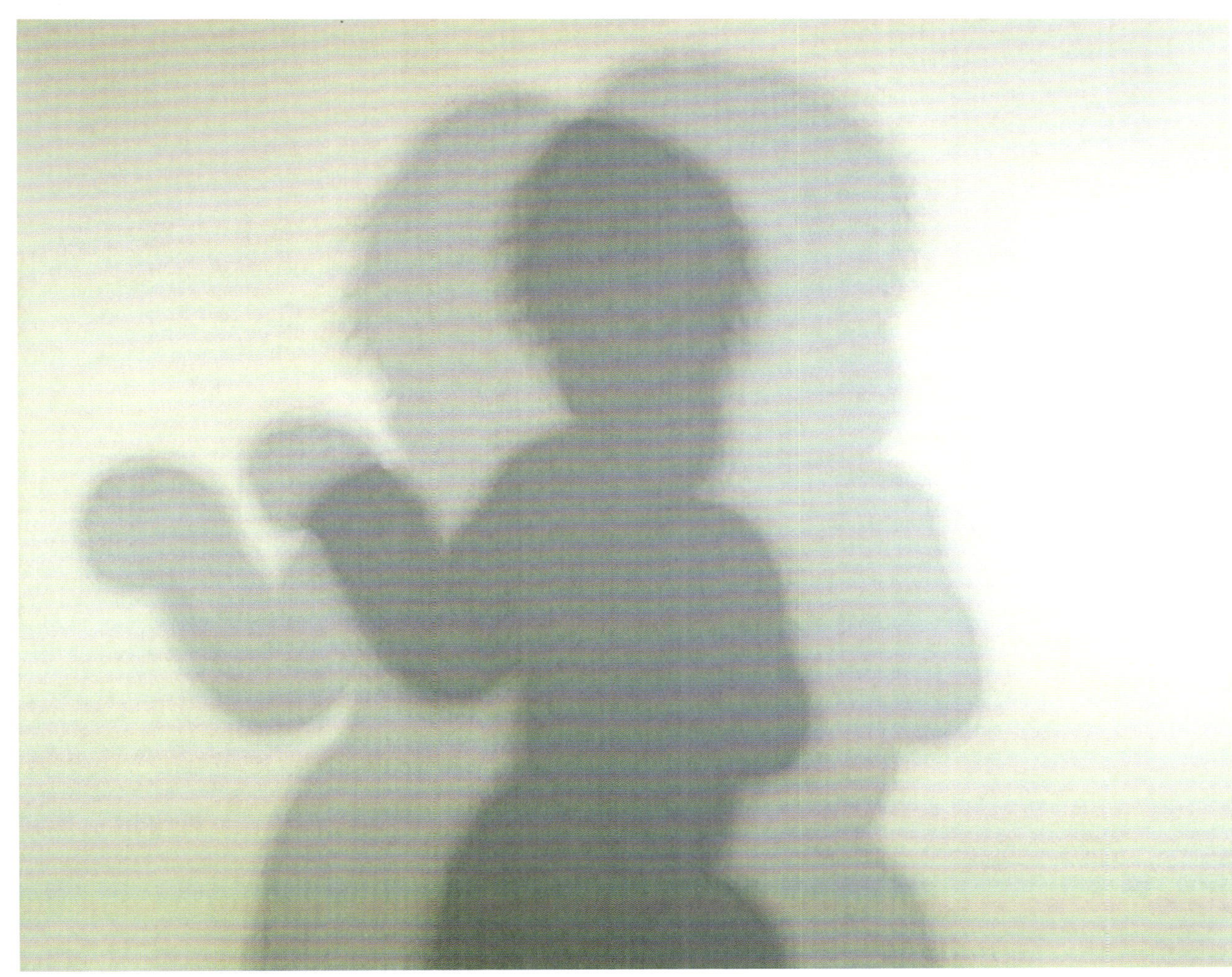

McKEE

McKee Gallery
US-New York, NY 10151 | 745 Fifth Avenue
Phone +1 212 688 59 51 | Fax +1 212 752 56 38
info@mckeegallery.com | www.mckeegallery.com
Directors David McKee
Renee Conforte McKee

Artists at Art Basel Miami Beach | **Vija Celmins**
Philip Guston
Franz Kline
Richard Learoyd
Leonid Lerman
Loren Madsen
Martin Puryear
Harvey Quaytman
Kit Rank
Jeanne Silverthorne
William Tucker
Lucy Williams
Daisy Youngblood

Gallery Information | Vija Celmins:
Lifelike, Walker Art Center, Minneapolis, MN, February 25-May 27, 2012, travels to New Orleans Museum of Art, LA, November 10, 2012-January 27, 2013, Museum of Contemporary Art, San Diego, CA, February 24-May 26, 2013, The Blanton Museum of Art, Austin, TX, June 23-September 29, 2013

Philip Guston:
Encounters with the 1930s, Museo Nacional Centro de Arte Reina Sofía, Madrid, Spain, October 2, 2012-January 7, 2013 (2 paintings)
El Factor Grotesco, Museo Picasso, Málaga, October 22, 2012-February 10, 2013 (2 paintings)
Philip Guston: Late Works, Schirn Kunsthalle Frankfurt, Frankfurt am Main, November 2013
Biographical Forms. Construction and Individual Mythologies, Museo Nacional Centro de Arte Reina Sofía, Madrid, November 2013-February 2014 (4 paintings)

Richard Learoyd:
Seduced by Art: Photography Past and Present, The National Gallery, London, October 31, 2012-January 20, 2013

Martin Puryear:
Martin Puryear: Prints and Drawings, The Art Institute of Chicago, IL, 2013

Jeanne Silverthorne:
Jeanne Silverthorne, The Phillips Collection, Washington DC, February 2013
Jeanne Silverthorne, Galerie de France, Paris, March 2013

William Tucker:
William Tucker, Steel and Wood Constructions from the 1970s, The Margulies Collection at the Warehouse, Miami, FL, November 2012-April 2013

Richard Learoyd
Tatiana in Red, with New Red Chair, 2012
Unique Ilfochrome photograph, 48 x 48 inches

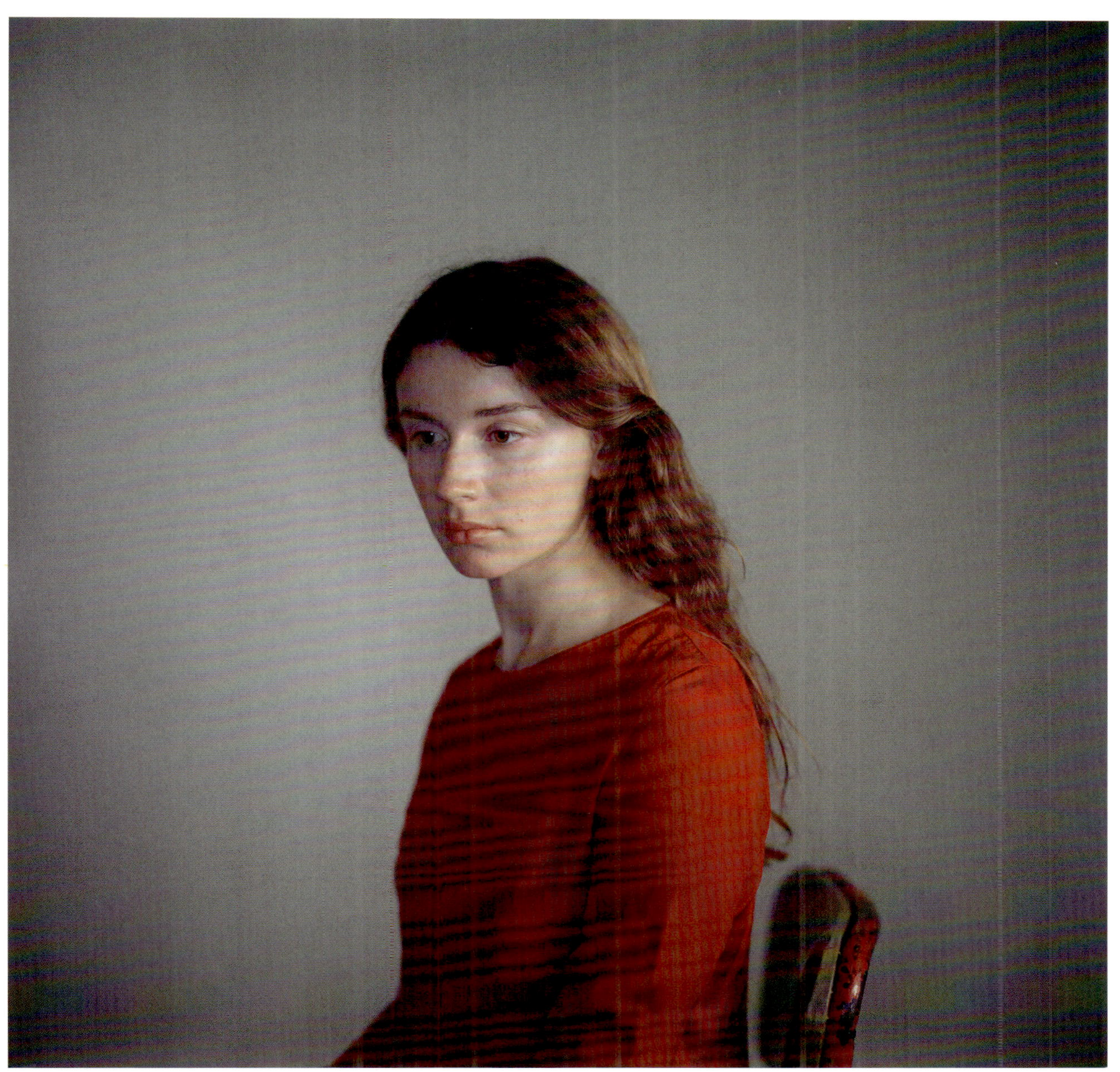

MEESSEN DE CLERCQ

Meessen De Clercq
BE-1000 Brussels | Abdijstraat 2a Rue de l'Abbaye
Phone +32 2 644 34 54
info@meessendeclercq.be | www.meessendeclercq.com
Directors Olivier Meessen
Jan De Clercq

Artists at Art Nova | Evariste Richer
Fabrice Samyn
José María Sicilia

Gallery Information | Meessen De Clercq is an internationally oriented platform dedicated to defending and promoting the practice of a group of contemporary artists. The gallery occupies three floors in a house built in 1911, including a separate video space and a 'Wunderkammer' offering a particular view of the theater of the world. The gallery also publishes catalogs and editions in close collaboration with the represented artists, in order to promote and distribute their work.

Further artists represented:
Ignasi Aballí
Sarah Bostwick
Jordi Colomer
Lieven de Boeck
Hreinn Fridfinnsson
Ellen Harvey
Jorge Méndez Blake
Claudio Parmiggiani
Bruno Perramant
Sarah Pickering
Kelly Schacht
Katrín Sigurdardóttir
Maarten Vanden Eynde

In reaction to the extent of materialism, Meessen De Clercq questions a phrase attributed to André Malraux, who in 1975 stated: 'I am reported as saying: the 21st century will be religious… I never said that… I do not rule out the possibility of a spiritual event on a global scale.'

Now that we are well into the 21st century, it is relevant to subject this to critical questioning. Removing all reference to religion in the literal sense, the project focuses on spirituality in a broader sense. How can a material work transcend matter to open up a spiritual dimension? How can one combine substance and immaterial thought? How can one go beyond this paradox? The project presents works that attempt to overcome the appearance of things to provoke an inner questioning.

Since the dawn of civilization, one material par excellence has conveyed a spiritual dimension: gold. A precious metal that has always fascinated and fueled the desire to possess it, gold is nonetheless a symbol of the divine. Three artists of different generations aim to redirect the visitor's gaze towards the ambiguous aspect of gold in contemporary art. They emphasize the necessity that still exists today to challenge the status of excess apparent in today's society and not to be deceived by the visible when it is important to cherish the spiritual that animates all beings.

Fabrice Samyn (*1981) presents *Untitled,* a ready-made ladder spattered with drops of gold paint, producing a metaphor of the artist as creator while referring to the Biblical story of Jacob and the celestial ladder, a motif that recurs throughout the history of art, from Romanesque paintings to Byzantine art and Gothic illuminations.

Evariste Richer (*1969) offers a diptych as two prophylactic presences. This large work represents two sides of a survival blanket. One is gold and the other silver. The piece plays on duality (gold–silver/hot–cold/retaining–dissipating heat) and the notion of preserving the very essence of life.

Another duality is explored by José María Sicilia (*1954), who shows vertical plates of gilded bronze polished so intensely that they become as reflective as mirrors. On each plate the artist has etched aphorisms bearing metaphysical connotations.

Evariste Richer
South Face, North Face, 2010
Lambda print, framed:
231 x 156 x 5 cm
Part of a diptych

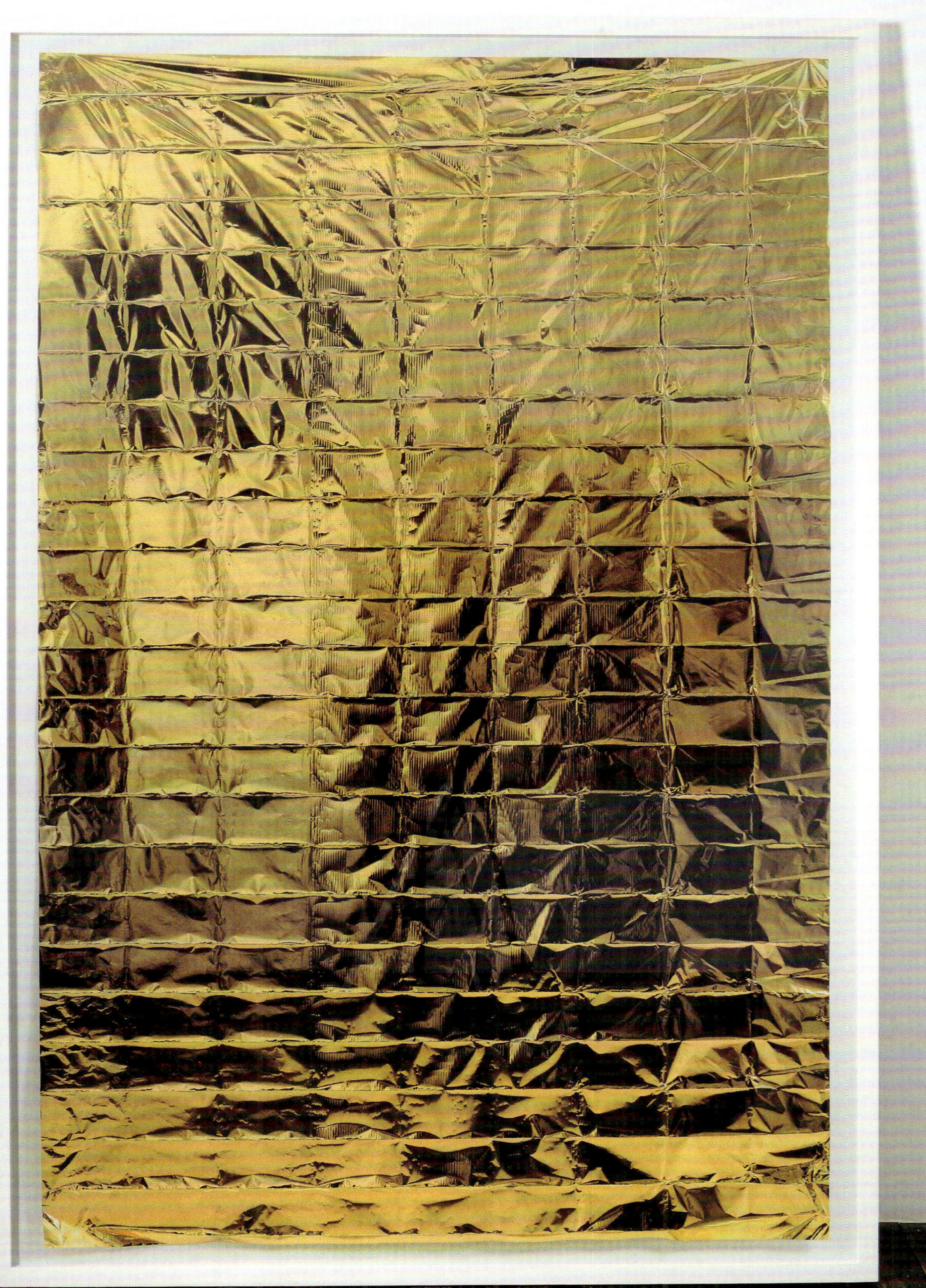

MEIER

Mobile +1 415 264 27 45

Anthony Meier Fine Arts
US-San Francisco, CA 94109 | 1969 California Street
Phone +1 415 351 14 00 | Fax +1 415 351 14 37
gallery@anthonymeierfinearts.com | www.anthonymeierfinearts.com
Directors Sarah Bryan
Rebecca Camacho
Megan McConnell

Artists at
Art Basel Miami Beach | **Hurvin Anderson**
Carl Andre
Janine Antoni
Georg Baselitz
Alighiero Boetti
Nicholas Byrne
Sarah Cain
Rosana Castrillo Diaz
John Chamberlain
Jeremy Dickinson
Leonardo Drew
Cecilia Edefalk
Tony Feher
Teresita Fernández
Dan Flavin
Lucio Fontana
Barnaby Furnas
Robert Gober
Jim Hodges
Donald Judd
Yayoi Kusama
Robert Mangold
Brice Marden
Agnes Martin
Roy McMakin
Donald Moffett
Dave Muller
Bruce Nauman
Jockum Nordström
Sigmar Polke
Rob Reynolds
Gerhard Richter
Ed Ruscha
Robert Ryman
Kate Shepherd
Jasmin Sian
Gary Simmons
Cy Twombly
Tam Van Tran
Andy Warhol

Gallery Information | Anthony Meier Fine Arts was established in 1984 as a private dealer in the secondary market. Working with both public and private collections, Anthony Meier built a highly regarded international reputation specializing in post-World War II contemporary masters. After twelve years as a private dealer, Anthony Meier opened a public gallery in the fall of 1996.

As a public forum, Anthony Meier Fine Arts mounts five shows per year dedicated to emerging and mid-career artists. The work shown in the gallery is consistent with the quality and visual aesthetic for which the business has become known.

Leonardo Drew
Number 23S, 2012
Wood and mixed media,
96 x 96 x 20 inches

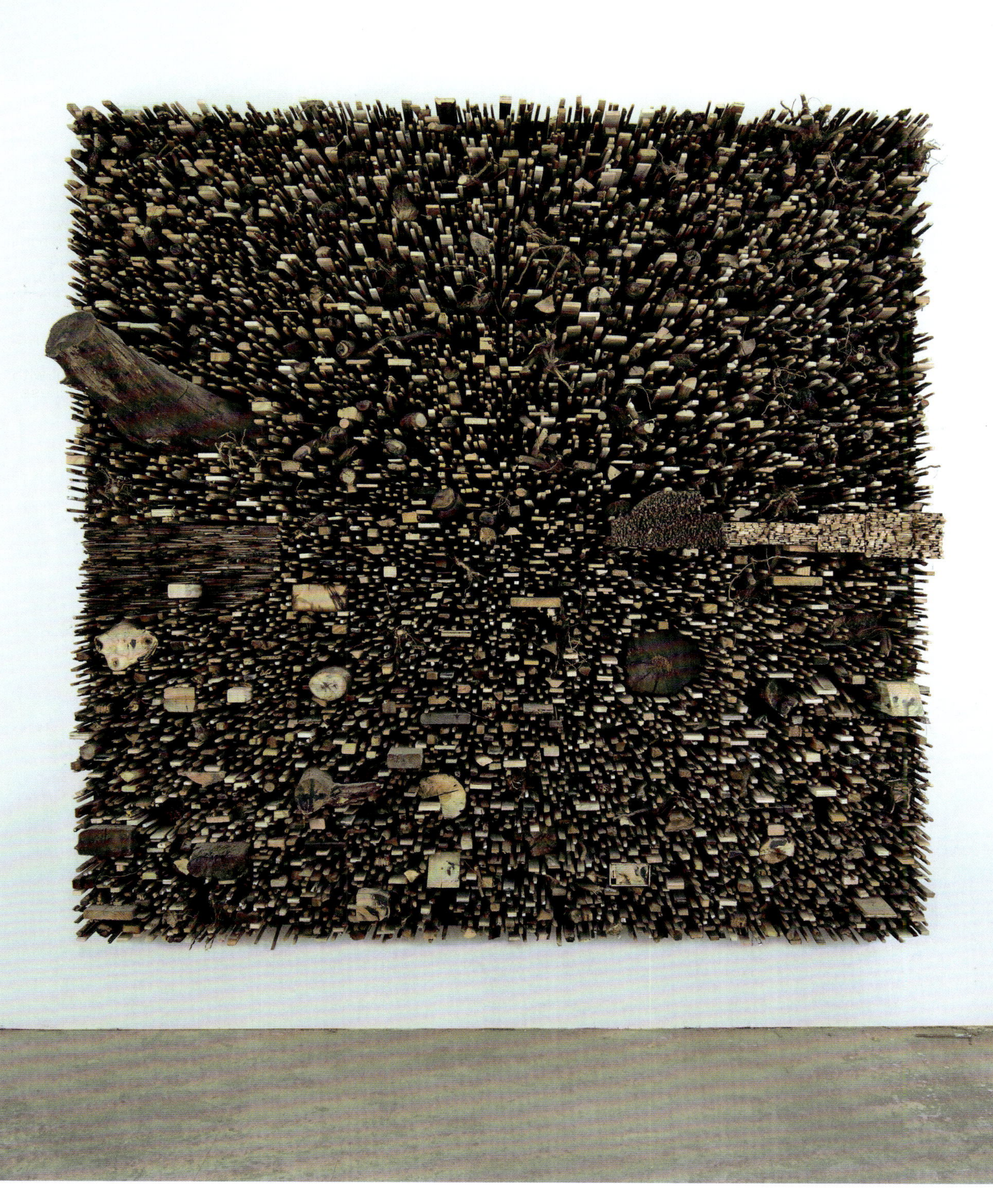

MEILE

Galerie Urs Meile, Beijing-Lucerne
CH-6004 Lucerne | Rosenberghöhe 4
Phone +41 41 420 33 18 | Fax +41 41 420 21 69
galerie@galerieursmeile.com | www.galerieursmeile.com
Director Karin Seiz

Galerie Urs Meile, Beijing-Lucerne
CN-100015 Beijing | no. 104, Caochangdi Cun, Cui Gezhuang Xiang, Chaoyang District
Phone +86 10 64 33 33 93 | Fax +86 10 64 33 02 03
beijing@galerieursmeile.com | www.galerieursmeile.com
Director Nataline Colonnello

Artists at
Art Basel Miami Beach | **Ai Weiwei**
Hu Qingyan
Li Gang
Qiu Shihua
Christian Schoeler
Shao Fan
Julia Steiner
Not Vital
Wang Xingwei
Xie Nanxing
Yan Xing

Further artists represented | Chen Hui
Cheng Ran
Wim Delvoye
Andreas Golder
L/B
Li Dafang
Li Zhanyang
Liu Ding
Meng Huang
Shan Fan
Anatoly Shuravlev
Xia Xiaowan

Xie Nanxing
Self Portrait, 2011
Oil on canvas, 100 x 80 cm

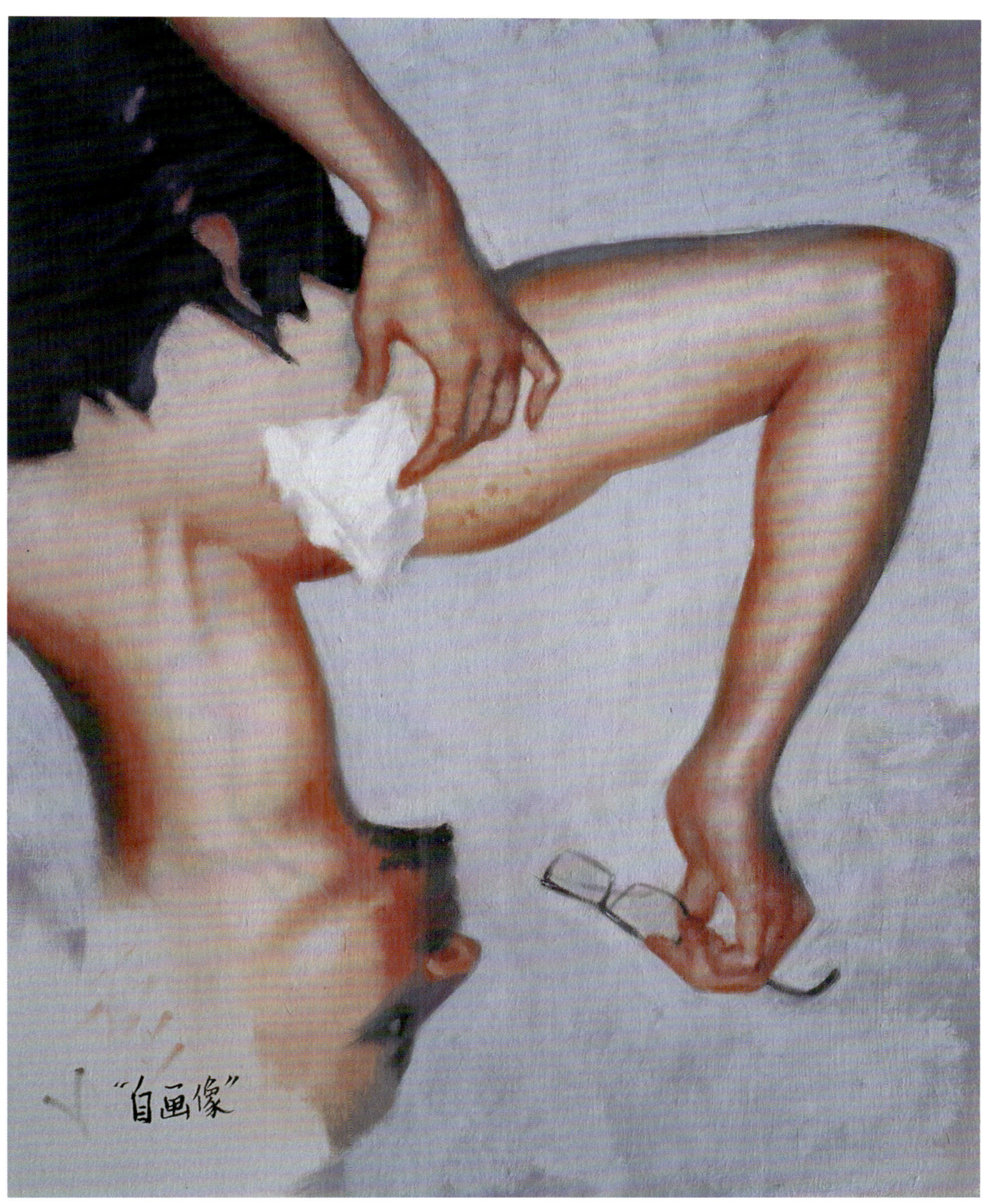
“自画像”

MENDES WOOD

Mendes Wood
BR-São Paulo 01416-000 | Rua da Consolação 3358
Phone +55 11 30 81 17 35 | Fax +55 11 30 60 96 62
info@mendeswood.com | www.mendeswood.com
Directors Felipe Dmab
Pedro Mendes
Matthew Wood

Artists at Art Nova | Adriano Costa
Tunga

Gallery Information | Directed by Pedro Mendes, Matthew Wood, and Felipe Dmab, Mendes Wood was established in São Paulo in 2009 with the intention of exhibiting both Brazilian and international artists in a context of critical dialogue and cross-pollination.

One of the central concerns of the program has been the exploration of regional differences and personal individuation while promoting cosmopolitanism and collaboration. Motivated by a belief in the new convergence of art, music, performance, design, architecture, and video, the gallery is committed to an interdisciplinary program – one that celebrates conceptualism, political resistance, and intellectual rigor.

Further artists represented:
Lucas Arruda
Theo Craveiro
Jen Denike
Ana Dias Batista
Kota Ezawa
Kevin Francis Gray
Deyson Gilbert
Patricia Leite
Thiago Martins Melo
Paulo Nazareth
Leticia Ramos
Marina Simão
Diego Singh
Daniel Steegmann

Adriano Costa
O Quadrado Campo, 2012
Tissue, concrete, and iron,
110 x 92 cm

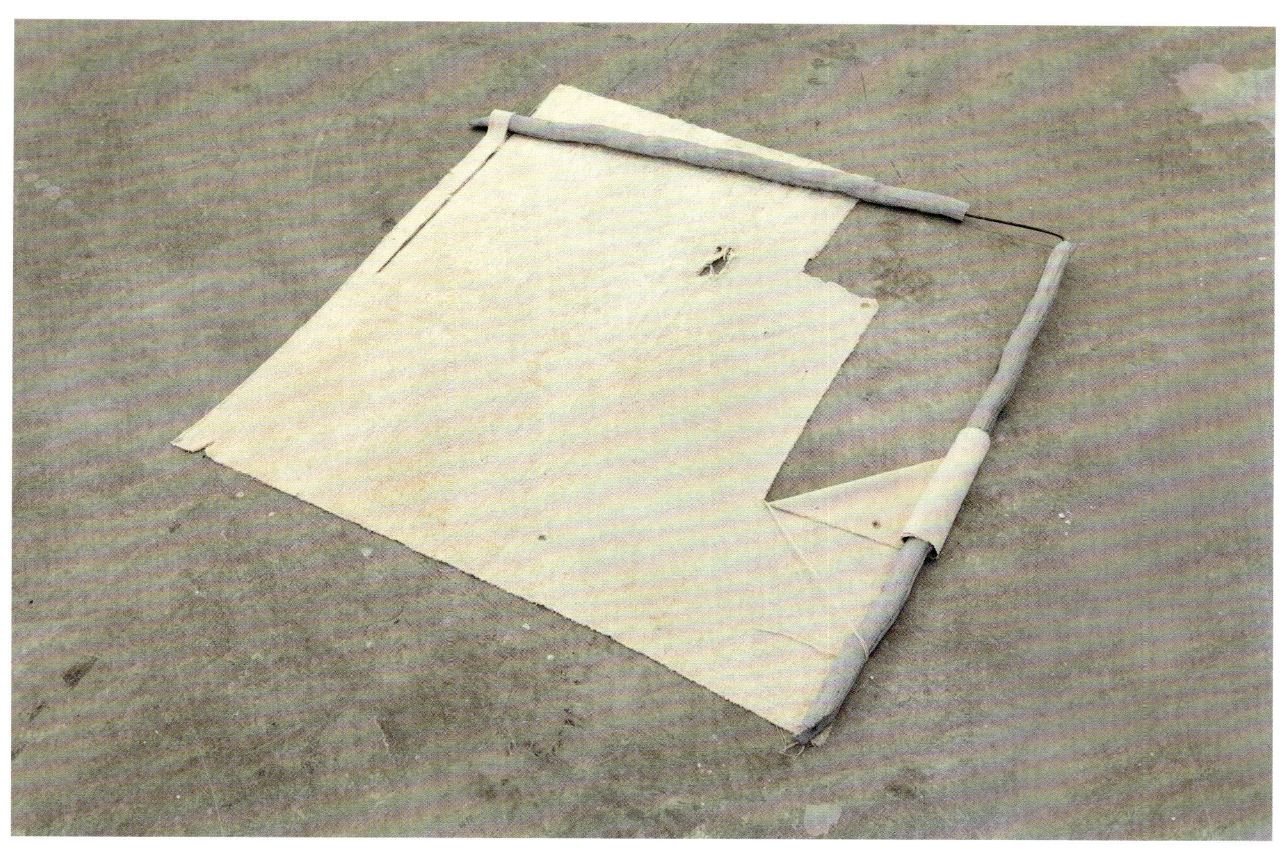

MENNOUR

kamel mennour
FR-75006 Paris | 47, rue Saint-André-des-Arts
Phone +33 1 56 24 03 63 | Fax +33 1 40 46 80 20
galerie@kamelmennour.com | www.kamelmennour.com
Directors Kamel Mennour
Marie-Sophie Eiché
Jessy Mansuy-Leydier

Artists at Art Basel Miami Beach | **Mohamed Bourouissa**
Marie Bovo
Daniel Buren
Latifa Echakhch
Dario Escobar
Michel François
Yona Friedman
Alberto Garcia-Alix
Camille Henrot
David Hominal
Huang Yong Ping
Alfredo Jaar
Tadashi Kawamata
Sigalit Landau
Claude Lévêque
François Morellet
Martial Raysse
Zineb Sedira
Miri Segal
Shen Yuan

Latifa Echakhch
Tkaf/Mer d'encre/Tambour, 2012
Exhibition view, kamel mennour, Paris

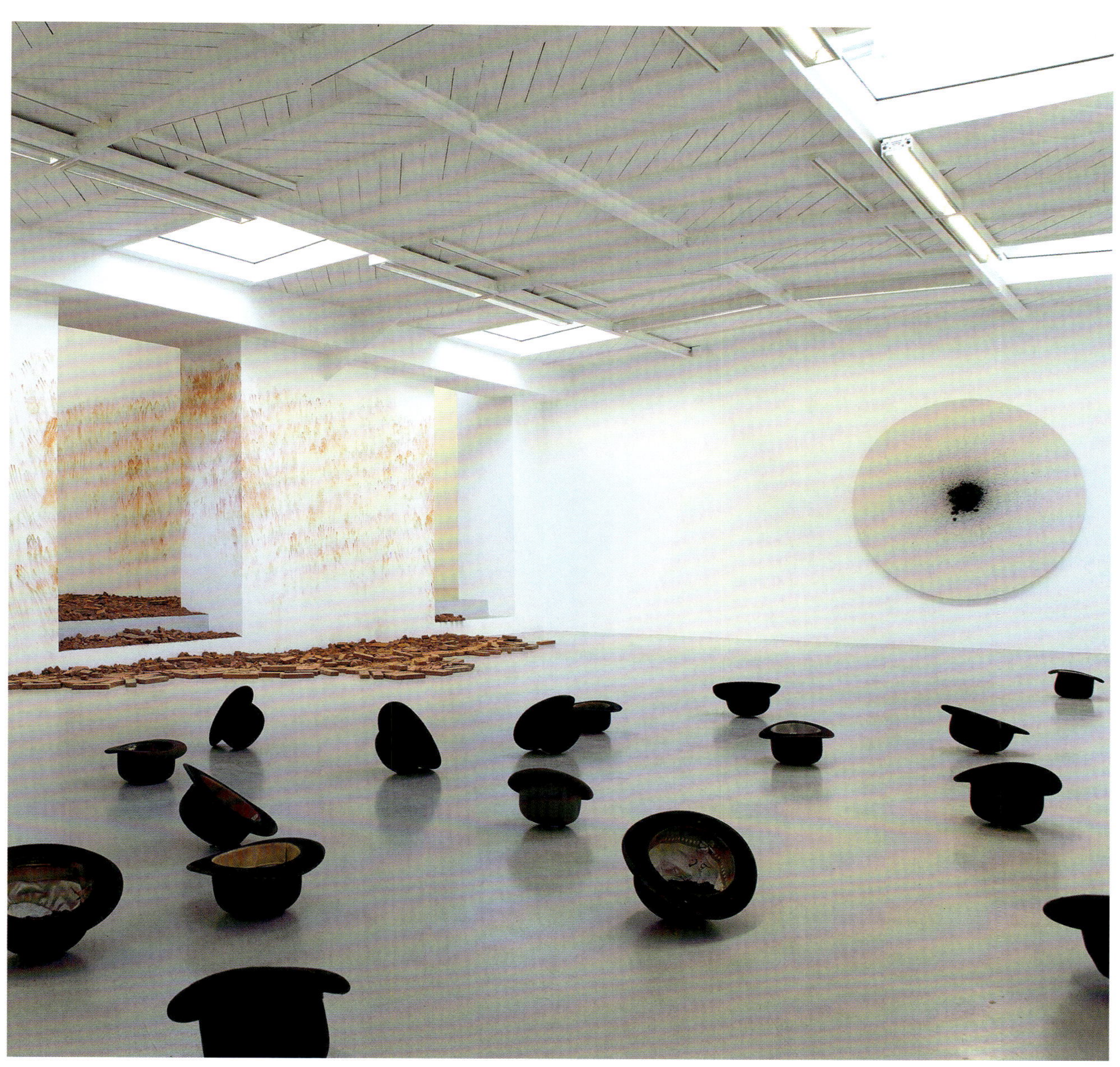

METRO PICTURES

Mobile +1 917 576 14 06

Metro Pictures
US-New York, NY 10011 | 519 West 24th Street
Phone +1 212 206 71 00 | Fax +1 212 337 00 70
gallery@metropictures.com | www.metropictures.com
Directors Janelle Reiring
Helene Winer
Tom Heman
Allison Card
Manuela Mozo

Artists at
Art Basel Miami Beach | **Olaf Breuning**
André Butzer
Claire Fontaine
Andy Hope 1930
Isaac Julien
Louise Lawler
Robert Longo
David Maljkovic
John Miller
Paulina Olowska
Tony Oursler
Trevor Paglen
Stephen G. Rhodes
Jim Shaw
Cindy Sherman
Gary Simmons
Andreas Slominski
Catherine Sullivan
Sara VanDerBeek
Tris Vonna-Michell
T.J. Wilcox
B. Wurtz

Gary Simmons
Mural at 262 Bowery, New York,
2011

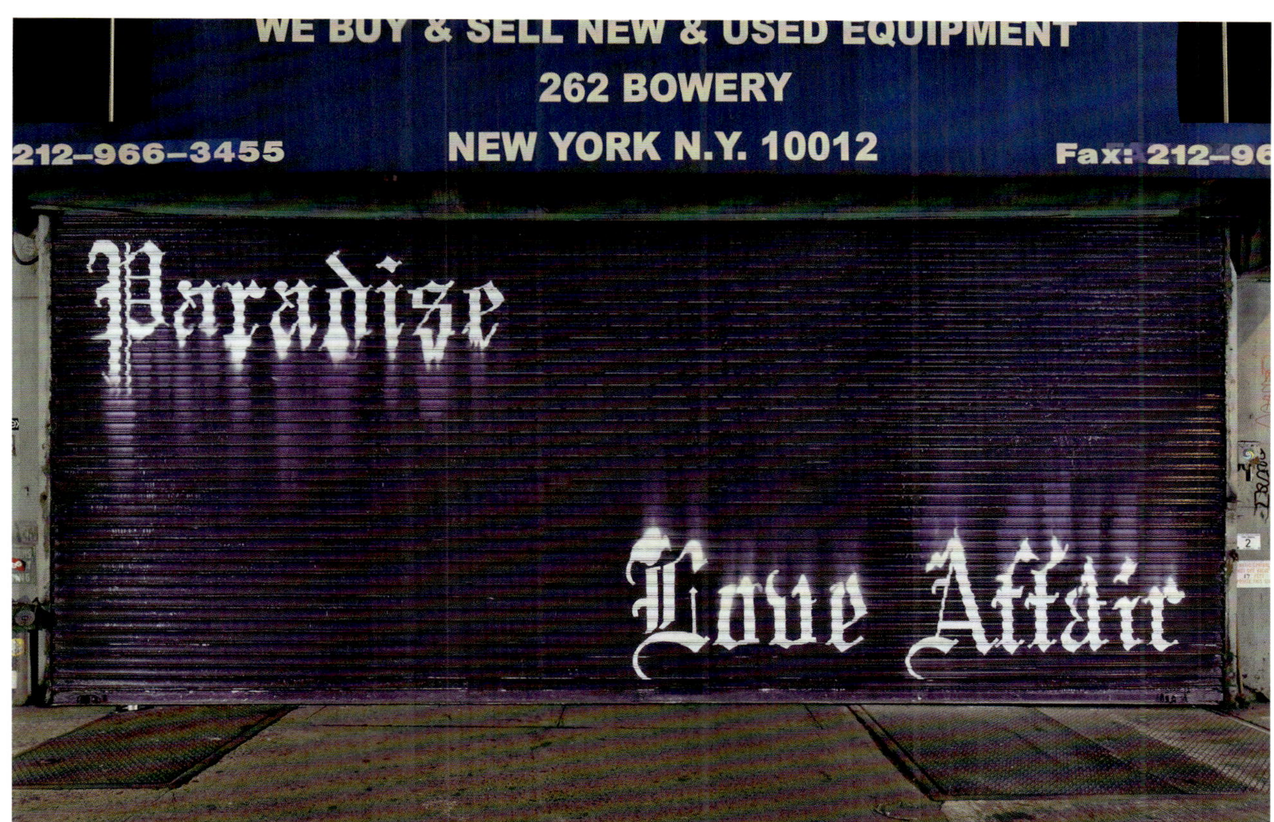
WE BUY & SELL NEW & USED EQUIPMENT
262 BOWERY
212-966-3455
NEW YORK N.Y. 10012
Paradise
Love Affair

MEYER RIEGGER

Mobile +49 172 678 22 62, +49 173 665 62 58

Meyer Riegger
DE-76137 Karlsruhe | Klauprechtstrasse 22
Phone +49 721 82 12 92 | Fax +49 721 982 21 41
info@meyer-riegger.de | www.meyer-riegger.de
Directors Jochen Meyer
Thomas Riegger

Meyer Riegger
DE-10969 Berlin | Friedrichstrasse 235
Phone +49 30 31 56 65 80 | Fax +49 30 31 56 65 81
info@meyer-riegger.de | www.meyer-riegger.de

Artists at Art Basel Miami Beach | **Franz Ackermann**
Katinka Bock
Armin Boehm
Björn Braun
Miriam Cahn
Henrik Håkansson
Uwe Henneken
Jamie Isenstein
Eva Kotatkova
Jan Mančuška
Meuser
John Miller
Helen Mirra
Jonathan Monk
Melvin Moti
Scott Myles
Julia Schmidt
David Thorpe
Gabriel Vormstein
Waldemar Zimbelmann

Waldemar Zimbelmann
Untitled, 2012
Mixed media on canvas,
71 x 50 cm

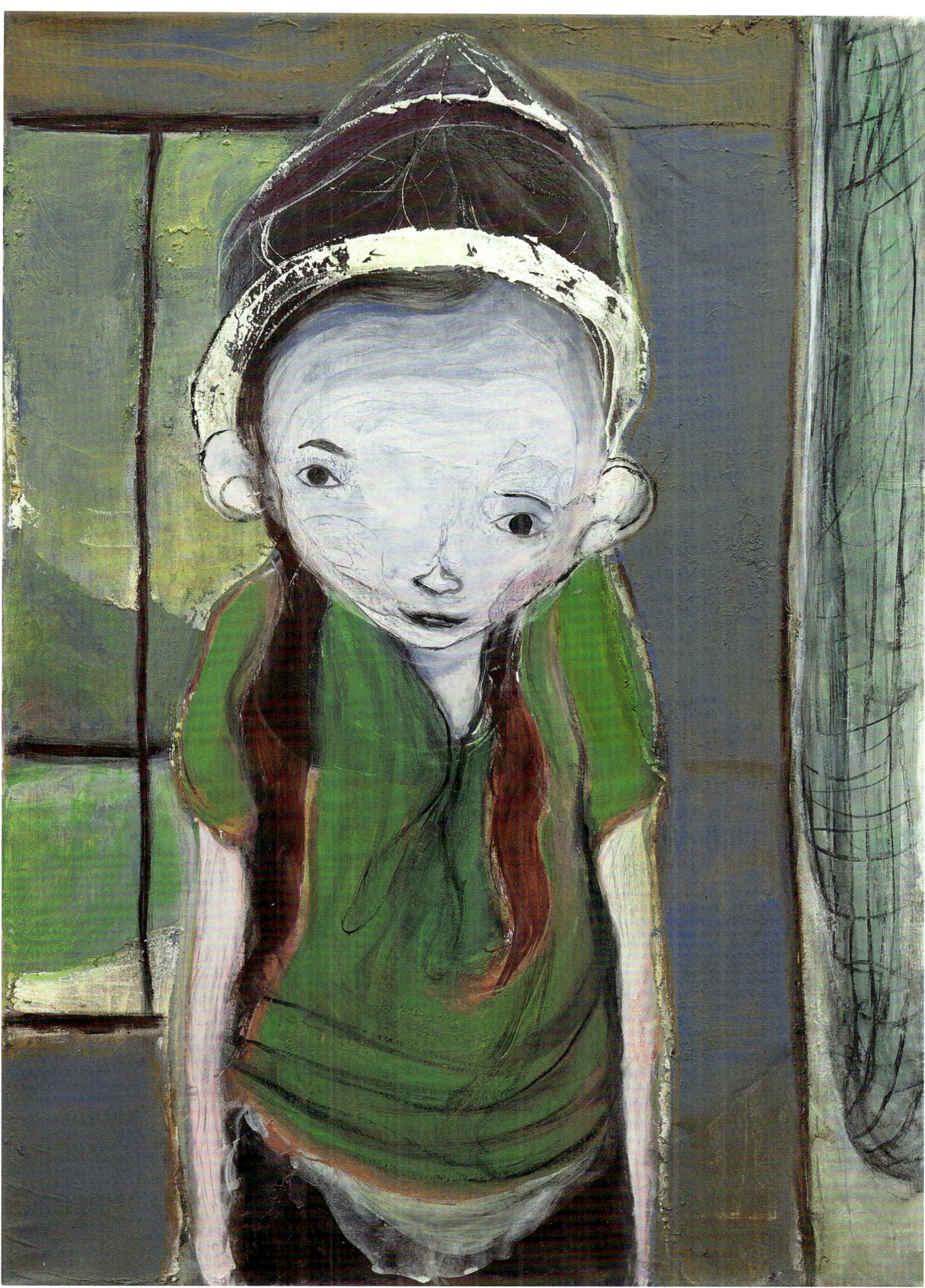

MEZZANIN

Galerie Mezzanin
AT-1010 Vienna | Getreidemarkt 14/Eschenbachgasse
Phone +43 1 5264356 | Fax +43 1 5269187
office@galeriemezzanin.com | www.galeriemezzanin.com
Director Karin Handlbauer

Artists at Art Nova | Thomas Bayrle
Peter Kogler
Mandla Reuter

Further artists represented | Gerald Domenig
Bernhard Frue
Manuel Gorkiewicz
Michael Hakimi
Lisa Lapinski
Christian Mayer
Marzena Nowak
Michelangelo Pistoletto
Katrin Plavcak
Stephen Prina
Sturtevant
Santos R. Vasquez
Alexander Wolff
Christina Zurfluh

'The weaving room trembled under the rhythmic pounding of the looms – in a wailing, frantic machine monotony. In utter fatigue, I often dozed off in front of my machine there... I lost myself in the rhythm of the repetition of the always similar program – for a few seconds I sunk away... At a particular frequency, my loom's motor began to sing almost like a human... In this phase, I heard the whimpering voice of the rosary singing directly out of the engine block... and suddenly the praying women from my childhood village church were back. I was frightened – but at the same time, I almost languorously abandoned myself to the situation.' (Thomas Bayrle, 2009)

Peter Kogler finds metaphors for the individual and his social positioning in arrangements that he liberates to create a kind of modern ornament. He portrays the image of an engineered and technologically devout community, which is trapped in the net of a structure made from the superimposition of different archetypes.

Mandla Reuter's works often deal with the correlation of artwork and architecture, which – in most cases – houses it. *The Plot* in Los Angeles serves as point of departure for a series of works, which often have a narrative circling around architectural projects and how space can be defined, which often turn out as utopias.

A+B | **Mandla Reuter**
The Agreement, Vienna, 2011
Armoire, 198 x 129 x 85 cm
Installation view,
Galerie Mezzanin, 2011

A

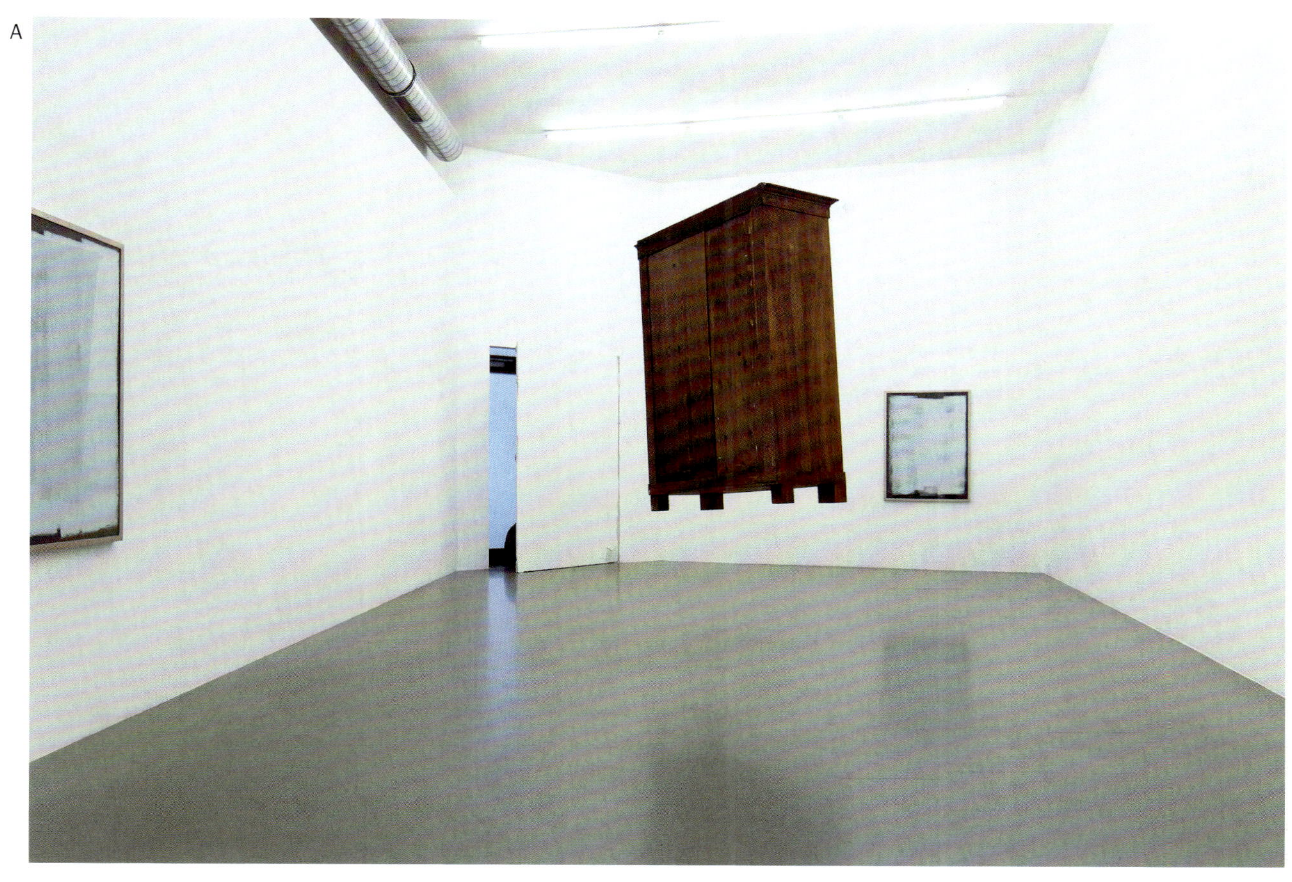

B

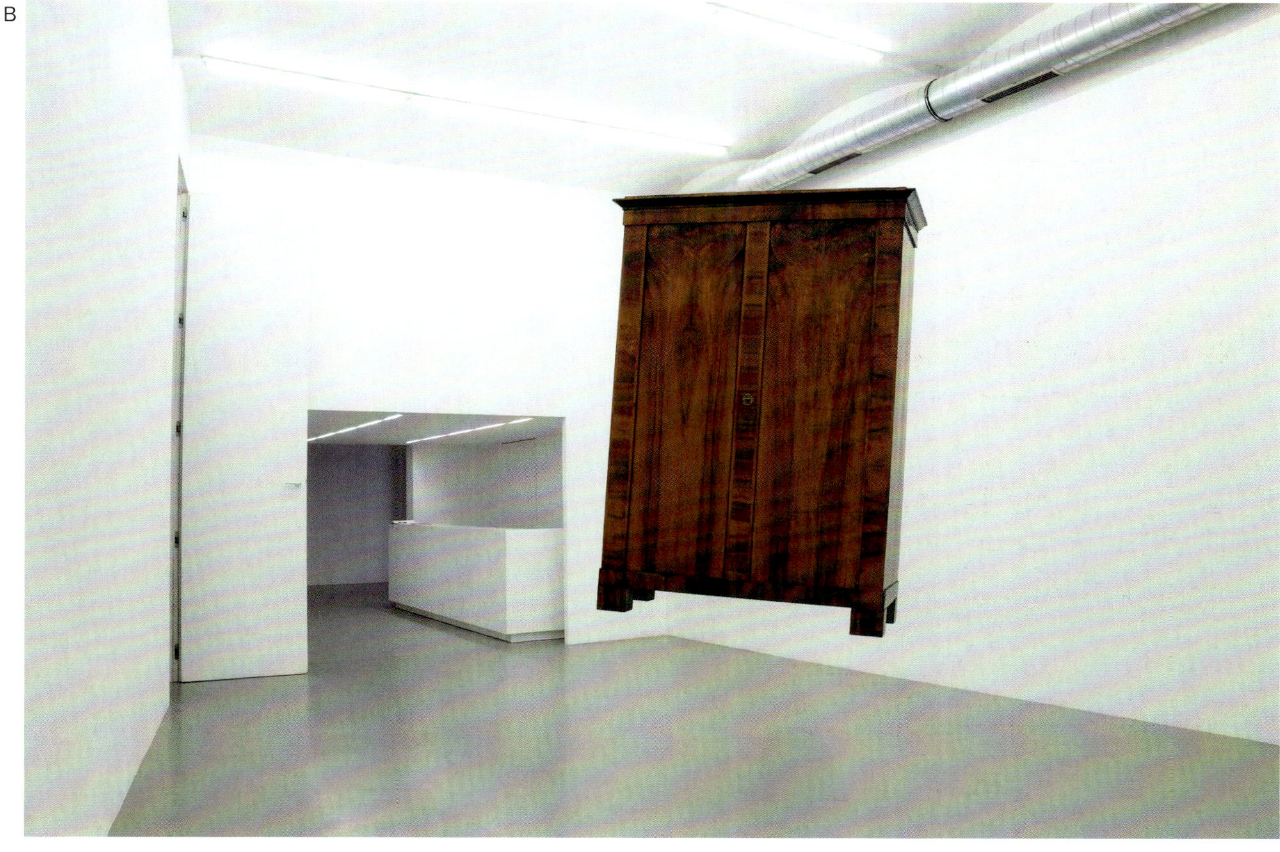

MILLAN

Galeria Millan
BR-São Paulo 05416-001 | Rua Fradique Coutinho, 1360
Phone +55 11 30 31 60 07 | Fax +55 11 30 31 60 07
galeria@galeriamillan.com.br | www.galeriamillan.com.br
Directors André Millan
Socorro de Andrade Lima

Artists at Art Basel Miami Beach | **Rodrigo Andrade**
Artur Barrio
Rodrigo Bivar
Tatiana Blass
Sofia Borges
Paulo Climachauska
Felipe Cohen
Lenora de Barros
Nelson Felix
Dudi Maia Rosa
Anna Maria Maiolino
Rubens Mano
Lais Myrrha
Emmanuel Nassar
Henrique Oliveira
Paulo Pasta
Miguel Rio Branco
Thiago Rocha Pitta
Mira Schendel
Bob Wolfenson

Gallery Information | Sofia Borges/Thiago Rocha Pitta, *A iminência das poéticas,* 30th São Paulo Biennial, September 7-December 9, 2012

Henrique Oliveira, *Inside Out and From the Ground Up,* MOCA Cleveland, OH, October 6, 2012-January 27, 2013

Rodrigo Andrade
A | *Tsunami Landscape*, 2011
Oil on canvas on MDF,
60 x 105 cm

B | *Libyan Landscape*, 2011
Oil on canvas on MDF,
60 x 105 cm

A

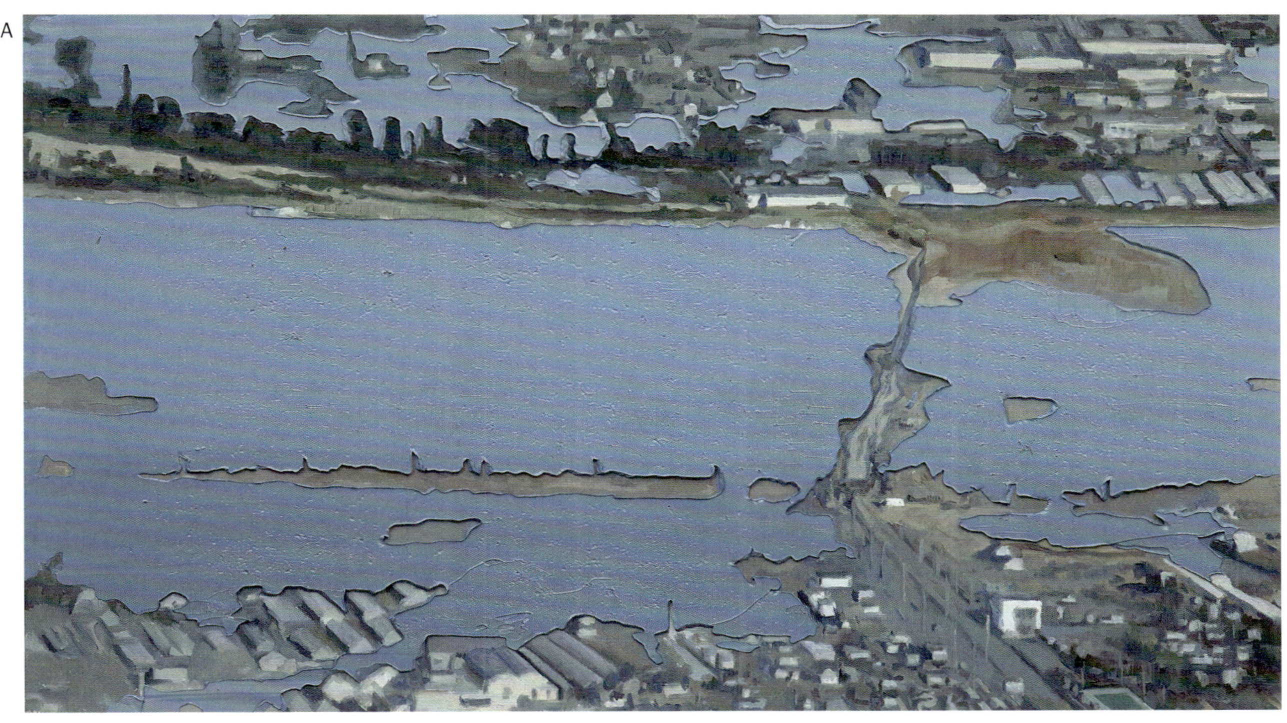

B

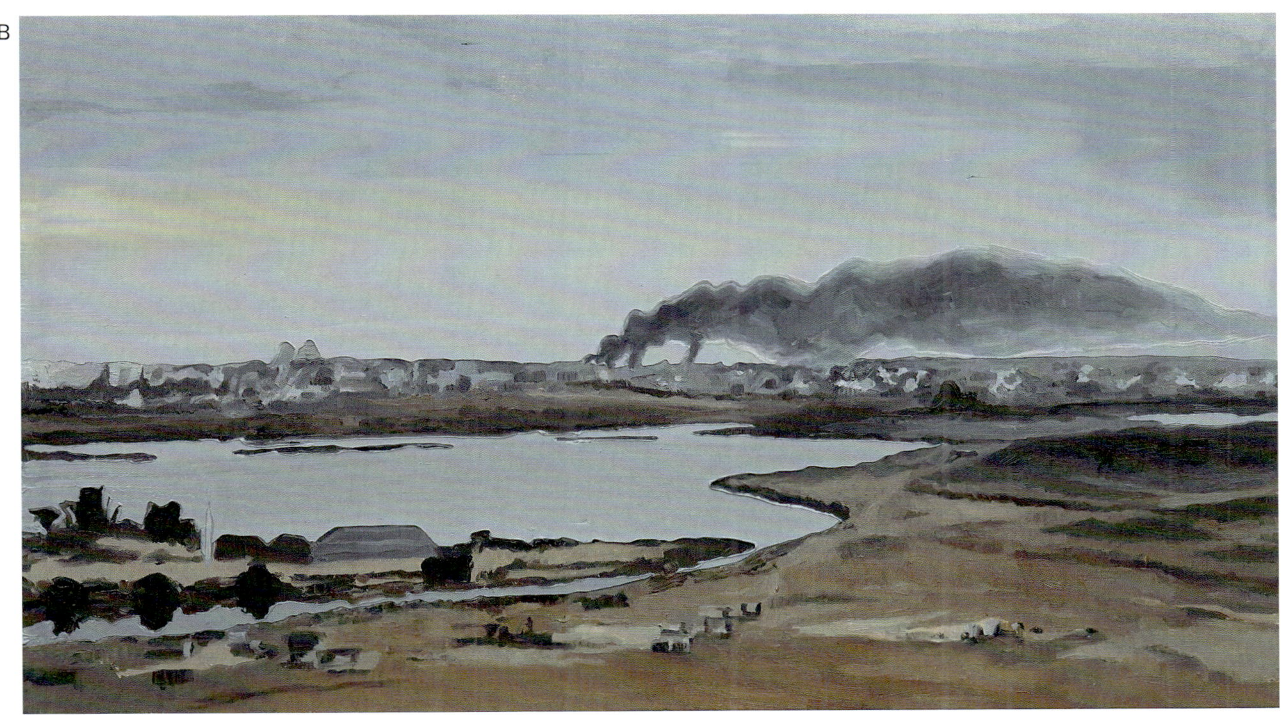

MILLER

Robert Miller Gallery
US-New York, NY 10001 | 524 West 26th Street
Phone +1 212 366 47 74 | Fax +1 212 366 44 54
rmg@robertmillergallery.com | www.robertmillergallery.com
Director Betsy Wittenborn Miller

Artists represented | Ai Weiwei
Justin Allen
Diane Arbus
Jean-Michel Basquiat
Louise Bourgeois
Dirk Braeckman
Robert Greene
Bill Henson
Lee Krasner
Yayoi Kusama
Robert Mapplethorpe
Alice Neel
Willem Oorebeek
Milton Resnick
Glen Rubsamen
Patti Smith
Mayumi Terada

Yayoi Kusama
Painted Player Piano, 1971
Piano and bench,
53 x 56½ x 28 inches

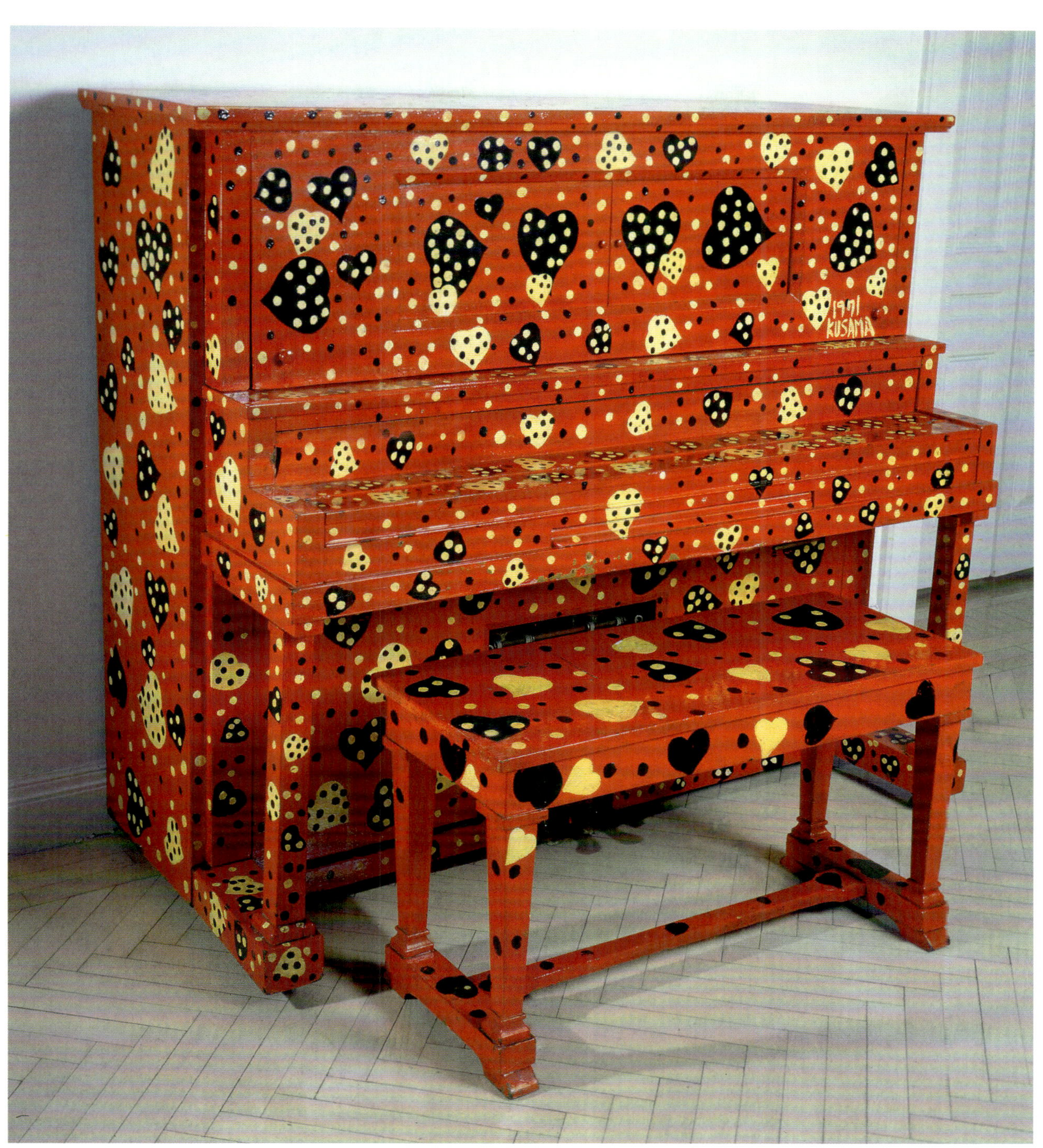
1971
KUSAMA

MININI

Mobile +39 335 784 35 43

Francesca Minini
IT-20134 Milan | Via Massimiano 25
Phone +39 02 26 92 46 71 | Fax +39 02 21 59 64 02
info@francescaminini.it | www.francescaminini.it
Directors Francesca Minini
Alessandra Minini

Artists at Art Nova | Becky Beasley
Simon Dybbroe Møller

Further artists represented | Ghada Amer
Matthias Bitzer
Armin Boehm
Tobias Buche
Alessandro Ceresoli
Paolo Chiasera
Jan De Cock
Giulio Frigo
Dan Graham
Ali Kazma
Deborah Ligorio
Jonas Lipps
Gabriele Picco
Riccardo Previdi
Mandla Reuter
Francesco Simeti

According to the dictionary, to 'design' something means taking decisions concerning the look and the function of a particular object. But design can also be about intention and purpose.

Becky Beasley and Simon Dybbroe Møller deliver poignantly different takes on the importance of making shape and function. Whereas Beasley's works take their starting point in the dreamy individualism of the designs of Carlo Mollino – where the personality of its maker seems to seep out of every detail, material, and surface – Dybbroe Møller looks at things in either a so general or so iconic way that the things seem to have shaped themselves.

Both artists re-design already-existing objects, but with different results. While Dybbroe Møller takes the objects and reinvents them to become new versions of themselves that have different meanings and different emotions in regards to their usefulness, Beasley's works offer us something new but deeply enshrouded by a mysterious presence, poetical and immaterial. Soulless objects versus transcendental ones.

A | **Becky Beasley**
The Outside, 2011
Exhibition view,
Francesca Minini, Milan

B | **Simon Dybbroe Møller**
'O', 2011
Exhibition view,
Francesca Minini, Milan

A

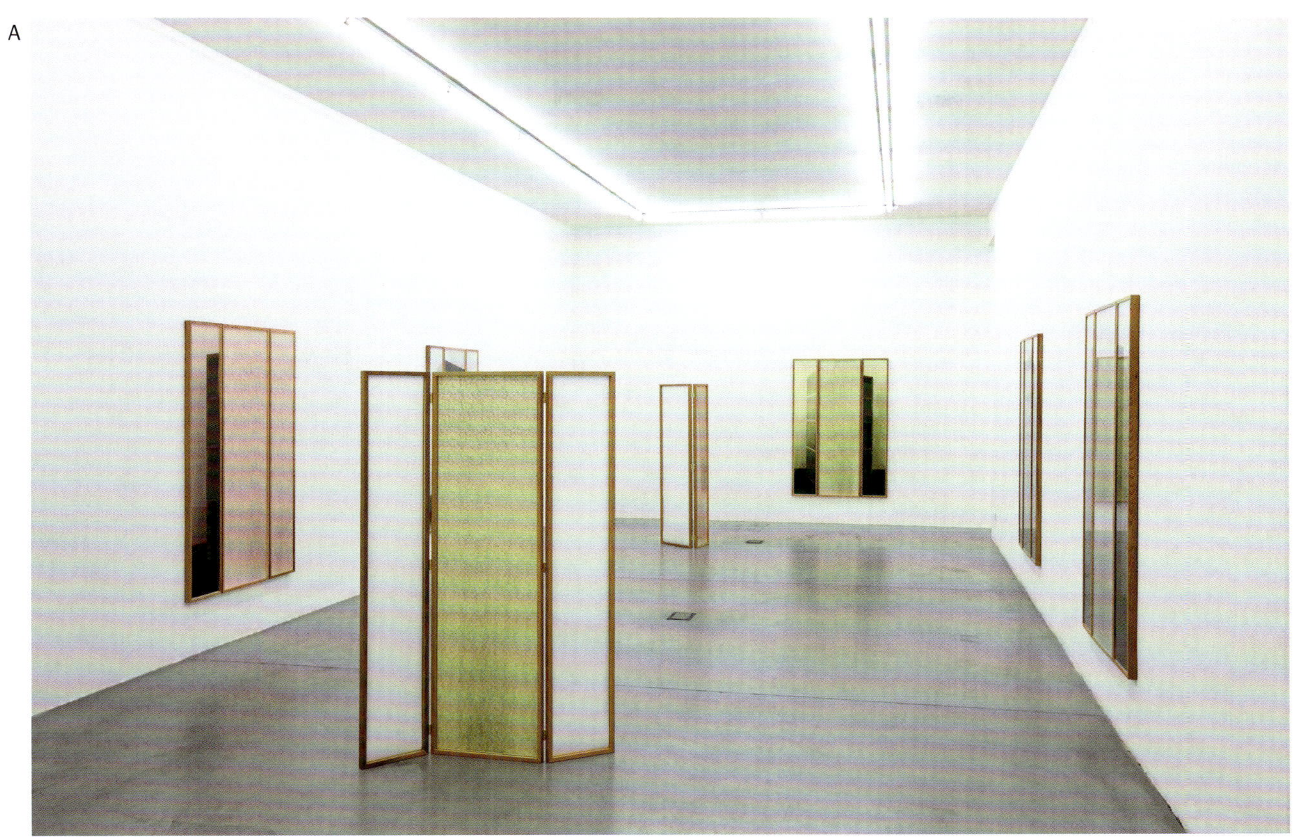

B

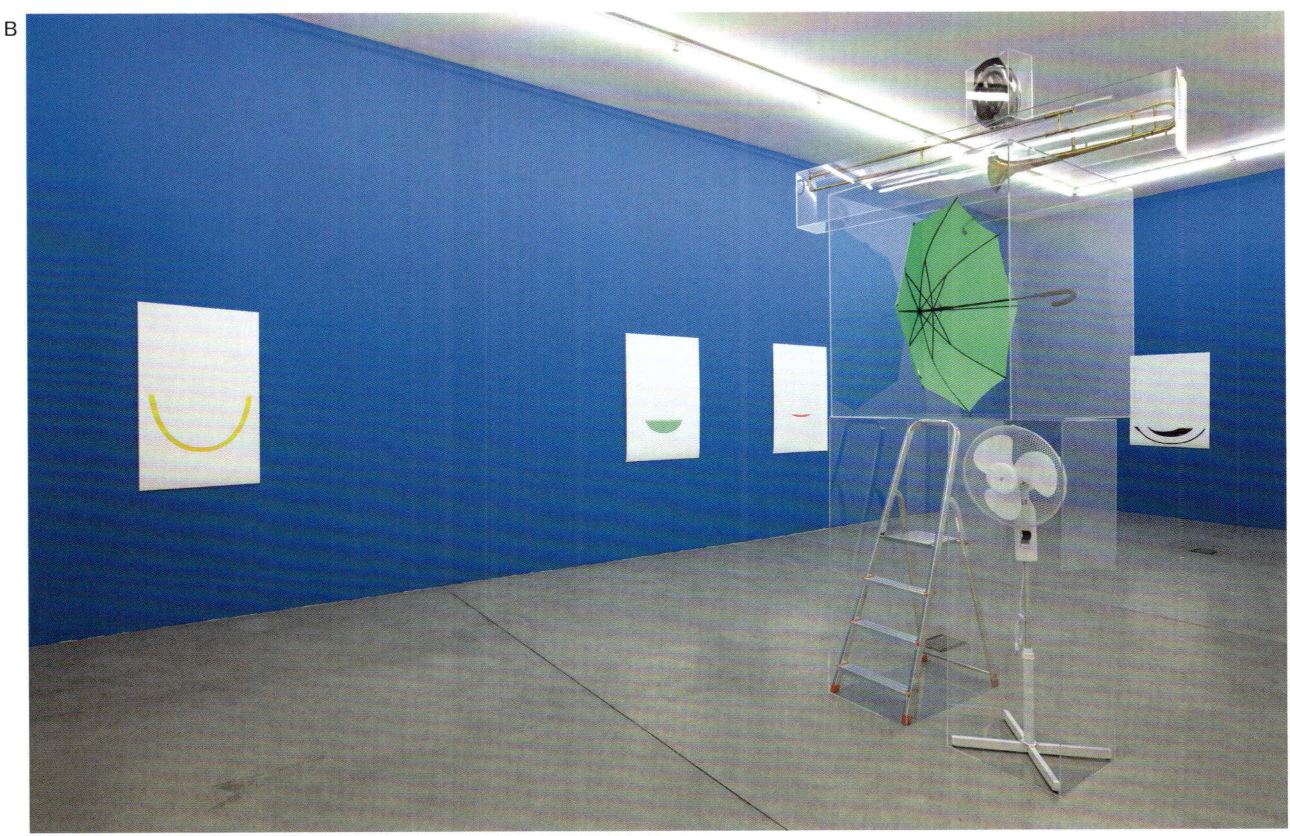

MIRO

Victoria Miro
GB-London N1 7RW | 16 Wharf Road
Phone +44 20 73368109 | Fax +44 20 72515596
info@victoria-miro.com | www.victoria-miro.com
Directors Victoria Miro
W.P. Miro
Glenn Scott Wright

Artists at Art Basel Miami Beach | **Doug Aitken**
Hernan Bas
Varda Caivano
Verne Dawson
Jules de Balincourt
Peter Doig
Stan Douglas
William Eggleston
Elmgreen & Dragset
Inka Essenhigh
Ian Hamilton Finlay
Barnaby Furnas
David Harrison
NS Harsha
Alex Hartley
Christian Holstad
Chantal Joffe
Isaac Julien
Idris Khan
John Kørner
Udomsak Krisanamis
Yayoi Kusama
Wangechi Mutu
Alice Neel
Maria Nepomuceno
Chris Ofili
Jacco Olivier
Grayson Perry
Tal R
Conrad Shawcross
Sarah Sze
Adriana Varejão
Suling Wang
Stephen Willats
Francesca Woodman

Barnaby Furnas
The Flenser, 2012
Water dispersed pigments, pencil, and acrylic on linen,
40⅛ x 28⅛ inches,
101.9 x 71.4 cm

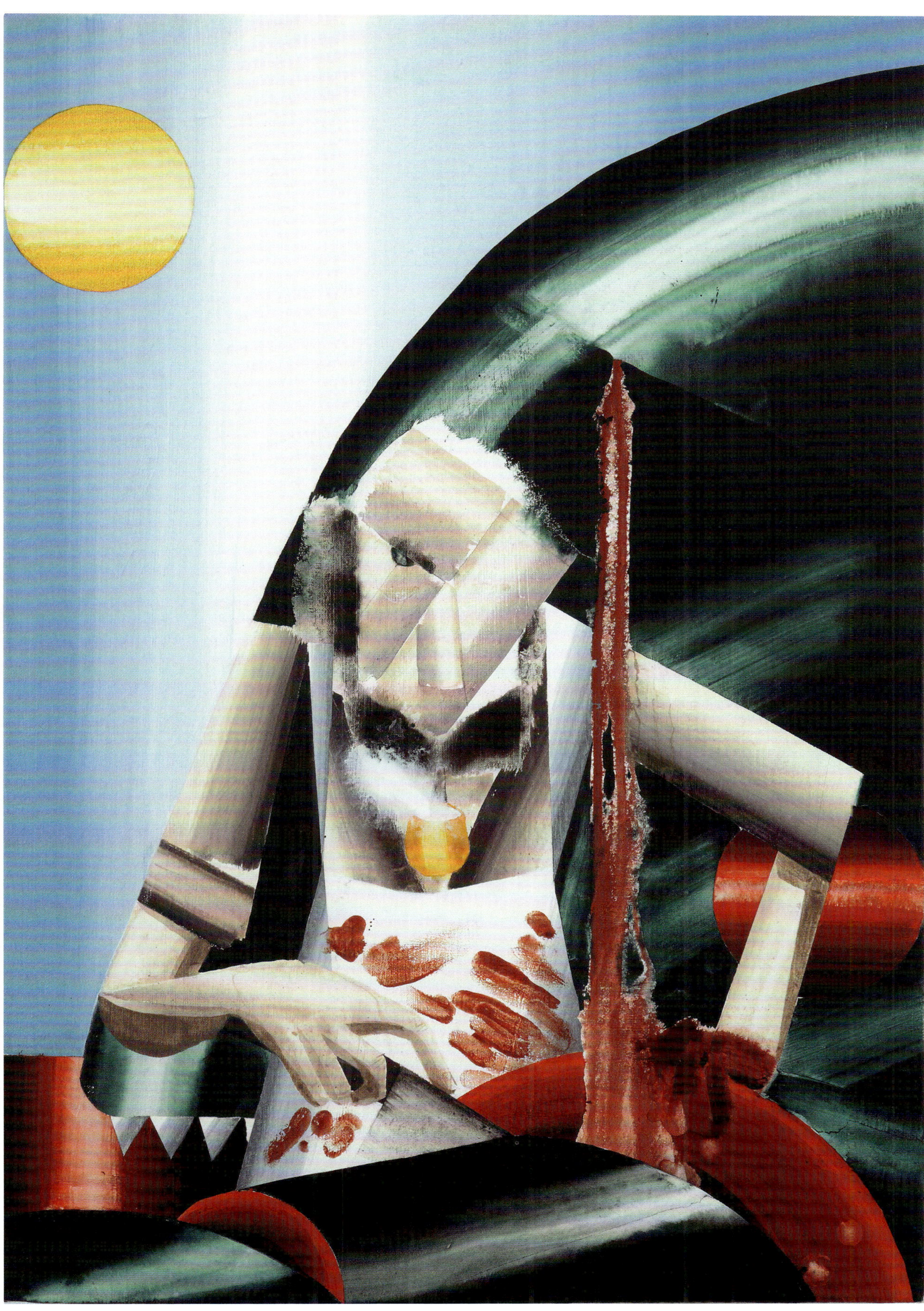

MITCHELL-INNES & NASH

Mitchell-Innes & Nash
US-New York, NY 10075 | 1018 Madison Avenue
Phone +1 212 744 74 00 | Fax +1 212 744 74 01
info@miandn.com | www.miandn.com
Directors David Nash
Lucy Mitchell-Innes

Mitchell-Innes & Nash
US-New York, NY 10001 | 534 West 26th Street
Phone +1 212 744 74 00 | Fax +1 212 744 74 01
info@miandn.com | www.miandn.com
Director Jay Gorney

Artists at
Art Basel Miami Beach | **Sarah Braman**
Keltie Ferris
Chris Johanson
Martin Kersels
Justine Kurland
Daniel Lefcourt
Chris Martin
Christopher Miner
Catherine Opie
Virginia Overton
William Pope.L
Martha Rosler
Amanda Ross-Ho
Norbert Schwontkowski
Jessica Stockholder
Paul Winstanley

Further artists represented | Alberto Burri
Anthony Caro
Allan D'Arcangelo
Leon Kossoff
Alexander Liberman
Roy Lichtenstein
Kenneth Noland
Jack Tworkov

Keltie Ferris
*: **, 2012
Oil, acrylic, and pastel on canvas,
90 x 80 inches

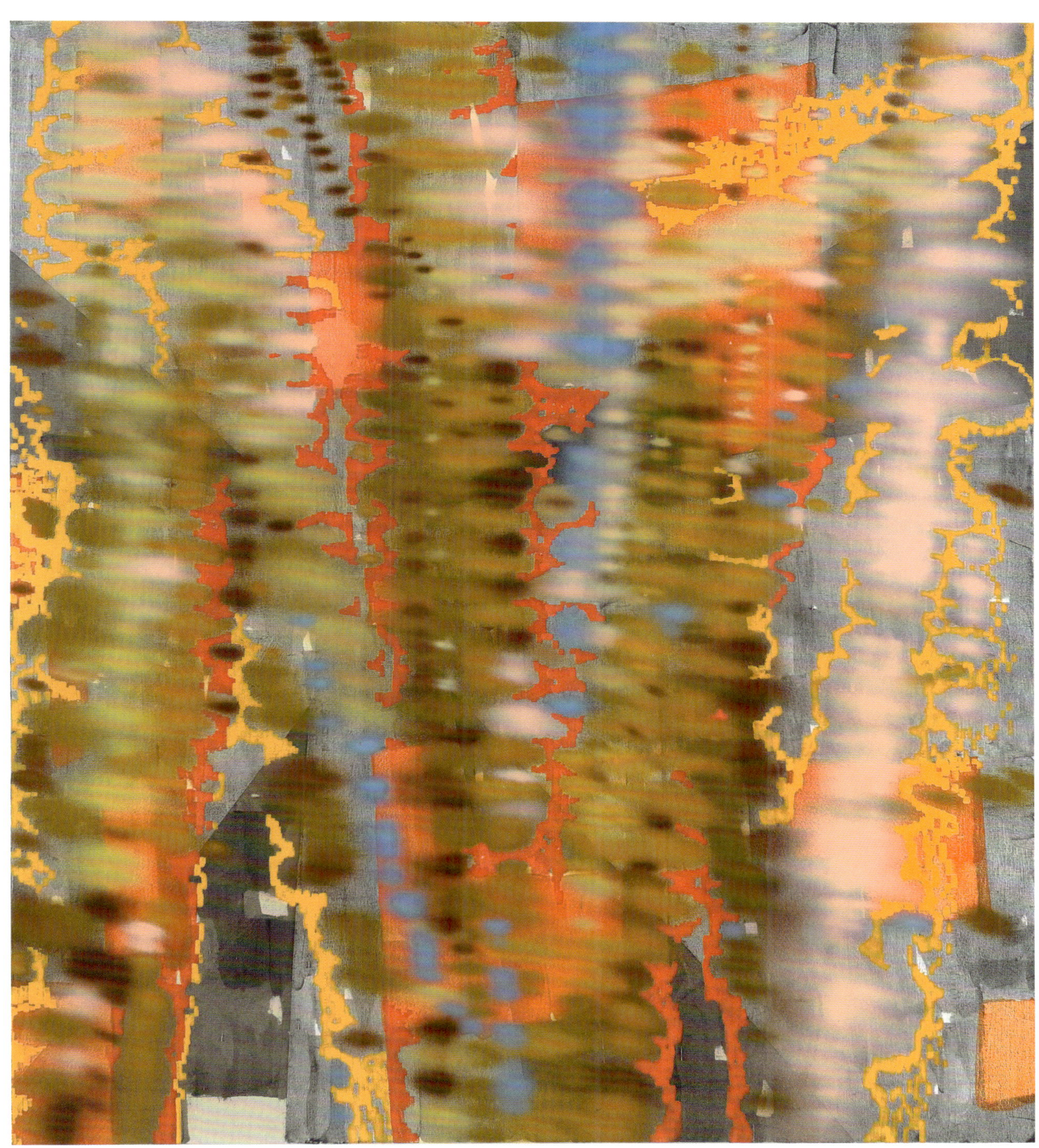

MODERN ART

Stuart Shave/Modern Art
GB-London W1W 8DF | 23/25 Eastcastle Street
Phone +44 20 72997950 | Fax +44 20 72997951
info@modernart.net | www.modernart.net
Directors Stuart Shave
Jimi Lee
Kirk McInroy
Ryan Moore

Artists at Art Basel Miami Beach | **David Altmejd**
Karla Black
Tom Burr
Nigel Cooke
Tim Gardner
Lothar Hempel
Jacqueline Humphries
Ansel Krut
Phillip Lai
Paul Lee
Linder
Barry McGee
Jonathan Meese
Matthew Monahan
Katy Moran
Oscar Murillo
David Noonan
Eva Rothschild
Bojan Šarčević
Lara Schnitger
Collier Schorr
Steven Shearer
Ricky Swallow
Richard Tuttle
Clare Woods

Oscar Murillo
work! #3, 2012
Oil, tape, spray, oil stick, dirt on canvas, 314 x 279 cm

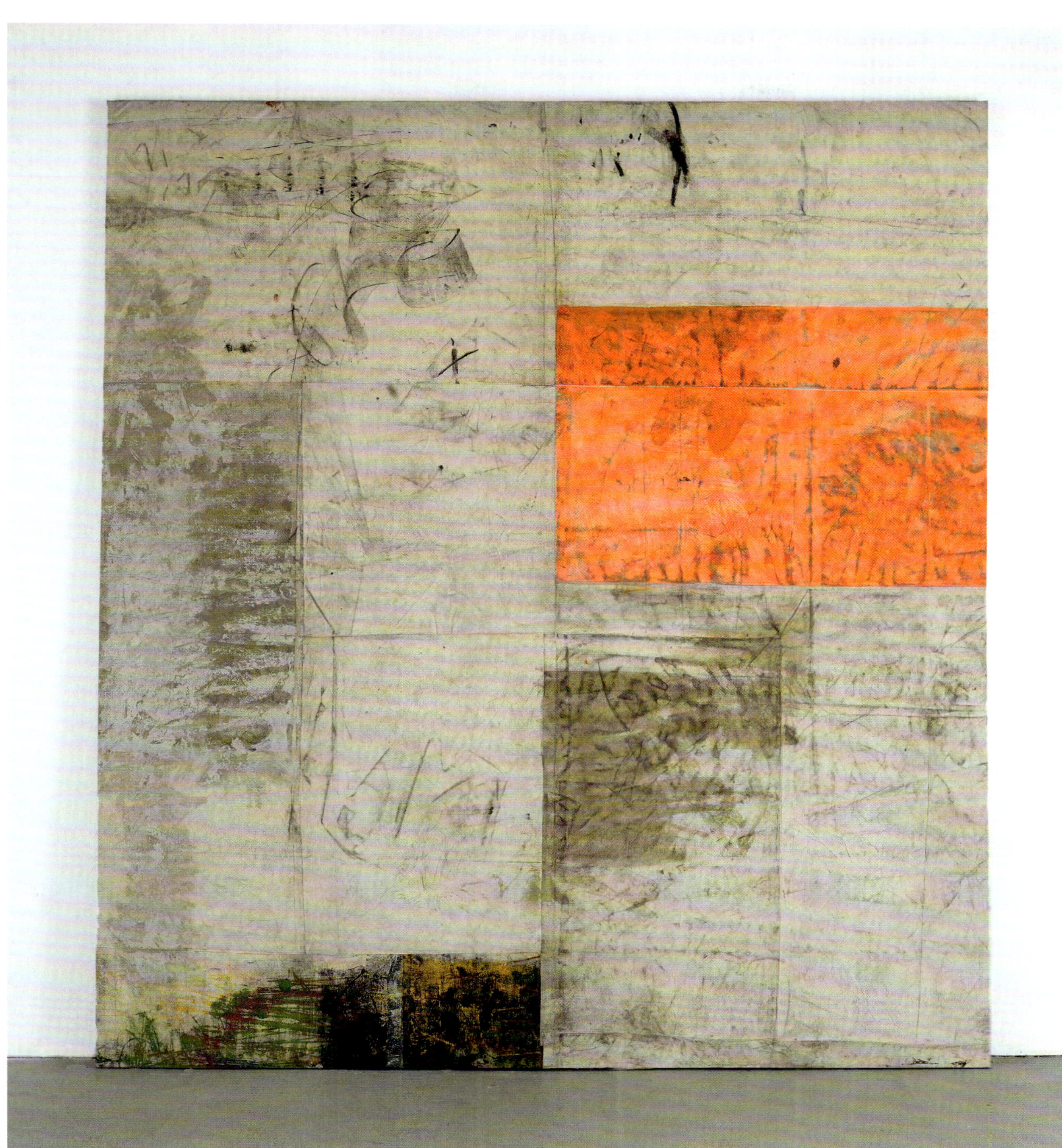

MODERN INSTITUTE

The Modern Institute
GB-Glasgow G1 5QN | 14-20 Osborne Street
Phone +44 141 248 37 11 | Fax +44 141 552 59 88
mail@themoderninstitute.com | www.themoderninstitute.com
Directors Toby Webster
Andrew Hamilton

Artists at Art Basel Miami Beach | **Dirk Bell**
Martin Boyce
Jeremy Deller
Alex Dordoy
Urs Fischer
Kim Fisher
Luke Fowler
Henrik Håkansson
Mark Handforth
Thomas Houseago
Richard Hughes
Chris Johanson
Andrew Kerr
Jim Lambie
Duncan MacQuarrie
Victoria Morton
Scott Myles
Nicolas Party
Toby Paterson
Simon Periton
Manfred Pernice
Mary Redmond
Anselm Reyle
Eva Rothschild
Monika Sosnowska
Simon Starling
Katja Strunz
Tony Swain
Spencer Sweeney
Joanne Tatham & Tom O'Sullivan
Pádraig Timoney
Hayley Tompkins
Sue Tompkins
Cathy Wilkes
Michael Wilkinson
Gregor Wright
Richard Wright

Hayley Tompkins
Chair, 2011
Chair, watercolor, 79 x 48 x 43 cm

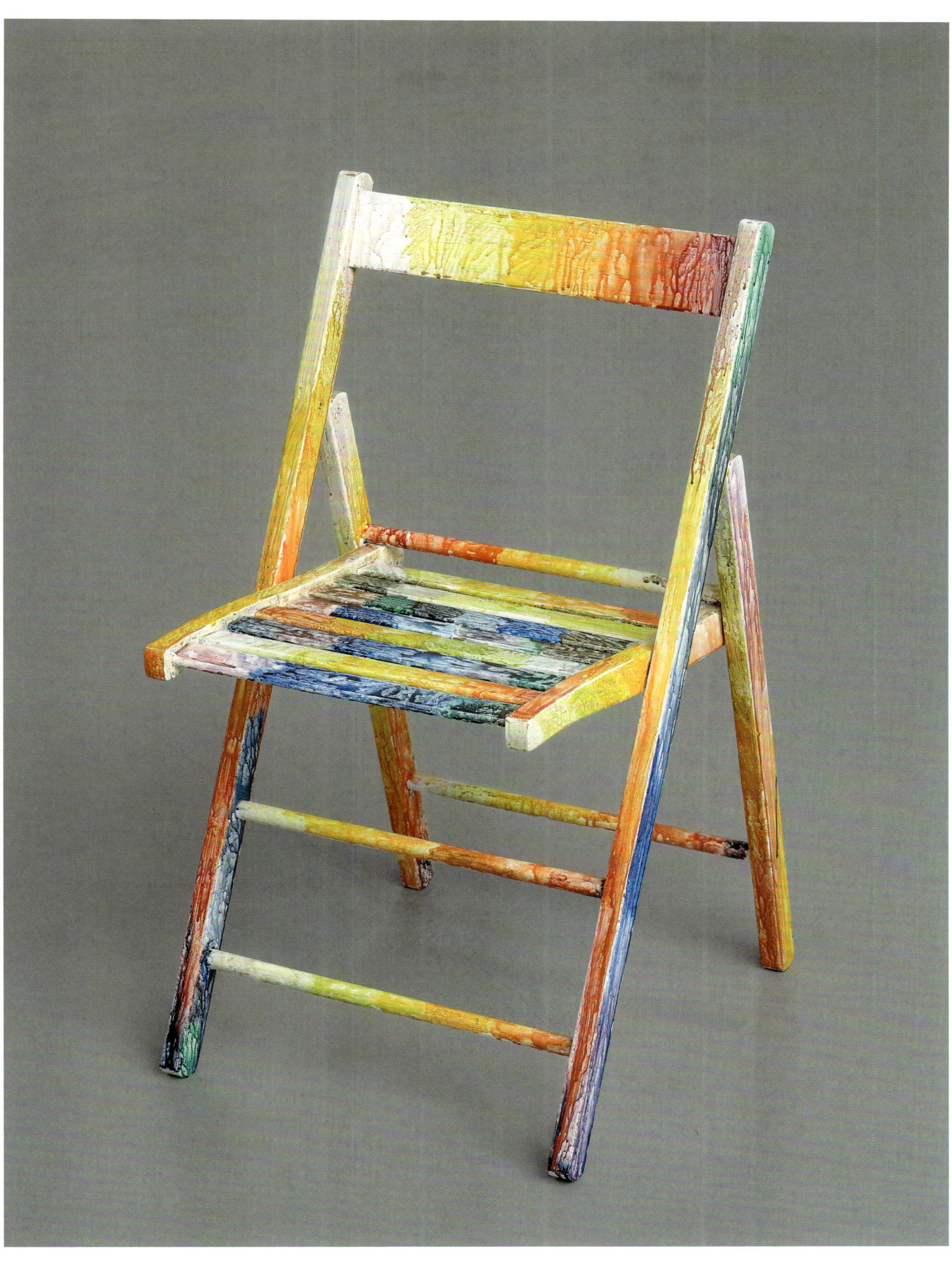

MONCLOVA

Mobile +52 1 55 18 00 41 50

Proyectos Monclova
MX-06700 Mexico City | Colima 55, Colonia Roma
Phone +52 55 55 25 97 15 | +52 55 47 54 35 46
info@proyectosmonclova.com | www.proyectosmonclova.com
Director José García

Artists at Art Nova | Nina Beier
Tania Pérez Córdova

Further artists represented | Edgardo Aragón
Nina Beier & Marie Lund
François Bucher
Mario García Torres
Christian Jankowski
Eduardo Sarabia
Tercerunquinto
Eduardo Terrazas

Following the notion of breaking an object in order to truly experience it, Nina Beier (*1975, Denmark) presents *The Demonstrators,* a group of artworks that portrays futility as a state of pure presence.

At the core of Beier's sculptures are images purchased from various stock photography agencies that come from online sources. These found images are then merged with found objects: poster print-outs are dipped in glue and hung to dry on different sorts of objects that constitute the support.

These *ensembles,* although apparently simplistic, allow a complete merging of sign, support, and *that which is signified,* although – at the same time – they could suggest a collapse of language, instead of its configuration. They seek recognizable symbolical value while remaining open metaphors, and have the ability to refer to many things, while left to reflect upon their own sense of 'being.' While the poster and its object support are firmly glued together, Beier takes an interest in how they remain without an adhesive that cements subject and object together so that the intentional experience is one.

The work Tania Pérez Córdova (*1979, Mexico City, Mexico) is inspired by her interest in the way that the certainty of an object is created and in the relation between vision and conviction. She explores the situation of objects, paying special attention to the way in which they exist. Pérez Córdova does not believe in the autonomy of objects but in their circumstantial existence and significance. A very important part of her work consists in being really close to the production process, where she can closely analyze the materials and the way in which one thing leads to the other, experiencing the invisible content of a work of art through the space between one object and another.

Nina Beier
The Demonstrators, 2011
Mixed media

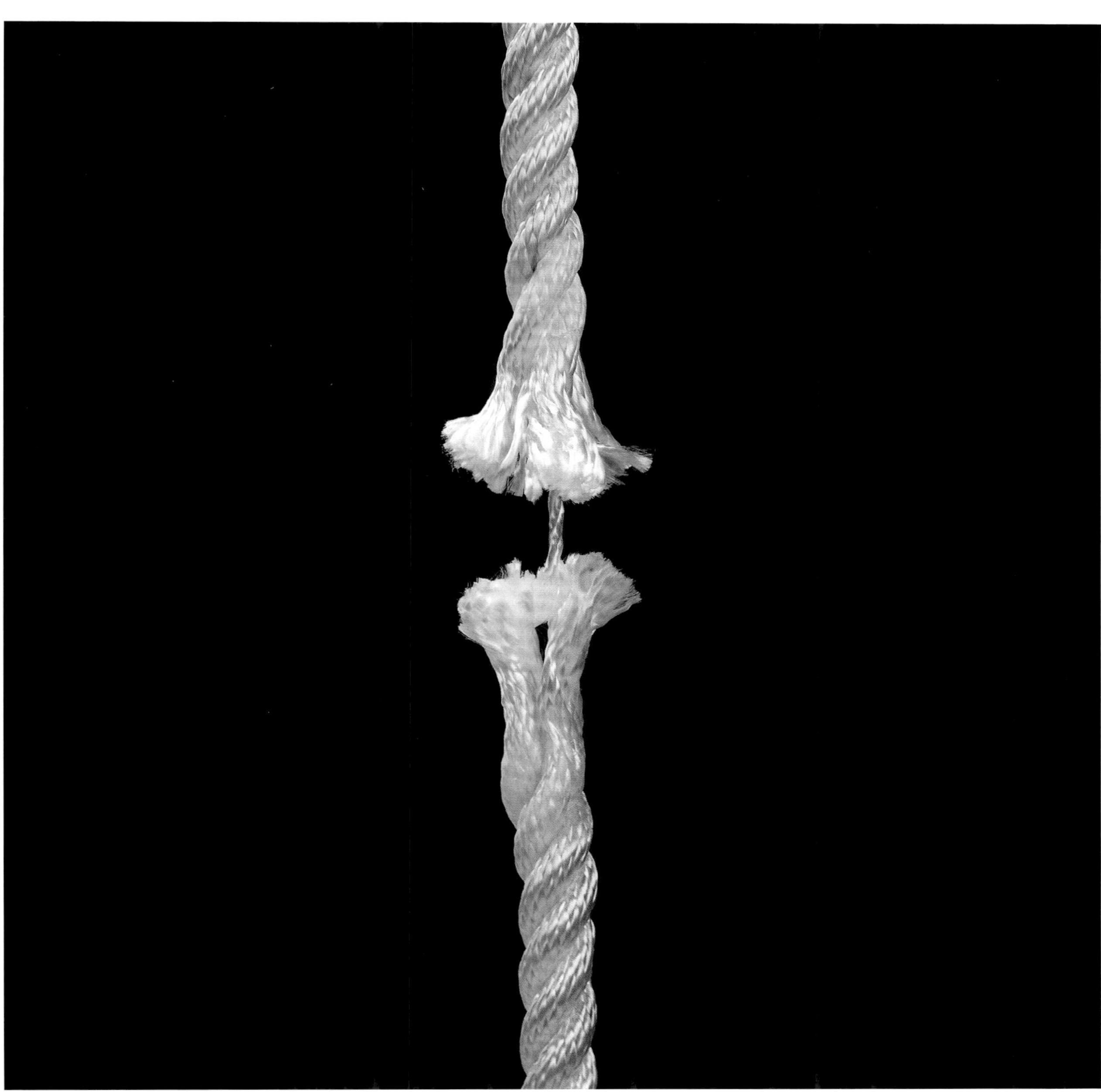

MOR CHARPENTIER

Mobile +33 7 60 63 41 71

Galerie Mor Charpentier
FR-75003 Paris | 8, rue Saint-Claude
Phone +33 1 44 54 01 58
contact@mor-charpentier.com | www.mor-charpentier.com
Directors Alex Mor
Philippe Charpentier

One-Person Show | Artist Information

Julieta Aranda

*1975, Mexico City, Mexico
Lives and works in Berlin, Germany, and New York, NY, United States

Selected exhibitions:
2012 *dOCUMENTA (13),* Kassel
n.n.k., Berlin
Fondazione Giuliani, Rome
2011 Biennale di Venezia, Venice
Stroom Den Haag, The Hague
Living as Form, Creative Time, New York, NY
Istanbul Biennial
Portikus, Frankfurt am Main
2010 New Museum of Contemporary Art, New York, NY
Kunstverein, Arnsberg
MUSAC, Léon
2009 Solomon R. Guggenheim Museum, New York, NY
Museum of Contemporary Art, Miami, FL
Witte de With, Rotterdam
2007 Museum of Contemporary Art, Chicago, IL
2nd Moscow Biennial
2006 MUSAC, Léon
2000 VII Havanna Biennial

Central to Aranda's multidimensional practice are her involvement with circulation mechanisms and the idea of a 'poetics of circulation,' the possibility of a politicized subjectivity through the perception and use of time, and the notion of power over the imaginary.

As a co-director of e-flux together with Anton Vidokle, Julieta Aranda has developed the projects *Time/Bank, Pawnshop,* and *e-flux video rental,* all of which started in the e-flux storefront in New York and have traveled to many venues worldwide.

But they look like anyone else, usually, and tend not to announce themselves is a project that explores Aranda's interest in science fiction and dystopian architecture. Taking as a point of departure the Le Corbusier-inspired multifamily buildings that were built in Mexico City in the 1940s, 50s, and 60s (mostly by architect Mario Pani), the Roosevelt Island complex in New York City, and the 1966 high school social studies book *Living as Neighbors,* Aranda uses archival material, original photographs, video, and sculptural elements to create a speculative narrative that responds to these spaces.

The story of the film *Living as Neighbors,* based on the book by the same name, is interrupted by the heavily altered images of brutalist buildings and the potential sideline narratives that might be taking place within their walls. These images are also presented in the booth, outside the projection space, together with a sculptural display made out of construction materials ranging from the cheap, mundane, build-it-quick materials that are often used to build multifamily buildings to the more elusive, poetic materials that the social body inhabiting these buildings can use to create its own identity.

Gallery Information | Exhibition summary:

2012: Voluspa Jarpa, solo show, November/December 2012
The Colour Red, Liliana Porter, solo show, September/October 2012
A Pilgrimage through Light & Spells, Charwei Tsai, solo show, May-July 2012
Cartographie du Désastre, Oscar Muñoz, Teresa Margolles, Julieta Hanono, January/February 2012
Poulpe, Yoshua Okón, solo show, March/April 2012

2011: *The Riot Act,* Athanasios Argianas, Cevdet Erek, Inci Eviner, Jan Freuchen, Deniz Gül, November 2011-January 2012
Customary Beauty, Alexander Apostol, José Dàvila, Mateo Lòpez, Terence Gower, Laura Gannon, Milena Bonilla, Pablo Leòn de la Barra, September/October 2011
La Mala Educaciòn, Priscilla Monge & Mohamed Namou, June/August 2011

2010: *Tentative d'expansion d'un lieu Parisen,* Cadu Costa, Charwei Tsai, Ignacio Uriarte, Daniel Medina, Nicolàs Paris, November/December 2010
Anarchive, Oscar Muñoz, opening show, October/November 2010

Fair participation: ARCO, Madrid, 2011 & 2012
Zona MACO, 2012
Loop, Barcelona, 2012
Art-O-Rama, Marseille, 2012
ArtBo (Bogotá), 2011 & 2012
Frame Section, Frieze London, 2012

Further artists represented:
Milena Bonilla
Voluspa Jarpa
Oscar Muñoz
Mohamed Namou
Yoshua Okón
Charwei Tsai

Julieta Aranda
I wanted to give it to someone else, 2012
Giclée print on cotton paper, unframed: 85 x 65 cm

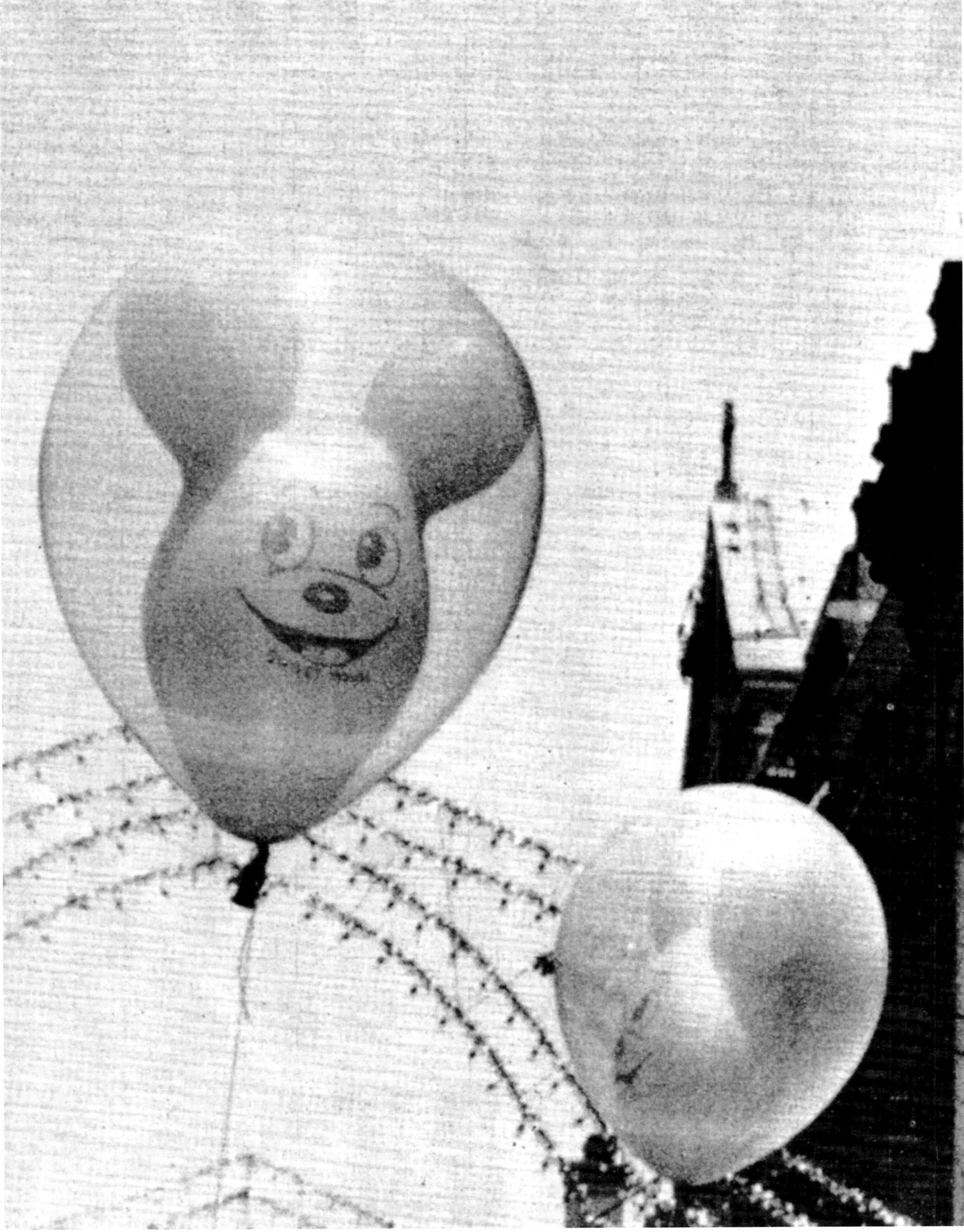

MOTHER'S TANKSTATION

mother's tankstation
IE-Dublin 8 | 41-43 Watling Street, Usher's Island
Phone +353 1 6717654
gallery@motherstankstation.com | www.motherstankstation.com
Director Finola Jones

One-Person Show | Artist Information

Atsushi Kaga

*1978, Tokyo, Japan
Lives and works in New York, NY, United States, and Dublin, Ireland

Selected solo and group exhibitions:
2012 *One and Many,* Location One, New York, NY
2011 *Astatic,* Sandra & David Bakalar Gallery, MassArt, Boston, MA
Art Futures, Art HK 11, with mother's tankstation
2010 *Rest with Us in Peace,* mother's tankstation, Dublin
Kantor Gallery, Los Angeles, CA
Process Room, Artists Residency Program, Irish Museum of Modern Art, Dublin
2009 *Why Can We Keep Going Forward? Because We Forget The Problem of Yesterday,* Galeria Leme, São Paulo
2008 *I Want to Give Love to Socially Neglected Parts of You, That's My Mission,* Butler Gallery, Kilkenny
Consolations for Bunny, Nicolas Krupp, Basel
2007 *Bunny's Darkness and Other Stories,* mother's tankstation, Dublin

Residencies:
2011/12 Location One, New York, NY, awarded by The Arts Council of Ireland
2011 ISCP International Studio & Curatorial Program, New York, NY
2010 Artist's Residency Program, Irish Museum of Modern Art, Dublin
2009 Galeria Eduardo Leme, São Paolo, residency and project space exhibition
Fountainhead Residency, Miami, FL

Further artists represented | Uri Aran
Ian Burns
Nina Canell
Kevin Cosgrove
Brendan Earley
Shane McCarthy
Locky Morris
Mairead O'hEocha
Matt Sheridan Smith
David Sherry

Nerd Bag Factory
Atsushi Kaga's work is a compelling fusion of East and West; visually spectacular, his unmistakably Japanese stylings are extended by caustic wit and an astute manipulation of bilingual (Japanese-to-Irish/English) text. Confronting complex sociological concerns of identity and social identification, Kaga's work exploits familiarity with the form of the talking 'funny animal' derived from comics and animation. His cast of stylized 'avatars' appears repeatedly throughout his drawings, sculptures, and animations. This subterranean world pivots around two main protagonists: Usacchi (a lovable, but roguish, Aesopian rabbit – importantly, Kaga's alter-ego) and Kumacchi (a drug-addicted amputee bear and soul mate). Kaga recounts that, when he was a child, his mother habitually handmade fabric bags, out-supplying need or purpose. Counter to peer-driven identification with the dominant culture of 'designer goods,' the junior Kagas were obliged to use these 'unique' artifacts produced from scraps of patterned fabrics and Kimono remnants as school bags. *Nerd Bag Factory,* an accumulative project conducted with the participation of the artist's mother, establishes a busy production facility to output exclusive 'replicas' of these eccentrically handcrafted utilitarian objects. On numerous levels, the installation is conceived as cultural payback.

Atsushi Kaga
Usacchi Sewing, 2012
Acrylic on board, 20x20cm

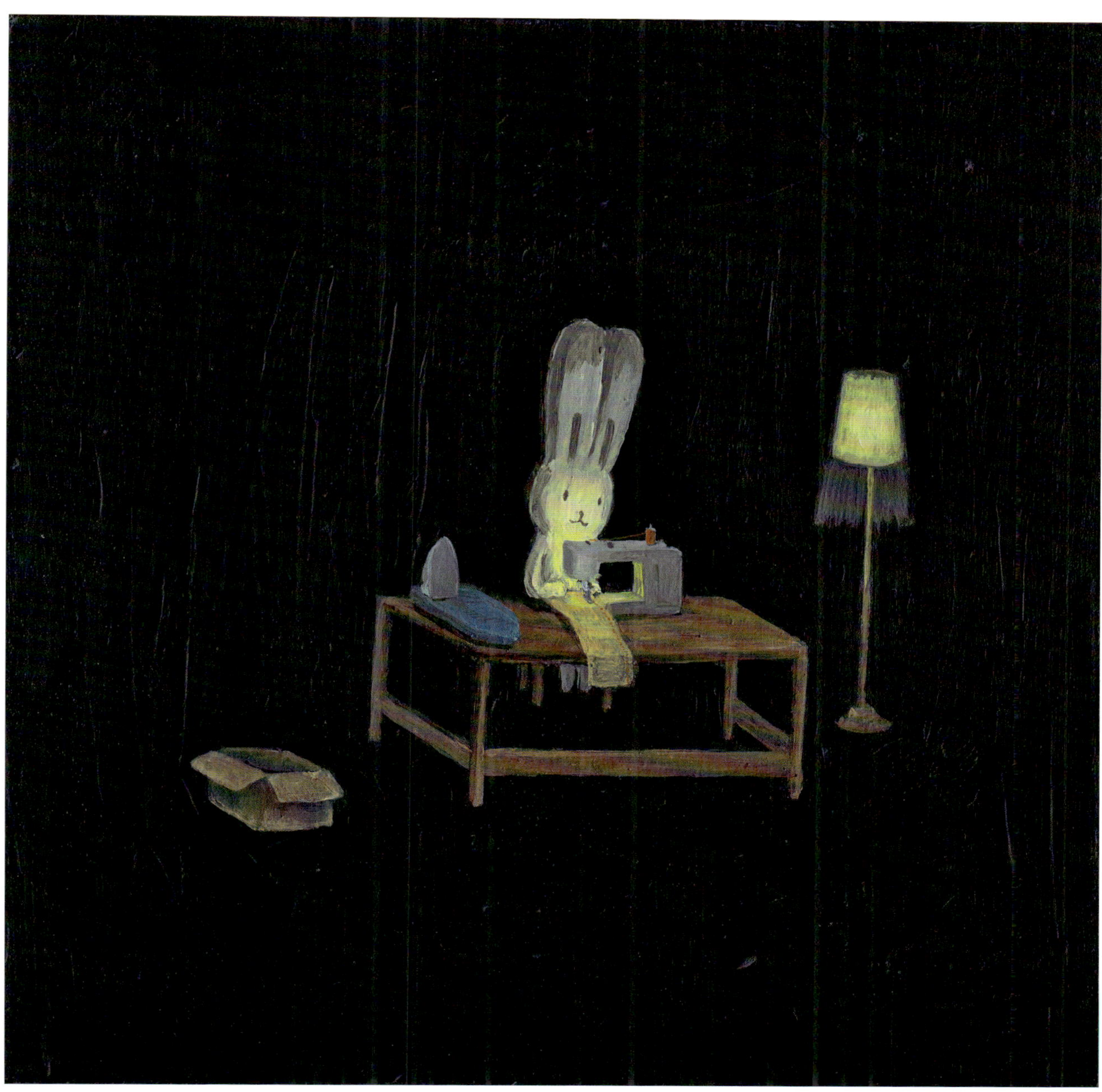

NÄCHST ST. STEPHAN

Mobile +43 664 338 8173

Galerie nächst St. Stephan
Rosemarie Schwarzwälder
AT-1010 Vienna | Grünangergasse
Phone +43 1 512 12 66 | Fax +43 1 513 43 07
galerie@schwarzwaelder.at | www.schwarzwaelder.at
Director Rosemarie Schwarzwälder

Artists at
Art Basel Miami Beach | **Adam Adach**
Polly Apfelbaum
Herbert Brandl
Michał Budny
Ernst Caramelle
Helmut Federle
Bernard Frize
Katharina Grosse
Imi Knoebel
Daniel Knorr
Lee Ufan
Isa Melsheimer
Manfred Pernice
Karin Sander
Jörg Sasse
Adrian Schiess
Jessica Stockholder
Joëlle Tuerlinckx
Günter Umberg
James Welling

Further artists represented | Sabine Boehl
Heinrich Dunst
Rainer Ganahl
Aneta Grzeszykowska
Agnieszka Kalinowska
Luisa Kasalicky
Sonia Leimer
Christoph Weber

Adrian Schiess
Untitled, 2012
Acrylic on polyester, 230 x 235 cm

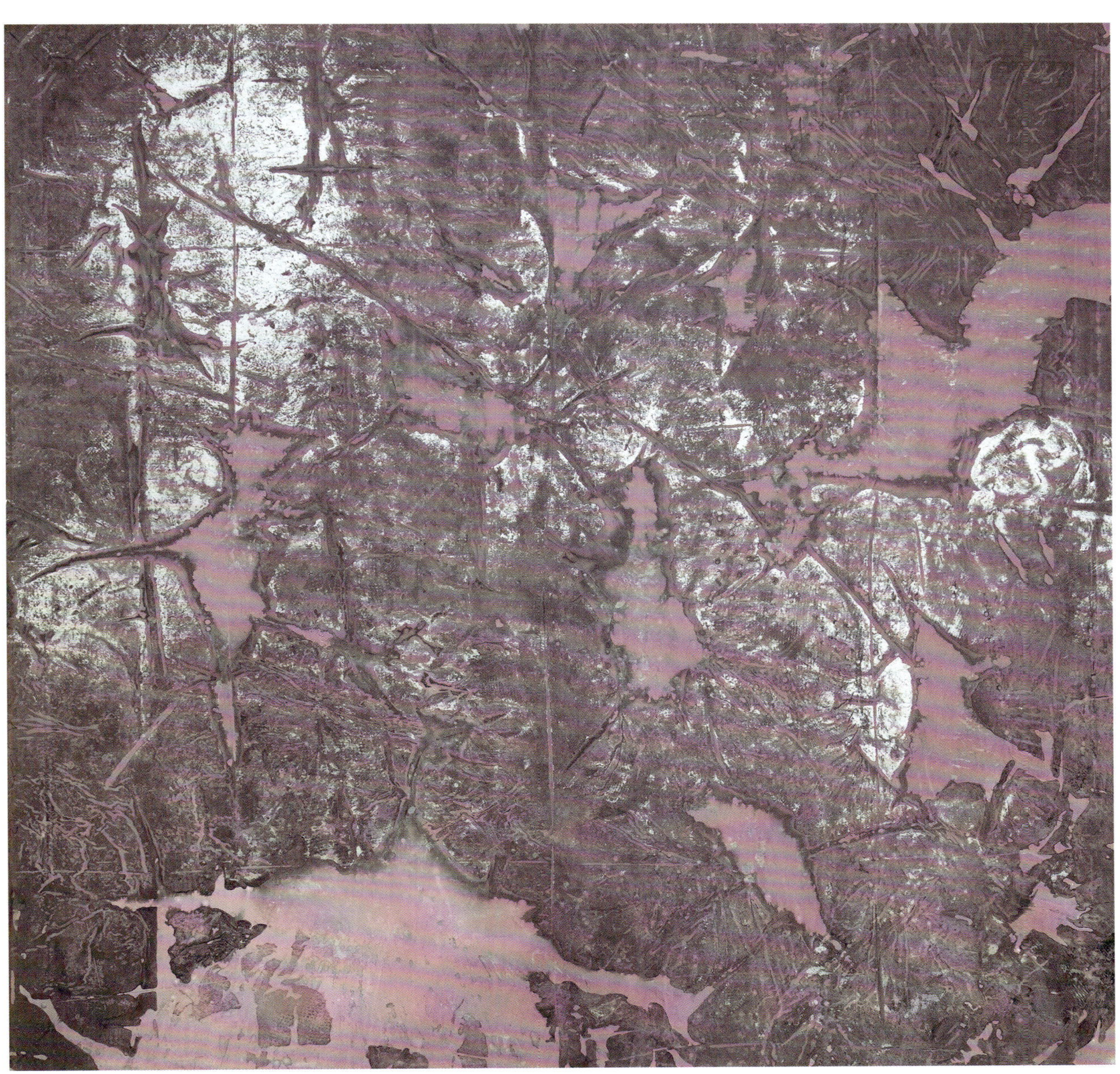

NAHEM

Edward Tyler Nahem Fine Art LLC
US-New York, NY 10019 | 37 West 57th Street
Phone +1 212 517 24 53 | Fax +1 212 861 35 66
info@etnahem.com | www.etnahem.com
Directors Edward Nahem
Kristen Chiacchia
Janis Gardner Cecil
Paloma Martin Llopis

Artists at Art Basel Miami Beach | **Jean-Michel Basquiat**
Alighiero Boetti
Alexander Calder
John Chamberlain
Willem de Kooning
Sam Francis
Keith Haring
Ellsworth Kelly
Anselm Kiefer
Franz Kline
Roy Lichtenstein
René Magritte
Joan Miró
Joan Mitchell
Pablo Picasso
Richard Prince
Robert Rauschenberg
Gerhard Richter
Mark Rothko
Ed Ruscha
Frank Stella
Cy Twombly
Andy Warhol
Tom Wesselmann

Keith Haring
Untitled, 1986
Acrylic on canvas, 60 x 60 inches

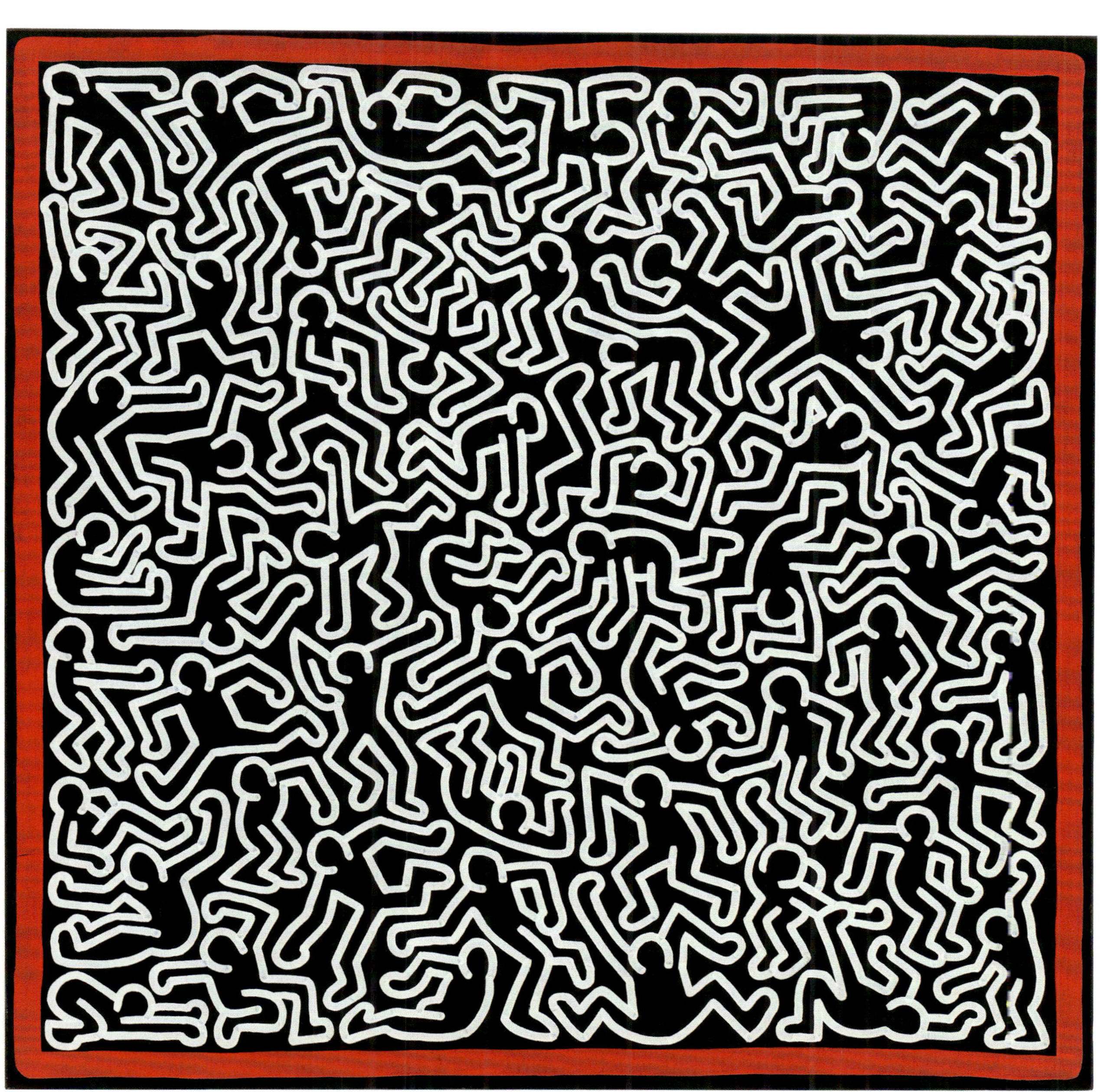

HELLY NAHMAD

Helly Nahmad Gallery
US-New York, NY 10075 | 975 Madison Avenue
Phone +1 212 879 20 75 | Fax +1 212 737 14 83
info@hellynahmadgallery.com | www.hellynahmadgallery.com
Director Marzina Marzetti

Artists at Art Basel Miami Beach | **Georges Braque**
Alexander Calder
Marc Chagall
Salvador Dalí
Giorgio de Chirico
Edgar Degas
Jean Dubuffet
Max Ernst
Lucio Fontana
Sam Francis
Alberto Giacometti
Juan Gris
Wassily Kandinsky
Wifredo Lam
Fernand Léger
René Magritte
Marino Marini
Henri Matisse
Roberto Matta
Joan Miró
Amedeo Modigliani
Claude Monet
Giorgio Morandi
Francis Picabia
Pablo Picasso
Camille Pissarro
Pierre Auguste Renoir
Alfred Sisley
Chaïm Soutine
Yves Tanguy
Kees van Dongen

Gallery Information | The Helly Nahmad Gallery is a leading commercial gallery located in New York City on the corner of 76th Street and Madison Avenue. The gallery, which opened in January 2000, specializes in works by Impressionist and Modern masters. The collection includes such artists as Chagall, Dubuffet, Ernst, Kandinsky, Léger, Matisse, Miró, Modigliani, Monet, and Picasso, among others.

Twice a year, the gallery produces a major exhibition as a means of increasing its presence in the New York art scene. Among the most recent were:

2011: *Soutine/Bacon*
2010: *Sam Francis*
2009: *Jean Dubuffet*
2008: *Picasso's Bodegones*
2007: *Picasso Themes & Variations from the Mourlot Collection 1949-1958*
2006: *Max Ernst*
2005: *Fernand Léger*
Amedeo Modigliani: A Bohemian Myth
2004: *Kandinsky: Sounds of Color*

Aside from the semi-annual exhibitions, the gallery maintains a permanent collection. Through enhancing our inventory, we have also created significant private collections, and we lend regularly to major museums around the world.

Pablo Picasso
Double portrait de mousquetaire, 1969
Pastel and grease pencil on lithograph, 74.4 x 52.9 cm

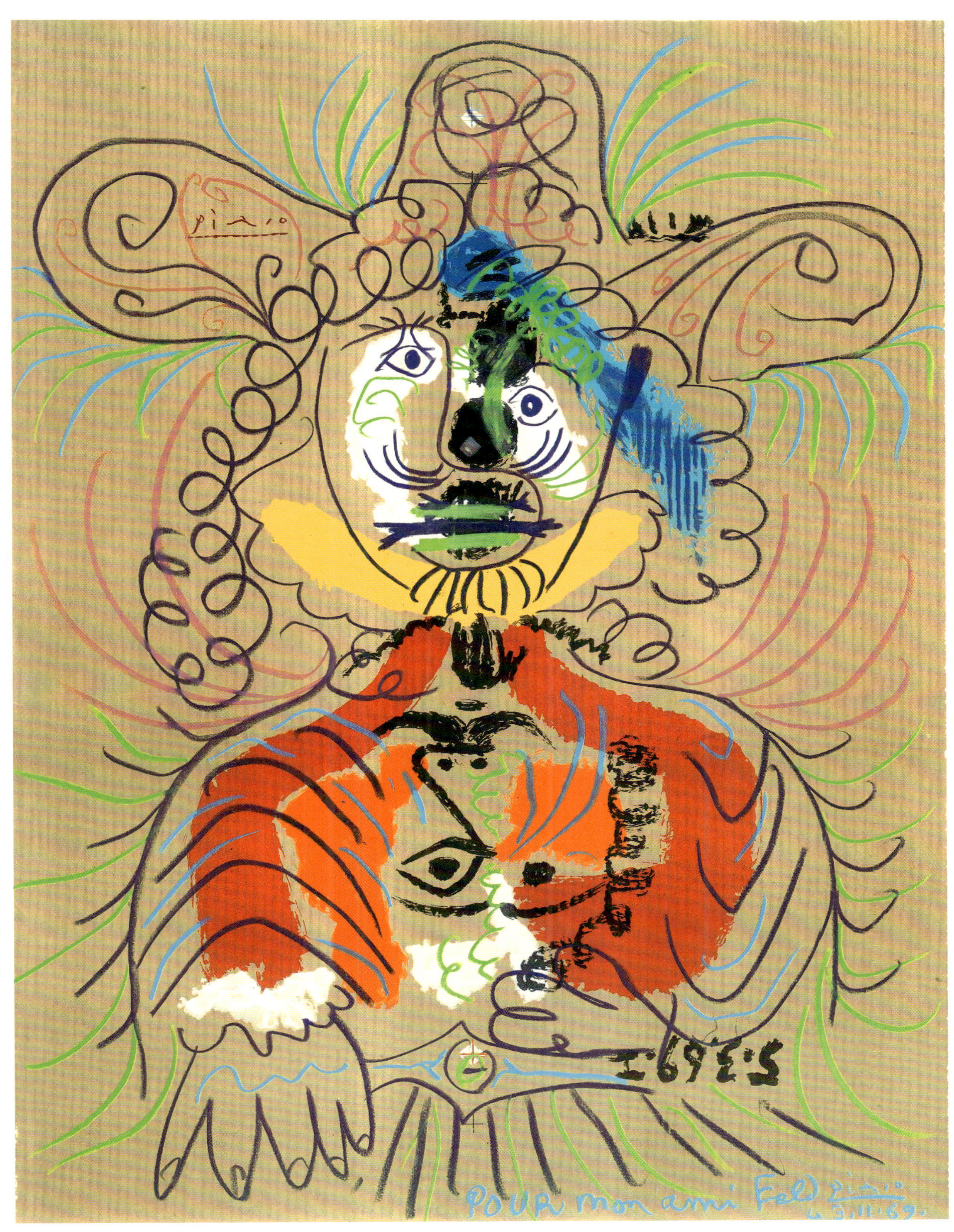
POUR mon ami Feld
3.11.69.

NAUMANN

Francis M. Naumann Fine Art
US-New York, NY 10019 | 24 West 57th Street, Suite 305
Phone +1 212 582 32 01
LHOOQ@francisnaumann.com | www.francisnaumann.com
Director Francis M. Naumann

Artists at
Art Basel Miami Beach | **Jean Crotti**
Katherine S. Dreier
Marcel Duchamp
Suzanne Duchamp
Raymond Duchamp-Villon
Stanley William Hayter
Leon Kelly
Man Ray
Gordon Onslow Ford
Walter Pach
Francis Picabia
Naomi Savage
Dorothea Tanning
Jacques Villon
Elsa von Freytag-Loringhoven
Beatrice Wood

Gallery Information | Francis M. Naumann Fine Art specializes in the art of the Dada and Surrealist periods, as well as a selection of contemporary artists whose work displays related aesthetic sensibilities.

Of special interest are works by Jean Crotti (1878-1958), Marcel Duchamp (1887-1968), Stanley William Hayter (1901-1988), Leon Kelly (1901-1982), Man Ray (1890-1976), Francis Picabia (1879-1953), and Beatrice Wood (1893-1998), artists who made their most important contribution to the history of art during the first half of the 20th century, but who continue to be of relevance for countless contemporary artists who seek inspiration from their pioneering example.

Among the artists who currently exhibit at the gallery are: Nancy Becker, Mike Bidlo, Robert Forman, Kathleen Gilje, Don Joint, Pamela Joseph, Sophie Matisse, Jacques Moitoret, André Raffray, Douglas Vogel, and Tetsuya Yamada.

Further artists represented: Nancy Becker
Robert Brinker
Robert Forman
Don Joint
Pamela Joseph
Sophie Matisse
Wallace Putnam
André Raffray
Tom Shannon
Douglas Vogel

Katherine S. Dreier
Untitled, 1932
Oil on canvas, 28 x 12 inches

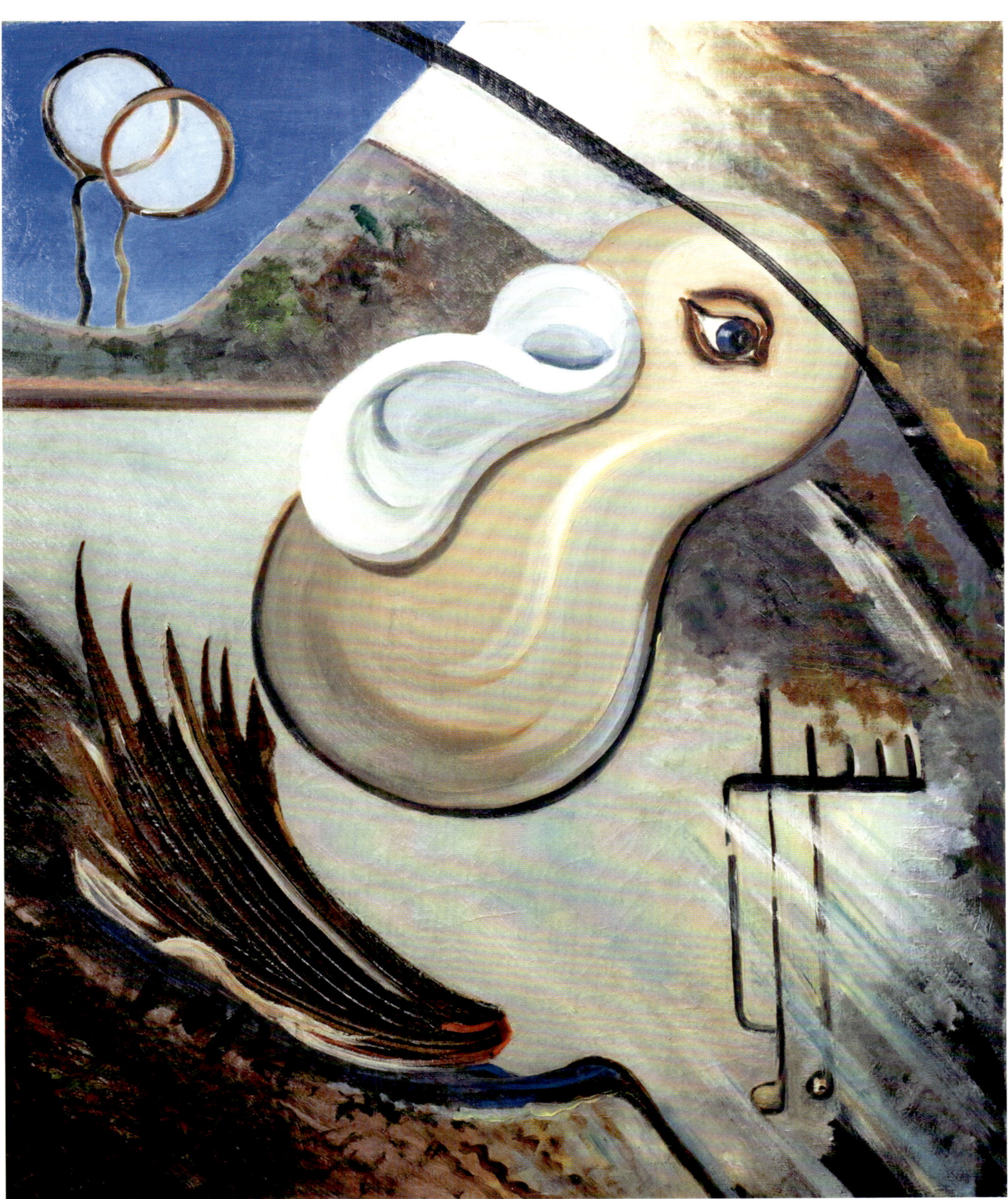

NAVARRO

Galeria Leandro Navarro
ES-28014 Madrid | Amor de Dios, 1
Phone +34 91 4298955 | Fax +34 91 4299155
galeria@leandro-navarro.com | www.leandro-navarro.com
Director Iñigo Navarro

Artists at
Art Basel Miami Beach | **Francisco Bores**
Marc Chagall
Oscar Domínguez
Pablo Gargallo
Baltasar Lobo
Manolo Millares
Joan Miró
Pablo Picasso
Manuel Rivera
Kurt Schwitters
Joaquín Torres García
Maria Helena Vieira da Silva

Gallery Information | Founded in 1978, the gallery specializes in the historical avant-garde within international modern art. Shows representing art movements like Cubism, Purism, Dadaism, and Constructivist painting have taken place from the start.

Solo exhibitions of artists like Giorgio Morandi and Kurt Schwitters were shown here for the first time in a private Spanish gallery.

The gallery represents the estates, of some important avant-garde artists, like M. Millares, M. Rivera, P. Gargallo, and J. Torres García. Season 2012/13 will feature Millares and Picasso solo shows.

Further artists represented: Juan Barjola
Juan Gris
Giorgio Morandi
Benjamin Palencia
Antoni Tàpies
Georges Valmier

Manolo Millares
Excavacion, 1971
Mixed media on burlap, 110 x 130 cm
Manolo Millares, Paintings, Catalogue raisonné, Museo Nacional Centro de Arte Reina Sofía, Madrid, p. 586, no. 517 P-71-11; exhibited: Museo Sen-Oku, Hakuko Kan, Tokyo, 2003; Chelsea Art Museum, New York, NY, 2003

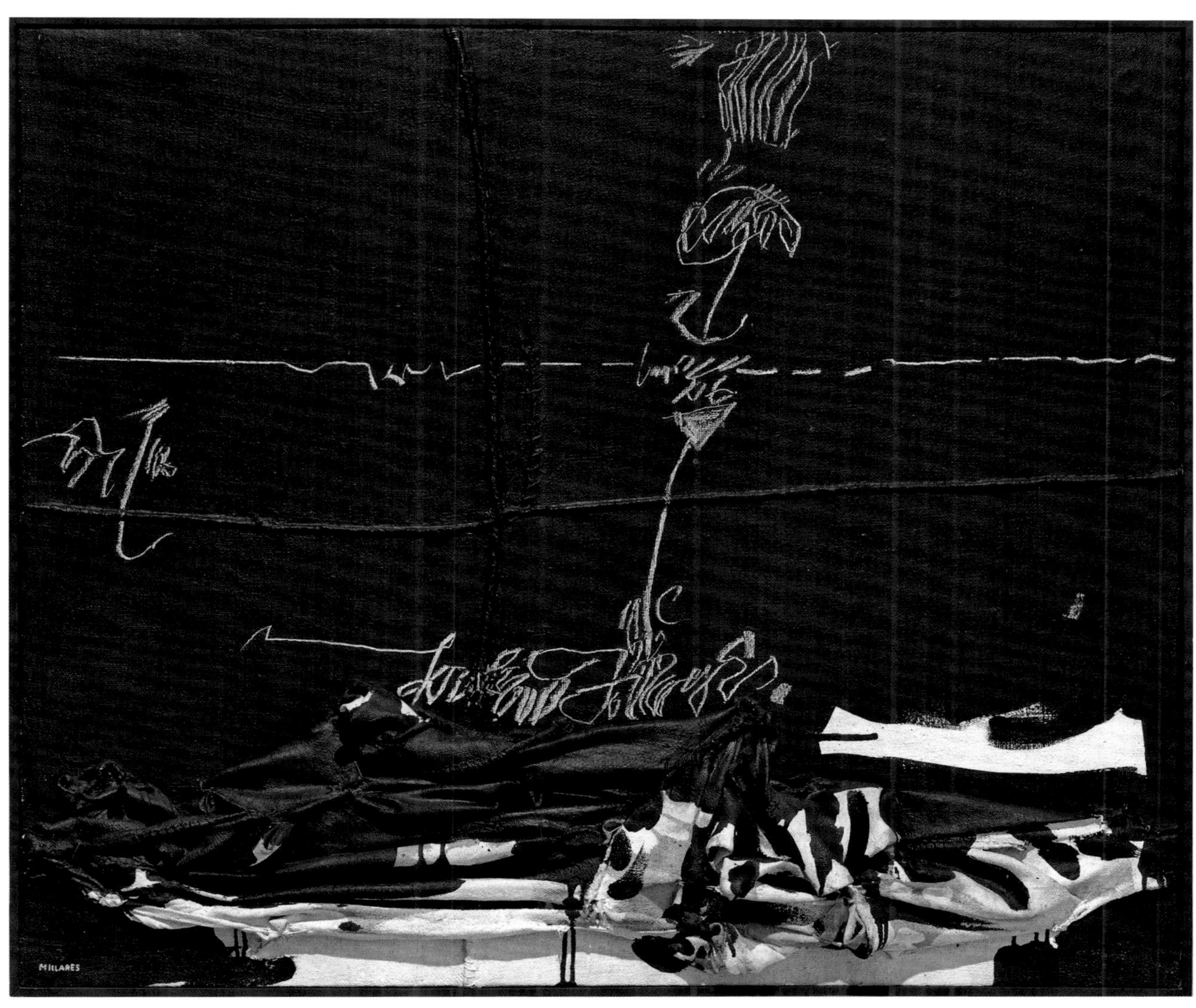
MILLARES

NELSON-FREEMAN

Mobile +33 6 80 28 78 24

Galerie Nelson-Freeman
FR-75004 Paris | 59, rue Quincampoix
Phone +33 1 42 71 74 56 | Fax +33 1 42 71 74 58
info@galerienelsonfreeman.com | www.galerienelsonfreeman.com
Directors Peter Freeman
Cécile Barrault

Gallery Information | In 1982 Philip Nelson opened Galerie Nelson in Villeurbanne, France. Eleven years later, the gallery moved to Paris, where commitment to its artists remained the gallery's top priority through close relationships with artists, exhibitions that allow for significant creative development, and participation in prestigious international art fairs, including Art Basel, Art Basel Miami Beach, and FIAC.

Galerie Nelson's founder formed a partnership with American gallerist Peter Freeman in 2006 in order to maintain and perpetuate Galerie Nelson's success. The partnership transformed the gallery into Galerie Nelson-Freeman, a gallery that continues to uphold the traditions of Galerie Nelson while welcoming new artists into its family, most recently Charlotte Posenenske, Richard Wentworth, Lucy Skaer, David Adamo, and Josephine Halvorson.

Further artists represented: David Adamo
Silvia Bächli
Joseph Bartscherer
Mel Bochner
Marie José Burki
Pedro Cabrita Reis
Ernst Caramelle
Helmut Dorner
Lili Dujourie
Robert Filliou
Pia Fries
Josephine Halvorson
Alex Hay
Harald Klingelhöller
Ken Lum
Helen Mirra
Matt Mullican
Eric Poitevin
Charlotte Posenenske
Fred Sandback
Anne-Marie Schneider
Thomas Schütte
Lucy Skaer
Mitja Tušek
James Welling
Richard Wentworth
Rachel Whiteread

Josephine Halvorson
Kiln, 2012
Oil on linen, 122 x 102 cm

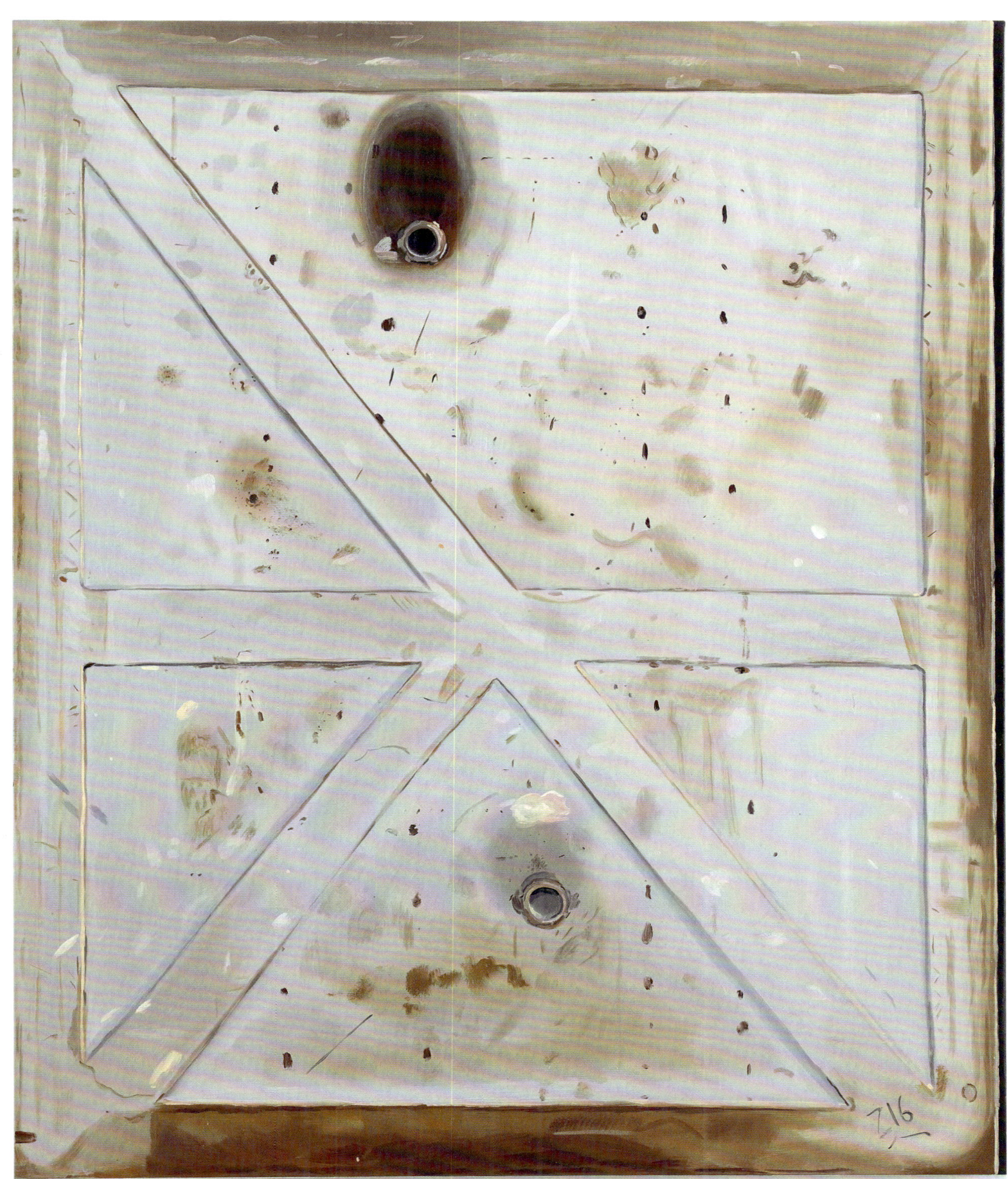

NEUGERRIEMSCHNEIDER

neugerriemschneider
DE-10115 Berlin | Linienstrasse 155
Phone +49 30 28 87 72 77 | Fax +49 30 28 87 72 78
mail@neugerriemschneider.com | www.neugerriemschneider.com
Directors Tim Neuger
Burkhard Riemschneider

Artists at Art Basel Miami Beach | **Franz Ackermann**
Ai Weiwei
Pawel Althamer
James Benning
Billy Childish
Keith Edmier
Olafur Eliasson
Noa Eshkol
Isa Genzken
Sharon Lockhart
Michel Majerus
Antje Majewski
Mike Nelson
Jorge Pardo
Elizabeth Peyton
Tobias Rehberger
Simon Starling
Thaddeus Strode
Rirkrit Tiravanija
Pae White

Pawel Althamer
Peter, 2011
Plaster and plastic on a metal construction, 197 x 74 x 73 cm

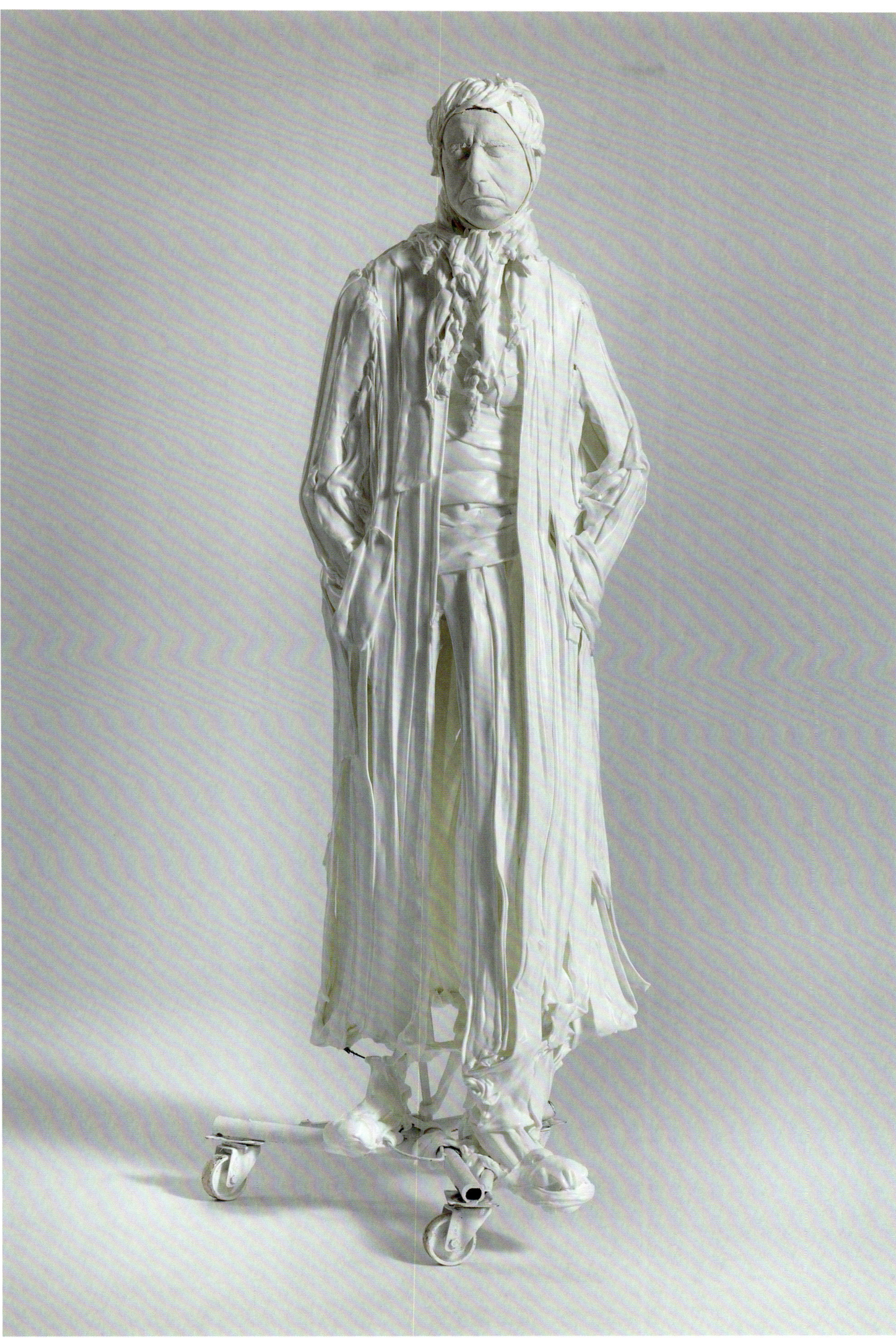

NITSCH

Carolina Nitsch
US-New York, NY 10012 | 101 Wooster Street
Phone +1 212 4630610 | Fax +1 212 4630614
info@carolinanitsch.com | www.carolinanitsch.com
Directors Carolina Nitsch
Brian Rumbolo

Carolina Nitsch Project Room
US-New York, NY 10011 | 534 West 22nd Street
Phone +1 212 6452030 | Fax +1 212 4630614
info@carolinanitsch.com | www.carolinanitsch.com

Artists at
Art Basel Miami Beach | **Ai Weiwei**
Richard Artschwager
Tauba Auerbach
Louise Bourgeois
E.V. Day
Spencer Finch
Richard Hamilton
Carsten Höller
Jenny Holzer
Donald Judd
Martin Kippenberger
Sherrie Levine
Vera Lutter
Olaf Nicolai
Raymond Pettibon
Thomas Schütte
Cindy Sherman
Alyson Shotz
Aaron Spangler
Sarah Sze
Jeff Wall
Christopher Wool

Gallery Information | Carolina Nitsch specializes in drawings and editions, including prints and monotypes, multiples, photographs, artist books, and installations. We actively publish editions with a growing roster of international artists, ranging from traditional etching on paper or silkscreen to large installations.

While we are a member of the IFPDA – The International Fine Print Dealers Association – our aim in publishing is to encourage the artist to explore new possibilities that stretch the boundaries of printmaking per se, and thus we work with many different printers and fabricators to achieve the most innovative and original quality.

Furthermore, we publish editions annually for institutions including the New Museum of Contemporary Art and the Whitney Museum of American Art.

Sarah Sze
Eyechart, 2011
Silkscreen and laser engraving,
7 x 12 x 2 inches
Edition of 29

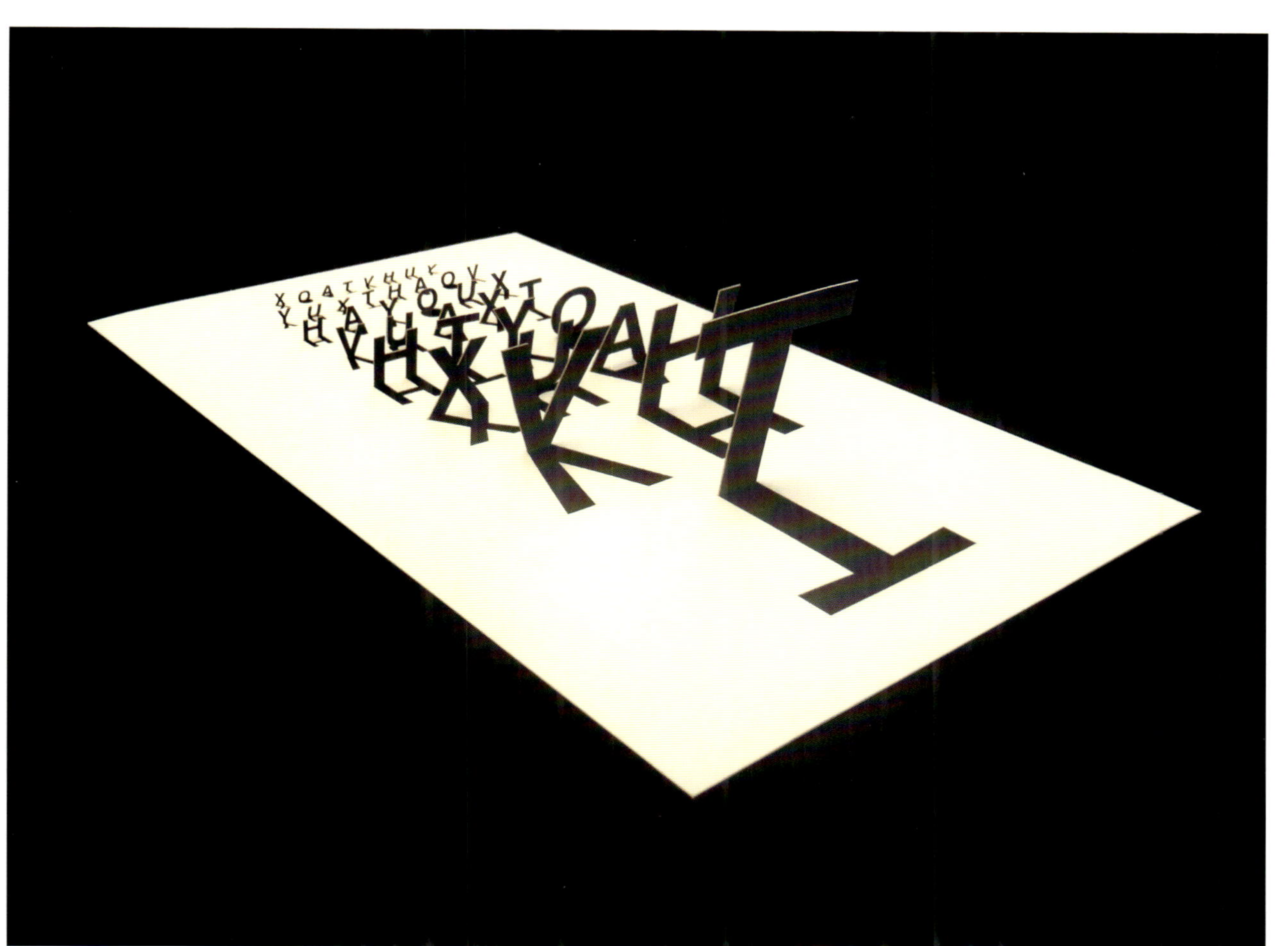

NOERO

Mobile +39 335 6250 95 77

Galleria Franco Noero
IT-10124 Turin | Via Giulia di Barolo, 16/D
Phone +39 011 88 22 08 | Fax +39 011 19 83 74 08
info@franconoero.com | www.franconoero.com
Director Franco Noero

Artists at Art Basel Miami Beach | **Darren Bader**
Pablo Bronstein
Tom Burr
Jeff Burton
Neil Campbell
Andrew Dadson
Jason Dodge
Lara Favaretto
Martino Gamper
Henrik Håkansson
Arturo Herrera
Gabriel Kuri
Phillip Lai
Jim Lambie
Robert Mapplethorpe
Mike Nelson
Henrik Olesen
João Onofre
Kirsten Pieroth
Steven Shearer
Simon Starling
Costa Vece
Francesco Vezzoli

Jim Lambie
Stairway to Heaven, 2012
Wood, paint, mirrors, overall dimensions: 250 x 160 x 650 cm
Installation view, *Everything Louder Than Everything Else,* February 9-March 15, 2012, Galleria Franco Noero, Turin

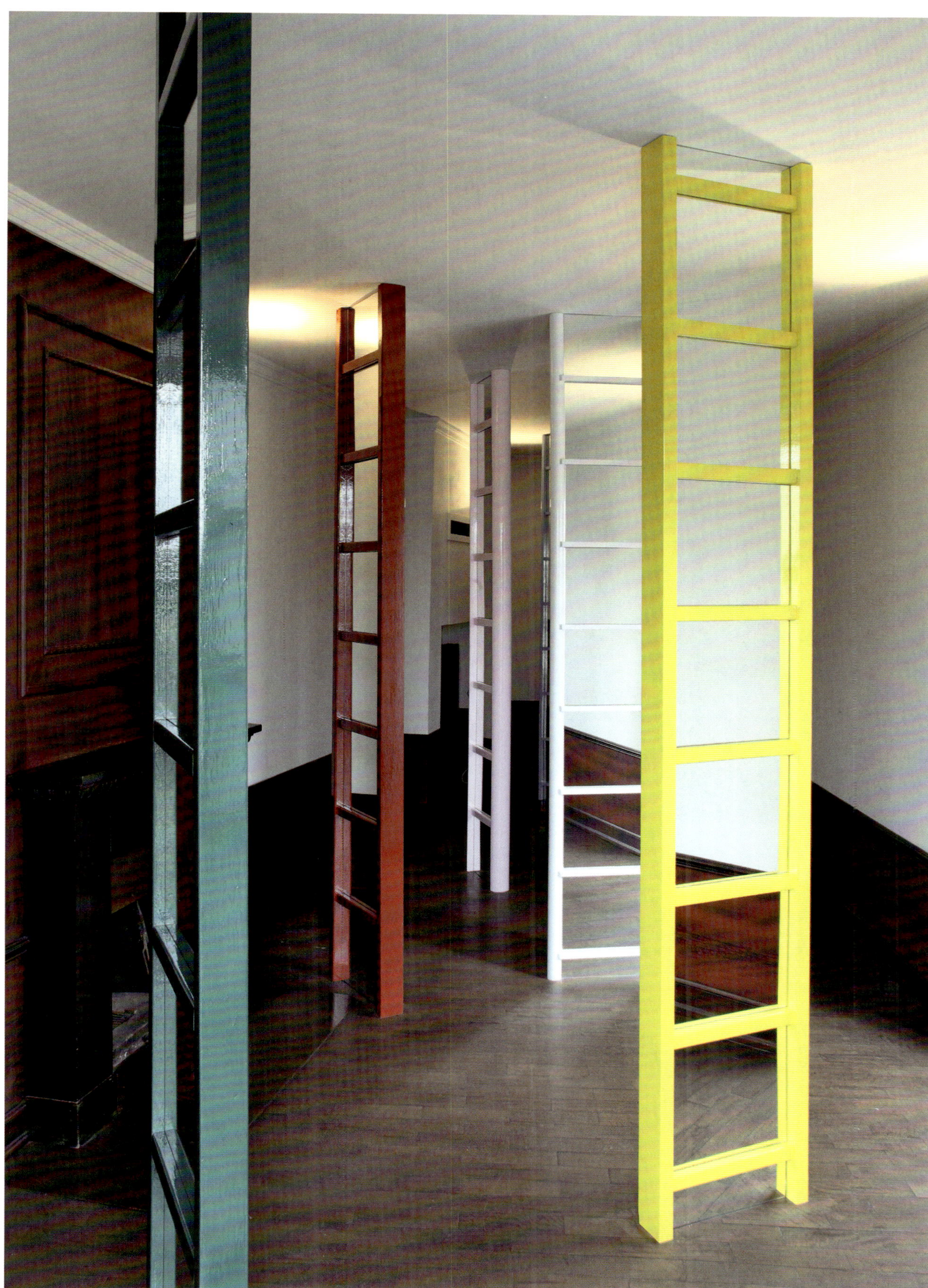

NOGUERAS BLANCHARD

NoguerasBlanchard
ES-08001 Barcelona | Xuclà 7
Phone +34 93 342 57 21 | Fax +34 93 342 57 22
info@noguerasblanchard.com | www.noguerasblanchard.com
Directors Alex Nogueras
Rebeca Blanchard

Artists at Art Nova | Anne-Lise Coste
Rubén Grilo
Ignacio Uriarte

Gallery Information | Nogueras Blanchard opened its space in Barcelona in 2004. The gallery is located next to Las Ramblas, in the historic, multi-ethnic Raval neighborhood. In this context we are strongly committed to developing an exhibition program with emerging international artists whose work shows strong conceptual concerns and participates in the dialogue between art and broader currents in contemporary society.

Further artists represented:
Rafel G. Bianchi
Leandro Erlich
Marine Hugonnier
Michael Lin
Juan López
David Maljkovic
Fran Meana
Ester Partegàs
Wilfredo Prieto
Shimabuku

The use of language in art practice is commonly related to the production of knowledge. The increasing role of language has been progressively intended less as an aesthetic product, to be looked at, and increasingly as an intellectual activity, to be read. Under this conceptual framework we are presenting a group of works that break down language to its most elementary form: the letters of the alphabet.

The booth is a stage of painted, sculpted, and recited letters, a space free of statements and open to the visitor's interpretation. The sound installation *ASDFGHJKLÖ* by Ignacio Uriarte runs on a continuous loop, in which one hears the German punk musician Blixa Bargeld reciting rhythmically the letters of the keyboard, a, s, d, f, g, h, j, k, l, ö with varying tonalities.

Words, slogans, quotations, and fragments of phrases play a central role in Anne-Lise Coste's work, where text and images are combined to comment on political, social, and personal issues as well as emotional states that fluctuate between idealism, irony, and despair. The freedom of the sprayed airbrush lends itself perfectly to the artist's childlike handwriting applied directly on the canvas.

In the case of Rubén Grilo, whose recent practice reflects upon the technology of images through PowerPoint presentations, we will show sculptures made with projections on screen canvas in the shape of the letters of the alphabet. Faithful to the narratives of conceptual art, his works look closely at the modern idea of image autonomy by means of a channel whose codes are familiar to the viewer.

Rubén Grilo
P-Scr 'PeaScreen' from 'Screen Alphabet', 2011
High-gain screen projection foil stretched on painted steel tube, approx. 79 x 44 x 23 cm

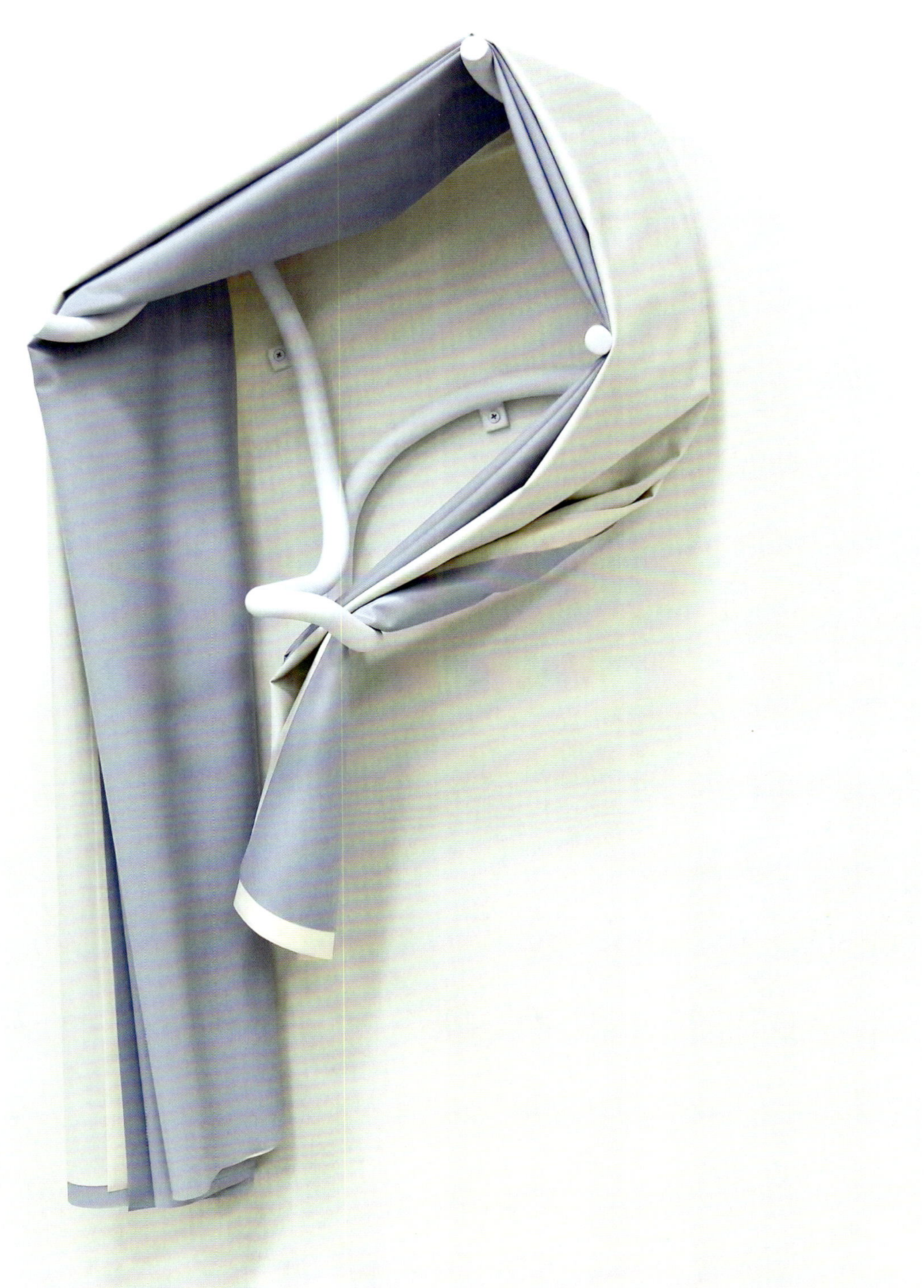

NOLAN

Mobile +1 917 5825958

David Nolan Gallery
US-New York, NY 10001 | 527 West 29th Street
Phone +1 212 9256190 | Fax +1 212 3349139
info@davidnolangallery.com | www.davidnolangallery.com
Director Katherine Chan

Artists at
Art Basel Miami Beach | **Richard Artschwager**
Steve DiBenedetto
Neil Gall
Victoria Gitman
Mel Kendrick
Barry Le Va
Ciprian Muresan
Jim Nutt
Alexander Ross
Serban Savu
Sandra Vásquez de la Horra
Jorinde Voigt

Gallery Information | Since 1987, David Nolan Gallery has been on the forefront of bringing important contemporary pieces and master-works to the international art scene. Works on paper were the initial focus of the gallery's program, featuring artists from Europe and the United States. In recent years, the roster of artists has expanded to a global level to include cutting-edge emerging artists from South America and Eastern Europe working in all media from painting and drawings to sculpture and video. The carefully tailored program of the gallery and its reputation for expertly curated exhibitions makes it one of the most unique venues for art in New York.

Jorinde Voigt
Horizont (Berlin VII), 2011
Ink, oil crayon, and graphite
on paper

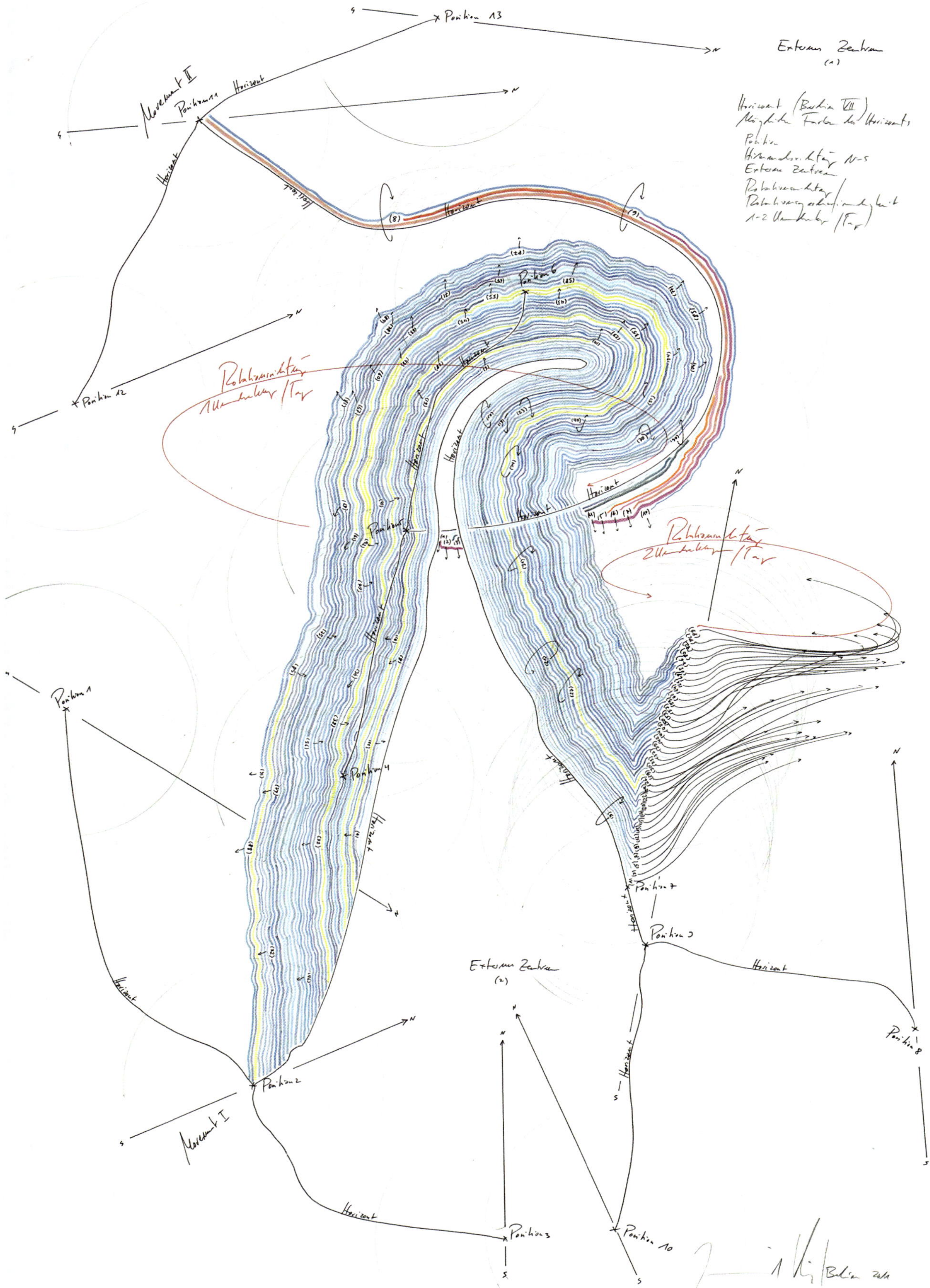

Position 13
Externes Zentrum (1)
Movement II
Position 11
Horizont
Position 12
Rotationsrichtung
1 Umdrehung / Tag
Rotationsrichtung
2 Umdrehungen / Tag
Position 6
Position 5
Position 4
Position 1
Position 7
Position 9
Position 8
Externes Zentrum (2)
Position 2
Movement I
Position 3
Position 10

NON

NON
TR-34430 Istanbul | Istiklal Caddesi 163/4 Beyoglu
Phone +90 212 249 87 74 | Fax +90 212 249 87 74
info@galerinon.com | www.galerinon.com
Director Derya Demir

One-Person Show | Artist Information

Asli Çavusoglu

*1982, Istanbul, Turkey
Lives and works in Istanbul, Turkey

Selected recent group exhibitions:
2012 *Frieze Projects,* Frieze Art Fair, London
Mindaugas Triennial, Contemporary Art Centre, Vilnius
2011 *Performa 11,* New York, NY
Seven New Works, Borusan Contemporary, Perili Köşk, Istanbul
We Have Woven The Motherlands With Nets of Iron, Giza Hejaz Railway Station, Amman
Who Do You Admire?, La Box, École Nationale Supérieure d'Art de Bourges, Bourges
2010 *Transient Spaces – The Tourist Syndrome,* Neue Gesellschaft für Bildende Kunst, Berlin
When Ideas Become Crime, DEPO, Istanbul
Voices From Silence – Truths Unveiled By Time, Galerie Opdahl, Berlin
Fantasy & Island, FRAC Corse, Corsica
2009 *This Place You See Has No Size At All,* Kadist Art Foundation, Paris
Everyday Challengers, HISK, Ghent
Interferencia, Bogota
Kein Ding, ACC Galerie, Weimar
End Game, Gallery Loop, Seoul

Further artists represented | Gökçen Cabadan
Erdem Ergaz
Annika Eriksson
Extrastruggle
Sefer Memisoglu
Karen Mirza/Brad Butler
Meriç Algün Ringborg
Günes Terkol

By means of an installation of interrelated works, Asli Çavusoglu will transform NON's Art Basel Miami Beach booth into an exhibition in which the specter of history is ever-present yet subtly buried within a range of works that parallel the complex interplay of subjectivities and knowledge production in historical contexts, especially during times of political or social rupture. Taken as a whole, this radical transformation of source material, both editorial and physical, seeks to illuminate the discrepancies inherent in the study of history. Though at times history serves its function as a recorded past marked by important events deemed worthy of remembrance, its transformations are never without their alternate effects, namely the demise of cultural objects and rituals, which are henceforth relegated to the cultural dustbin. Çavusoglu's grouping of three projects shows different facets of this phenomenon, whether they be the removal of the prophetic power of an ancient material, the literal re-molding of history books into purely functional objects, or the loss of visual detail in important relics of another empire.

Further information on illustrations A + B:
Çavusoglu has collected various textbooks that have been, or are currently, employed to teach national history in Turkish high schools. Diving head-on into this huge compendium, the artist has chosen to lessen its size by excerpting a few pedagogical diagrams – which attempt to distill and instill the complex Modernization project through simple and culturally approved didactics – so as to provide an introduction of sorts to the subject and its study materials.

Further information on illustrations C + D:
The effacement of history is further explored in the artist's works dealing with Ottoman jewelry. Now produced as cheap imitations and sold in mass quantities at outdoor markets in consequence of the extreme popularity of the soap opera *Muhteşem Yuzyıl* (Magnificent Century), the jewels have already been robbed of the unique, exquisite, precious qualities that once made them important signifiers of wealth and power. In accordance with procedures used during the Ottoman Empire to photograph and archive sets of jewelry, the artist has arranged these modern reproductions in the same configurations. However, as they are produced as photograms, the images retain only the empty, blank shapes of the jewels, rendering them mere outlines completely divorced from their former context of social prestige. Rather than acting as evidence of the preservation or appreciation of the past, they now convey a heightened sense of absence and loss, as though an already inaccessible chapter of material history had now been completely hidden from modern eyes. Their blankness echoes the feelings of emptiness and nostalgia that accompany losses of historical information during times of political rupture.

Asli Çavusoglu
A + B | *How to Teach Transformation,* 2011
Marker on paper, 34.5 x 53 x 1 cm

C + D | *Pawnbroker Series,* 2012
Photograms, 30 x 40.5 x 1 cm each

A

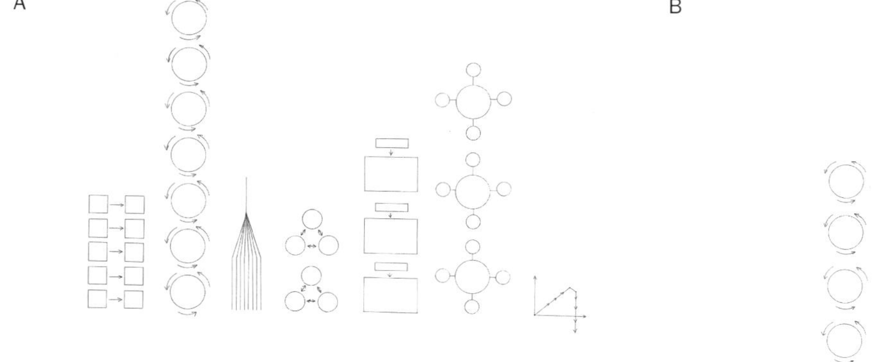

B

C

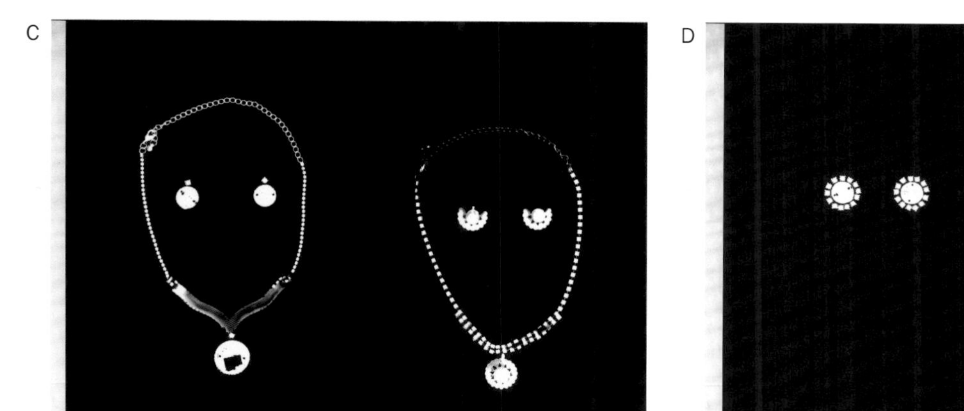

D

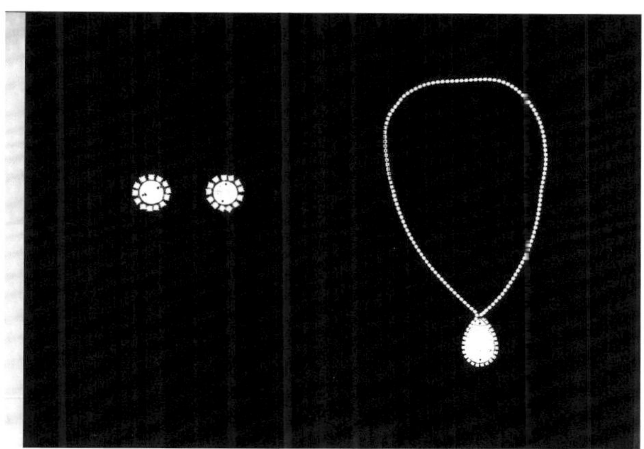

NORDENHAKE

Mobile +49 176 18 86 66 80, +49 176 18 86 66 81

Galerie Nordenhake
DE-10969 Berlin | Lindenstrasse 34
Phone +49 30 206 14 83 | Fax +49 30 206 14 8 48
berlin@nordenhake.com | www.nordenhake.com
Directors Claes Nordenhake
Claudia Sorhage

Galerie Nordenhake
SE-11330 Stockholm | Hudiksvallsgatan 8
Phone +46 8 21 18 92 | Fax +46 8 31 18 95
stockholm@nordenhake.com | www.nordenhake.com
Director Ben Loveless

Artists at
Art Basel Miami Beach | **Miroslaw Balka**
Gerard Byrne
Sarah Crowner
Ann Edholm
Spencer Finch
Hreinn Fridfinnsson
Esko Männikkö
Helen Mirra
Sirous Namazi
Walter Niedermayr
Marjetica Potrč
Håkan Rehnberg
Michael Schmidt
Florian Slotawa
Johan Thurfjell
Günter Umberg
Not Vital
Magnus Wallin

Gallery Information | Galerie Nordenhake presents contemporary art in various media and with an international focus, exhibiting emerging, mid-career, and established artists. The gallery has exhibition spaces in Berlin and in Stockholm.

Esko Männikkö & Pekka Turunen
Untitled (From the Series 'Pemoht'), 1989-1995/2012
Archival inkjet print, framed by the artist, 132 x 111 x 4 cm
Edition of 6

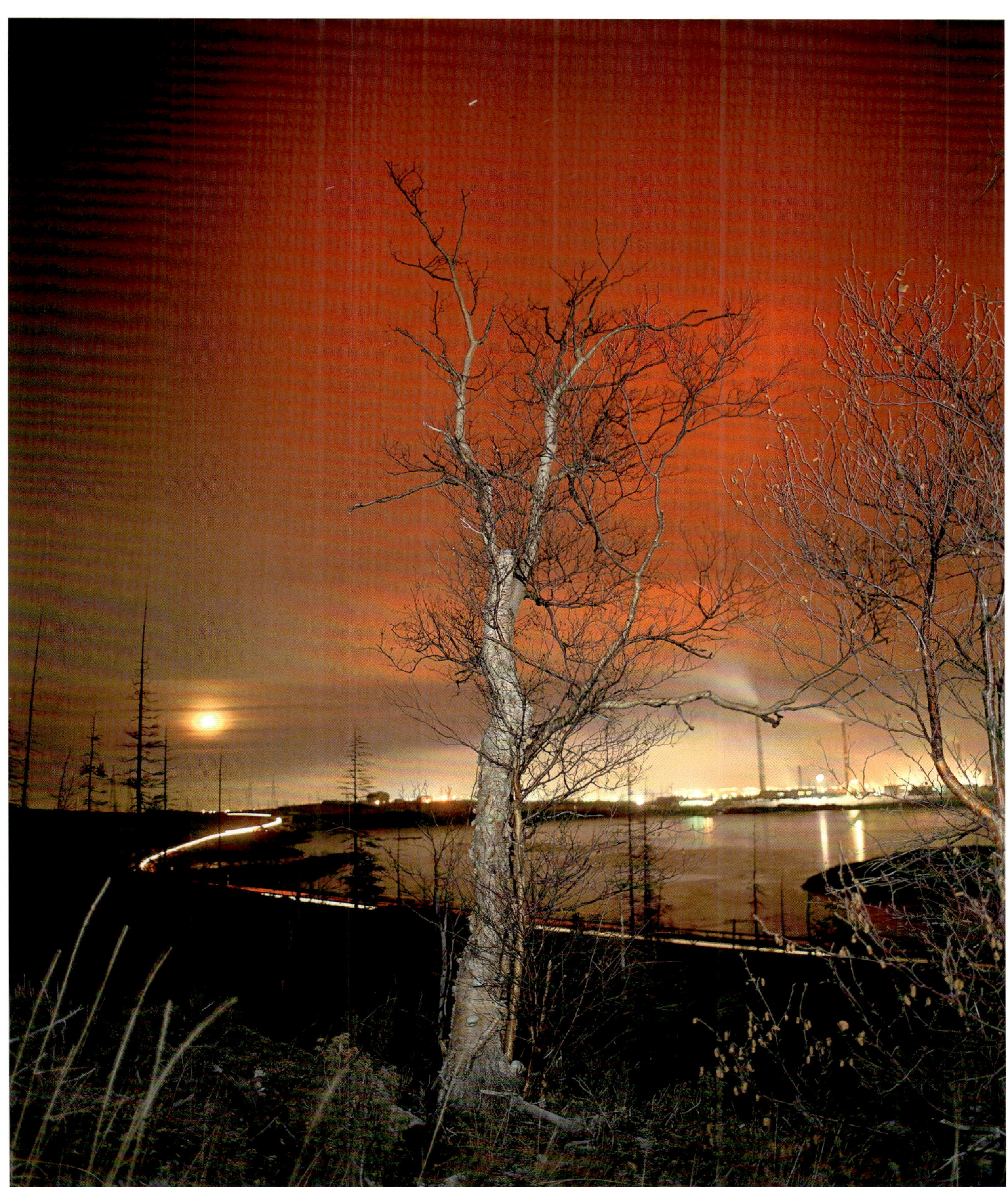

OMR

Mobile +52 1 55 54 00 17 78, +52 1 55 54 19 94 60, +52 1 55 27 28 39 03

Galería OMR
MX-06700 Mexico City | Plaza Río de Janeiro 54
Phone +52 55 55 11 11 79 | +52 55 55 25 30 95 | +52 55 52 07 10 80 | Fax +52 55 55 33 42 44
info@galeriaomr.com | www.galeriaomr.com
Directors Jaime Riestra
Patricia Ortiz Monasterio
Cristobal Riestra

Artists at
Art Basel Miami Beach | **Julieta Aranda**
José Arnaud-Bello
Atelier Van Lieshout
Iñaki Bonillas
Aldo Chaparro
Félix Curto
Jose Dávila
Gabriel de la Mora
Candida Höfer
Yishai Jusidman
Artur Lescher
Rafael Lozano-Hemmer
Jorge Méndez Blake
Theo Michael
Rubén Ortiz Torres
Random International
Adolfo Riestra
Laureana Toledo
Torolab
Troika

Gallery Information | Patricia Ortiz Monasterio and Jaime Riestra, owners and directors, founded Galería OMR in 1983. The gallery is located in a spacious early-twentieth-century house in the heart of the Roma district in Mexico City. From its beginnings, OMR has sought to promote the latest artistic tendencies as well as Mexican and international contemporary art. It has a schedule of six to eight exhibitions per year in its Mexico City location, having produced over 400 exhibitions since 1983. OMR represents a broad spectrum of prominent artists of both the Mexican and international art scene without neglecting the emerging group of talented young creators. It is the exclusive representative of the estates of Adolfo Riestra and Luis Ortiz Monasterio.

In April 2009 OMR opened an alternative space next door: el52, a 4-story-high 1940s house converted into exhibition space with living space for artists' residencies, under the direction of Cristobal Riestra. Its mission is to present young artists, both national and international, who can take over the space for a period of one to two months to produce an event, whether it is an exhibition, a performance, or an installation. On the first floor el52 hosts a shop selling multiples and editions by different national and international artists.

Gabriel de la Mora
8, 2011
Human hair, blood, paper, graphite, 71 x 54.5 x 11 cm
The work consists of eight 1 : 1-scale mosquitos made from human hair, blood, paper, and graphite, inside an acrylic vitrine.

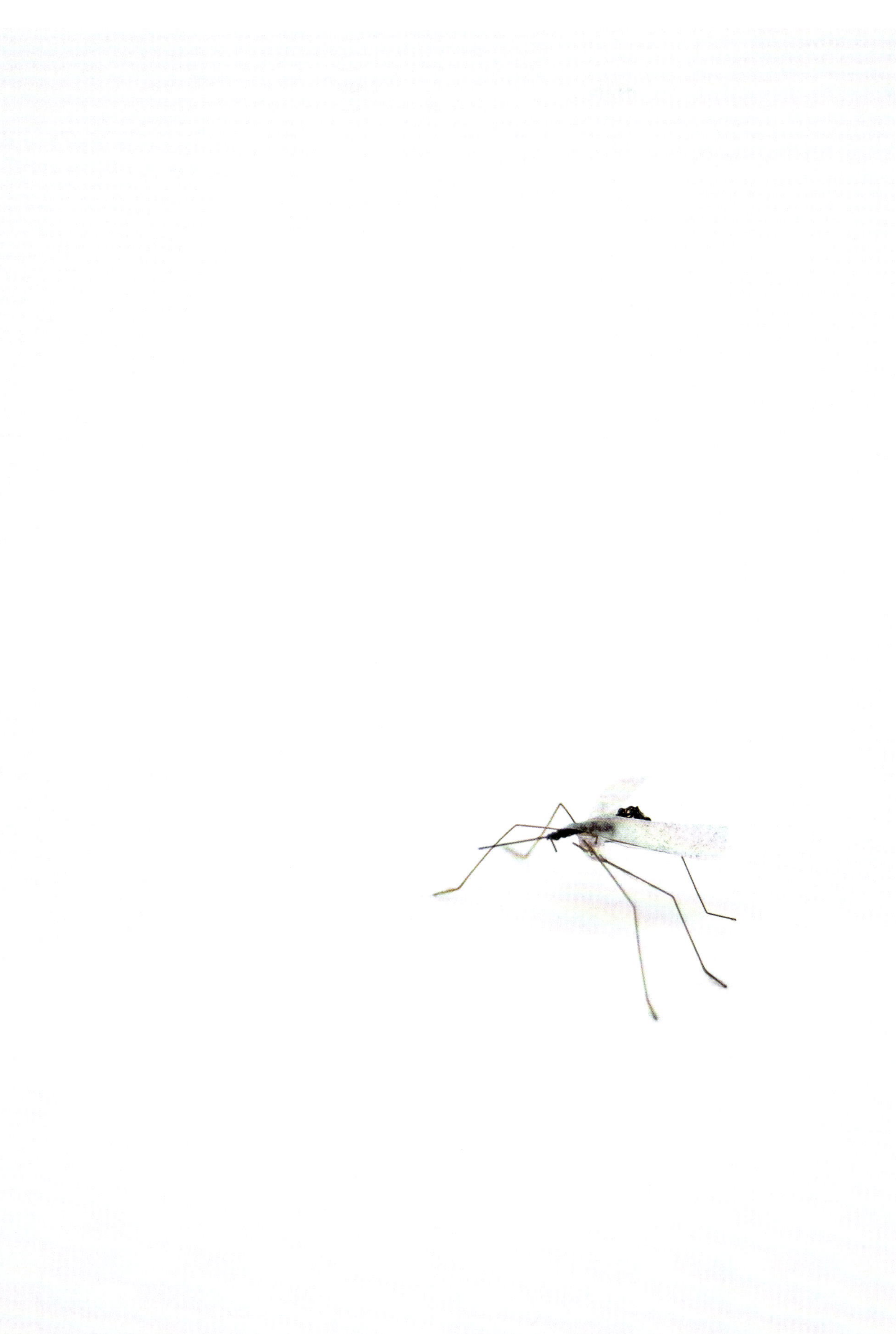

OVERDUIN AND KITE

Overduin and Kite
US-Los Angeles, CA 90028 | 6693 Sunset Blvd.
Phone +1 323 464 36 00 | Fax +1 323 464 36 07
info@overduinandkite.com | www.overduinandkite.com
Directors Lisa Overduin
Kristina Kite

Artists at Art Nova | Ei Arakawa
Nikolas Gambaroff

Further artists represented | Frank Benson
Merlin Carpenter
Marc Camille Chaimowicz
Maureen Gallace
Barry Johnston
Dianna Molzan
Scott Olson
Silke Otto-Knapp
Eileen Quinlan
Nick Relph
Stephen G. Rhodes
Haim Steinbach
Cheyney Thompson
Kaari Upson
Erika Vogt
Tris Vonna-Michell

Ei Arakawa
and Nikolas Gambaroff
Cardman (AL/LA), 2012
Fabric and acrylic woodblock print, 75 x 25 x 12 inches
Unique

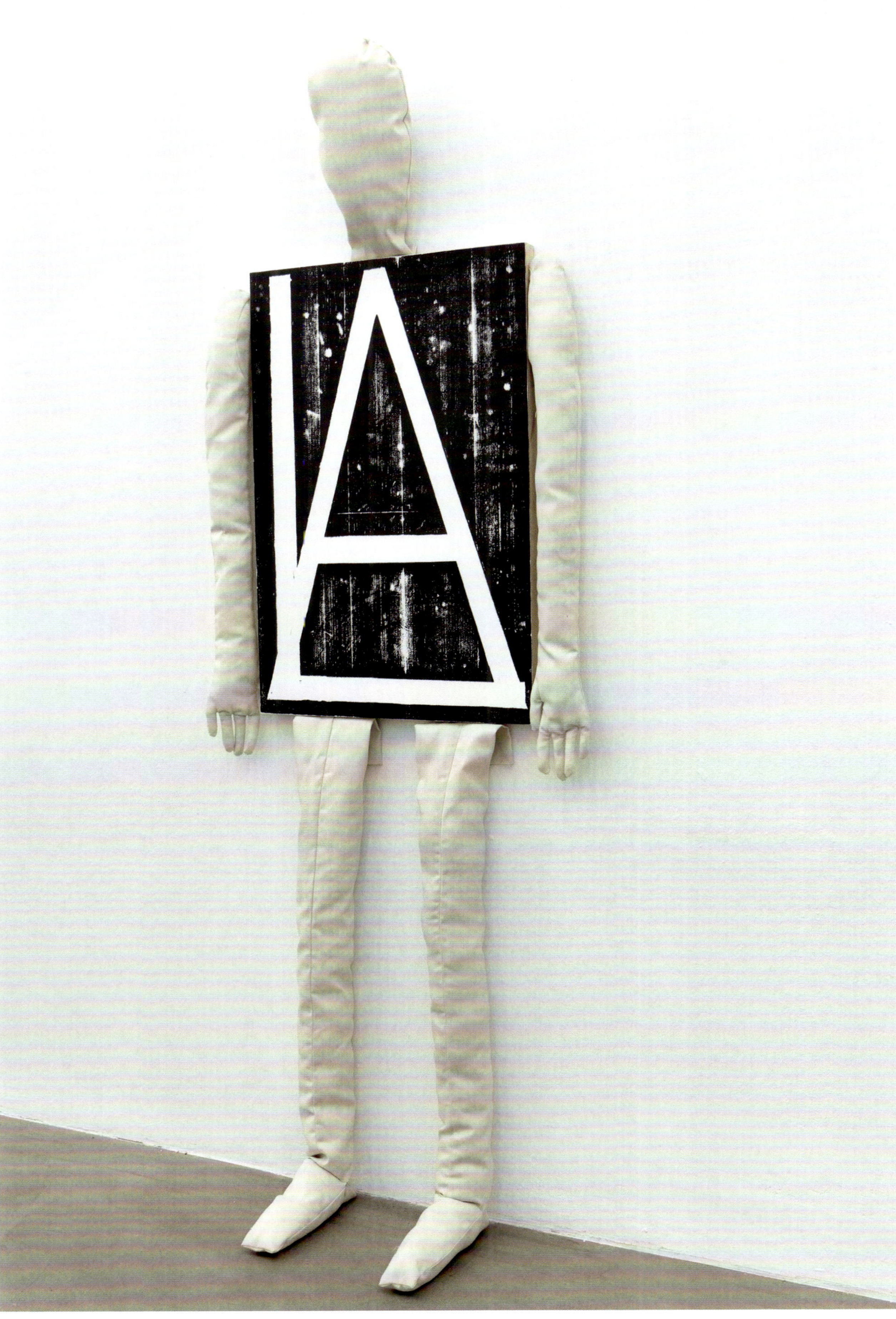
LA

PACE

Pace
US-New York, NY 10022 | 32 East 57th Street
Phone +1 212 421 32 92 | Fax +1 212 421 08 35
newyork@pacegallery.com | www.pacegallery.com

Pace
US-New York, NY 10001 | 534 West 25th Street
Phone +1 212 929 70 00 | Fax +1 212 929 70 01
newyork@pacegallery.com | www.pacegallery.com

Pace
US-New York, NY 10001 | 510 West 25th Street
Phone +1 212 255 40 44 | Fax +1 212 659 00 96
newyork@pacegallery.com | www.pacegallery.com

Pace
US-New York, NY 10001 | 508 West 25th Street
Phone +1 212 989 42 58 | Fax +1 212 989 42 63
newyork@pacegallery.com | www.pacegallery.com

Pace Beijing
CN-100015 Beijing | 798 Art District, No. 2 Jiuxianqiao Road
Phone +86 10 59 78 97 81 | Fax +86 10 59 78 97 82
beijing@pacegallery.com | www.pacegallery.com

Pace London
GB-London W1S 3ET | 6 Burlington Gardens
Phone +44 20 74 37 10 50 | Fax +44 20 774 40 17 49
london@pacegallery.com | www.pacegallery.com

Pace London
GB-London W1F 0LB | 6-10 Lexington Street
Phone +44 20 74 37 10 50 | Fax +44 20 774 40 17 49
london@pacegallery.com | www.pacegallery.com

Artists at Art Basel Miami Beach | **Josef Albers**
Alexander Calder
Chuck Close
Willem de Kooning
Jim Dine
Tara Donovan
Jean Dubuffet
Tim Eitel
Tony Feher
Lee Friedlander
Adrian Ghenie
Adolph Gottlieb
Paul Graham
Loris Gréaud
Tim Hawkinson
Barbara Hepworth
David Hockney
Robert Irwin
Alfred Jensen
Donald Judd
Ilya & Emilia Kabakov
Lee Ufan
Sol LeWitt
Li Songsong
Maya Lin
Robert Mangold
Agnes Martin
Roberto Matta
Elizabeth Murray
Yoshitomo Nara
Louise Nevelson
Carsten Nicolai
Isamu Noguchi
Thomas Nozkowski
Claes Oldenburg
Adam Pendleton
Pablo Picasso
Fiona Rae
Robert Rauschenberg
Ad Reinhardt
Bridget Riley
Mark Rothko
Michal Rovner
Robert Ryman
Lucas Samaras
Joel Shapiro
Raqib Shaw
James Siena
Kiki Smith
Bosco Sodi
Keith Sonnier
Saul Steinberg
Hiroshi Sugimoto
Antoni Tàpies
James Turrell
Richard Tuttle
Keith Tyson
Coosje van Bruggen
Corban Walker
Robert Whitman
Fred Wilson
Zhang Huan
Zhang Xiaogang

Antoni Tàpies
Terra del Montseny, 2008
Mixed media on wood,
200 x 225 cm

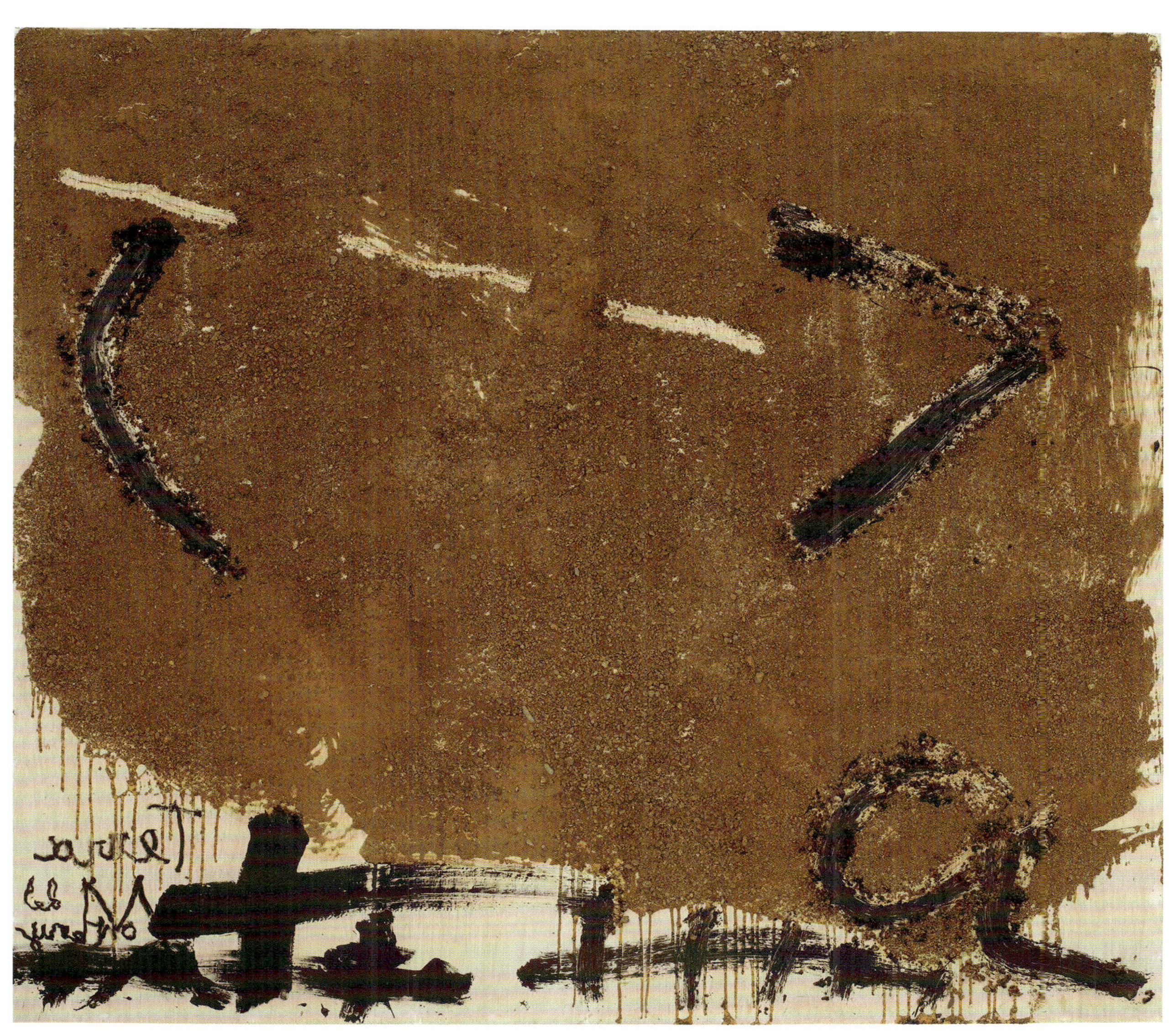

PARAGON

Paragon
GB-London SW5 0JN | 6 Wetherby Gardens
Phone +44 20 73 70 12 00 | Fax +44 20 73 70 12 29
info@paragonpress.co.uk | www.paragonpress.co.uk
Directors Charles Booth-Clibborn
Florian Oliver Simm

Artists at
Art Basel Miami Beach | **Jake & Dinos Chapman**
Richard Deacon
Damien Hirst
Gary Hume
Anish Kapoor
Grayson Perry
Ged Quinn
Jonathan Yeo

Gallery Information | Publishers of contemporary art in print since 1986

Further artists represented: Kai Althoff
Hurvin Anderson
Georg Baselitz
Victor Burgin
Gillian Carnegie
Alan Charlton
Grenville Davey
Alan Davie
Peter Doig
Sir Terry Frost
Hamish Fulton
Antony Gormley
Eberhard Havekost
Patrick Heron
John Hilliard
Shirazeh Houshiary
Michael Landy
Langlands & Bell
Christopher Le Brun
Richard Long
Elizabeth Magill
Ian McKeever
Sarah Morris
Paul Morrison
Chris Ofili
Marc Quinn
George Shaw
Corinne Wasmuht
Richard Wathen
Rachel Whiteread
Bill Woodrow
Thomas Zipp

Gary Hume
Paradise Printing Four, 2012
Linocut, 128 x 93 cm
Edition of 56

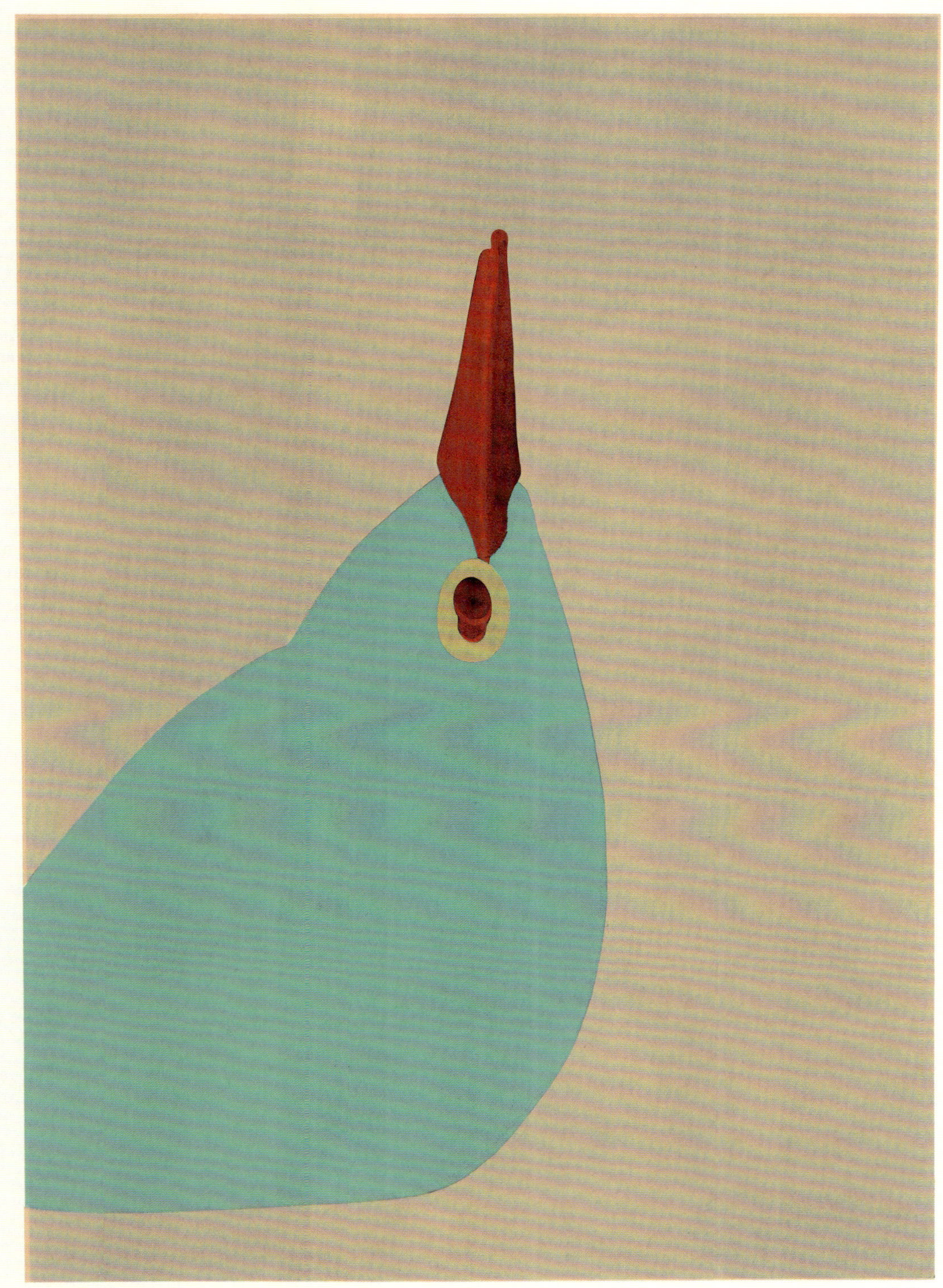
PARADISE PRINTING FOUR
HUME 12

PARKETT

Parkett Publishers
US-New York, NY 10013 | 145 Avenue of the Americas
Phone +1 212 673 26 60 | Fax +1 212 271 07 04
info@parkettart.com | www.parkettart.com
Directors Dieter von Graffenried (Publisher)
Andrea Urban (Editions, New York)
Beatrice Fässler (Editions, Zurich)
Bice Curiger (Editor-in-Chief)

Parkett Publishers
CH-8031 Zurich | Quellenstrasse 27
Phone +41 44 271 81 40 | Fax +41 44 272 43 01
info@parkettart.com | www.parkettart.com

Artists at
Art Basel Miami Beach | **Yto Barrada**
Kerstin Brätsch
Paul Chan
Nicole Eisenman
Dominique Gonzalez-Foerster
Carsten Höller
Maria Lassnig
Liu Xiadong
Monika Sosnowska
Oscar Tuazon
Cosima von Bonin
Charline von Heyl
Andro Wekua
Franz West
Haegue Yang

Gallery Information | A Small Museum and a Large Library of Contemporary Art

Parkett collaborates directly with compelling international artists. Each artist creates a special signed and numbered edition exclusively for Parkett, which may take any form, from prints, photographs, and objects to unique works of art. More than 200 works made by contemporary artists have joined Parkett's 'Musée en Appartement,' a unique collection of the art of our times.

Since 1984, Parkett has published 91 volumes with some 200 monographic portraits and more than 1,400 essays, making Parkett a small museum and a large library of contemporary art.

Parkett's editions and works have been presented in numerous museum exhibitions including the Museum of Modern Art, New York; UCCA Beijing; the Centre Pompidou, Paris; and the Kunsthaus Zurich. Recent Parkett exhibitions were held at the Kanazawa Museum, Japan; the Singapore Tyler Print Institute (STPI); and Seoul Arts Center, Korea.

The catalogue raisonnée *200 Art Works – 25 Years* features all works made by artists for Parkett, artists' documents, sketches, letters, and an index by authors to all 1,400 texts published.

Please visit www.parkettart.com.

Dominique Gonzalez-Foerster
Calendario 2020, 2007
Silkscreen, 42 x 46.6 cm
Calendar for 12 months in 12 years (January 2008-December 2019), unique collection of 14 calendars to simultaneously display all 14 prints, including two by Philippe Parreno (for Parkett 80)

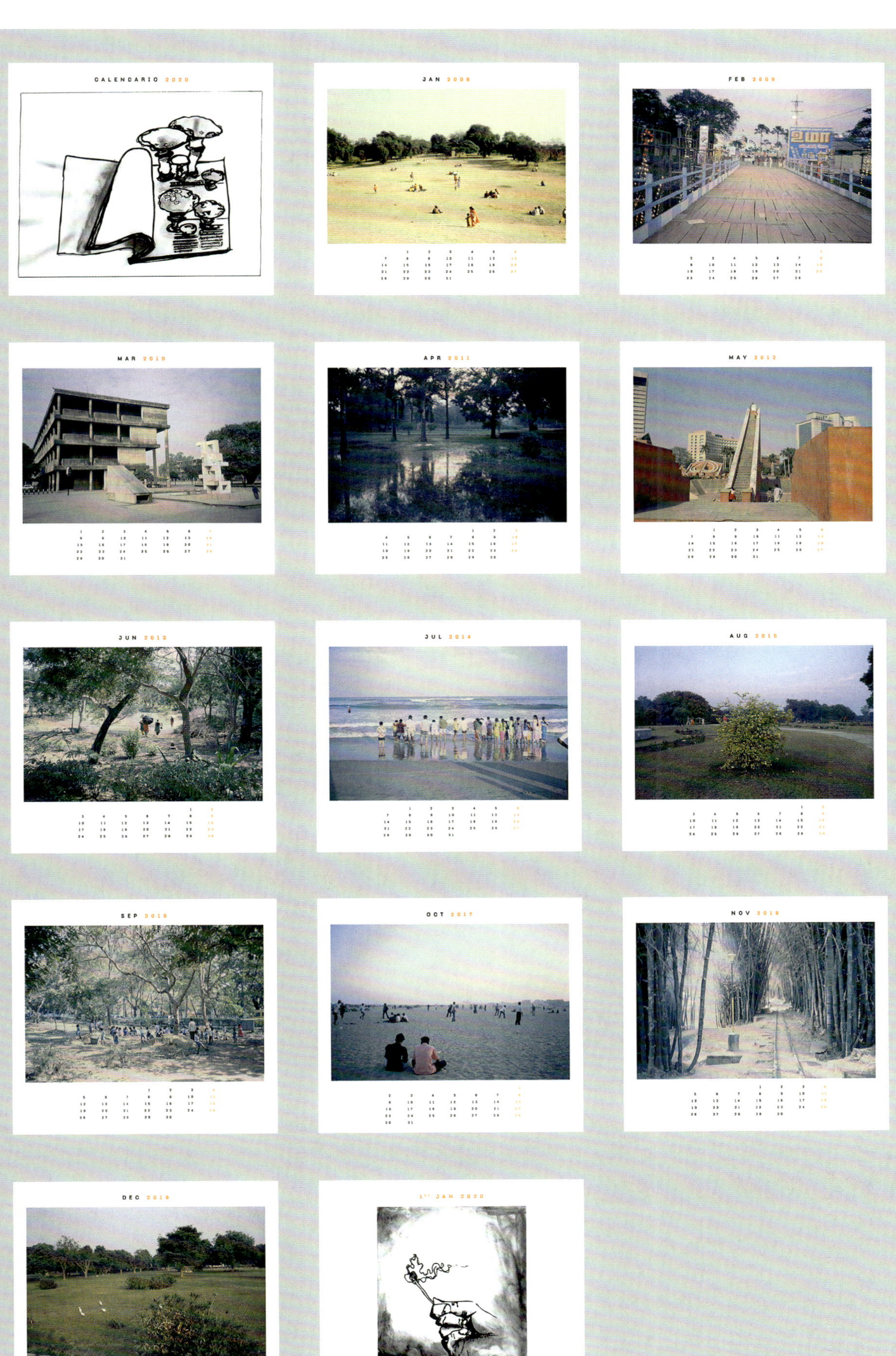
CALENDARIO 2020
JAN 2008
FEB 2009
MAR 2010
APR 2011
MAY 2012
JUN 2013
JUL 2014
AUG 2015
SEP 2016
OCT 2017
NOV 2018
DEC 2019
1st JAN 2020

PARRASCH

Mobile +1 917 533 38 66

Franklin Parrasch Gallery
US-New York, NY 10019 | 20 West 57th Street
Phone +1 212 246 53 60 | Fax +1 212 246 53 91
info@franklinparrasch.com | www.franklinparrasch.com
Directors Katharine Overgaard
Franklin Parrasch

Franklin Parrasch Gallery
US-New York, NY 10001 | 548 West 22nd Street
Phone +1 212 246 53 60 | Fax +1 212 246 53 91

Artists at
Art Basel Miami Beach | **Mary Corse**
Joe Goode
Craig Kauffman
Agnes Martin
John McCracken
John McLaughlin
Bruce Nauman
Ken Price
Ed Ruscha

Gallery Information | Franklin Parrasch Gallery began in 1986, with a program guided by a conscious reflection upon the process of creativity as it relates to human evolution.

Over the past two decades, the gallery has established a profile of exhibiting Los Angeles artists whose careers emerged in the 1960s and whose aesthetic alignment with Minimalism developed independently from that of their East Coast contemporaries. Throughout numerous group exhibitions, the gallery has explored artistic philosophies specific to West Coast subcultures, including hot-rodding and surfing, and how these sensibilities informed the works of Los Angeles artists of this time period.

Our project space in Chelsea presents new art by contemporary artists, pairings of material by like-spirited artists from a variety of periods, ephemeral installations, and historical works grouped in contexts designed to bend preconceptions.

The gallery consistently organizes shows that consider diverse evolutionary theories, with a focused sensitivity to the migration of ideas and aesthetic development as expressed by a wide range of artists who employ innovative practices.

Further artists represented: John Altoon
Chris Churchill
Jason Fox
Mark Gonzales
Justin Lieberman
Ed Paschke
Jesse Wine

John McLaughlin
#38, 1958
Oil on board, 9½ x 5¼ inches

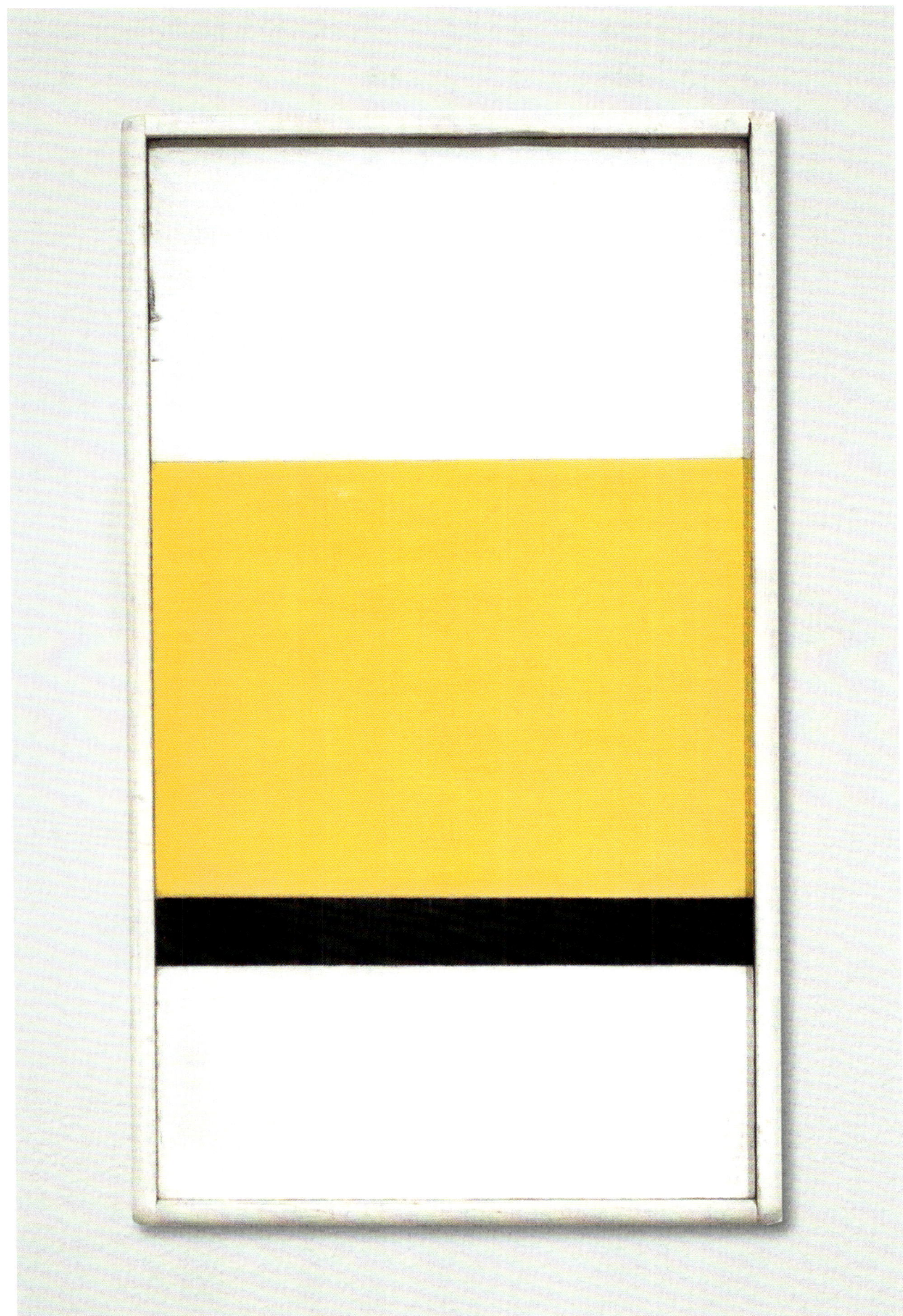

PERROTIN

Galerie Perrotin
FR-75003 Paris | 76, rue de Turenne
Phone +33 1 42 16 79 79 | Fax +33 1 42 16 79 74
info@perrotin.com | www.perrotin.com
Directors Emmanuel Perrotin
Peggy Leboeuf
Emmanuelle Orenga de Gaffory
Julie Morhange
Philippe Joppin
Clara Ustinov

Galerie Perrotin
CN-Hong Kong | 17th Floor, 50 Connaught Road, Central
Phone +852 37 58 21 80 | Fax +852 37 58 21 86
hongkong@perrotin.com
Directors Etsuko Nakajima
Alice Lung

Artists at
Art Basel Miami Beach | **Chiho Aoshima**
Ivan Argote
Daniel Arsham
Hernan Bas
Sophie Calle
Maurizio Cattelan
Johan Creten
Wim Delvoye
Gelitin
Duane Hanson
JR
Jesper Just
Kaws
Bharti Kher
Kolkoz
Klara Kristalova
Guy Limone
Jin Meyerson
Farhad Moshiri
Mr.
Takashi Murakami
Kaz Oshiro
Jean-Michel Othoniel
Paola Pivi
Claude Rutault
Michael Sailstorfer
Aya Takano
Tatiana Trouvé
Piotr Uklanski
Xavier Veilhan
Peter Zimmermann

Farhad Moshiri
Fan, 2012
Hand embroidery on canvas,
169 x 127 x 6 cm

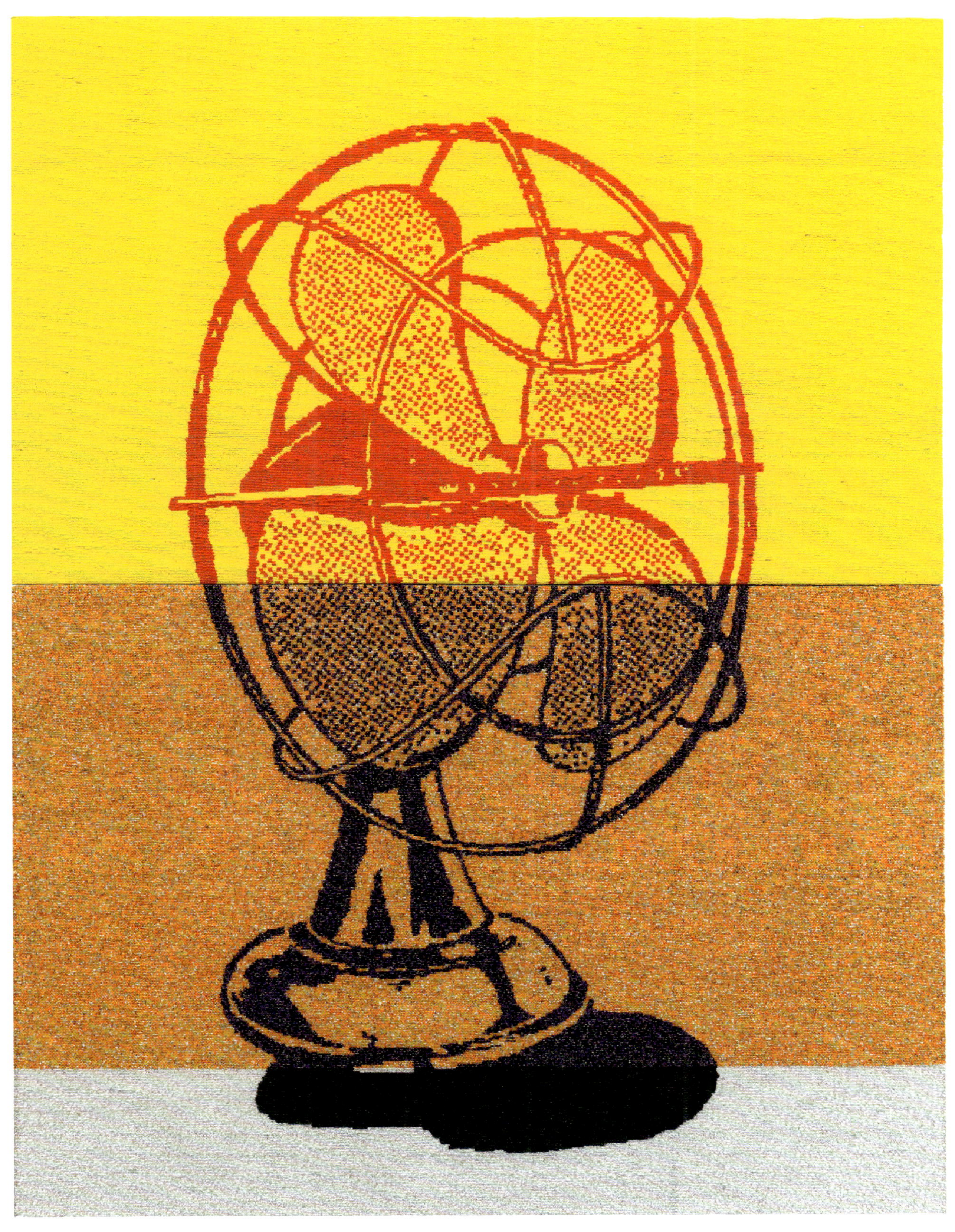

PETZEL

Mobile +1 917 528 11 16

Friedrich Petzel Gallery
US-New York, NY 10011 | 456 West 18th Street
Phone +1 212 680 94 67 | Fax +1 212 680 94 73
info@petzel.com | www.petzel.com
Directors Andrea Teschke
Sam Tsao
Jason Murison
Kat Parker

Artists at
Art Basel Miami Beach | **Yael Bartana**
Troy Brauntuch
Willem de Rooij
Simon Denny
Keith Edmier
Thomas Eggerer
Wade Guyton
Robert Heinecken
Georg Herold
Dana Hoey
Christian Jankowski
Sean Landers
Maria Lassnig
Allan McCollum
Sarah Morris
Jorge Pardo
Philippe Parreno
Joyce Pensato
Seth Price
Stephen Prina
Jon Pylypchuk
Dana Schutz
Dirk Skreber
John Stezaker
Nicola Tyson
Rezi van Lankveld
Cosima von Bonin
Charline von Heyl
Corinne Wasmuht
Heimo Zobernig

Gallery Information | Current and upcoming exhibitions by Wade Guyton:

Wade Guyton, Whitney Museum of American Art, New York, NY, opening October 4, 2012

Wade Guyton-Guyton\Walker-Kelley Walker, curated by Yilmaz Dziewior, Kunshaus Bregenz, Spring 2013

Wade Guyton, curated by Beatrix Ruf, Kunsthalle Zürich, Zurich, Summer 2013

Further information on the illustration:

Exhibition history:
The Painting Factory: Abstraction After Warhol, group exhibition, curated by Jeffrey Deitch, The Museum of Contemporary Art, Los Angeles, CA, April 29-August 20, 2012

Wade Guyton
Untitled, 2012
Epson UltraChrome inkjet on linen,
198 x 414 inches,
502.9 x 1051.6 cm (overall),
6 panels: each 198 x 69 inches,
502.9 x 175.3 cm

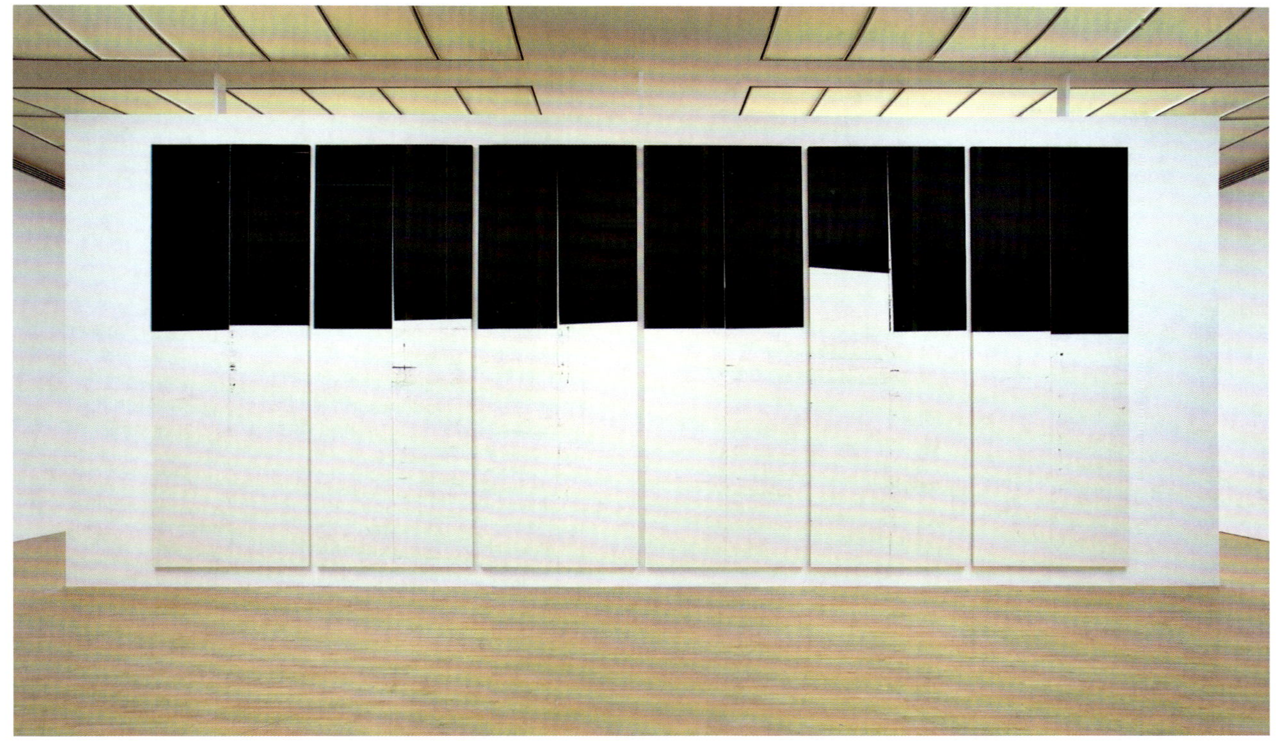

POLÍGRAFA

Mobile +34 666 43 71 11

Polígrafa Obra Gràfica, S.L.
ES-08007 Barcelona | Balmes, 54
Phone +34 93 488 23 81 | Fax +34 93 487 73 92
aloy@poligrafa.net | www.poligrafa.net
Directors José Aloy
Joan de Muga
Álvaro Puigdengolas

Artists at
Art Basel Miami Beach | **Carlos Cruz-Díez**
Atsushi Kaga
Nelson Leirner
Mateo López
Jorge Pardo
Enoc Perez
Gary Simmons
Luis Tomasello

Gallery Information | Polígrafa Obra Gráfica was launched in 1961 by Manuel de Muga and has published editions featuring over 300 artists since then.

In the 1970s Joan de Muga, son of the founder, opened Polígrafa's own workshop with facilities for etching, lithography, woodcuts, and other traditional print techniques.

Current partners Joan de Muga, José Aloy, and Álvaro Puigdengolas continue the business, inviting artists to the workshop in Barcelona to develop new projects with other renowned contemporary artists.

Further artists represented: Vito Acconci
Yaacov Agam
Carlos Amorales
Francis Bacon
Donald Baechler
Iain Baxter&
José Bedia
Lynda Benglis
Olaf Breuning
Joan Brossa
Stefan Brüggemann
Fernando Bryce
Eduardo Chillida
Christo
George Condo
Jan Dibbets
León Ferrari
Eric Fischl
Helen Frankenthaler
Sandra Gamarra
Liam Gillick
Luis Gordillo
Ana Mercedes Hoyos
Leiko Ikemura
Ilya Kabakov
Kcho
André Komatsu
Guillermo Kuitca
Jorge Macchi
Fabián Marcaccio
Bernhard Martin
Enrique Martínez Celaya
Aleksandra Mir
Joan Miró
Jonathan Monk
Robert Motherwell
Matt Mullican
Scott Myles
Tony Oursler
Paul P.
Nicolas Paris
Jaume Plensa
George Segal
Daniel Senise
Donald Sultan
Antoni Tàpies
Wang Huai-Qing
Zao Wou-Ki

Enoc Perez
Hearst Tower, New York, 2012
Hand-colored lithograph,
100 x 70 cm
Edition of 20

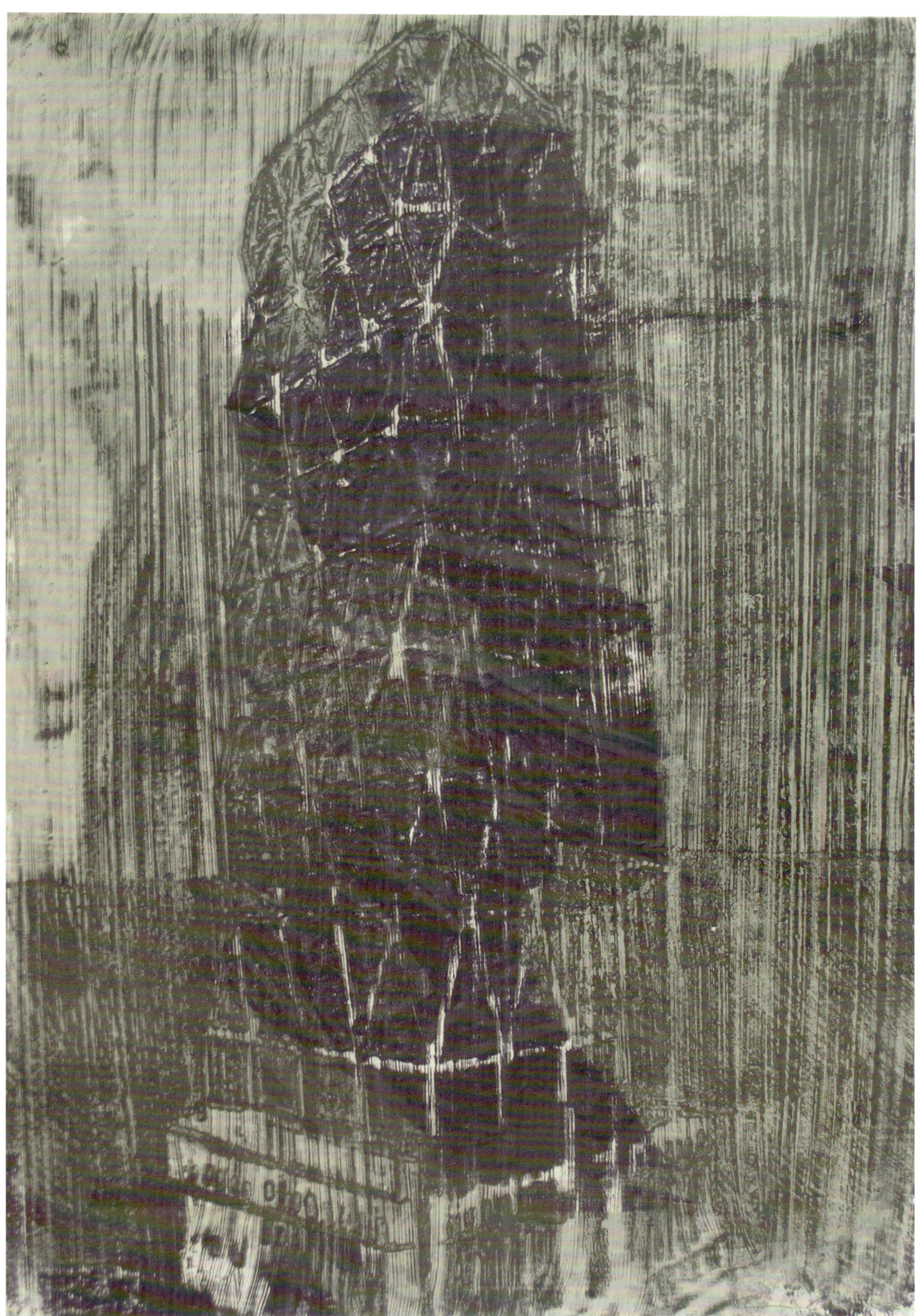

PRAZ-DELAVALLADE

Praz-Delavallade
FR-75003 Paris | 5, rue des Haudriettes
Phone +33 1 45 86 20 00 | Fax +33 1 45 86 20 10
info@praz-delavallade.com | www.praz-delavallade.com
Directors Bruno Delavallade
René-Julien Praz
Silvia Ammon

Artists at Art Basel Miami Beach | **Edgar Arceneaux**
Amy Bessone
Andrea Bowers
Philippe Decrauzat
Sam Durant
Thomas Fougeirol
Gabriel Hartley
Julian Hoeber
Jim Isermann
Nathan Mabry
Fabien Merelle
John Miller
Adi Nes
Robyn O'Neil
Amy O'Neill
Mai-Thu Perret
Dario Robleto
Antoine Roegiers
Brett Cody Rogers
Analia Saban
Erik Schmidt
Jim Shaw
Marnie Weber
Johannes Wohnseifer

Philippe Decrauzat
Untitled, 2012
Acrylic on canvas, 155 x 134 cm

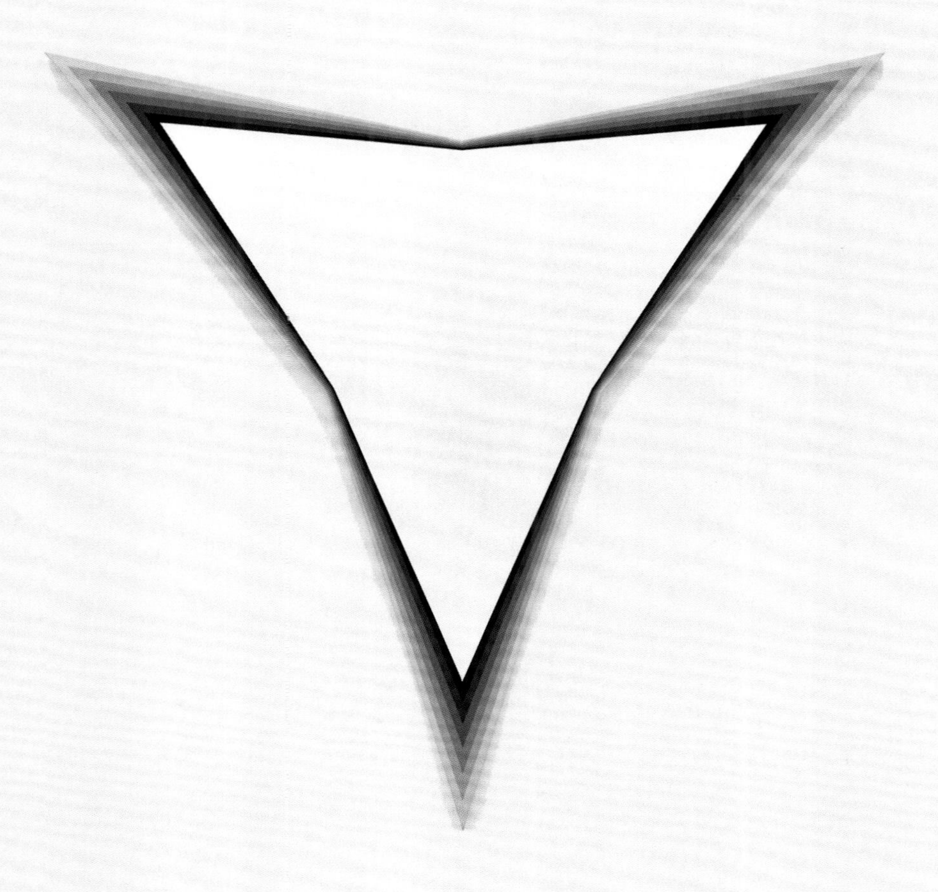

PRESENHUBER

Galerie Eva Presenhuber
CH-8005 Zurich | Diagonal Building, Zahnradstrasse 21
Phone +41 43 444 70 50 | Fax +41 43 444 70 60
info@presenhuber.com | www.presenhuber.com
Directors Eva Presenhuber
Markus Rischgasser

Artists at Art Basel Miami Beach | **Doug Aitken**
Emmanuelle Antille
Martin Boyce
Joe Bradley
Angela Bulloch
Valentin Carron
Verne Dawson
Jay DeFeo
Trisha Donnelly
Carroll Dunham
Maria Eichhorn
Matias Faldbakken
Urs Fischer
Peter Fischli/David Weiss
Sylvie Fleury
Liam Gillick
Douglas Gordon
Amy Granat
Mark Handforth
Candida Höfer
Alex Hubbard
Karen Kilimnik
Andrew Lord
Richard Prince
Gerwald Rockenschaub
Tim Rollins and K.O.S.
Ugo Rondinone
Dieter Roth
Eva Rothschild
Jean-Frédéric Schnyder
Steven Shearer
Josh Smith
Beat Streuli
Oscar Tuazon
Franz West
Sue Williams

Gallery Information | Swiss and international contemporary art

Oscar Tuazon
A Lamp, 2012
Hull, steel profile, concrete, lamps, 472 x 472 x 472 cm

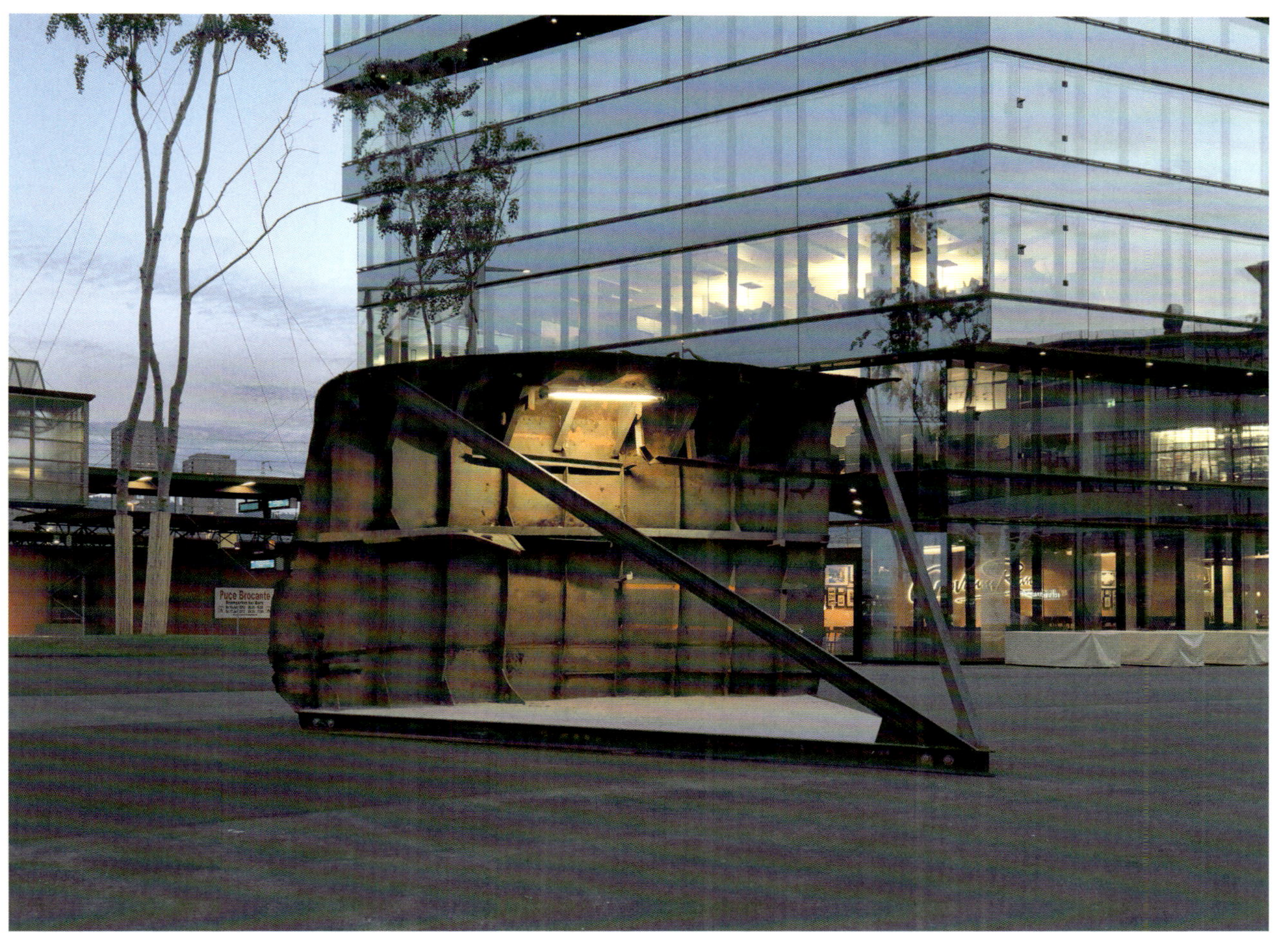
Puce Brocante

PRESTON

Simon Preston
US-New York, NY 10002 | 301 Broome Street
Phone +1 212 431 11 05
office@simonprestongallery.com | www.simonprestongallery.com
Directors Simon Preston
Paula Naughton

Artists at Art Nova | John Gerrard
Michelle Lopez
Hans Schabus

Gallery Information | Located on the Lower East Side in New York since 2008, the gallery presents a program of exploratory work by emerging and established artists. The gallery has a particular dedication to fostering strong intergenerational dialogue, presenting a series of solo exhibitions alongside curated group shows.

Further artists represented:
Carlos Bevilacqua
Nick Goss
Daniel Joseph Martinez
Jessica Mein
Marco Rios
Kara Tanaka
Caragh Thuring
Josh Tonsfeldt

Hans Schabus
Let's Call It Heimat, 2012
Installation view, Simon Preston, New York, NY

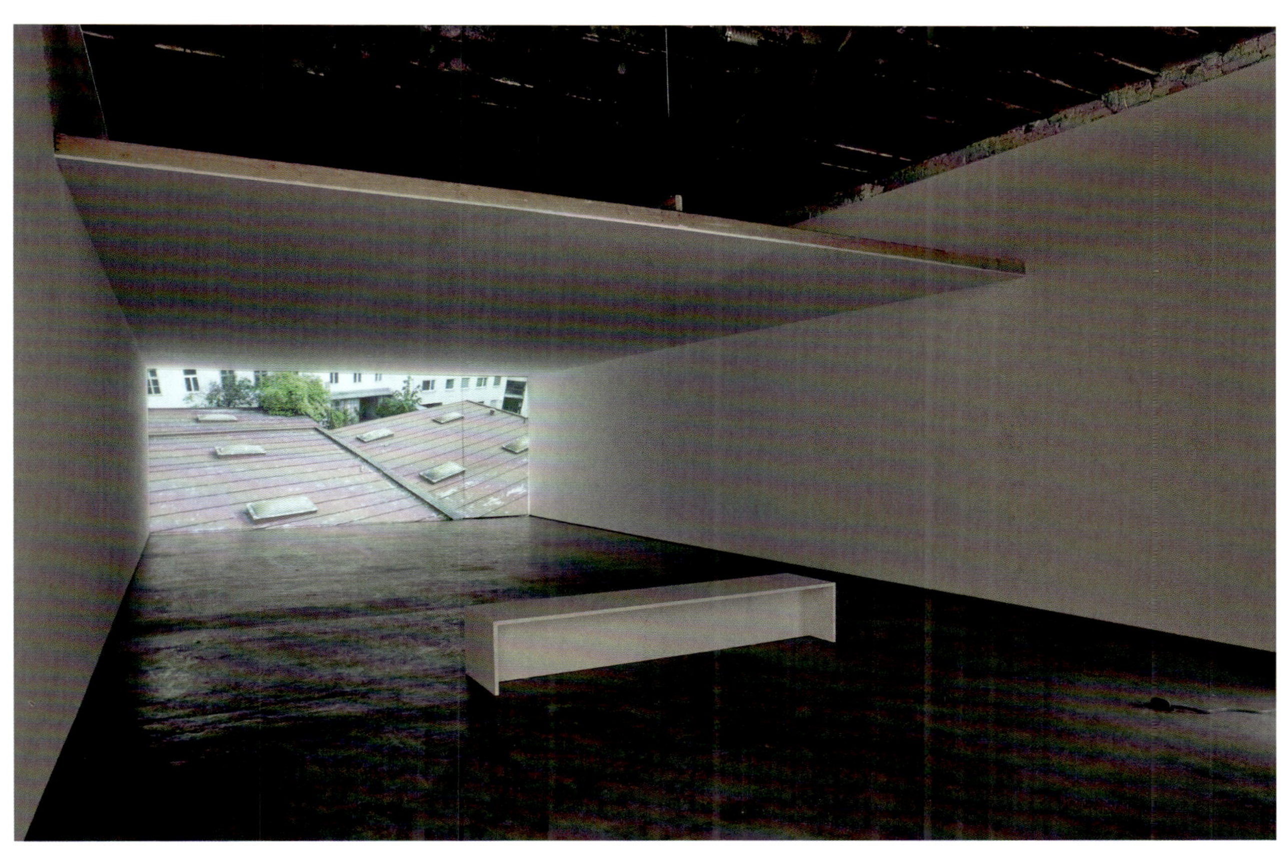

PROJECTE SD

Mobile +34 630 822868

ProjecteSD
ES-08008 Barcelona | Passatge Mercader, 8
Phone +34 93 4881360 | Fax +34 93 4881360
info@projectesd.com | www.projectesd.com
Director Silvia Dauder

Artists at Art Nova | Raimond Chaves
Gilda Mantilla

The work of Gilda Mantilla (*1967, Los Angeles, CA, United States) and Raimond Chaves (*1963, Bogotá, Colombia) is built upon their interest in the Latin American context. Through various media, Mantilla and Chaves interpret the traditions associated with the concepts of drawing, cartography, landscape or portraiture, and, with irony, Latin American imagery.

An Uncomfortable Eagerness, the work presented at Art Basel Miami Beach, is a wide-ranging project composed of drawings, video work, and archival material, which has been extracted and edited by the artists from two main sources: the Amazonian Library dependent on the Order of St. Augustine and the library of the Instituto de Investigaciones de la Amazonía Peruana (Institute of Research of the Peruvian Amazon), both in the Peruvian village of Iquitos.

An Uncomfortable Eagerness aims at a counter-reading, or a reading in a critical fashion, of the pool of images and texts about the Amazon area found in these specialized libraries. Mantilla and Chaves's approach is to question the archive and its privileged position with respect to an idea of 'knowledge.' They are also interested in the roles of those who have access to the archive, the specialist researcher or the general audience, while confronting their own expectations of this *Other* Amazon jungle, both construed and implemented by the archives and libraries.

An Uncomfortable Eagerness is not about the images of the Amazonia per se, but about the production, storage, and distribution of the images 'about' the idea of Amazonia.

Gallery Information | Based in Barcelona, ProjecteSD cultivates a program aimed at generating a dialogue between renowned and young artists and likewise between works from different times and contexts, as a way of setting artistic value over trends, classifications, or generations. The gallery goes out from a Minimalist and Conceptual standpoint, and aims to promote the artists it represents in the international field, as well as introducing international artists to a Spanish audience. ProjecteSD has been recognized as home to a new gallery concept within the Spanish contemporary art gallery scene. The consistency of its program, its specific selection of artists – unmotivated by commercial concerns and rising above the trends and demands of the market – and its personal approach have contributed to the gallery's recognition and uniqueness.

Exhibitions and art fairs 2012:
Art Basel Miami Beach 2012
Asier Mendizabal, November 2012-January 2013
Pierre Leguillon: In the Series of the Umbrella Corner (2/7), November 2012
FIAC art fair, Paris, October 2012
Patricia Dauder: The Big Circle, September/October 2012
Willem Oorebeek: In the Series of the Umbrella Corner (1/7), September 2012
Art 43 Basel, June 2012
Christoph Weber: 10, 25, 80, May-July 2012
Peter Piller: Noch immer Sturm (Still Storming), February-April 2012
ARCO Madrid, February 2012
Matt Mullican: City, November 2011-February 2012

Further artists represented:
Iñaki Bonillas
Patricia Dauder
Koenraad Dedobbeleer
Hans-Peter Feldmann
Dora García
Guillaume Leblon
Jochen Lempert
Asier Mendizabal
Matt Mullican
Marc Nagtzaam
Peter Piller
Xavier Ribas
Pieter Vermeersch
Christoph Weber

A-D | **Raimond Chaves and Gilda Mantilla**
An Uncomfortable Eagerness, 2011
QuickTime video animation with sound, 20 min 33 sec
Edition of 3+1 AP

A

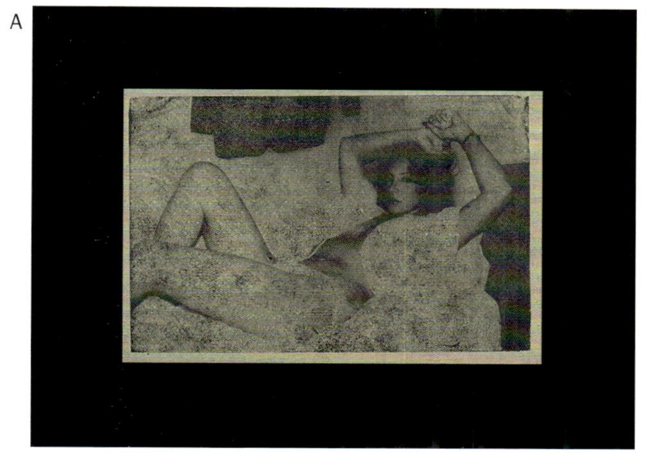

B

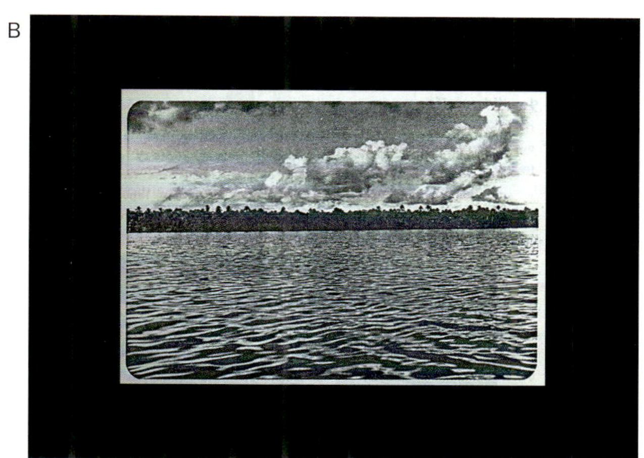

C

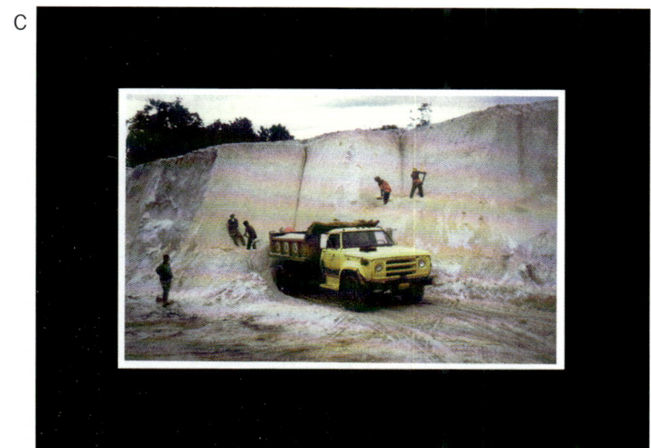

D

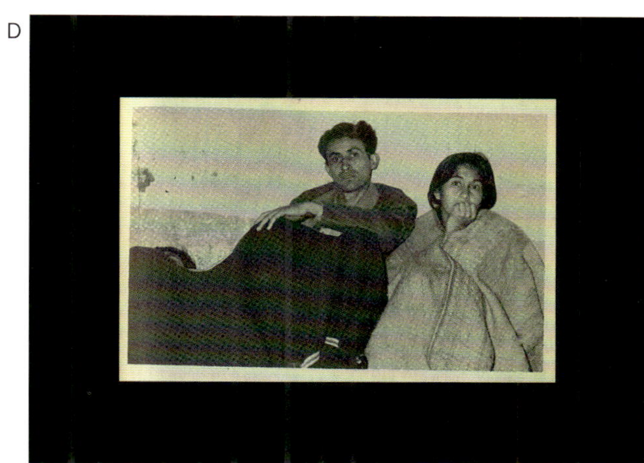

PSM

Mobile +49 178 785 51 67

PSM
DE-10405 Berlin | Strassburger Strasse 6-8
Phone +49 30 75 52 46 26 | Fax +49 30 75 52 46 25
office@psm-gallery.com | www.psm-gallery.com
Director Sabine Schmidt

One-Person Show | Artist Information

Nathan Peter

*1978, Minneapolis, MN, United States
Lives and works in Berlin, Germany

Further artists represented | Øystein Aasan
Eduardo Basualdo
Thomas Chapman
Paolo Chiasera
Sophie Erlund
Christian Falsnaes
Nadira Husain
Daniel Jackson
Ujino Muneteru
Anca Munteanu Rimnic
Ariel Reichman

Nathan Peter is not interested in an iconographic trade with the past. Any formal or thematic influence is continuously abstracted and absorbed in a haptic process of material abrading that appears to court and avoid destruction at the same time. By revealing layers in this way and making real space by folding, piecing, and suspending canvas as a contour, painting is both reduced and opened up. Peter has, for example, previously referenced the peeled lemon seen in paintings by seventeenth-century Dutch painter Pieter Claesz. In a Claesz Vanitas painting, the peeled lemon acts both chromatically, as a strong visual accent, and as a metaphor of revelation. Peter's installation again returns to this reference, but this time it is painting that is the Vanitas. The yellow canvas edges of several paintings are cut and spiraled free to make the booth itself a temporal volumetric painting specific to the space. The physical structure of painting is exposed, laid bare for all to see – unspooled three-dimensionally, like a fractured, temporal web.

Nathan Peter
detail: peel, 2012
Bitumen lacquer, enamel, paint, tape, wood, and canvas, dimensions of canvas peel are variable, 25 x 45 x 92 cm

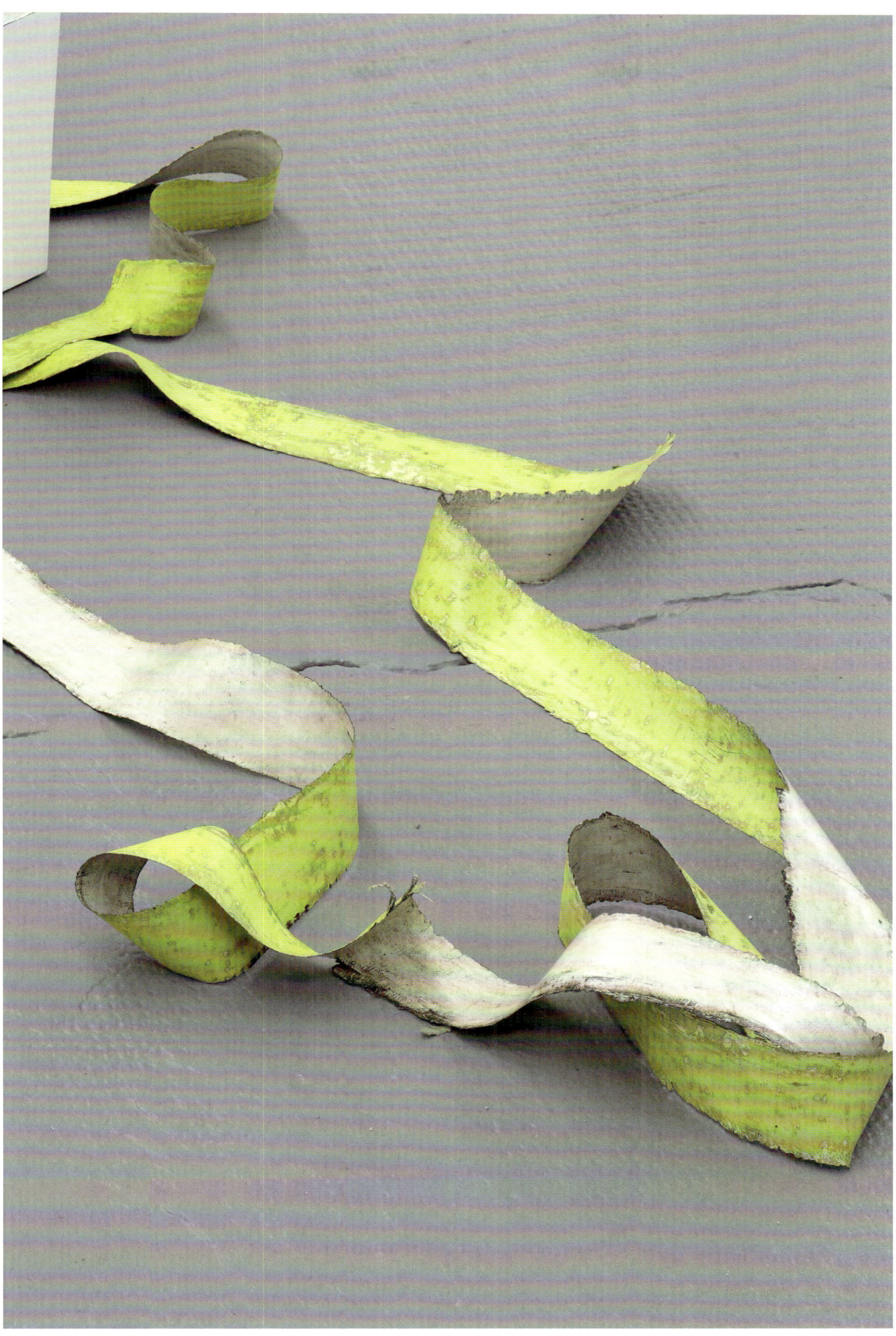

RAEBERVONSTENGLIN

Mobile +41 76 200 54 20, +41 76 441 55 50

RaebervonStenglin
CH-8005 Zurich | Pfingstweidstrasse 23
Phone +41 43 818 21 00
info@raebervonstenglin.com | www.raebervonstenglin.com
Directors Beat Raeber
Matthias von Stenglin

One-Person Show | Artist Information

Ivan Seal

*1973, Manchester, United Kingdom
Lives and works in Berlin, Germany

Further artists represented | Saâdane Afif
Karsten Födinger
Sofia Hultén
David Keating
Robert Kinmont
Susanne Kriemann
Manuela Leinhoss
Taiyo Onorato & Nico Krebs
Kilian Rüthemann
Alexander Wagner

Once, when I was a teenager, I bought some cheap white trousers, a pastel blue t-shirt, slip-on shoes, and a speckled grey suit jacket. These were worn to look like Don Johnson from *Miami Vice;* at the time I was quite fat but that seemed not to deter me from the look-alike attempt. The first and only time I wore this combination of clothes, I went out just to walk the streets of my home village, check out some girls who hung out by the school and see if I could finally impress. Between my house and the girls it rained heavily, as it tends to do in Manchester. Consequently, by the time I got to my destination my cheap white trousers had turned completely transparent and I was left standing there with my very bright red underpants showing through.

Ivan Seal
bloonkomibicrul sne sosegponkies om flassss (groping hand), 2012
Oil on canvas, 30 x 40 cm

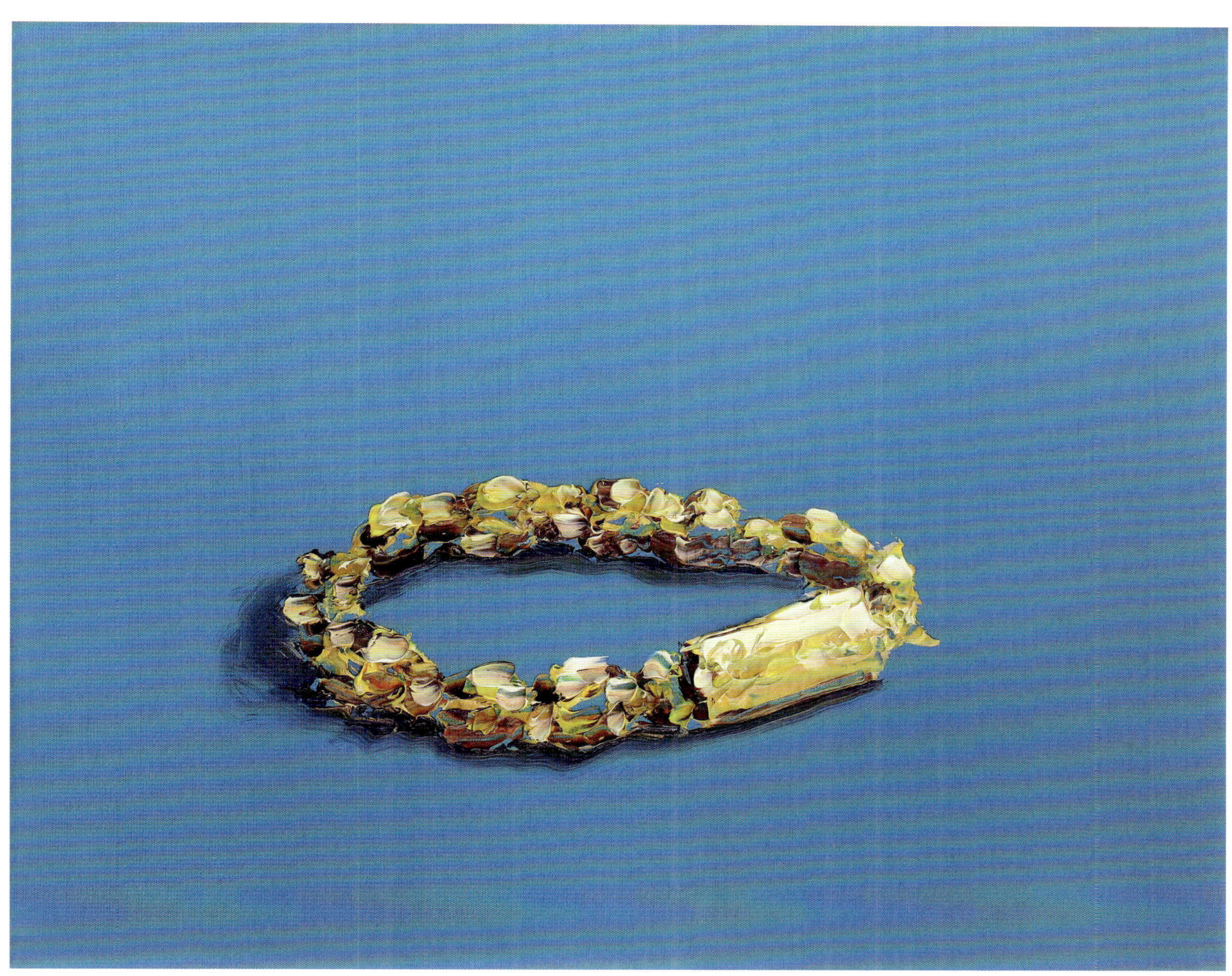

RAMIKEN CRUCIBLE

Mobile +1 917 434 42 45

Ramiken Crucible
US-New York, NY 10002 | 389 Grand Street
Phone +1 917 328 46 56
ramiken@ramikencrucible.com | www.ramikencrucible.com
Directors Mike Egan
Blaize Lehane

One-Person Show | Artist Information

Andra Ursuta

*1979, Salonta, Romania
Lives and works in New York, NY, United States

Further artists represented | Lucas Blalock
Elaine Cameron-Weir
Borden Capalino
Nolan Hendrickson
Gavin Kenyon

Andra Ursuta's sculptures and drawings articulate elaborate narratives of self-annihilation, in which notions of tradition and subjectivity turn on themselves with the enthusiasm of an arcane propaganda. *Pole Woman* is a series of anthropomorphic steel sculptures standing on vandalized fake rock formations. The tubular polished steel figures recast sexualized Paleolithic female figures as impossible stripper poles and coin-operated cult objects that do not work, collapsing the body of the strip club worker with the tool of its trade. The pedestals mimic petrified women in a style that undermines the sculptures they support, creating an incongruous cave environment where notions of exoticism clash in superimposed layers of sedimented female bodies.

Andra Ursuta
Pole Woman 1, 2012
Stainless steel, chicken wire, foam, clay, concrete, dirt, paint,
96 x 8 x 5 inches

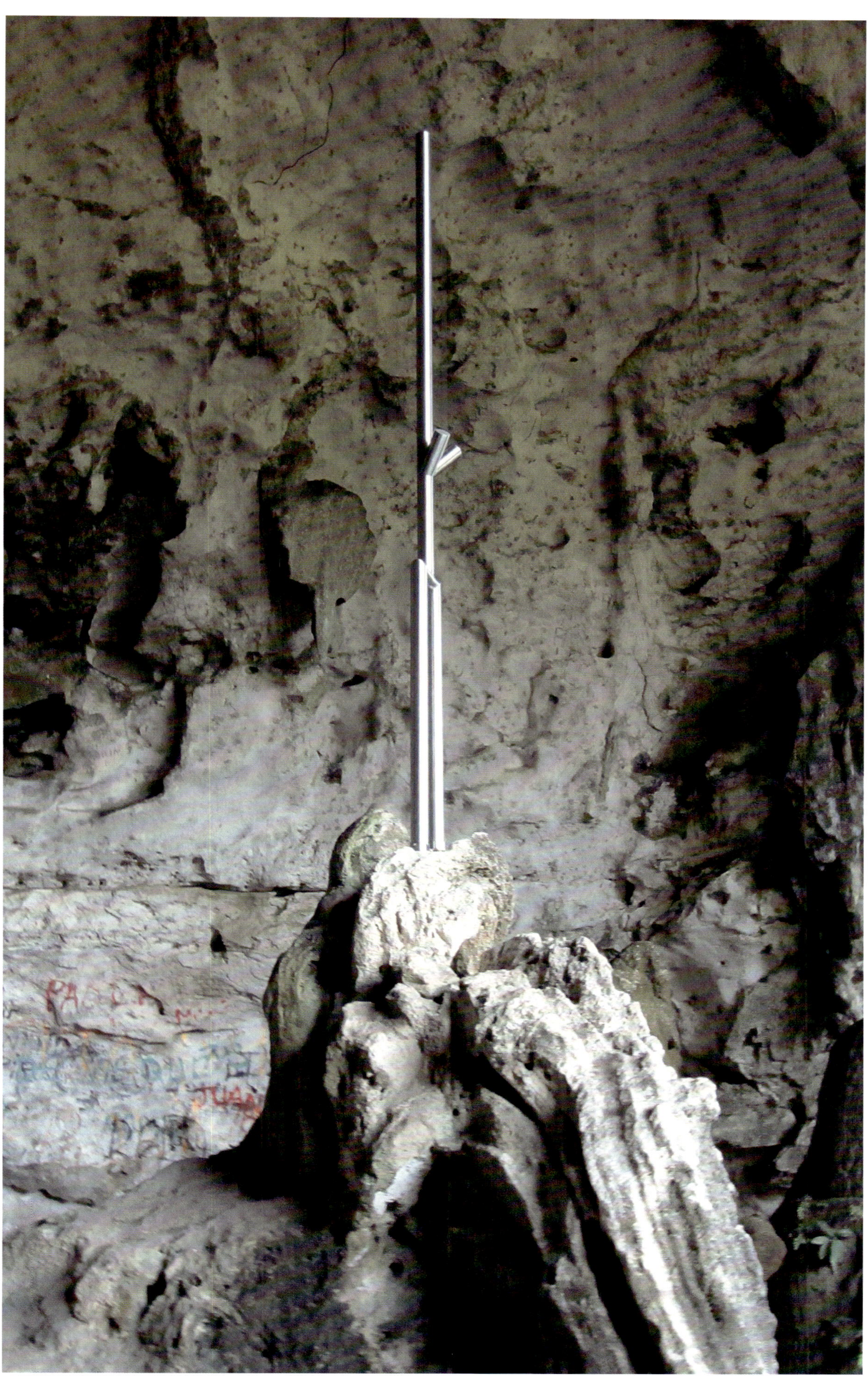

RAMPA

Mobile +90 530 7836056

Rampa
TR-34357 Istanbul | Sair Nedim Cad 21A Akaretler Besiktas
Phone +90 212 3270800 | Fax +90 212 3270801
info@rampaistanbul.com | www.rampaistanbul.com
Directors Leyla Tara Suyabatmaz
Özkan Cangüven

Artists at Art Nova | Nevin Aladağ
Güçlü Öztekin

Gallery Information | Exhibitions:
Nevin Aladağ, April 19-June 9, 2012
Servet Koçyigit, September 8-October 20, 2012
Erinç Seymen, November 13-December 22, 2012

Further artists represented:
Hüseyin Bahri Alptekin
Vahap Avşar
Cengiz Çekil
İnci Furni
Leyla Gediz
Hatice Güleryüz
Selma Gürbüz
Nilbar Güreş
Servet Koçyigit
Ahmet Oran
Erinç Seymen

Berlin-based artist Nevin Aladağ's performative work employs video, photography, and sculpture as media, renegotiating the delineations of identity, social and cultural norms, with a comparatively specific yet poetically general sensibility. Istanbul-based Güçlü Öztekin's work is heavily anchored in the process of production – the artist takes issue with the very physical means with which he works.

The forms that Öztekin's work represent become secondary to the actual method with which he 'exposes' the inherent nature of his media, similar to a sculptural process that attains form through diminishment, not addition. The un-finished and non-precious nature of his work is in clear contrast with Aladağ's finished works, which transform the indescribable and chaotic into finessed forms. Yet both artists' processes are performative – temporality and indexicality are critical to understanding what remains both of Öztekin's sheets of craft paper and of Aladağ's rugs, tin plates, and videos. The impulse constantly to re-configure the very means with which contemporary art finds form foregrounds the two artists' self-expansion, exploration, and interrogation.

Nevin Aladağ
Makramé, 2012
Aluminum stick, 1.5 mm wire cable, 123 x 180 cm
The knotting patterns of the macrame are visualizations of the pattern inherent in the cable itself.

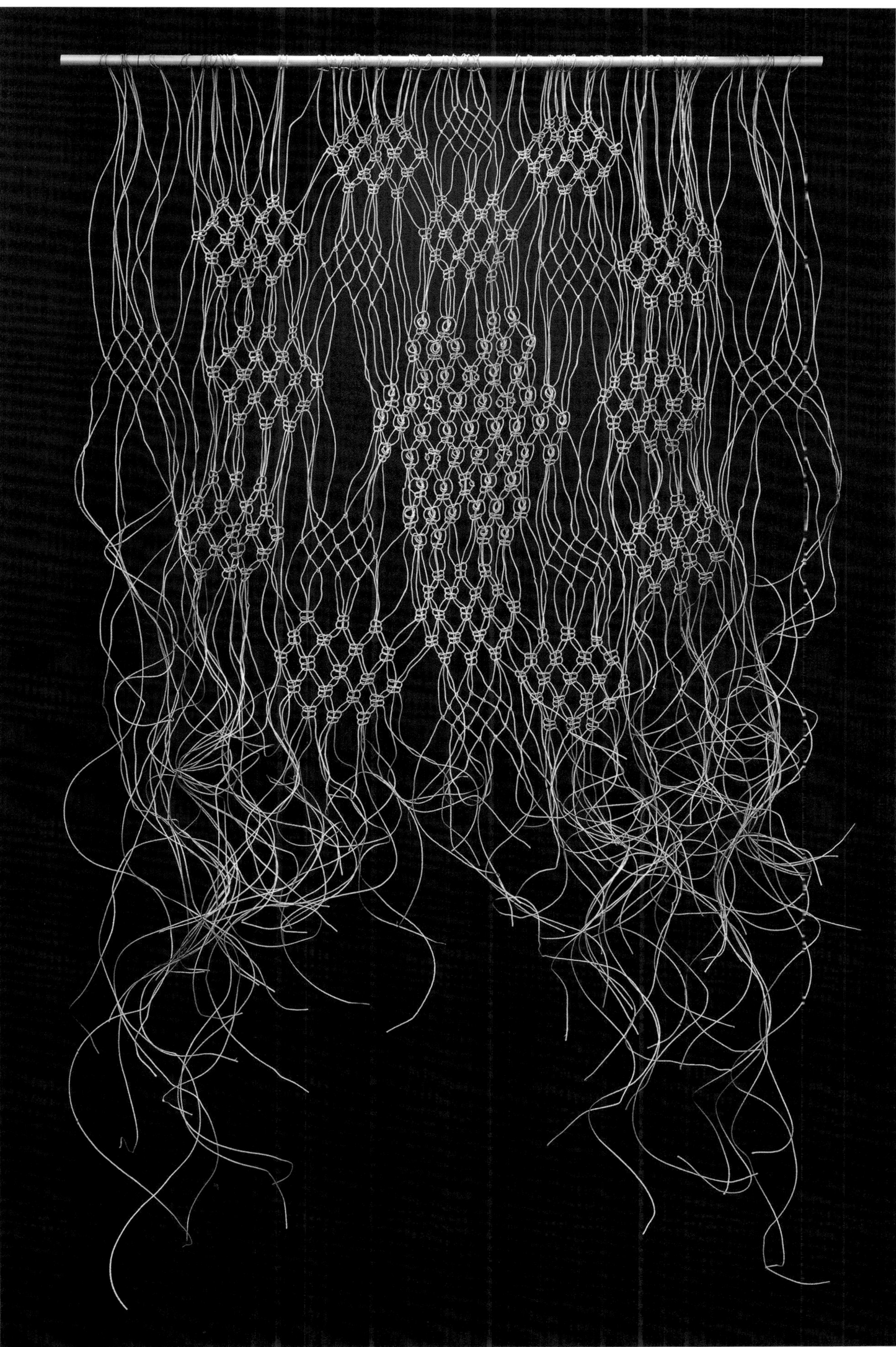

RAZUK

Mobile +55 11 999 76 15 50

Galeria Marília Razuk
BR-São Paulo 04536-000 | Rua Jeronimo da Veiga, 62 and 131
Phone +55 11 30 79 08 53 | Fax +55 11 30 79 08 53
info@galeriamariliarazuk.com.br | www.galeriamariliarazuk.com.br
Directors Marília Razuk
Marcela Razuk

Artists at Art Nova | Débora Bolsoni
Raquel Garbelotti
Wagner Malta Tavares

Further artists represented | José Bechara
Flávia Bertinato
Cabelo
Joaquín Cociña
Cláudio Cretti
Marlon de Azambuja
Amilcar de Castro
Rodrigo de Castro
Caetano Dias
Bruno Dunley
Mariana Galender
Zlatko Kopljar
Cristóbal Léon
Vanderlei Lopes
Maria Lynch
Fabio Miguez
Germana Monte-Mór
Gustavo Rezende
Hilal Sami Hilal
Mariana Serri
Angelo Venosa
Marina Weffort

Wagner Malta Tavares (*1964) presents *Bermudas* and *Oblivio,* part of a series of works in relief, monotypes, photographs, and sculptures in which aircrafts, ships, and submarines are enshrouded by what the artist calls an 'oblivious fog.' In the photographs, the fog covers everything, leaving only traces of these vehicles lost in time. In the sculpture, a sunken submarine has accumulated layers of oblivion, while the specular surface of the glass walls invites us to rescue it with our own gaze.

The work of Débora Bolsoni (*1975) concentrates on an assortment of images made with mundane objects such as wrapping paper, construction materials, sand, and paraffin. Her concern is always about the degree of simplicity of the constructive procedures, leaving the impression that much has been done with scant resources, which, in many instances, gives Bolsoni's work a magical, unexpected aspect.

Raquel Garbelotti (*1973) presents *Movimento Involuntário,* consisting of two photographs and a video, in which one witnesses a simulation of the sprouting of a real fern. *Juntamentz* is the result of academic research and an open ethnographic study conducted by the artist and some of her students. It could be categorized as a poetic mapping of the Pomeranian community present in the Brazilian state of Espirito Santo.

Débora Bolsoni
Biblioteca (Library), 2011
Tile and cement, 27 x 37 x 21 cm

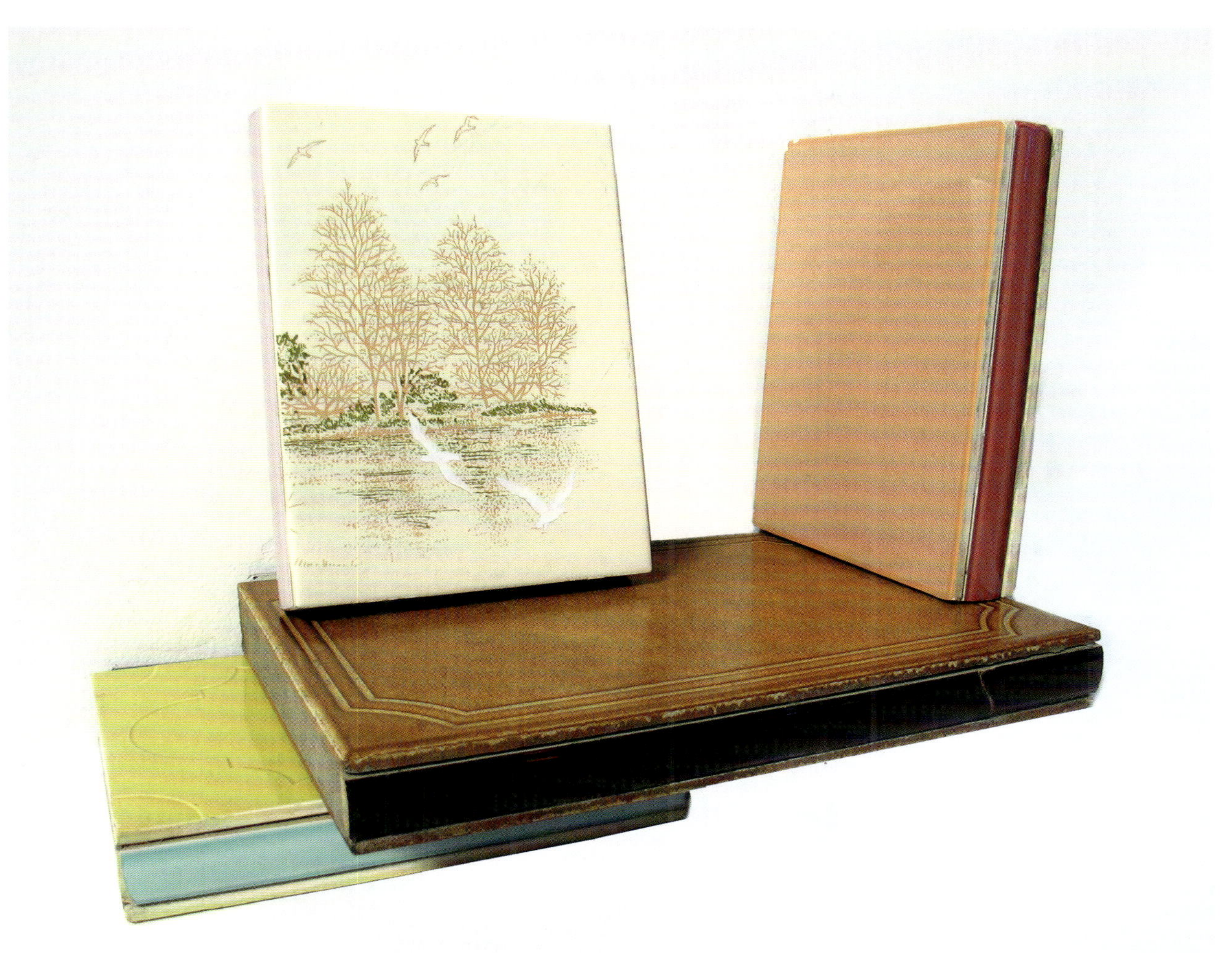

RECH

Almine Rech Gallery
FR-75003 Paris | 19 rue de Saintonge
Phone +33 1 45 83 71 90 | Fax +33 1 45 70 91 30
contact.paris@alminerech.com | www.alminerech.com
Directors Carlos Cardenas
Amélie Reisinger

Almine Rech Gallery
BE-1050 Brussels | Abdijstraat 20 Rue de l'Abbaye
Phone +32 2 648 56 84 | Fax +32 2 648 44 84
contact.brussels@alminerech.com | www.alminerech.com
Directors Jason Cori
Anna Fisher

Artists at
Art Basel Miami Beach | **Matthias Bitzer**
Joe Bradley
Don Brown
Tom Burr
Aaron Curry
Sylvie Fleury
John Giorno
Gregor Hildebrandt
Alex Israël
Isaac Julien
Jeff Koons
Joseph Kosuth
Ange Leccia
Erik Lindman
Liu Wei
Joel Morrison
Richard Prince
Anselm Reyle
Ugo Rondinone
Taryn Simon
Katja Strunz
Ida Tursic & Wilfried Mille
Franz West
Tsuruko Yamazaki

Gallery Information | Exhibitions Paris:
Semyon Faibisovich/Sergey Bratkov, January/February 2013
Alex Israël, October/November 2012
John Giorno, September/October 2012
Erik Lindman, September/October 2012
Taryn Simon, June/July 2012

Exhibitions Brussels:
Francesco Vezzoli, December 2012/January 2013
Jeff Koons, October/November 2012
Angel Vergara, September 2012
Aaron Curry, June/July 2012

Further artists represented: Ziad Antar
Beatrice Caracciolo
Johan Creten
Philip-Lorca diCorcia
Teresita Fernández
Mark Hagen
Mark Handforth
Patrick Hill
Xylor Jane
Barbara Kasten
Thomas Kiesewetter
Daniel Lergon
Curtis Mann
John McCracken
Peter Peri
Matthieu Ronsse
Hedi Slimane
Tatiana Trouvé
Gavin Turk
James Turrell
Not Vital
Gabriel Vormstein
Yeesookyung
Aaron Young

Joel Morrison
There Will Be Blood and Waffles,
2012
Stainless steel,
77.5 x 41.9 x 40.6 cm

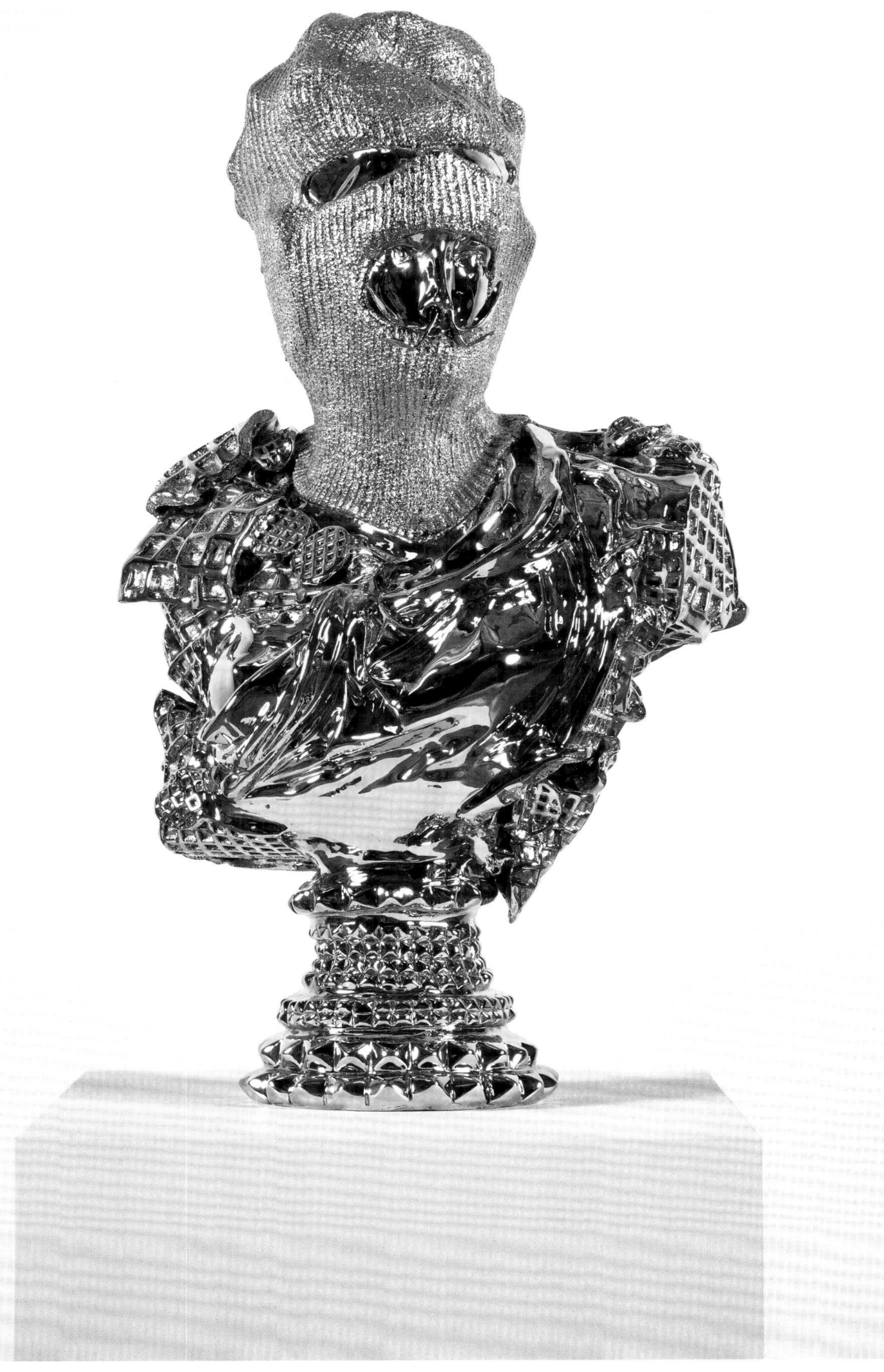

REGEN PROJECTS

Regen Projects
US-Los Angeles, CA 90038 | 6750 Santa Monica Boulevard
Phone +1 310 276 54 24 | Fax +1 310 276 74 30
office@regenprojects.com | www.regenprojects.com
Directors Shaun Caley Regen
Jennifer Loh
Heather Harmon

Artists at
Art Basel Miami Beach | **Doug Aitken**
Matthew Barney
Walead Beshty
John Bock
Abraham Cruzvillegas
Willem de Rooij
Dan Graham
Rachel Harrison
Elliott Hundley
Sergej Jensen
Anish Kapoor
Toba Khedoori
Gabriel Kuri
Liz Larner
Glenn Ligon
Scott McFarland
Marilyn Minter
Catherine Opie
Jennifer Pastor
Manfred Pernice
Raymond Pettibon
Elizabeth Peyton
Jack Pierson
Lari Pittman
Richard Prince
Daniel Richter
Gary Simmons
Wolfgang Tillmans
Ryan Trecartin
Gillian Wearing
Lawrence Weiner
James Welling
Sue Williams
Andrea Zittel

Lawrence Weiner
AROUND & AROUND HIGH & LOW,
2012
Language + the materials
referred to, dimensions variable
Installation view, Regen Projects II,
Los Angeles

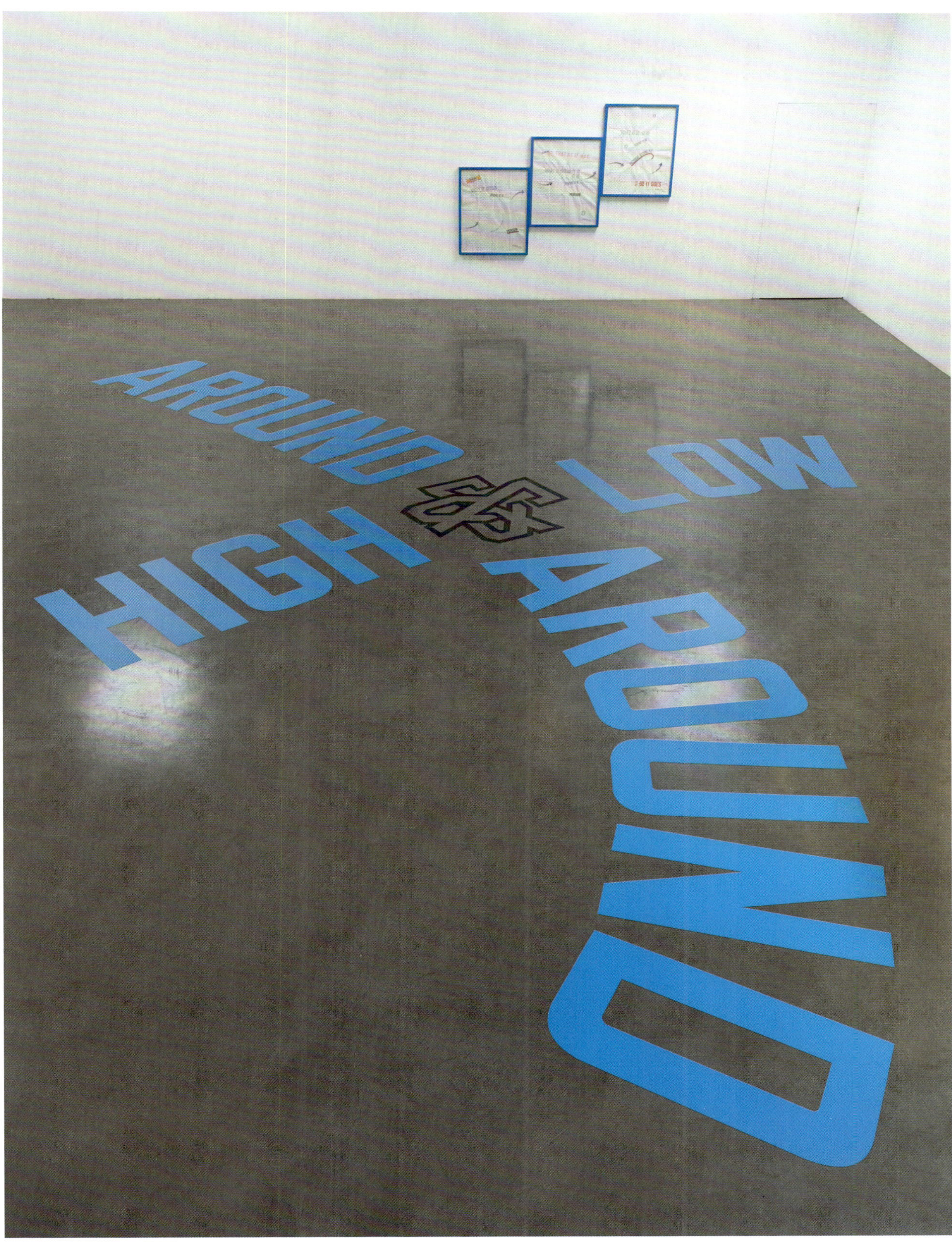
AROUND
&
LOW
HIGH
AROUND

REGINA

Regina Gallery
RU-105120 Moscow | 1, 4th Syromyatnichesky pereulok
Phone +7 495 228 13 30 | Fax +7 495 228 13 32
moscow@reginagallery.com | www.reginagallery.com
Directors Vladimir Ovcharenko
Nadia Totskaya

Regina Gallery
GB-London W1W 8DE | 22 Eastcastle Street
Phone +44 207 636 77 68 | Fax +44 207 636 77 68
london@reginagallery.com | www.reginagallery.com
Directors Romilly Eveleigh
Mike Ovcharenko

Artist at
Art Basel Miami Beach | **Sergey Bratkov**

Gallery Information | Established in 1990 by Regina and Vladimir Ovcharenko, Regina Gallery has distinguished itself as one of the most pioneering contemporary art galleries on the Russian art scene.

A wide international program provides a unique platform to present Russian artists to the world public as well as introduce latest developments of contemporary Western art in Russia. Regina currently represents around 30 established and emerging artists.

In April 2010 Regina Gallery inaugurated its new space in London. The venue is the first permanent space run by a Russian gallery abroad and will develop the gallery's activities.

Further artists represented: Victor Alimpiev
Evgeniy Antufiev
Nikolay Bakharev
Ivan Chuikov
Semyon Faibisovich
Claire Fontaine
Oleg Golosiy
Tigran Khachatryan
Egor Koshelev
Olya Kroytor
Eli Kuka
Oleg Kulik
Vlad Kulkov
Vladimir Logutov
Jonathan Meese
Slava Mogutin
Andrei Monastyrski
Pavel Pepperstein
Jack Pierson
Kerim Ragimov
Daniel Richter
Andrei Roiter
Maria Serebriakova
Natasha Struchkova
Jorinde Voigt
Stas Volyazlovsky
Erwin Wurm
Rose Wylie
Sergey Zarva
Arseniy Zhilyaev
Constantin Zvezdochotov

Sergey Bratkov
#1 from the Series
ШАПИТО MOSCOW, 2011
Color photo, 200 x 220 cm
Edition of 5

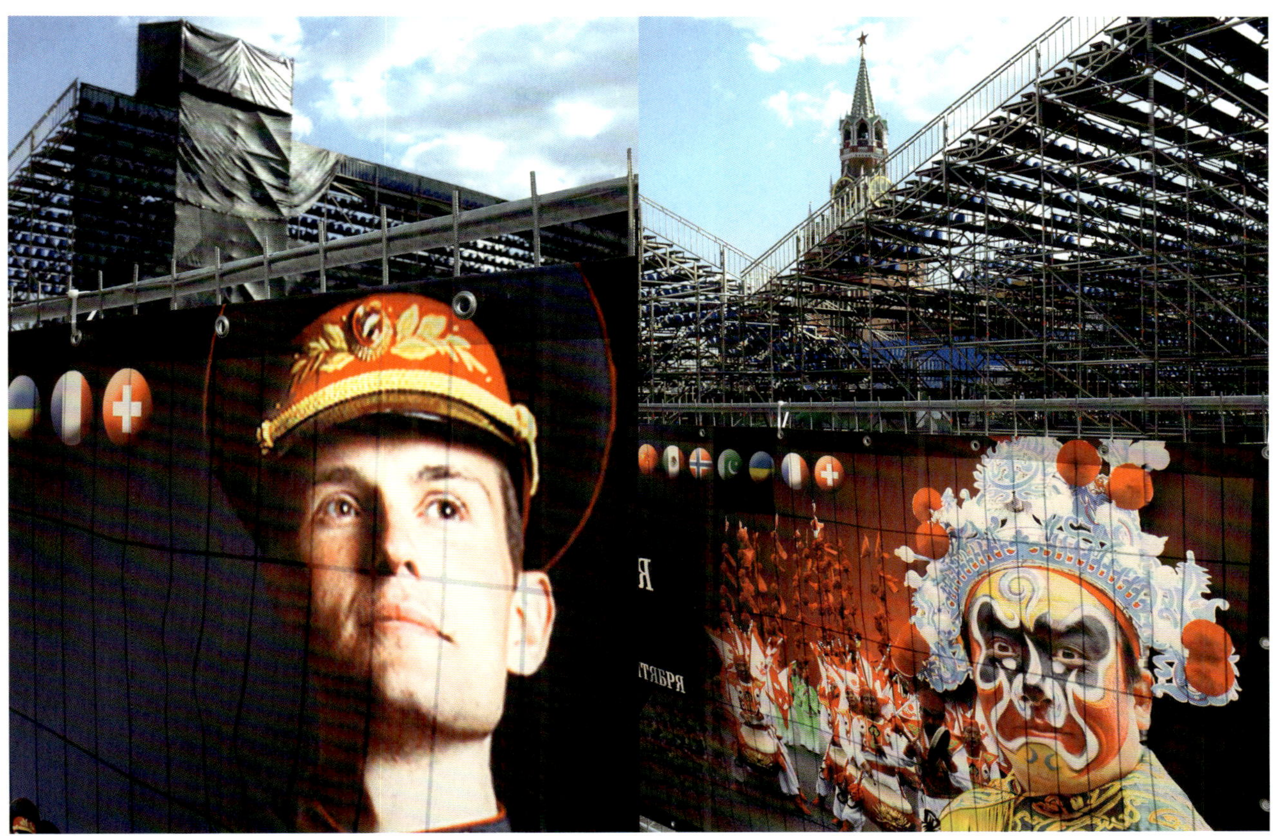

REIN

Mobile +33 6 63686813

Galerie Michel Rein
FR-75003 Paris | 42, rue de Turenne
Phone +33 1 42726813 | Fax +33 1 42728194
galerie@michelrein.com | www.michelrein.com
Director Michel Rein

One-Person Show | Artist Information

LaToya Ruby Frazier

*1982, Braddock, PA, United States
Lives and works in Braddock, PA, New Brunswick, NY, and New York, NY, United States

Selected solo shows:
2013 Contemporary Arts Museum, Houston, TX
Brooklyn Museum, New York, NY
2012 Indianapolis Museum of Contemporary Art, Indianapolis, IN

Selected group shows:
2012 Whitney Biennial, Whitney Museum of American Art, New York, NY
Galerie Michel Rein, Paris
2011 Incheon Women Artists' Biennial, Korea
Pittsburgh Biennial, Andy Warhol Museum, Pittsburgh, PA
2010 *Greater New York,* P.S.1 MoMA, New York, NY
2009 New Museum Triennial, New York, NY

Further artists represented | Saâdane Afif
Maria Thereza Alves
Maja Bajevic
Jean-Pierre Bertrand
Jordi Colomer
Jimmie Durham
Didier Faustino
Dora Garcia
Mathew Hale
Christian Hidaka
Jean-Charles Hue
Armand Jalut
Yuri Leiderman
Didier Marcel
Stefan Nikolaev
ORLAN
Dan Perjovschi
Elisa Pône
Mark Raidpere
Michael Riedel
Franck Scurti
Allan Sekula
Raphaël Zarka

LaToya Ruby Frazier's work explores the psychological connections of intergenerational relationships within her family and community through photographs and videos that blur the line between self-portraiture and social documentary.

Her work is informed by late-19th- and early-20th-century modes of representation in documentary practice. With an emphasis on postmodern conditions, class, and capitalism, Frazier investigates issues of propaganda, politics, and the importance of subjectivity.

LaToya Ruby Frazier
Self Portrait (March 10am), 2009
Gelatin silver print, 20 x 16 inches

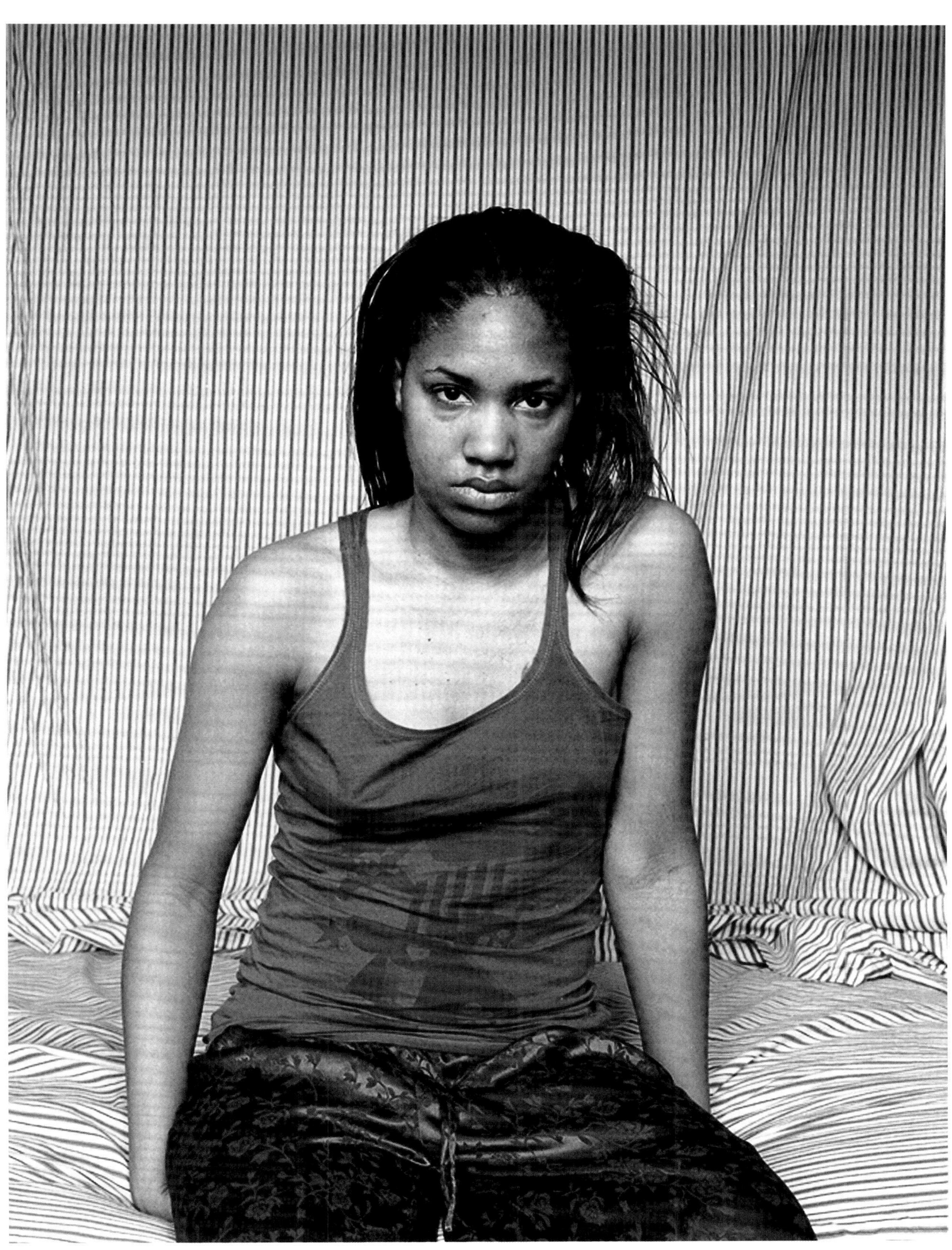

REVOLVER

Mobile +51 1 987 98 96 14

Revolver Galería
PE-Miraflores, Lima 18 | Calle Recavarren 261
Phone +51 1 255 85 71
contacto@revolvergaleria.com | www.revolvergaleria.com
Director Giancarlo Scaglia

Artists at Art Nova | Jerry B. Martin
José Carlos Martinat
Giancarlo Scaglia

Gallery Information | Revolver Gallery was established in 2008 in the heart of the historically wounded district of Miraflores, Lima, Peru. Since its inception, Revolver has set clear targets in its mission as a private platform for the exhibition, promotion, and management of contemporary artists – a young generation with a common and conscious background. It strives to redirect from the trajectory of the local scene – with more than a decade of sustained development peaking at the turn of the century – and to aim towards exchange and connection with the international, reinforcing the idea that it is the active trade of discourses that will articulate further development independent from the gallery's spatial physicality.

Revolver is committed to supporting the individuality of its artists and enhancing their experimentation through any media and genre. It likewise maintains a self-managed program of international residencies, inviting selected emerging artists from abroad to produce an exhibit in the gallery, hence redirecting the international into the local. Focused on its role as the catalyzing nexus between artists, critics, museum directors, curators, and collectors, Revolver reaffirms that the sum of these – resulting in intelligent art collection – will trigger the development of a wide-ranging scenario.

Further artists represented:
Miguel Andrade Valdez
Elena Damiani
Matias Duville
Philippe Gruenberg
Pablo Hare
Gilda Mantilla
Andrés Marroquín Winkelmann
Ishmael Randall Weeks
Juan Salas Carreño
José Vera Matos

A | **José Carlos Martinat**
Experimental Prototype Community of Tomorrow: Epcot, 2012
Photograph
Prototype for Art Basel (installation), image taken from Internet

B | **Jerry B. Martin**
Piezas y emblemas, 2009
Typewritten text drawing on paper, 86 x 61 cm

C | **Giancarlo Scaglia**
No title (From 'Nunca fuimos la revolución' Series), 2011
Oil on canvas, 200 x 150 cm

A

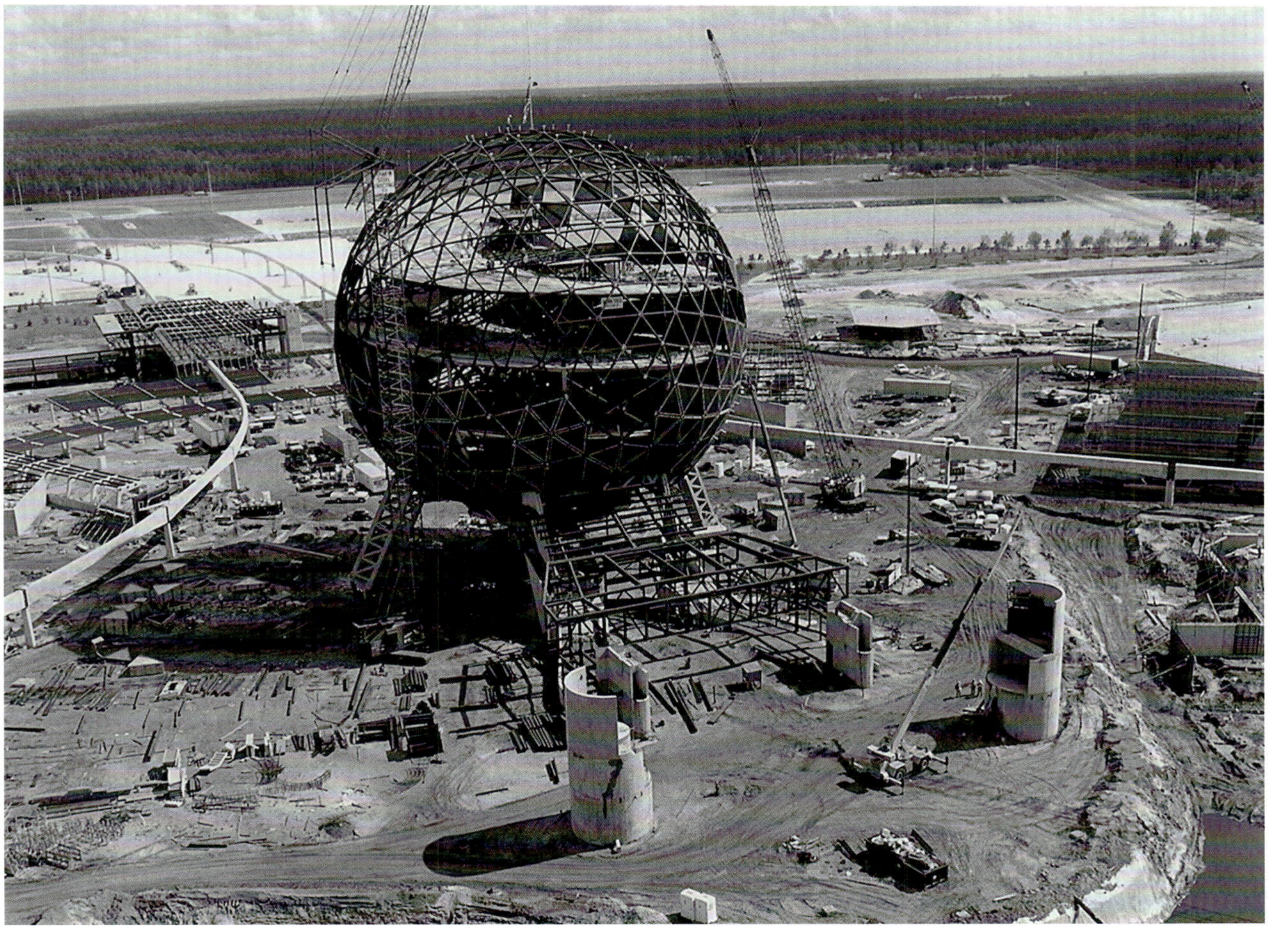

B

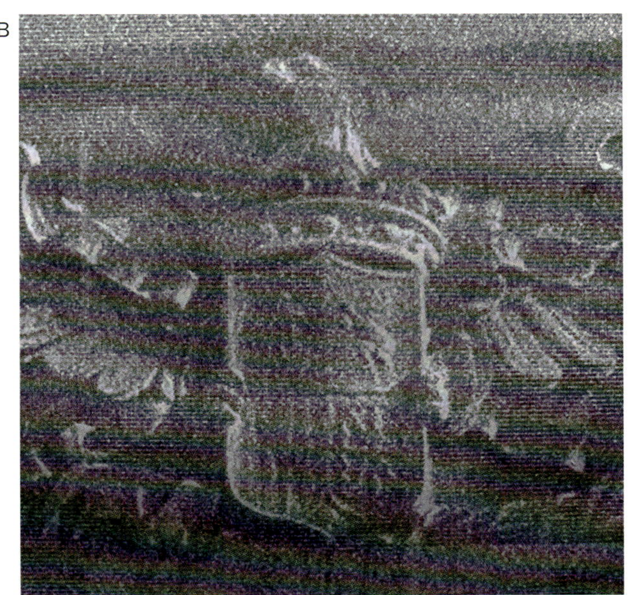

C

REYNOLDS

Mobile +44 77 98606343

Anthony Reynolds Gallery
GB-London W1F 7BG | 60 Great Marlborough Street
Phone +44 20 74392201 | Fax +44 20 74391869
info@anthonyreynolds.com | www.anthonyreynolds.com
Director Anthony Reynolds

Artists at Art Basel Miami Beach | **David Austen**
Ian Breakwell
Peter Gallo
Leon Golub
Paul Graham
Lucy Harvey
Emily Jacir
Kai Kaljo
Andrew Mansfield
Asier Mendizabal
Lucia Nogueira
Walid Raad
Georgia Sagri
Nancy Spero
Sturtevant
Jon Thompson
Amikam Toren
Nobuko Tsuchiya
Mark Wallinger

Asier Mendizabal
Untitled (Syntagmatic and Paradigmatic), 2012
Chestnut wood, 30 x 325 x 25 cm

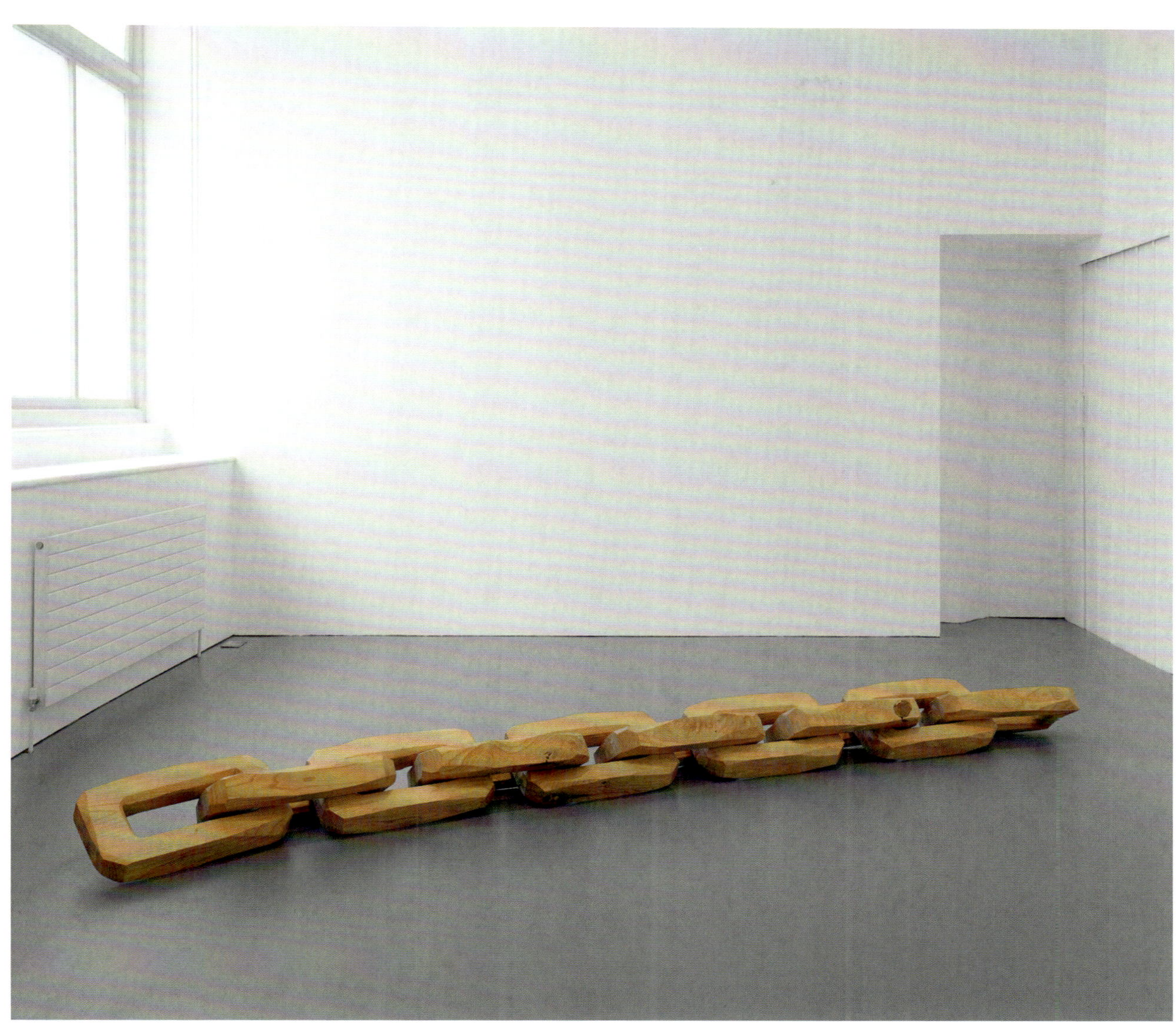

ROBERTS & TILTON

Roberts & Tilton
US-Culver City, CA 90232 | 5801 Washington Blvd
Phone +1 323 549 02 23 | Fax +1 323 549 02 24
info@robertsandtilton.com | www.robertsandtilton.com
Directors Bennett Roberts
Julie Roberts
Jack Tilton
Mary Skarbek

Artists at Art Basel Miami Beach | **Noah Davis**
Ellen De Meutter
Eberhard Havekost
Thomas Kiesewetter
Daniel Joseph Martinez
Barry McGee
Betye Saar
Ed Templeton
Kehinde Wiley
Ai Yamaguchi

Daniel Joseph Martinez
Present & Future, 2012
Mixed media with white neon,
37 x 20¼ x 3 inches,
94 x 51.4 x 7.6 cm
Edition of 3 + 2 AP

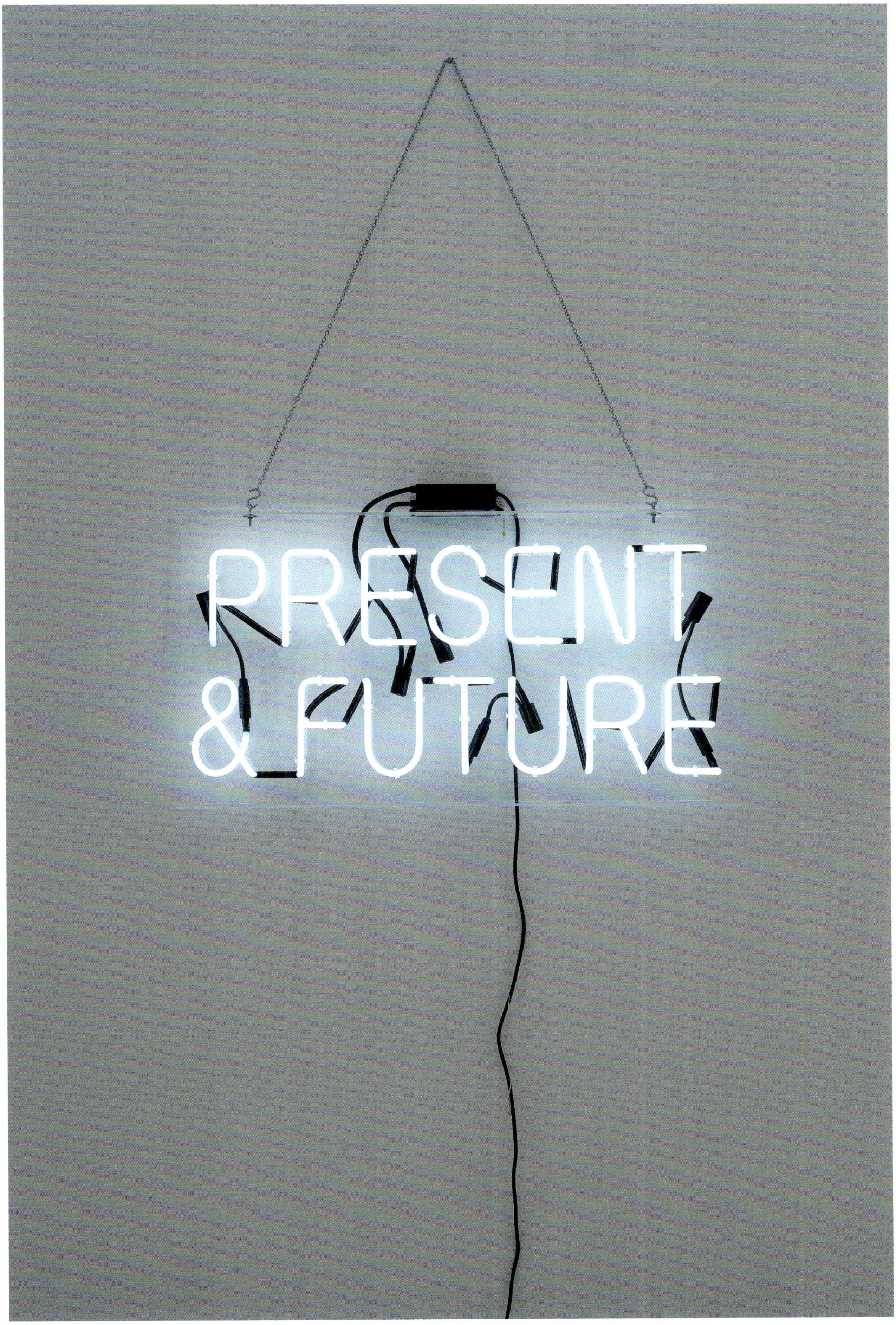

PRESENT
& FUTURE

ROESLER

Mobile +55 11 85421146

Galeria Nara Roesler
BR-São Paulo 01449-001 | Av Europa 655
Phone +55 11 30632344 | Fax +55 11 30880593
info@nararoesler.com.br | www.nararoesler.com.br
Directors Nara Roesler
Daniel Roesler
Alexandre Roesler
Alexandra Garcia

Artists at Art Nova | Brígida Baltar
Lucia Koch
Melanie Smith

Gallery Information | For over thirty years, Nara Roesler has continuously promoted Latin American art to a local and international body of collectors, curators, and scholars. In 1989, she founded Galeria Nara Roesler in São Paulo, Brazil, as an arena to expand the boundaries of art practice and create a dialogue between Latin American and Brazilian artists nationally and abroad. Representing some of the most interesting artists in Latin America, such as Hélio Oiticica, Antonio Dias, Paulo Bruscky, Cao Guimarães, Melanie Smith, and Alberto Baraya, the gallery directs much of its interest towards confronting art practices from the late 60s onwards with their contemporaneous and convergent ramifications.

In 2010, four years after the gallery began to represent Antonio Dias, a towering figure in conceptual art in Brazil, Galeria Nara Roesler welcomed Alice Miceli, whose project *Chernobyl* garnered overwhelming critical acclaim at the 29th São Paulo Biennial. In the following year, the gallery not only renovated its 350 square meters of exhibition space but also integrated Carlito Carvalhosa and Melanie Smith into its growing roster of artists. Now, in 2012, the gallery welcomes Vik Muniz and doubles its exhibition space to over 800 square meters to foster collaboration and enable a diverse body of curators to produce dynamically curated shows.

Further artists represented:
Alberto Baraya
Paulo Bruscky
Cristina Canale
Carlito Carvalhosa
Marcos Chaves
Eduardo Coimbra
Antonio Dias
Cao Guimarães
Jonathan Hernández
Paul Ramirez Jonas
Karin Lambrecht
Julio Le Parc
Artur Lescher
Milton Machado
Marco Maggi
Alice Miceli
Raul Mourão
Vik Muniz
O Grivo
Tomie Ohtake
Hélio Oiticica
Abraham Palatnik
Rodolpho Parigi
José Patrício
Marcelo Silveira
Luzia Simons
Sérgio Sister
Laura Vinci

'Completed over the course of the two years it took to work on the film (*Xilitla,* 2010), these paintings are different from the photographic relationship to painting seen in her previous works. Her most recent paintings are the product of processes of erasure, sanding, and surface destruction that bring them closer to the notion of a palimpsest, revealing textures and layers of memory that enter into relationships, sometimes with the place and others with elements that come from the artist's psyche. The painting of monkeys in an apocalyptic landscape expands the scope of the piece's action further still. Thus dismantlings and different conceptions of the world find themselves in dialog with each other.' (Paola Santoscoy, 2010)

Melanie Smith
Monkeys III, 2010
Oil on canvas, 75x60cm

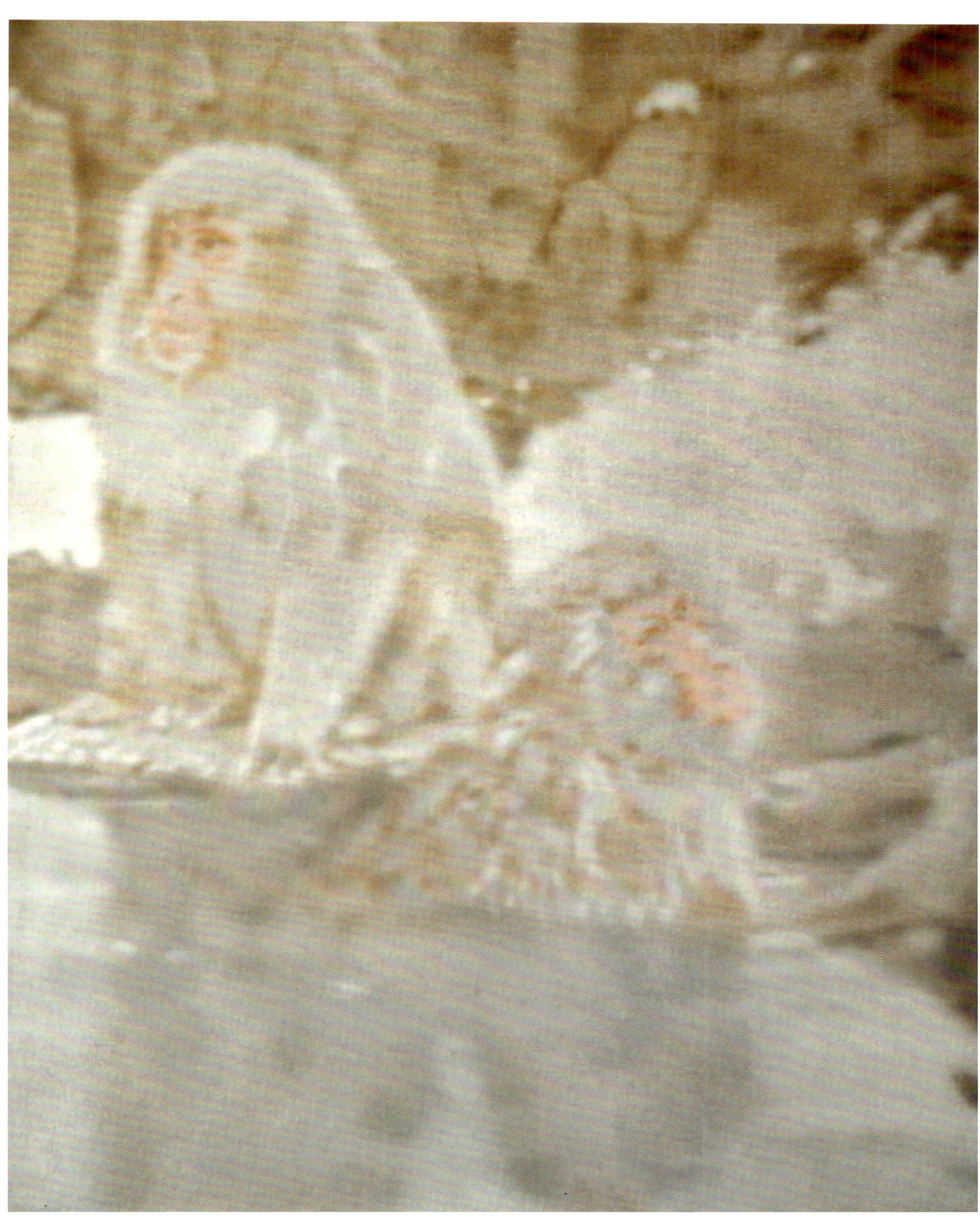

ROPAC

Galerie Thaddaeus Ropac
FR-75003 Paris | 7, rue Debelleyme
Phone +33 1 42729900 | Fax +33 1 42726166
galerie@ropac.net | www.ropac.net
Director Thaddaeus Ropac

Galerie Thaddaeus Ropac
AT-5020 Salzburg | Mirabellplatz 2
Phone +43 662 881393 | Fax +43 662 8813939
office@ropac.at | www.ropac.net
Directors Thaddaeus Ropac
Arne Ehmann

Artists at
Art Basel Miami Beach | **Ali Banisadr**
Georg Baselitz
Joseph Beuys
Tony Cragg
Jules de Balincourt
Richard Deacon
Antony Gormley
Ilya & Emilia Kabakov
Alex Katz
Anselm Kiefer
Imi Knoebel
Terence Koh
Robert Longo
Liza Lou
Robert Mapplethorpe
Jason Martin
Farhad Moshiri
Jack Pierson
Marc Quinn
Gerwald Rockenschaub
Tom Sachs
Raqib Shaw
Andreas Slominski
Sturtevant
Banks Violette
Not Vital
Andy Warhol
Erwin Wurm

Gallery Information | International contemporary art

Further artists represented: Cory Arcangel
Art & Language
Donald Baechler
Stephan Balkenhol
Marc Brandenburg
Jean-Marc Bustamante
Francesco Clemente
Elger Esser
Harun Farocki
Sylvie Fleury
Lori Hersberger
Wolfgang Laib
Jonathan Lasker
Lee Bul
Lee Ufan
Nick Oberthaler
Rona Pondick
David Salle
Sandra Vásquez de la Horra
Lawrence Weiner

Georg Baselitz
Oh, wie nahe, 2012
Oil on canvas, 290 x 208 cm

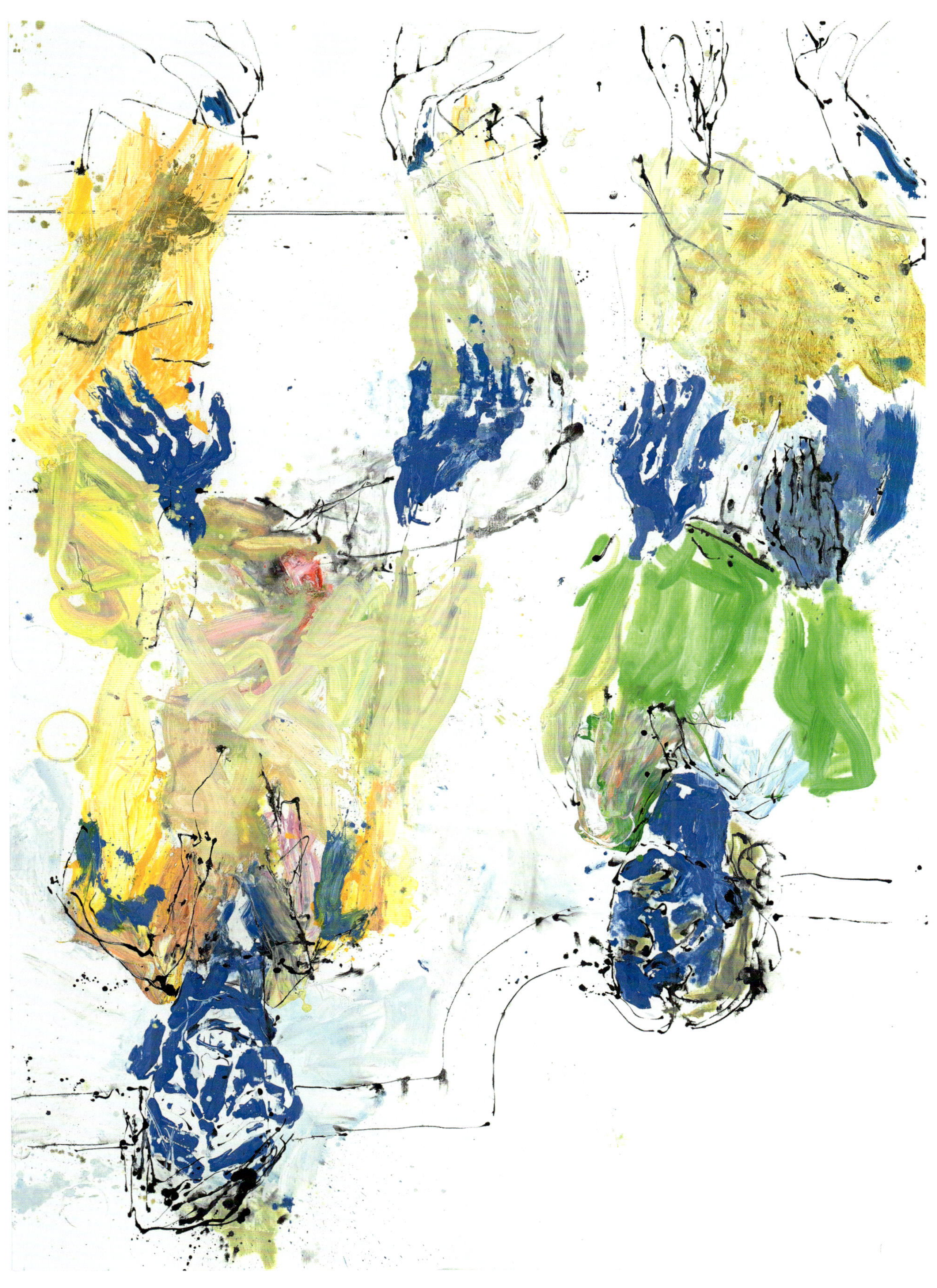

ROSEN

Mobile +1 646 528 30 44

Andrea Rosen Gallery
US-New York, NY 10011 | 525 West 24th Street
Phone +1 212 627 60 00 | Fax +1 212 627 54 50
andrea@rosengallery.com | www.andrearosengallery.com
Directors Branwen Jones
Andrea Cashman

Artists at Art Basel Miami Beach | **David Altmejd**
Gillian Carnegie
Nigel Cooke
Walker Evans
Lizzie Fitch/Ryan Trecartin
Felix Gonzalez-Torres
Al Hansen
Elliott Hundley
Tetsumi Kudo
Friedrich Kunath
José Lerma
Josiah McElheny
Josephine Meckseper
László Moholy-Nagy
Katy Moran
Dan Peterman
Michael Raedecker
Matthew Ritchie
Matthew Ronay
Mika Rottenberg
Wolfgang Tillmans
Ryan Trecartin
Andrea Zittel

Gallery Information | Andrea Rosen Gallery was inaugurated in January 1990 with a seminal exhibition of work by Felix Gonzalez-Torres. This exhibition would set the pace and agenda for the entire program of the gallery: conceptually rigorous, fully aware of the responsibility of putting one's subjectivity in the public realm, and unafraid of actually being beautiful.

It has always been the goal of the gallery to retain a specific territory for each artist that we represent. What defines the artists as a group is that each, independently, is fully responsible to the medium of their choice and is fully questioning of the role that art plays in the contemporary social-political and/or cultural arena.

We see the responsibility of the gallery as threefold; to work for the long-term development of each artist's career, acting as a liaison to international galleries and museums as well as placing works in collections; to create a historical archive for each artist; and to act as an accessible public space in which the exhibitions become an exemplary gesture of the power of subjectivity to the audience at large.

Ryan Trecartin,
Lizzie Fitch/Ryan Trecartin
Public Crop, 2011
Built around: *P.opular S.ky (section ish),* 2009, HD video
Unique sculptural theater
Installation view, Musée d'Art Moderne de la Ville de Paris

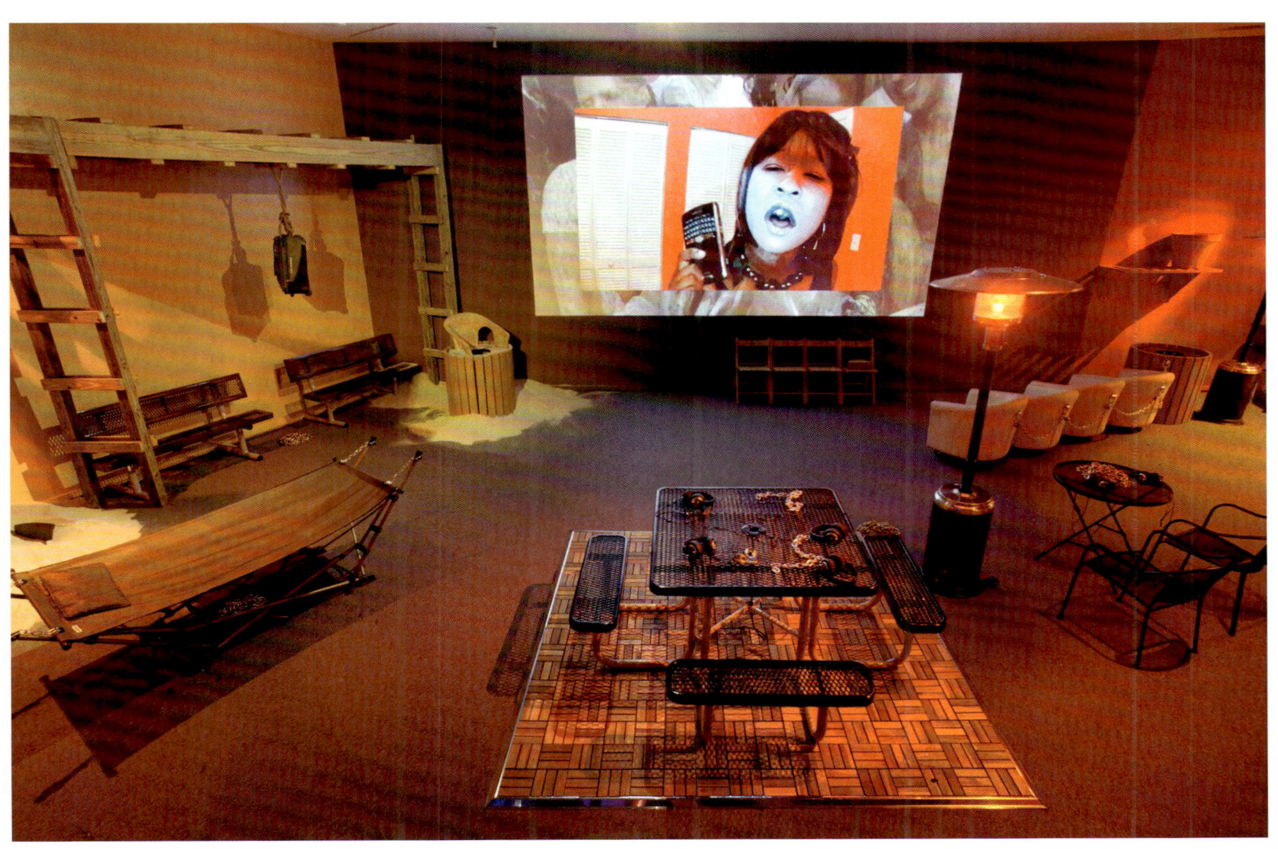

ROSENFELD

Mobile +1 917 701 61 87

Michael Rosenfeld Gallery
US-New York, NY 10011 | 100 Eleventh Avenue at 19th Street
Phone +1 212 247 00 82 | Fax +1 212 247 04 02
info@michaelrosenfeldart.com | www.michaelrosenfeldart.com
Directors Michael Rosenfeld
halley k harrisburg

Artists at
Art Basel Miami Beach | **Romare Bearden**
Lee Bontecou
Jay DeFeo
Beauford Delaney
Marcel Duchamp
John Ferren
Nancy Grossman
Conrad Kramer
Norman Lewis
Seymour Lipton
Conrad Marca-Relli
André Masson
Alfonso Ossorio
Francis Picabia
Richard Pousette-Dart
Irene Rice-Pereira
Mark Rothko
Charles Shaw
Dorothea Tanning
Pavel Tchelitchew
Bob Thompson
Mark Tobey

Gallery Information | Michael Rosenfeld Gallery is now located in Chelsea, occupying the ground floor of the Jean Nouvel tower (100 Eleventh Avenue at 19th Street).

Established in 1989, Michael Rosenfeld Gallery specializes in 20th-century American art. Over the past 23 years, the gallery has organized over one hundred and sixty exhibitions and published more than one hundred scholarly exhibition catalogs. Gallery programming focuses on Abstract Expressionism, early American abstraction (AAA & TPG groups), figurative expressionism, social realism, and surrealism.

A member of the Art Dealers Association of America, since 2000, Michael Rosenfeld Gallery currently represents sixteen artists.

Marcel Duchamp
Nu descendant un escalier, 1915
Graphite gouache and ink over a photograph of *Nude Descending a Staircase #2* mounted to luan plywood, 14³⁄₈ x 8³⁄₄ inches
Signed and dated

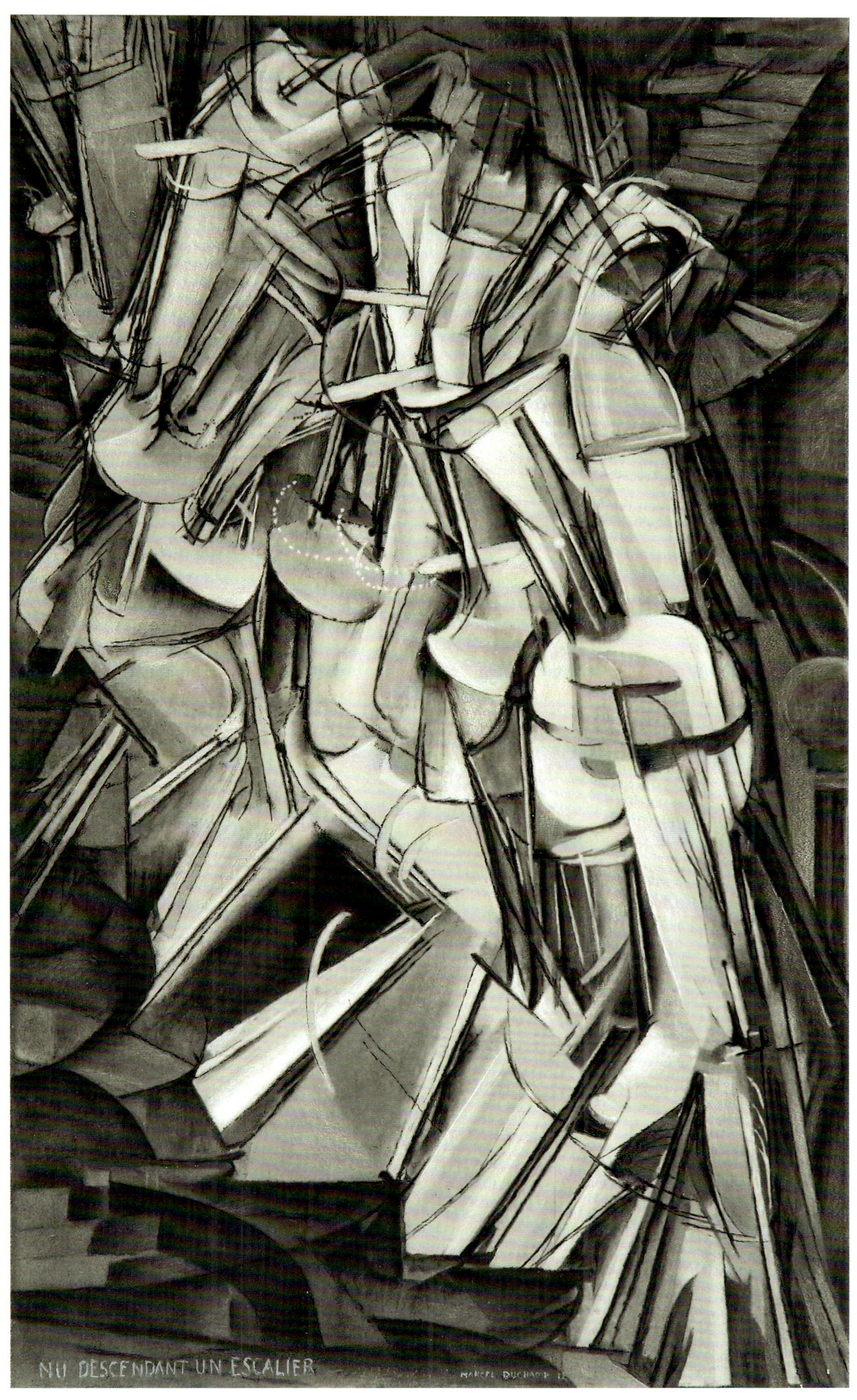
NU DESCENDANT UN ESCALIER
MARCEL DUCHAMP 12

RUMMA

Mobile +39 335 618 86 40

Lia Rumma
IT-20154 Milan | Via Stilicone 19
Phone +39 02 29 00 01 01 | Fax +39 02 36 51 17 02
info@liarumma.it | www.liarumma.it
Directors Lia Rumma
Paola Potena

Lia Rumma
IT-80121 Naples | Via Vannella Gaetani 12
Phone +39 081 19 81 23 54 | Fax +39 081 19 81 24 06
info@liarumma.it | www.liarumma.it
Directors Lia Rumma
Paola Potena

Artists at Art Basel Miami Beach | **Marina Abramovic**
Vanessa Beecroft
Alfredo Jaar
Ilya & Emilia Kabakov
William Kentridge
Joseph Kosuth
Marzia Migliora
Michelangelo Pistoletto
Thomas Ruff
Ettore Spalletti
Haim Steinbach
Tobias Zielony

Gallery Information | Anselm Kiefer, *Der fruchtbare Halbmond – La Mezzaluna fertile,* solo show, Lia Rumma, Milan, September-November 2012
Haim Steinbach, solo show, Lia Rumma, Milan, November 2012-February 2013
Alfredo Jaar, solo show, Lia Rumma, Naples, October 2012-January 2013

Further artists represented: Alberto Burri
Enrico Castellani
Clegg & Guttmann
Gino De Dominicis
Andreas Gursky
Gary Hill
Douglas Huebler
Anselm Kiefer
Hendrik Krawen
Mocellin – Pellegrini
Reinhard Mucha
Sabah Naim
Franco Scognamiglio
Dré Wapenaar

Marina Abramovic
The Communicator, 2012
Clear wax with malachite, kayanite cristal quartz stones, glass pedestal,
head: 60 x 60 x 60 cm,
pedestal: 130 x 24 x 24 cm
Detail

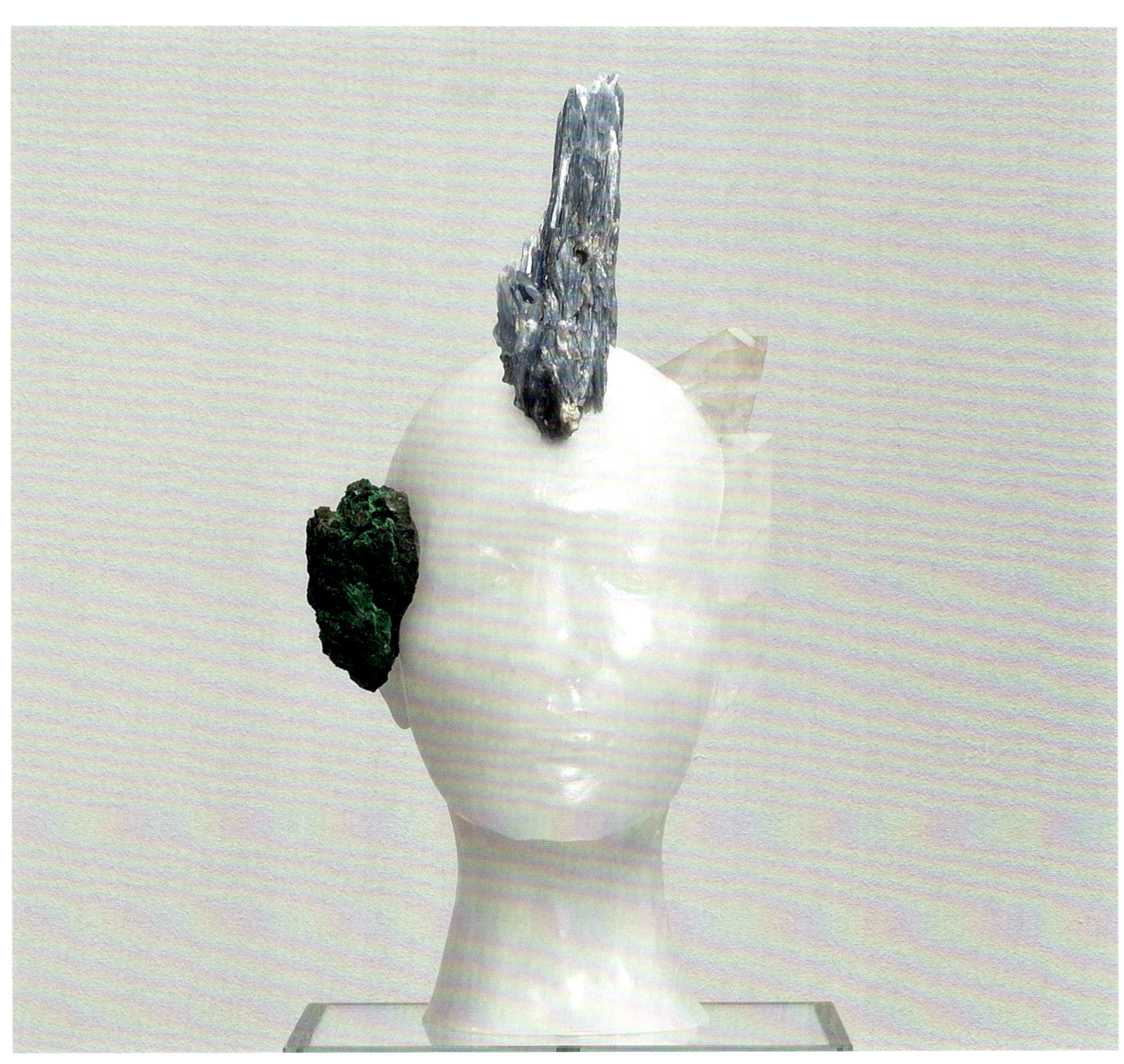

SALON 94

Salon 94 Freemans
US-New York, NY 10002 | 1 Freeman Alley
Phone +1 212 529 74 00 | Fax +1 212 529 74 01
info@salon94.com | www.salon94.com
Directors Fabienne Stephan
Alissa Friedman

Salon 94
US-New York, NY 10128 | 12 East 94th Street
Phone +1 646 672 92 12 | Fax +1 646 672 92 17
info@salon94.com | www.salon94.com
Directors Fabienne Stephan
Alissa Friedman

Salon 94 Bowery
US-New York, NY 10002 | 243 Bowery
Phone +1 212 979 00 01 | Fax +1 212 979 00 04
info@salon94.com | www.salon94.com
Directors Fabienne Stephan
Alissa Friedman

Artist at
Art Basel Miami Beach | **Jon Kessler**

Further artists represented | Amy Bessone
Huma Bhabha
Carter
Liz Cohen
Gerald Davis
Jules de Balincourt
Francesca DiMattio
Dzine
Katy Grannan
Kara Hamilton
Marilyn Minter
Carlo Mollino
Takeshi Murata
Jayson Musson
Aïda Ruilova
David Benjamin Sherry
Lorna Simpson
Francis Upritchard
Betty Woodman

Jon Kessler
A | *Ear*, 2012
Sculpture: plastic hot dogs, rubber ear, motor, electronics, ear buds, and placemat, 27 x 13 x 9 inches

B | *Foot*, 2012
Sculpture: boot, steel, motor, inkjet print, and string, 12 x 12 x 16 inches

C | *Eye*, 2012
Sculpture: glass eye, aluminum, steel, ping pong ball, and enamel, 14 x 19 x 10 cm

A

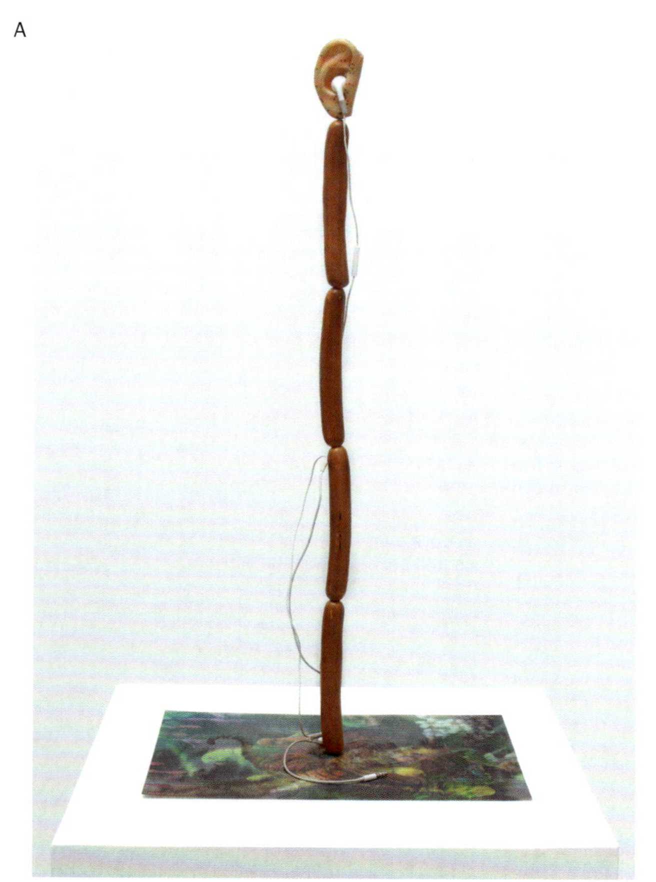

B

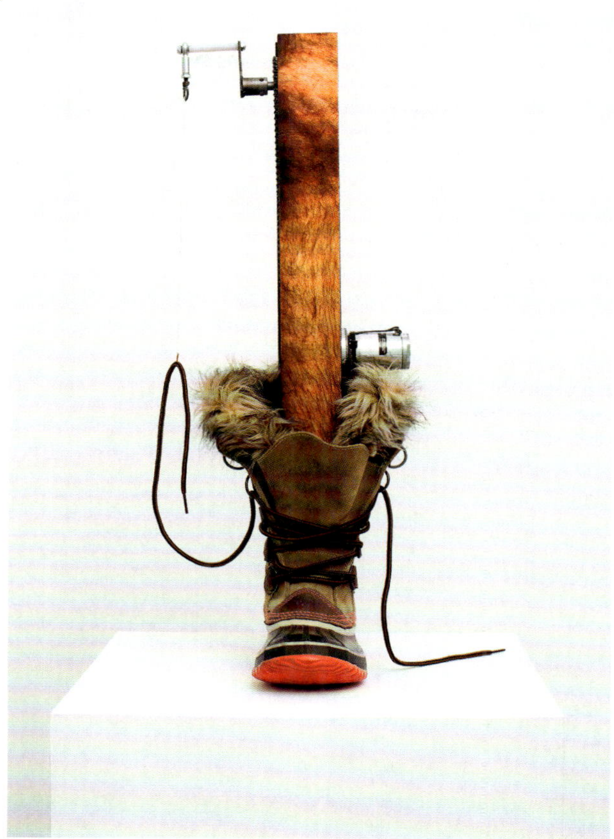

C

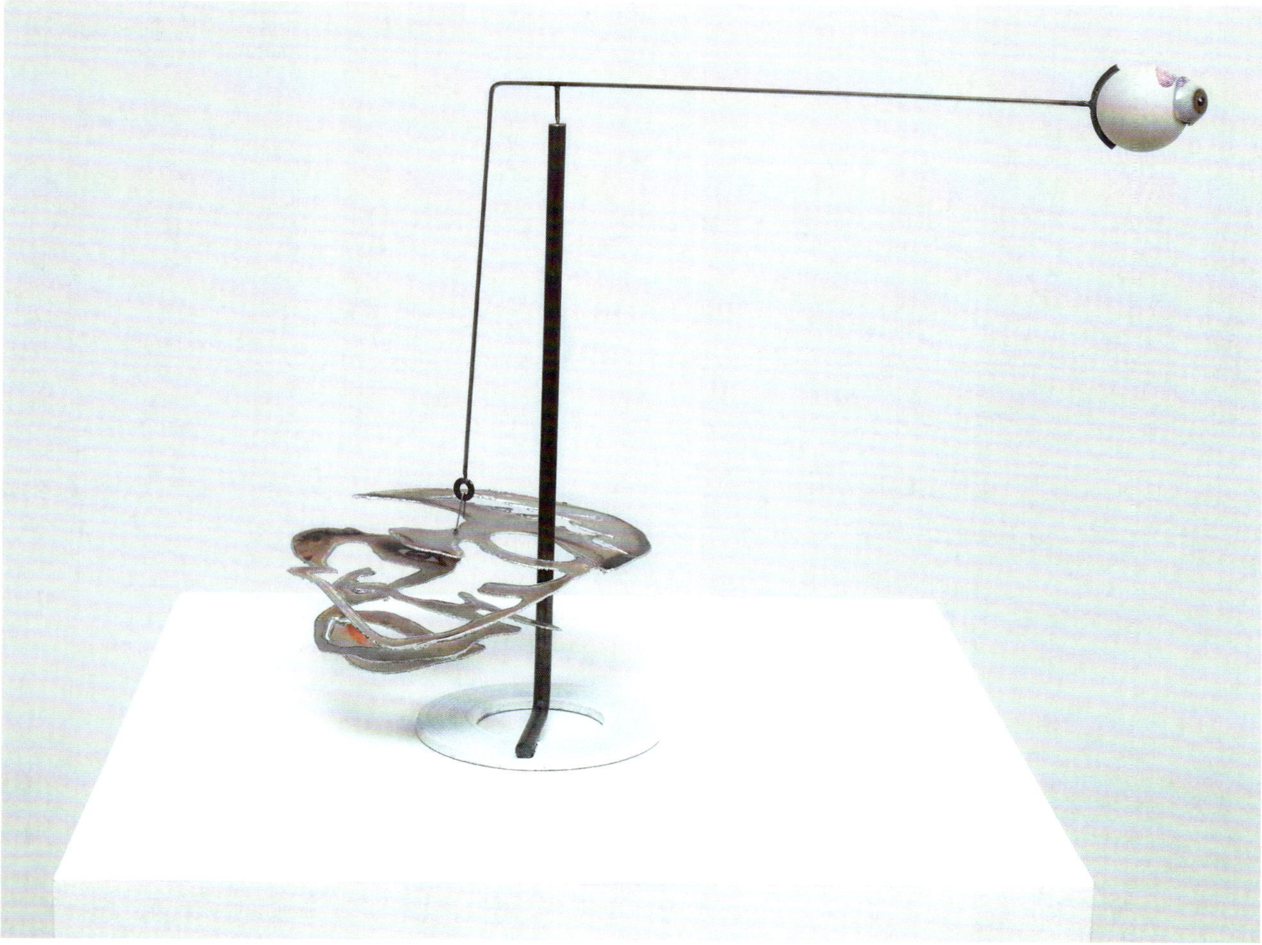

SCAI

SCAI The Bathhouse
JP-Tokyo 110-0001 | 6-1-23 Yanaka Taito-ku
Phone +81 3 38 21 11 44 | Fax +81 3 38 21 35 53
info@scaithebathhouse.com | www.scaithebathhouse.com
Directors Masami Shiraishi
Maho Kubota

Artists at
Art Basel Miami Beach | **Genpei Akasegawa**
Noriko Ambe
Kaoru Hirano
Anish Kapoor
Yusuke Komuta
Lee Ufan
Tatsuo Miyajima
Natsuyuki Nakanishi
Kohei Nawa
Martin Puryear

Gallery Information | Exhibitions 2012 at SCAI The Bathhouse:
Daisuke Ohba, November 27-December 21
Tatsuo Miyajima, October 12-November 17
Tadanori Yokoo, September 7-October 6
Kaoru Hirano, June 29-July 28

Others:
Rebirth, Royal Academy of Arts, London, December 2012-March 2013: Mariko Mori
Tokyo 1955-1970, MoMA P.S.1, New York, NY, November 18, 2012-February 25, 2013: Genpei Akasegawa, Natsuyuki Nakanishi, Tadanori Yokoo

Further artists represented: Brian Alfred
Darren Almond
Dzine
William Eggleston
Toshikatsu Endo
Jeppe Hein
Jenny Holzer
Naoki Ishikawa
Jeon Joonho
Kentaro Kobuke
Mariko Mori
Yurie Nagashima
Miwa Ogasawara
Daisuke Ohba
Julian Opie
Tomoko Shioyasu
Sputniko!
Tomoaki Suzuki
Nobuko Tsuchiya
Choe U Ram
Apichatpong Weerasethakul
Tadanori Yokoo

Yusuke Komuta
Plane_Space Shuttle, 2012
Acrylic on cotton, 168 x 238 cm

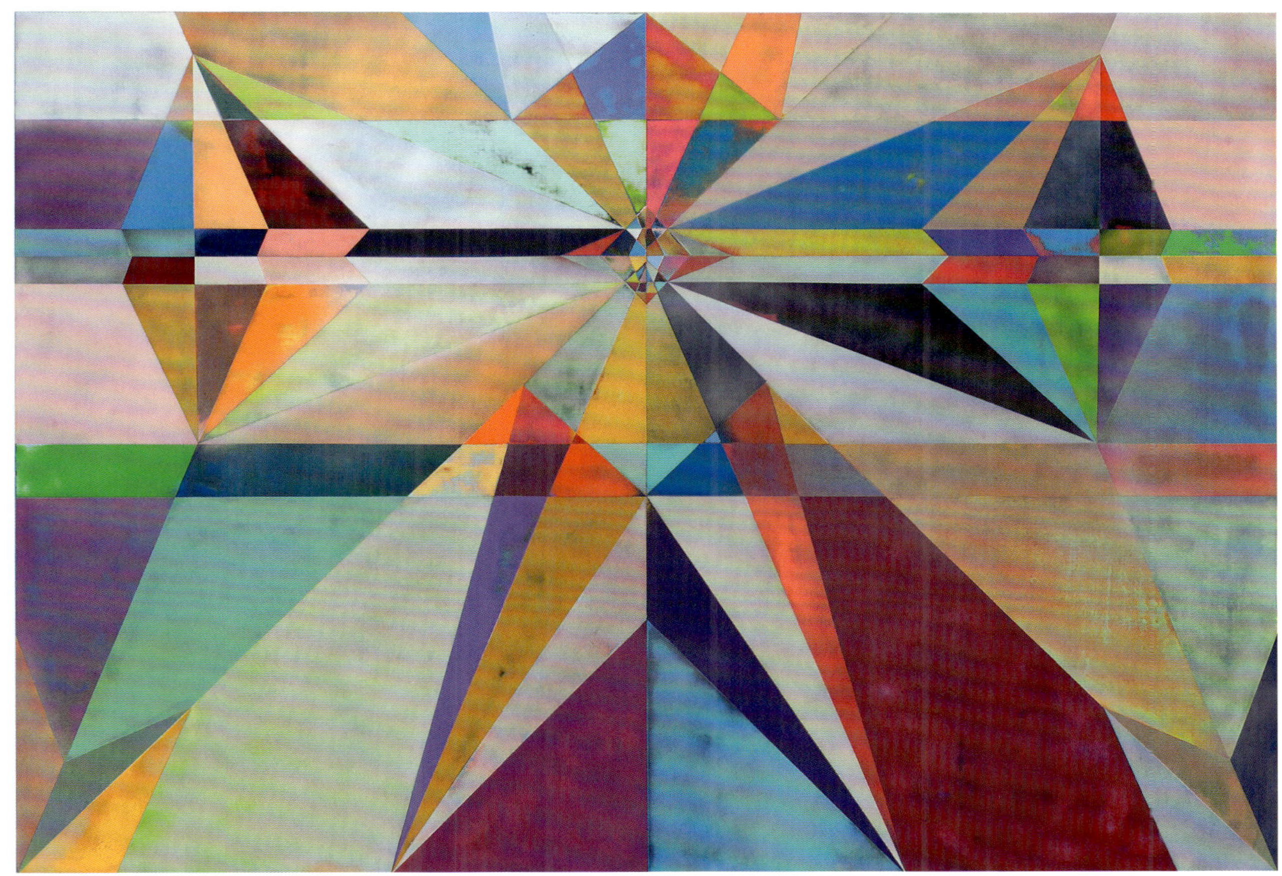

SCHIPPER

Esther Schipper
DE-10785 Berlin | Schöneberger Ufer 65
Phone +49 30 374 43 31 33 | Fax +49 30 374 43 31 34
office@estherschipper.com | www.estherschipper.com

Artists at
Art Basel Miami Beach | **AA Bronson**
Angela Bulloch
Nathan Carter
Thomas Demand
Ceal Floyer
Gabriel Kuri
Philippe Parreno
Ugo Rondinone
Karin Sander

Further artists represented | Matti Braun
General Idea
Liam Gillick
Dominique Gonzalez-Foerster
Grönlund-Nisunen
Pierre Huyghe
Ann Veronica Janssens
Christoph Keller
Isa Melsheimer
Christopher Roth
Julia Scher

Nathan Carter
The Deep Freeze Industry Park Static Connection Bridge Antenna Listening Loud To The Wait, 2012
Wood, metal, paint,
150 x 240 x 50 cm

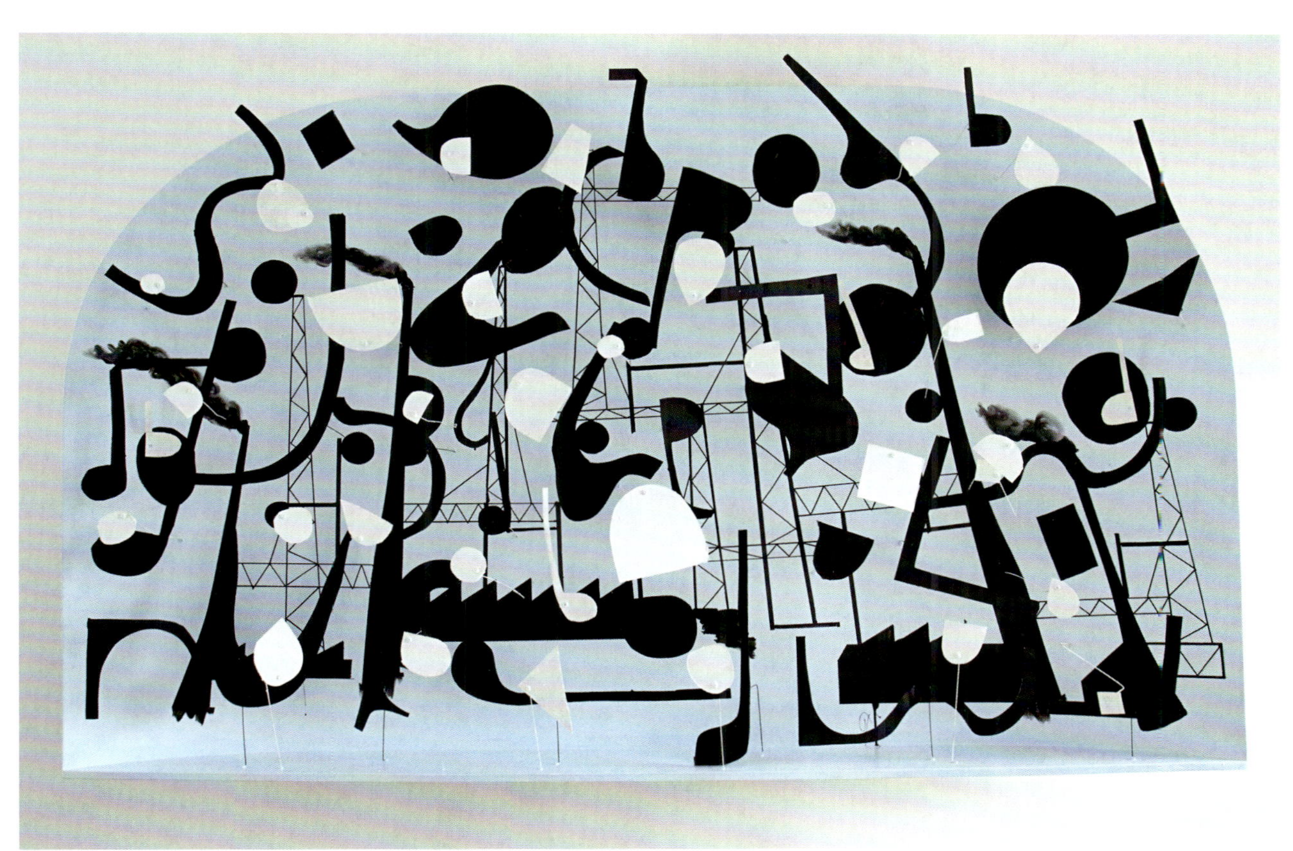

SCHUBERT

Mobile +49 177 8640173

Galerie Micky Schubert
DE-10557 Berlin | Bartningallee 2-4
Phone +49 30 49808487 | Fax +49 30 49808487
info@mickyschubert.de | www.mickyschubert.de
Director Micky Schubert

Artists at Art Nova | Ketuta Alexi-Meskhishvili
Marieta Chirulescu
Lydia Gifford

Further artists represented | Thea Djordjadze
Graham Fagen
Manuela Leinhoss
Carolin Leszczinski
Barry MacGregor Johnston
Alan Michael
Gerda Scheepers
Daniel Sinsel
Stephen Sutcliffe
Sue Tompkins
Mark Van Yetter
Maximilian Zentz Zlomovitz

Marieta Chirulescu's paintings seem to evade subjectivity through a process of reproduction using analogue as well as digital technologies. The repetitive scanning process results in technical irregularities and distortions that disrupt any fixed 'image' or surface, pointing to, as Adam Szymczyk writes, 'afterimages or reflections of the mechanical unconscious.'

Ketuta Alexi-Meskhishvili also uses photography, but her works are imbued with an existential abstraction that is created through collage, mirroring, and chance. Her apparently 'snapped shots' are, in fact, layered compositions, where each work consists of several different photographs taken at different times.

Lydia Gifford's work rests in the space 'between': between media and between completion and dissolution. Her paintings, often made on voluminous forms, do not foreground a finished creative act, but rather underscore a continuing activity and movement. The works perform, question, and improvise, opening up a space for interpretation and theatricality.

Ketuta Alexi-Meskhishvili
American Night, 2012
C-type print, 56 x 46.5 cm

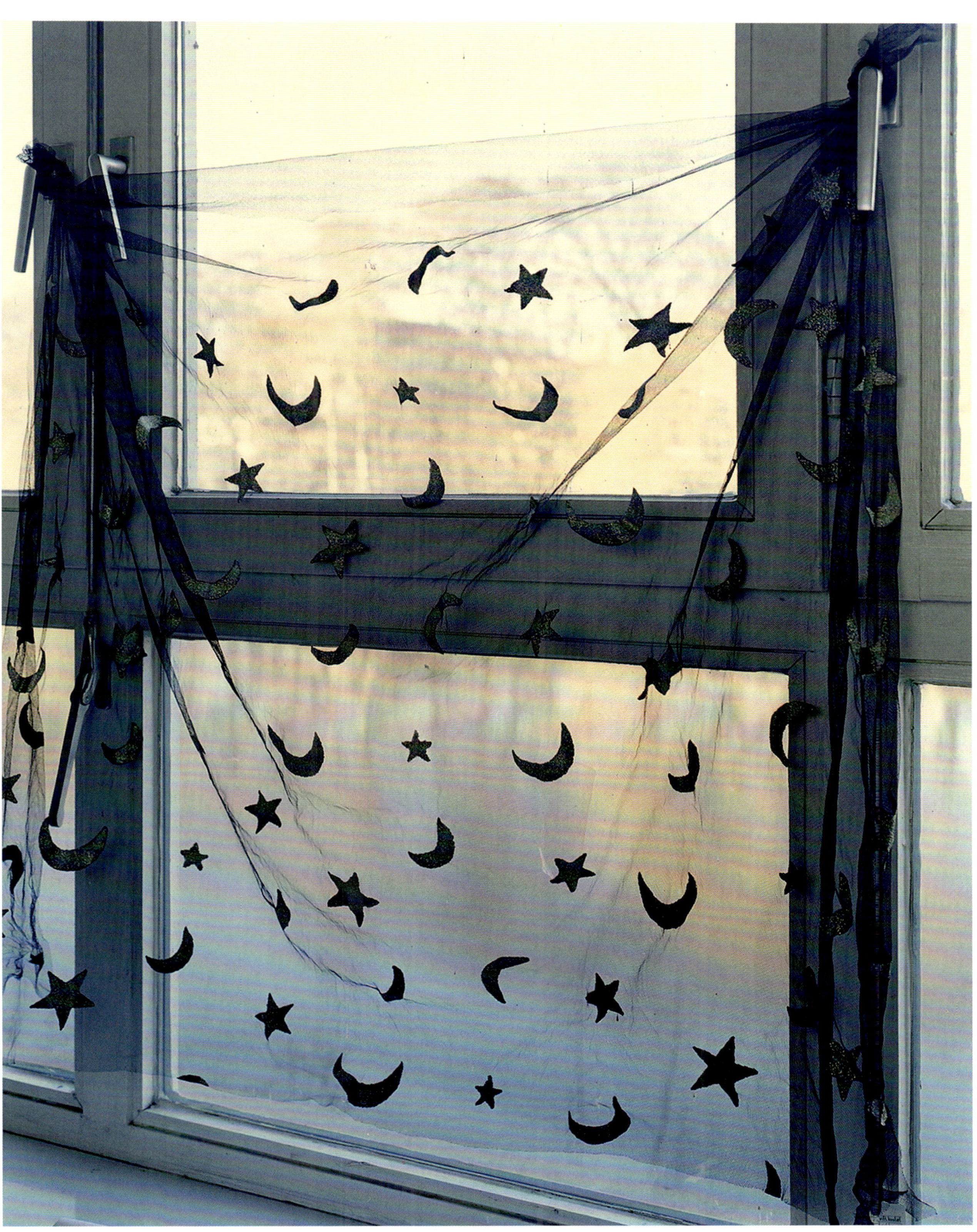

SCHULTE

Mobile +49 172 3220795

Galerie Thomas Schulte
DE-10117 Berlin | Charlottenstrasse 24
Phone +49 30 20608990 | Fax +49 30 20608 9910
mail@galeriethomasschulte.de | www.galeriethomasschulte.de
Directors Thomas Schulte
Eike Dürrfeld
Gonzalo Alarcón

Artists at
Art Basel Miami Beach | **Alice Aycock**
Richard Deacon
Mark Francis
Alfredo Jaar
Idris Khan
Jonathan Lasker
Iñigo Manglano-Ovalle
Robert Mapplethorpe
Fabian Marcaccio
Bernhard Martin
Allan McCollum
Peter Rogiers
Albrecht Schnider
Iris Schomaker
Juan Uslé
Stephen Willats

Gallery Information | Galerie Thomas Schulte was established in 1991 as Galerie Franck+Schulte. It was the first major newcomer to the reawakening art scene of the reunited German capital and received high critical acclaim from its very start.

The program of represented artists centers around conceptual art and focuses on the contemporary scene since 1960. Among the best-known positions of the gallery are: Alice Aycock, Richard Deacon, Alfredo Jaar, Jonathan Lasker, Iñigo Manglano-Ovalle, Robert Mapplethorpe, Fabian Marcaccio, Gordon Matta-Clark, Allan McCollum, Katharina Sieverding, Juan Uslé, Stephen Willats, and Robert Wilson.

Aside from its current program, the gallery has over the years dedicated one or more solo exhibitions to numerous artists, including Bas Jan Ader, Dieter Appelt, Richard Artschwager, Alighiero e Boetti, Chuck Close, Helmut Federle, Michael Heizer, Johannes Kahrs, Joseph Kosuth, Jannis Kounellis, Sol LeWitt, Mark Lombardi, Roxy Paine, Pipilotti Rist, and Robert Smithson.

Since its founding, Galerie Thomas Schulte has regularly participated in major international art fairs, including Art Basel, Art Basel Miami Beach, Armory Show, ARCO, FIAC, Art Forum Berlin, Art Cologne, Art Chicago, Art Brussels, and others.

Further artists represented: Paco Knöller
Gordon Matta-Clark
Michael Müller
Jacco Olivier
João Penalva
Hermann Pitz
Julio Rondo
Katharina Sieverding
Pat Steir
Robert Wilson

Peter Rogiers
Geen Titel, 2012
Aluminum and stainless steel,
650 x 500 x 500 cm

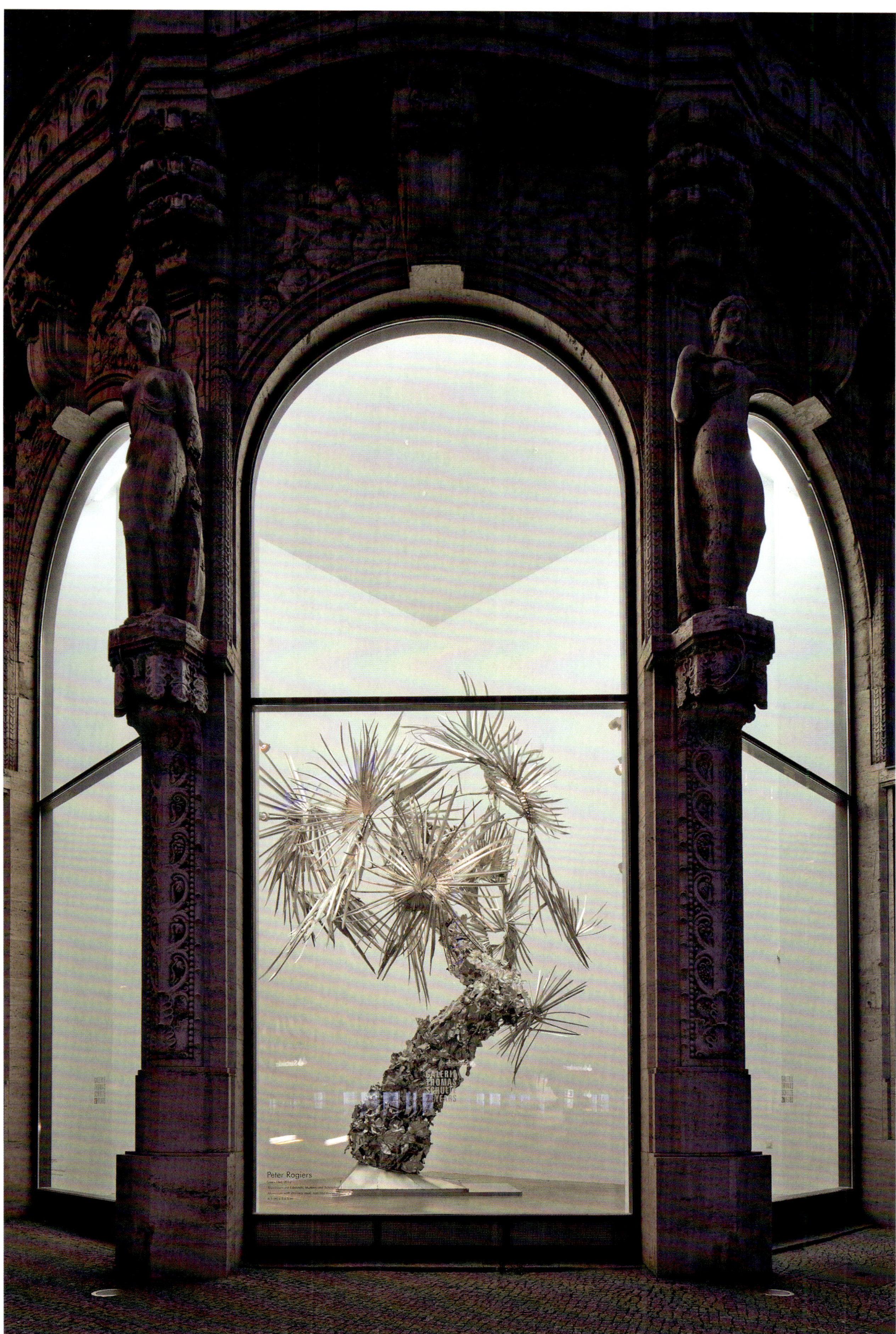
Peter Rogiers

SHAINMAN

Mobile +1 646 541 29 54

Jack Shainman Gallery
US-New York, NY 10011 | 513 West 20th Street
Phone +1 212 645 17 01 | Fax +1 212 645 83 16
info@jackshainman.com | www.jackshainman.com
Directors Jack Shainman
Claude Simard
Tamsen Greene

Artists at
Art Basel Miami Beach | **El Anatsui**
Radcliffe Bailey
Yoan Capote
Nick Cave
Gehard Demetz
Vibha Galhotra
Barkley L. Hendricks
Hayv Kahraman
Tallur L.N.
Kerry James Marshall
Richard Mosse
Zwelethu Mthethwa
Odili Donald Odita
Toyin Odutola
Arlene Shechet
Michael Snow
Hank Willis Thomas
Carlos Vega
Carrie Mae Weems
Lynette Yiadom-Boakye

Further artists represented | Shimon Attie
Tim Bavington
Pierre Dorion
Jean-Pierre Gauthier
Pascal Grandmaison
Anton Kannemeyer
Deborah Luster
Adi Nes
Jackie Nickerson
Robert & Shana ParkeHarrison
Jonathan Seliger
Malick Sidibé
Leslie Wayne

Kerry James Marshall
Red Hot Deal, 2012
Acrylic on board,
71⅝ x 59¾ x 2¾ inches

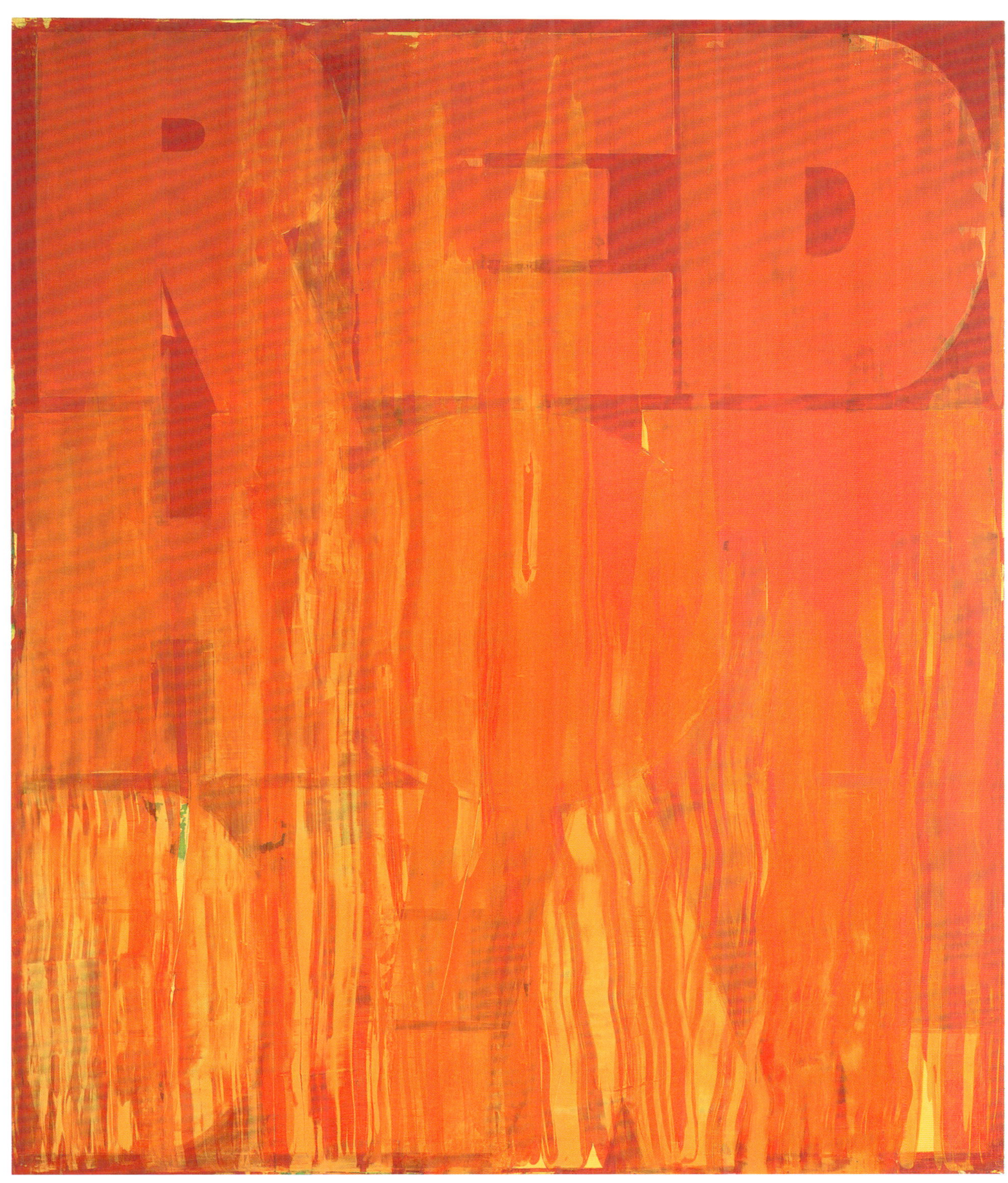
RED

SHANGHART

Mobile +86 1350 1934595

ShanghART & H Space
CN-200060 Shanghai | Bldg. 16, Moganshan Rd. 50
Phone +86 21 63593923 | Fax +86 21 63594570
info@shanghartgallery.com | www.shanghartgallery.com
Directors Lorenz Helbling
Chen Yan

ShanghART Beijing
CN-100015 Beijing | 261 Cao Chang Di, Old Airport Road, Chaoyang District
Phone +86 10 64323202 | Fax +86 10 64324395
infobj@shanghartgallery.com | www.shanghartgallery.com
Directors Lorenz Helbling
Chen Yan

ShanghART Taopu
CN-200433 Shanghai | Bldg. 8, No. 18 Wu Wei Road (near Qilianshan Road)
Phone +86 21 63593923 | Fax +86 21 63594570
info@shanghartgallery.com | www.shanghartgallery.com
Directors Lorenz Helbling
Chen Yan

Artists at
Art Basel Miami Beach |
Birdhead
Chen Xiaoyun
Ding Yi
Geng Jianyi
Hu Jieming
Huang Kui
Ji Wenyu & Zhu Weibing
Li Pinghu
Li Shan
Liang Shaoji
Liang Yue
Liu Weijian
MadeIn Company
Pu Jie
Shen Fan
Shi Qing
Shi Yong
Sun Xun
Tang Maohong
Wei Guangqing
Wu Yiming
Xiang Liqing
Xue Song
Yang Fudong
Yang Zhenzhong
Yu Youhan
Zeng Fanzhi
Zhang Ding
Zhang Enli
Zhang Qing
Zhou Tiehai
Zhou Zixi
Zhu Jia

Gallery Information | ShanghART gallery was inititated in 1996 in Shanghai and has since grown to become one of China's most influential contemporary art institutions. The gallery has established itself as a leading gallery representing established figures whilst continuing to support the work of younger artists. As a gallery, producer, supporter, and point of reference, ShanghART contributes, as a vital resource, to the development of contemporary art in China.

Today ShanghART occupies several spaces in Shanghai and Beijing and represents over forty artists working in different media, ranging from painting, sculpture, and installation to video art and performance. Situated at M50 (50 Moganshan Rd.), which has developed to become Shanghai's artistic center, ShanghART Main Gallery (in building 16) serves as the office and a showroom for smaller exhibitions, while the larger ShanghART H-Space just next door (in building 18) operates as a flexible white-cube exhibition hall for the display of extensive shows and grand-scale projects. ShanghART Beijing is located in Cao Chang Di, in Beijing's most interesting gallery district.

ShanghART Taopu Warehouse: ShanghART's newest venture is a large-scale open warehouse in the new Taopu art district in the industrial west of Shanghai.

Zhang Ding
Buddha Jumps over the Wall-Pig,
2012
Photograph, color inkjet,
93 x 140 cm

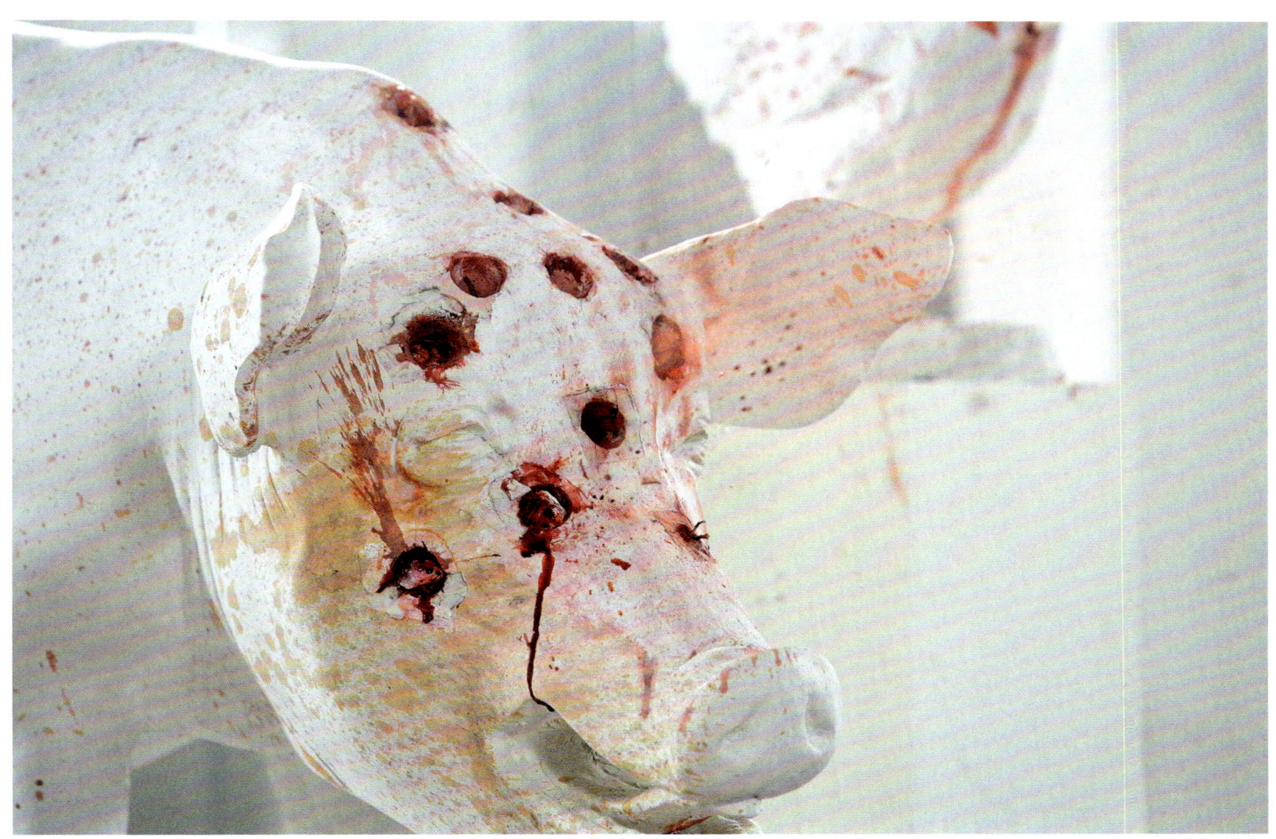

SICARDI

Mobile +1 281 827 38 13

Sicardi
US-Houston, TX 77006 | 1506 West Alabama Street
Phone +1 713 529 13 13 | Fax +1 713 529 04 43
info@sicardi.com | www.sicardigallery.com
Directors Allison Ayers
Maria Ines Sicardi

Artists at
Art Basel Miami Beach | **Antonio Asis**
Martin Blaszko
Carlos Cruz-Diez
Geraldo de Barros
Sérvulo Esmeraldo
Manuel Espinosa
León Ferrari
Gego
Francisco Sobrino
Jesús Rafael Soto
Luis Tomasello

Further artists represented | Maria Fernanda Cardoso
Gabriel de la Mora
Dias & Riedweg
Thomas Glassford
Graciela Hasper
Marco Maggi
Oscar Muñoz
Liliana Porter
Miguel Angel Rojas
Regina Silveira
Pablo Siquier

Antonio Asis
Vibraciones linéaires en cercles,
1964
Gouache on paper, 21 x 29.7 cm

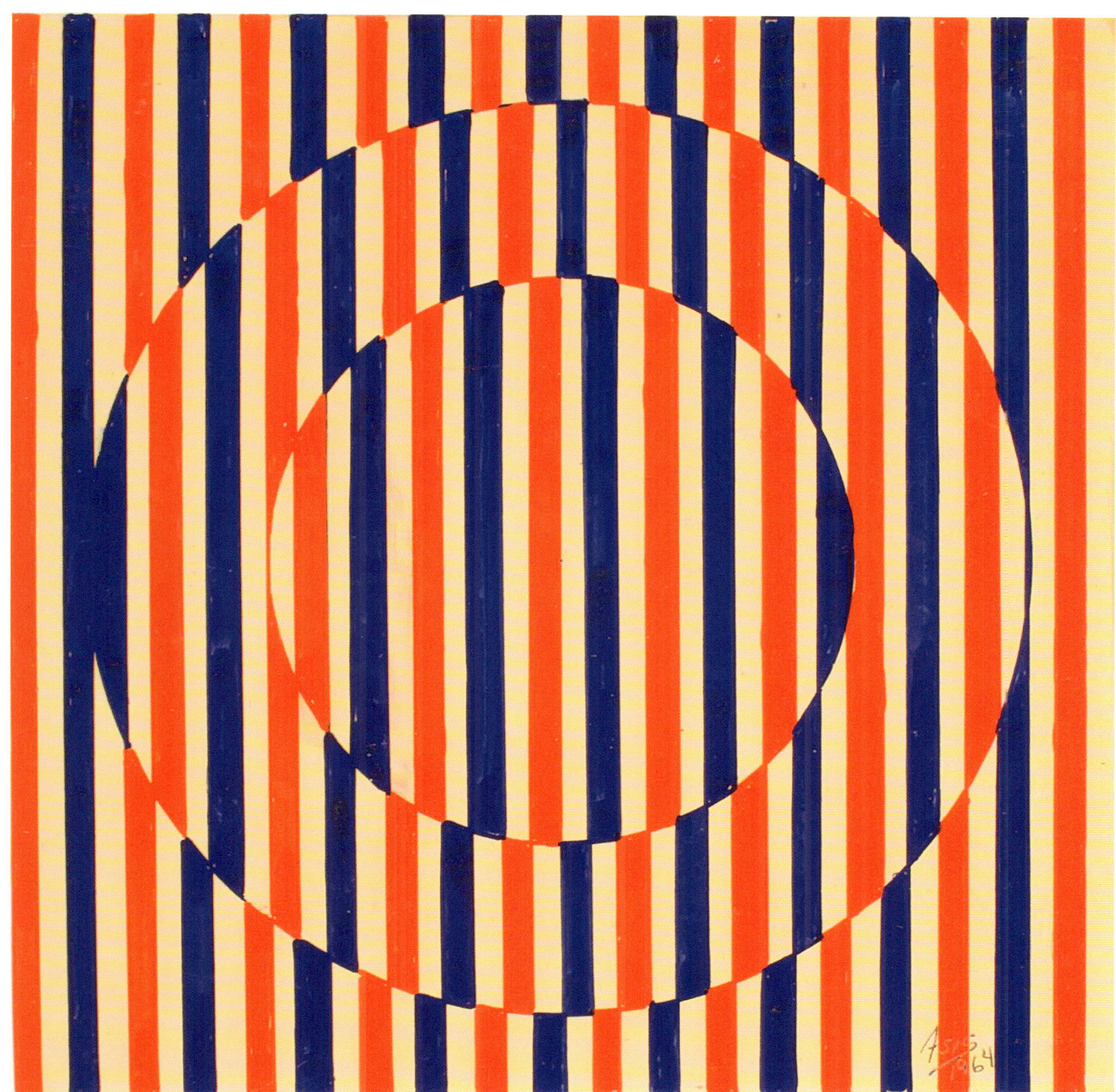

SIES + HÖKE

Mobile +49 177 7730289

Sies + Höke
DE-40213 Düsseldorf | Poststrasse 2 + 3
Phone +49 211 3014360 | Fax +49 211 135668
post@sieshoeke.com | www.sieshoeke.com
Directors Nina Höke
Alexander Sies

Artists at Art Basel Miami Beach | **Etienne Chambaud**
Talia Chetrit
Björn Dahlem
Marcel Dzama
João Maria Gusmão & Pedro Paiva
Federico Herrero
Thomas Kiesewetter
Kris Martin
Jonathan Meese
Fabrice Samyn
Florian Slotawa
Neal Tait
Michael van Ofen
Claudia Wieser
Sam Windett

Björn Dahlem
Magellansche Wolke, 2012
Wood, fluorescents, site-specific dimensions

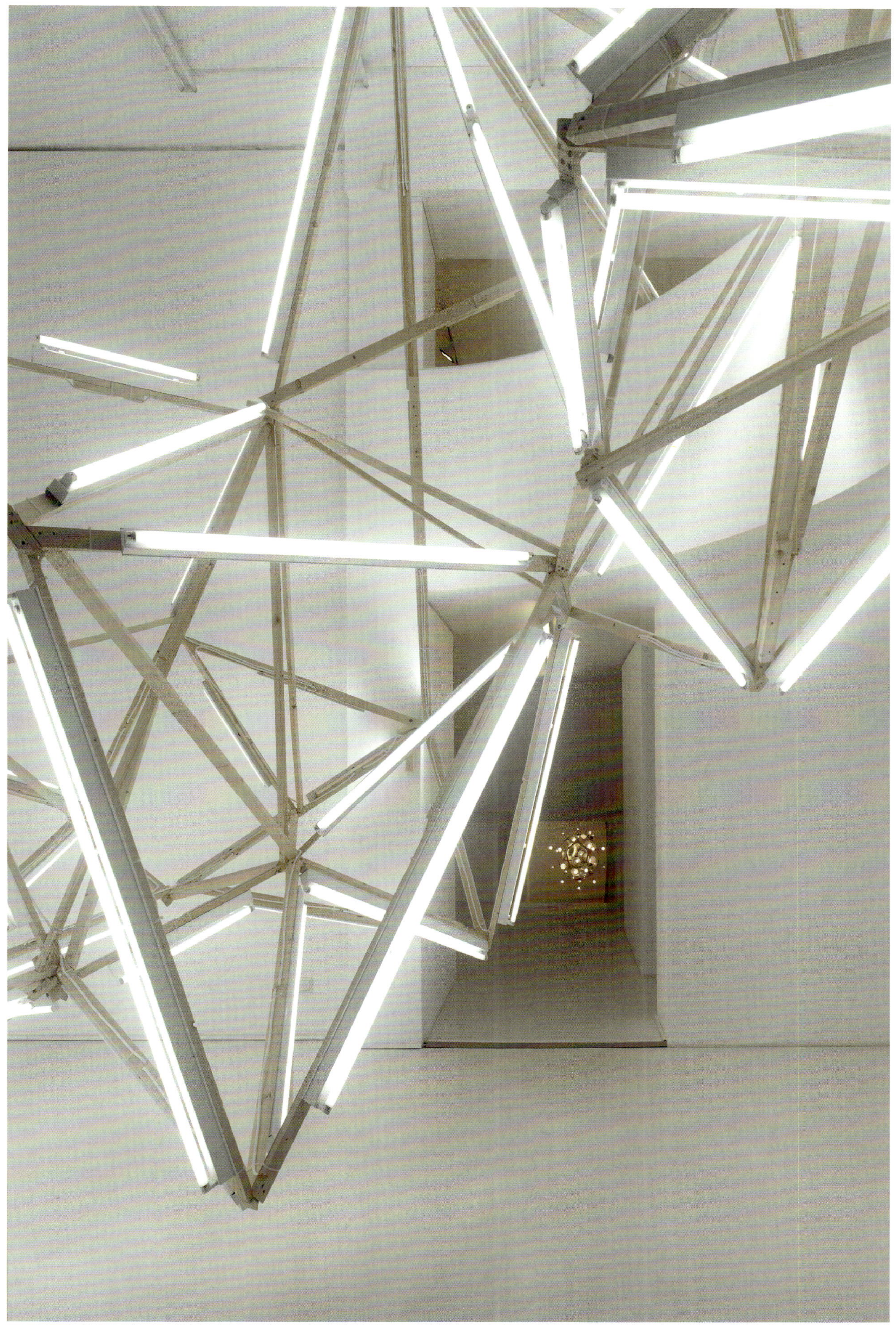

SIKKEMA JENKINS

Mobile +1 917 518 89 89

Sikkema Jenkins & Co.
US-New York, NY 10011 | 530 West 22nd Street
Phone +1 212 929 22 62 | Fax +1 212 929 23 40
gallery@sikkemajenkinsco.com | www.sikkemajenkinsco.com
Directors Brent Sikkema
Michael Jenkins
Meg Malloy
Katie Rashid

Artists at Art Basel Miami Beach | **Burt Barr**
Mark Bradford
Trisha Brown
William Cordova
Leonardo Drew
Mitch Epstein
Josephine Halvorson
Marc Handelman
Jan Henle
Arturo Herrera
Leslie Hewitt
Sheila Hicks
Merlin James
Nikki S. Lee
Marlene McCarty
Vik Muniz
Jorge Queiroz
Kay Rosen
Shahzia Sikander
Amy Sillman
Janaina Tschäpe
Kara Walker

Kara Walker
Fountain of You, 1993
Ink on paper, 50 x 38 inches

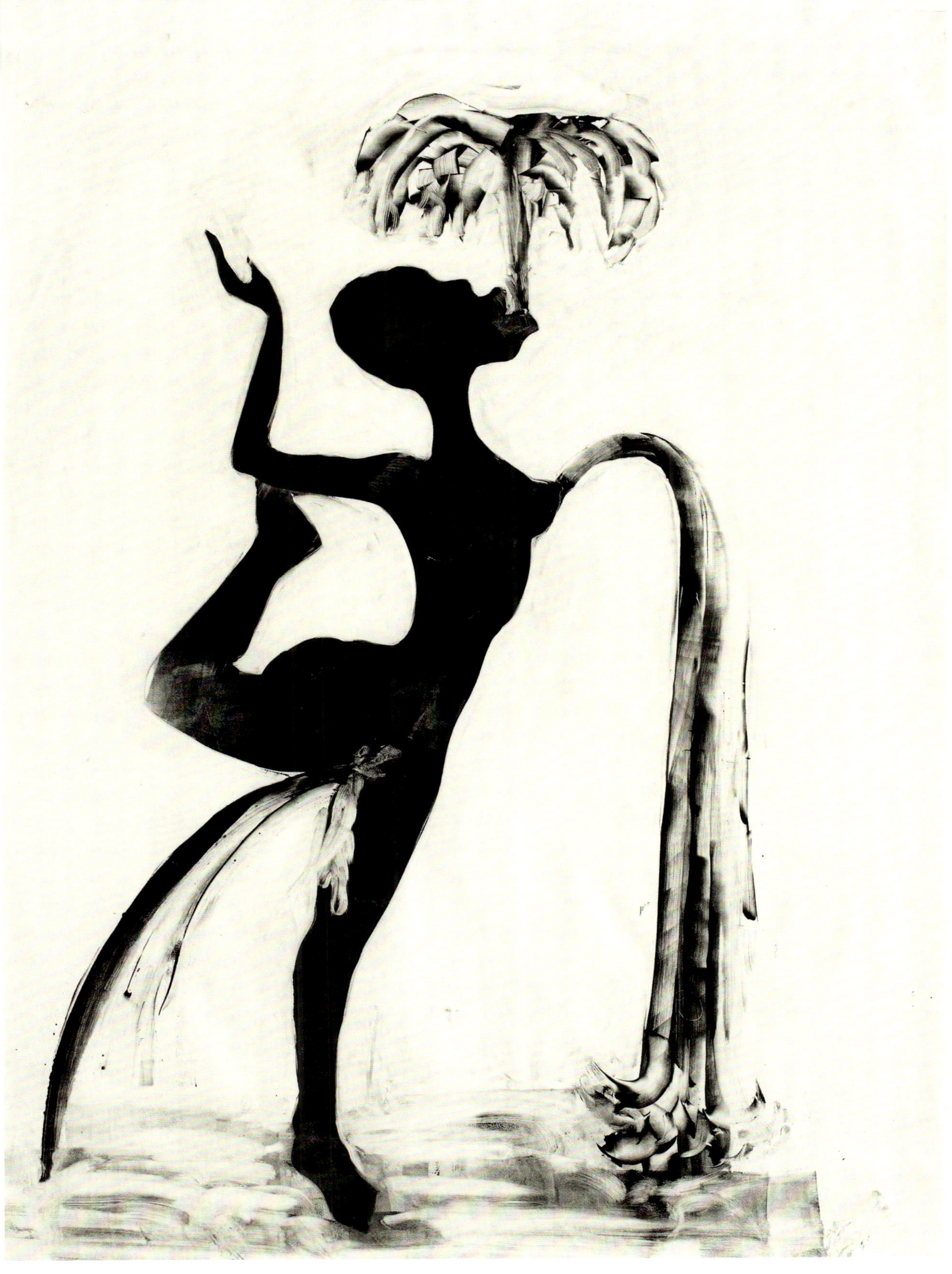

SILVERSTEIN

Bruce Silverstein
US-New York, NY 10011 | 535 West 24th Street
Phone +1 212 627 39 30 | Fax +1 212 691 55 09
inquiries@brucesilverstein.com | www.brucesilverstein.com
Directors Bruce Silverstein
Liam Derik van Loenen

Artists at Art Basel Miami Beach | **Diane Arbus**
Constantin Brancusi
Bill Brandt
Mark Cohen
Martin Denker
Robert Doisneau
Robert Frank
Leonard Freed
Todd Hido
Nicolai Howalt
André Kertész
Dorothea Lange
Lu Yao
Nathan Lyons
Maria Antonietta Mameli
Shinichi Maruyama
Lisette Model
Barbara Morgan
Max Neumann
Marvin E. Newman
Frank Paulin
Larry Silver
Aaron Siskind
Keith Smith
Rosalind Solomon
Frederick Sommer
Trine Søndergaard
Alfred Stieglitz
Zoe Strauss
Randy West
Joel-Peter Witkin
Michael Wolf
Silvio Wolf
John Wood

Silvio Wolf
RCA Self Portrait, 2012
C-print mounted to Dibond,
190 x 125 cm

SKARSTEDT

Skarstedt Gallery
US-New York, NY 10075 | 20 East 79th Street
Phone +1 212 737 20 60 | Fax +1 212 737 41 71
info@skarstedt.com | www.skarstedt.com
Directors Per Skarstedt
Brady Doty
Atalanti Martinou

Skarstedt Gallery
GB-London W1S 4PZ | 23 Old Bond Street
Phone +1 212 737 20 60 | Fax +1 212 737 41 71
info@skarstedt.com | www.skarstedt.com

Artists at Art Basel Miami Beach | **George Condo**
Carroll Dunham
Eric Fischl
Peter Fischli/David Weiss
Keith Haring
Jenny Holzer
Mike Kelley
Martin Kippenberger
Barbara Kruger
Louise Lawler
Sherrie Levine
Juan Muñoz
Albert Oehlen
Richard Prince
Thomas Schütte
Cindy Sherman
Rosemarie Trockel
Andy Warhol
Christopher Wool

Cindy Sherman
Untitled #113, 1982
Color photograph, 45 x 30 inches

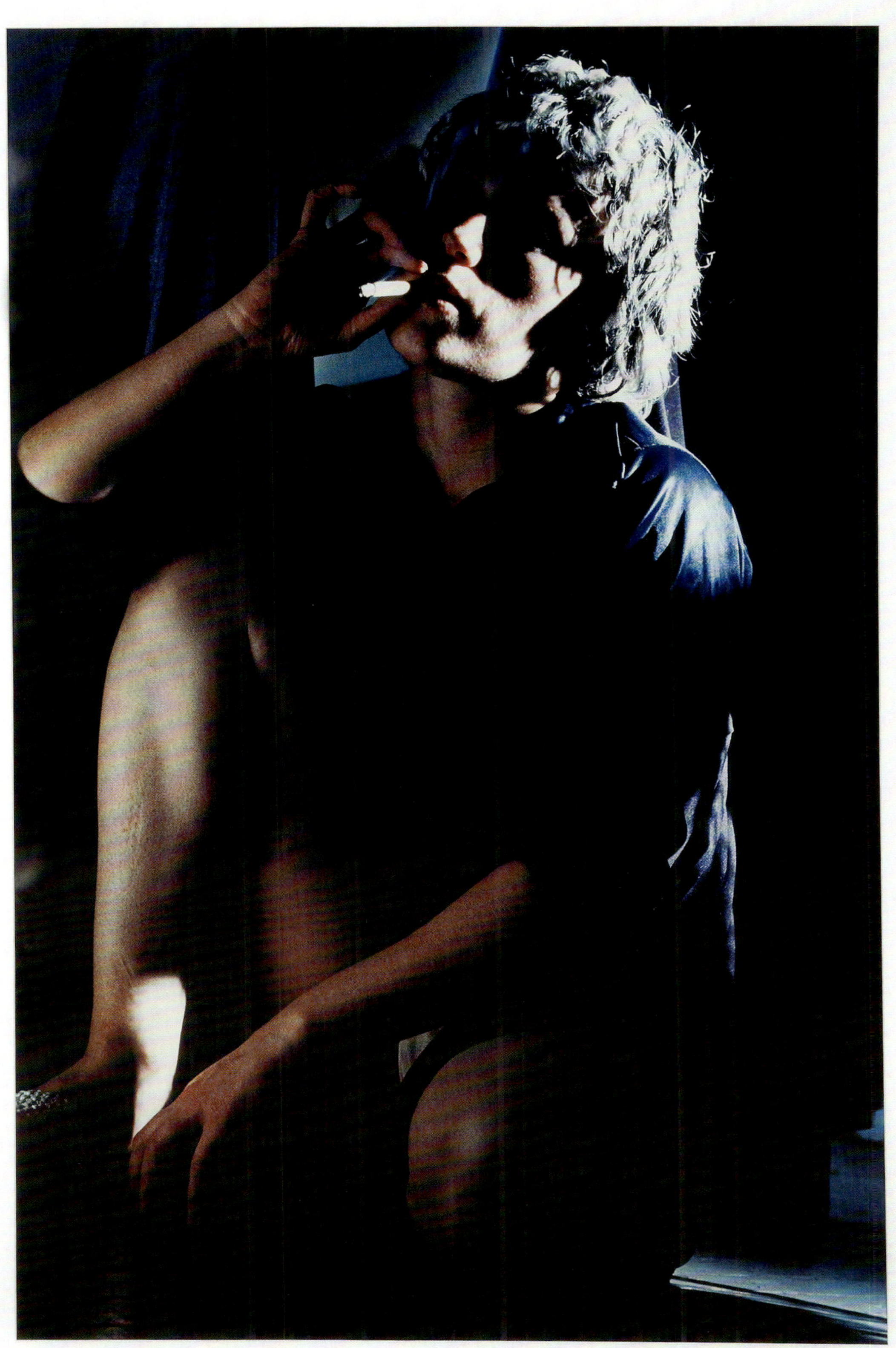

SNITZER

Mobile +1 786 271 09 32

Fredric Snitzer Gallery
US-Miami, FL 33127 | 2247 Northwest 1st Place
Phone +1 305 448 89 76 | Fax +1 305 573 58 10
info@snitzer.com | www.snitzer.com
Directors Fredric Snitzer
Richard Arregui

Artists at Art Basel Miami Beach | **Alice Aycock**
Hernan Bas
José Bedia
Merlin Carpenter
Zhivago Duncan
Mauricio Gonzalez
Jon Pylypchuk
Robert Reed
Bert Rodriguez
Cristina Lei Rodriguez
Georgia Sagri
Diego Singh
Michael Vasquez

Zhivago Duncan
Shadow Claw, The Devil of Hierarchy, 2011/12
Ink, Rabbit size, and oil on linen, 200 x 240 cm

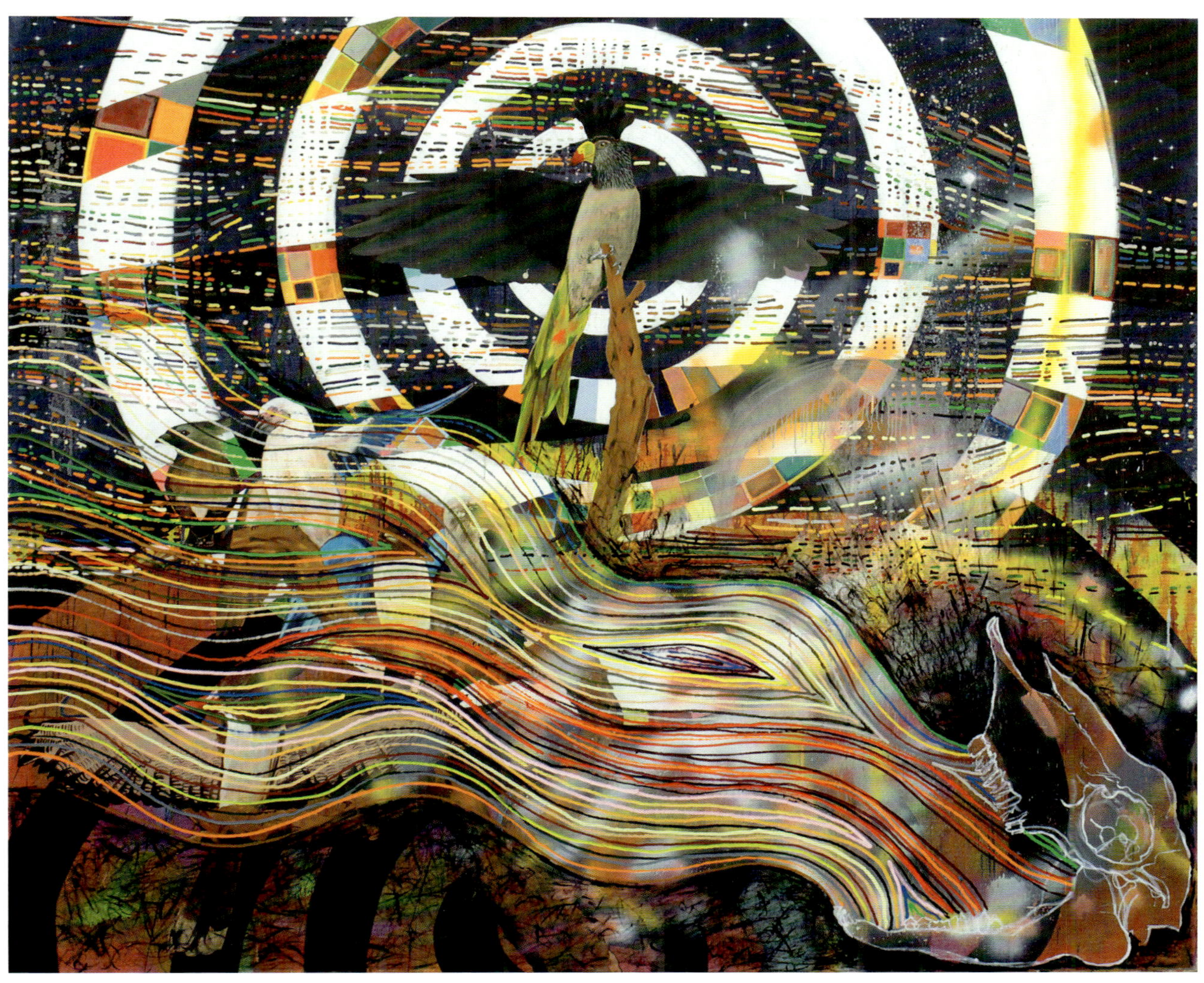

SOLOMON

Thomas Solomon Gallery
US-Los Angeles, CA 90012 | 427 Bernard Street
Phone +1 323 275 16 87
info@thomassolomongallery.com | www.thomassolomongallery.com
Directors Thomas Solomon
Tif Sigfrids

Artists at Art Nova | Ry Rocklen
Analia Saban
Ulrich Wulff

Further artists represented | Robert Barry
Brad Eberhard
Bart Exposito
Peter Harkawik
Vishal Judgeo
Josh Mannis
Dennis Oppenheim
Miljohn Ruperto
Mitchell Syrop
Rosha Yaghmai

Analia Saban is a Los Angeles-based artist whose practice explores the deconstruction of various modes of artmaking, often connecting disciplines. In a recent body of work, she illuminates the representational ability of painting by working from casts of household objects ranging from towels to bed sheets, which are then draped over the surface of a canvas so that the work becomes what might be considered a hybrid of painting and sculpture. Through various working methods this question of image-making is consistently addressed.

Ulrich Wulff is a Berlin-based artist who works primarily with painting and drawing, but employs other mediums, including sculpture, poetry, and performance, to promote his balanced idea of a conceptual-intuitive approach to artmaking. In his work, Wulff examines the borders of perception in humble acceptance of the poetic Zen-way of the painter, and in the context of history and his story. He is also engaged in collaborative pursuits as a co-founder of both European Fine Art Gallery and the Heckler und Koch Publishing Company, Berlin.

Ry Rocklen is a Los Angeles-based sculptor whose work champions cast-aside objects, giving their second lives new meaning and challenging the definition of a thrift store find. In a state of complete devotion, these one-time derelict vessels undergo effulgent makeovers and become transformed into sculptures bearing a witty relationship to minimalism. Rocklen's careful selection of objects invites viewers to consider their personal relationships to the items, while at the same time diffusing these associations through his ability to transfer them into matters of pure form.

A | **Ulrich Wulff**
THE BLUE ONE, 2012
Oil on canvas, 180 x 140 cm

B | **Ry Rocklen**
Steve, 2012
Found ceramic head, wood, 56 x 13 x 22 inches

C | **Analia Saban**
Erosion (Geometric Cubes within Circle; Two-Point Perspective with Guidelines), 2012
Laser-sculpted acrylic paint on canvas, diameter 40 cm

A

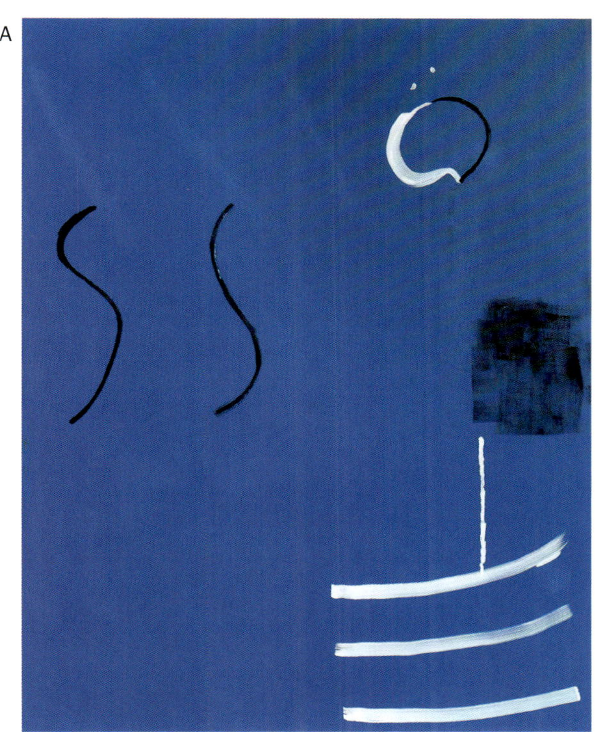

B

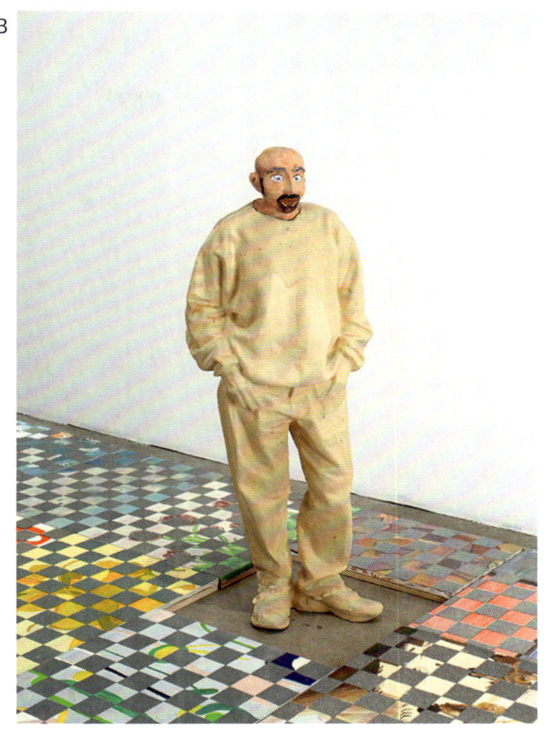

C

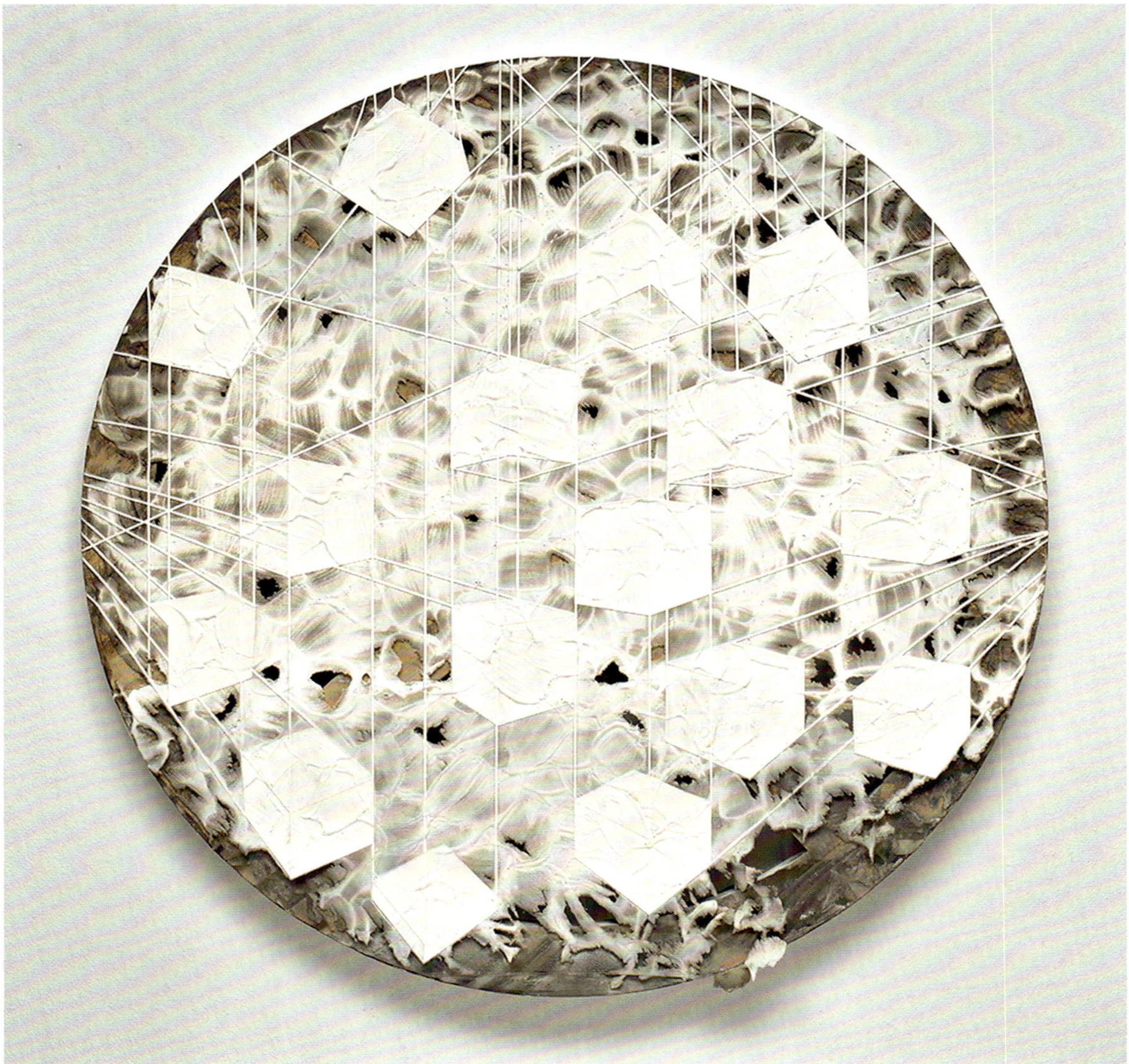

SOMMER

Sommer Contemporary Art
IL-66881 Tel Aviv | 13 Rothschild Boulevard
Phone +972 3 516 64 00 | Fax +972 3 516 86 77
info@sommergallery.com | www.sommergallery.com
Director Tamar Zagursky

Artists at Art Nova | Yael Bartana
Tom Burr
Tal R

Further artists represented | Darren Almond
Boyan
Rineke Dijkstra
Ofir Dor
Karl Haendel
Alona Harpaz
Tamar Harpaz
Michal Helfman
Gregor Hildebrandt
Itzik Livneh
Muntean & Rosenblum
Adi Nes
Ugo Rondinone
Christoph Ruckhäberle
Wilhelm Sasnal
Yehudit Sasportas
Netally Schlosser
Efrat Shvily
Doron Solomons
Eliezer Sonnenschein
Wolfgang Tillmans
Paloma Varga Weisz
Sharon Ya'ari
Rona Yefman
Guy Zagursky
Thomas Zipp

The group exhibition at our booth of this year's Art Basel Miami Beach – Art Nova, stems from a theoretical investigation of the concept of leadership and power, both present and absent. The title of the show, 'We Shall Be Strong in our Weakness,' challenges the viewer to investigate the tension between power and domination, on the one hand, and subordination, struggle, and persistence to pursue change, on the other. The exhibition will include work by Yael Bartana, Tom Burr, and Tal R.

Tom Burr is an artist whose genre – photographs, drawings, sculptures, and installations – revisits Minimalism and post-Minimalism, and mixes together Pop iconography, homosexual cultures, underground aesthetics, with musical, cinematographic, and literary influences, as well as contemporary architecture and design. The artist investigates the way in which identity is constrained by society and its physical spaces.

Tal R collects a wide range of imagery, figurative and abstract, from high and low culture, to create his works. Whether in paintings, drawings, prints, or textiles, his resourceful and energetic elements express a spirit and sentiment that can be interpreted on many levels. Tal R continues to pursue his unique way of writing history, eroticism, citations of nature, and political commentary as important themes in his work.

Yael Bartana
We Shall Be Strong In Our Weakness, 2012
Neon, 40 x 110 cm

We Shall be Strong
in our Weakness

SPERONE WESTWATER

Mobile +1 917 916 03 80

Sperone Westwater
US-New York, NY 10002 | 257 Bowery
Phone +1 212 999 73 37 | Fax +1 212 999 73 38
info@speronewestwater.com | www.speronewestwater.com
Directors Gian Enzo Sperone
Angela Westwater
David Leiber

Artists at
Art Basel Miami Beach | **Carla Accardi**
Kutlug Ataman
Barry X Ball
Bertozzi & Casoni
Alighiero Boetti
Wim Delvoye
Kim Dingle
Lucio Fontana
Andrew Grassie
Mark Greenwold
Guillermo Kuitca
Charles LeDray
Liu Ye
Richard Long
Emil Lukas
Heinz Mack
Piero Manzoni
Mario Merz
Frank Moore
Malcolm Morley
Nabil Nahas
Bruce Nauman
Evan Penny
Otto Piene
Susan Rothenberg
Tom Sachs
Julian Schnabel
Not Vital
William Wegman
Martin Wilner
Jan Worst

Gallery Information | Current exhibitions:

Barry X Ball, Bass Museum of Art, 2100 Collins Avenue, Miami, FL 33139, December 2012

Guillermo Kuitca: Diarios, The Drawing Center, 35 Wooster Street, New York, NY 10013, November 2-December 9, 2012

Malcolm Morley: On Paper, Parrish Art Museum, 279 Montauk Highway, Water Mill, NY 11976, November 10, 2012-January 13, 2013

Toxic Beauty: The Art of Frank Moore, Grey Art Gallery, New York University, 100 Washington Square East, New York, NY 10003, September 6-December 8, 2012

Evan Penny: Re Figured, Art Gallery of Ontario, 317 Dundas Street West, Toronto, ON, M5T 1G4, September 19, 2012-January 6, 2013

Barry X Ball
Matthew Barney/BXB Dual-Dual Portrait, 2000-2009
Mexican onyx, stainless steel,
55 x 5¼ x 8 inches each

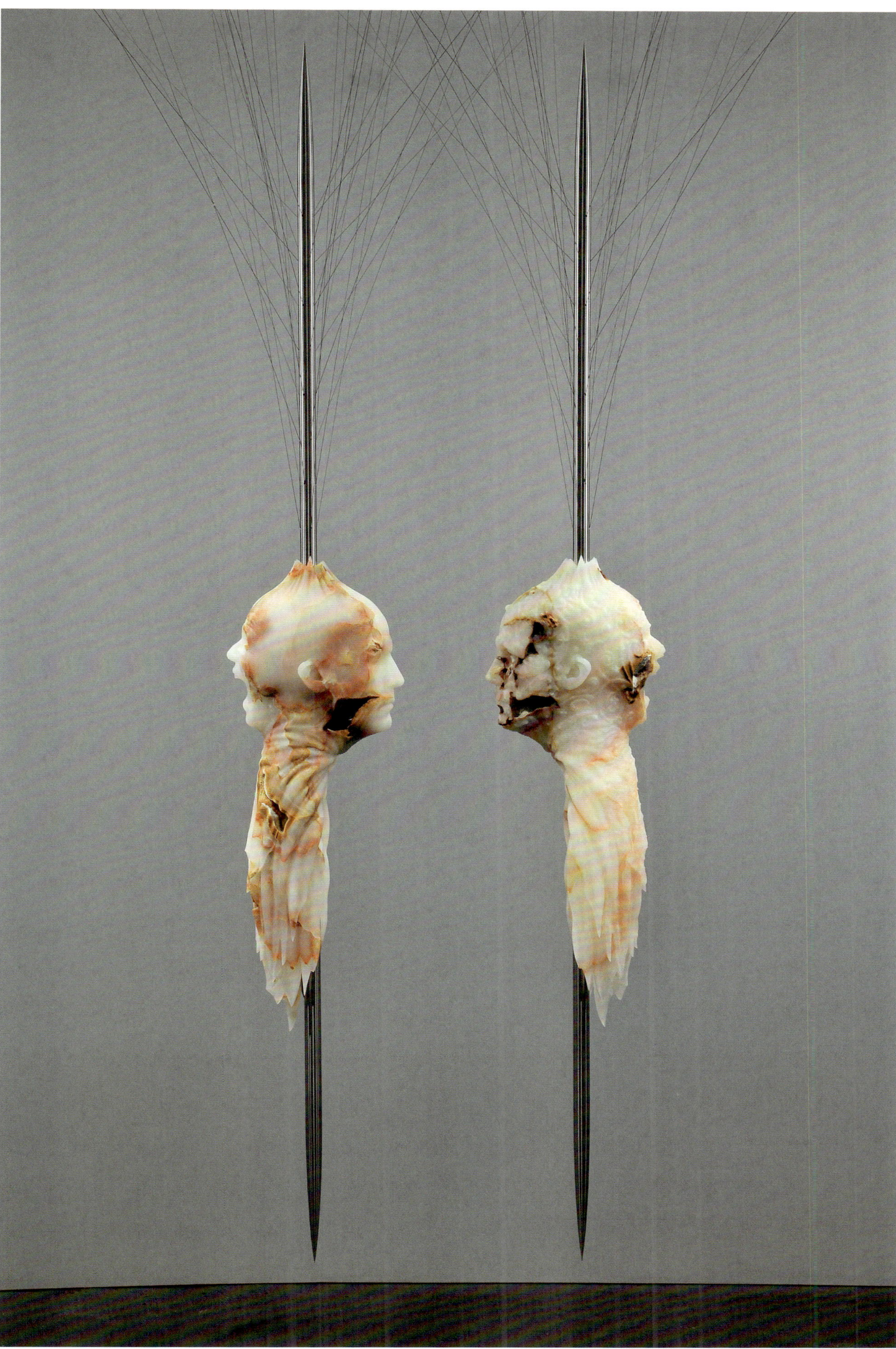

SPINELLO

Spinello Projects
US-Miami, FL 33127 | 2930 NW 7th Avenue
Phone +1 786 271 42 23 | Fax +1 786 271 42 23
info@spinelloprojects.com | spinelloprojects.com
Director Anthony Spinello

One-Person Show | Artist Information

Agustina Woodgate

*1981, Buenos Aires, Argentina
Lives and works in Miami, FL, United States

Gallery Information | Spinello Projects is a Miami-based contemporary art venture founded in 2005.

Spinello Projects prides itself on exhibiting intelligent works of art in every conceivable medium by local and international artists. It has become a playground for unorthodox and experimental artists not easily placed into the confines of a traditional gallery space.

Its mission: to represent, support, and collaborate with contemporary artists – initiating groundbreaking change in Miami's cultural landscape and beyond.

Further artists represented:
Abby Double
Farley Aguilar
Sandra Bermudez
Kris Knight
Sinisa Kukec
Manny Prieres
Santiago Rubino
TYPOE

Multidisciplinary artist Agustina Woodgate focuses her practice on concepts of building, expanding, and expounding upon new landscapes in the physical and metaphysical spheres. Like the iconic bayonet's barrel stuffed with a flower, Woodgate actively shifts the patterns of violent ends and, instead, provokes beginnings.

In her most recent body of work, *New Landscapes,* Agustina Woodgate takes three representations of the planet Earth: an outdated copy of *The Times Atlas of the World,* a Planisphere world map, and a vintage world globe. She creates positive and negative matter from a single action. The negative is produced by sanding away the topographical and political markers of the nations of the world down to homogeneous landmasses: a cartographic implosion – a proposal for a new kind of territorial exploration. Rather than nations or countries taking precedence as the visual anchor, the Earth as a whole (all at once rendered mute, but equal) becomes the primary focus. Through the gesture of erasing political borders and imagined national spaces, Woodgate offers a signal of hope: an optimistic realization of a world both beautiful to behold and comforting to imagine.

Agustina Woodgate
Untitled (World Globe), 2011
Sanded found world globe,
diameter 12 inches

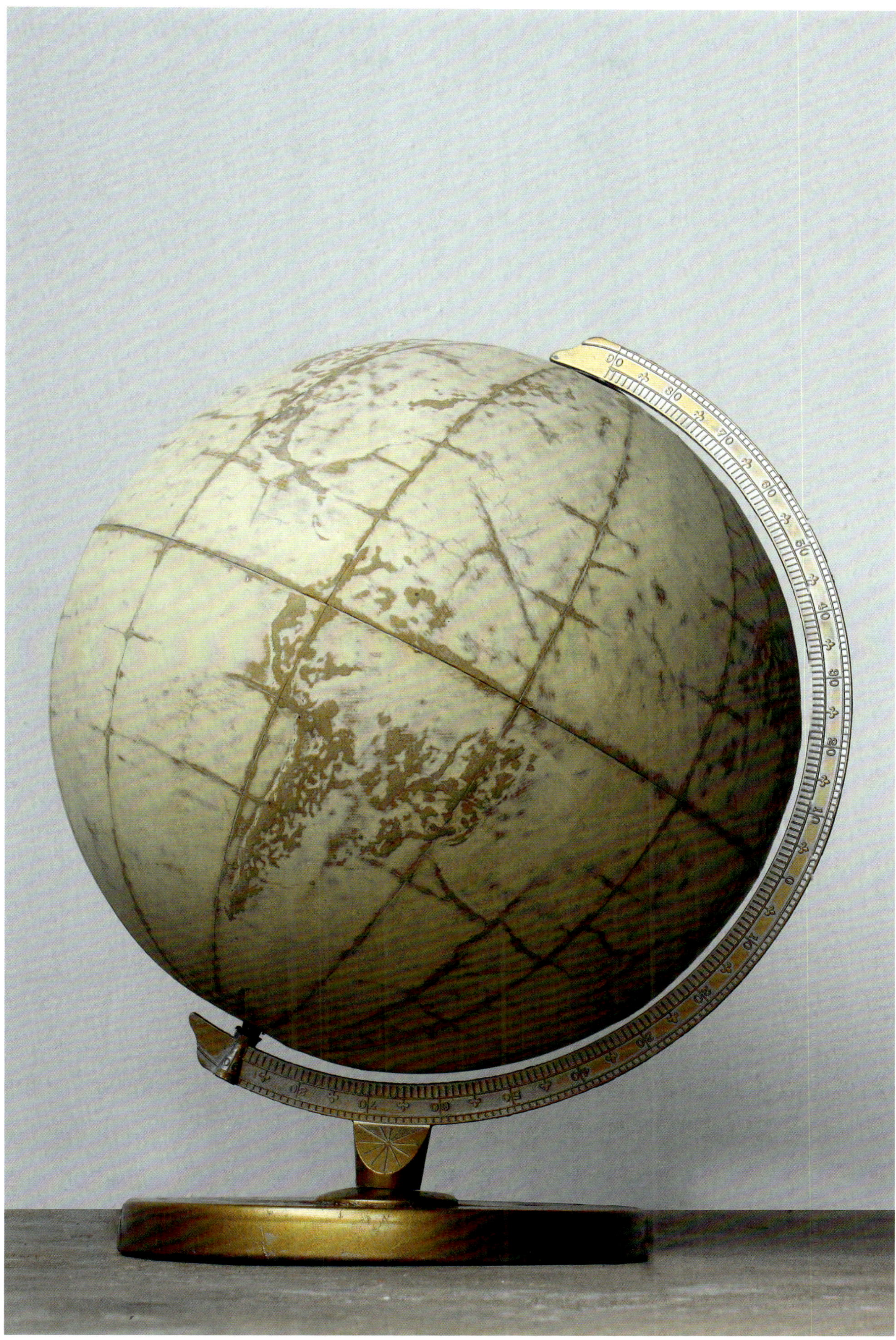

SPRÜTH MAGERS

Sprüth Magers Berlin
DE-10178 Berlin | Oranienburger Strasse 18
Phone +49 30 28884030 | Fax +49 30 28884052
info@spruethmagers.com | www.spruethmagers.com
Directors Monika Sprüth
Philomene Magers
Franziska von Hasselbach
Iris Scheffler

Sprüth Magers London
GB-London W1S 4EJ | 7A Grafton Street
Phone +44 20 74081613 | Fax +44 20 74994531
info@spruethmagers.com | www.spruethmagers.com
Directors Monika Sprüth
Philomene Magers
Andreas Gegner
Andrew Silewicz
Patricia Pratas

Artists at
Art Basel Miami Beach | **Richard Artschwager**
John Baldessari
Alighiero Boetti
George Condo
Thomas Demand
Thea Djordjadze
Peter Fischli/David Weiss
Cyprien Gaillard
Andreas Gursky
Jenny Holzer
Gary Hume
Karen Kilimnik
Joseph Kosuth
Barbara Kruger
David Lamelas
Louise Lawler
Robert Morris
Jean-Luc Mylayne
Michail Pirgelis
Sterling Ruby
Ed Ruscha
Thomas Scheibitz
Andreas Schulze
Cindy Sherman
Robert Therrien
Rosemarie Trockel
Andrea Zittel

Further artists represented | Siegfried Anzinger
Walter Dahn
Philip-Lorca diCorcia
Robert Elfgen
Sylvie Fleury
Donald Judd
Axel Kasseböhmer
Astrid Klein
Kraftwerk
David Maljkovic
Anthony McCall
Nina Pohl
Richard Prince
Gerda Scheepers
Frances Scholz
Stephen Shore
Alexandre Singh
Marcel van Eeden

Jenny Holzer
Secret 2, Text: U.S. government document, 2012
Oil on linen, 58 x 44 x 1½ inches,
147.3 x 111.8 x 3.8 cm
Unique

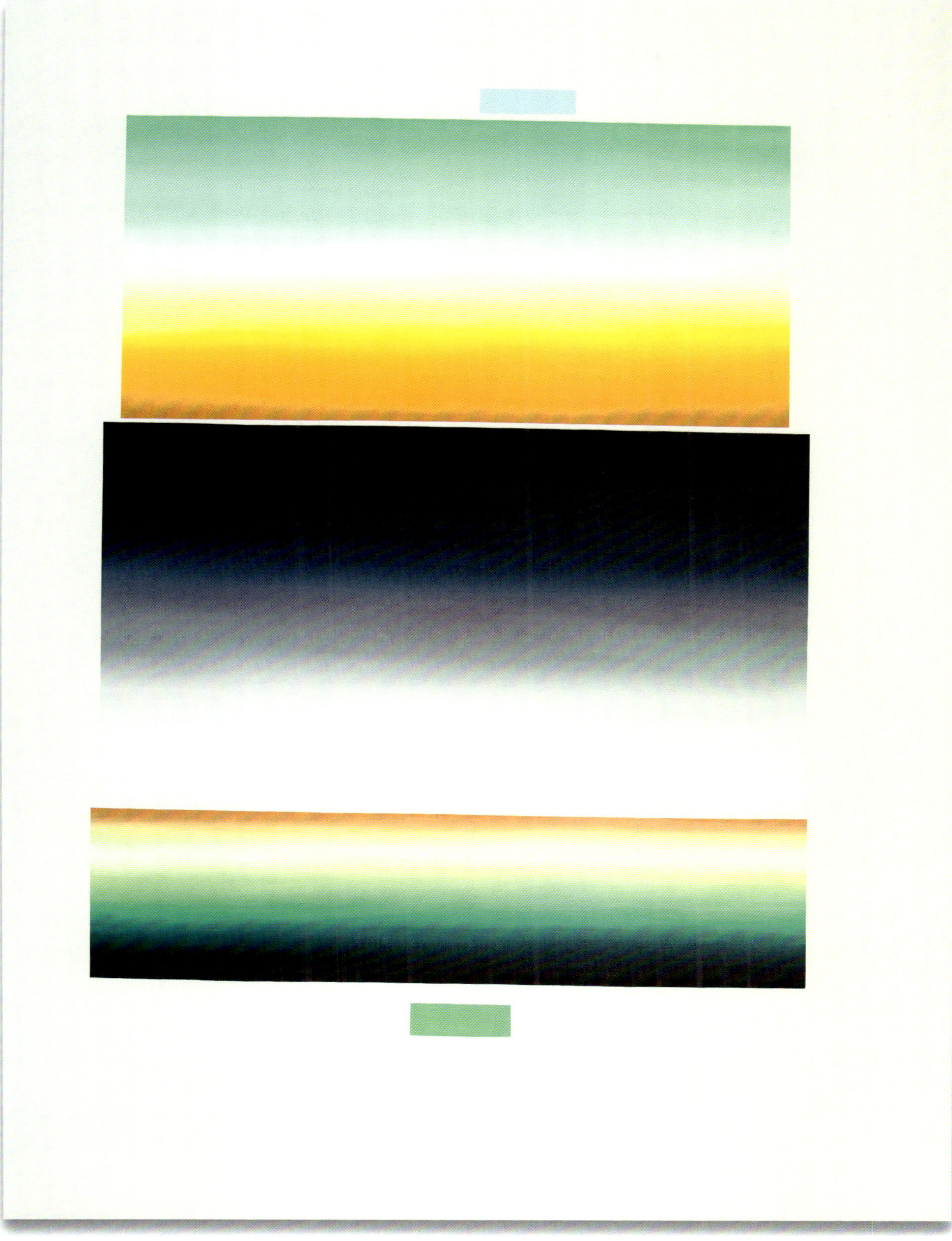

STÆRK

Mobile +45 40 88 77 66

Nils Stærk
DK-1760 Copenhagen | Ny Carlsberg Vej 68
Phone +45 32 54 45 62
gallery@nilsstaerk.dk | www.nilsstaerk.dk
Directors Nils Stærk
Caroline Bøge

Artists at Art Basel Miami Beach | **Miriam Bäckström**
Olaf Breuning
Ingvar Cronhammar
Mads Gamdrup
Nils Erik Gjerdevik
Jone Kvie
Michael Kvium
Runo Lagomarsino
Torbjørn Rødland
Matthew Ronay
Tom Sandberg
Tove Storch
Thaddeus Strode
Superflex
Ed Templeton

Runo Lagomarsino
OtherWhere, 2011
168 postcards and stones,
6 painted wood tables

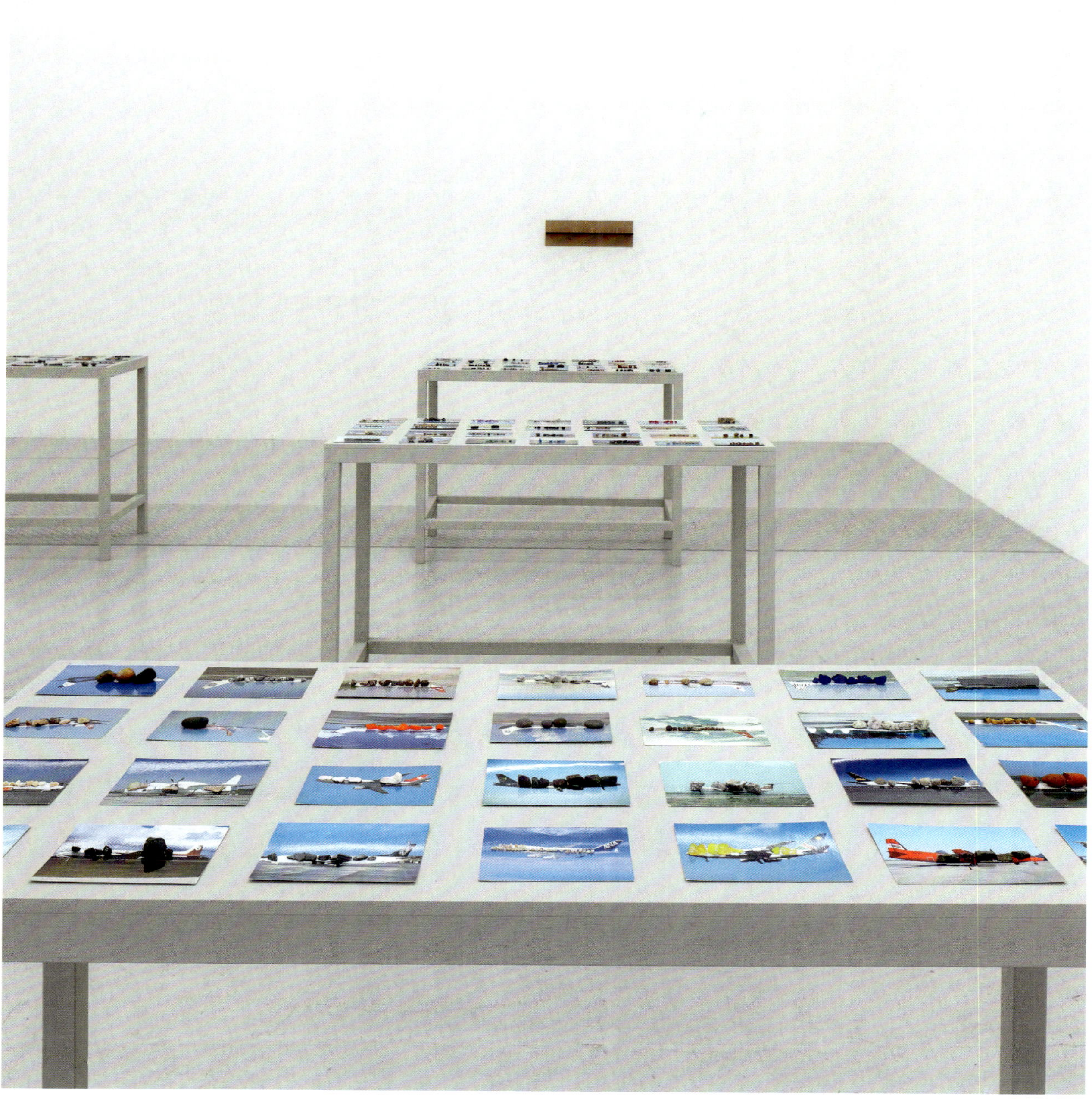

STANDARD (OSLO)

Mobile +47 917 074 29

Standard (Oslo)
NO-0175 Oslo | Waldemar Thranes gate 86c
Phone +47 22 60 13 10 | Fax +47 22 60 13 11
info@standardoslo.no | www.standardoslo.no
Director Eivind Furnesvik

Artists at
Art Basel Miami Beach | **Matias Faldbakken**
Josh Smith
Fredrik Værslev

Gallery Information | Exhibitions:
Gardar Eide Einarsson/Marius Engh/Matias Faldbakken/Anders Nordby/Josh Smith/Oscar Tuazon/Fredrik Værslev, November 9-December 15, 2012
Nina Beier, January 18-February 16, 2013
Kim Hiorthøy, February 22-March 23, 2013

Further artists represented: Tauba Auerbach
Nina Beier
Johanna Billing
Gardar Eide Einarsson
Marius Engh
Ane Graff
Kim Hiorthøy
Ann Cathrin November Høibo
Alex Hubbard
Michaela Meise
Anders Nordby
Chadwick Rantanen
Nick Relph
Torbjørn Rødland
Oscar Tuazon
Emily Wardill

Fredrik Værslev
Untitled (Canopy Painting: White, Purple and Blue), 2012
Primer, spray paint, house paint, and white spirit on canvas on wooden stretcher,
220 x 198 x 3.3 cm

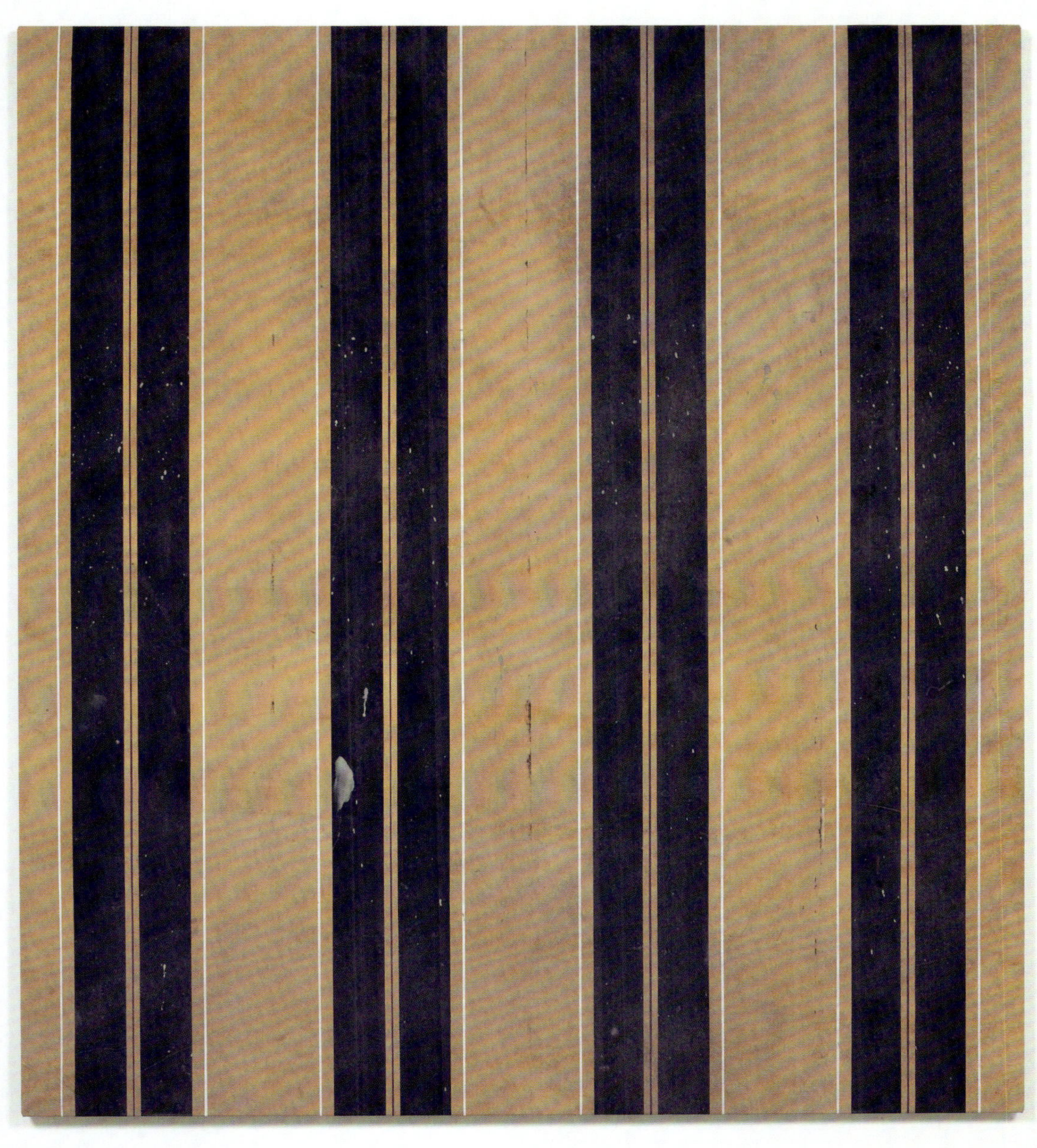

STARR

Craig F. Starr Gallery
US-New York, NY 10021 | 5 East 73rd Street
Phone +1 212 570 17 39 | Fax +1 212 570 68 48
info@starr-art.com | www.starr-art.com
Directors Craig F. Starr
Emily Whitley Larson
Alexander P. Jarolim

Artists at
Art Basel Miami Beach |

Alexander Calder
Chuck Close
Richard Diebenkorn
Helen Frankenthaler
Eva Hesse
Edward Hopper
Jasper Johns
Donald Judd
Sol LeWitt
Brice Marden
Agnes Martin
Robert Morris
Bruce Nauman
Barnett Newman
Robert Rauschenberg
Dorothea Rockburne
Susan Rothenberg
Ed Ruscha
Richard Serra
David Smith
Rudolf Stingel
Richard Tuttle
Cy Twombly

Gallery Information | Exhibitions:

Transparencies: Richard Serra Recent Drawings, November/December 2012

Dorothea Rockburne: Works 1967-1972, September/October 2012

Robert Rauschenberg: North African Collages and Scatole Personali c. 1952, June-August 2012

Surface/Infinity: Vija Celmins, Brice Marden, Agnes Martin, April/May 2012

Donald Judd: Cadmium Red, February/March 2012

Barnett Newman Paintings, November/December 2011

Chuck Close
Marta/Fingerprint, 1986
Oil-based ink on Mylar,
58 3/8 x 42 inches (sheet size)

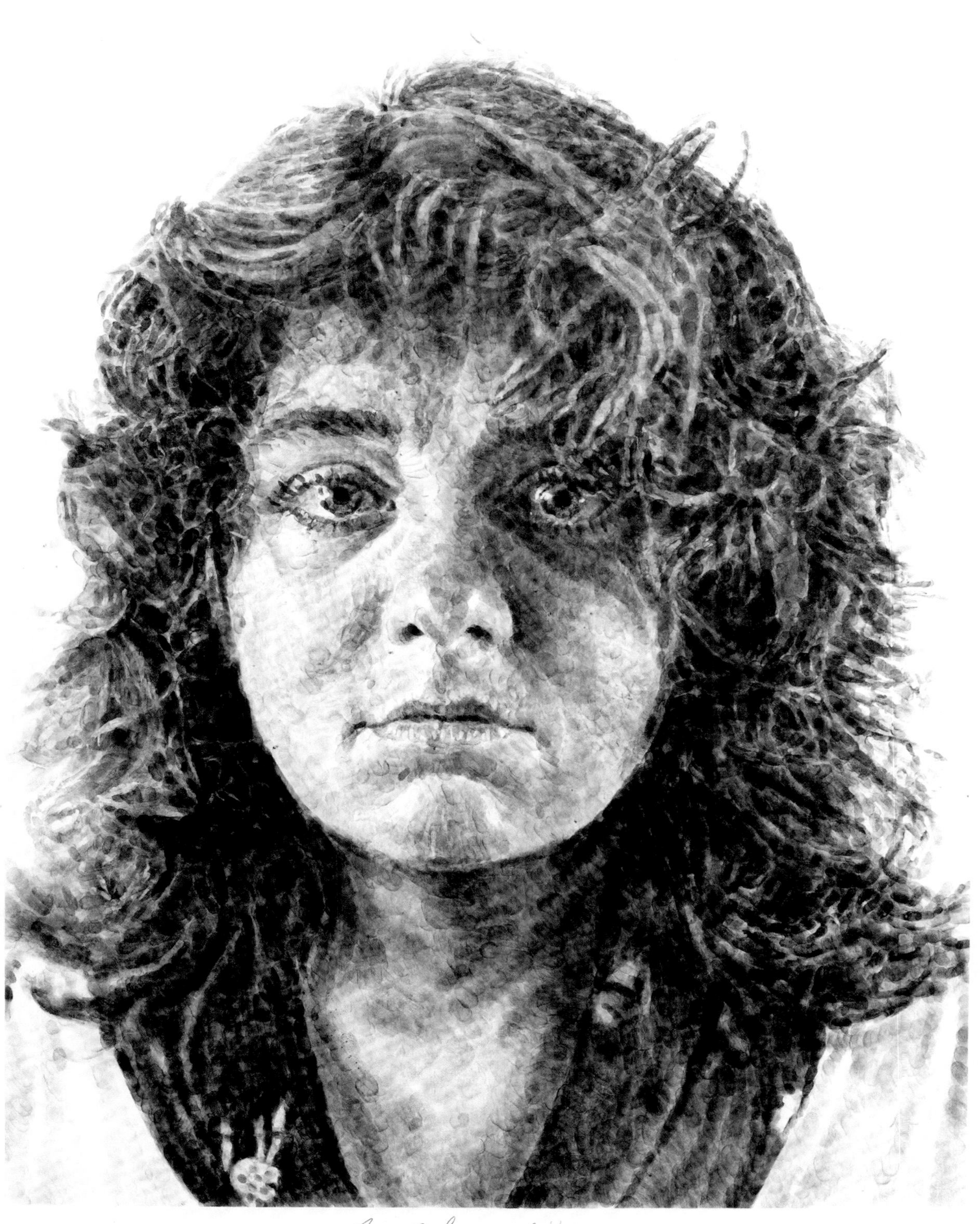

STEIN

Christian Stein
IT-20122 Milan | Corso Monforte, 23
Phone +39 02 76 39 33 01 | Fax +39 02 76 00 71 14
christianstein@iol.it
Director Gianfranco Benedetti

Artists at
Art Basel Miami Beach | **Domenico Bianchi**
Alighiero Boetti
Pier Paolo Calzolari
Paolo Canevari
Luciano Fabro
Lucio Fontana
Bernard Frize
Jannis Kounellis
Piero Manzoni
Fausto Melotti
Mario Merz
Marisa Merz
Mimmo Paladino
Giulio Paolini
Jack Pierson
Michelangelo Pistoletto
Remo Salvadori
Christopher Wool

Gallery Information | Christian Stein Gallery was founded in 1966 in Turin.

Pier Paolo Calzolari
Untitled, 1971
Leather straps, neon elements, freezing structure, lead, freezing motor, transformer,
330 x 150 x 35 cm

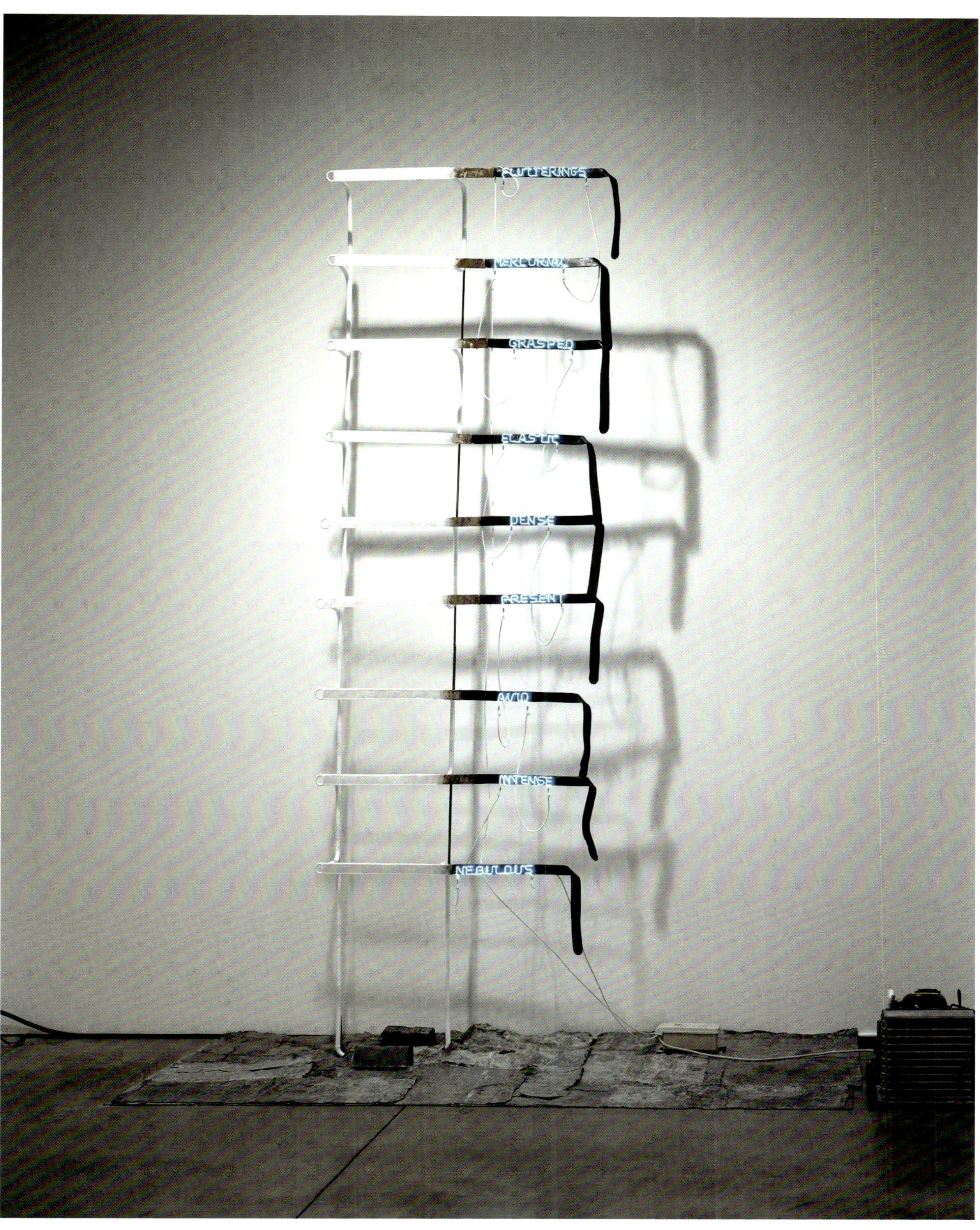
FLUTTERINGS
MERCURIAL
GRASPED
ELASTIC
DENSE
PRESENT
AVID
INTENSE
NEBULOUS

STEVENSON

Stevenson
ZA-7925 Cape Town | 160 Sir Lowry Road, Woodstock
Phone +27 21 462 15 00 | Fax +27 21 462 15 01
info@stevenson.info | www.stevenson.info
Directors Federica Angelucci
Joost Bosland
Andrew da Conceicao
Sophie Perryer
David Brodie
Michael Stevenson

Stevenson
ZA-2001 Johannesburg | 62 Juta Street, Braamfontein
Phone +27 11 326 00 34/41 | Fax +27 86 275 19 18
jhb@stevenson.info | www.stevenson.info

Artists at
Art Basel Miami Beach | **Zander Blom**
Nicholas Hlobo
Serge Alain Nitegeka

Further artists represented | Dineo Seshee Bopape
Conrad Botes
Wim Botha
Steven Cohen
Paul Edmunds
Ângela Ferreira
Meschac Gaba
Simon Gush
Pieter Hugo
Anton Kannemeyer
Michael MacGarry
Sabelo Mlangeni
Nandipha Mntambo
Zanele Muholi
Daniel Naudé
Odili Donald Odita
Deborah Poynton
Jo Ractliffe
Viviane Sassen
Claudette Schreuders
Berni Searle
Lerato Shadi
Penny Siopis
Guy Tillim
Frohawk Two Feathers
Lynette Yiadom-Boakye

Zander Blom
Untitled, 2012
Oil on canvas, 198 x 140 cm

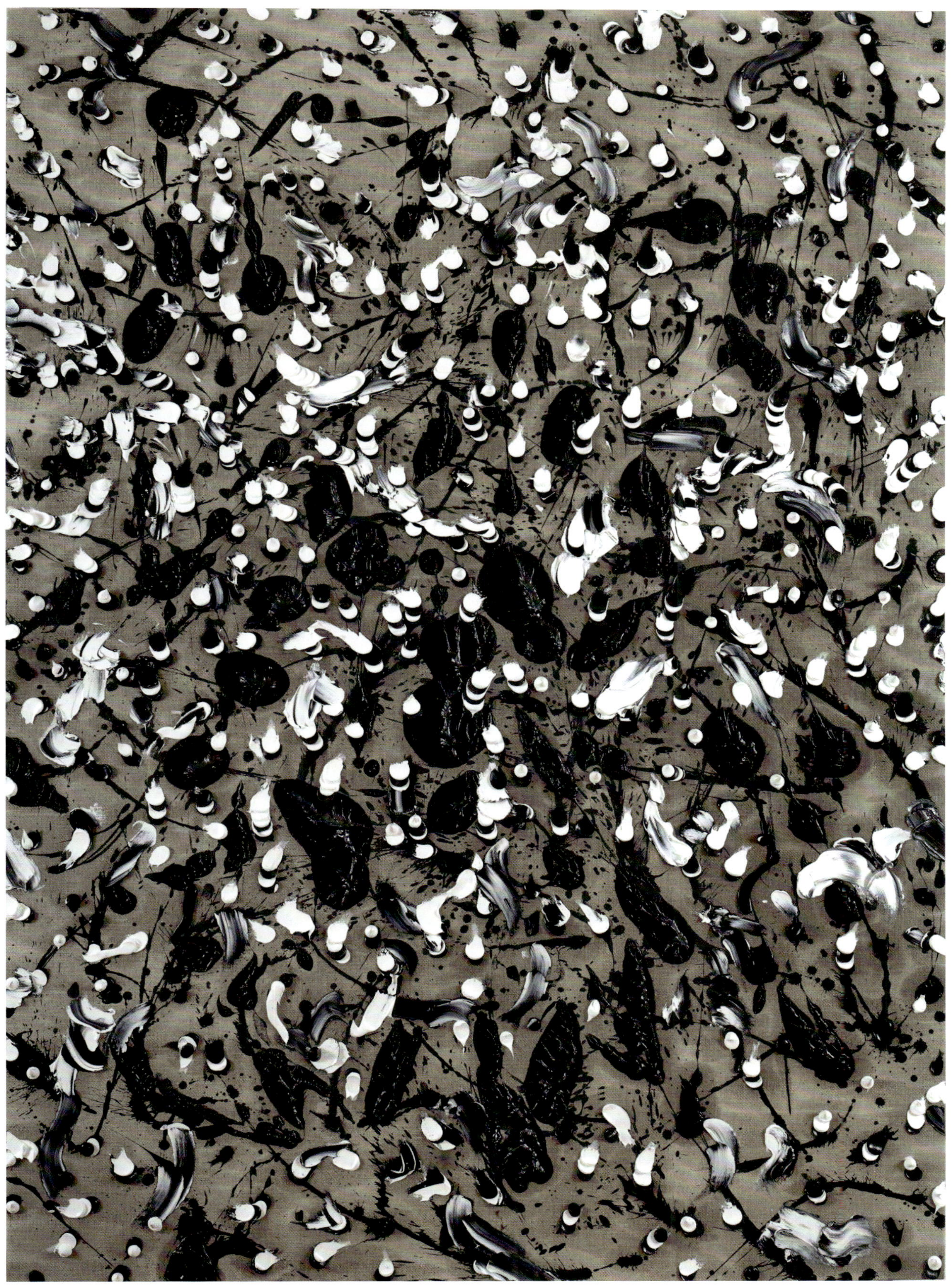

STRINA

Mobile +55 11 81 11 02 33

Galeria Luisa Strina
BR-São Paulo SP 01411-001 | Rua Padre João Manuel, 755
Phone +55 11 30 88 24 71 | Fax +55 11 30 64 63 91
info@galerialuisastrina.com.br | www.galerialuisastrina.com.br
Directors Luisa Malzoni Strina
Marli Matsumoto
Maria Quiroga

Artists at
Art Basel Miami Beach | **Pablo Accinelli**
Juan Araujo
Alessandro Balteo Yazbeck
Laura Belém
Erick Beltrán
Alexandre da Cunha
Caetano de Almeida
Edgard de Souza
Matías Duville
Olafur Eliasson
Marcius Galan
Carlos Garaicoa
Fernanda Gomes
Brian Griffiths
David Haines
Federico Herrero
Magdalena Jitrik
Marcellvs L.
Luisa Lambri
Tonico Lemos Auad
Laura Lima
Armin Linke
Jarbas Lopes
Jazmin López
Mateo López
Renata Lucas
Jorge Macchi
Antonio Manuel
Marepe
Gilberto Mariotti
Cildo Meireles
Pedro Motta
Muntadas
Lygia Pape
Nicolás Paris
Pedro Reyes
Marina Saleme
Gabriel Sierra
Adrian Villar Rojas

Gallery Information | Established in 1974, Galeria Luisa Strina specializes in contemporary Brazilian and international art.

Lygia Pape
Book of Time, 1961
Paint on wood, 42 x 50 x 9 cm

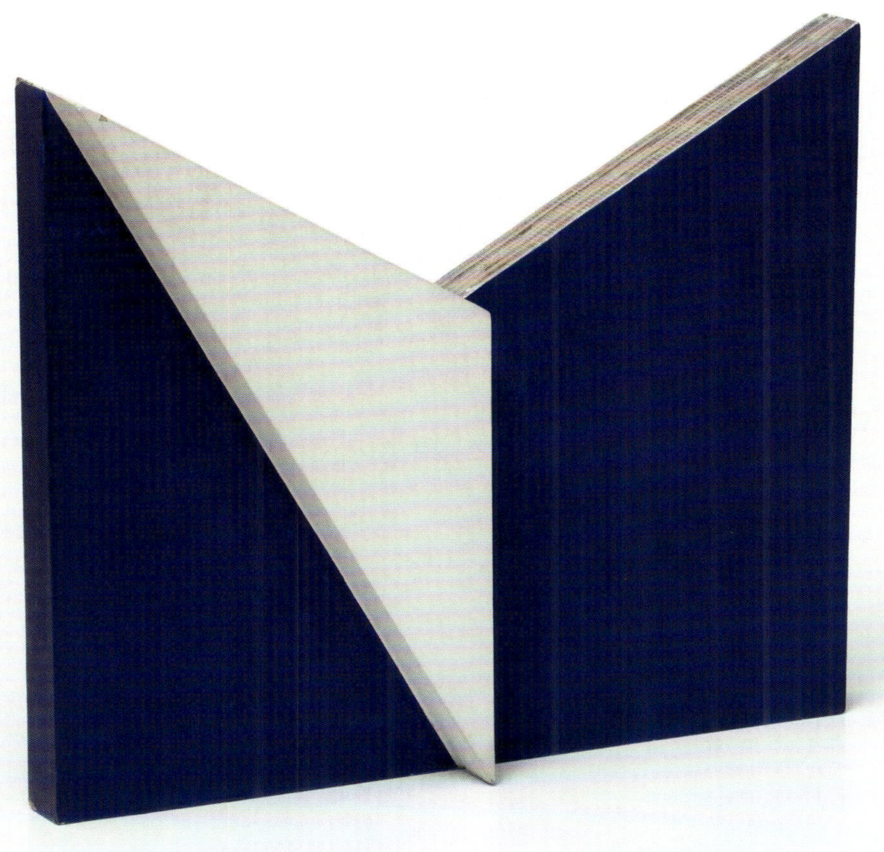

SUR

Mobile +598 99 68 40 99

Galería Sur
UY-Punta del Este | Ruta 10, Parada 46, La Barra
Phone +59 827 10 13 36 | Fax +59 827 10 25 04
sur@montevideo.com.uy | www.galeriasur.com.uy
Directors Jorge Castillo
Martin Castillo

Artists at
Art Basel Miami Beach | **Pablo Atchugarry**
Rafael Barradas
Antonio Berni
Fernando Botero
José Gurvich
Victor Magariños D.
Joaquín Torres García

Gallery Information | Galería Sur started its activities in 1984 in Punta del Este, Uruguay. The gallery specializes in the historic avant-garde of Rio de la Plata, with its relationship to the European and American movements of the 1920s, 1930s, and 1940s (Joaquín Torres García, Rafael Barradas, Pedro Figari); in Latin American masters (Antonio Berni, Roberto Matta, Fernando Botero, Wifredo Lam, Portinari); in the Escuela del Sur (Gurvich, Fonseca, Matto, Augusto Torres); and in abstract and concrete movements in Rio de la Plata (Pareja, Costigliolo, Hilda Lopez, Maria Freire), or, for example, the Madi Group.

Galería Sur also works with contemporary artists from Rio de la Plata, such as Iturria, Atchugarry, Vila, Cardozo, and Legrand.

Further artists represented: Eduardo Cardozo
José Pedro Costigliolo
Pedro Figari
Gonzalo Fonseca
Alfredo Hlito
Marcelo Legrand
Hilda Lopez
Raúl Pavlotzky
Claudio Tozzi

Pablo Atchugarry
Untitled, 2001
Pink Portugal marble,
238 x 37 x 28 cm

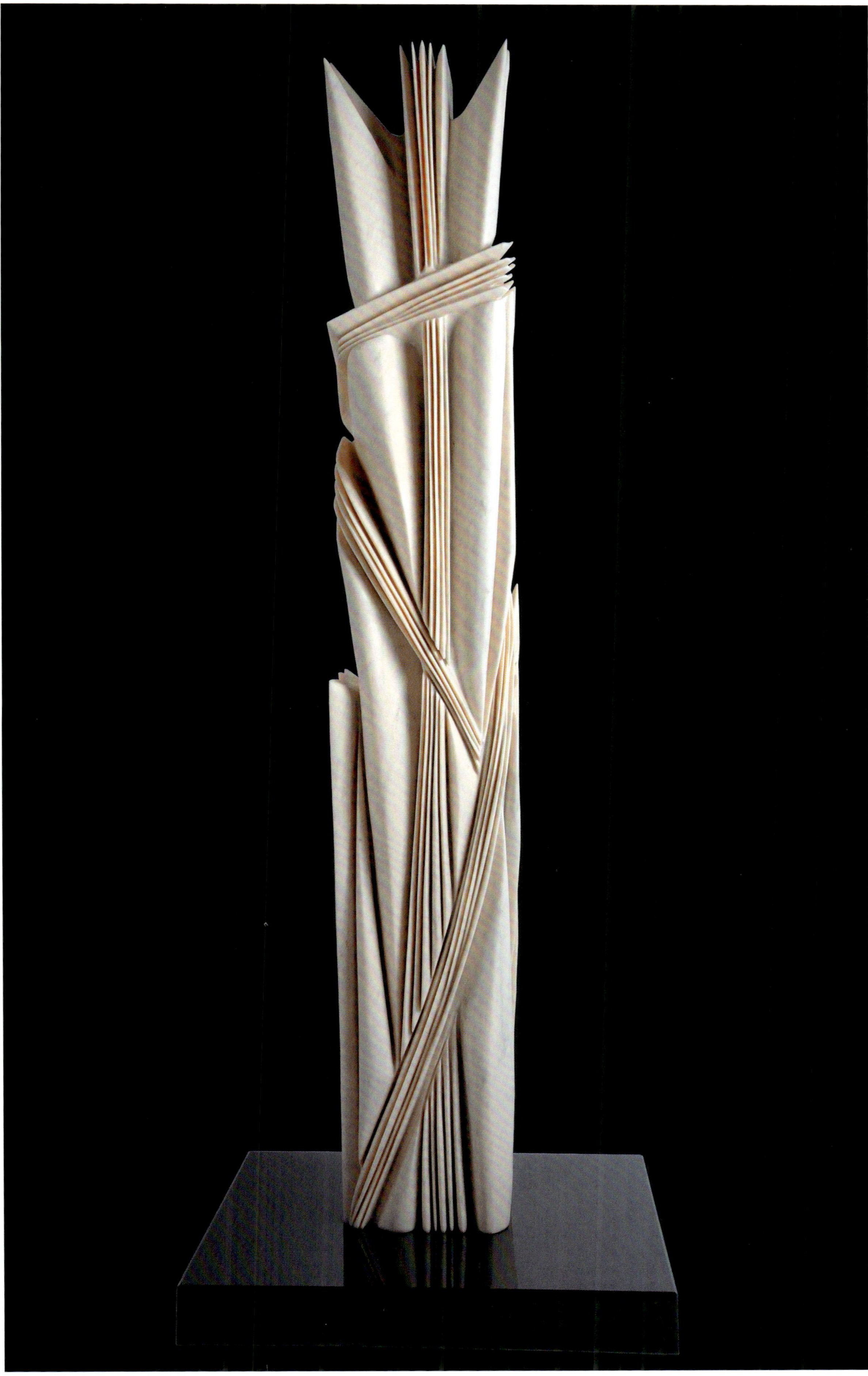

TEAM

Team Gallery
US-New York, NY 10013 | 83 Grand Street
Phone +1 212 2799219 | Fax +1 212 2799220
office@teamgal.com | www.teamgal.com
Directors Jose Freire
Miriam Katzeff

Artists at Art Basel Miami Beach | **Cory Arcangel**
Alex Bag
Pierre Bismuth
Vlassis Caniaris
Brice Dellsperger
Maria Eichhorn
Gardar Eide Einarsson
Massimo Grimaldi
Marc Hundley
Ross Knight
Jakob Kolding
Ryan McGinley
Muntean/Rosenblum
Tam Ochiai
David Ratcliff
Davis Rhodes
Sam Samore
Andreas Schulze
Santiago Sierra
Gert & Uwe Tobias
Chris Vasell
Banks Violette
Stanley Whitney

Marc Hundley
Joan Baez Is Alive, 2011
Installation view

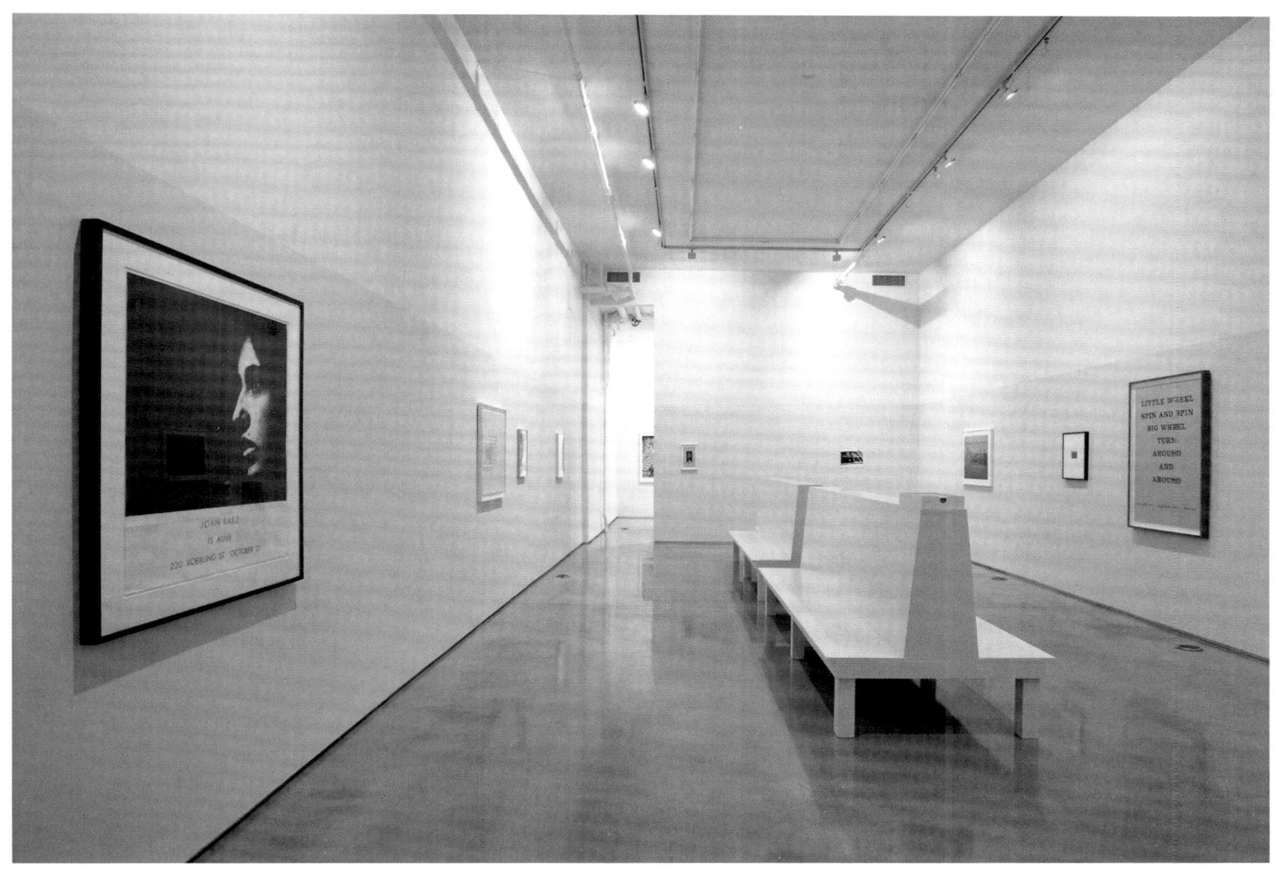
LITTLE WHEEL
SPIN AND SPIN
BIG WHEEL
TURN
AROUND
AND
AROUND

TEMPLON

Galerie Daniel Templon
FR-75003 Paris | 30, rue Beaubourg
Phone +33 1 42 72 14 10 | Fax +33 1 42 77 45 36
info@danieltemplon.com | www.danieltemplon.com
Directors Daniel Templon
Anne-Claudie Coric

Artists at
Art Basel Miami Beach | **Jan Fabre**
He An
Jonathan Meese
Iván Navarro
Sudarshan Shetty
Chiharu Shiota
Tunga
Kehinde Wiley

Further artists represented | Valerio Adami
Jean-Michel Alberola
Larry Bell
Ben
Norbert Bisky
Anthony Caro
James Casebere
Saint Clair Cemin
Philippe Cognée
Will Cotton
Gregory Crewdson
Daniel Dezeuze
Jim Dine
Anju Dodiya
Atul Dodiya
Eric Fischl
Gérard Garouste
Oda Jaune
Clay Ketter
Ulrich Lamsfuss
Loïc Le Groumellec
Mao Yan
Philip Pearlstein
Julião Sarmento
Joel Shapiro
Frank Stella
Claude Viallat

Iván Navarro
Nowhere Man III, 2009
Fluorescent tubes, electricity,
74 x 70½ inches

Man Hole (Icon), 2011
LED, mirror, one-way mirror, wood,
electricity, 9½ x Ø 30 inches

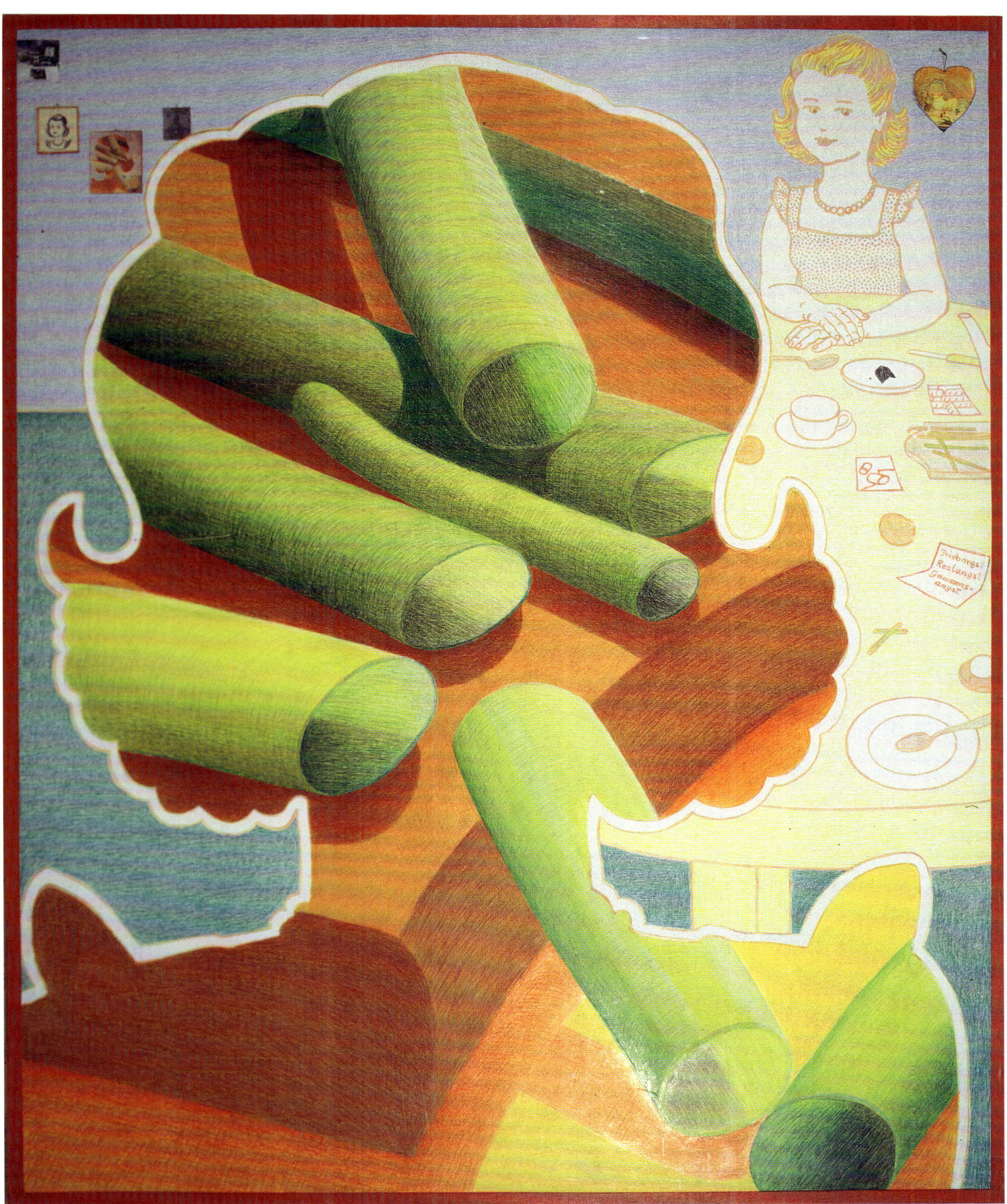
Triebangst
Realangst
Gewissens-
angst

TILTON

Tilton Gallery
US-New York, NY 10021 | 8 East 76th Street
Phone +1 212 737 22 21 | Fax +1 212 396 17 25
info@jacktiltongallery.com | www.jacktiltongallery.com
Director Jack Tilton

Artists at Art Basel Miami Beach | **Derrick Adams**
Njideka Akunyili
Noel Anderson
Noah Davis
Chitra Ganesh
David Hammons
Fred Holland
Simone Leigh
Jarbas Lopes
David Lynch
John Outterbridge
Rebecca Purdum
Sudarshan Shetty
Jeff Sonhouse
Berend Strik
Felandus Thames
Ruth Vollmer
Brenna Youngblood
Zhang Peili
Zhao Gang

Simone Leigh
Cowrie (Blue), 2012
Terra cotta, porcelain, cobalt, epoxy, 11½ x 19½ x 11½ inches

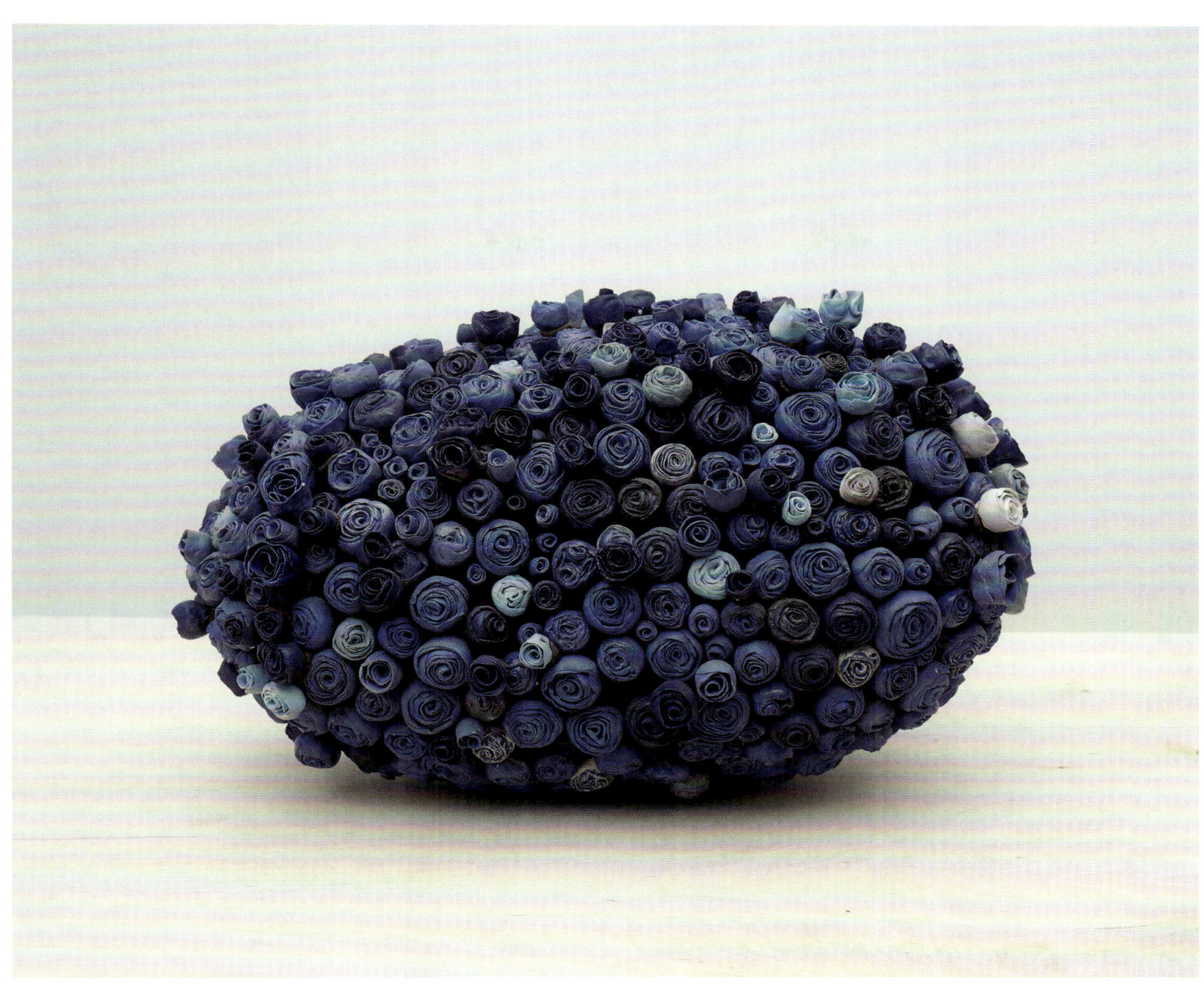

TONKONOW

Leslie Tonkonow Artworks + Projects
US-New York, NY 10011 | 535 West 22nd Street
Phone +1 212 255 84 50 | Fax +1 212 414 87 44
info@tonkonow.com | www.tonkonow.com
Directors Leslie Tonkonow
Tyler Auwarter

Artists at Art Basel Miami Beach | **Dean Byington**
Agnes Denes
Laurel Nakadate
Michelle Stuart
Kunié Sugiura
Robert Watts

Gallery Information | Leslie Tonkonow Artworks + Projects specializes in contemporary art in all media and works on paper from the 1960s to the present. The gallery represents an international group of established and emerging artists, including selected works by Wolfgang Laib, Nikki S. Lee, James Welling, and Yves Klein.

The gallery is a member of the Art Dealers Association of America.

Further artists represented: Tracey Baran
Amy Cutler
Ian Davis
Danny Jauregui
Betsy Kaufman
Julia Oschatz
Tokihiro Sato

Agnes Denes
Wheatfield – A Confrontation (The Harvest), 1982
Vintage Cibachrome print, 16 x 20 inches
From the series documenting *Wheatfield – A Confrontation,* 1982, a site-specific work in which the artist planted and harvested two acres of wheat on a landfill in Manhattan's financial district; commissioned by The Public Art Fund, New York, NY

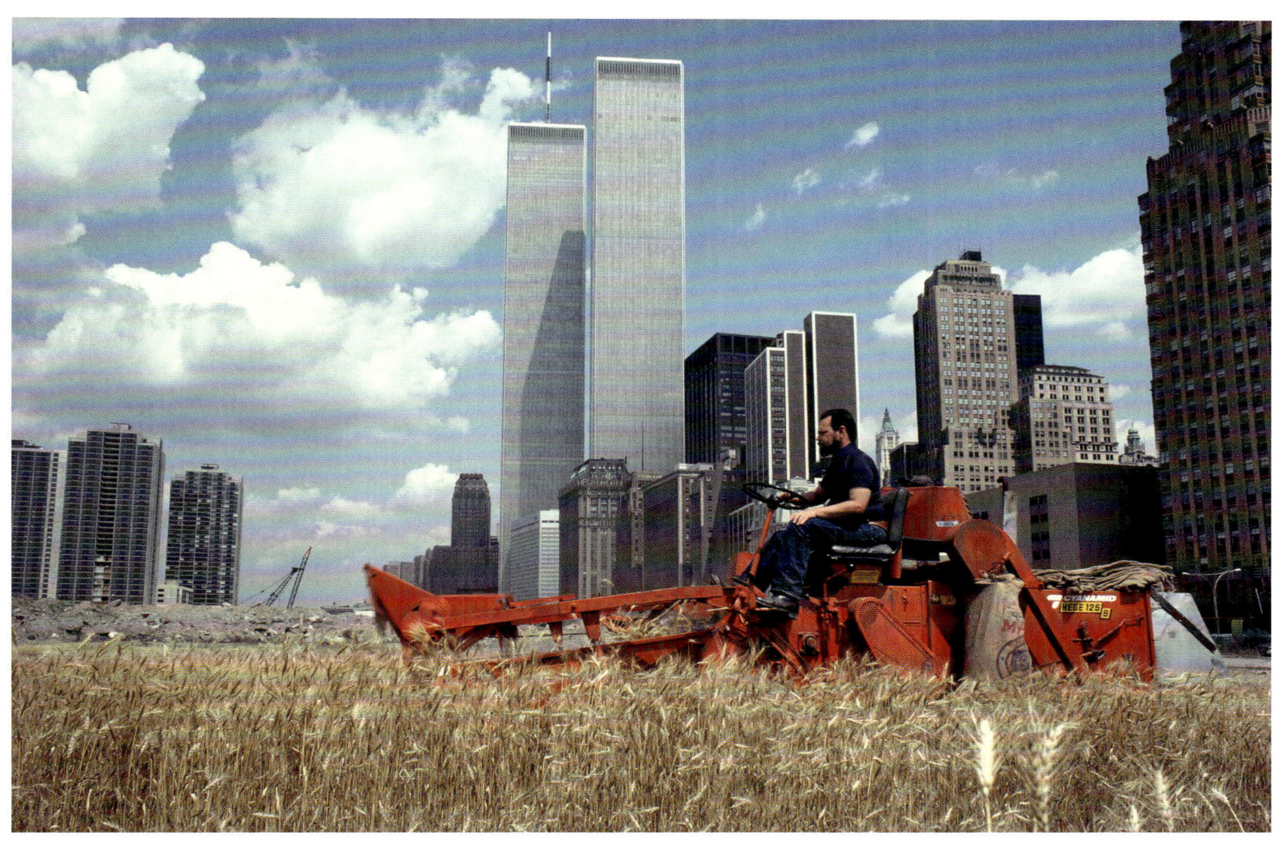
CYANAMID
HEGE 125 B

TORNABUONI

Tornabuoni Art
FR-75008 Paris | 16 Avenue Matignon
Phone +33 1 53535151 | Fax +33 1 53535150
info@tornabuoniart.fr | www.tornabuoniart.fr
Director Roberto Casamonti

Artists at
Art Basel Miami Beach | **Enrico Castellani**
Lucio Fontana

Gallery Information | Highly specialized in Italian art from the second half of the 20th century (Alighiero Boetti, Agostino Bonalumi, Enrico Castellani, Dadamaino, Piero Dorazio, Lucio Fontana, and Piero Manzoni), Tornabuoni Art also features a permanent stock of works by international avant-garde artists of the 20th century (Picasso, Miró, Kandinsky, Hartung, Poliakoff, Dubuffet, Lam, Matta, Christo, Wesselmann, Warhol, and Basquiat, to name only a few) as well as by the main artists of the Italian Novecento (de Chirico, Morandi, Balla, Severini, and Sironi).

The Tornabuoni Art Gallery in Paris opened October 1, 2009 with an exhibition dedicated to Lucio Fontana. Each year the gallery presents a meticulous program of four exhibitions, including two solo shows and two group shows.

Further artists represented: Carla Accardi
Jean-Michel Basquiat
Alighiero Boetti
Agostino Bonalumi
Alberto Burri
Christo
Dadamaino
Giorgio de Chirico
Piero Dorazio
Keith Haring
Hans Hartung
Wassily Kandinsky
Piero Manzoni
Joan Miró
Giorgio Morandi
Pablo Picasso
Arnaldo Pomodoro
Robert Rauschenberg
Andy Warhol
Tom Wesselmann

Lucio Fontana
Concetto Spaziale, 1964
Oil and scratches on canvas, 82 x 65 cm

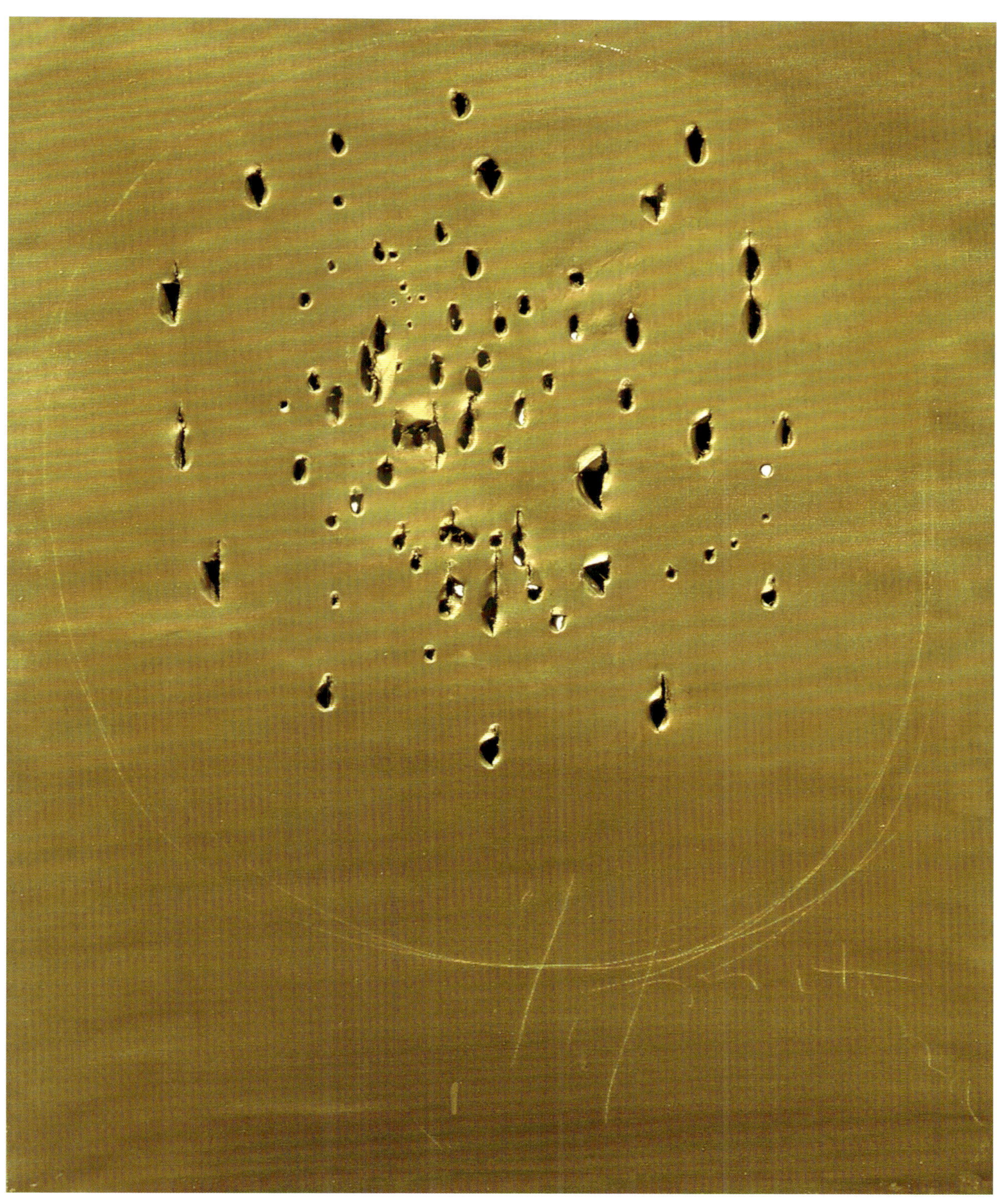

TRAVESÍA CUATRO

Mobile +34 661 334352

Travesía Cuatro
ES-28004 Madrid | San Mateo, 16
Phone +34 91 3100098 | Fax +34 91 3199817
galeria@travesiacuatro.com | www.travesiacuatro.com
Directors Inés López-Quesada
Silvia Ortiz

Artists at Art Nova | Jose Dávila
Jorge Méndez Blake

Gallery Information | Exhibitions 2011/12:

Vicky Uslé, *Absence + Deployment,* June 20-July 21, 2012

The Exact Weight of Lightness, group show: Laura Buckley, Marcius Galan, João Maria Gusmão & Pedro Paiva, Ann Veronica Janssens, Maria Loboda, Navid Nuur, Goran Petercol, Bradley Pitts & Dominick Talvacchio, Gonçalo Sena, April 14-June 2, 2012

Gonzalo Lebrija/Yuri Masnyj, *La vida no vale nada/X,* February 17-March 31, 2012

Jorge Méndez Blake, *Biblioteca Mallarmé,* November 5, 2011-February 15, 2012

Carolina Silva, *La verdad es,* September 15-October 28, 2011

Further artists represented:
Juan De Sande
Máximo González
John Isaacs
Gonzalo Lebrija
Yuri Masnyj
Marco Rountree
Carolina Silva
Vicky Uslé

For Art Nova, Travesía Cuatro presents a project by Mexican artists Jorge Méndez Blake and Jose Dávila (both *1974, Guadalajara, México), who are from the same generation and have been good friends since they embarked on their careers. Both studied architecture and have experienced a similar professional development.

With this program, Travesía Cuatro seeks to emphasize the commonalities of these two artists and the way that, within parallel universes and pursuing similar paths, they produce conceptually different artworks. What is really interesting about this project is to see the particularities and common features of their creative process. Méndez Blake spins his work from influences from the history of literature, architecture, and art. Dávila does it through a review of the history of art and architecture.

Jorge Méndez Blake presents four works connected with his interests in literature, architecture, and history. All of them relate, in one way or the other, to a classic theme in art history and literature: the sea and the shipwreck, a metaphor of progress and modernity.

Jose Dávila presents three works, all of them related to his interest in the history of art and architecture from the perspective of an intimate view and poetic re-interpretation. One work is about an iconic painting and its dichotomy to sculpture; the second is about an iconic building and its comprehensive links to art; the third one is about its auteurs and their creative processes and influence. Through Davila's own influences and aspirations, all of these works dwell on the realms of imagination and memory, translation and reference, reinterpretation and creativity, as brought together by the poetic nature of these forces.

Jorge Méndez Blake
Naufragio, 2011
Vinyl on wall, dimensions variable

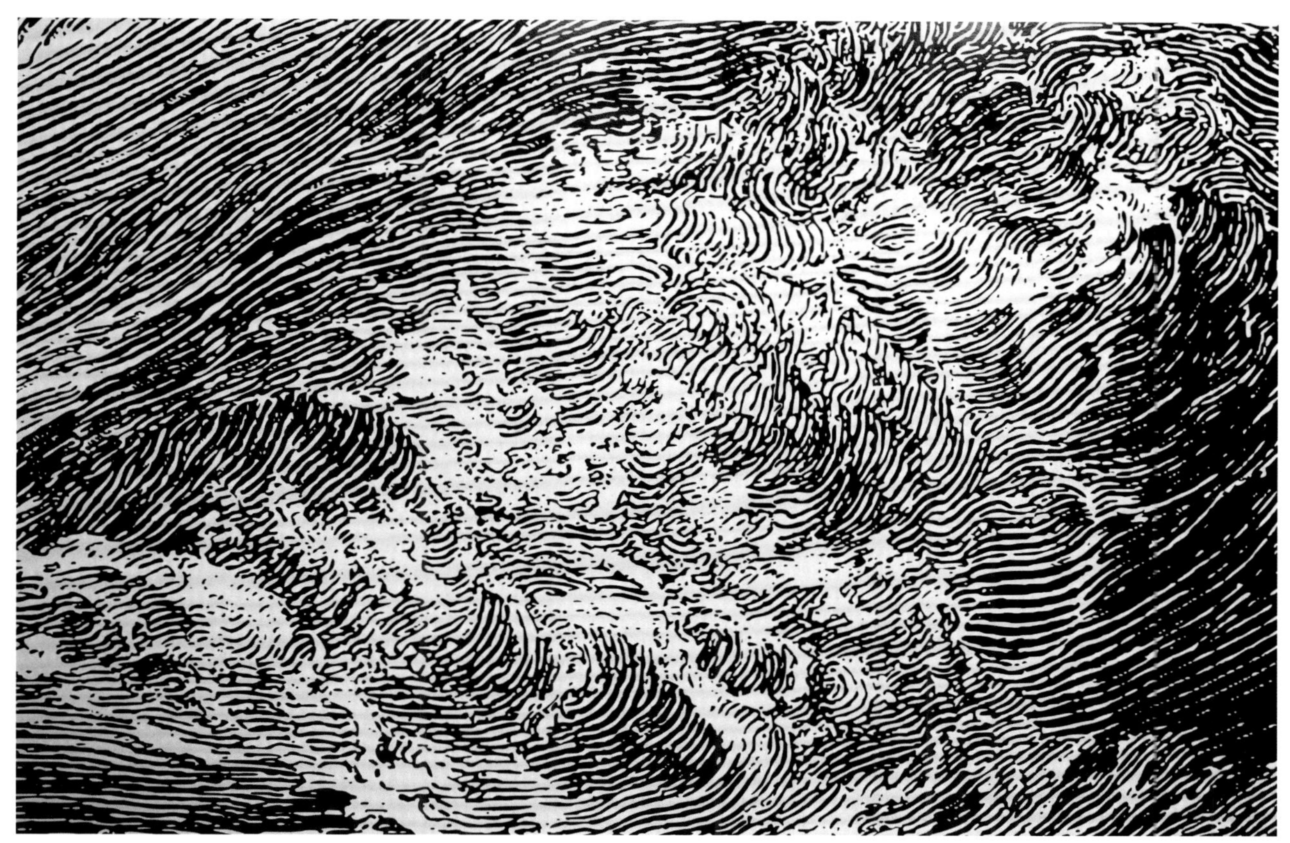

TWO PALMS

Mobile +1 917 583 05 08

Two Palms
US-New York, NY 10013 | 476 Broadway
Phone +1 212 965 85 98 | Fax +1 212 965 80 67
info@twopalms.us | www.twopalms.us
Directors David Lasry
Evelyn Day Lasry

Artists at
Art Basel Miami Beach | **Mel Bochner**
Cecily Brown
Carroll Dunham
Chris Ofili
Elizabeth Peyton
Dana Schutz
Terry Winters

Further artists represented | Chuck Close
Peter Doig
Ellen Gallagher
Per Kirkeby
Sol LeWitt
Richard Prince
Matthew Ritchie
Kiki Smith
Jessica Stockholder

Mel Bochner
Everybody Is Full of Shit, 2012
Etching with aquatint,
56.5 x 76.8 cm
Edition of 20

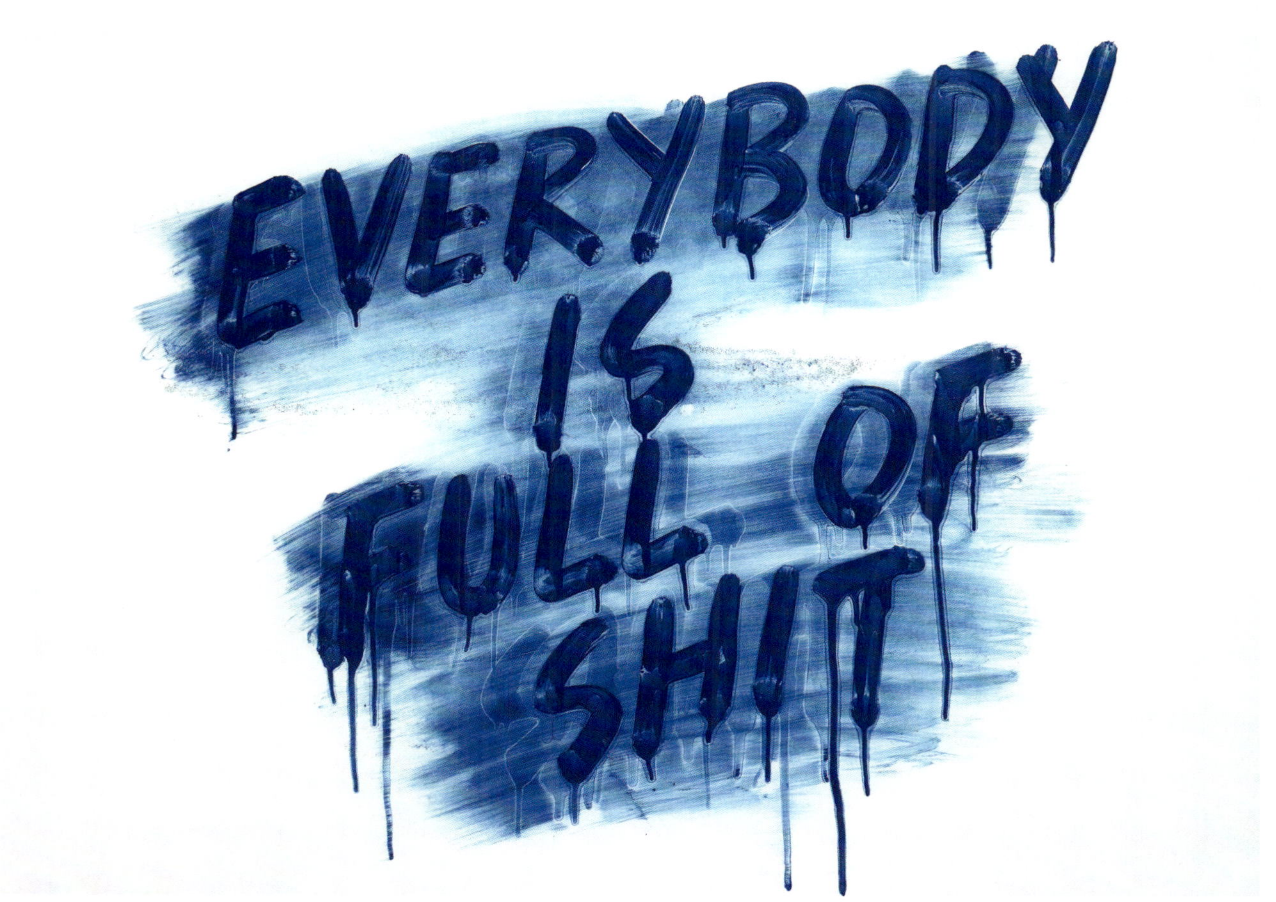
EVERYBODY
IS
FULL OF
SHIT

UNTITLED

Untitled
US-New York, NY 10002 | 30 Orchard Street
Phone +1 212 608 60 02 | Fax +1 212 608 60 02
info@nyuntitled.com | www.nyuntitled.com
Directors Carol Cohen
Joel Mesler

Artists at Art Nova | N. Dash
Ian Tweedy

Gallery Information | Exhibitions 2011/12:

Fall 2011: Ry Rocklen

Fall/Winter 2011: Joshua Neustein/ Sergej Jensen/N. Dash

Winter 2012: Ian Tweedy

Winter/Spring 2012: Henry Taylor

Spring 2012: N. Dash

Summer 2012: Sean Kennedy/Chadwick Rantanen

Fall 2012: Phil Wagner

Fall/Winter 2012: Joshua Neustein

Further artists represented:
David Adamo
Matthew Chambers
Brendan Fowler
Ry Rocklen
Henry Taylor
Phil Wagner

A | **N. Dash**
Groundings (SE), 2012
Adobe, jute, linen, wood support, 36 x 56 inches

B | **Ian Tweedy**
Fredrix, 2011
Oil on found canvas, 60 x 48 inches

A

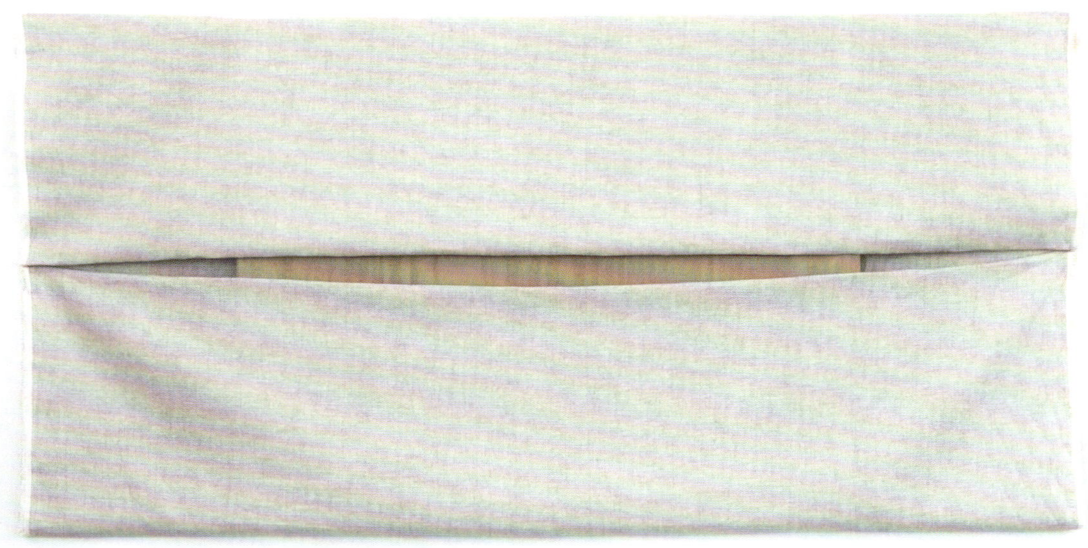

B

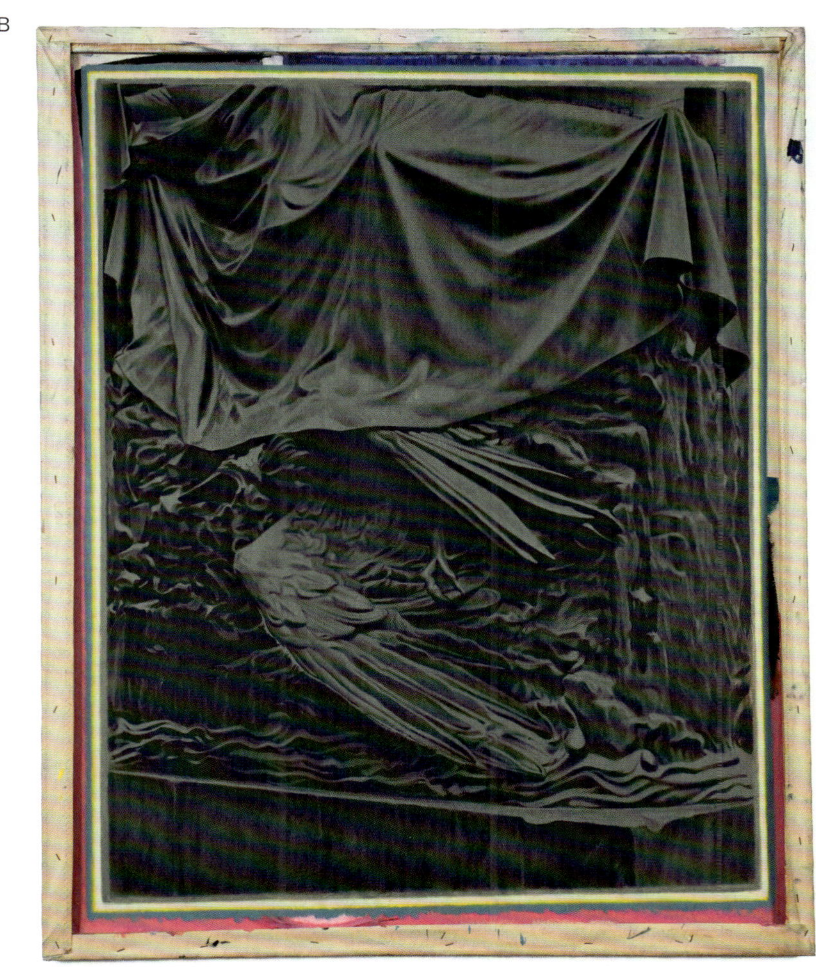

VALENTIN

Valentin
FR-75003 Paris | 9, rue Saint-Gilles
Phone +33 1 48 87 42 55 | Fax +33 6 12 06 24 02
galeriechezvalentin@noos.fr | www.galeriechezvalentin.com
Directors Frédérique Valentin
Philippe Valentin

Artists at Art Nova | David Douard
Luca Francesconi

Further artists represented | Pierre Ardouvin
Cécile Bart
Eric Baudart
Etienne Bossut
Babak Ghazi
Dominique Ghesquière
Aloïs Godinat
Laurent Grasso
George Henry Longly
Andrew Mania
Nicolas Moulin
Anne Neukamp
David Renggli
Joe Scanlan
Veit Stratmann
Niels Trannois
Donelle Woolford

Luca Francesconi (*1979, Milan, Italy) first presented this work at the 2011 Venice Biennale. In general, the work of Luca Francesconi is centered upon the search for the absolute, bringing art back to its most sacred intentions, whilst at the same time summoning our very immediate environment. Motivated by the idea of natural cycles, Luca Francesconi's installations seem to rebuild an ideal space where the primitive comes into dialogue with the present and where intuition's own pulse mimics the organic movement of the stars. This instinctive practice is deployed through the poetic usage of objects and forms that seem to have been eroded by time, constructing a primitive, spontaneous form of language which is kept at a distance from one's intellect.

David Douard (*1983, Paris, France) has been selected by Elena Filipovic for the Fondation d'entreprise Ricard Prize 2012. David Douard produces forms that play on current but outmoded means of modern communication and creativity, such as blogs, social networks, and advertising. Developed out of a profusion of materials, or fragments of manufactured objects, texts, images, advertising posters, raw and organic materials, his hybrid devices shift from the register of the most trivial low culture to that of the greater history of art and ideas. Having no hang-ups in relation to the references he manipulates with an often humorous or ironic irreverence, his radical artistic gestures are something of an appropriation or taking possession of reality as raw material, as a reservoir of pure forms.

David Douard
True Vision, 2012
Plaster, metal, wood, computer, ropes, glue, magazines, poster, 138 x 150 x 30 cm

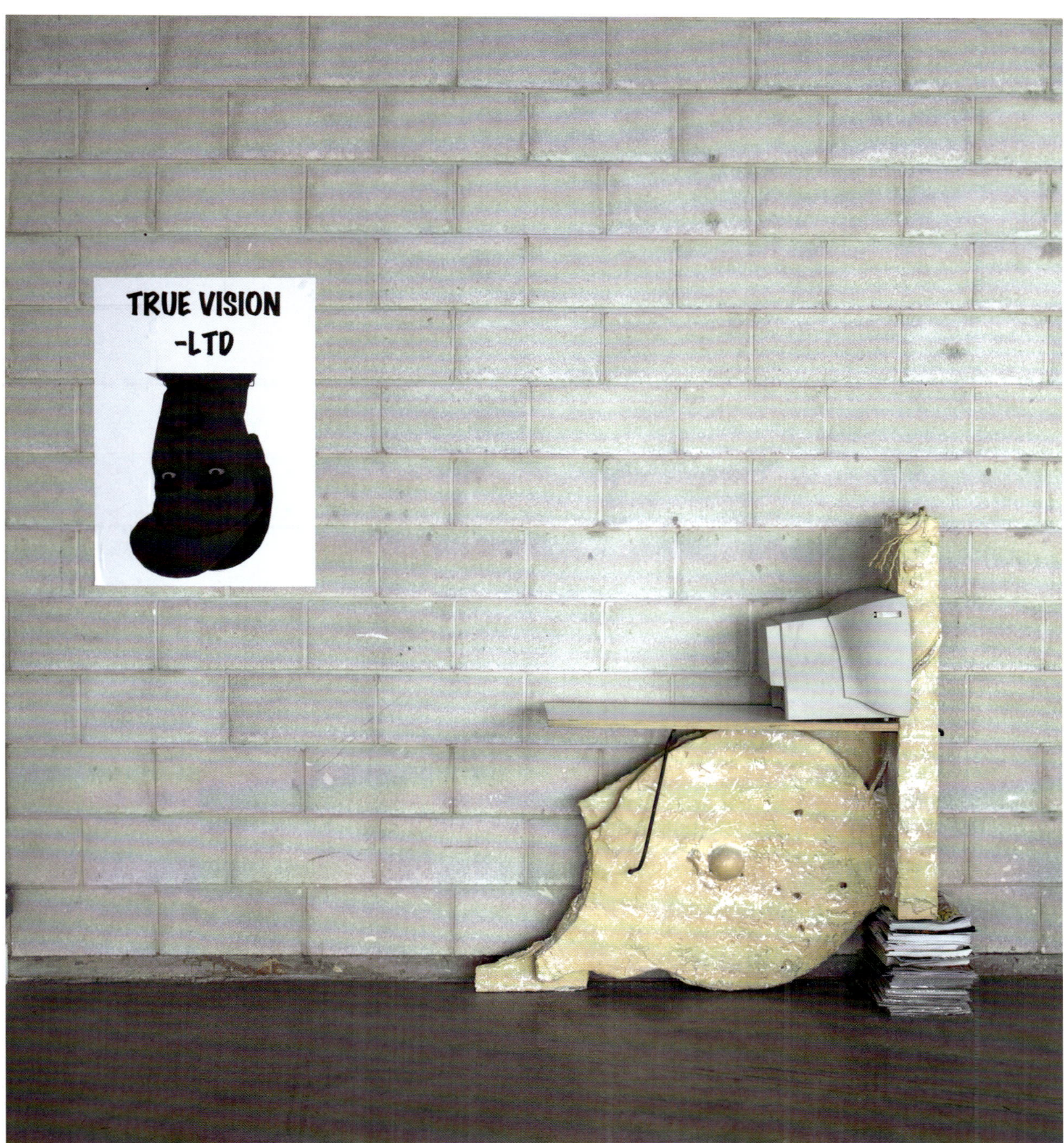
TRUE VISION
-LTD

VAN DE WEGHE

Van de Weghe Fine Art
US-New York, NY 10075 | 1018 Madison Avenue at 78th Street
Phone +1 212 744 19 00 | Fax +1 212 744 19 19
info@vdwny.com | www.vdwny.com
Director Christophe Van de Weghe

Artists at
Art Basel Miami Beach |
Jean-Michel Basquiat
Alexander Calder
Lucio Fontana
Duane Hanson
Damien Hirst
Donald Judd
Roy Lichtenstein
René Magritte
Bruce Nauman
Pablo Picasso
Richard Prince
Gerhard Richter
Ed Ruscha
Frank Stella
Rudolf Stingel
Cy Twombly
Andy Warhol
Tom Wesselmann
Christopher Wool

Gallery Information | Exhibitions:
Ed Ruscha Stains, 2011
With One Color, curated by Paul McCabe, 2011
Donald Judd, 2010
Alexander Calder, 2010
Jean-Michel Basquiat/Jean Dubuffet, 2010
Keith Haring, 2010
Duane Hanson, 2009
Frank Stella: Works on Canvas from the '60s, 2008
Duane Hanson: Housepainter, 2008
Warhol/Basquiat: Collaboration Paintings, 2008
Duane Hanson: Sculpture, 2007
Jean-Michel Basquiat: Works on Paper, 2007
René Magritte Paintings, 2006
Jean-Michel Basquiat: Heads, 2006
Andy Warhol: Black & White Paintings, 2005
Andy Warhol: Self-Portraits, 2005
Andy Warhol: Dollar Signs, 2004
Richard Long: Little Tejunga Canyon Line, 2004
Donald Judd: Single Stacks, 1964-1969, 2004
Ellsworth Kelly: Paintings, 2003
Jean Tinguely: The Witches, 2003
Alexander Calder: A Modern Definition of Space, 2003
Bruce Nauman: Neons, Sculptures, Drawings, 2002
Keith Haring: Tarps, 2002
Richard Serra: Prop Sculptures, 1969-1987, 2002
Alexander Calder, Richard Serra, Frank Stella, 2002
Andy Warhol: Guns, 2001
Andy Warhol: Works on Paper from the Early '60s, 2000

The Estate of Duane Hanson is represented by
Van de Weghe Fine Art.

Jean-Michel Basquiat
Bap, 1983
Acrylic, oilstick, and paper collage
on canvas mounted on tied wood
supports, 72 x 72 inches

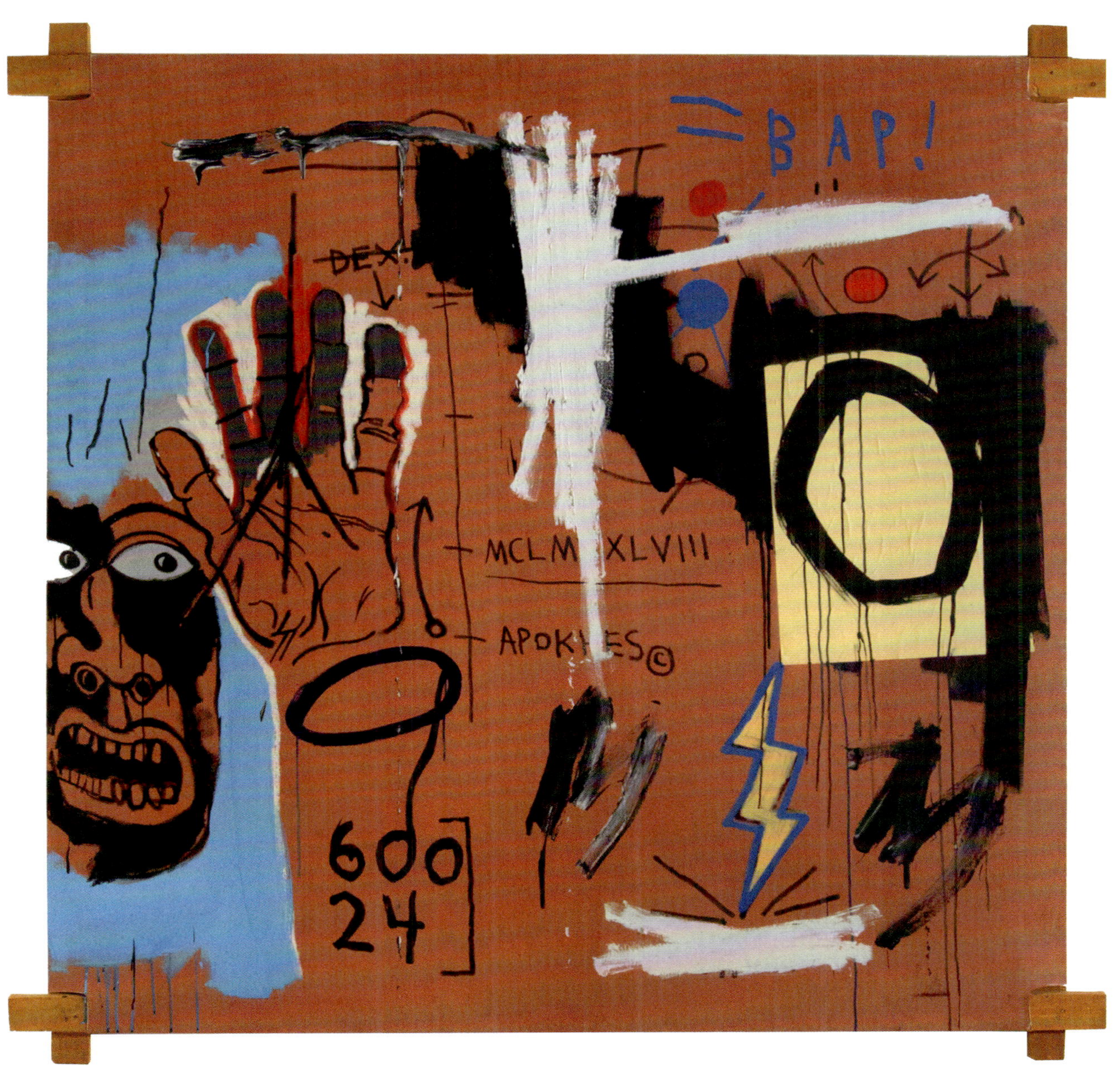
BAP!
DEX
600
24

VERMELHO

Mobile +55 11 996 31 02 50

Vermelho
BR-São Paulo 01244-010 | Rua Minas Gerais, 350
Phone +55 11 31 38 15 20 | Fax +55 11 31 38 15 29
info@galeriavermelho.com.br | www.galeriavermelho.com.br
Directors Eduardo Brandão
Eliana Finkelstein
Akio Aoki
Jan Fjeld

Artists at
Art Basel Miami Beach | **Chiara Banfi**
Marcelo Cidade
Marilá Dardot
Jonathas de Andrade
André Komatsu
Cinthia Marcelle
Odires Mlászho
Rosângela Rennó
Nicolás Robbio
Daniel Senise

Further artists represented | Gabriela Albergaria
Claudia Andujar
Rafael Assef
Nicolás Bacal
Rodrigo Braga
Cadu
Lia Chaia
Cia. Da Foto
Angela Detanico/Rafael Lain
Mauricio Dias/Walter Riedweg
Chelpa Ferro
Carmela Gross
Maurício Ianês
Dora Longo Bahia
João Loureiro
Leya Mira Brander
Fabio Morais
Gisela Motta/Leandro Lima
Guilherme Peters
Marco Paulo Rolla
Ana Maria Tavares
Carla Zaccagnini
Marcelo Zocchio

Chiara Banfi
Fireglo Tradicional, 2012
Paint and coat on ash wood,
160 x 110 x 7 cm

A

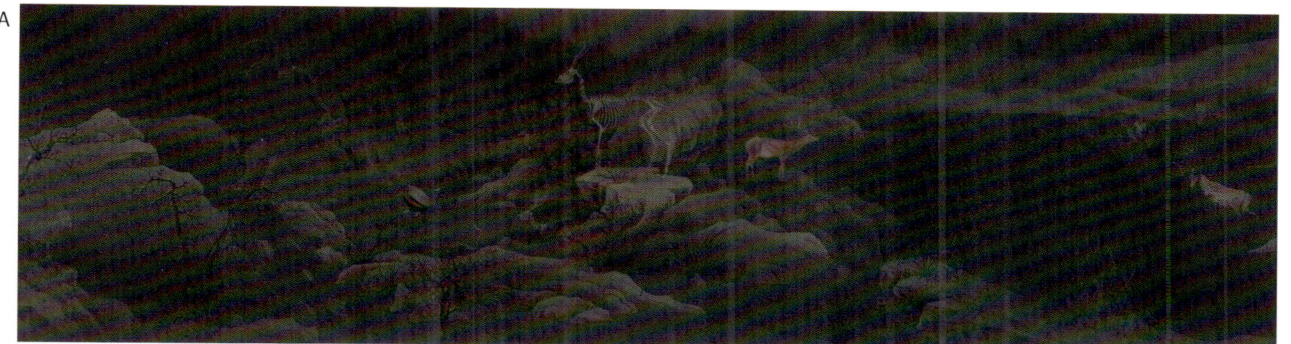

B

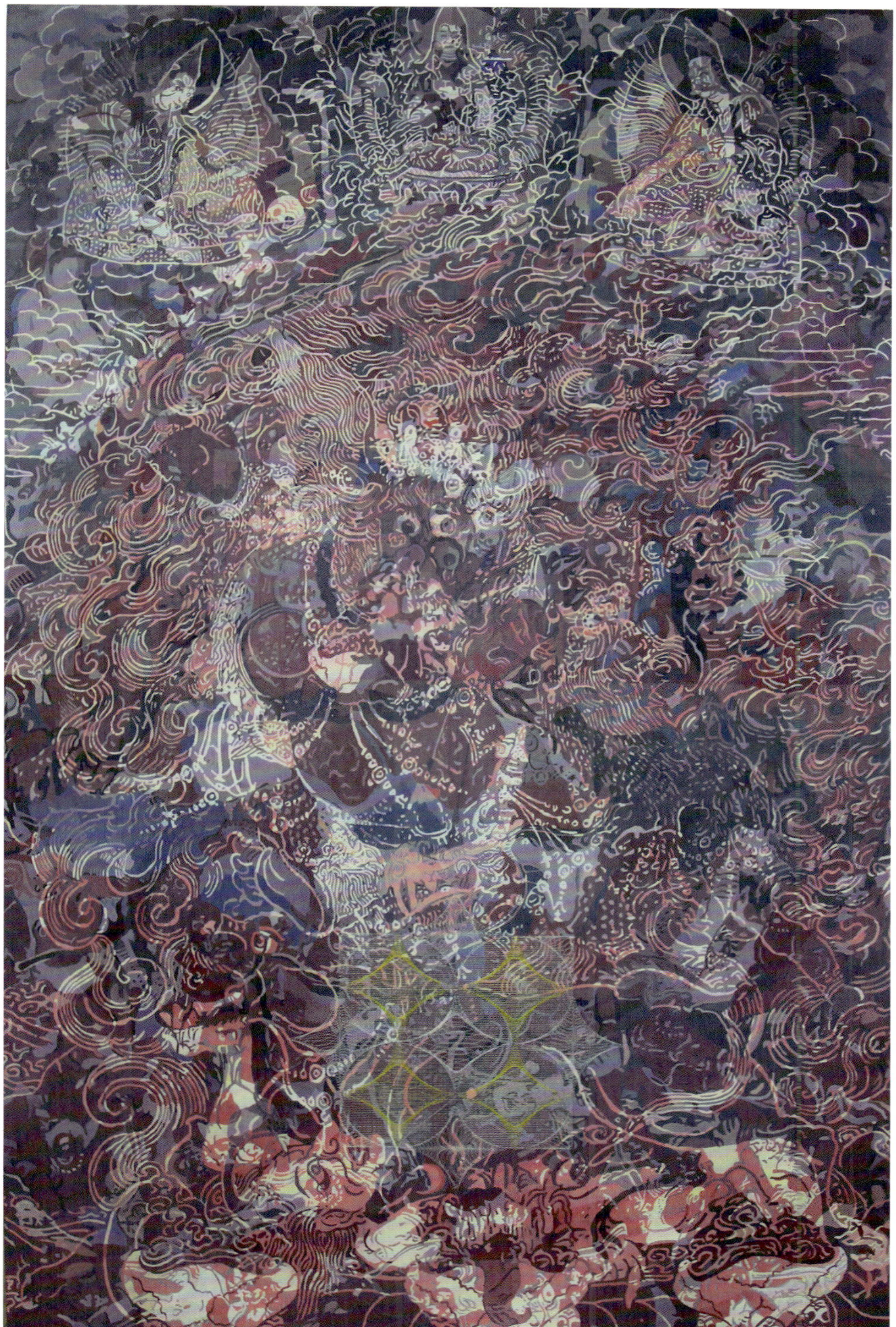

WADDINGTON CUSTOT

Mobile +44 78 24 77 20 28

Waddington Custot Galleries
GB-London W1S 3LT | 11 Cork Street
Phone +44 20 78 51 22 00 | Fax +44 20 77 34 41 46
mail@waddingtoncustot.com | www.waddingtoncustot.com
Directors Leslie Waddington
Stephane Custot

Artists at Art Basel Miami Beach | **Josef Albers**
Carl Andre
Milton Avery
Peter Blake
Patrick Caulfield
John Chamberlain
Ian Davenport
Jean Dubuffet
Barry Flanagan
Dan Flavin
Julio González
Peter Halley
Patrick Heron
Axel Hütte
Robert Indiana
Donald Judd
Sol LeWitt
Agnes Martin
Henri Matisse
Fausto Melotti
Joan Miró
Henry Moore
Ben Nicholson
Claes Oldenburg & Coosje van Bruggen
Mimmo Paladino
Francis Picabia
Pablo Picasso
Robert Rauschenberg
Susan Rothenberg
Lucas Samaras
Haim Steinbach
Frank Stella
Antoni Tàpies
Joe Tilson
William Turnbull
Andy Warhol
John Wesley
Bill Woodrow

Robert Indiana
LOVE
Violet Red, 1966-2000
Polychrome aluminum,
36 x 36 x 18 inches
Copy no. 4 of 6 + 4 AP

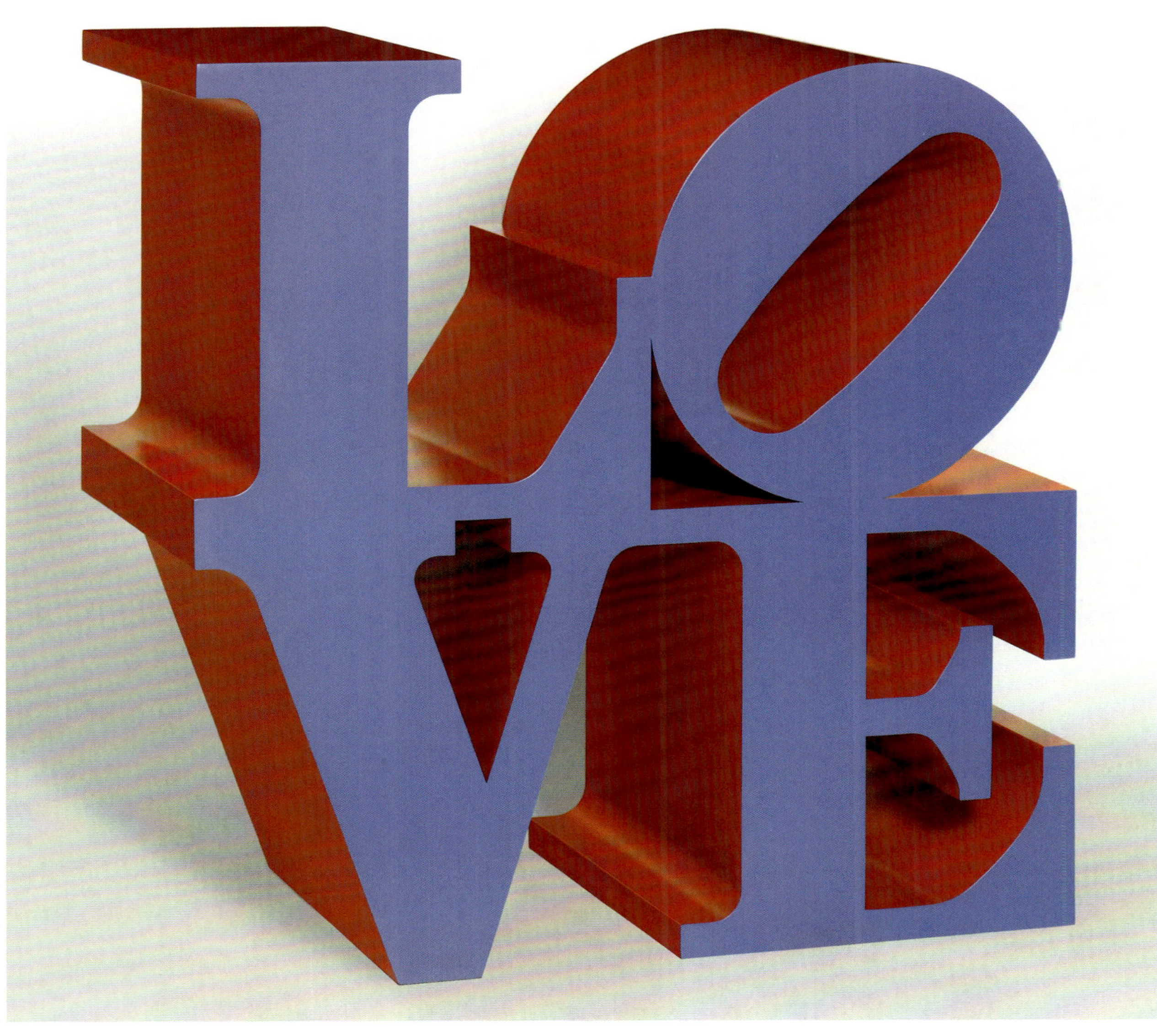
LOVE

WALLNER

Galleri Nicolai Wallner
DK-1760 Copenhagen | Ny Carlsberg Vej 68 OG
Phone +45 32 57 09 70 | Fax +45 32 57 09 71
nw@nicolaiwallner.com | www.nicolaiwallner.com
Directors Gitte Skjødt Madsen
Marie Gellert Jensen

Artists at Art Basel Miami Beach | **Michael Elmgreen & Ingar Dragset**
Dan Graham
Jeppe Hein
Chris Johanson
Jesper Just
Joachim Koester
Jakob Kolding
Peter Land
Jonathan Monk
Christoph Ruckhäberle
Christian Schmidt-Rasmussen
David Shrigley
Glenn Sorensen
Alexander Tovborg
Richard Tuttle
Gitte Villesen

Jonathan Monk
The World in Denim, 2012
Textile, 136 x 187 cm
Unique

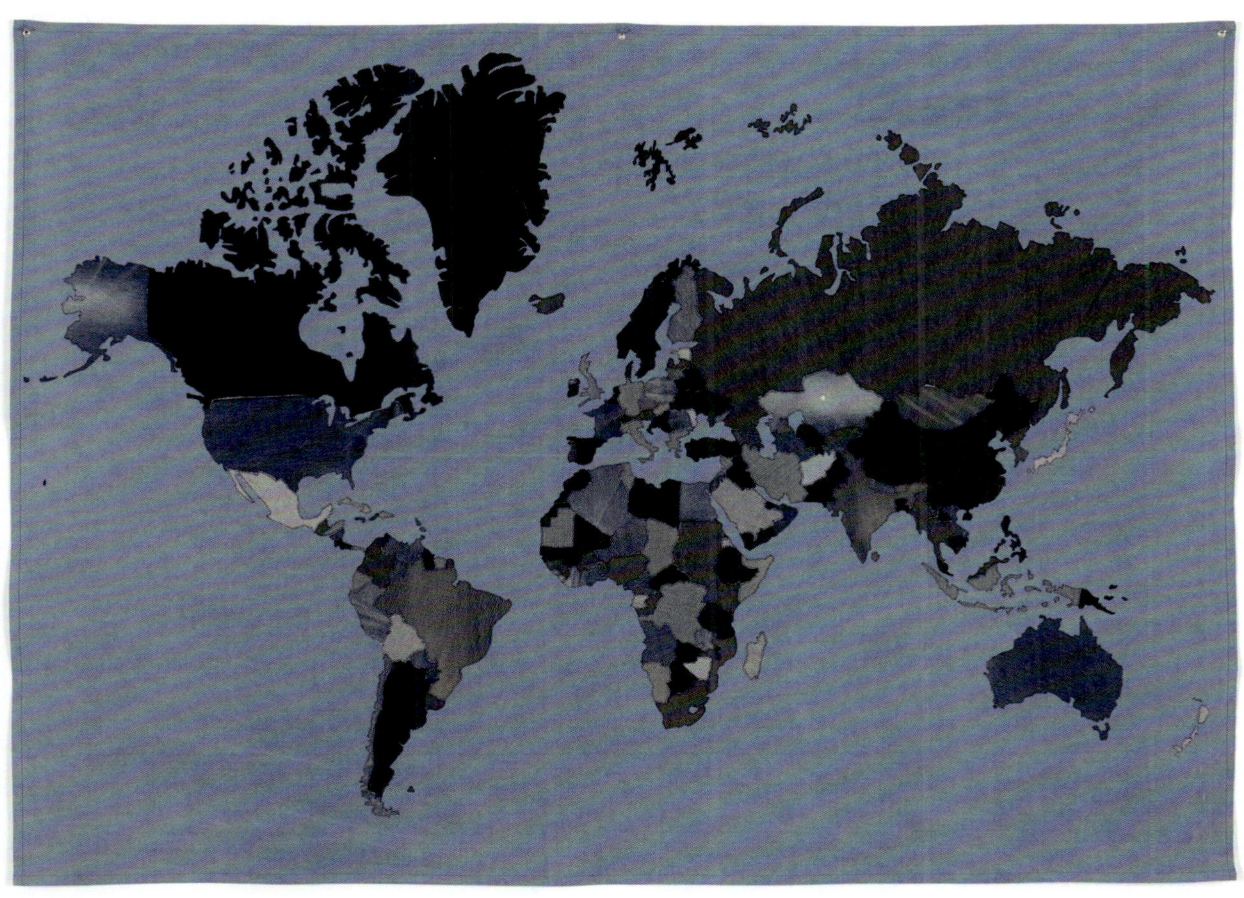

WALLSPACE

Mobile +1 917 355 96 35, +1 917 518 92 74

Wallspace
US-New York, NY 10001 | 619 West 27th Street
Phone +1 212 594 94 78 | Fax +1 212 594 98 05
info@wallspacegallery.com | www.wallspacegallery.com
Directors Janine Foeller
Jane Hait

Artists at Art Nova | John Divola
Harry Dodge

Harry Dodge
The Twin Paradox (In Six Dimensions), 2011
Zebra wood, paint, clamp, clear plastic sheeting, urethane,
24 x 30 x 8 cm

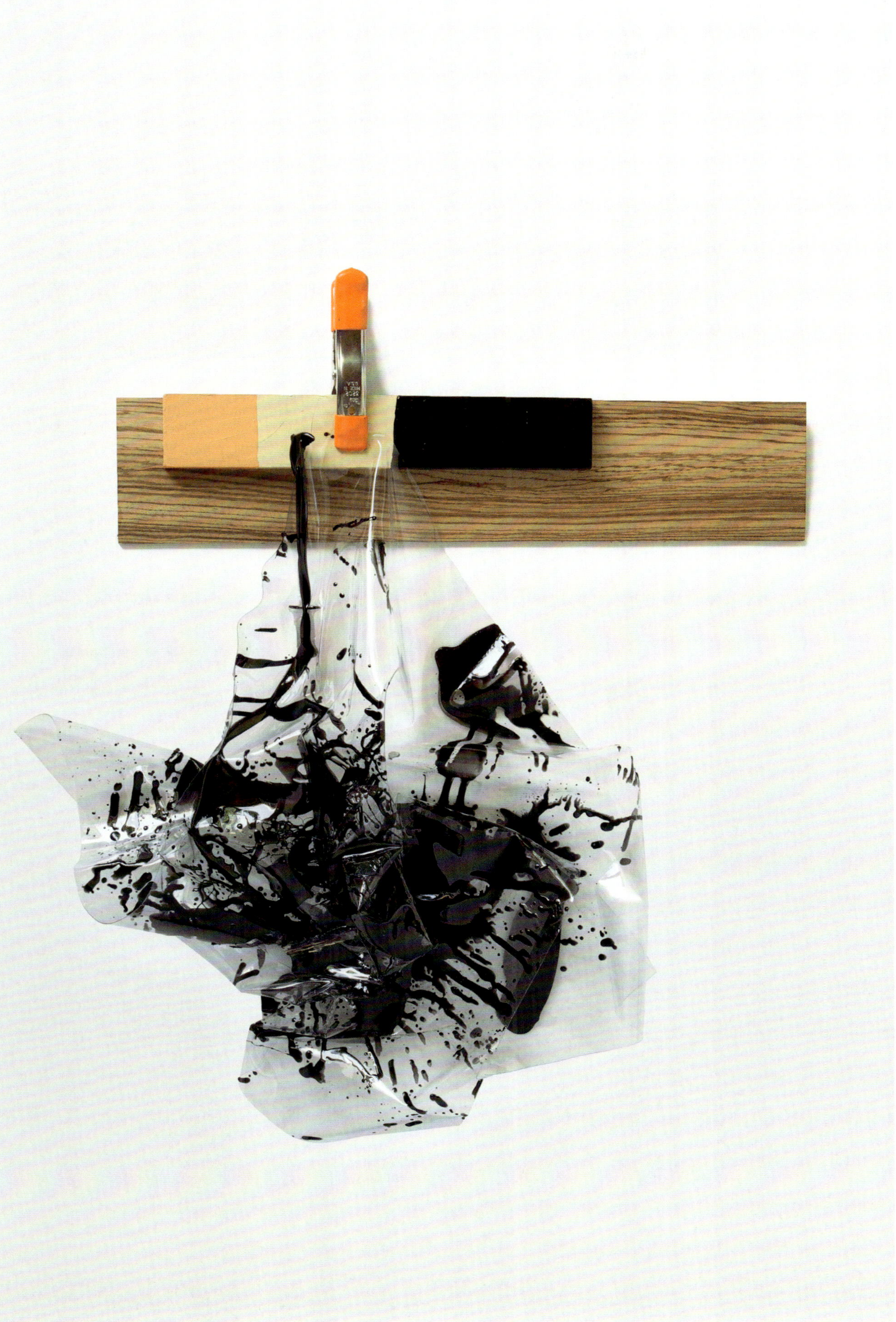

WASHBURN

Mobile +1 917 881 38 91

Washburn Gallery
US-New York, NY 10019 | 20 West 57th Street
Phone +1 212 397 67 80 | Fax +1 212 397 48 53
jwashburn@earthlink.net | www.washburngallery.com
Directors Joan Washburn
Brian Washburn

Artists at Art Basel Miami Beach | **Ilya Bolotowsky**
Nicolas Carone
Tom Levine
Gwynn Murrill
Doug Ohlson
Ray Parker
Jackson Pollock
Robert Rauschenberg
David Smith
Leon Polk Smith

Gallery Information | Founded in 1971, the Washburn Gallery exclusively represents works by Jackson Pollock from the Pollock-Krasner Foundation; the estates of Ilya Bolotowsky, Nicolas Carone, Alice Trumbull Mason, Doug Ohlson, Ray Parker, Anne Ryan, Myron Stout, Leon Polk Smith, and David Smith (1930s and 1940s paintings). The gallery also represents contemporary artists including Tom Levine, Gwynn Murrill, and Jack Youngerman.

Exhibitions 2010-2012:

Gwynn Murrill: Sixty-Five Animal Maquettes: Cats, Dogs, Birds, Deer and Bighorn Rams
May 17-July 20, 2012

Jackson Pollock Graphic Work: Intaglios and Screenprints
April 5-May 12, 2012

Nicolas Carone – Paintings from the 1950s
February 2-March 31, 2012

Ray Parker (1922-1990) – Simple Paintings from the 1960s
November 17, 2011-January 28, 2012

Doug Ohlson (1936-2010) – Panel Paintings from the 1960s
September 15-November 12, 2011

Leon Polk Smith – 50 Years of Separation: Paintings from the 1940s and the 1990s
April 7-June 30, 2011

Jackson Pollock – Drawings on Paper and Canvas
January 13-March 26, 2011

Stuart Davis and George Sugarman – 'Shapes' of the Space
October 1-December 18, 2010

Nicolas Carone – Paintings from the 1950s
Gallery II: *Jackson Pollock – Works on Paper*
April 1-May 29, 2010

Tom Levine – String Instruments & Other Recent Works
January 21-March 27, 2010

Further artists represented:
James Abbe
Rosalind Bengelsdorf
Oscar Bluemner
Norman Bluhm
Patrick Henry Bruce
Alexander Calder
Mary Callery
Arthur B. Carles
Marjorie Content
Stuart Davis
Willem de Kooning
Burgoyne Diller
Arthur Dove
Werner Drewes
Albert E. Gallatin
Fritz Glarner
Arshile Gorky
John Graham
Balcomb Greene
Gertrude Greene
Marsden Hartley
William Hill
Harry Holtzman
Joshua Johnson
Paul Kelpe
Conrad Kramer
Man Ray
John Marin
Alice Trumbull Mason
George L.K. Morris
Georgia O'Keeffe
Ammi Phillips
Richard Pousette-Dart
Mark Rothko
Morgan Russell
Anne Ryan
Rolph Scarlett
Louis Schanker
John Sennhauser
Niles Spencer
Alfred Stieglitz
Myron Stout
Jean Xceron
Jack Youngerman

Ray Parker
Untitled, 1963
Oil on canvas, 49 x 54 cm

WENTRUP

Wentrup
DE-10963 Berlin | Tempelhofer Ufer 22
Phone +49 30 48 49 36 00 | Fax +49 30 48 49 36 01
mail@wentrupgallery.com | www.wentrupgallery.com
Directors Jan Wentrup
Tina Wentrup
Sascha Welchering

Artists at Art Nova | Cristian Andersen
Florian Meisenberg

Further artists represented | Nevin Aladag
Miriam Böhm
Axel Geis
Mathew Hale
Gregor Hildebrandt
Jen Ray
David Renggli
Wawrzyniec Tokarski
Timm Ulrichs

Florian Meisenberg's paintings – mainly oil on canvas, sometimes on a stretcher, and often just suspended on a wall – are united in their bright colors and an unmistakably comic yet everyday poetic visual language. Cristian Andersen's sculptures also use everyday objects which are put into new grotesque contexts. The two artists not only share common ground in their playful approach to the *conditio humana,* but also their practice of deconstructing the plethora of objects of this world into their parts.

In Meisenberg's works, the beholder is confronted with individual body parts – arms, legs, eyes, noses, mustaches. His grotesque faces dissolve into pastel patchwork rugs or mere smudges left by the oil paints on the untreated canvas. With a playful flippancy, Meisenberg produces paintings that engage in a casual manner with their own medium. Part of this is manifest in the paintings' presentation on small cornices, which thus consciously simulate (both real and metaphoric) weightiness, making fun of the notion of their sublimity.

Cristian Andersen, on the other hand, brings together scattered fragments of the material world into the fixed form of sculpture. Here, the medium of ceramics plays a key role: the porcelain-white sculptures are fragile and at risk. Yet, the value of the ceramics stands in contrast with the depiction of trash and objects that seem banal and random. Figurative and abstract elements are piled on top of one another to form an unstable assemblage. The issue, for the artist, lies in the tension between figuration and abstraction, and in the question of how to bring these fragments into balance without having them collapse.

Both artists are quite aware of the material as the precondition of their medium. The canvas, which Meisenberg likes to replace with printed lengths of fabric, always remains visible in terms of structure: it peeps through and sometimes functions as a foundation and then as a surface for playful formal experiments. On the whole, Meisenberg's works in their generous colorfulness are steeped in a perceptible dynamism. In Andersen's sculptures, the dynamism is given a contour, and at the same time, the individual objects oscillate between stasis and movement.

Florian Meisenberg
from the series: magic moments of homeopathy, 2011
Oil on canvas, 245 x 200 cm

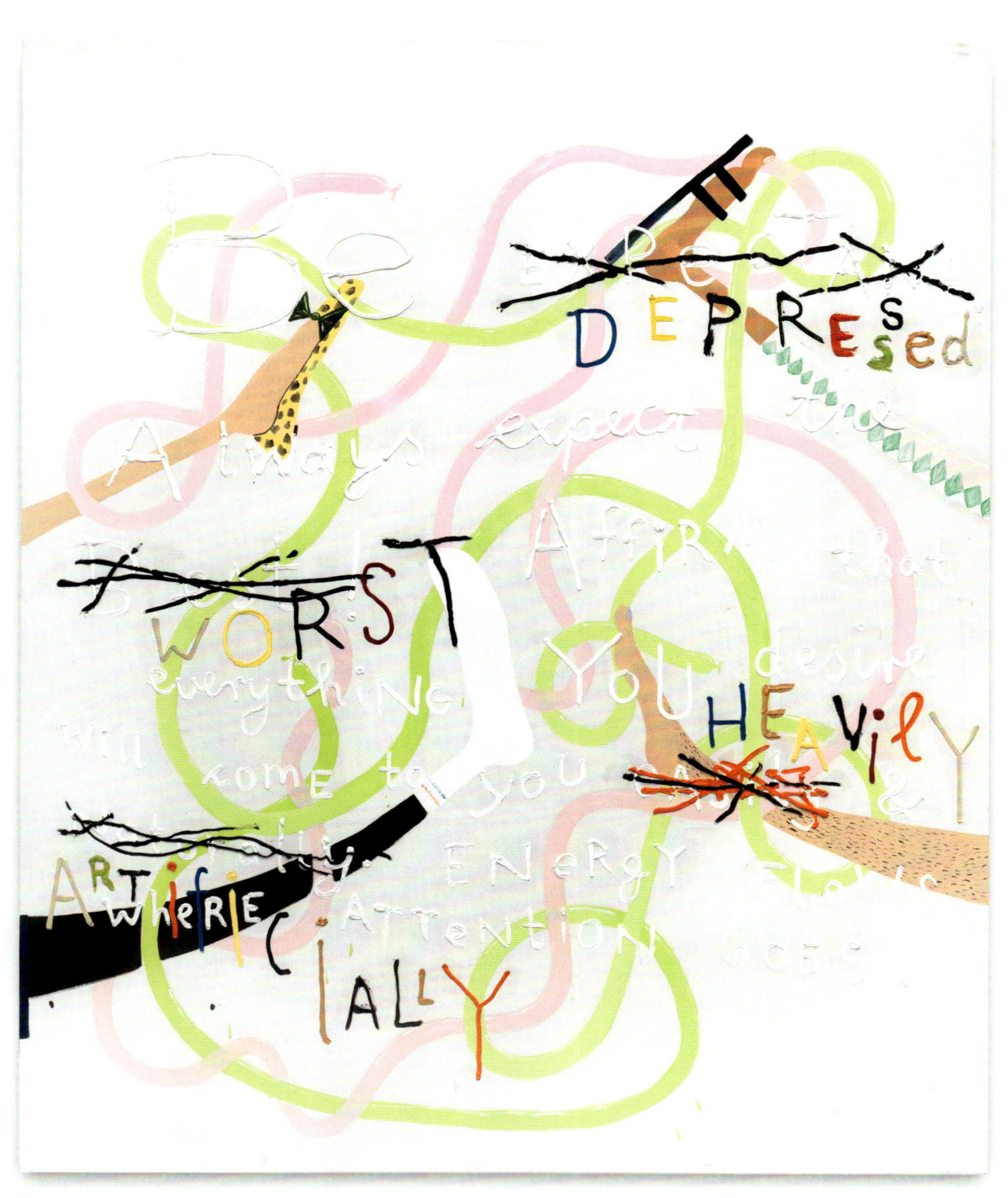
Always expect the
WORST
everything
YOU
desire
HEAVily
come to you
Energy
Attention goes
ALLY

WERNER

Michael Werner
US-New York, NY 10075 | 4 East 77th Street
Phone +1 212 988 16 23 | Fax +1 212 988 17 74
info@michaelwerner.com | www.michaelwerner.com
Directors Justine Birbil
Birte Kleemann
Kadee Robbins
Harry Scrymgeour
Gordon VeneKlasen

Michael Werner
GB-London W1K 7PZ | 22 Upper Brook Street
Phone +44 20 74 95 68 55
info@michaelwerner.com | www.michaelwerner.com

Artists at
Art Basel Miami Beach | **Hurvin Anderson**
Georg Baselitz
Marcel Broodthaers
James Lee Byars
Aaron Curry
Enrico David
Peter Doig
Jörg Immendorff
Per Kirkeby
Eugène Leroy
Markus Lüpertz
Ernst Wilhelm Nay
A.R. Penck
Sigmar Polke
Don Van Vliet

Further artists represented | Hans Arp
Joseph Beuys
Ernst Ludwig Kirchner
Wilhelm Lehmbruck
Piero Manzoni
Francis Picabia
Kurt Schwitters

Per Kirkeby
Untitled, 2011
Oil on canvas, 200 x 140 cm

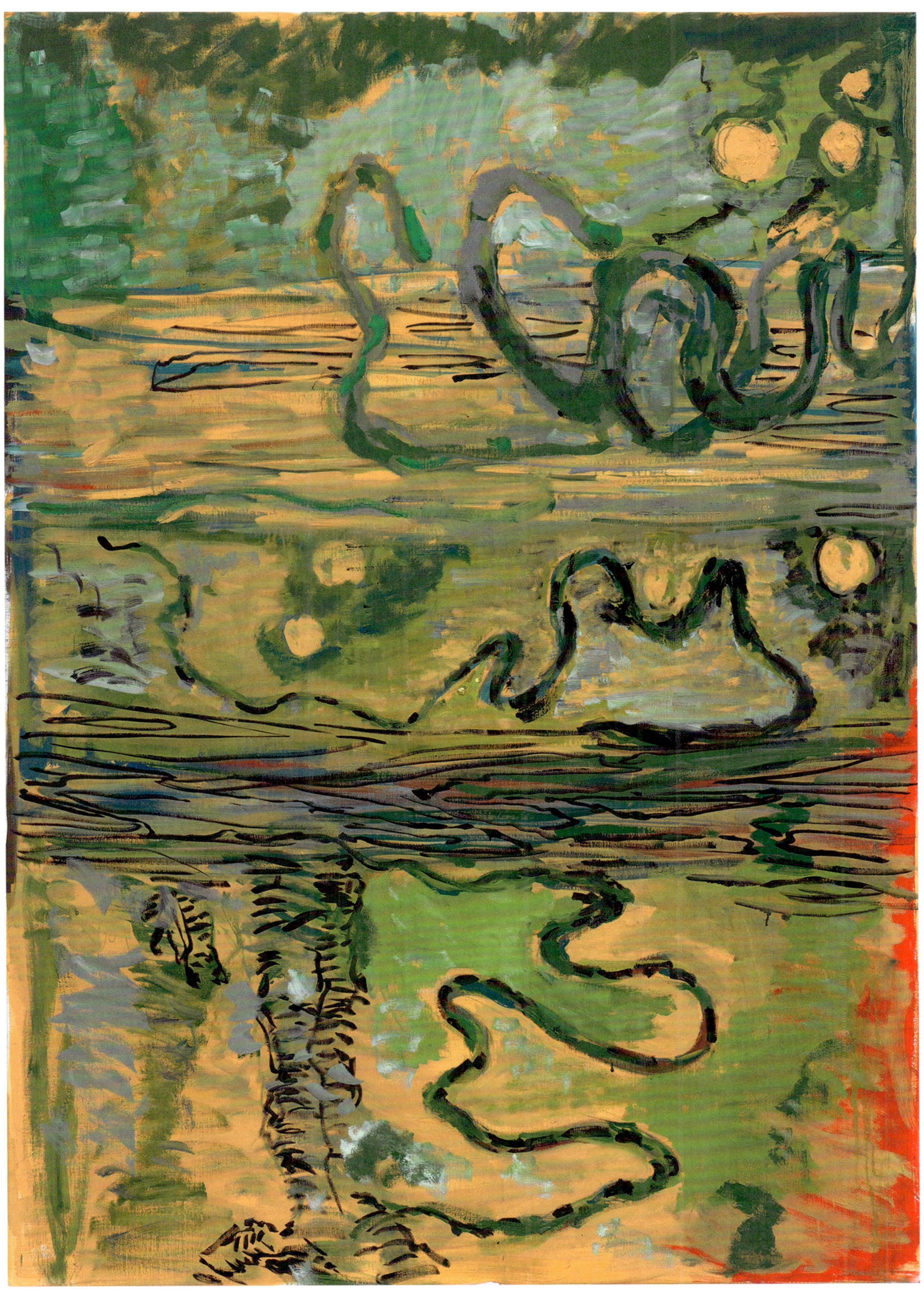

WHITE CUBE

White Cube
GB-London N1 6PB | 48 Hoxton Square
Phone +44 20 79 30 53 73 | Fax +44 20 77 49 74 80
enquiries@whitecube.com | www.whitecube.com
Directors Jay Jopling
Daniela Gareh
Tim Marlow
Susan May
Andrea Schlieker

White Cube
GB-London SW1Y 6BU | 25-26 Mason's Yard St James's
Phone +44 20 79 30 53 73 | Fax +44 20 77 49 74 80
enquiries@whitecube.com | www.whitecube.com
Directors Jay Jopling
Daniela Gareh
Tim Marlow
Susan May
Andrea Schlieker

White Cube
GB-London SE1 3TQ | 144-152 Bermondsey Street
Phone +44 20 79 30 53 73 | Fax +44 20 77 49 74 80
enquiries@whitecube.com | www.whitecube.com
Directors Jay Jopling
Daniela Gareh
Tim Marlow
Susan May
Andrea Schlieker

White Cube
CN-Hong Kong | 50 Connaught Road, Central
Phone +852 25 92 20 00
enquiries@whitecube.com | www.whitecube.com
Directors Jay Jopling
Daniela Gareh
Tim Marlow
Susan May
Graham Steele
Laura Zhou

Artists represented | Franz Ackermann
Darren Almond
Ellen Altfest
Miroslaw Balka
Georg Baselitz
Ashley Bickerton
Mark Bradford
Candice Breitz
Ernesto Caivano
Jake & Dinos Chapman
Chuck Close
Gregory Crewdson
Tracey Emin
Katharina Fritsch
Theaster Gates
Gilbert & George
Antony Gormley
Andreas Gursky
Mona Hatoum
Eberhard Havekost
Damien Hirst
Gary Hume
Robert Irwin
Runa Islam
Sergej Jensen
Anselm Kiefer
Rachel Kneebone
Friedrich Kunath
Elad Lassry
Liza Lou
Christian Marclay
Kris Martin
Josiah McElheny
Julie Mehretu
Harland Miller
Sarah Morris
Gabriel Orozco
Damián Ortega
Richard Phillips
Magnus Plessen
Marc Quinn
Jessica Rankin
Robin Rhode
Doris Salcedo
Raqib Shaw
Haim Steinbach
Neal Tait
Sam Taylor-Wood
Fred Tomaselli
Jeff Wall
Cerith Wyn Evans
Zhang Huan

Antony Gormley
Stay III, 2012
6mm square key steel,
dimensions variable

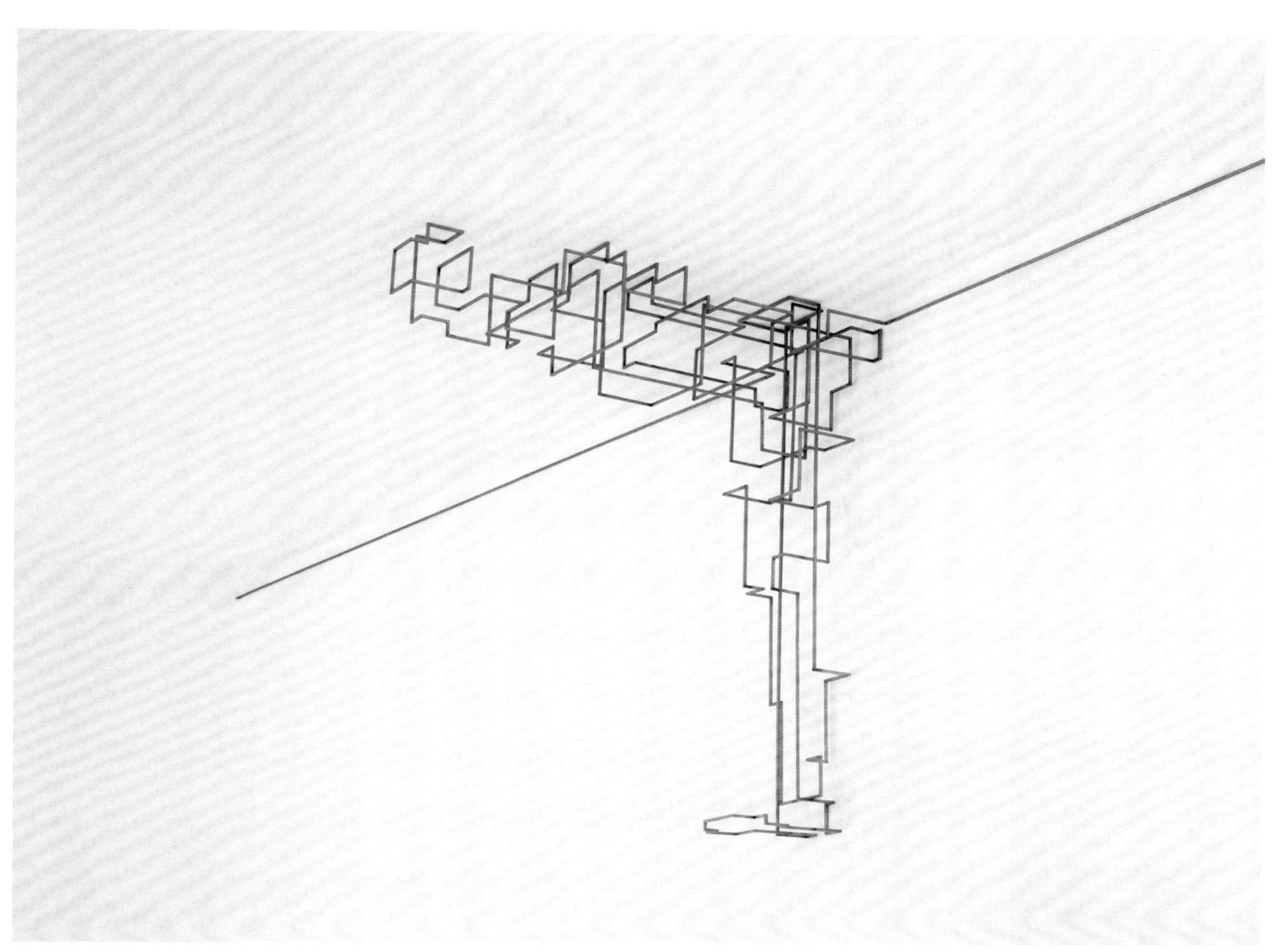

ZENO X

Zeno X Gallery
BE-2000 Antwerp | Leopold De Waelplaats 16
Phone +32 3 216 38 88 | Fax +32 3 216 09 92
info@zeno-x.com | www.zeno-x.com
Director Frank Demaegd

Zeno X Storage
BE-2140 Antwerp | Appelstraat 37
Phone +32 3 216 38 88 | Fax +32 3 216 09 92
info@zeno-x.com | www.zeno-x.com
Director Frank Demaegd

Artists at Art Basel Miami Beach | **Michaël Borremans**
Dirk Braeckman
Raoul De Keyser
Jan De Maesschalck
Stan Douglas
Marlene Dumas
Kees Goudzwaard
Noritoshi Hirakawa
Ji Yun-Fei
Kim Jones
Johannes Kahrs
Naoto Kawahara
John Körmeling
Mark Manders
Jockum Nordström
Jenny Scobel
Maria Serebriakova
Bart Stolle
Luc Tuymans
Patrick Van Caeckenbergh
Anne-Mie Van Kerckhoven
Jack Whitten
Cristof Yvoré

Jack Whitten
Loop # 29 (Broken Circle), 2012
Acrylic on panel, 20.3 x 20.3 cm

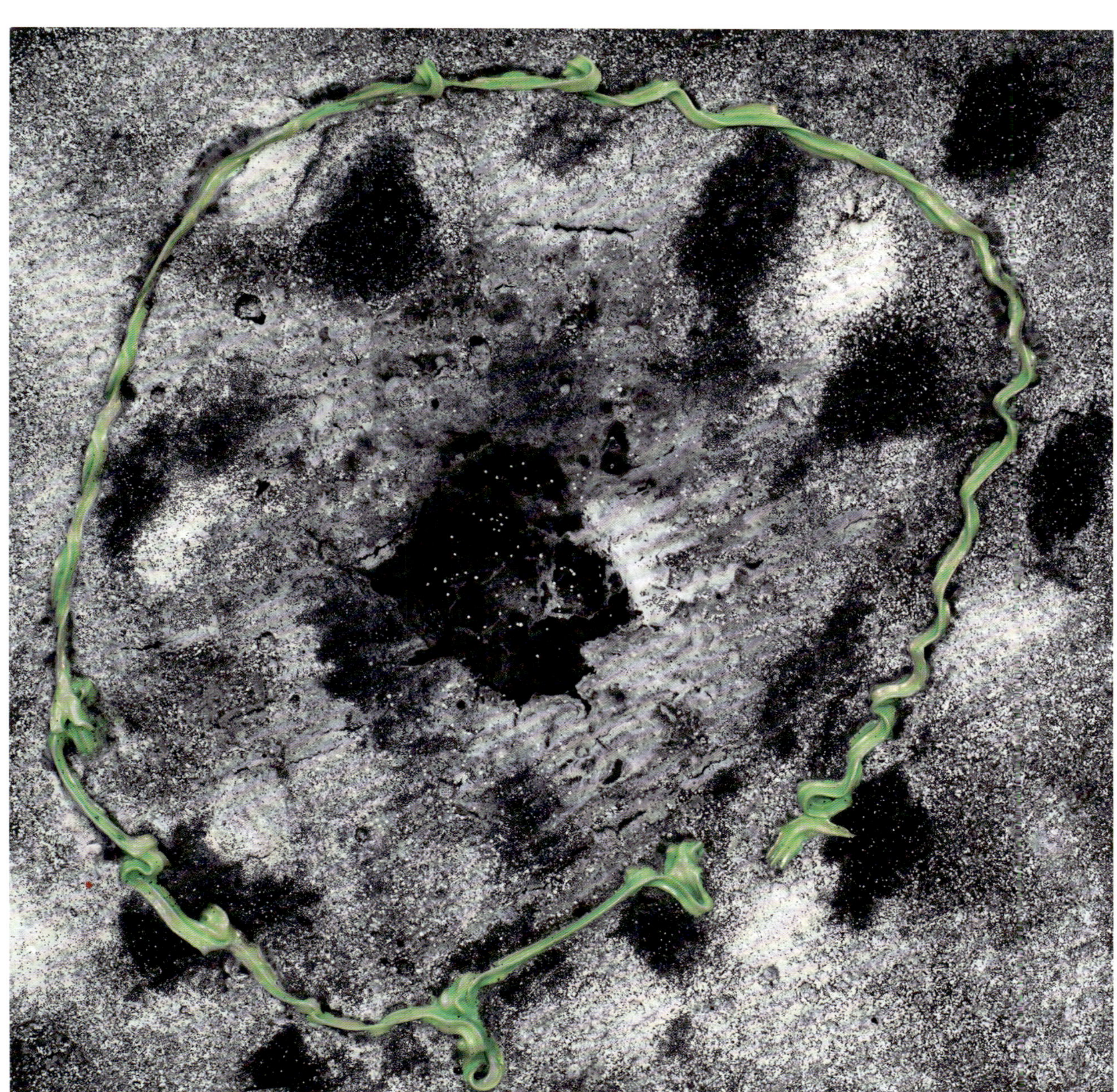

ZERO

ZERO...
IT-20124 Milan | Via Tadino 20
Phone +39 02 87 23 45 77 | Fax +39 02 87 23 45 80
info@galleriazero.it | www.galleriazero.it
Director Paolo Zani

Artists at Art Basel Miami Beach | **Giorgio Andreotta Calò**
Micol Assaël
Mark Barrow
Neïl Beloufa
Cezary Bodzianowski
Anthony Burdin
Hubert Duprat
Christian Frosi
Giuseppe Gabellone
Francesco Gennari
Massimo Grimaldi
João Maria Gusmão & Pedro Paiva
Thomas Houseago
Andrea Kvas
Victor Man
Pietro Roccasalva
Michael Sailstorfer
Hans Schabus
Shimabuku
Gedi Sibony
Michael E. Smith

Victor Man
Untitled, 2011
Pencil on paper, 29.7 x 21 cm

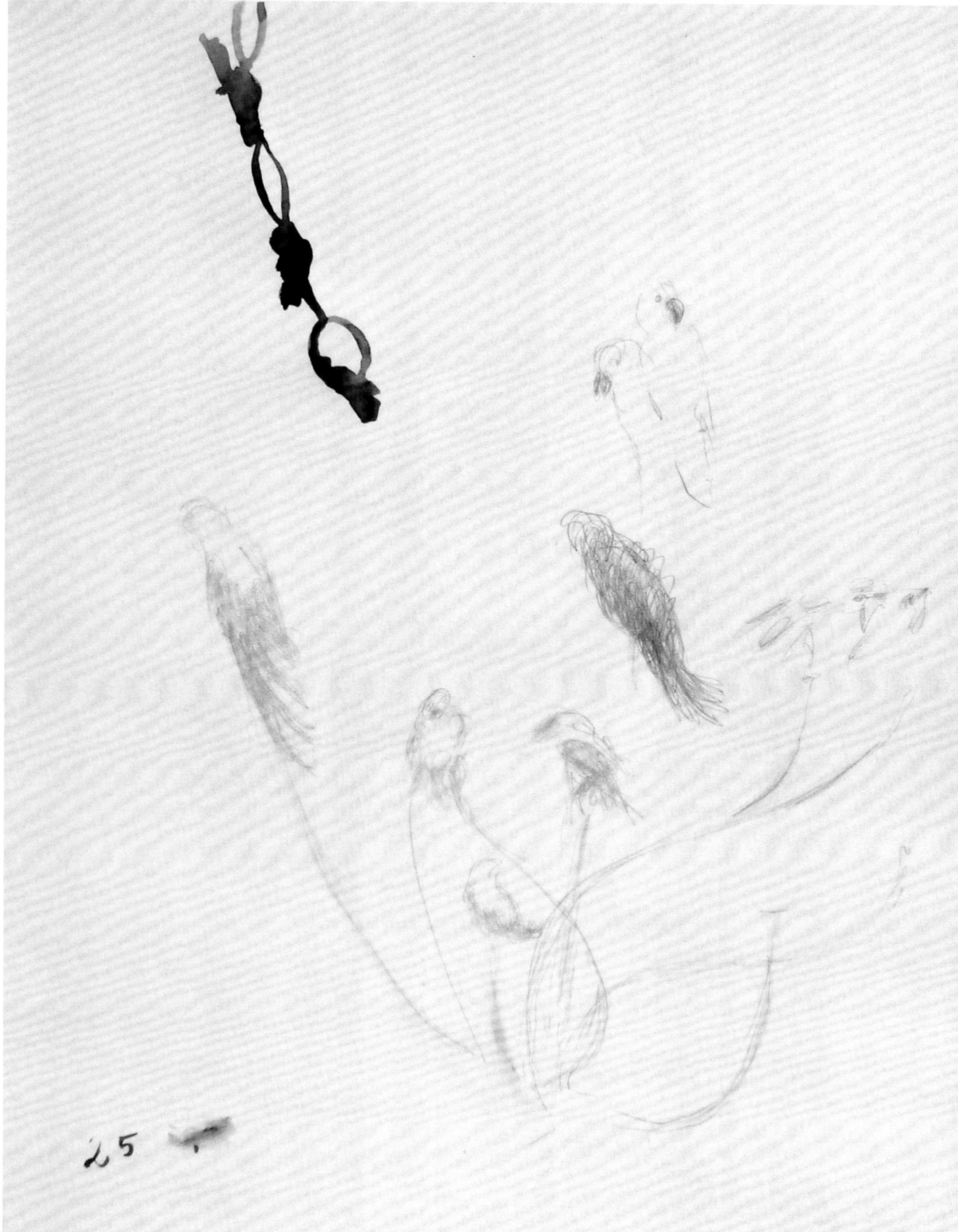
25

ZWIRNER

Mobile +1 917 297 82 34

David Zwirner
US-New York, NY 10011 | 525 West 19th Street
Phone +1 212 727 20 70 | +1 212 517 86 77 | Fax +1 212 727 20 72 | +1 212 517 89 59
information@davidzwirner.com | www.davidzwirner.com
Directors Kristine Bell
Angela Choon
Justine Durrett
Bellatrix Hubert
Greg Lulay
Ales Ortuzar
Hanna Schouwink

David Zwirner
GB-London W1S 4EZ | 24 Grafton Street
Phone +44 20 35 38 31 65
www.davidzwirner.com

Artists at
Art Basel Miami Beach | **Adel Abdessemed**
Francis Alÿs
Mamma Andersson
Michaël Borremans
Carol Bove
Raoul De Keyser
Philip-Lorca diCorcia
Stan Douglas
Marlene Dumas
Marcel Dzama
Dan Flavin
Suzan Frecon
Isa Genzken
Donald Judd
John McCracken
Alice Neel
Neo Rauch
Jason Rhoades
Michael Riedel
Thomas Ruff
Fred Sandback
Al Taylor
Luc Tuymans
James Welling
Christopher Williams
Lisa Yuskavage

Gallery Information | Further artists represented: Tomma Abts
R. Crumb
On Kawara
Toba Khedoori
Gordon Matta-Clark
Jockum Nordström
Chris Ofili
Raymond Pettibon
Daniel Richter
Katy Schimert
Yutaka Sone
Diana Thater
Doug Wheeler
Yan Pei-Ming

Works by: Carl Andre
John Baldessari
Georg Baselitz
Bernd & Hilla Becher
Larry Bell
Joseph Beuys
Marcel Broodthaers
Chris Burden
John Chamberlain
Christo
Bruce Conner
Joseph Cornell
Hanne Darboven
Jan Dibbets
Robert Gober
Felix Gonzalez-Torres
Dan Graham
Rodney Graham
Andreas Gursky
David Hammons
Mary Heilmann
Eva Hesse
Konrad Klapheck
Jeff Koons
Joseph Kosuth
Lee Lozano
Brice Marden
Agnes Martin
Claes Oldenburg
Francis Picabia
Richard Prince
Gerhard Richter
Dieter Roth
Ed Ruscha
Thomas Schütte
Richard Serra
Andy Warhol

Michael Riedel
Untitled (Circle), 2012
Silkscreen on linen,
90½ x 67 x 2¼ inches

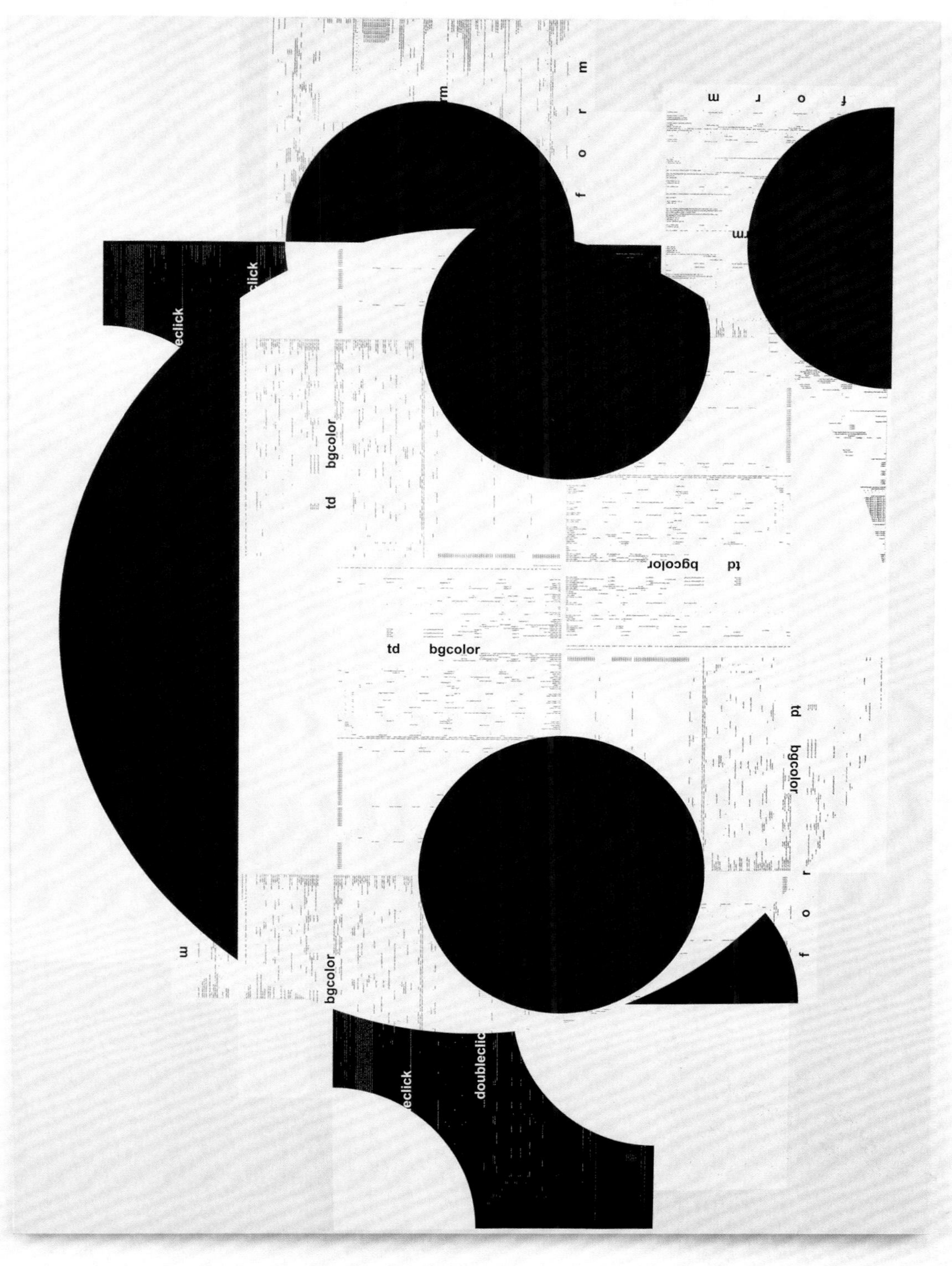
td bgcolor
td bgcolor
td bgcolor
td bgcolor
bgcolor
f o r m
f o r
eclick
doubleclic

Art | Magazines

ART MAGAZINES Booth **Q1-Q24**

Aesthetica | Aesthetica Magazine | Aesthetica Magazine Ltd
GB-York YO1 7HE | Exhibition Square
Phone +44 1904 629137 | Fax +44 1904 622831
bethany@aestheticamagazine.com | www.aestheticamagazine.com

AGMA | AGMA | AGMA
AT-1040 Vienna | Trappelgasse 9/9
Phone +39 335 475633
info@agmamagazine.com | www.agmamagazine.com

Annual | Annual | A.P.C. Trading Limited
CY-1703 Nicosia | 12 Kennedy Avenue
Phone +357 22 767630 | Fax +357 22 760918
pk@annualartmagazine.com | www.annualartmagazine.com

Art & Deal | Art & Deal | Art & Deal Publications
IN-110016 New Delhi | 23, Hauz Khas Village
Phone +91 11 26531819
siddhartathagore@gmail.com | artanddeal@gmail.com | www.artanddealmagazine.com

Art + Antiques | Art + Antiques | Art + Antiques World Wide Media, LLC
US-Wilmington, NC 28405 | 1319 cc Military Cutoff Road, Suite 192
Phone +1 910 6794402 | Fax +1 919 8691864
info@artandantiquesmag.com | www.artandantiquesmag.com

Art + Auction | Art + Auction | Louise Blouin Media
US-New York, NY 10001 | 601 West 26th Street
Phone +1 917 8044642 | Fax +1 212 627 41 75
kshanley@artinfo.com | www.artinfo.com

Art in America | Art in America | Brant Publications
US-New York, NY 10012 | 110 Greene Street
Phone +1 212 9412800 | Fax +1 212 9412870
dreddy@brantpub.com | www.artinamericamagazine.com

Art in China | Art in China | IAC Foundation
CN-100015 Beijing | E06, 798 Art Zone, No. 4 Jiuxianqiao Road, Chaoyang District
Phone +86 10 51031 3654 | +34 61 8696 4631 | Fax +86 10 59789041
artinchinaredaccion@hotmail.com | www.artinchina.es

Art Issue | Art Issue | Art Issue Project
CN-100015 Beijing | No. A1 Beigao, Cuigezhuang County, Chaoyang District
Phone +86 10 64340266 | Fax +86 10 64333266
info@art-issue.com | www.art-issue.com

art ltd. | art ltd. magazine | Lifescapes Publishing, Inc.
US-Los Angeles, CA 91364 | 5525 Oakdale Avenue, Suite 160
Phone +1 818 3160900 | Fax +1 818 7022500
peterf@artltdmag.com | www.artltdmag.com

ART PAPERS | ART PAPERS | ART PAPERS, Inc.
US-Atlanta, GA 30307 | 1083 Austin Avenue, NE, Suite 206
Phone +1 404 5881837-18 | Fax +1 404 5881836
director@artpapers.org | www.artpapers.org

Art Ukraine | Art Ukraine | Art Ukraine LTD
UA-01010 Kiev | 10, Lavszka st
Phone +38 44 2885225 | Fax +38 44 2885225
editor@artukraine.com.ua | nastyaplatonova@yandex.ru | www.artukraine.com.ua

artam | artam Global Art & Design | Artam Antik A.S.
TR-34357 Istanbul | Suleyman Seba Cad., Talimyeri Sok., No. 2, Beşiktaş
Phone +90 212 2362460 | Fax +90 212 2362773
ummuhan@antikpalace.com.tr | www.artam.com

ArtAsiaPacific | ArtAsiaPacific | ArtAsiaPacific Holdings LTD
HK-Hong Kong | GPO Box 10084
Phone +852 25535586 | Fax +852 25531199
info@aapmag.com | www.artasiapacific.com

Artchronika | Artchronika | Art-Media
RU-127051 Moscow | Neglinnaya st, 15-1-37
Phone +7 495 6510537 | Fax +7 495 6510538
aguschina@artchronika.ru | www.artchronika.ru

Arte al Dia International | Arte al Dia International | American Art Corporation
US-Miami, FL 33131 | 1110 Brickell Avenue, Suite 800
Phone +1 305 3738110 | Fax +1 305 3738114
contact@artealdia.com | www.artealdia.com

Arte al Límite | Arte al Límite | Arte al Límite
CL-7700890 Santiago de Chile | Camino Agua del Carrizal 9497, Lo Barnechea
Phone +56 2 9553261
cduch@arteallimite.com | anamariamatthei@arteallimite.com | www.arteallimite.com

Arte e Critica | Arte e Critica | Associazione Arte e Critica
IT-00196 Rome | Via dei Tadolini 26
Phone +39 06 45554880 | Fax +39 06 45551617
redazione@arteecritica.it | www.arteecritica.it

Arte por Excelencias | Arte por Excelencias | Grupo Excelencias
ES-28020 Madrid | Capitán Haya 16
Phone +34 91 556 00 40 | Fax +34 91 555 37 64
arte@arteporexcelencias.com | www.arteporexcelencias.com

ARTE!Brasileiros | ARTE!Brasileiros | Editora Brasileiros
BR-São Paulo 05417-001 | Rua Mourato Coelho, 798
Phone +55 11 38 17 48 02 | Fax +55 11 38 17 48 02
emilia@artebrasileiros.com.br | www.artebrasileiros.com.br

ARTEin | ARTEin – International Art Magazine | International Art Magazine Group s.r.l.
IT-30171 Venezia Mestre | Viale Stazione 20
Phone +39 041 93 50 78 | Fax +39 041 538 87 99
artein@artein.it | www.artein.it

artfacts.net | artfacts.net
GB-London W5 5TL | 109 Uxbridge Road
Phone +44 20 81 80 85 66 | Fax +44 20 75 04 81 40
info@artfacts.net | artevents@artfacts.net | www.artfacts.net

Artforum International | Artforum International | Artforum International
US-New York, NY 10001 | 350 7th Avenue
Phone +1 212 475 40 00 | Fax +1 212 529 12 57
generalinfo@artforum.com | www.artforum.com

Artillery | Artillery
US-Los Angeles, CA 90026 | P.O. Box 26234
Phone +1 213 250 70 81 | +1 323 243 06 58 | Fax +1 213 250 70 81
publisher@artillerymag.com | www.artillerymag.com

ArtNexus | ArtNexus | ArtNexus
US-Miami, FL 33160 | 12500 NE 8th Avenue, 2nd Floor
Phone +1 305 891 72 70-110 | Fax +1 305 891 64 08
zroca@artnexus.com | www.artnexus.com

artports.com | artports.com | artports.com
DE-76135 Karlsruhe | Sophienstrasse 156
Phone +49 721 750 86 45 | Fax +49 721 750 86 46
info@artports.com | www.artports.com

ArtPremium | ArtPremium | ArtPremium
FR-75012 Paris | 100, rue de Charenton
Phone +33 6 61 20 61 90
info@artpremium.com | www.artpremium.com

ArtPulse | ArtPulse | W Media LLC
US-Miami, FL 33296 | P.O. Box 960008
Phone +1 786 274 32 36 | Fax +1 305 456 93 64
jlopez@artpulsemagazine.com | www.artpulsemagazine.com

ArtReview | ArtReview | ArtReview Ltd.
GB-London EC1R 0BE | 1 Sekforde Street
Phone +44 20 71 07 27 60 | Fax +44 20 71 07 27 61
office@artreview.com | www.artreview.com

Baku | Baku | Condé Nast
GB-London W1G 0ER | 8 Cavendish Square
Phone +44 20 72 99 34 13
maria.webster@condenast.co.uk

Border Crossings | Border Crossings | Arts Manitoba Publications Inc.
CA-Winnipeg R3B 1G7 | 500-70 Arthur Street
Phone +1 204 942 57 78 | Fax +1 204 949 07 93
ads@bordercrossingsmag.com | www.bordercrossingsmag.com

Camera Austria | Camera Austria International
AT-8020 Graz | Lendkai 1
Phone +43 316 81 55 50 | Fax +43 316 81 55 09
press@camera-austria.at | www.camera-austria.at

Canvas | Canvas | Mixed Media Publishing
AE-Dubai | P.O. Box 500487
Phone +97 14 367 16 93 | Fax +97 14 367 26 45
info@mixed-media.com | www.canvasonline.com

Capricious | Capricious Magazine | Capricious Publishing
US-Brooklyn, NY 11211 | 285 North 6th Street
Phone +1 718 384 12 08
anika@becapricious.com | www.becapricious.com

Caviar Izquierda | Caviar Izquierda | Franklin Callao
MX-06140 Mexico City | Alfonso Reyes 23
Phone +52 55 56 05 36 27
franklin@caviarizquierda.com | www.caviarizquierda.com

Chinese Contemporary Art News | Chinese Contemporary Art News | Beijing Cans Culture Communication Media Ltd.
CN-100022 Beijing | Room 302, Bldg B, No. 16, Jianguomenwai St., Chao Yang District
Phone +86 10 65 69 63 05 | Fax +86 10 65 69 63 07
cans_bj@yahoo.com.cn | www.canart.com.tw

Crash | Crash | Armelle Leturcq
FR-75001 Paris | 257 rue Saint Honoré, 1er
Phone +33 1 43 45 74 61 | Fax +33 1 43 45 76 87
armelleleturcq@crash.fr | www.crash.fr

cura | cura.magazine | Moving Produzioni soc. coop.
IT-00195 Rome | Via Nicola Ricciotti, 4
Phone +39 06 96 03 96 72 | Fax +39 06 96 03 96 73
info@curamagazine.com | www.curamagazine.com

Dardo | Dardo Magazine | ArteDardo S.L.
ES-15702 Santiago de Compostela | Rúa Severino Riveiro Tomé No. 3, Baixo
Phone +34 881 97 69 86
dardo@dardomagazine.com | www.dardomagazine.com

Dasartes | Dasartes | Indexa Editora
BR-Rio de Janeiro 22420-041 | Prudente de Morais 889 C 204
Phone +55 21 82 93 00 08 | Fax +55 21 22 66 17 56
liege@dasartes.com | www.dasartes.com

Dear Dave | Dear Dave Magazine | David Rhodes
US-New York, NY 10010 | 209 East 23rd Street
Phone +1 212 592 23 57 | Fax +1 212 592 23 36
info@deardavemagazine.com | www.deardavemagazine.com

Drome | Drome Magazine | Phlegmatics
IT-00182 Rome | Piazza Camerino,15
Phone +39 06 87 76 51 04 | Fax +39 06 87 76 51 05
drome@dromemagazine.com | www.dromemagazine.com

BE-1000 Brussels | Rue Notre-Dame du Sommeil, 2
Phone +32 2 511 91 12 | Fax +32 2 511 91 12

ELSE | ELSE | Musée de l'Elysée
CH-1014 Lausanne | 18, Avenue de l'Elysée
Phone +41 21 316 99 11 | +41 21 316 96 95
www.elsemag.ch

esse | esse arts + opinions | Les éditions esse
CA-Montreal H2K 3T2 | c.p. 56 succursale De Lorimier
Phone +1 514 521 85 97 | Fax +1 514 521 85 98
publicite@esse.ca | www.esse.ca

Eyeline | Eyeline | Eyeline Publishing Limited
AU-4059 Kelvin Grove | c/- Visual Arts QUT, Victoria Park Road
Phone +61 7 31 38 55 21 | Fax +61 7 31 38 39 74
info@eyelinepublishing.com | www.eyelinepublishing.com

Fantom | Fantom Photographic Quarterly | Boiler Corporation
IT-20123 Milan | Via Lanzone 22
Phone +39 02 805 77 10
info@fantomeditions.com | www.fantomeditions.com

Fillip | Fillip
CA-Vancouver V6B 2N4 | 305 Cambie Street
Phone +1 604 781 44 17
fillip@fillip.ca | www.fillip.ca

Fine Arts Literature | Fine Arts Literature | Hubei Classic Publishing House
CN-430061 Wuhan | SF, No. 368, Zhongshan Road
Phone +86 27 88 91 89 49 | Fax +86 27 88 86 05 45
meishuwenxian@126.com | www.meishuwenxian.com

Fisheye | Fisheye | Carlo Cambi Editore
IT-53036 Poggibonsi (Siena) | Via San Gimignano, 108
Phone +39 05 77 93 65 80 | Fax +39 05 77 97 41 47
press@carlocambieditore.it | www.carlocambieditore.it

Flash Art | Flash Art | Giancarlo Politi Editore SRL
IT-20159 Milan | Via Carlo Farini 68
Phone +39 02 688 73 42
marialuisa@flashart.it | www.flashartonline.com

frieze | frieze
GB-London E2 7EU | 1 Montclare Street
Phone +44 20 33 72 61 11
adair.lentini@frieze.com | www.frieze.com

futuro | futuro contemporaryart | Del Mese-Fischer Verlag
CH-5616 Meisterschwanden | Seefeldstrasse 10
Phone +41 56 667 18 28 | Fax +41 56 667 18 04
info@futuro-magazin.ch | www.futuro-magazin.ch

Gallery.spb | Gallery.spb | 24 Moyka
RU-191186 St. Petersburg | emb. Moyka 24
Phone +7 812 315 02 51 | Fax +7 812 312 75 41
galleryspb@gmail.com | www.spb-gallery.info

Harper's Bazaar Art | Harper's Bazaar Art | Trends Group
CN-100021 Beijing | 21F, Trends Building, 9th Guang Hua Road
Phone +86 10 65 89 52 78 | Fax +86 10 65 87 21 66
liupinyu@gmail.com | www.trends.com.cn

Harper's Bazaar Arabia | Harper's Bazaar Arabia | ITP Publishing Group
AE-Dubai | P.O. Box 500024
Phone +971 4 444 30 00 | Fax +971 4 444 30 30
www.itp.com

Iberoamericana | Iberoamericana International Magazine | Empresacom EIRL
PE-Lima | Las Avellanas 190 Urb. Los Recaudadores – Salamanca ATE Lima
Phone +51 957 88 81 66
sonniavaldivia@hotmail.com | editor@iberointernacional.com | www.iberointernacional.com

ice | ice Magazine | Contemporary Istanbul
TR-34437 Istanbul | Mete Cad. Yeni Apt. No. 10/11, Taksim
Phone +90 212 244 71 71 | Fax +90 212 244 71 81
zeynep@contemporaryistanbul.com | www.iceartmag.com

Kaleidoscope | Kaleidoscope | Asso s.r.l.
IT-20124 Milan | Galleria Buenos Aires, 10
Phone +39 02 36 53 55 63
magazine@kaleidoscope-press.com | www.kaleidoscope-press.com

KQ KUNSTQUARTAL | KQ KUNSTQUARTAL | Hatje Cantz Verlag
DE-73760 Ostfildern | Zeppelinstrasse 32
Phone +49 711 440 52 26 | Fax +49 711 440 52 28
contact@kqkunstquartal.de | www.kq-daily.de

LEAP | LEAP | Modern Media Group
CN-100027 Beijing | No. A2, Gongti East Road, Chaoyang District
Phone +86 10 65 61 55 50-849 | Fax +86 10 65 61 08 19
cailixin@modernmedia.com.cn | www.modernmedia.com

LLEI D'ART | LLEI D'ART 'La Revista Independiente' | Editorial LLEI D'ART
ES-25110 Alpicat-Lleida | Pau Casals, 10
Phone +34 973 73 80 56 | Fax +34 973 73 69 26
info@lleidart.com | www.lleidart.com

M | the M magazine | in the art world
US-New York, NY 11101 | 143-01, 22nd Street, No. 442
Phone +1 212 956 06 14
editor@intheartworld.com | www.intheartworld.com

masdearte.com | masdearte.com | masdearte contenidos digitales
ES-28020 Madrid | Sor Angela de la Cruz, 10 7º C
Phone +34 91 530 29 73
martag@masdearte.com | www.masdearte.com

Modern Matter | Modern Matter | OMO Creates
GB-London N1 7JQ | 16-24 Underwood Street
office@amodernmatter.com | www.amodernmatter.com

Modern Painters | Modern Painters | Louise Blouin Media
US-New York, NY 10001 | 601 West 26th Street, #410
Phone +1 646 348 63 36
kmurphy@artinfo.com | www.artinfo.com

Mousse | Mousse | Mousse Magazine & Publishing
IT-20123 Milan | Via De Amicis 53
Phone +39 02 835 66 31 | Fax +39 02 49 53 14 00
info@moussemagazine.it | www.moussemagazine.it

Nero | Nero | Produzioni Nero
IT-00153 Rome | Lungotevere degli Artigiani 8B
Phone +39 06 97 27 12 52 | Fax +39 06 97 27 12 52
info@neromagazine.it | www.neromagazine.it

Next Level | Next Level | Next Level Projects
GB-London E9 7TT | 23 Royal Gate, 1 Rutland Road
Phone +44 79 56 31 26 08
sheyi@nextleveluk.com | www.nextleveluk.com

Peeping Tom's Digest | Peeping Tom's Digest | Peeping Tom
FR-75018 Paris | 64, rue Philippe de Girard
contact@peepingtomgalerie.com | www.peepingtomgalerie.com

photography-now.com | photography-now.com
DE-10117 Berlin | Ziegelstrasse 29
Phone +49 30 24 34 27 80 | Fax +49 30 24 34 27 89
contact@photography-now.com | www.photography-now.com

Pipeline | Pipeline | Double Pipe Publishers Limited
HK-Hong Kong | 26C, 235 Wing Lok Street, Sheung Wan
Phone +852 25 68 07 77 | Fax +852 28 56 25 78
hello@pipelinemag.com | www.pipelinemag.com

RES | RES Art World/World Art | Dirimart
TR-34367 Istanbul | Abdi Ipekçi Cad. 7/4
Phone +90 212 291 34 34 | Fax +90 212 219 64 00
info@resartworld.com | www.resartworld.com

Revista Codigo | Revista Codigo | Editorial Codigo
MX-06170 Mexico City | Amsterdam 219A, Di. 202
Phone +52 55 64 96 10-121 | Fax +52 55 64 96 10-116
adrian@editorialcodigo.com | www.revistacodigo.com

Rooms | Rooms Magazine | Rooms Art Uncovered Limited
GB-London E5 8EE | 135 Clarence Road
Phone +44 78 40 69 02 52
ana@roomsmagazine.com | www.roomsmagazine.com

Segno | Segno | Associazione Culturale Segno
IT-65127 Pescara | Corso Manthoné, 57
Phone +39 085 617 12 | Fax +39 085 943 04 67
info@rivistasegno.eu | www.rivistasegno.eu

sleek | sleek magazine | BBE Group
DE-10178 Berlin | Alexanderstrasse 7
Phone +49 30 288 86 75 20 | Fax +49 30 288 86 75 29
amy@sleekmag.com | www.sleekmag.com

Some/Things | Some/Things
FR-75011 Paris | 16, Villa Gaudelet
Phone +33 1 47 00 91 90
contact@someslashthings.com | www.someslashthings.com

tasj | tasj | tasj magazine
US-Culver City, CA 90232 | 5797 Washington Blvd.
Phone +1 323 939 06 00
info@tasjmagazine.com | www.tasjmagazine.com

The Art Newspaper | The Art Newspaper | Umberto Allemandi Publishing
GB-London SW8 1RL | 70 South Lambeth Road
Phone +44 20 34 16 90 00 | Fax +44 20 77 35 33 32
s.ollivier@theartnewspaper.com | www.theartnewspaper.com

(t)here | (t)here | There Media, Inc.
US-New York, NY 10014 | 410 West 14th Street
Phone +1 212 366 41 40 | Fax +1 212 202 47 91
info@theremedia.com | www.theremag.com

Vellum | Vellum Magazine
US-Brooklyn, NY 11232 | 164 23rd Street
Phone +1 347 523 24 41
thirdman3@netzero.com | www.vellumonline.com

White Zinfandel | White Zinfandel | White Zinfandel
US-New York, NY 10002 | 157 Bowery #2B
Phone +1 610 217 16 80
david@withnyc.org | www.whitezinf.org

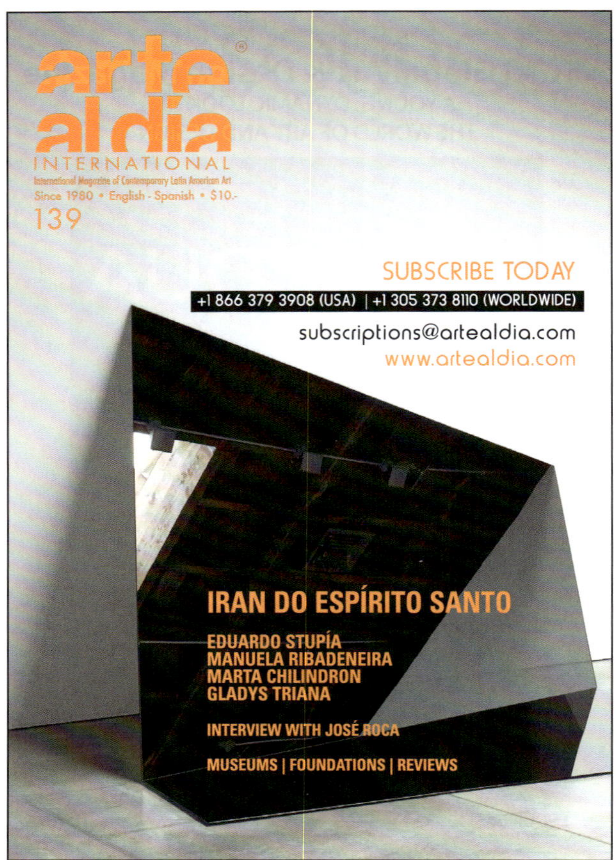

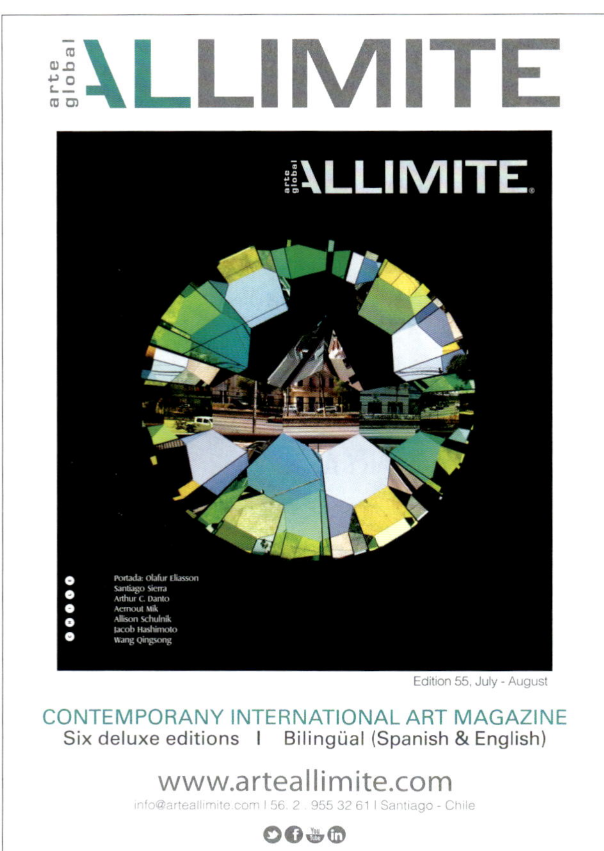

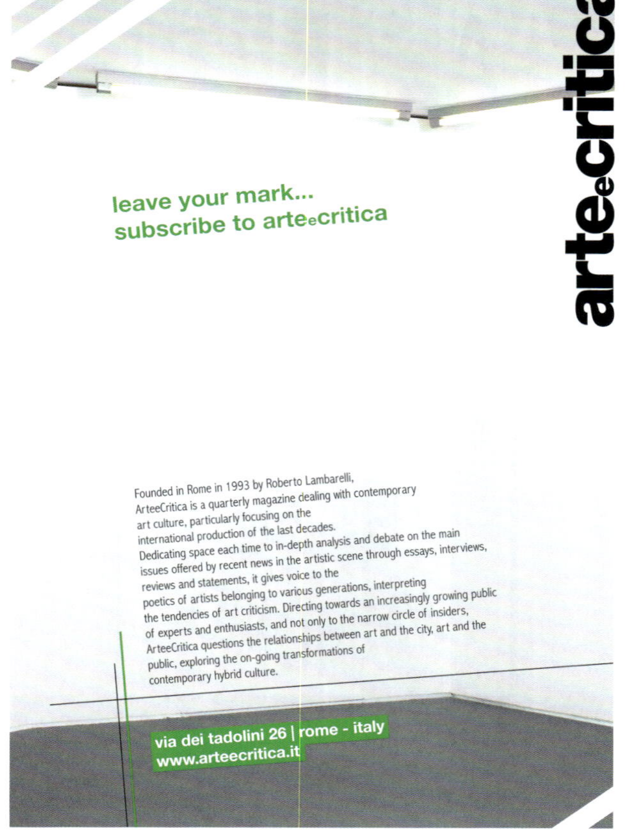

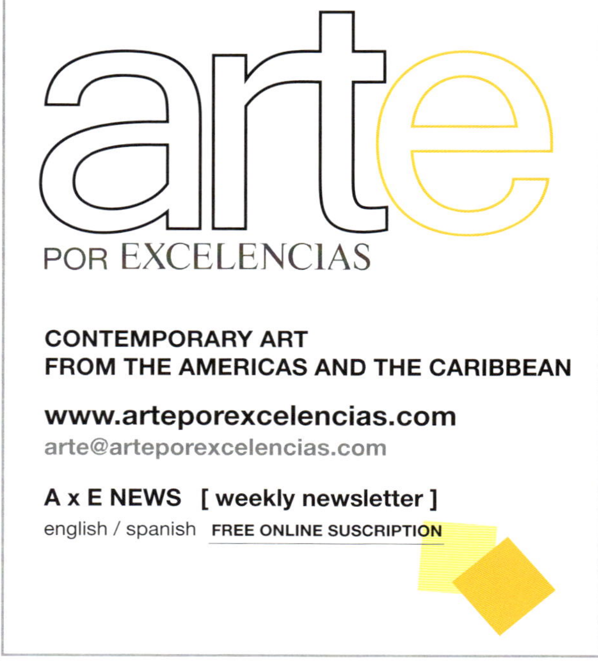

Excelencias Cultural Space
Magdalena 8, Madrid 28012, Spain
+34 915560040 / +34 635603188
Caravaggio for sale

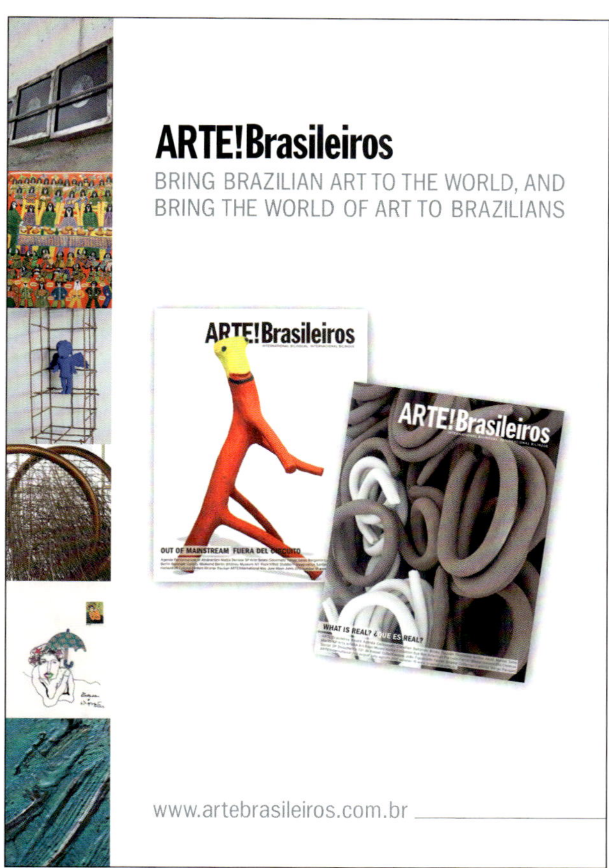
ARTE!Brasileiros
BRING BRAZILIAN ART TO THE WORLD, AND
BRING THE WORLD OF ART TO BRAZILIANS
ARTE!Brasileiros
ARTE!Brasileiros
www.artebrasileiros.com.br

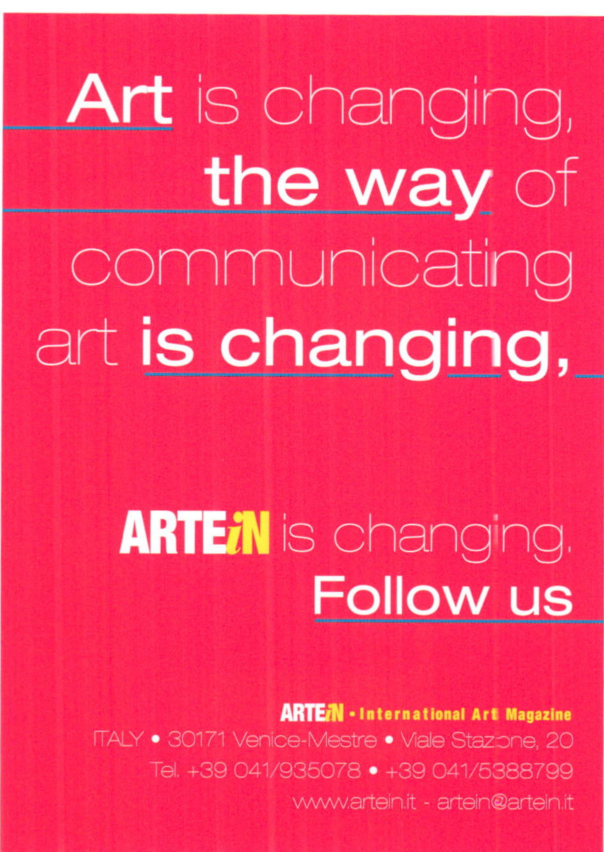
Art is changing,
the way of
communicating
art is changing,
ARTEiN is changing.
Follow us
ARTEiN • International Art Magazine
ITALY • 30171 Venice-Mestre • Viale Stazione, 20
Tel. +39 041/935078 • +39 041/5388799
www.artein.it - artein@artein.it

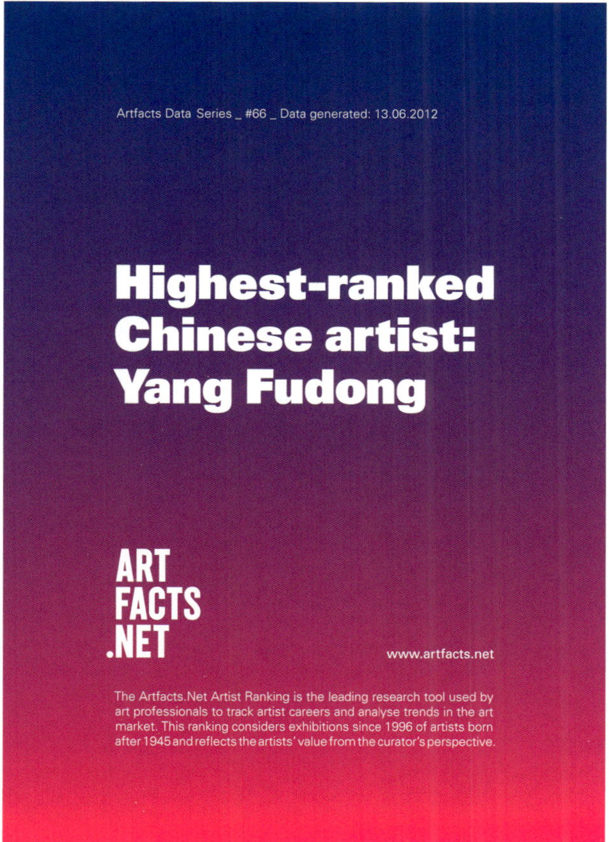
Artfacts Data Series _ #66 _ Data generated: 13.06.2012
Highest-ranked
Chinese artist:
Yang Fudong
ART
FACTS
.NET
www.artfacts.net
The Artfacts.Net Artist Ranking is the leading research tool used by art professionals to track artist careers and analyse trends in the art market. This ranking considers exhibitions since 1996 of artists born after 1945 and reflects the artists' value from the curator's perspective.

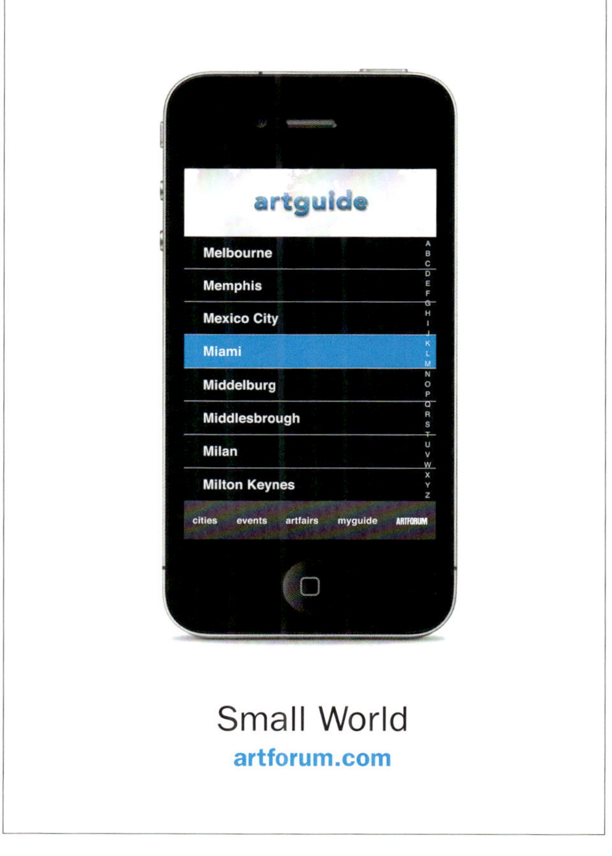
artguide
Melbourne
Memphis
Mexico City
Miami
Middelburg
Middlesbrough
Milan
Milton Keynes
cities
events
artfairs
myguide
Small World
artforum.com

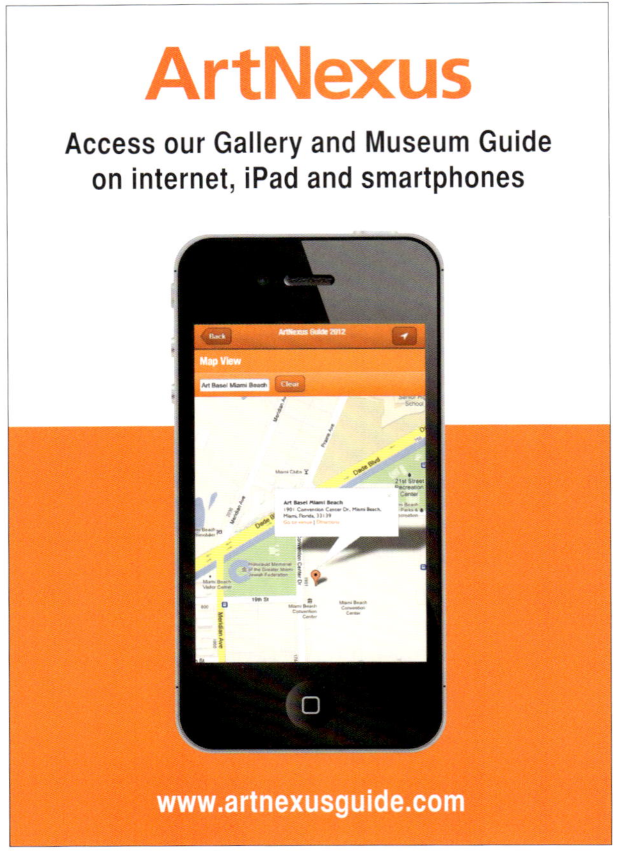
ArtNexus
Access our Gallery and Museum Guide
on internet, iPad and smartphones
www.artnexusguide.com

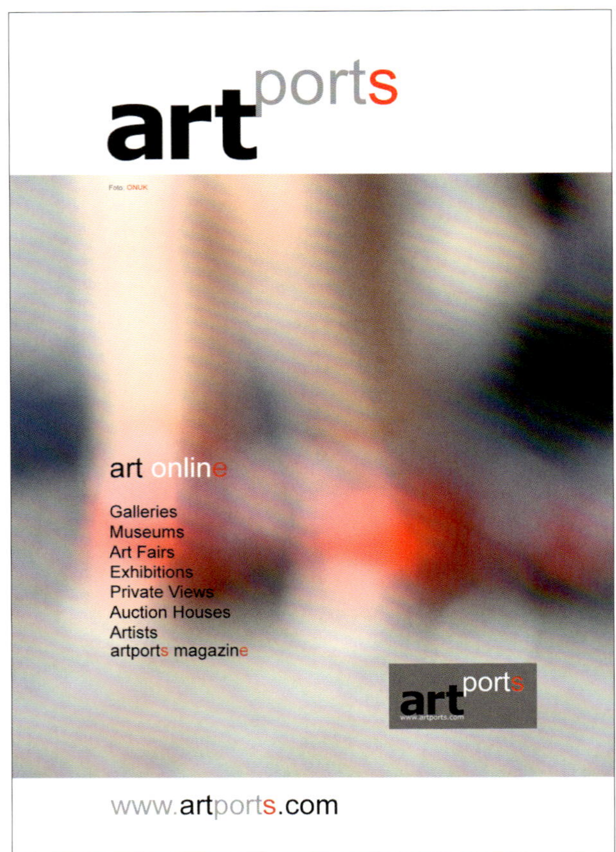
artports
art online
Galleries
Museums
Art Fairs
Exhibitions
Private Views
Auction Houses
Artists
artports magazine
www.artports.com

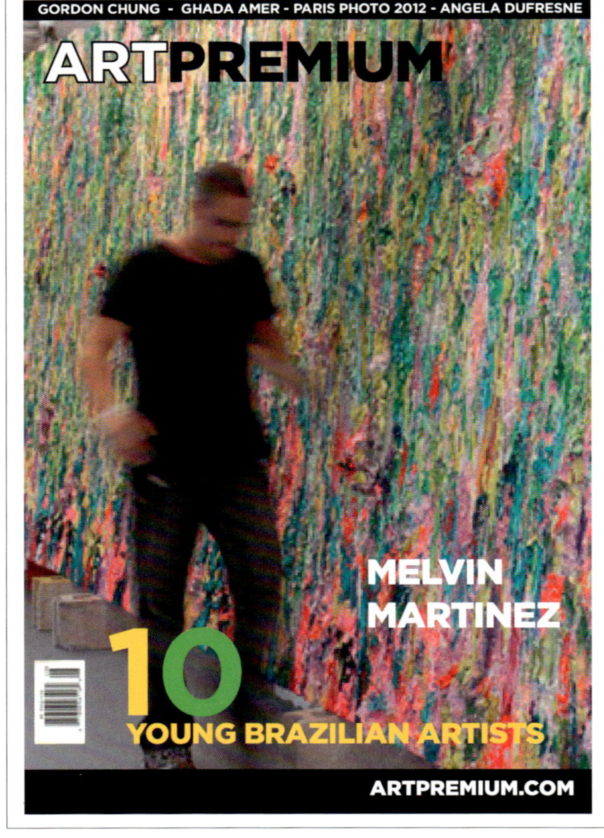
GORDON CHUNG - GHADA AMER - PARIS PHOTO 2012 - ANGELA DUFRESNE
ARTPREMIUM
MELVIN
MARTINEZ
10
YOUNG BRAZILIAN ARTISTS
ARTPREMIUM.COM

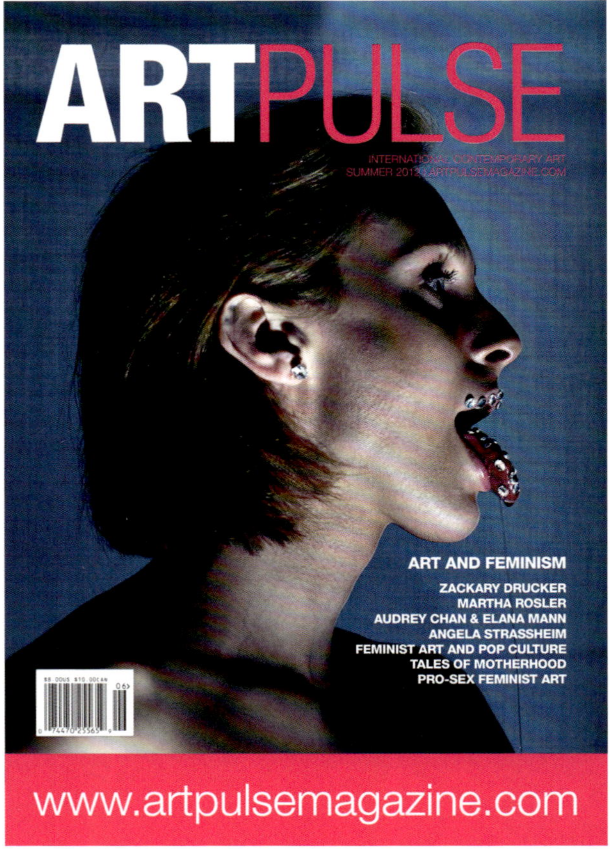
ARTPULSE
ART AND FEMINISM
ZACKARY DRUCKER
MARTHA ROSLER
AUDREY CHAN & ELANA MANN
ANGELA STRASSHEIM
FEMINIST ART AND POP CULTURE
TALES OF MOTHERHOOD
PRO-SEX FEMINIST ART
www.artpulsemagazine.com

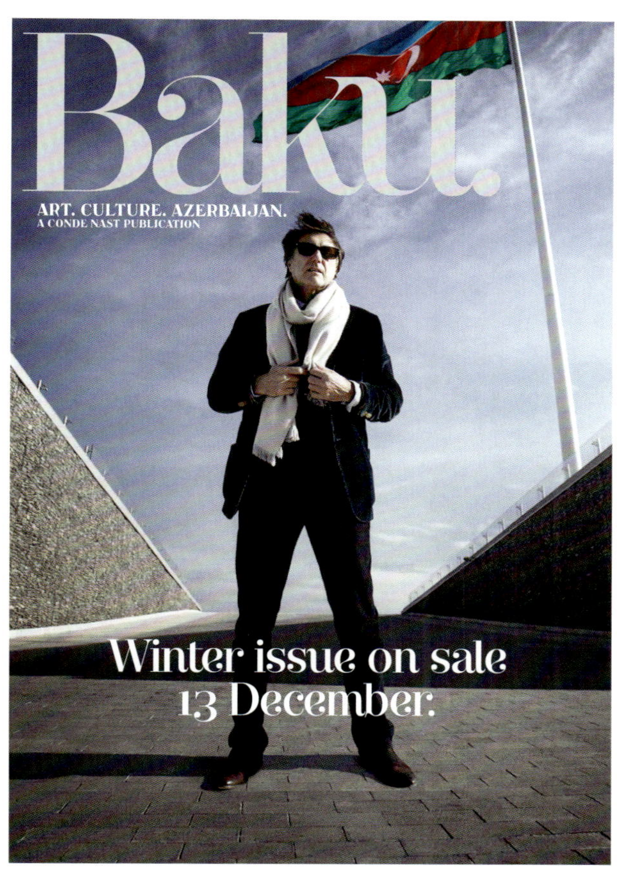
Baku.
ART. CULTURE. AZERBAIJAN.
A CONDE NAST PUBLICATION
Winter issue on sale
13 December.

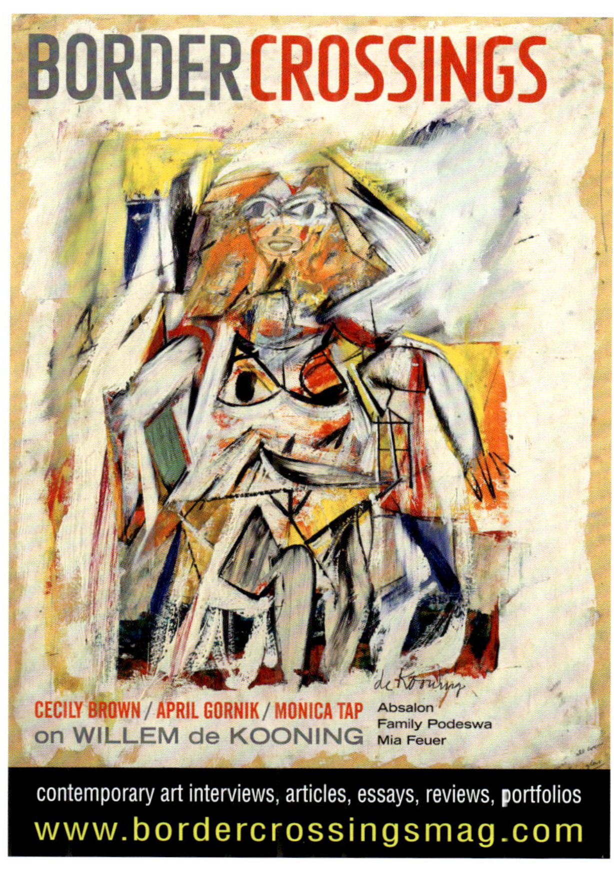
BORDERCROSSINGS
CECILY BROWN / APRIL GORNIK / MONICA TAP
on WILLEM de KOONING
Absalon
Family Podeswa
Mia Feuer
contemporary art interviews, articles, essays, reviews, portfolios
www.bordercrossingsmag.com

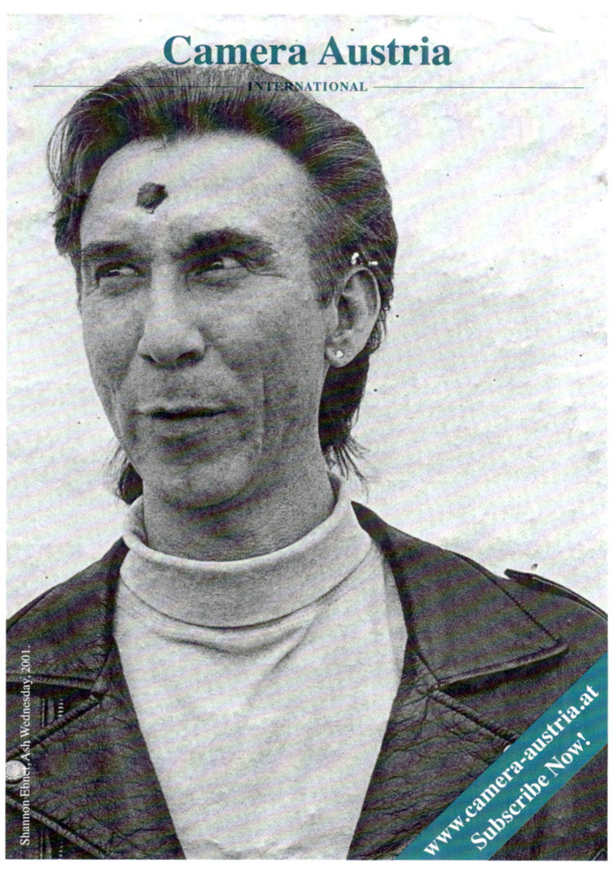
Camera Austria
INTERNATIONAL
Shannon Ebner, Ash Wednesday, 2001.
www.camera-austria.at
Subscribe Now!

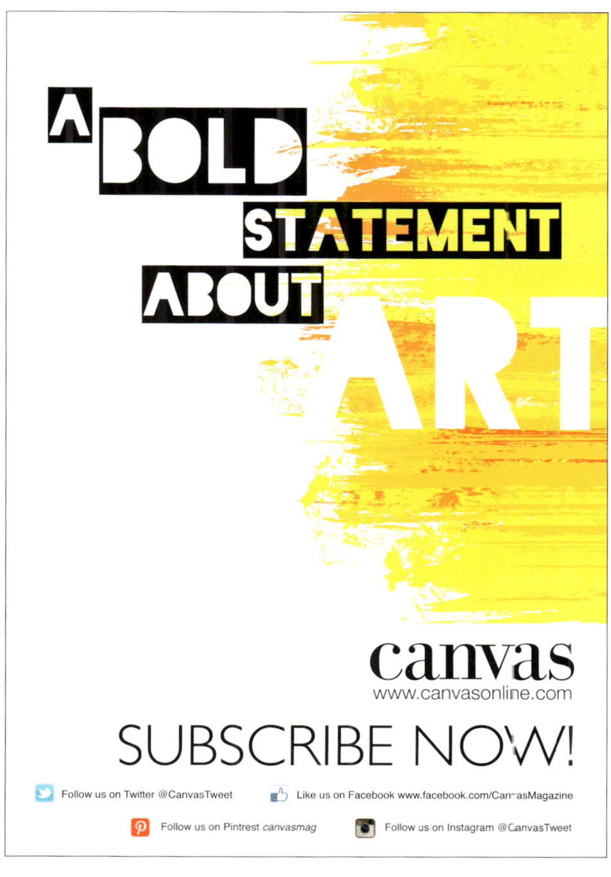
A BOLD
STATEMENT
ABOUT
ART
canvas
www.canvasonline.com
SUBSCRIBE NOW!
Follow us on Twitter @CanvasTweet
Like us on Facebook www.facebook.com/CanvasMagazine
Follow us on Pintrest canvasmag
Follow us on Instagram @CanvasTweet

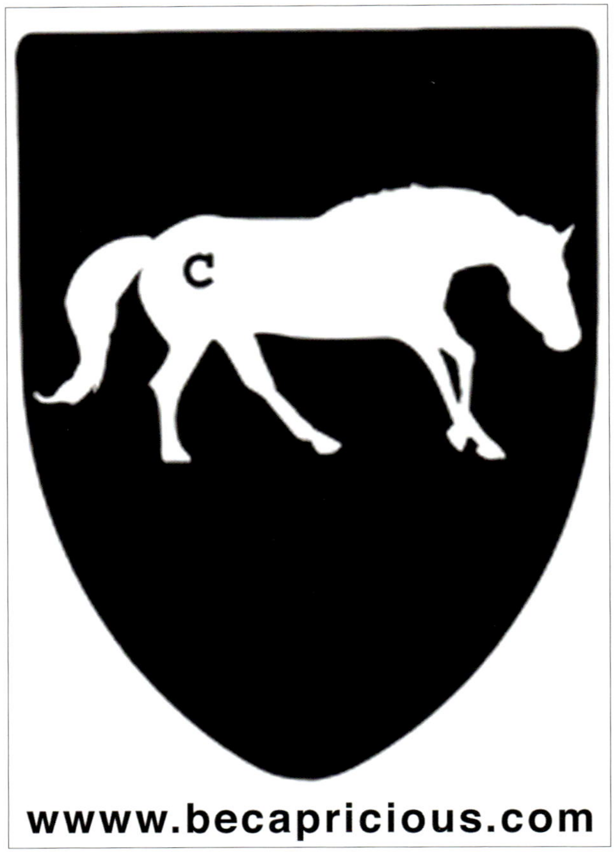
c
wwww.becapricious.com

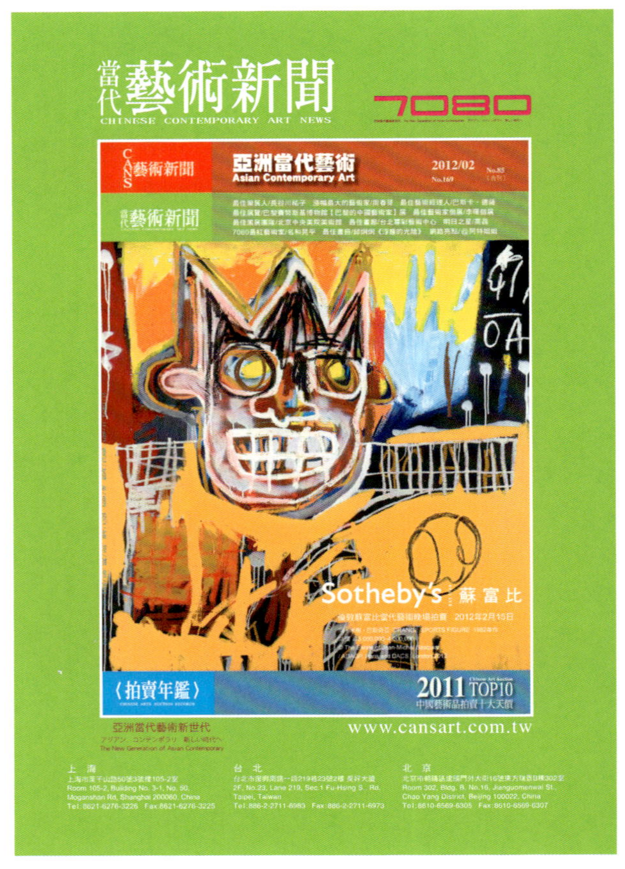
當代藝術新聞
CHINESE CONTEMPORARY ART NEWS
7080
CANS 藝術新聞
亞洲當代藝術
Asian Contemporary Art
2012/02
No.169
No.85
當代藝術新聞
Sotheby's 蘇富比
〈拍賣年鑑〉
2011 TOP10
中國藝術品拍賣十大天價
亞洲當代藝術新世代
The New Generation of Asian Contemporary
www.cansart.com.tw
上海
Room 105-2, Building No. 3-1, No. 50, Moganshan Rd, Shanghai 200060, China
Tel:8621-6276-3226 Fax:8621-6276-3225
台北
2F, No.23, Lane 219, Sec.1 Fu-Hsing S. Rd. Taipei, Taiwan
Tel:886-2-2711-6983 Fax:886-2-2711-6973
北京
Room 302, Bldg. B, No.16, Jianguomenwai St. Chao Yang District, Beijing 100022, China
Tel:8610-6569-6305 Fax:8610-6569-6307

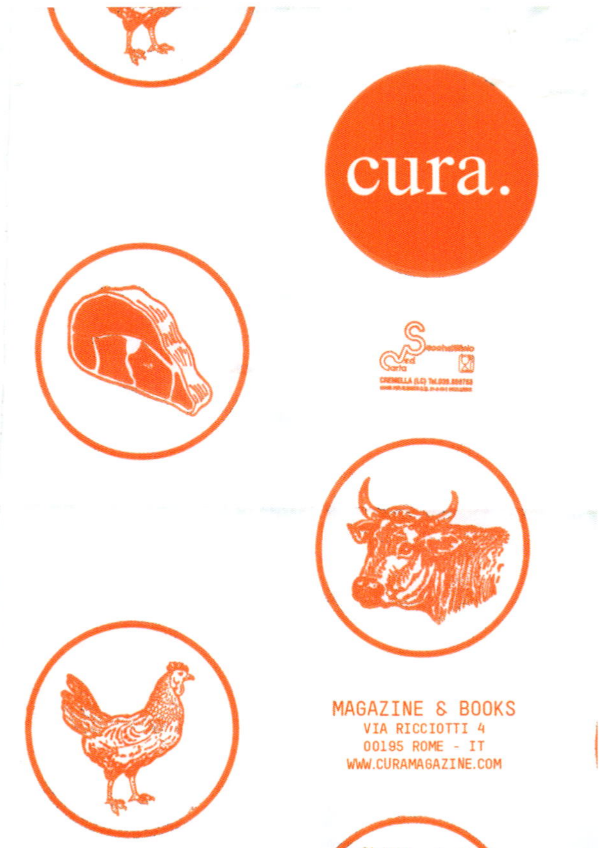
cura.
MAGAZINE & BOOKS
VIA RICCIOTTI 4
00195 ROME - IT
WWW.CURAMAGAZINE.COM

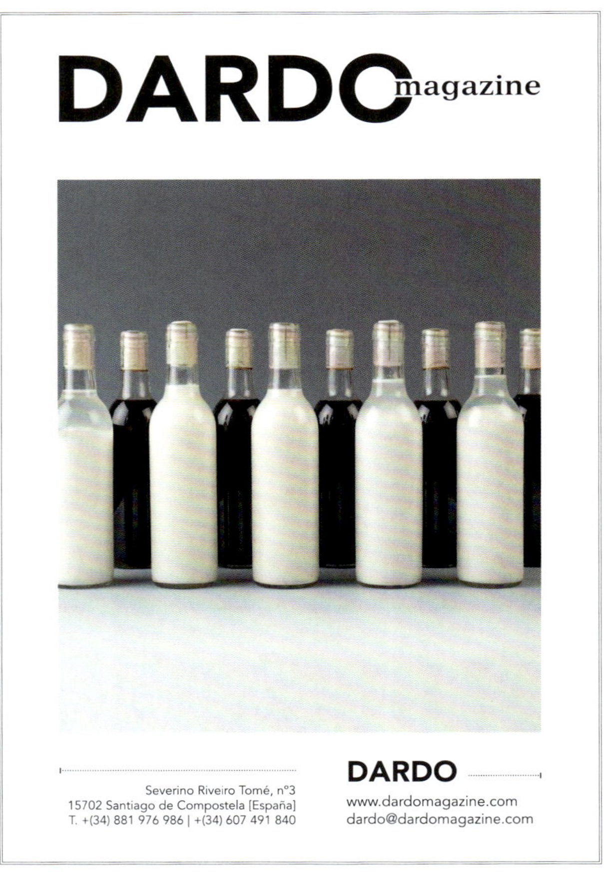
DARDO magazine
Severino Riveiro Tomé, nº3
15702 Santiago de Compostela [España]
T. +(34) 881 976 986 | +(34) 607 491 840
DARDO
www.dardomagazine.com
dardo@dardomagazine.com

FANTOM
PHOTOGRAPHIC QUARTERLY

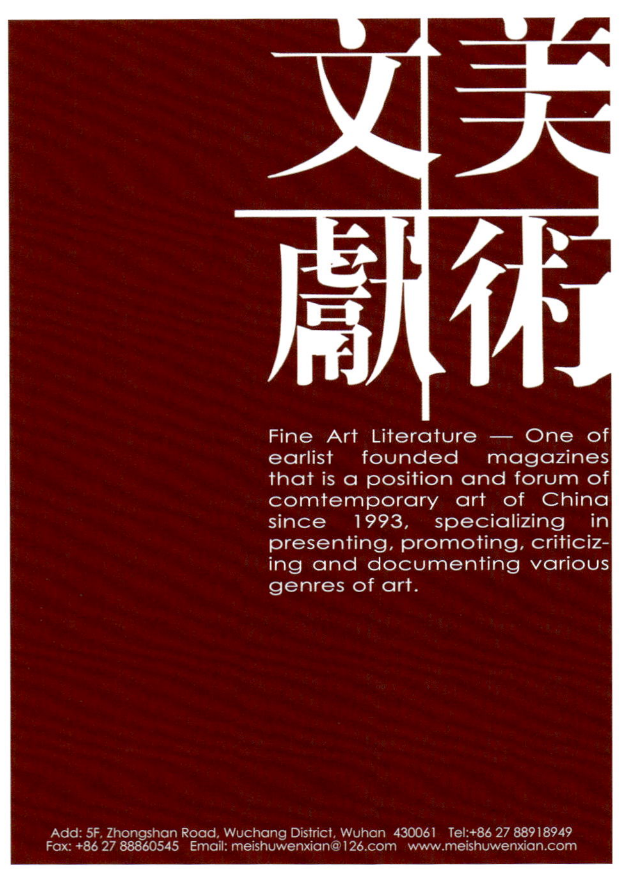
美術
文獻
Fine Art Literature — One of earlist founded magazines that is a position and forum of comtemporary art of China since 1993, specializing in presenting, promoting, criticizing and documenting various genres of art.
Add: 5F. Zhongshan Road, Wuchang District, Wuhan 430061 Tel:+86 27 88918949
Fax: +86 27 88860545 Email: meishuwenxian@126.com www.meishuwenxian.com

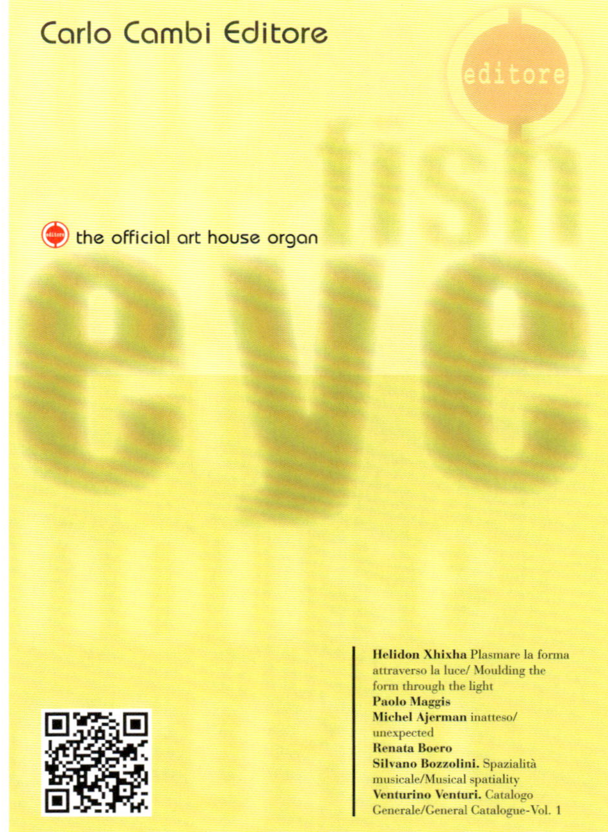
Carlo Cambi Editore
editore
fish
the official art house organ
eye
Helidon Xhixha Plasmare la forma attraverso la luce/ Moulding the form through the light
Paolo Maggis
Michel Ajerman inatteso/ unexpected
Renata Boero
Silvano Bozzolini. Spazialità musicale/Musical spatiality
Venturino Venturi. Catalogo Generale/General Catalogue-Vol. 1

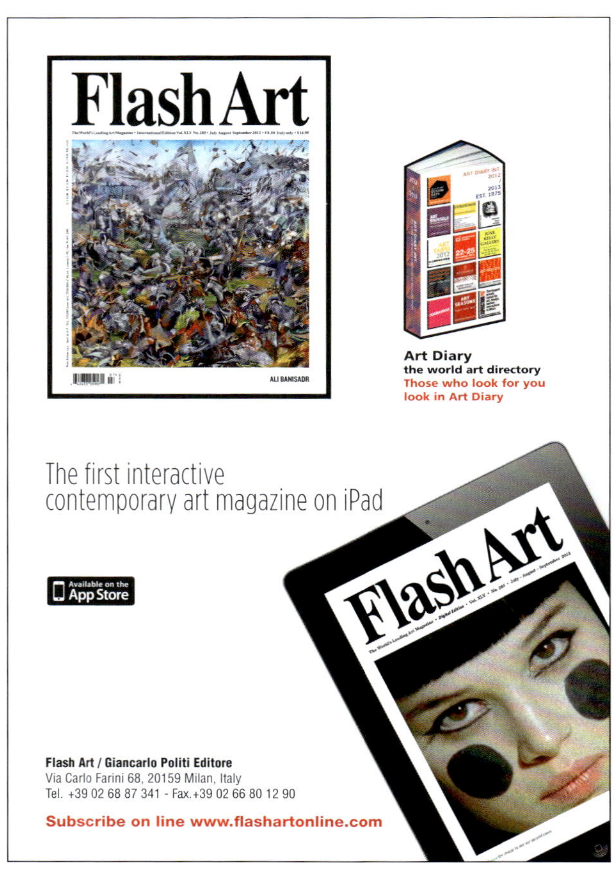
Flash Art
ALI BANISADR
Art Diary
the world art directory
Those who look for you look in Art Diary
The first interactive contemporary art magazine on iPad
Available on the App Store
Flash Art
Flash Art / Giancarlo Politi Editore
Via Carlo Farini 68, 20159 Milan, Italy
Tel. +39 02 68 87 341 - Fax.+39 02 66 80 12 90
Subscribe on line www.flashartonline.com

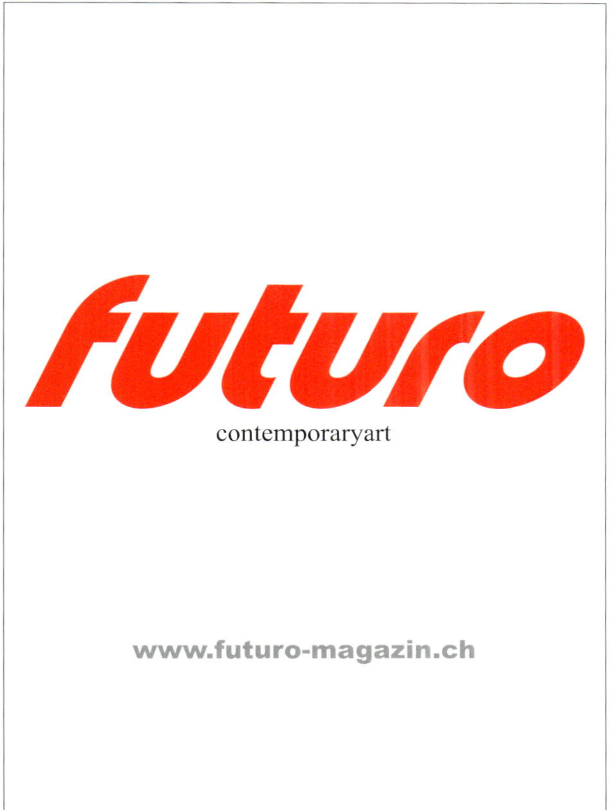
futuro
contemporaryart
www.futuro-magazin.ch

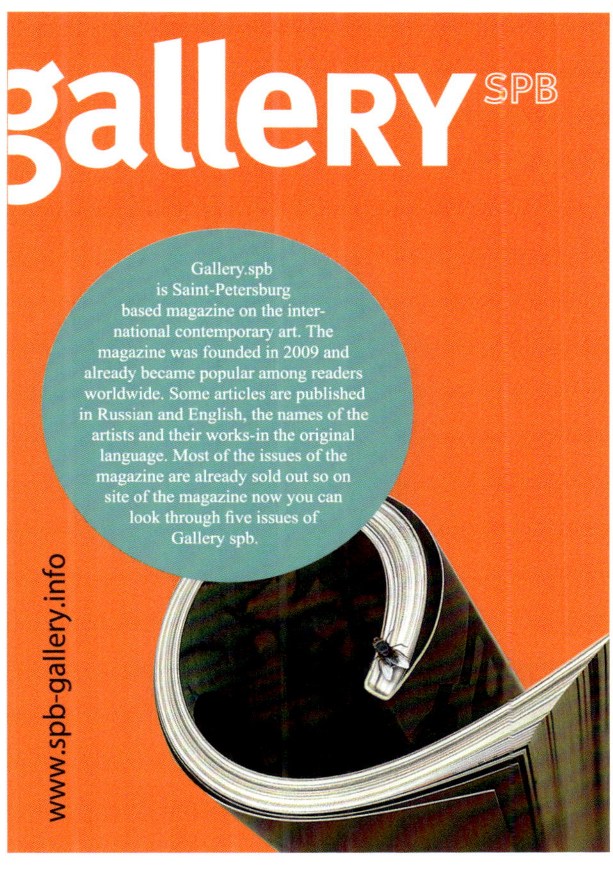
gallery SPB
Gallery.spb is Saint-Petersburg based magazine on the international contemporary art. The magazine was founded in 2009 and already became popular among readers worldwide. Some articles are published in Russian and English, the names of the artists and their works-in the original language. Most of the issues of the magazine are already sold out so on site of the magazine now you can look through five issues of Gallery spb.
www.spb-gallery.info

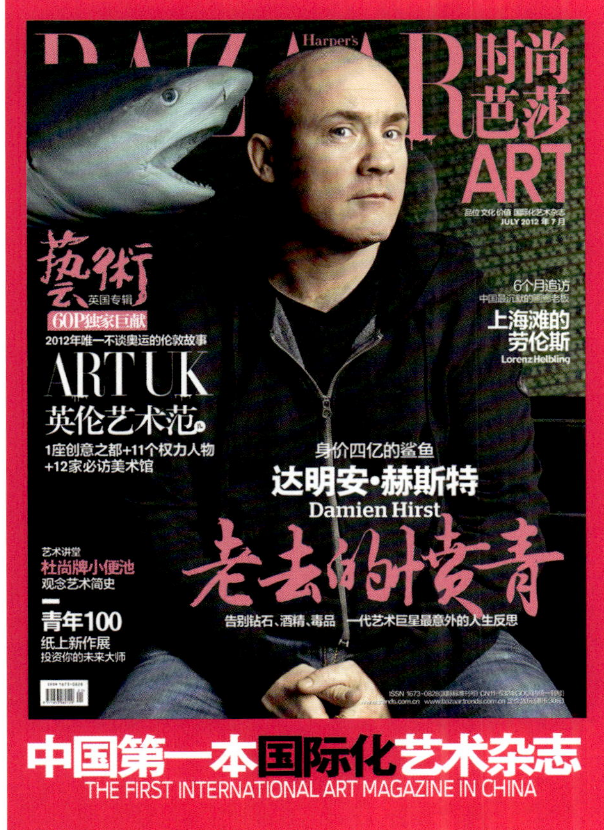
Harper's BAZAAR 时尚芭莎 ART
JULY 2012 年 7 月
藝術 英国专辑
60P独家巨献
2012年唯一不谈奥运的伦敦故事
ARTUK
英伦艺术范
1座创意之都+11个权力人物
+12家必访美术馆
6个月追访
上海滩的劳伦斯
Lorenz Helbling
身价四亿的鲨鱼
达明安·赫斯特
Damien Hirst
老去的愤青
告别钻石、酒精、毒品 一代艺术巨星最意外的人生反思
艺术讲堂
杜尚牌小便池
观念艺术简史
青年100
纸上新作展
投资你的未来大师
中国第一本国际化艺术杂志
THE FIRST INTERNATIONAL ART MAGAZINE IN CHINA

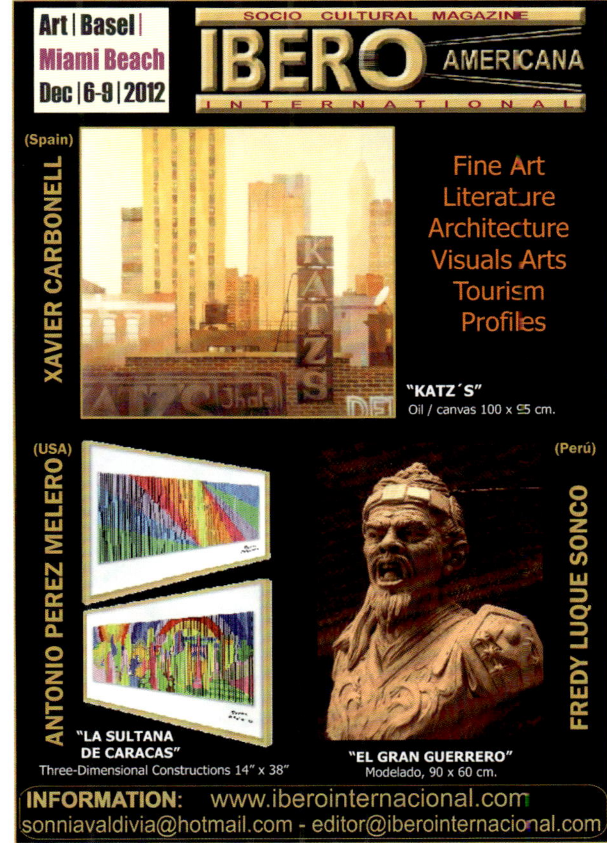
Art | Basel | Miami Beach Dec | 6-9 | 2012
SOCIO CULTURAL MAGAZINE
IBERO AMERICANA
INTERNATIONAL
(Spain)
XAVIER CARBONELL
Fine Art
Literature
Architecture
Visuals Arts
Tourism
Profiles
"KATZ´S"
Oil / canvas 100 x 95 cm.
(USA)
ANTONIO PEREZ MELERO
"LA SULTANA DE CARACAS"
Three-Dimensional Constructions 14" x 38"
(Perú)
FREDY LUQUE SONCO
"EL GRAN GUERRERO"
Modelado, 90 x 60 cm.
INFORMATION: www.iberointernacional.com
sonniavaldivia@hotmail.com - editor@iberointernacional.com

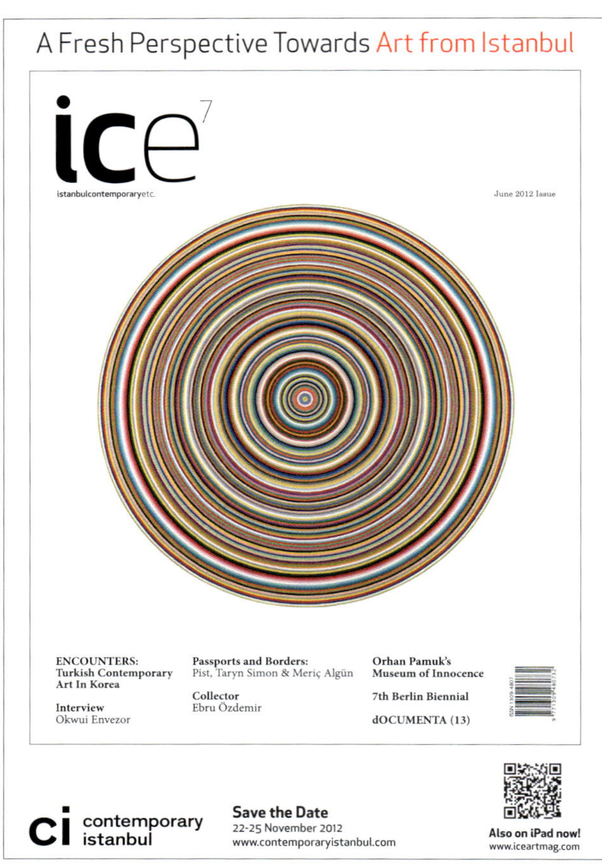
A Fresh Perspective Towards Art from Istanbul
ice7
istanbulcontemporaryetc.
June 2012 Issue
ENCOUNTERS: Turkish Contemporary Art In Korea
Interview Okwui Envezor
Passports and Borders: Pist, Taryn Simon & Meriç Algün
Collector Ebru Özdemir
Orhan Pamuk's Museum of Innocence
7th Berlin Biennial
dOCUMENTA (13)
ci contemporary istanbul
Save the Date
22-25 November 2012
www.contemporaryistanbul.com
Also on iPad now!
www.iceartmag.com

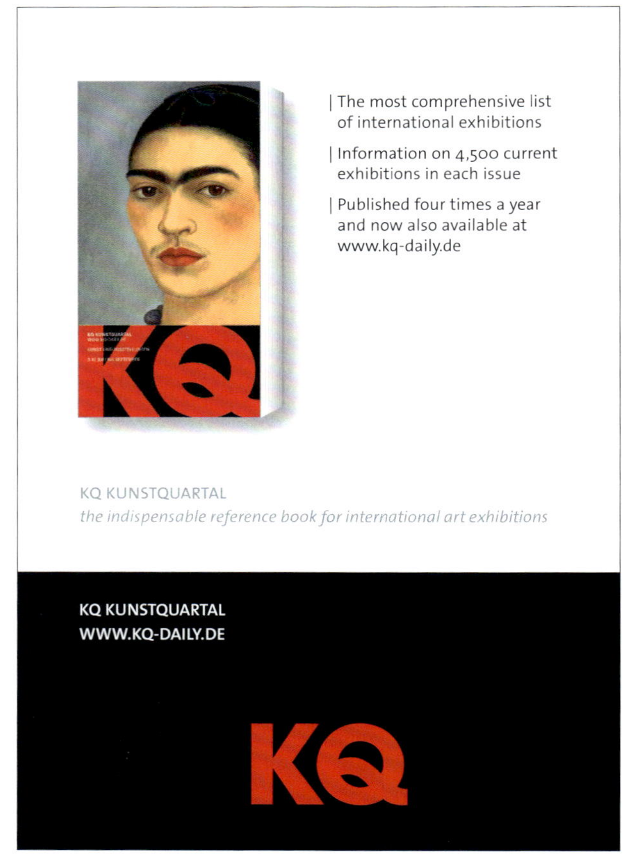
| The most comprehensive list of international exhibitions
| Information on 4,500 current exhibitions in each issue
| Published four times a year and now also available at www.kq-daily.de
KQ
KQ KUNSTQUARTAL
the indispensable reference book for international art exhibitions
KQ KUNSTQUARTAL
WWW.KQ-DAILY.DE
KQ

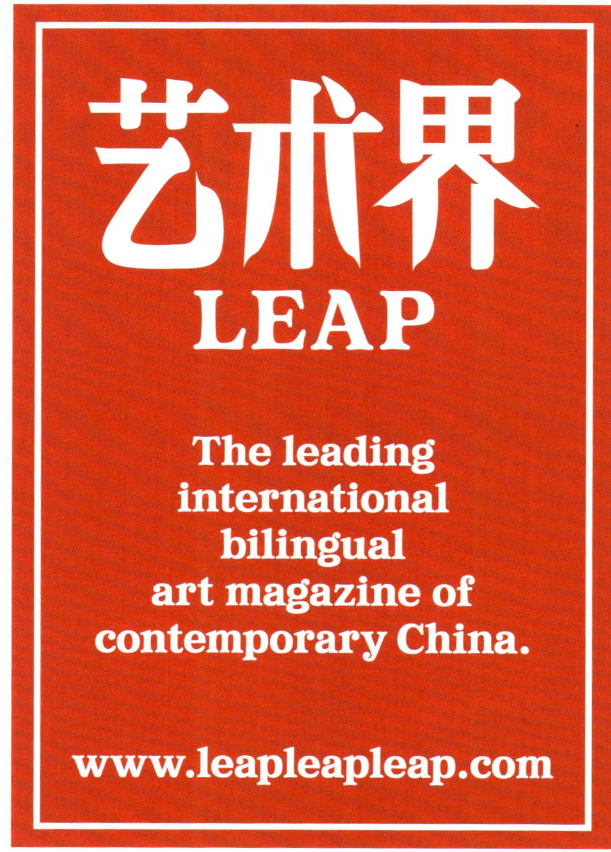
艺术界
LEAP
The leading international bilingual art magazine of contemporary China.
www.leapleapleap.com

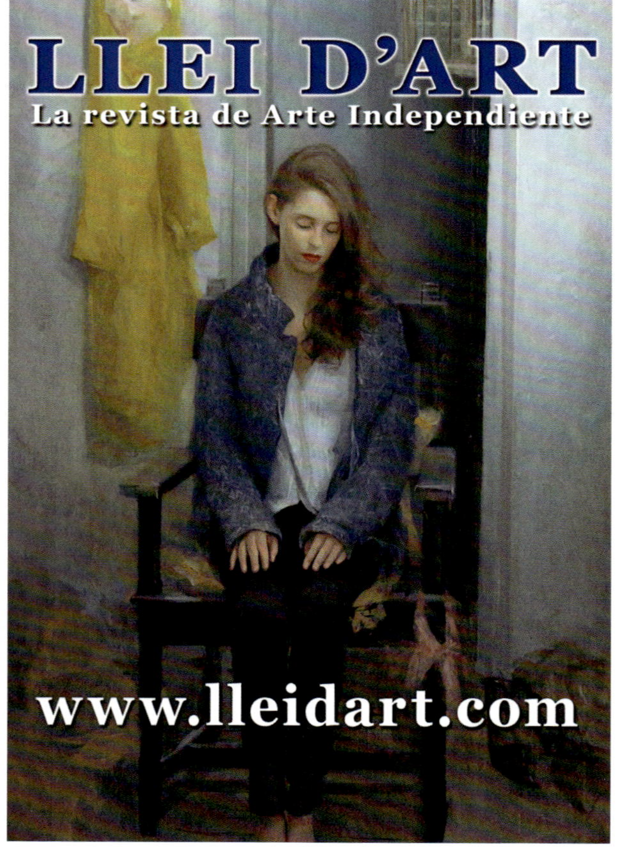
LLEI D'ART
La revista de Arte Independiente
www.lleidart.com

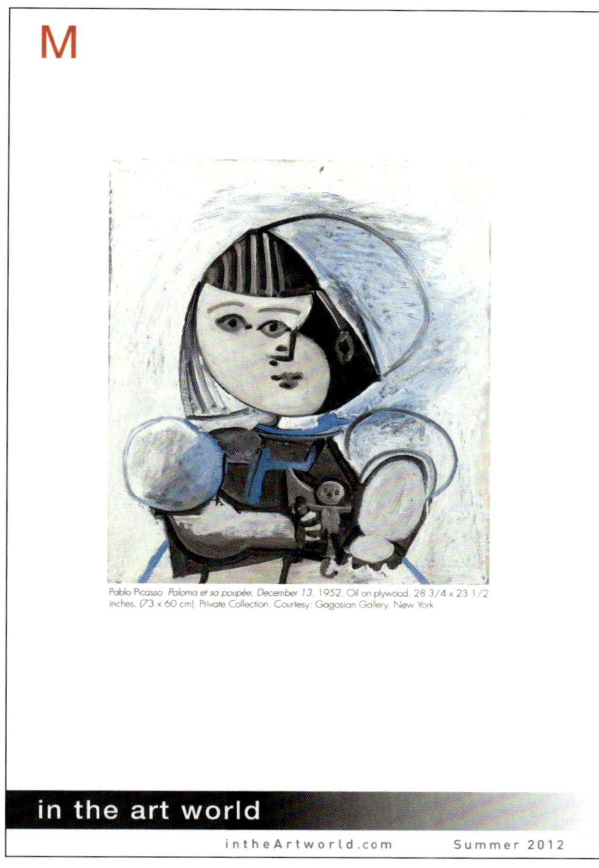

Pablo Picasso *Paloma et sa poupée*, December 13, 1952. Oil on plywood. 28 3/4 x 23 1/2 inches. (73 x 60 cm). Private Collection. Courtesy: Gagosian Gallery, New York

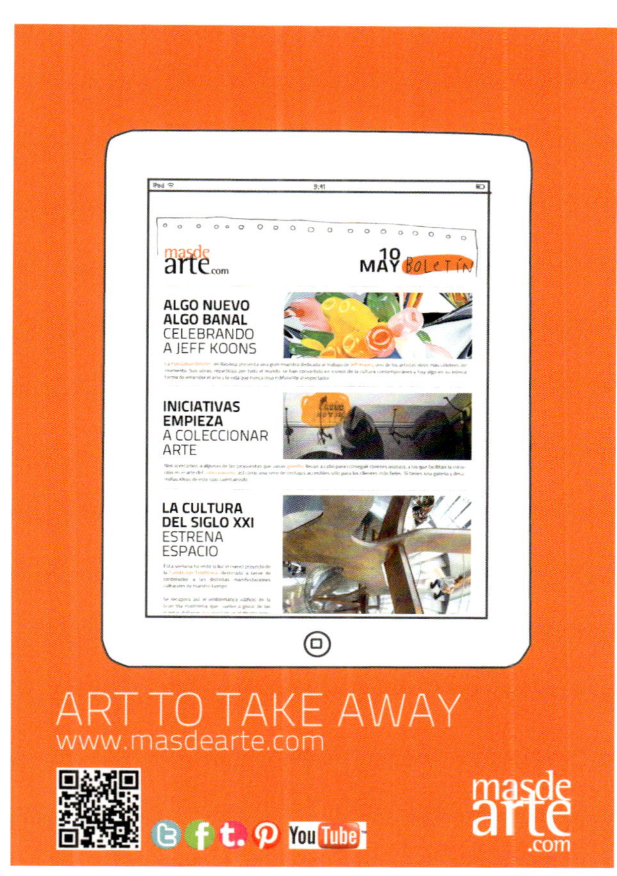

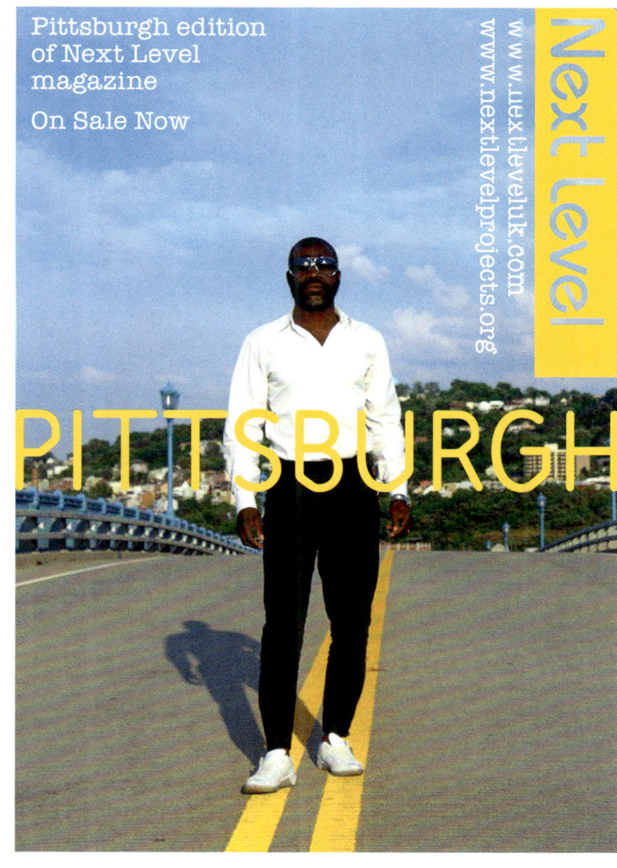

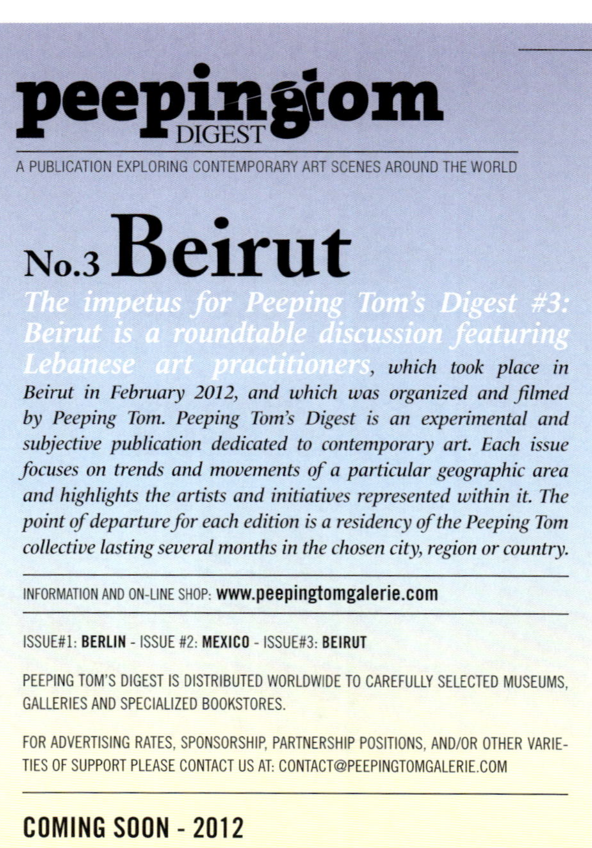
peepingtom
DIGEST
A PUBLICATION EXPLORING CONTEMPORARY ART SCENES AROUND THE WORLD
No.3 Beirut
The impetus for Peeping Tom's Digest #3: Beirut is a roundtable discussion featuring Lebanese art practitioners, which took place in Beirut in February 2012, and which was organized and filmed by Peeping Tom. Peeping Tom's Digest is an experimental and subjective publication dedicated to contemporary art. Each issue focuses on trends and movements of a particular geographic area and highlights the artists and initiatives represented within it. The point of departure for each edition is a residency of the Peeping Tom collective lasting several months in the chosen city, region or country.
INFORMATION AND ON-LINE SHOP: www.peepingtomgalerie.com
ISSUE#1: BERLIN - ISSUE #2: MEXICO - ISSUE#3: BEIRUT
PEEPING TOM'S DIGEST IS DISTRIBUTED WORLDWIDE TO CAREFULLY SELECTED MUSEUMS, GALLERIES AND SPECIALIZED BOOKSTORES.
FOR ADVERTISING RATES, SPONSORSHIP, PARTNERSHIP POSITIONS, AND/OR OTHER VARIETIES OF SUPPORT PLEASE CONTACT US AT: CONTACT@PEEPINGTOMGALERIE.COM
COMING SOON - 2012

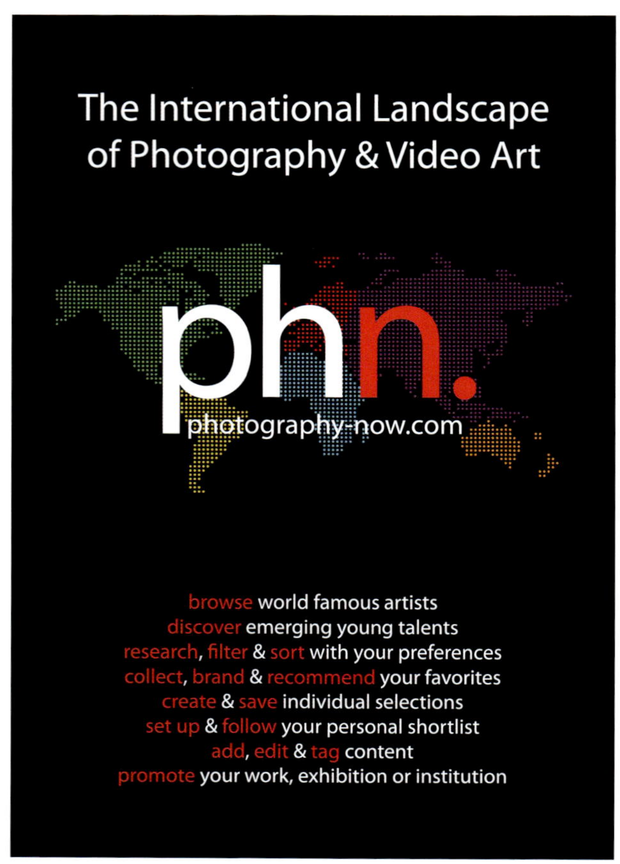
The International Landscape
of Photography & Video Art
phn.
photography-now.com
browse world famous artists
discover emerging young talents
research, filter & sort with your preferences
collect, brand & recommend your favorites
create & save individual selections
set up & follow your personal shortlist
add, edit & tag content
promote your work, exhibition or institution

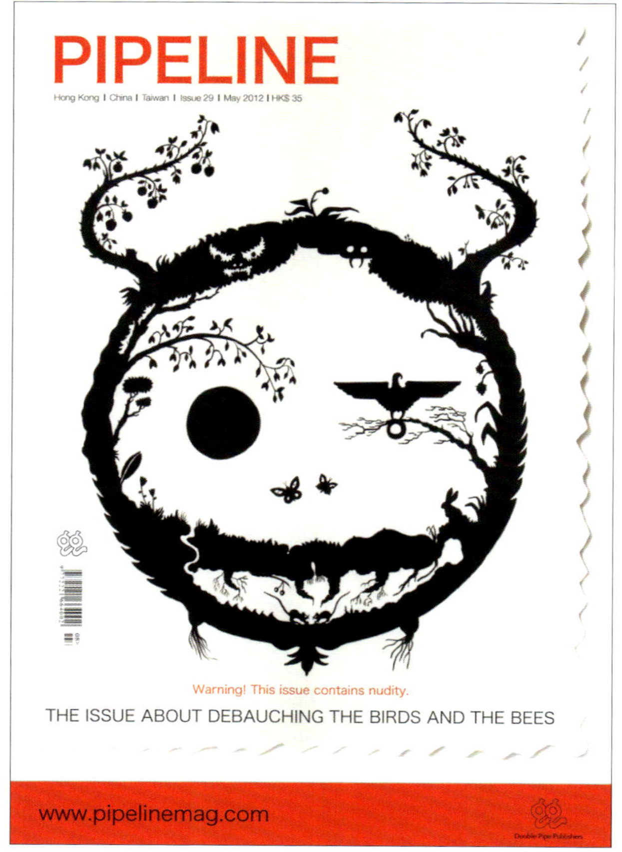
PIPELINE
Hong Kong | China | Taiwan | Issue 29 | May 2012 | HK$ 35
Warning! This issue contains nudity.
THE ISSUE ABOUT DEBAUCHING THE BIRDS AND THE BEES
www.pipelinemag.com

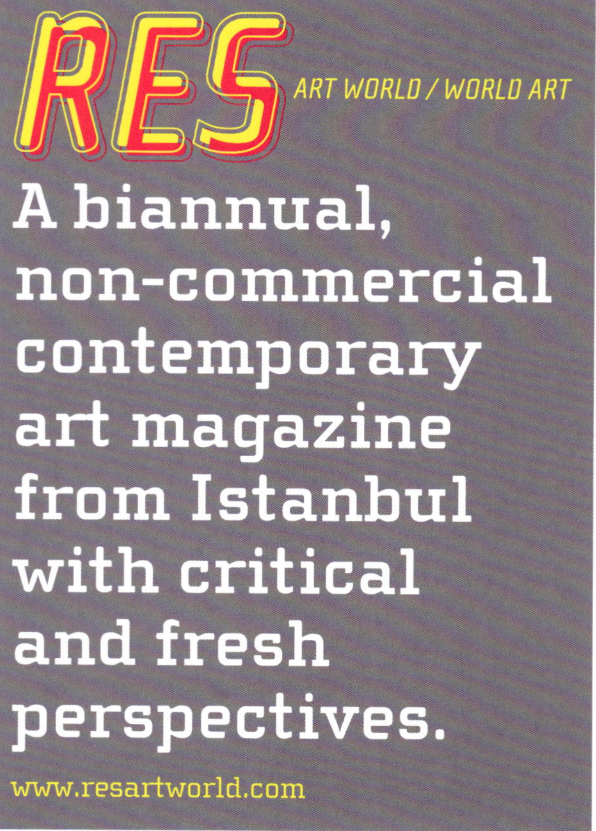
RES
ART WORLD / WORLD ART
A biannual, non-commercial contemporary art magazine from Istanbul with critical and fresh perspectives.
www.resartworld.com

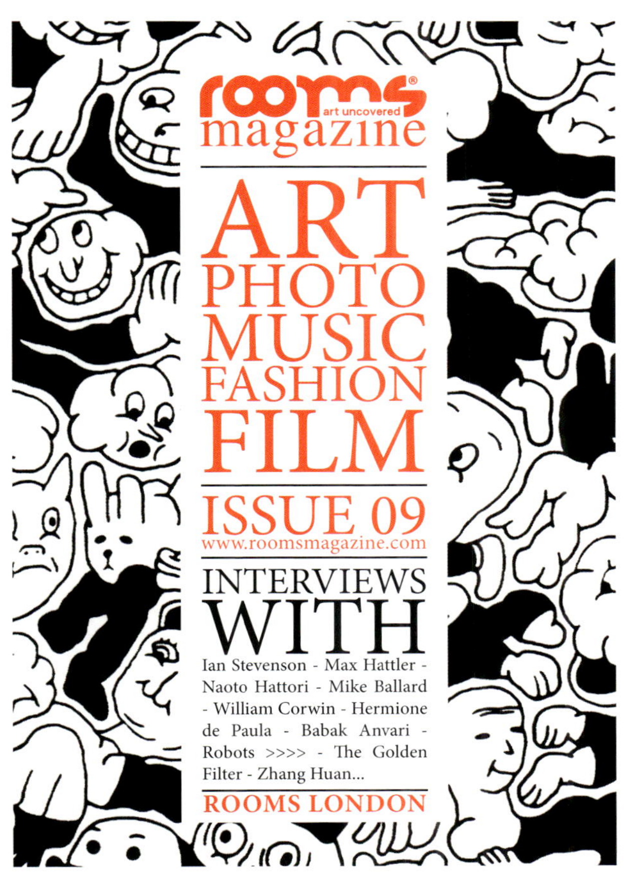
rooms
art uncovered
magazine
ART
PHOTO
MUSIC
FASHION
FILM
ISSUE 09
www.roomsmagazine.com
INTERVIEWS
WITH
Ian Stevenson - Max Hattler - Naoto Hattori - Mike Ballard - William Corwin - Hermione de Paula - Babak Anvari - Robots >>>> - The Golden Filter - Zhang Huan...
ROOMS LONDON

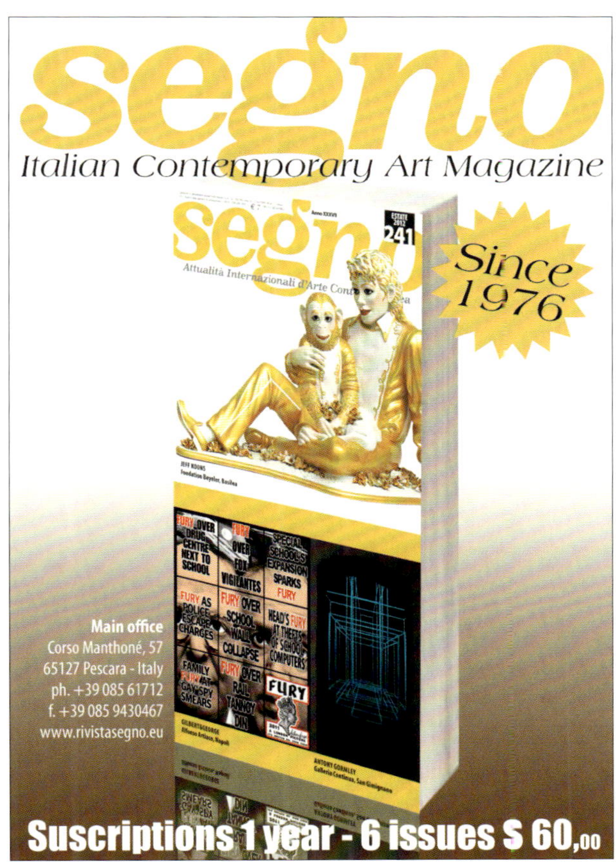
segno
Italian Contemporary Art Magazine
segno
241
Attualità Internazionali d'Arte Contemporanea
Since 1976
Main office
Corso Manthoné, 57
65127 Pescara - Italy
ph. +39 085 61712
f. +39 085 9430467
www.rivistasegno.eu
Suscriptions 1 year - 6 issues $ 60,00

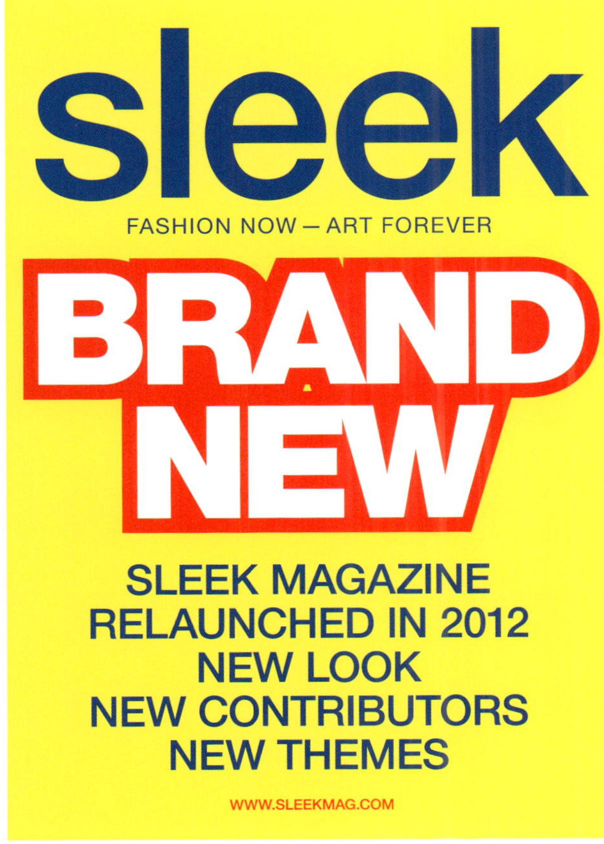
sleek
FASHION NOW — ART FOREVER
BRAND
NEW
SLEEK MAGAZINE
RELAUNCHED IN 2012
NEW LOOK
NEW CONTRIBUTORS
NEW THEMES
WWW.SLEEKMAG.COM

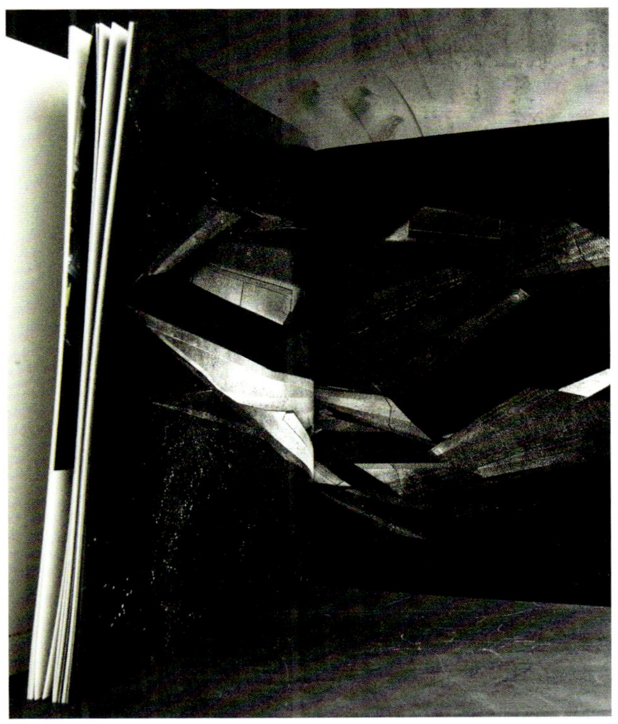
SOME/THINGS
SOME/THINGS MAGAZINE— CURATED PROJECT IN THE FORM OF A LUXURY BOOK.

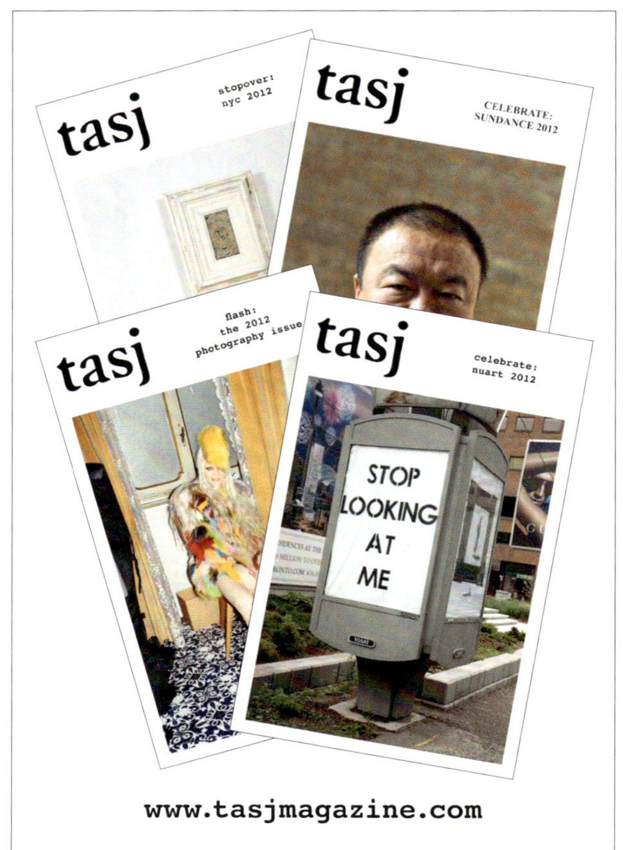

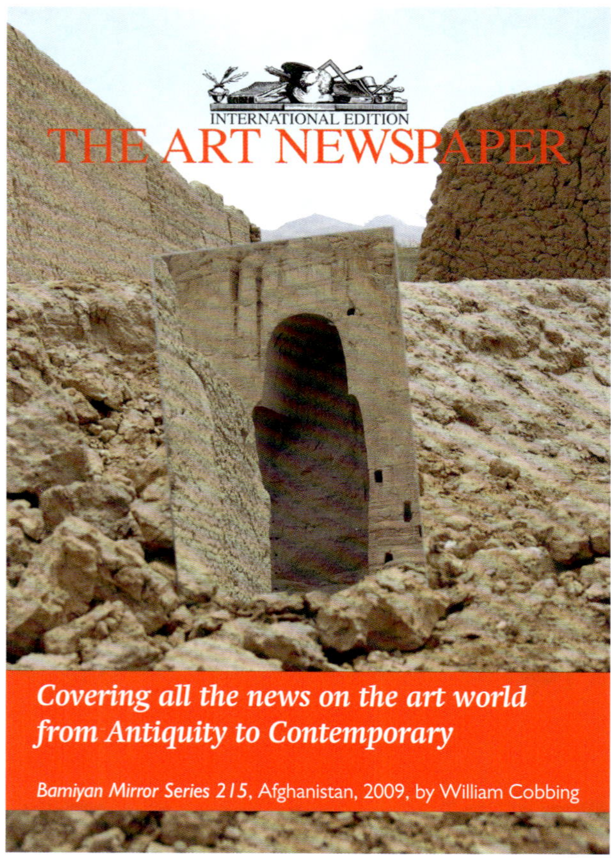

Bamiyan Mirror Series 215, Afghanistan, 2009, by William Cobbing

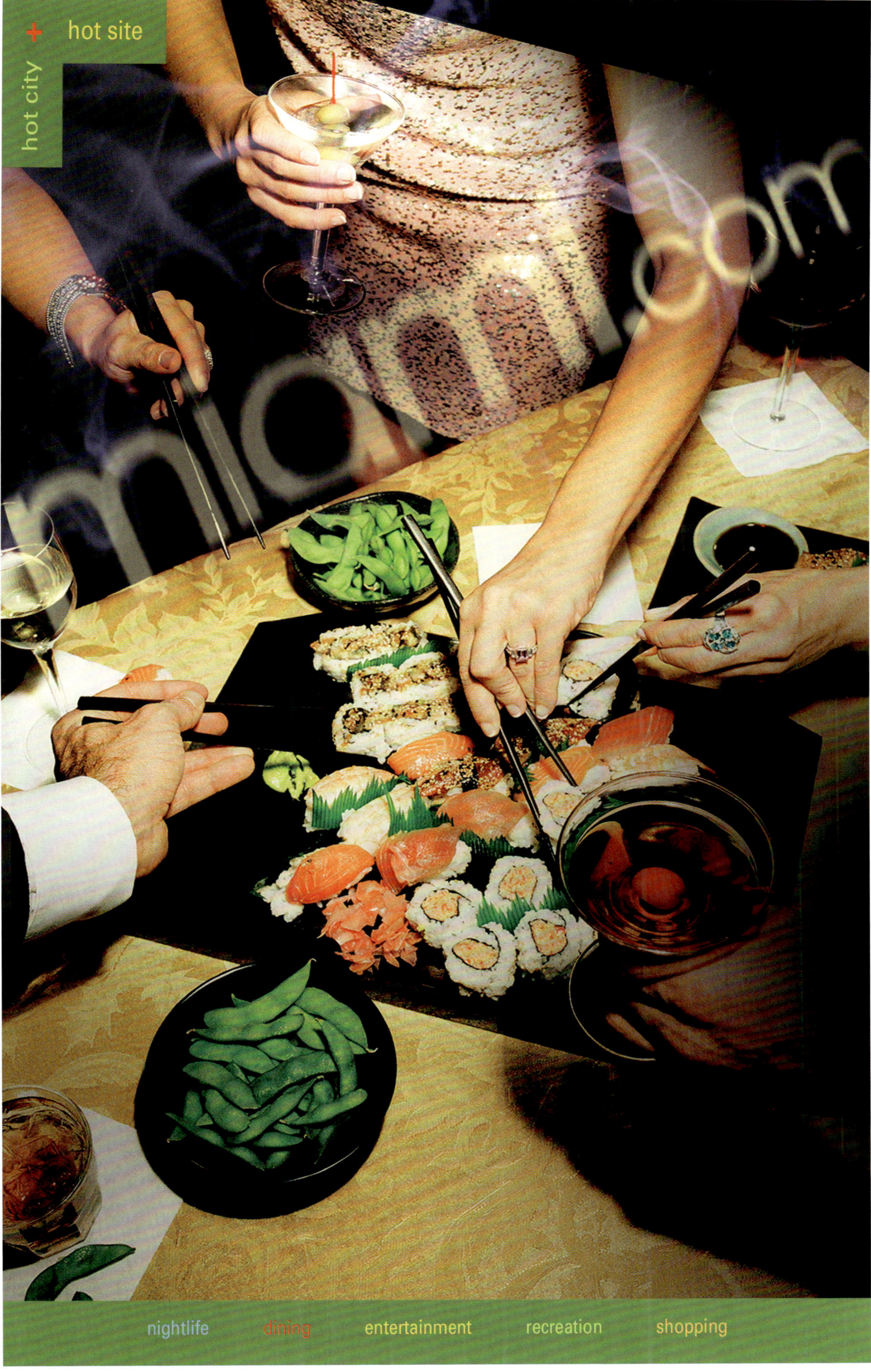
hot city
+
hot site
miami.com
nightlife
dining
entertainment
recreation
shopping

Art | Museums

KNIGHT MASTERWORKS PRINT COLLECTION
and inaugural artist
DONALD SULTAN

As part of its mission to enlighten, educate and entertain our community, the Adrienne Arsht Center will annually commission world-class artists to produce limited-edition prints that capture the spirit of the Center, the performing artists that appear on its stages and the Center's unique role in its diverse community. Uniting the performing and visual arts, this initiative begins a new, distinguished art collection worthy of the Adrienne Arsht Center and Miami's growing presence in the global arts scene.

Art works commissioned for this collection will seek inspiration from the power of the performing arts to nourish and challenge the human spirit and from Miami as the diverse, international crossroads where creative forces passionately connect.

ADRIENNE ARSHT CENTER TOUR
Saturday, December 8 @ Noon | Free

Tour features a viewing of Donald Sultan's Red Poppies, 2012, the inaugural work of the Knight Masterworks Print Collection.

For more information on Arsht Center Art Basel Miami Beach activities, visit arshtcenter.org/basel

The Knight Masterwork's Print Collection is generously funded in part by

Knight Foundation

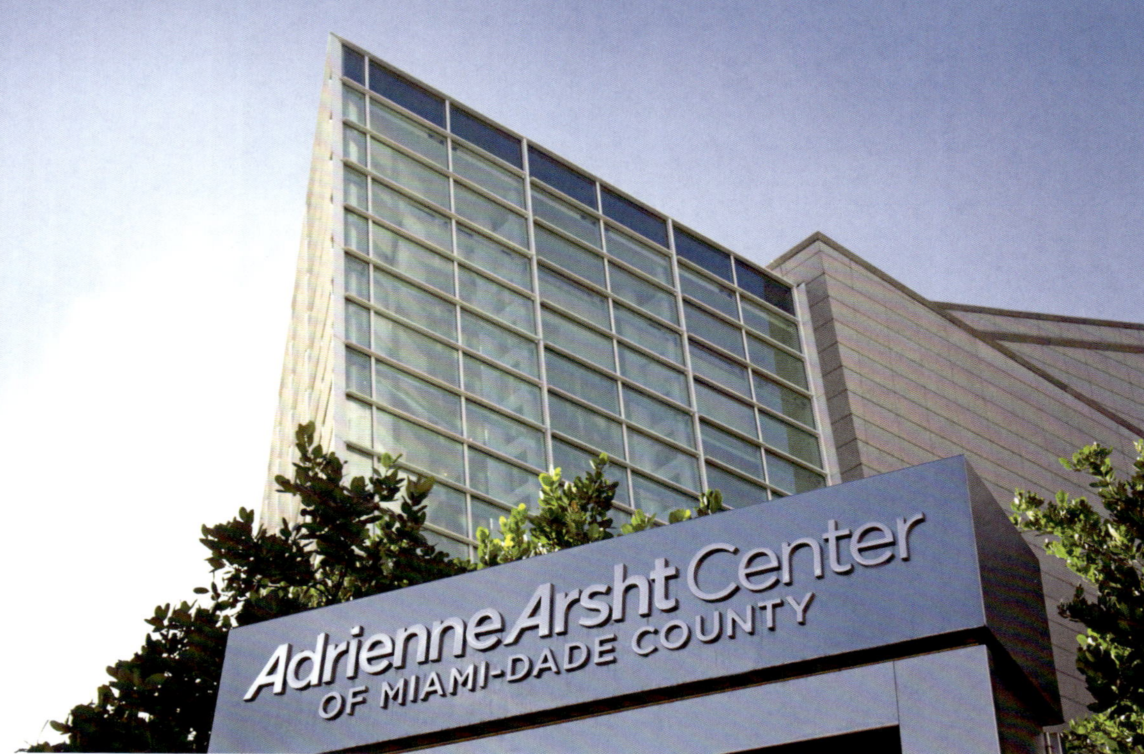

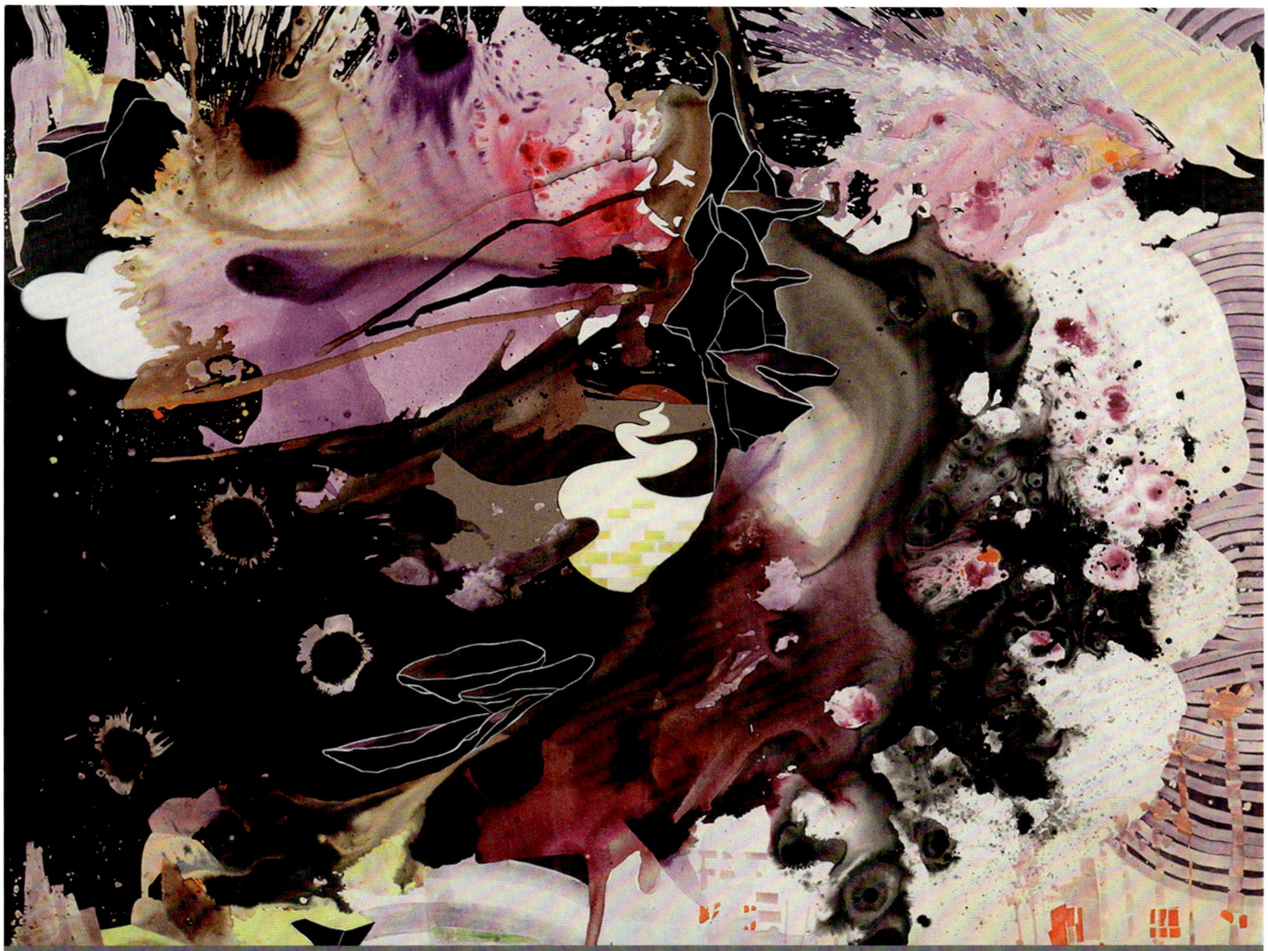

Art and Culture Center of Hollywood

2012/2013 Exhibition Season

Nov. 10 – Jan. 13
- Elisabeth Condon: The Seven Seas
- Millree Hughes and Peter Boyd McLean: Lummox
- Antonia Wright: Be
- Rosemarie Chiarlone/Susan Weiner: Obstruction

Jan. 25 – Feb. 22
- Abracadabra: Sixth Annual Exhibition and Fund-raiser
- David Leroi: Amusez La Galerie
- Matu Croney: BRAVELION & THE CLASS OF 2000
- Perry Pandrea: If I've said it once, I've said it a thousand times...

March 9 – April 14
- Don Lambert: Lawn Jobs
- Brandon Opalka: Janigan's
- Jenny Brillhart: Accumulation

April 27 – May 26
- Sixth Annual All-Media Juried Biennial
- Elaine Defibaugh: Illuminated Collage

June 8 – Sept. 1
- Charles M. Schulz: Pop Culture in Peanuts

Art and Culture Center of Hollywood
1650 Harrison Street
Hollywood, FL 33020
954. 921. 3274
ArtAndCultureCenter.org

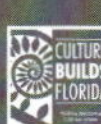

BROWARD COUNTY FLORIDA HOLLYWOOD

The Art and Culture Center of Hollywood is a 501(c)(3) non-profit organization supported in part by its members, admissions, private entities, the City of Hollywood, the Broward County Board of County Commissioners as recommended by the Broward Cultural Council; the State of Florida, Department of State, Division of Cultural Affairs, the Florida Council on Arts and Culture; and the Kresge Foundation. We welcome donations from all members of the community who wish to support our work.

Image: Elisabeth Condon, *White Lines* (detail), Acrylic on linen, 84 x 90 inches, Courtesy of Lesley Heller Workspace

Curated Studio Visits

December 6 - 9, 2012 | 9am to 12pm
800-810 Lincoln Road at Meridian Ave.
Miami Beach. Space is limited.
RSVP to exhibitions@artcentersf.org

AfterHours ArtLounge *@ Project 924*

December 5 - 8, 2012 | 9pm to 12am
924 Lincoln Road, Second Floor.
Miami Beach. Free public access.

ART BASEL HOURS:
WED - THU | 9am - 10pm
FRI - SAT | 9am - 11pm
SUN | 9am - 9pm

REGULAR HOURS:
MON - THU | 12pm - 9pm
FRI - SAT | 11am - 10pm
SUN | 11am - 9pm

Exhibitions and programs at ArtCenter/South Florida are made possible through grants from the Miami-Dade County Department of Cultural Affairs, the Cultural Affairs Council, The Children's Trust; the Miami-Dade Mayor and Board of County Commissioners; the City of Miami Beach Cultural Arts Council; the Miami Beach Mayor and City Commissioners; and the State of Florida, Florida Department of State, Division of Cultural Affairs, the Florida Arts Council and the National Endowment for the Arts. Additional funding provided by the Walgreens Company, Celebrity Cruises, Wells Fargo, WLRN, Arts for Learning, and The Center at Miami Dade College.

ArtCenter
SOUTH FLORIDA

800-810 & 924 Lincoln Road
www.artcentersf.org
305.674.8278

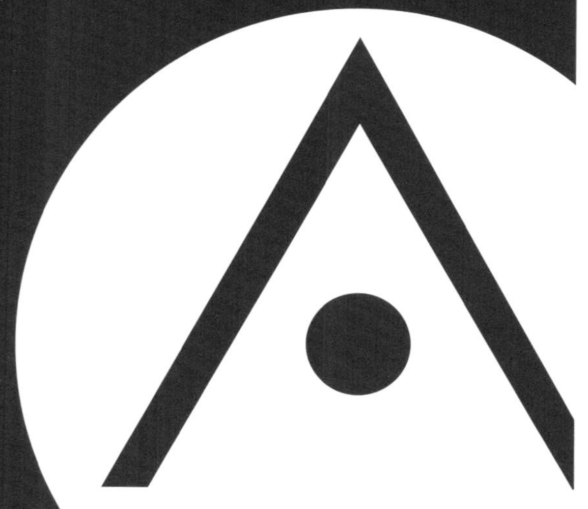

the endless renaissance

six solo artist projects

Eija-Liisa Ahtila

Barry X Ball

Walead Beshty

Hans-Peter Feldmann

Ged Quinn

Araya Rasdjarmrearnsook

dec 6 2012 – mar 17 2013

bassmuseum*of***art**

2100 collins avenue | miami beach fl 33139 | t 305.673.7530 | www.bassmuseum.org

hours during art basel: dec 6-10 (thurs-mon) 10am-6pm | regular hours thereafter: wed-sun 12-5pm

The Bass Museum of Art is a nonprofit, tax-exempt organization accredited by the American Association of Museums. The Bass Museum of Art is generously funded by the City of Miami Beach, Cultural Affairs Program, Cultural Arts Council; Miami-Dade County Department of Cultural Affairs and the Cultural Affairs Council, the Miami-Dade County Mayor and Board of County Commissioners; John S. and James L. Knight Foundation; and sponsored in part by the State of Florida, Department of State, Division of Cultural Affairs and the Florida Council on Arts and Culture and the Bass Museum of Art membership.

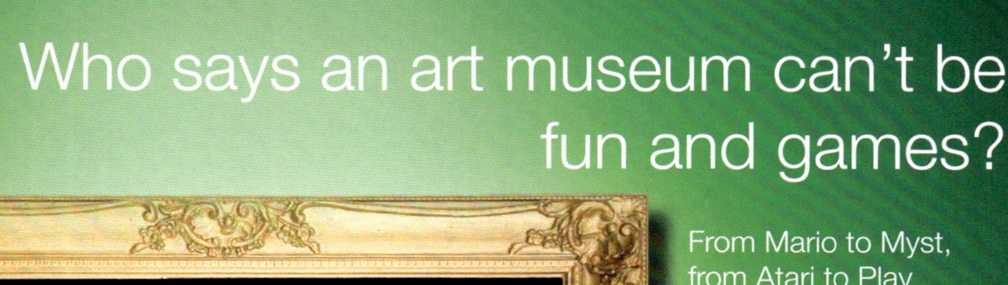

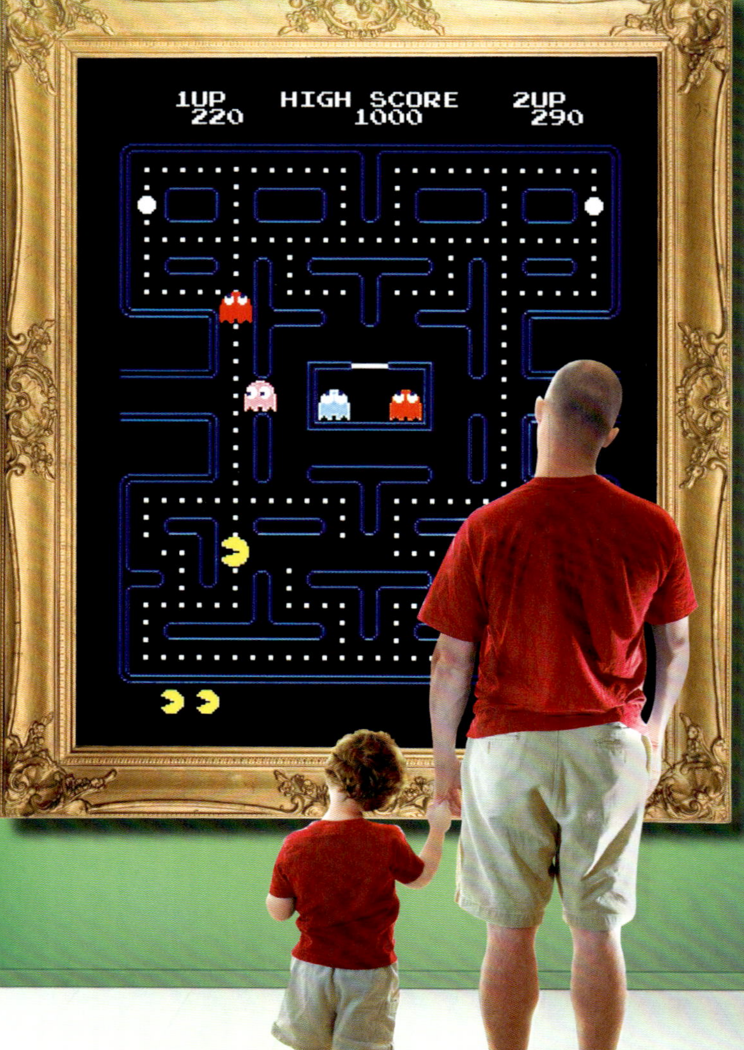

From Mario to Myst, from Atari to Play Station, *The Art of Video Games* brings you a fascinating look into the 40-year evolution of digital design, story-telling and interactivity of video games.

Organized by the Smithsonian American Art Museum, the exhibition displays 80 games selected for their creative visual effects and use of technologies **with all-time greats set up for visitors to play.**

Don't miss this fun and enlightening exhibition. For more information contact the Boca Raton Museum of Art.

Presented in Boca Raton by
fmsbonds, Inc.
Municipal Bond Specialists

The Art of Video Games | 10.24.12–1.13.13

The Art of Video Games is organized by the Smithsonian American Art Museum with generous support from the Entertainment Software Association Foundation; Sheila Duignan and Mike Wilkins; Shelby and Frederick Gans; Mark Lamia; Ray Muzyka and Greg Zeschuk; Rose Family Foundation; Betty and Lloyd Schermer; and Neil Young. The C.F. Foundation in Atlanta supports the museum's traveling exhibition program, Treasures to Go.

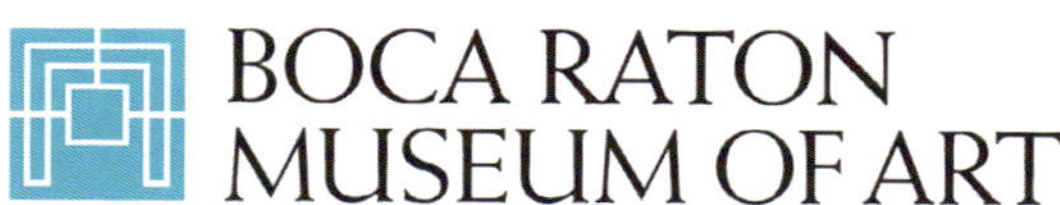

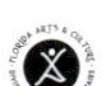
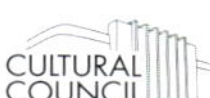

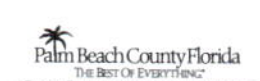

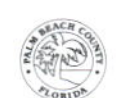

above: Pac-Man (arcade), 1980, Tōru Iwatani. TM & (C) NAMCO BANDAI Games Inc.

501 Plaza Real, Boca Raton, FL
www.bocamuseum.org
561.392.2500

Follow us
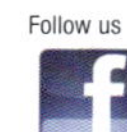

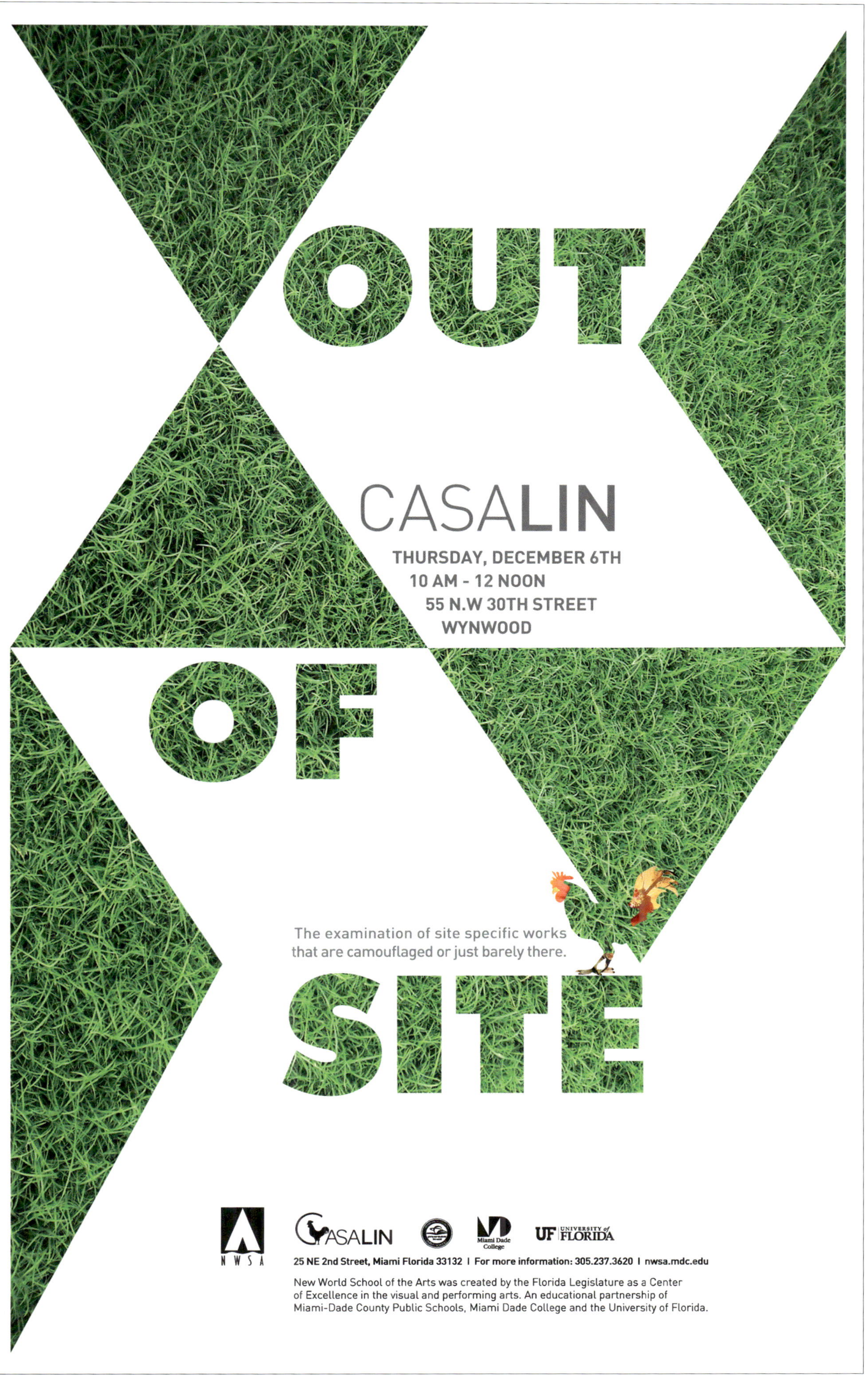
OUT
CASALIN
THURSDAY, DECEMBER 6TH
10 AM - 12 NOON
55 N.W 30TH STREET
WYNWOOD
OF
The examination of site specific works
that are camouflaged or just barely there.
SITE
NWSA
CASALIN
Miami Dade College
UF UNIVERSITY of FLORIDA
25 NE 2nd Street, Miami Florida 33132 | For more information: 305.237.3620 | nwsa.mdc.edu
New World School of the Arts was created by the Florida Legislature as a Center
of Excellence in the visual and performing arts. An educational partnership of
Miami-Dade County Public Schools, Miami Dade College and the University of Florida.

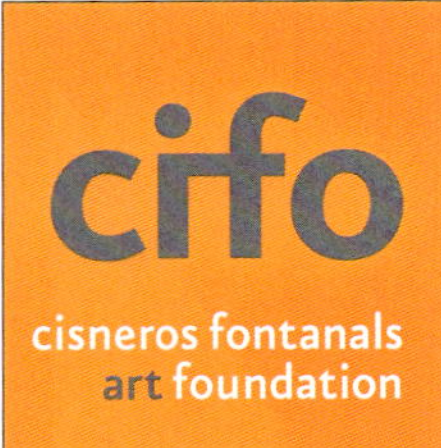

Unsaid/Spoken

Selected works from The Ella Fontanals-Cisneros Collection and The CIFO Collection

Curated by Moacir dos Anjos and José Roca

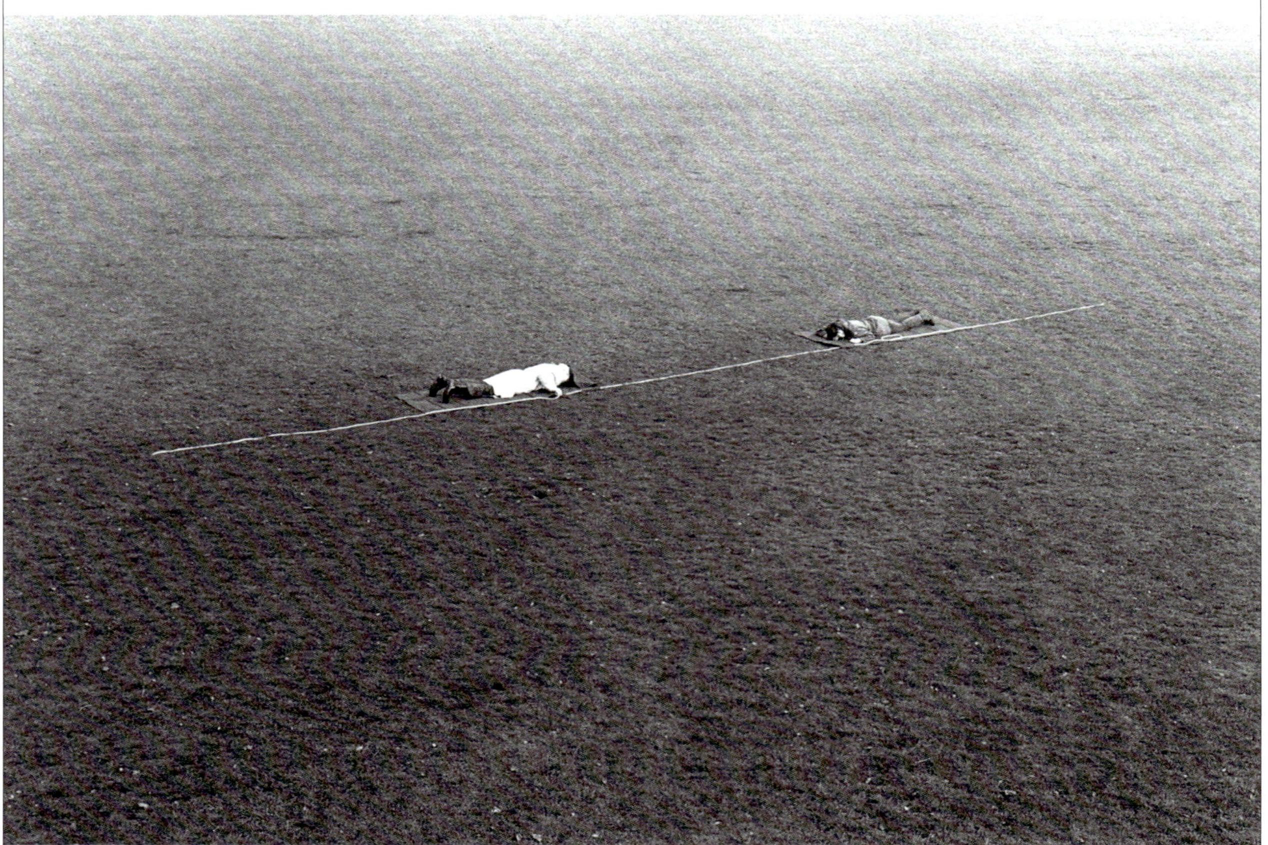

Franz Erhard Walther, *Gegenuber (Area - distance - cord - cord as "language medium") Single Element n°.28 of 1. Werksatz*, 1967.

Photo ©Tim Rautert. All rights reserved. Courtesy Stiftung Franz Erhard Walther and Tim Rautert.

December 5, 2012 - March 3, 2013

Thursday - Friday: Noon - 6pm; Saturday-Sunday: 10am - 4pm

Special hours during **Art Basel Miami Beach:**

Wednesday, Dec. 5 – Sunday, Dec. 9, 2012: 9am - 4pm

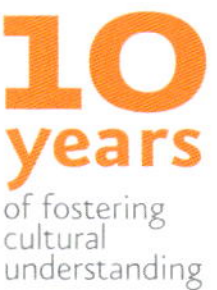

1018 N. Miami Avenue | Miami, Florida 33136

T: 305.455.3380 | E: info@cifo.org | **www.cifo.org**

2012

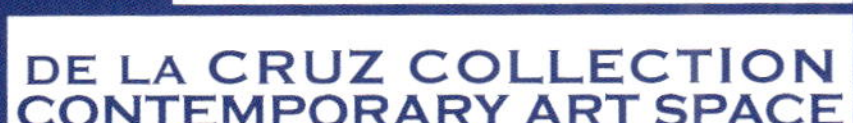

23 NE 41 STREET
MIAMI DESIGN DISTRICT, 33137
TEL- 305 576 6112
WWW.DELACRUZCOLLECTION.ORG
CONTACT: IBETT YANEZ, DIRECTOR

FROM THE COLLECTION

PROJECT ROOM - "PLEAT CONSTRUCTION" BY JIM DRAIN

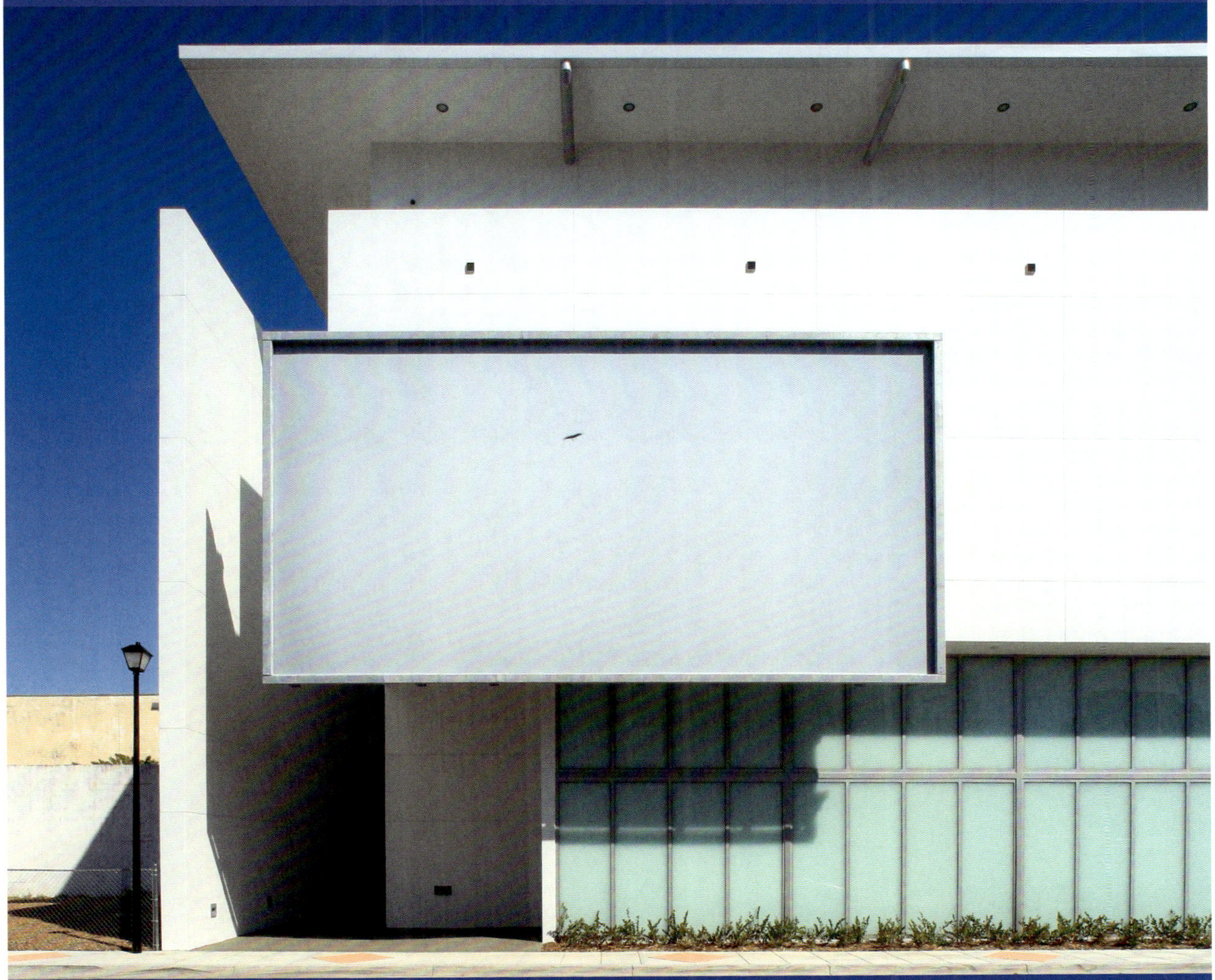

HOURS DURING ART BASEL MIAMI BEACH

TUES DEC 4 THROUGH SAT DEC 8
FROM 9 AM TO 4 PM - ADMISSION FREE OF CHARGE

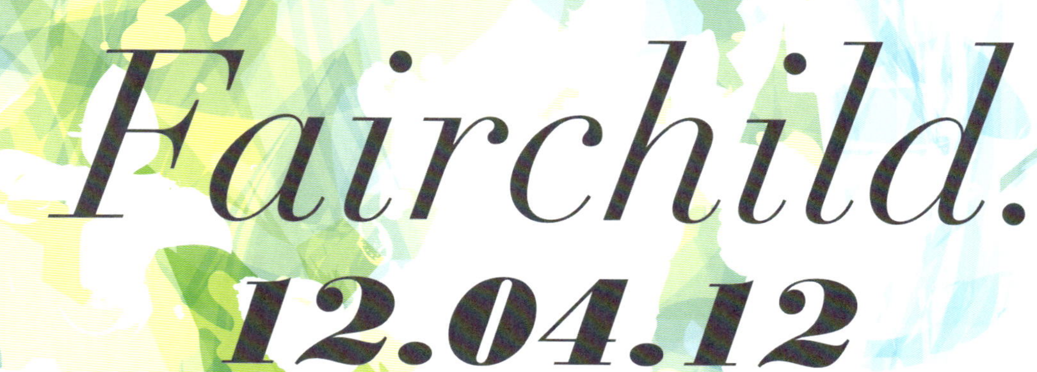

10 Years of Art + Nature

Botero • Chihuly • Di Suvero • Dion • Gainer • Kusama • Les Lalanne • Levine
Lichtenstein • Martin • Oka Doner • Ono • Rennert • Rodriguez-Casanova • Ryman
SICIS • Tschumy • van Dalen • von Rydingsvard • West • Youngblood

FAIRCHILD TROPICAL BOTANIC GARDEN
Exploring, Explaining and Conserving the World of Tropical Plants
10901 Old Cutler Road, Coral Gables, Florida 33156-4296 USA • 305.667.1651 • www.fairchildgarden.org

University Galleries

Florida Atlantic University

New Art: South Florida

Cultural Consortium Visual and Media Artists Fellowship Exhibition

September 22 – December 15, 2012
Opening Reception: Friday, September 21, 6 – 9 pm

Eleven artists from Florida's five southeastern counties that have received a highly competitive grant.
Artists: Nellie Appleby, Domingo Castillo, Clifton Childree, Phillip Estlund, Jiae Hwang, Eric Landes, Nicolas Lobo, Mark Moormann, Ernesto Oroza, John Sanchez and Tom Scicluna.

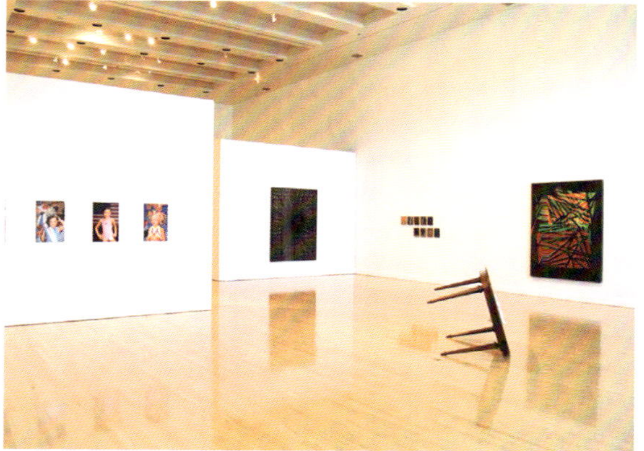

Installation view of *New Art: 2009 South Florida Cultural Consortium Visual and Media Arts Fellowship Exhibition* with photography by Colby Katz, paintings by Gavin Perry and a sculpture by Francis Trombly.

Papercuts

January 19 – March 2, 2013
Opening Reception: Friday, January 18, 6 – 9 pm

Works in manipulated, bent and cut paper create pieces that range from visual narratives to complex sculptural abstractions.
Artists: Jaq Belcher, Béatrice Coron, Michelle Forsyth, Reni Gower, Lenka Konopasek, Lauren Scanlon and Daniella Woolf.

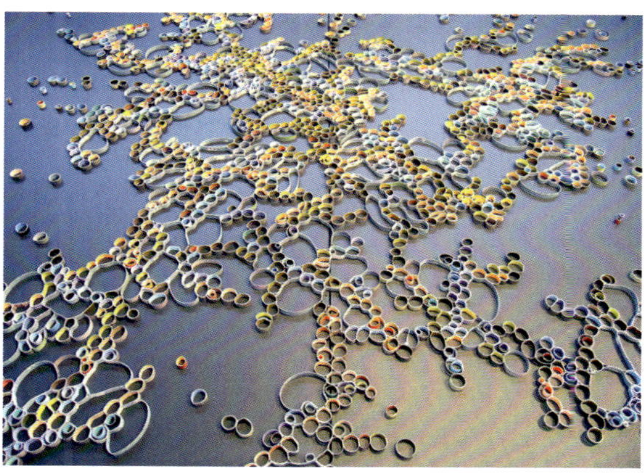

Michelle Forsyth, *For March 24, 1989*, 2011, paper, watercolor, screenprint and ColorAid paper 120 x 120 x 8".

Pour

February 5 – March 23, 2013
Pour (paint): a Symposium
Saturday, February 23, 2 – 5 pm

Fluid painting techniques and the influence of digital culture blend in abstract paintings.
Artists: Ingrid Calame, Kris Chatterson, Roland Flexner, Angelina Gualdoni, Carrie Moyer, Carolanna Parlato, David Reed, Jackie Saccoccio and Carrie Yamaoka.

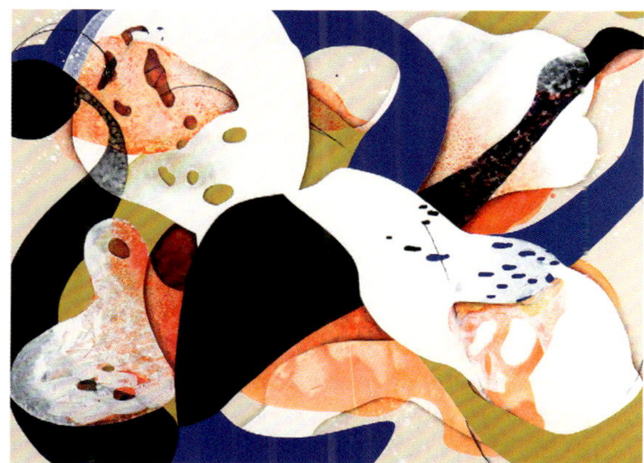

Carrie Moyer, *Diver*, 2011, acrylic on canvas, 48 x 60", courtesy CANADA, LLC.

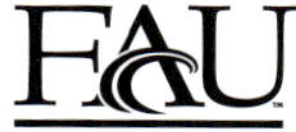

University Galleries, School of the Arts
Dorothy F. Schmidt College of Arts and Letters
www.fau.edu/galleries • 561.297.2661

Florida Atlantic University
777 Glades Road
Boca Raton, FL 33431

Hours:
Monday - Friday 1:00 - 4:00 pm
Saturday 1:00 - 5:00 pm

Breakfast in the Park

The Patricia & Phillip Frost Art Museum

Celebrate
Art Basel Miami Beach with

ALBERT PALEY

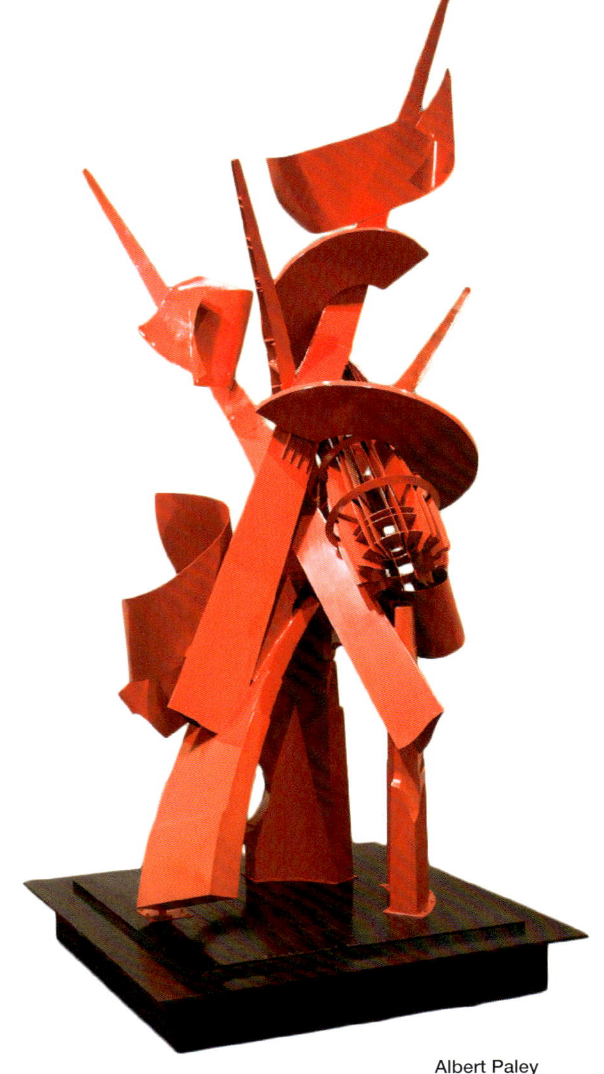

Sunday, December 9, 2012
9:30am - 12:00pm
For more information, call 305.348.2890
or visit http://thefrost.fiu.edu

Complimentary
Outdoor Breakfast

Informal talk with
Albert Paley

Guided Tours
of the Sculpture Park

Also on view:
Ivan Navarro: *Fluorescent Light Sculptures*
Reflections Across Time: *Seminole Portraits*
to beauty: A Tribute to Mike Kelley
American Sculpture in the Tropics
Mark Messersmith: *Fragile Nature*
Material and Meaning

Albert Paley
Clay Center Model, 2009
Mild Steel, 12' × 6' × 7' 3"
Paley Studios, Ltd. Archive

The Patricia & Phillip Frost Art Museum at
Florida International University
10975 SW 17th Street
Miami, Florida 33199

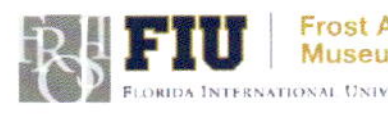

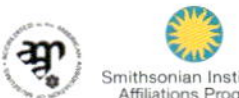

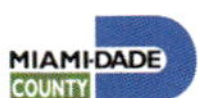

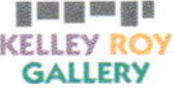

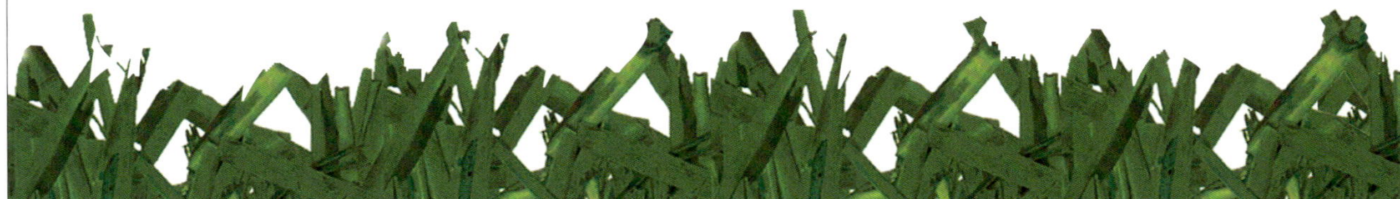

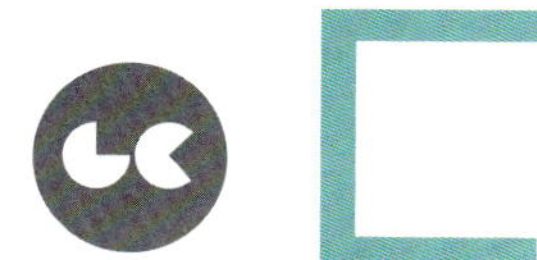

Girls' Club presents
Following the Line
Contemporary drawings from the collection
of Francie Bishop Good & David Horvitz
Curated by Carol Jazzar

Works by
Louise Bourgeois/ Lou Anne Colodny/
William Cordova/ Tracey Emin/
Naomi Fisher/ Joanne Greenbaum/
Klara Kristalova/ Julie Mehretu/
Wangechi Mutu/ Beatriz Monteavaro/
Alice Neel/ Jorge Pantoja and more.
Catalog available

Girls' Club
Contemporary Art by Women

117 NE 2nd St.
Fort Lauderdale, FL 33301
954. 828. 9151
www.girlsclubcollection.org

Free & open to the public
Regular hours:
Wed - Fri 1-5 pm
and by appt.

Directions from Miami:
30 min. North on I-95
Exit East on Broward Blvd.
L on Andrews Av.
R on 2nd St.
Parking across the st.

The exhibition and catalog
are made possible by
Funding Arts Broward and
private donors

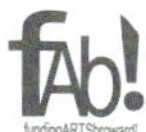

Art Basel | Miami Beach 2012
Wed - Sun 9am - 1pm
VIP Brunch Sun, Dec 9

On view
Nov 2, 2012 - Sep 30, 2013

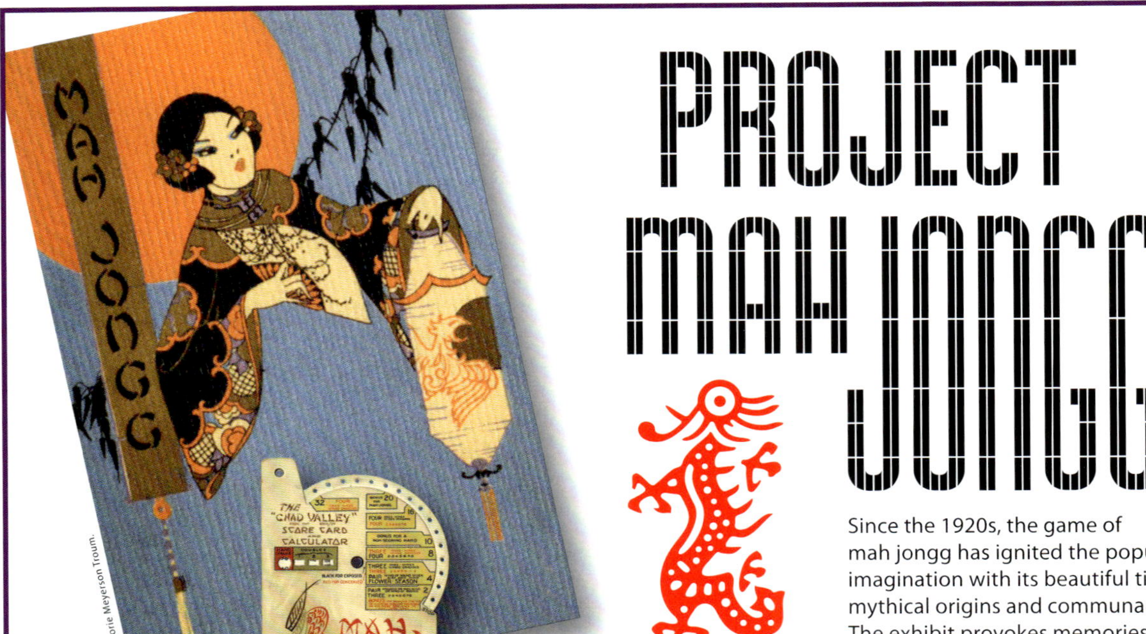

Courtesy of Marjorie Meyerson Troum.

Score card for mah jongg, c. 1923
Courtesy the Museum of Jewish Heritage — A Living Memorial to the Holocaust

PROJECT MAH JONGG

Since the 1920s, the game of mah jongg has ignited the popular imagination with its beautiful tiles, mythical origins and communal spirit. The exhibit provokes memories of the intergenerational tradition of this game, and illuminates mah jongg's influence on contemporary design, art, literature, theater, fashion and cuisine.

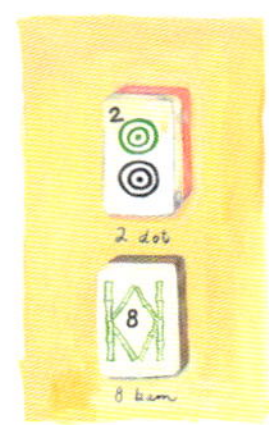

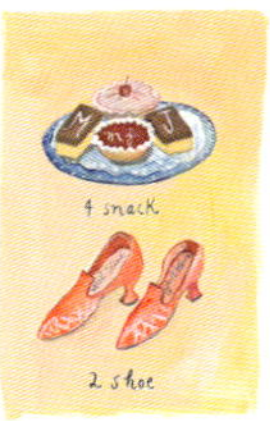

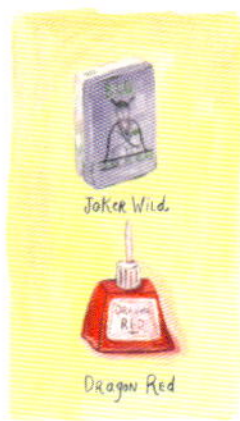

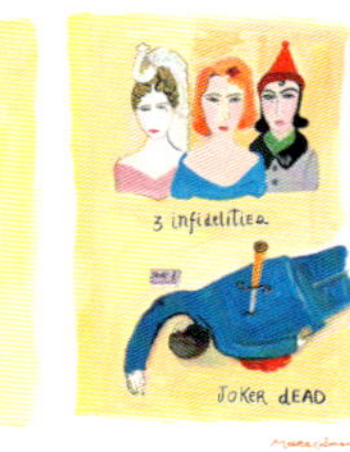

Mah Jongg Murder

Illustration by Maira Kalman for *Mah Jongg: Crak, Bam, Dot*, a 2wice Books publication.

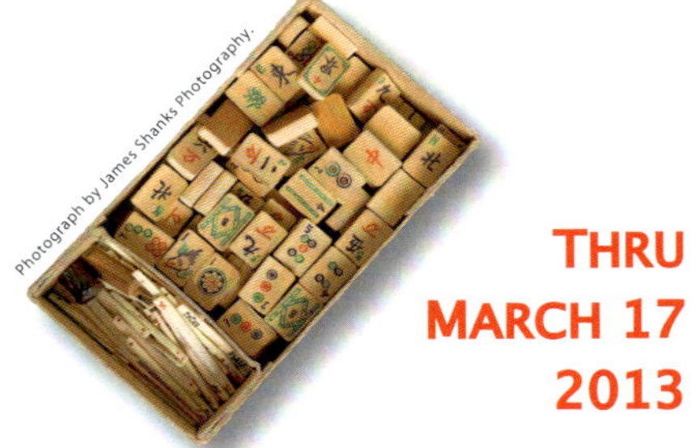

Photograph by James Shanks Photography.

THRU MARCH 17 2013

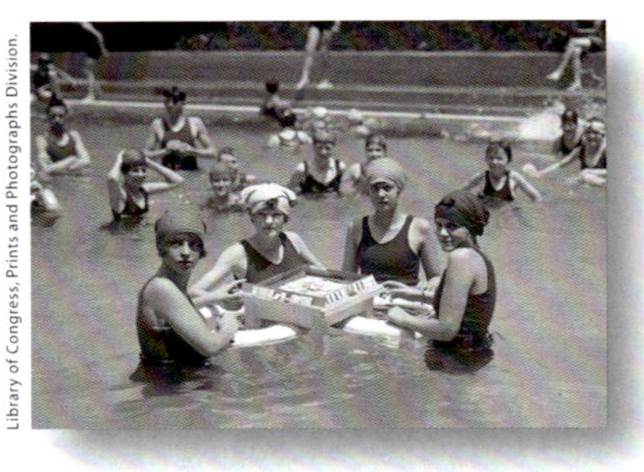

Library of Congress, Prints and Photographs Division.

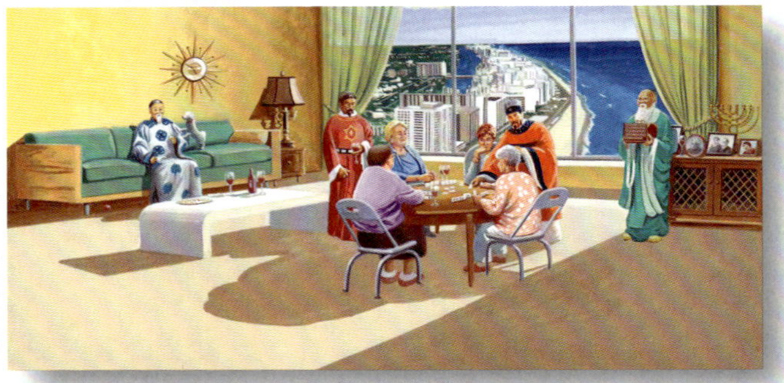

Bruce McCall, 2010, used with permission.

Project Mah Jongg was curated and is circulated by the Museum of Jewish Heritage—A Living Memorial to the Holocaust, New York. The exhibition is made possible through the generosity of the National Mah Jongg League. Additional support is provided by Sylvia Hassenfeld and 2wice Arts Foundation.

Local funders for Project Mah Jongg include: Robert Arthur Segall Foundation, Funding Arts Network, Charles & Sandra Simon, Joni & Stanley Tate. As of 8/8/12.

Also on exhibit: Core Exhibit: *MOSAIC: Jewish Life in Florida 1763 - Present.* *FROM HOME TO HOME: Immigration to America* - Hands-on exhibit for children and families that brings to life the experience of moving to a new country. Thru January 27, 2013.

Housed in two internationally acclaimed and lovingly restored historic former synagogues, discover 250 years of unique Florida history.

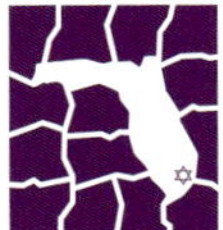

Jewish Museum of Florida
301 Washington Avenue
Miami Beach, FL 33139
305-672-5044 • Fax 305-672-5933
www.jewishmuseum.com

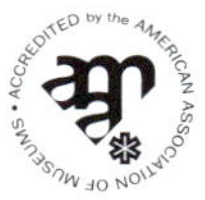

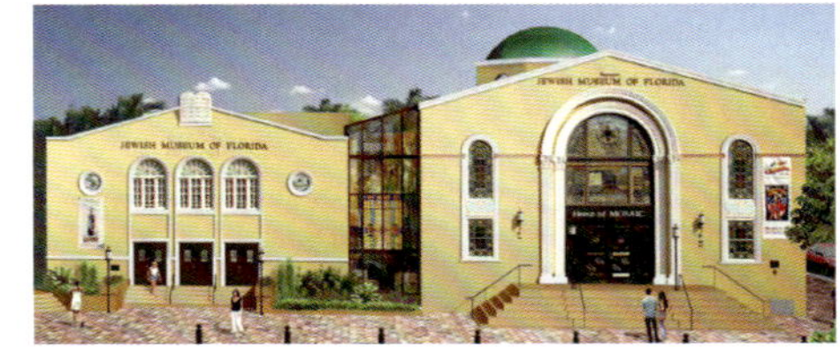

The Museum is supported by individual contributions, foundations, memberships and grants from the State of Florida, Department of State, Division of Cultural Affairs and the Florida Council on Arts and Culture, the Miami-Dade County Tourist Development Council, the Miami-Dade County Department of Cultural Affairs and the Cultural Affairs Council, the Miami-Dade County Mayor and Board of County Commissioners and the City of Miami Beach, Cultural Affairs Program, Cultural Arts Council. Open daily 10 a.m. to 5 p.m. except Mondays and Civil and Jewish holidays.

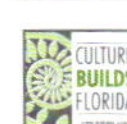

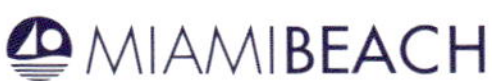

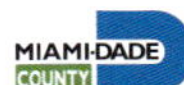

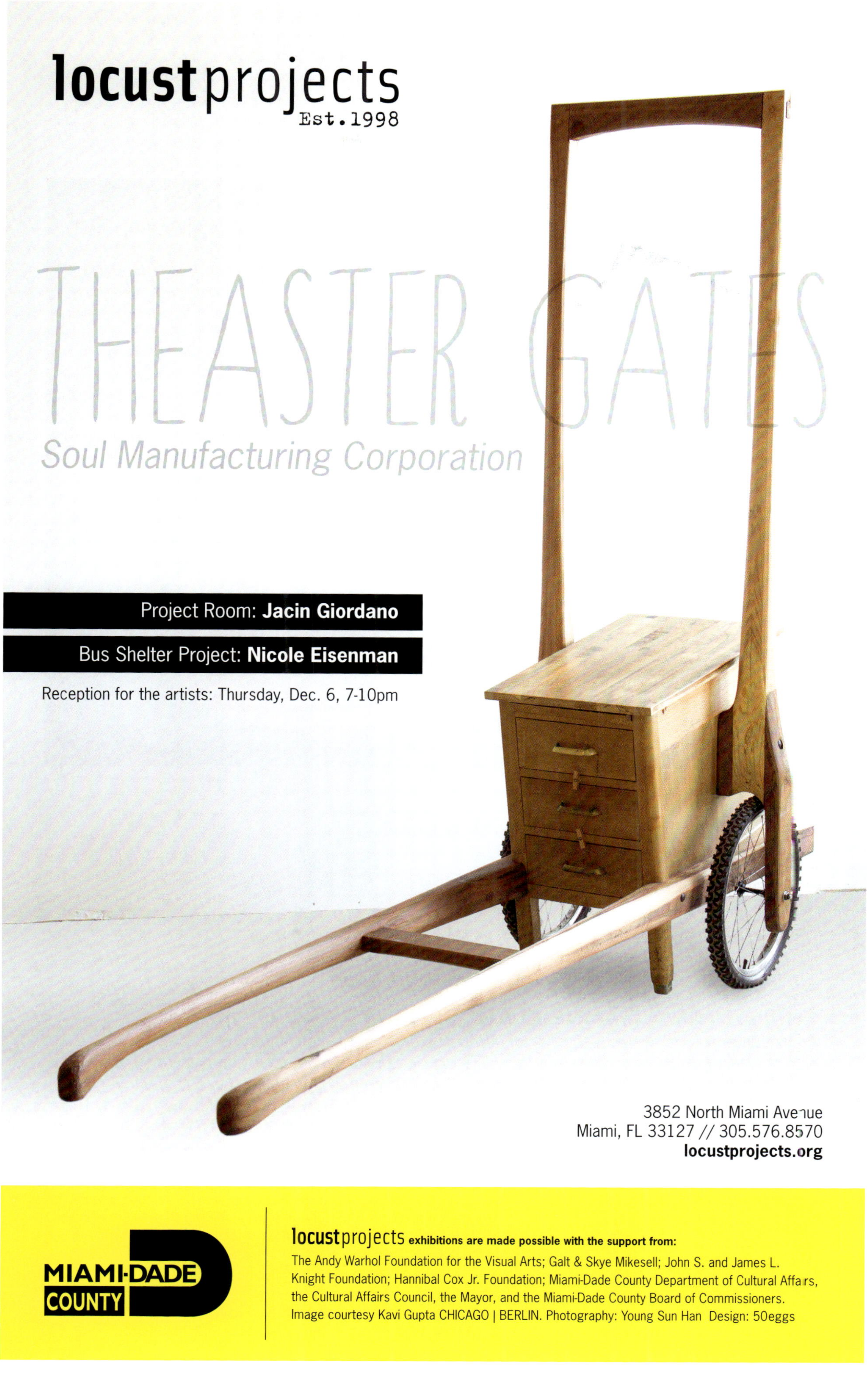

locustprojects
Est.1998

THEASTER GATES
Soul Manufacturing Corporation

Project Room: **Jacin Giordano**

Bus Shelter Project: **Nicole Eisenman**

Reception for the artists: Thursday, Dec. 6, 7-10pm

3852 North Miami Avenue
Miami, FL 33127 // 305.576.8570
locustprojects.org

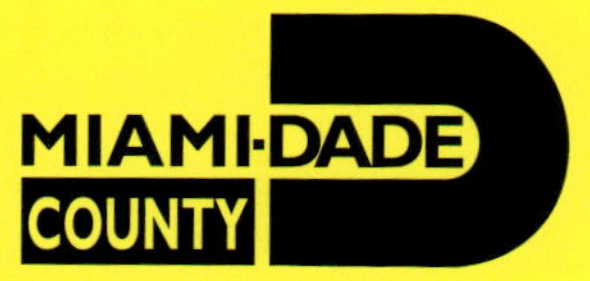

locustprojects exhibitions are made possible with the support from:
The Andy Warhol Foundation for the Visual Arts; Galt & Skye Mikesell; John S. and James L. Knight Foundation; Hannibal Cox Jr. Foundation; Miami-Dade County Department of Cultural Affairs, the Cultural Affairs Council, the Mayor, and the Miami-Dade County Board of Commissioners.
Image courtesy Kavi Gupta CHICAGO | BERLIN. Photography: Young Sun Han Design: 50eggs

University of Miami Lowe Art Museum

ANNUAL ART BASEL CHAMPAGNE BRUNCH

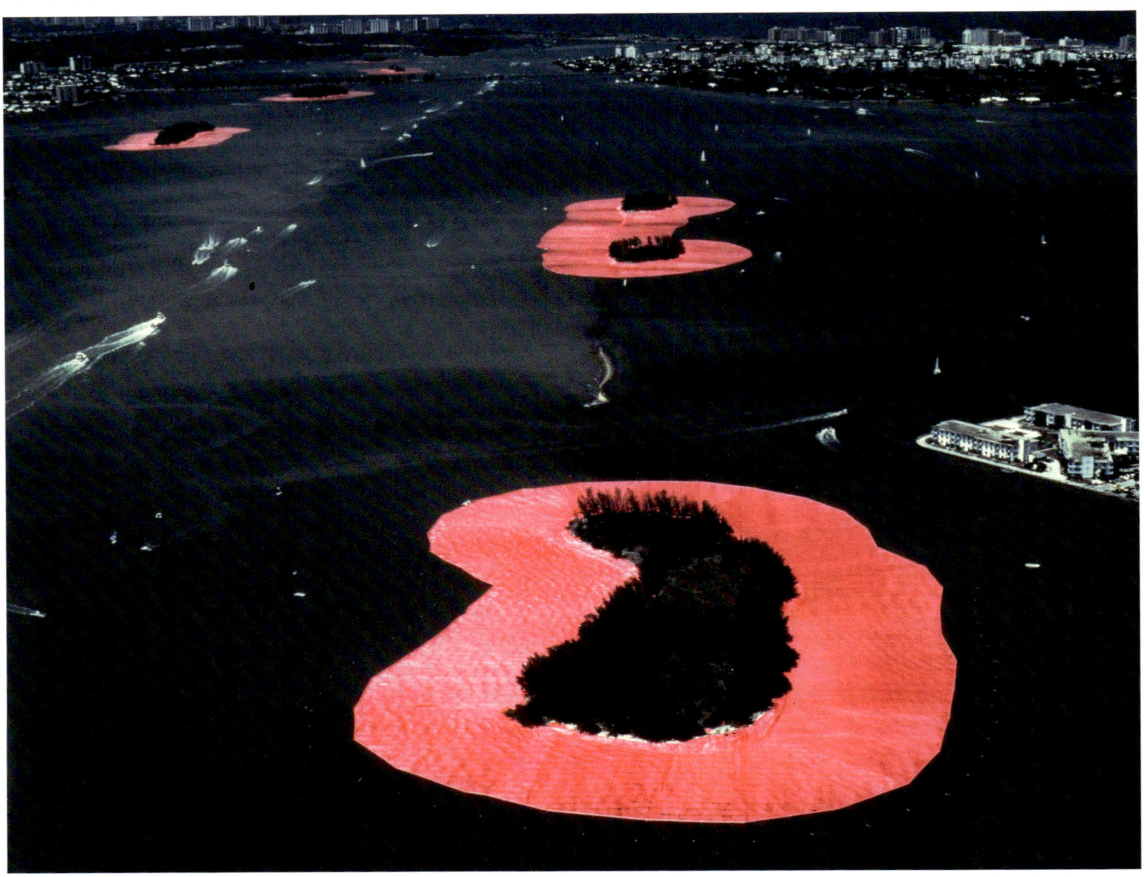

CHRISTO AND JEANNE-CLAUDE: SURROUNDED ISLANDS, BISCAYNE BAY, GREATER MIAMI, FLORIDA, 1980-83, 1984. Portfolio with 4 dye-transfer color photographs, mounted on rag paper, and sample of fabric used in the project. Photograph by Wolfgang Volz. © Christo 1984.

SUNDAY, DECEMBER 9, 2012

BRUNCH: 10 AM - 12 PM

Sponsored by Stella M. Holmes

LECTURE: 12 PM, EUGENIO LÓPEZ

"A Collector's Art: Highlights from the Jumex Collection"

CHRISTO AND JEANNE-CLAUDE: PRINTS AND OBJECTS

An exhibition of more than 130 original numbered editions of prints and objects by Christo and photographic editions by Wolfgang Volz of works by Christo and Jeanne-Claude. Varied in content and technique, the collection represents more than 40 years of Christo and Jeanne-Claude's versatile artistic career, and includes works of art that date from as early as 1962 through 2004. The exhibition is being toured in the United States for this first time in more than 15 years. Organized by Metropolitan State College of Denver, Center for Visual Art, Denver, CO. Christo derives no income from this exhibition. On view through January 13, 2013.

UNIVERSITY OF MIAMI
LOWE ART MUSEUM

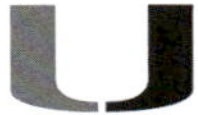

Lowe Art Museum exhibitions and programs are sponsored in part by The State of Florida, Division of Cultural Affairs, The Florida Arts Council, and the National Endowment for the Arts, with the support of the Miami-Dade County Department of Cultural Affairs and the Cultural Affairs Council, the Miami-Dade County Mayor and Board of County Commissioners.

Free for Art Basel VIP card holders and exhibitors. RSVP 305.284.5587 or lowersvp@as.miami.edu

1301 Stanford Drive • Coral Gables, FL • 33124-6310 • www.lowemuseum.org • 305.284.3535

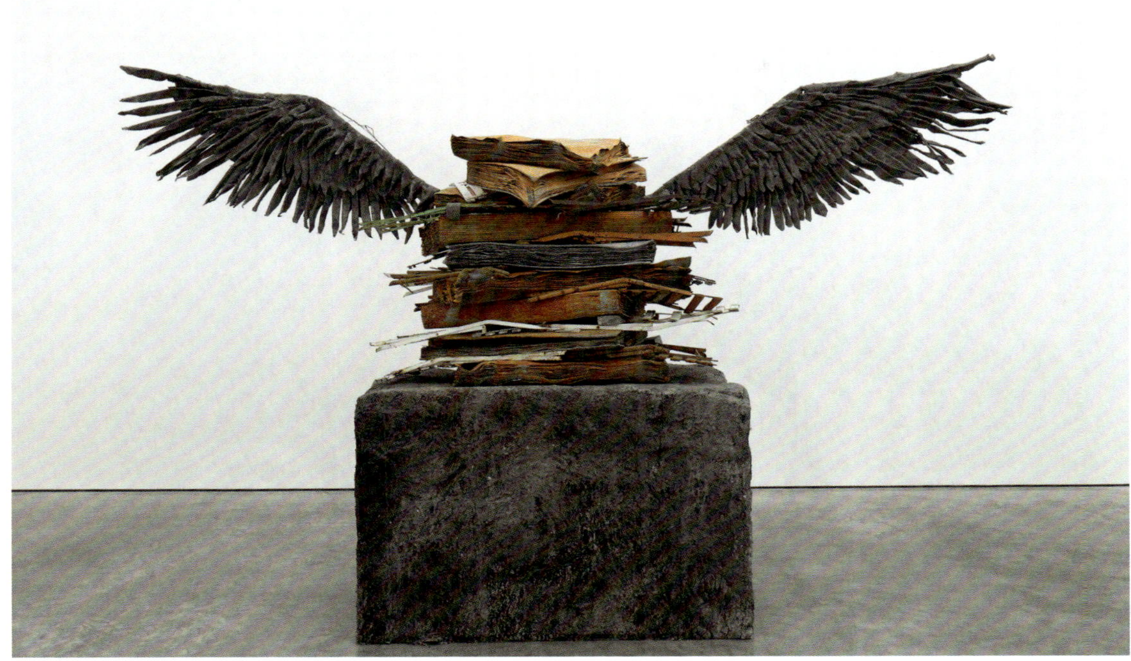

Anselm Kiefer *Sprache der Vögel* 1989

the margulies collection at the WAREhOUSE

ART BASEL MIAMI BEACH 2012
OPEN TO THE PUBLIC
DECEMBER 4 - 9, 2012
TUESDAY - SATURDAY 9AM - 4PM
SUNDAY 9AM - 2PM

FEATURE EXHIBITIONS

SCULPTURE
Anselm Kiefer
Richard Long
William Tucker
Simryn Gill

INSTALLATION
Amar Kanwar
Doug Aitken
David Ellis &
Roberto Lange

VIDEO
Kader Attia
Nathalie Djurberg
Leandro Erlich

PHOTOGRAPHY
Sabelo Mlangeni
Barbara Probst
Wael Shawky

PERMANENT INSTALLATION

Olafur Eliasson
Donald Judd
George Segal

Michael Heizer
Richard Serra
Sol LeWitt

Isamu Noguchi
Tony Smith
Michelangelo Pistoletto

Franz West
John Chamberlain
Willem de Kooning

Martin Z. Margulies
Foundation, Inc.

591 NW 27th Street, Miami, FL 33127 | p: 305.576.1051 f: 305.576.4963
email: mcollection@bellsouth.net | www.margulieswarehouse.com
Curator: Katherine Hinds

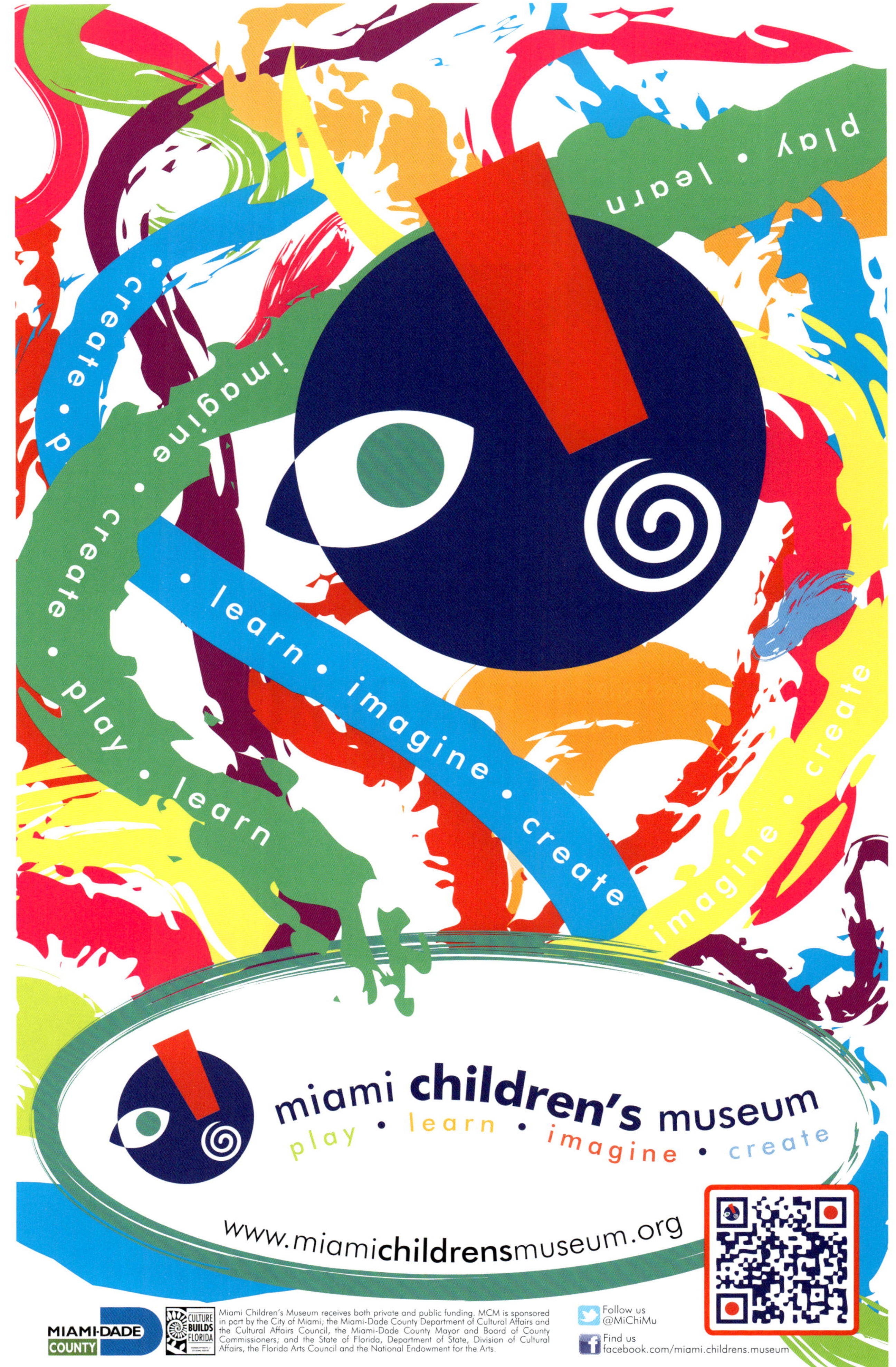
play • learn
create • p
imagine
• create
• learn • imagine • create
create • play • learn
imagine • create
miami children's museum
play • learn • imagine • create
www.miamichildrensmuseum.org
MIAMI-DADE COUNTY
CULTURE BUILDS FLORIDA
Miami Children's Museum receives both private and public funding. MCM is sponsored in part by the City of Miami; the Miami-Dade County Department of Cultural Affairs and the Cultural Affairs Council, the Miami-Dade County Mayor and Board of County Commissioners; and the State of Florida, Department of State, Division of Cultural Affairs, the Florida Arts Council and the National Endowment for the Arts.
Follow us @MiChiMu
Find us facebook.com/miami.childrens.museum

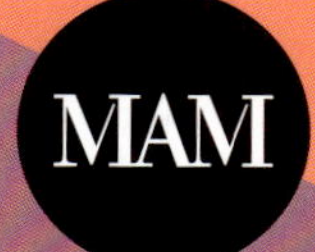

Miami Art Museum

Celebrates Art Basel Miami Beach 2012

On view:

New Work Miami 2013

A salute to Miami's arts community

Tuesday - Friday: 10am - 5pm
Saturday & Sunday: noon - 5pm

Featuring a number of recent and newly commissioned projects
General museum admission.

Party on the Plaza

Celebrating the opening of *New Work Miami 2013*

Thursday, December 6, 2012
7pm - 11pm

Music by Spam Allstars, dancing, cocktails
Access with MAM invitation, MAM members at the Contributing ($250) and above level, and MAM Contemporaries or ABMB VIP card, exhibitor pass, press pass. Shuttle provided between Convention Center and MAM.

Miami Art Museum Ball and Crash the Ball

After Party

Saturday, December 8, 2012
7pm - 11pm

Black tie dinner, Music by Steve Chase Society
Seats begin at $1,000. Crash the Ball included. Advance ticket purchase required.

Begins 10pm

DJ, dancing, cocktails
Crash the Ball tickets presale $100, door $150.

Currency, Value, Hype

Parodi Lecture in the Philosophy of Art

Sunday, December 9, 2012
11:30 am (Doors open 11am)

Miami Art Museum and University of Miami, Department of Philosophy present Martha Buskirk, Professor of art history and criticism at Montserrat College of Art, Beverly, Massachusetts. Free to the public.

For information, or to purchase tickets, contact events@miamiartmuseum.org or 305 375 5935

Pérez Art Museum Miami 2013

Join us next year for MAM's momentous reopening as the Pérez Art Museum Miami

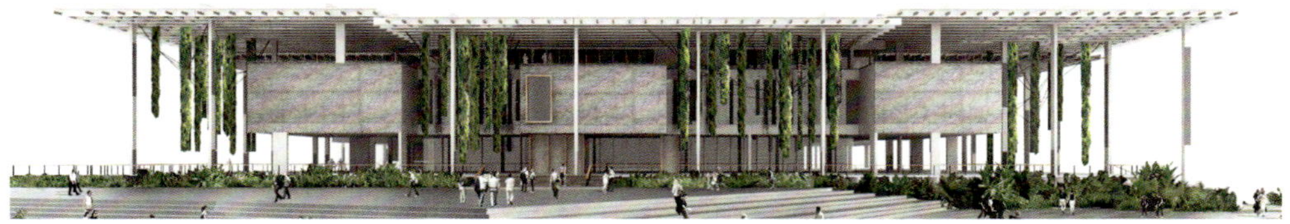

For more information: **newpamm@miamiartmuseum.org, or 305 375 3018**

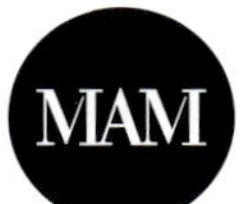

Miami Art Museum
Reopening as the Pérez Art Museum Miami in downtown Miami's Museum Park fall 2013

101 West Flagler Street • Miami, FL 33130 • 305 375 3000 • miamiartmuseum.org

Image: The new Pérez Art Museum Miami at Museum Park, © Herzog & de Meuron. Support for *New Work Miami 2013* is provided by Nedra and Mark Oren. Accredited by the American Association of Museums, Miami Art Museum is sponsored in part by the State of Florida, Department of State, Division of Cultural Affairs and the Florida Arts Council; with the support of Miami-Dade County Department of Cultural Affairs, the Cultural Affairs Council, the Mayor and the Board of County Commissioners. This project is supported by the Building Better Communities Bond Program and the Mayor and Board of County Commissioners of Miami-Dade County.

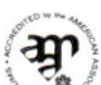
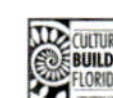

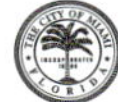
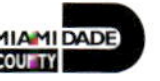

Join us for a

"Where the Boys Are"

VIP breakfast celebrating our new exhibition
Warhol and Cars: American Icons

December 9, 2012
9 am to 12 noon
Museum of Art | Fort Lauderdale

For VIP Card holders and Museum members at the Director's Circle level and above.

Hosted by William R. Stanton, Interim Executive Director, Museum of Art | Fort Lauderdale and Eric C. Shiner, Director of The Andy Warhol Museum

Information and RSVP | Roberta Kjelgaard, Tel. +1 954 262 0233, rkjelgaard@moafl.org

Also on view:

- ***Pop Art in America***
  selections from the Museum of Art | Fort Lauderdale Collection
- ***Elliott Erwitt: Personal Best Photography***
  from the Cricket Taplin Collection
- ***A Return to the Ashcan***
- ***Associations and Inspiration: The CoBrA Movement and the Arts of Africa and New Guinea***
- ***SHARK*** curated by noted marine artist and author, Richard Ellis
- Commissioned wall paintings by **Arturo Herrera, Jen Stark, Roberto Behar** and **Rosario Marquardt**.

MUSEUM of ART | FORT LAUDERDALE
NOVA SOUTHEASTERN UNIVERSITY
One East Las Olas Boulevard
Fort Lauderdale, FL 33301
954.525.5500 | moafl.org

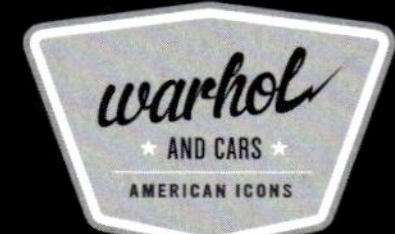

FUELED BY PNC BANK

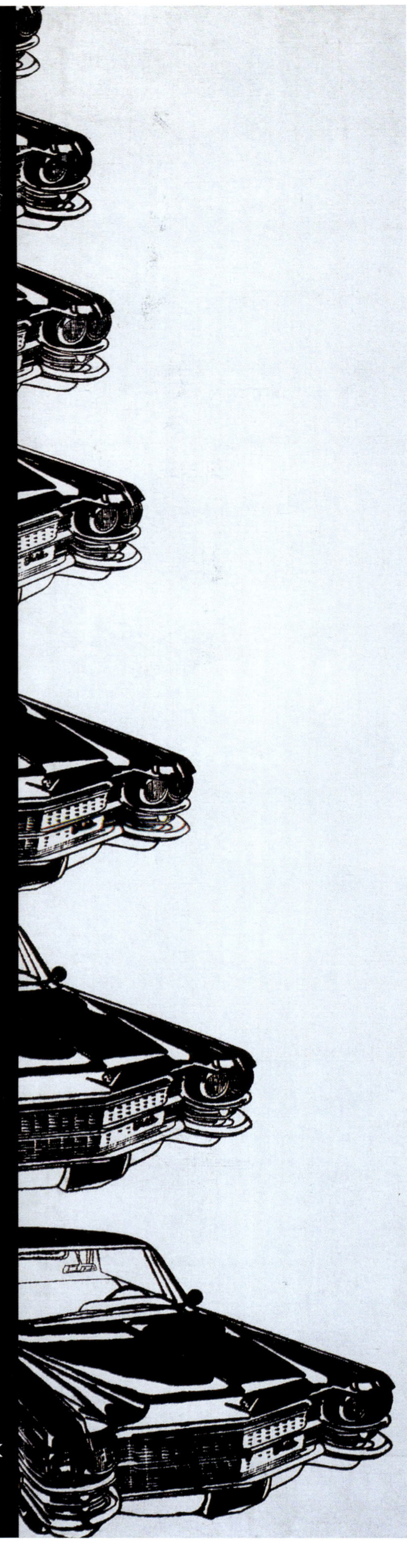

Andy Warhol, Seven Cadillacs, 1962, © AWF

Norton Museum of Art
WEST PALM BEACH, FLORIDA | www.norton.org

Sylvia Plimack Mangold

LANDSCAPE AND TREES

DEC. 9, 2012–MARCH 3, 2013

The second exhibition of RAW — Recognition of Art by Women — made possible by the Leonard and Sophie Davis Fund/ML Dauray Arts Initiative. Organized by the Norton Museum of Art.

The Maple Tree (Summer) (detail), 2011. Oil on linen, 20 x 36 in. Photograph taken by Joerg Lohse Courtesy Alexander and Bonin, New York

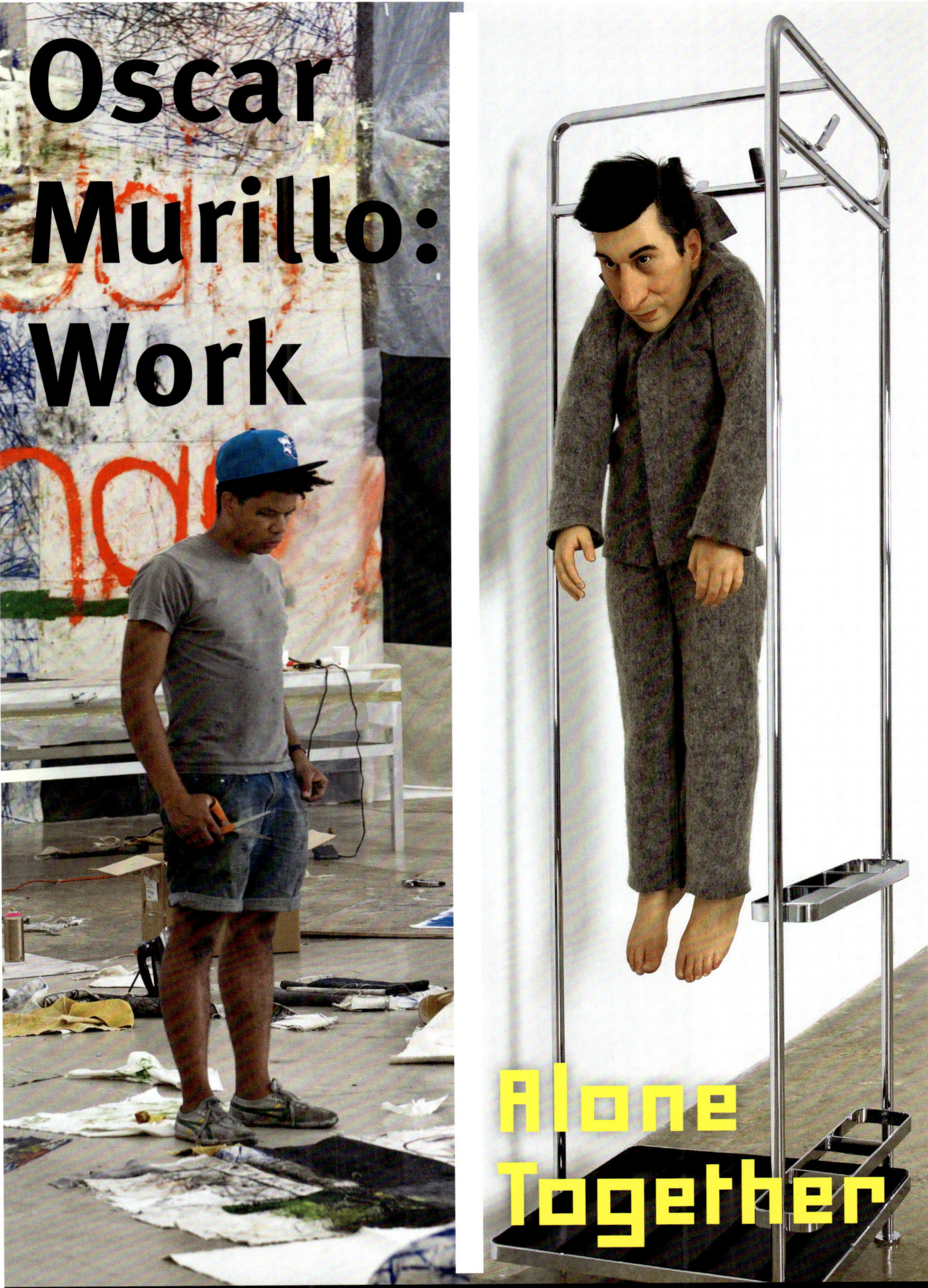
Oscar Murillo: Work
Alone Together

PREVIEW

INDEX OF EXHIBITORS

Index of Exhibitors | Indice de expositores

ALPHABETICAL INDEX Indice alfabético

BY EXHIBITION SECTOR
por sector de exhibición

Roberts & Tilton
Ropac
Rosen
Rosenfeld
Rumma
Salon 94
SCAI
Schipper
Schulte
Shainman
ShanghART
Sicardi
Sies + Höke
Sikkema Jenkins
Silverstein
Skarstedt
Snitzer
Sperone Westwater
Sprüth Magers
Stærk
Standard (Oslo)
Starr
Stein
Stevenson
Strina
Sur
Team
Templon
Thomas
Thumm
Tilton
Tonkonow
Tornabuoni
Two Palms
Van de Weghe
Vermelho
Vielmetter
Waddington Custot
Wallner
Washburn
Werner
White Cube
Zeno X
ZERO
Zwirner

Art Nova | **Bradley**
Bugada & Cargnel
Cherry and Martin
Cintra + Box4
Corrias
Elbaz
Eleven Rivington
Gaudel de Stampa
Gupta
i8
IBID
Michael Janssen
Kamm
Karma International
Leme
Liprandi
Lombard Freid
Maisterravalbuena
Meessen De Clercq
Mendes Wood
Mezzanin
Minini
Monclova
Nogueras Blanchard
Overduin and Kite
Preston
ProjecteSD
Rampa
Razuk
Revolver
Roesler
Schubert
Solomon
Sommer
Travesía Cuatro
Untitled
Valentin
Vitamin
Wallspace
Wentrup

Art Positions | **Altman Siegel**
Arratia Beer
Casas Riegner
Fitzroy
Fonti
La Central
Labor
Marsiaj
Mor Charpentier
mother's tankstation
NON
PSM
RaebervonStenglin
Ramiken Crucible
Rein
Spinello

BY COUNTRY por país

Japan | **Koyama** | Kyoto, Tokyo, Singapore
SCAI | Tokyo

Mexico | **kurimanzutto** | Mexico City
Labor | Mexico City
Monclova | Mexico City
OMR | Mexico City

Monaco | **Marlborough** | Monte Carlo, Barcelona, London, Madrid, New York, Vitacura

Norway | **Standard (Oslo)** | Oslo

Peru | **Revolver** | Miraflores

Portugal | **Graça Brandão** | Lisbon
Guerra | Lisbon

Russia | **Regina** | Moscow, London

Singapore Rep. | **Koyama** | Singapore, Kyoto, Tokyo

South Africa | **Goodman Gallery** | Johannesburg, Woodstock
Stevenson | Cape Town, Johannesburg

South Korea | **Kukje** | Seoul, New York

Spain | **benítez** | Madrid
de Osma | Madrid
González | Madrid
Kewenig | Palma de Mallorca, Berlin
Maisterravalbuena | Madrid
Marlborough | Barcelona, Madrid, London, Monte Carlo, New York, Vitacura
Navarro | Madrid
Nogueras Blanchard | Barcelona
Polígrafa | Barcelona
ProjecteSD | Barcelona
Travesía Cuatro | Madrid

Sweden | **Andréhn-Schiptjenko** | Stockholm
Nordenhake | Stockholm, Berlin

Switzerland | **Buchmann** | Agra (Lugano), Berlin
Gagosian | Geneva, Athens, Beverly Hills, Hong Kong, London, New York, Paris, Rome
Gmurzynska | St. Moritz, Zug, Zurich
Greve | St. Moritz, Cologne, Paris
Hauser & Wirth | Zurich, London, New York
Houk | Zurich, New York
Karma International | Zurich
Kilchmann | Zurich
Mai 36 | Zurich
Meile | Lucerne, Beijing
Parkett | Zurich, New York
Presenhuber | Zurich
RaebervonStenglin | Zurich

Turkey | **NON** | Istanbul
Rampa | Istanbul

United Kingdom | **Campoli Presti** | London, Paris
Coles | London
Corrias | London
Dane | London
De Carlo | London, Milan
Friedman | London
Gagosian | London, Athens, Beverly Hills, Geneva, Hong Kong, New York, Paris, Rome
Hauser & Wirth | London, New York, Zurich
Herald St | London
IBID | London
Jacobson | London, New York
Jacques | London
Juda | London
Lee | London, Hong Kong
Lisson | London, Milan, New York
Marlborough | London, Barcelona, Madrid, Monte Carlo, New York, Vitacura
Miro | London
Modern Art | London
Modern Institute | Glasgow
Pace | London, Beijing, New York
Paragon | London
Regina | London, Moscow
Reynolds | London
Skarstedt | London, New York
Sprüth Magers | London, Berlin
Waddington Custot | London
Werner | London, New York
White Cube | London, Hong Kong
Zwirner | London, New York

Uruquay | **Sur** | Punta del Este

USA | **303 Gallery** | New York
Abreu | New York
Acquavella | New York
Alexander and Bonin | New York
Altman Siegel | San Francisco
Ameringer McEnery Yohe | New York
Berggruen | San Francisco
Blum & Poe | Los Angeles
Boesky | New York
Bonakdar | New York
Boone | New York
Bortolami | New York
Brown | New York
Carberry | Chicago
Cheim & Read | New York
Cherry and Martin | Los Angeles
Cohan | New York, Shanghai
Cooper | New York
CRG | New York
D'Amelio | New York
Davidson | New York
Eleven Rivington | New York
Faria | New York
Fitzroy | New York
Freeman | New York
Gagosian | Beverly Hills, New York, Athens, Geneva, Hong Kong, London, Paris, Rome
Gemini | Los Angeles
Gladstone | New York, Brussels
Marian Goodman | New York, Paris
Alexander Gray | New York
Richard Gray | Chicago, New York
Howard Greenberg | New York
Greenberg Van Doren | New York
Greene Naftali | New York
Gupta | Chicago, Berlin
Hammer | New York
Harris Lieberman | New York
Hauser & Wirth | New York, London, Zurich
Hirschl & Adler | New York
Hoffman | Chicago
Houk | New York, Zurich
Jacobson | New York, London
Kaplan | New York
Kasmin | New York
Kelly | New York
Kern | New York
Kohn | Los Angeles
Kordansky | Los Angeles
Kreps | New York
Kukje | New York, Seoul
L & M | Los Angeles, New York
Lehmann Maupin | New York
Lelong | New York, Paris
Lisson | New York, London, Milan
Lombard Freid | New York
Luhring Augustine | New York
Marks | Los Angeles, New York
Marlborough | New York, Barcelona, London, Madrid, Monte Carlo, Vitacura
Martin | New York
Mathes | New York
McCaffrey | New York
McKee | New York
Meier | San Francisco
Metro Pictures | New York
Miller | New York
Mitchell-Innes & Nash | New York
Nahem | New York
Helly Nahmad | New York
Naumann | New York
Nitsch | New York
Nolan | New York
Overduin and Kite | Los Angeles
Pace | New York, Beijing, London
Parkett | New York, Zurich
Parrasch | New York
Petzel | New York
Preston | New York
Ramiken Crucible | New York
Regen Projects | Los Angeles
Roberts & Tilton | Culver City
Rosen | New York
Rosenfeld | New York
Salon 94 | New York
Shainman | New York
Sicardi | Houston
Sikkema Jenkins | New York
Silverstein | New York
Skarstedt | New York, London
Snitzer | Miami
Solomon | Los Angeles
Sperone Westwater | New York
Spinello | Miami
Starr | New York
Team | New York
Tilton | New York
Tonkonow | New York
Two Palms | New York
Untitled | New York
Van de Weghe | New York
Vielmetter | Culver City
Wallspace | New York
Washburn | New York
Werner | New York, London
Zwirner | New York, London

INDEX OF ARTISTS

A

Assef Rafael | Vermelho

Assume Vivid Astro Focus | Casa
Triângulo

Ataman Kutlug | Dane
Sperone Westwater

Atay Fikret | Crousel

Atchugarry Pablo | Sur

Atelier Van Lieshout | Bonakdar
Krinzinger
OMR

Atlas Charles | Luhring Augustine

Attia Kader | Continua
Goodman Gallery
Krinzinger

Attie Shimon | Shainman

Auad Tonico Lemos | CRG

Audebert Julien | Art: Concept

Auder Michel | Fonti

Auerbach Frank | Marlborough

Auerbach Tauba | Cooper
Nitsch
Standard (Oslo)

Austen David | Reynolds

Avery Charles | Corrias

Avery Milton | Hirschl & Adler
Waddington Custot

Avini Andisheh | Boesky

Avora Emi | Greenberg Van Doren

Avotins Janis | IBID

AVPD (Aslak Vibæk & Peter Døssing) |
Leme

Aycock Alice | Schulte
Snitzer

B

Bacal Nicolás | Vermelho

Bachardy Don | Cheim & Read

Bächli Silvia | Freeman
Nelson-Freeman

Bäckström Miriam | Stærk

Bacon Francis | Richard Gray
Marlborough
Polígrafa

Bader Darren | Kreps
Noero

Baechler Donald | Cheim & Read
Polígrafa
Ropac

Baer Jo | Thumm

Bag Alex | Team

Baga Trisha | Greene Naftali

Baghramian Nairy | Buchholz

Bailey Radcliffe | Shainman

Bakharev Nikolay | Regina

Baldessari John | Berggruen
Bernier/Eliades
Gemini
Marian Goodman
Guerra
Knust
L & M
Mai 36
Sprüth Magers

Balka Miroslaw | Gladstone
Nordenhake
White Cube

Balkenhol Stephan | Berggruen
Friedman
Koyama
Mai 36
Ropac

Ball Barry X | Sperone Westwater

Ballester Moreno Antonio |
Maisterravalbuena

Baltar Brígida | Roesler

Balteo Yazbeck Alessandro | Faria
Janda
Strina

Baltz Lewis | Borch Jensen

Balula Davide | Elbaz

Bambozzi Lucas | Brito

Banfi Chiara | Cintra + Box4
Vermelho

Banisadr Ali | Ropac

Banner Fiona | Thumm

Baran Tracey | Tonkonow

Baraya Alberto | Roesler

Barba Rosa | carlier gebauer

Barcala Washington | de Osma

Barclay Claire | Friedman

Barjola Juan | Navarro

Barlow Phyllida | Hauser & Wirth

Barney Matthew | Coles
Gladstone
Regen Projects

Baroli Fábio | Marsiaj

Barr Burt | Sikkema Jenkins

Barrada Yto | Parkett

Barradas Rafael | Sur

Barrão | Fortes Vilaça
Marsiaj

Barré Martin | Kreps

Barrio Artur | Millan

Barrios Álvaro | Faria

Barrow Mark | ZERO

Barry Orla | Graça Brandão

Barry Robert | Artiaco
Lambert
Solomon

Barsotti Hércules | DAN

Bart Cécile | Valentin

Bartana Yael | Petzel
Sommer

Barth Uta | Andréhn-Schiptjenko
Bonakdar
González

Bartolini Massimo | D'Amelio
De Carlo
Magazzino

Bartscherer Joseph | Nelson-Freeman

Baruchello Gianfranco | Michael Janssen

Bas Hernan | Kilchmann
Lehmann Maupin
Miro
Perrotin
Snitzer

Basbaum Ricardo | A Gentil Carioca
Brito

Baselitz Georg | Borch Jensen
Contemporary Fine Arts
Richard Gray
Knust
Meier
Paragon
Ropac
Thomas
Werner
White Cube

Basquiat Jean-Michel | Miller
Nahem
Tornabuoni
Van de Weghe

Basualdo Eduardo | Benzacar
PSM

Batchelor David | Leme

Bates David | Berggruen

Baudart Eric | Valentin

Baudevin Francis | Art: Concept

Bauer Michael | Jacques
Kilchmann

Bauermeister Mary | Martin

Bauhaus | Kicken

Baumeister Willi | de Osma

Baumgarten Lothar | Marian Goodman

Bavington Tim | Shainman

Baxter& Iain | Polígrafa

Bayrle Thomas | Brown
Mezzanin

Bazak Ivan | Kewenig

Bearden Romare | Rosenfeld

Beasley Becky | Minini

Bechara José | Razuk

Becher Bernd & Hilla | Fischer
Kicken

Bechtle Robert | Berggruen
Gladstone

Bechtold Gottfried | Krinzinger

Becker Julie | Greene Naftali

Becker Nancy | Naumann

Beckley Bill | Mayer

Beckmann Max | Thomas

Bedford Whitney | Art: Concept
Vielmetter

Bedia José | Polígrafa
Snitzer

Beecroft Vanessa | Rumma

Beier Nina | Monclova
Standard (Oslo)

Beier Nina & Lund Marie | Monclova

Belém Laura | Strina

Belin Valérie | Houk

Bell Dirk | BQ
Brown
Coles
Modern Institute

Bell Larry | Jacobson
Mathes
Templon

B–C

C – D

Cordova William | Sikkema Jenkins
Cornell Joseph | Richard Gray
Greve
L&M
Mathes
Corse Mary | Lehmann Maupin
Parrasch
Corujeira Alejandro | DAN
Cosgrove Kevin | mother's tankstation
Costa Adriano | Mendes Wood
Costa Eduardo | Faria
Costa Luís Paulo | Guerra
Coste Anne-Lise | Nogueras Blanchard
Costi Rochelle | Brito
Costigliolo José Pedro | Sur
Cotton Will | Boone
Kohn
Templon
Coulis Holly | Cherry and Martin
Covarrubias Miguel | Martin
Coyne Petah | Lelong
Cragg Tony | Bernier/Eliades
Buchmann
Marian Goodman
Lisson
Ropac
Craig-Martin Jessica | Greenberg Van Doren
Cranston Meg | Michael Janssen
Craveiro Theo | Mendes Wood
Cravo Christian | DAN
Creed Martin | Brown
Hauser & Wirth
Creten Johan | Perrotin
Rech
Cretti Cláudio | Razuk
Crewdson Gregory | Templon
White Cube
Cronhammar Ingvar | Stærk
Crotti Jean | Naumann
Crotty Russell | CRG
Crowner Sarah | Nordenhake
Crumb R. | Zwirner
Cruz-Diez Carlos | DAN
Davidson
de Osma
Polígrafa
Sicardi
Cruzvillegas Abraham | Crousel
Dane
kurimanzutto
Regen Projects
Cucullu Santiago | Labor
Cuevas Minerva | kurimanzutto
Culbert Bill | DAN
Cuoghi Roberto | De Carlo
Cuquinha Lourival | A Gentil Carioca
Currin John | Coles
Curry Aaron | Kordansky
Rech
Werner
Curto Félix | OMR
Cutler Amy | Tonkonow
Cutrone Ronnie | Gmurzynska
Cytter Keren | Corrias
Czernin Adriana | Janda

D

D'Arcangelo Allan | Mitchell-Innes & Nash
Da Cunha Alexandre | CRG
Dane
Strina
Dack Sean | Fitzroy
Dadamaino | Mathes
Tornabuoni
Dadson Andrew | Noero
Dahlberg Jonas | Magazzino
Dahlem Björn | Baudach
Sies + Höke
Dahlgren Jacob | Andréhn-Schiptjenko
Dahn Walter | Sprüth Magers
Daifu Motoyuki | Lombard Freid
Dalí Salvador | Hammer
Helly Nahmad
Damasceno José | Dane
Fortes Vilaça
Damiani Elena | Revolver
Dammann Martin | Thumm
Daniels William | Luhring Augustine
Darboven Hanne | Fischer
Kewenig
Klosterfelde
Darbyshire Matthew | Herald St
Dardot Marilá | Vermelho
Dash N. | Untitled
Dauder Patricia | ProjecteSD
Dault Julia | Bradley
Davenport Ian | Kasmin
Waddington Custot
Davey Grenville | Paragon
David Enrico | Werner
Davidovich Jaime | Faria
Davidson Bruce | Howard Greenberg
Davie Alan | Paragon
Dávila Jose | OMR
Travesía Cuatro
Davis Gene | Ameringer McEnery Yohe
Davis Gerald | Salon 94
Davis Ian | Tonkonow
Davis Kate | Kamm
Davis Lynn | Greve
Davis Noah | Roberts & Tilton
Tilton
Davis Stuart | Hirschl & Adler
Washburn
Davis Tim | Eleven Rivington
Greenberg Van Doren
Dawood Shezad | Chemould
Dawson Sean | Buchmann
Dawson Verne | Brown
Miro
Presenhuber
Day E.V. | Nitsch
De Almeida Caetano | Eleven Rivington
Strina
De Andrade Jonathas | Vermelho
De Azambuja Marlon | Razuk
De Balincourt Jules | Miro
Ropac
Salon 94
De Barros Fabiana/Favre Michel | Brito
De Barros Geraldo | Brito
DAN
Sicardi
De Barros Lenora | Marsiaj
Millan
De Beer Sue | Boesky
De Beul Bert | Kewenig
De Boeck Lieven | Meessen De Clercq
De Bonis Renata | Marsiaj
De Bruyckere Berlinde | Continua
Hauser & Wirth
De Castro Amilcar | Cintra + Box4
Razuk
De Castro Hildebrando | Marsiaj
De Castro Rodrigo | Razuk
De Castro Willys | DAN
De Chirico Giorgio | Landau
Helly Nahmad
Tornabuoni
De Cock Jan | Minini
De Cointet Guy | Greene Naftali
De Cordier Thierry | Hufkens
De Dominicis Gino | Rumma
De Freitas Iole | Cintra + Box4
De Jong Folkert | Cohan
De Keyser Raoul | Janda
Zeno X
Zwirner
De Kooning Willem | Acquavella
Berggruen
Richard Gray
Greve
Hufkens
L&M
Nahem
Pace
Thomas
Washburn
De la Cruz Angela | Krinzinger
Lisson
De la Mora Gabriel | OMR
Sicardi
De Maesschalck Jan | Zeno X
De Meutter Ellen | Roberts & Tilton
De Miguel Regina | Maisterravalbuena
De Moraes Marcia | Leme
De Movellán Pedro S. | Davidson
De Obaldía Isabel | Martin
De Rijke Jeroen/de Rooij Willem | Buchholz
De Rivera José | Carberry
De Rooij Willem | Buchholz
Crousel
Petzel
Regen Projects
De Souza Edgard | Strina
De Toulouse-Lautrec Henri | Hammer
De Vlaminck Maurice | Hammer
Deacon Richard | Marian Goodman
Lisson
Paragon
Ropac
Schulte
Dean Michael | Herald St
Dean Stephen | Casa Triângulo
Dean Tacita | Borch Jensen
Marian Goodman
Decrauzat Philippe | Chouakri
Praz-Delavallade
Dedobbeleer Koenraad | Mai 36
ProjecteSD
DeFeo Jay | Presenhuber
Rosenfeld
Degaki Rogério | Casa Triângulo
Degas Edgar | Acquavella
Hammer
Landau
Helly Nahmad
Dehner Dorothy | Carberry
Deininger Svenja | Boesky
Janda
Deisler Guillermo | Faria
Del Rivero Elena | González
Del Santo Dionísio | DAN
Delafrouz Omid | Andréhn-Schiptjenko
Delaney Beauford | Rosenfeld
Delaunay Robert | Gmurzynska
Thomas
Delaunay Sonia | Gmurzynska
Deller Jeremy | Art : Concept
Brown
Modern Institute
Dellsperger Brice | Team
DeLucia Michael | Eleven Rivington

D – F

E

Earley Brendan | mother's tankstation
Early Jack | McCaffrey
Eastman Mari | Cherry and Martin
Eberhard Brad | Solomon
Ebner Shannon | Altman Siegel
Coles
kaufmann repetto
Echakhch Latifa | kaufmann repetto
mennour
Edefalk Cecilia | Gladstone
Meier
Eder Martin | Eigen + Art
Hauser & Wirth
Edholm Ann | Nordenhake
Edmier Keith | neugerriemschneider
Petzel
Edmunds Paul | Stevenson
Edwards Melvin | Alexander Gray
Eggerer Thomas | Buchholz
Petzel
Eggleston William | Cheim & Read
Hufkens
Miro
SCAI
Egreja Ana Elisa | Leme
Eichhorn Maria | Presenhuber
Team
Eichner Marcel | Contemporary Fine Arts
Eide Einarsson Gardar | Lambert
Standard (Oslo)
Team
Eisenman Nicole | Parkett
Vielmetter
Eitel Tim | Eigen + Art
Pace
Eizin Öijer Maya | Andréhn-Schiptjenko
Ekblad Ida | Gaudel de Stampa
Greene Naftali
Herald St
Karma International
Elespe Jeronimo | Eleven Rivington
Elfgen Robert | Boesky
Sprüth Magers
Eliasson Olafur | Bonakdar
Borch Jensen
González
i8
neugerriemschneider
Strina
Ellberg Carin | Andréhn-Schiptjenko
Elléouët Aube | Galerie 1900-2000
Ellis Sharon | Greenberg Van Doren
Elmgreen Michael & Dragset Ingar |
Borch Jensen
De Carlo
Miro
Wallner
Elzay Michelle | Fitzroy
Emin Tracey | Lehmann Maupin
White Cube
Endo Toshikatsu | SCAI
Engh Marius | Standard (Oslo)
Enokura Koji | McCaffrey
Ensor James | Freeman
Epstein Mitch | Rodolphe Janssen
Sikkema Jenkins
Ergaz Erdem | NON
Eriksson Andreas | Friedman
Eriksson Annika | NON
Erlich Leandro | Benzacar
Brito
Continua
Kelly
Nogueras Blanchard
Erlund Sophie | PSM
Ernesto Luiz | Cintra + Box4
Ernst Max | Haas
Landau
Helly Nahmad
Thomas
Erwitt Elliott | Houk
Escobar Dario | mennour
Escriba Xavier | Galerie 1900-2000
Eshkol Noa | neugerriemschneider
Esmeraldo Sérvulo | Sicardi
Espina Tomás | Liprandi
Espinosa Manuel | Sicardi
Espinoza Eugenio | Faria
Essaydi Lalla | Houk
Essenhigh Inka | Koyama
Miro
Esser Elger | Ropac
Essop Hasan & Husain | Goodman Gallery
Estes Richard | Marlborough
Estève Lionel | Bernier/Eliades
Estrada Adolfo | DAN
Mara La Ruche
Ethridge Roe | Campoli Presti
Kreps
Mai 36
Evans Simon | Cohan
Fortes Vilaça
Evans Walker | Houk
Rosen
Everett Liam | Altman Siegel
Exposito Bart | Solomon
Extrastruggle | NON
Ezawa Kota | Mendes Wood

F

Fabre Jan | Magazzino
Templon
Fabro Luciano | Stein
Fagen Graham | Schubert
Faibisovich Semyon | Regina
Fairhurst Angus | Coles
Faldbakken Matias | Lee
Presenhuber
Standard (Oslo)
Falsnaes Christian | PSM
Farassat Sissi | Houk
Farmer Geoffrey | Kaplan
Farocki Harun | Greene Naftali
Ropac
Fast Omer | Arratia Beer
Fatmi Mounir | Goodman Gallery
Lombard Freid
Fauguet Richard | Art : Concept
Favaretto Lara | Klosterfelde
Noero
Favre Valérie | Kilchmann
Thumm
Fecteau Vincent | Buchholz
Marks
Federle Helmut | nächst St. Stephan
Feher Tony | D'Amelio
Meier
Pace
Feiersinger Werner | Janda
Feininger Lyonel | Gmurzynska
Landau
Thomas
Feinstein Rachel | Boesky
Feldmann Hans-Peter | 303 Gallery
Chouakri
Lee
ProjecteSD
Feliciano João Paulo | Guerra
Felix Nelson | Millan
Ferber Herbert | Carberry
Fernández José Gabriel | Faria
Fernández Teresita | Lehmann Maupin
Meier
Rech
Fernández-Muro José Antonio | Mara La Ruche
Ferrari León | Mara La Ruche
Polígrafa
Sicardi
Ferraz Guga | A Gentil Carioca
Ferreira Ângela | Stevenson
Ferren John | Carberry
Rosenfeld
Ferris Keltie | Mitchell-Innes & Nash
Ferro Chelpa | Vermelho
Flaminghi Hermelindo | DAN
Figari Pedro | Sur
Filipe Carla | Graça Brandão
Filliou Robert | Nelson-Freeman
Filomeno Angelo | Lelong
Finch Spencer | Cohan
Hoffman
Lambert
Lisson
Nitsch
Nordenhake
Fingermann Sérgio | DAN
Finlay Ian Hamilton | Kewenig
Miro
Firmeza Yuri | Casa Triângulo
Fischer Arno | Kicken
Fischer Dan | Jacques
Fischer Urs | Brown
Coles
Modern Institute
Presenhuber

F–G

G

General Idea | Mai 36
Schipper
Geng Jianyi | ShanghART
Gennari Francesco | ZERO
Genovés Juan | Marlborough
Genzken Isa | Buchholz
Crousel
Hauser & Wirth
neugerriemschneider
Zwirner
Gerrard John | Dane
Preston
Gersht Ori | CRG
Gerszo Gunther | Martin
Gertsch Franz | Haas
Gharem Abdulnasser | Krinzinger
Ghazi Babak | Valentin
Ghenie Adrian | Pace
Ghesquière Dominique | Valentin
Ghirri Luigi | Mai 36
Marks
Ghost of a Dream | Davidson
Giacometti Alberto | Richard Gray
L & M
Landau
Helly Nahmad
Thomas
Gibbs Ewan | Richard Gray
Gifford Lydia | Schubert
Gilbert Deyson | Mendes Wood
Gilbert Stephen | DAN
Gilbert & George | Artiaco
Bernier/Eliades
Lehmann Maupin
White Cube
Gilbert-Rolfe Jeremy | Alexander Gray
Gilliam Sam | Kordansky
Gillick Liam | Kaplan
Knust
Polígrafa
Presenhuber
Schipper
Gilmore Kate | Maisterravalbuena
Gimhongsok | Kukje
Ginzburg Carlos | Faria
Giorno John | Rech
Gispert Luis | Boone
Hoffman
Gitlin Michael | Faria
Gitman Victoria | Nolan
Gjerdevik Nils Erik | Stærk
Glarner Fritz | Washburn
Glasner Kilian | Marsiaj
Glassford Thomas | Sicardi
Gobbetto Nicola | Fonti
Gober Robert | Gemini
Marks
Meier
Gobhai Mehlli | Chemould
Godinat Aloïs | Valentin
Goeritz Mathias | Martin
Goiris Geert | Art : Concept
Goldbach Philipp | Juda
Goldblatt David | Goodman Gallery
Marian Goodman
Howard Greenberg
Golder Andreas | Meile
Goldin Nan | Lambert
Marks
Goldstein Jack | Buchholz
Goldsworthy Andy | Lelong
Golia Piero | Bortolami
Bugada & Cargnel
Fonti
Golosiy Oleg | Regina
Golub Leon | Hoffman
Reynolds
Gomes Fernanda | Graça Brandão
Strina
Gómez Canle Max | Casa Triângulo
Gonper Fabiano | A Gentil Carioca
Gonzales Mark | Parrasch
Gonzales Wayne | Cooper
Friedman
Gonzalez Delia | Fonti
González Julio | González
Waddington Custot
Gonzalez Mauricio | Snitzer
Gonzalez Delia & Russom Gavin | Fonti
Gonzalez-Foerster Dominique | 303
Gallery
Parkett
Schipper
Gonzalez-Torres Felix | Rosen
Goode Joe | Kohn
Parrasch
Gordillo Luis | Polígrafa
Gordin Sidney | Carberry
Gordon Douglas | Borch Jensen
Lambert
Presenhuber
Gordon Melissa | Boesky
Gorkiewicz Manuel | Mezzanin
Gorky Arshile | Washburn
Gorlizki Alexander | Berggruen
Greenberg Van Doren
Gormley Antony | Continua
Hufkens
Kelly
Paragon
Ropac
White Cube
Goss Nick | Preston
Göthe Julian | Buchholz
Gottlieb Adolph | Carberry
González
Pace
Thomas
Goudzwaard Kees | Zeno X
Gower Terence | Labor
Graff Ane | Standard (Oslo)
Graham Dan | Marian Goodman
Hauser & Wirth
Lisson
Minini
Regen Projects
Wallner
Graham John | Washburn
Graham Paul | carlier gebauer
Pace
Reynolds
Graham Rodney | 303 Gallery
Borch Jensen
Hauser & Wirth
Lisson
Granat Amy | Kamm
Presenhuber
Grandmaison Pascal | Shainman
Granell Eugenio | de Osma
Grannan Katy | Salon 94
Grassie Andrew | Sperone Westwater
Grasso Laurent | Artiaco
Kelly
Valentin
Graubner Gotthard | Greve
Gréaud Loris | Lambert
Pace
Greely Hannah | Bernier/Eliades
Greenbaum Joanne | D'Amelio
Greene Balcomb | Washburn
Greene Gertrude | Washburn
Greene Robert | Miller
Greenfield-Sanders Isca | Berggruen
Greenfort Tue | König
Greenwold Mark | Sperone Westwater
Griffa Giorgio | Kaplan
Griffiths Brian | Strina
Grilo Rubén | Nogueras Blanchard
Grilo Sarah | de Osma
Mara La Ruche
Grimaldi Massimo | Team
ZERO
Grimm Kerstin | Haas
Grimonprez Johan | Kelly
Grippo Victor | Alexander and Bonin
Gris Juan | Landau
Helly Nahmad
Navarro
Grönlund-Nisunen | Schipper
Grooms Red | Marlborough
Gross Carmela | Vermelho
Grosse Katharina | König
nächst St. Stephan
Grossman Nancy | Rosenfeld
Grosvenor Robert | Cooper
Grosz George | Haas
Thomas
Gröting Asta | carlier gebauer
Grotjahn Mark | Blum & Poe
Kern
Gruenberg Philippe | Revolver
Grünewald Julius | Haas
Grünfeld Thomas | De Carlo
Michael Janssen
Grzeszykowska Aneta | nächst St.
Stephan
Gu Dexin | Continua
Gudmundsson Kristjan | i8
Gudmundsson Sigurdur | i8
Gueorguieva Iva | Ameringer McEnery
Yohe
Guez Dor | carlier gebauer
Guimarães Cao | Roesler
Guimarães Tamar | Fortes Vilaça
Gump Owen | BQ
Gundlach F.C. | Kicken
Gunning Lucy | Greene Naftali
Guo Fengyi | Long March
Gupta Sakshi | Krinzinger
Gupta Shilpa | Chemould
Continua
Lambert
Gupta Subodh | Continua
Hauser & Wirth
Gurkovska Antonia | Gupta
Gursky Andreas | Rumma
Sprüth Magers
White Cube
Gurvich José | de Osma
Sur
Gush Simon | Stevenson
Gusmão João Maria & Paiva Pedro |
Fortes Vilaça
Graça Brandão
Sies + Höke
ZERO
Guston Philip | Gemini
Richard Gray
McKee
Guyton Wade | Crousel
Petzel
Guyton \ Walker | Greene Naftali
Guzmán Daniel | Friedman
Harris Lieberman
kurimanzutto
Gygi Fabrice | Crousel

H–I

H

Hofmann Hans | Ameringer McEnery Yohe
Richard Gray
Thomas
Hohenbüchler Christine & Irene | Janda
Høibo Ann Cathrin November | Standard (Oslo)
Hoischen Christian | Thumm
Holland Fred | Tilton
Höller Carsten | Borch Jensen
De Carlo
Nitsch
Parkett
Hollingsworth Allyson | Kohn
Hollingsworth Dennis | Kohn
Koyama
Holloway Evan | Harris Lieberman
Hufkens
Holmer Emil | Michael Janssen
Holmwood Sigrid | Juda
Holstad Christian | De Carlo
Kreps
Miro
Holty Carl | Carberry
Holtzman Harry | Washburn
Holzapfel Olaf | Knust
Holzer Jenny | Cheim & Read
Hoffman
Kukje
Lambert
Nitsch
SCAI
Skarstedt
Sprüth Magers
Hominal David | Karma International
mennour
Honert Martin | Marks
Hong Seung-Hye | Kukje
Honório Thiago | Marsiaj
Hope 1930 Andy | Baudach
Hauser & Wirth
Knust
Metro Pictures
Hopf Judith | kaufmann repetto
Hopper Dennis | Mayer
Hopper Edward | Hirschl & Adler
Starr
Horn Rebecca | Kelly
Lelong
Horn Roni | Hauser & Wirth
Hufkens
i8
Kukje
Hornig Sabine | Bonakdar
Guerra
Horowitz Jonathan | Brown
Coles
Horsfield Craigie | Artiaco
Houseago Thomas | Hauser & Wirth
Hufkens
L & M
Modern Institute
ZERO
Houshiary Shirazeh | Lehmann Maupin
Lisson
Paragon
Howalt Nicolai | Silverstein
Howard Charles | Carberry
Hoyos Ana Mercedes | Polígrafa
Hsieh Tehching | Kelly
Hu Jieming | ShanghART
Hu Qingyan | Meile
Hu Xiangqian | Long March
Huang Yong Ping | Gladstone
mennour
Hubbard Alex | Lee
Presenhuber
Standard (Oslo)
Hubbard Teresa/Birchler Alexander | Bonakdar
Thumm
Huebler Douglas | Cooper
Rumma
Hueller Volker | Eleven Rivington
Hughes Richard | Kern
Modern Institute
Hugo Pieter | Stevenson
Hugonnier Marine | Fortes Vilaça
Nogueras Blanchard
Hujar Peter | Alexander and Bonin
Marks
Hultén Sofia | RaebervonStenglin
Hume Gary | Marks
Paragon
Sprüth Magers
White Cube
Humphries Jacqueline | Greene Naftali
Modern Art
Hundley Elliott | Regen Projects
Rosen
Hundley Marc | Team
Hunt William | IBID
Hurson Michael | Cooper
Husain Nadira | PSM
Hütte Axel | Waddington Custot
Hutzinger Christian | Janda
Huyghe Pierre | Marian Goodman
Hufkens
Schipper
Hylden Nathan | Art : Concept
König

I

Ianelli Thomaz | DAN
Ianês Maurício | Vermelho
Iglesias Cristina | Fischer
Marian Goodman
Ikemura Leiko | Greve
Haas
Polígrafa
Immendorff Jörg | Werner
Indiana Robert | Gmurzynska
Kasmin
Thomas
Waddington Custot
Innerst Mark | Kohn
Innes Callum | Kelly
Irwin Robert | González
Pace
White Cube
Isaacs John | Haas
Isenstein Jamie | Kreps
Meyer Riegger
Isermann Jim | Boone
Praz-Delavallade
Ishikawa Naoki | SCAI
Islam Runa | White Cube
Israël Alex | Rech
Ito Aya | Koyama
Ito Zon | Fischer
Izquierdo Maria | Martin
Izu Kenro | Howard Greenberg

J–K

Keating David | RaebervonStenglin
Keegan Matt | Altman Siegel
Keetman Peter | Kicken
Keïta Seydou | Kewenig
Kejriwal Suhasini | Chemould
Keller Christoph | Schipper
Kelley Mike | Skarstedt
Kelly Ellsworth | Freeman
Gemini
Marks
Nahem
Kelly Leon | Naumann
Kelm Annette | Herald St
König
Kreps
Kelpe Paul | Carberry
Washburn
Kempinas Zilvinas | Lambert
Leme
Kendrick Mel | Boone
Nolan
Kentridge William | Goodman Gallery
Marian Goodman
Rumma
Kenyon Gavin | Ramiken Crucible
Kerbel Janice | i8
Kerr Andrew | BQ
Modern Institute
Kersels Martin | Mitchell-Innes & Nash
Kertész André | Houk
Kicken
Silverstein
Kessler Jon | Salon 94
Ketter Clay | Borch Jensen
Templon
Khachatryan Tigran | Regina
Khakhar Bhupen | Chemould
Khan Hassan | Crousel
Khan Idris | Kelly
Lambert
Miro
Schulte
Khedoori Rachel | Hauser & Wirth
Khedoori Toba | Regen Projects
Zwirner
Kher Bharti | Hauser & Wirth
Perrotin
Kia Henda Kiluanji | Fonti
Kiaer Ian | Bonakdar
Jacques
Kiecol Hubert | Grässlin
Kiefer Anselm | Kukje
Lambert
Mathes
Nahem
Ropac
Rumma
Thomas
White Cube
Kiefhaber Christoph | Landau
Kienholz Edward & Nancy | Gemini
Kiesewetter Thomas | Contemporary
Fine Arts
Rech
Roberts & Tilton
Sies + Höke
Kilimnik Karen | 303 Gallery
Presenhuber
Sprüth Magers
Kim Byron | Cohan
Kimsooja | Continua
Kukje
King Scott | Bortolami
Herald St
Kinmont Robert | Alexander and Bonin
RaebervonStenglin
Kippenberger Martin | Borch Jensen
Grässlin
Nitsch
Skarstedt
Kirchner Ernst Ludwig | Thomas
Werner
Kirin | Mara La Ruche
Kirkeby Per | Borch Jensen
Knust
Two Palms
Werner
Kisling Annette | Kamm
Kit Lee | Lombard Freid
Vitamin
Kjartansson Ragnar | i8
Luhring Augustine
Klabin Maria | Cintra + Box4
Klapheck Konrad | Haas
Lelong
Klauke Jürgen | Baudach
Mayer
Kleberg Anna | Andréhn-Schiptjenko
Klee Paul | Haas
Landau
Thomas
Klein Astrid | Sprüth Magers
Klein Carla | Bonakdar
Klein Emil Michael | Gaudel de Stampa
Klein Jochen | Buchholz
Klein William | Howard Greenberg
Klein Yves | Gmurzynska
L & M
Kline Franz | Richard Gray
L & M
McKee
Nahem
Klingelhöller Harald | Fischer
Nelson-Freeman
Klippel Robert | Gmurzynska
Kluge Gustav | Haas
Kneebone Rachel | White Cube
Kneihsl Erwin | Baudach
Knifer Julije | Elbaz
Knight John | Greene Naftali
Knight Ross | Team
Knoebel Imi | Grässlin
Kewenig
Knust
nächst St. Stephan
Ropac
Thomas
Knöller Paco | Greve
Schulte
Knorr Daniel | Fonti
nächst St. Stephan
Knowles Christopher | Brown
Koberling Bernd | Kewenig
Kobuke Kentaro | SCAI
Koch Lucia | Cintra + Box4
Roesler
Koester Joachim | Greene Naftali
Wallner
Koether Jutta | Buchholz
Campoli Presti
Vielmetter
Kofmehl III William Earl | Lombard Freid
Koganezawa Takehito | Borch Jensen
Kogler Peter | Mezzanin
Koh Terence | Kelly
Ropac
Kohen Linda | DAN
Koide Naoki | Koyama
Kolding Jakob | Janda
Team
Wallner
Kolkoz | Perrotin
Koller Július | Janda
Koloane David | Goodman Gallery
Komad Zenita | Krinzinger
Komatsu André | Polígrafa
Vermelho
Komuta Yusuke | SCAI
Koo Jeong-A | Corrias
Koons Jeff | Hetzler
Rech
Kopelman Irene | Labor
Kopljar Zlatko | Razuk
Koppitz Rudolf | Kicken
Kordakis Yiorgos | Greve
Körmeling John | Zeno X
Kørner John | Miro
Korty David | Coles
Koshelev Egor | Regina
Koshimizu Susumu | Blum & Poe
Koshlyakov Valerie | Krinzinger
Kossoff Leon | Juda
Mitchell-Innes & Nash
Kosuth Joseph | Kelly
Rech
Rumma
Sprüth Magers
Kotatkova Eva | Meyer Riegger
Koumoundouros Olga | Vielmetter
Kounellis Jannis | Artiaco
Bernier/Eliades
Cheim & Read
Fischer
Greve
Kewenig
Lelong
Stein
Kowalski Tomasz | carlier gebauer
Kowski Uwe | Eigen + Art
Kraftwerk | Sprüth Magers
Kramer Conrad | Rosenfeld
Washburn
Krasinski Edward | Kern
Klosterfelde
Krasner Lee | Miller
Krauss Clemens | Marsiaj
Krawen Hendrik | Kewenig
Rumma
Krebber Michael | Buchholz
Crousel
Greene Naftali
Kretschmer Melissa | Artiaco
Fischer
Kriemann Susanne | RaebervonStenglin
Krinzinger Angelika | Krinzinger
Krisanamis Udomsak | Brown
Miro
Kristalova Klara | Jacques
Lehmann Maupin
Perrotin
Kriwet | BQ
Krokatsis Henry | Leme
Krone James | Gupta
Kroytor Olya | Regina
Kruger Barbara | Boone
L & M
Lambert
Skarstedt
Sprüth Magers
Kruglyanska Ella | Brown
Krut Ansel | Modern Art
Kudo Makiko | Koyama
Kudo Tetsumi | Galerie 1900-2000
Rosen
Kuehn Gary | Haas
Kühn Heinrich | Kicken
Kui Huang | ShanghART

K–L

Leiter Saul | Howard Greenberg
Lemos Auad Tonico | Strina
Lempert Jochen | ProjecteSD
Léon Cristóbal | Razuk
Leonard Zoe | D'Amelio
Leonardi Devin | Altman Siegel
Lergon Daniel | Rech
Lericolais Rainier | Elbaz
Lerma José | Hufkens
Rosen
Lerman Leonid | McKee
Lerooy Thomas | Rodolphe Janssen
Leroy Eugène | Werner
Lerski Helmar | Kicken
Lescher Artur | OMR
Roesler
Leszczinski Carolin | Schubert
Lethbridge Julian | Cooper
Letinsky Laura | Carberry
Leutenegger Zilla | Kilchmann
Lévêque Claude | mennour
Levine Sherrie | Boone
Cooper
Lee
Nitsch
Skarstedt
Levine Tom | Washburn
Lewandowski Edmund | Hirschl & Adler
Lewis Andrew | Art: Concept
Lewis Norman | Rosenfeld
Lewitt Sam | Abreu
Buchholz
LeWitt Sol | Artiaco
Cooper
De Carlo
Fischer
Hoffman
L & M
Lambert
Lisson
Mathes
Pace
Starr
Two Palms
Waddington Custot
Li Dafang | Meile
Li Gang | Meile
Li Pinghu | ShanghART
Li Shan | ShanghART
Li Songsong | Pace
Li Tianbing | Friedman
Long March
Li Zhanyang | Meile
Liang Shaoji | ShanghART
Liang Yue | ShanghART
Liberman Alexander | Mitchell-Innes & Nash
Lichtenstein Roy | Acquavella
Gemini
Richard Gray
L & M
Mitchell-Innes & Nash
Nahem
Thomas
Van de Weghe
Liddell Siobhan | CRG
Lieberman Justin | Bernier/Eliades
Rodolphe Janssen
Parrasch
Ligare David | Hirschl & Adler
Ligon Glenn | Dane
Luhring Augustine
Regen Projects
Ligorio Deborah | Minini
Lima Laura | A Gentil Carioca
Strina
Limone Guy | Kohn
Perrotin
Lin Maya | Pace
Lin Michael | Nogueras Blanchard
Lin Tianmiao | Lelong
Lincoln Paul Etienne | Alexander and Bonin
Lindbergh Peter | Mayer
Linder | Modern Art
Lindman Erik | Rech
Linke Armin | Klosterfelde
Strina
Linnenbrink Markus | Ameringer McEnery Yohe
Lipchitz Jacques | Landau
Marlborough
Lipps Jonas | Klosterfelde
Minini
Lipton Seymour | Rosenfeld
Lisa Esteban | de Osma
Lissitzky El | Gmurzynska
Little Graham | Jacques
Liu Ding | Meile
Liu Wei | Lehmann Maupin
Long March
Rech
Liu Weijian | ShanghART
Liu Xiadong | Boone
Parkett
Liu Ye | Sperone Westwater
Liversidge Peter | Kelly
Livneh Itzik | Sommer
Lloyd Hilary | Coles
Lobato Pablo | Brito
Lobo Baltasar | Navarro
Loboda Maria | Maisterravalbuena
Lockhart Sharon | Blum & Poe
Gladstone
neugerriemschneider
Loeb Damian | Acquavella
Löfström Katarina | Andréhn-Schiptjenko
Logutov Vladimir | Regina
Long Ben | Davidson
Long Charles | Bonakdar
Long Richard | Bernier/Eliades
Cohan
Crousel
Fischer
Paragon
Sperone Westwater
Longly George Henry | Valentin
Longo Robert | Mayer
Metro Pictures
Ropac
Longo Bahia Dora | Vermelho
Lonsdale-Hands Richard | Hirschl & Adler
Lopes Jarbas | A Gentil Carioca
Strina
Tilton
Lopes Vanderlei | Razuk
Lopez Hilda | Sur
López Jazmin | Strina
López Juan | Nogueras Blanchard
Lopez Lello | Artiaco
López Mateo | Casas Riegner
Polígrafa
Strina
Lopez Michelle | Preston
López Parra Rosario | Casas Riegner
Lord Andrew | Gladstone
Presenhuber
Los Carpinteros | Fortes Vilaça
Kelly
Kilchmann
Lou Liza | L & M
Ropac
White Cube
Louis Morris | Ameringer McEnery Yohe
Kasmin
Loureiro João | Vermelho
Loureiro José | Guerra
Louro João | Guerra
Lowman Nate | De Carlo
Loy Rosa | Kohn
Lozano Lee | Hauser & Wirth
Lozano-Hemmer Rafael | OMR
Lu Yao | Silverstein
Lucas Renata | A Gentil Carioca
Strina
Lucas Sarah | Coles
Gladstone
Lukas Emil | Sperone Westwater
Lum Ken | Nelson-Freeman
Lundqvist Rita | Bonakdar
Lundsager Eva | Greenberg Van Doren
Luongo Raffaele | Artiaco
Lüpertz Markus | Knust
Werner
Lupini Mauricio | Liprandi
Luster Deborah | Shainman
Lutes Jim | Carberry
Lutker Shana | Vielmetter
Lutter Vera | Artiaco
Hetzler
Nitsch
Lyall Scott | Abreu
Campoli Presti
Lynch David | Tilton
Lynch Maria | Razuk
Lyon Danny | Houk
Lyons Nathan | Silverstein

M

M

M–O

N

Newman Marvin E. | Silverstein
Newton Helmut | Kicken
Nguyen Christine | Kohn
Nguyen-Hatsushiba Jun | Lehmann
Maupin
Nhlengethwa Sam | Goodman Gallery
Nicholson Ben | Waddington Custot
Nicholson David | Haas
Nickerson Jackie | Shainman
Nicolai Carsten | Eigen + Art
Pace
Nicolai Olaf | Eigen + Art
Knust
Nitsch
Niederer Caro | Hauser & Wirth
Niedermayr Walter | Nordenhake
Nieto Amalia | Mara La Ruche
Ninagawa Mika | Koyama
Ninio Moshe | Crousel
Nitegeka Serge Alain | Stevenson
Nitsch Hermann | Krinzinger
Nitsche Frank | Hetzler
Noguchi Isamu | Gemini
Pace
Nogueira Lucia | Reynolds
Noland Cady | D'Amelio
Noland Kenneth | Mitchell-Innes & Nash
Nolde Emil | Thomas
Nomura Hitoshi | McCaffrey
Noonan David | Hufkens
Kordansky
Modern Art
Nordby Anders | Standard (Oslo)
Nordman Maria | Fischer
Marian Goodman
Nordström Jockum | Meier
Zeno X
Zwirner
Noro Gioberto | Artiaco
Norsten Todd | Fitzroy
Nowak Marzena | Mezzanin
Nozkowski Thomas | Friedman
Pace
Nugent Bob | DAN
Nugroho Eko | Lombard Freid
Nunca | Casa Triângulo
Núñez Jorge Pedro | Liprandi
Nutt Jim | Nolan

O

O Grivo | Roesler
O Zhang | CRG
O'Brien William | Boesky
O'Grady Lorraine | Alexander Gray
O'hEocha Mairead | mother's tankstation
O'Keeffe Georgia | Hirschl & Adler
Washburn
O'Neil Robyn | Praz-Delavallade
O'Neill Amy | Praz-Delavallade
Oberthaler Nick | Ropac
Ocampo Manuel | Grässlin
Ochiai Tam | Koyama
Team
Ochoa Ruben | Vielmetter
Odenbach Marcel | Kern
Odermatt Arnold | Buchmann
Odita Odili Donald | Shainman
Stevenson
Odutola Toyin | Shainman
Oehlen Albert | Artiaco
Borch Jensen
Grässlin
Hetzler
Skarstedt
Oehlen Markus | Grässlin
Mayer
Ofili Chris | Contemporary Fine Arts
Miro
Paragon
Two Palms
Zwirner
Ogasawara Miwa | SCAI
Oh Hein-Kuhn | Kukje
Ohanian Melik | Crousel
Ohba Daisuke | SCAI
Ohlson Doug | Washburn
Ohno Satoshi | Koyama
Ohtake Tomie | Roesler
Oiticica Hélio | Jacques
Lelong
Roesler
Okón Yoshua | kaufmann repetto
Oldenburg Claes | Freeman
Gemini
Pace
Oldenburg Claes & van Bruggen Coosje |
Cooper
Waddington Custot
Olesen Henrik | Buchholz
Noero
Oliveira Henrique | Cintra + Box4
Millan
Oliveira Nathan | Berggruen
Olivier Jacco | Boesky
Miro
Schulte
Olowska Paulina | Buchholz
Lee
Metro Pictures
Olson Megan | Davidson
Olson Scott | Overduin and Kite
Oltmann Walter | Goodman Gallery
Ondák Roman | Janda
kurimanzutto
Ono Yoko | Koyama
Onofre João | Guerra
Noero
Onorato Taiyo & Krebs Nico |
RaebervonStenglin
Onslow Ford Gordon | Naumann
Oorebeek Willem | Miller
Op de Beeck Hans | Boesky
Continua
Hufkens
Krinzinger
Opalka Roman | Lambert
Opie Catherine | Friedman
Mitchell-Innes & Nash
Regen Projects
Opie Julian | Kukje
Lisson
SCAI
Oppenheim Dennis | Solomon
Oppenheim Kristin | 303 Gallery
Oppenheim Lisa | Harris Lieberman
Klosterfelde
Oppenheim Meret | Krinzinger
Oppenheim Yves | Hetzler
Oppenheimer Sarah | Juda
Oppermann Anna | Thumm
Orozco Gabriel | Crousel
Marian Goodman
kurimanzutto
White Cube
Orozco José Clemente | Martin
Orr Christopher | Hauser & Wirth
IBID
Orta Lucy + Jorge | Continua
Ortega Damián | Fortes Vilaça
Gladstone
kurimanzutto
White Cube
Ortega Fernando | kurimanzutto
Ortiz Bernardo | Casas Riegner
Ortiz Torres Rubén | OMR
Oschatz Julia | Tonkonow
osgemeos | Fortes Vilaça
Oshiro Kaz | Elbaz
Perrotin
Osmond Kevin | Davidson
Osses Patrícia | Leme
Ossorio Alfonso | Rosenfeld
Ostoya Anna | Bortolami
Otake Rieko | Koyama
Otero Angel | Gupta
Lehmann Maupin
Othoniel Jean-Michel | Greve
Kukje
Perrotin
Otterness Tom | Berggruen
Marlborough
Otto-Knapp Silke | Brown
Buchholz
Overduin and Kite
Oursler Tony | Bernier/Eliades
Lehmann Maupin
Lisson
Mayer
Metro Pictures
Polígrafa
Outterbridge John | Tilton
Overby Robert | Hoffman
Kreps
Overton Virginia | Mitchell-Innes & Nash
Owens Bill | Cohan
Owens Laura | Brown
Coles
Ozbolt Djordje | Hauser & Wirth
Herald St
Öztekin Güçlü | Rampa
Ozzola Giovanni | Continua

P–Q

P

Plessen Magnus | Fischer
Gladstone
Mai 36
White Cube
Plimack Mangold Sylvia | Alexander and
Bonin
Plöger Wolfgang | Fischer
Pohl Nina | Sprüth Magers
Poirier Anne & Patrick | Artiaco
Poitevin Eric | Nelson-Freeman
Poledna Mathias | Buchholz
Poliakoff Serge | Thomas
Polidori Robert | Houk
Polke Sigmar | Crousel
Freeman
Mathes
McCaffrey
Meier
Thomas
Werner
Pollock Jackson | Acquavella
Richard Gray
Washburn
Pommerer Peter | Janda
Pomodoro Arnaldo | Marlborough
Tornabuoni
Pondick Rona | Ropac
Pope.L William | Mitchell-Innes & Nash
Popova Liubov | Gmurzynska
Porter Fairfield | Hirschl & Adler
Porter Liliana | Benzacar
Brito
Sicardi
Portnoy Michael | IBID
Posenenske Charlotte | Chouakri
Fischer
Freeman
Nelson-Freeman
Potrc Marjetica | Nordenhake
Pottorf Darryl | Gemini
Pousette-Dart Richard | Rosenfeld
Washburn
Pousttchi Bettina | Buchmann
Poynton Deborah | Stevenson
Prangenberg Norbert | Greve
Prego Sergio | Artiaco
Preheim Peggy | Bonakdar
Prekop Zak | Harris Lieberman
Prentice Tim | Davidson
Previdi Riccardo | Minini
Price Ken | Gemini
Hufkens
Marks
Parrasch
Price Seth | Petzel
Prieto Wilfredo | Nogueras Blanchard
Prina Stephen | Mezzanin
Petzel
Prince Richard | Coles
Richard Gray
Knust
Nahem
Presenhuber
Rech
Regen Projects
Skarstedt
Sprüth Magers
Two Palms
Van de Weghe
Pruitt Rob | Brown
De Carlo
Prvacki Ana | Lombard Freid
Pryde Josephine | Lee
Pu Jie | ShanghART
Puckette Elliott | Kasmin
Puente Alejandro | Faria
Pumhösl Florian | Buchholz
Lisson
Puppi Daniele | Magazzino
Purdum Rebecca | Tilton
Puryear Martin | Berggruen
Mathes
McKee
SCAI
Putnam Wallace | Naumann
Putrih Tobias | Brito
Pylypchuck Jonathan | Koyama
Petzel
Snitzer

Q

Qiu Shihua | Meile
Quabeck Cornelius | Friedman
Quaytman R. H. | Abreu
Buchholz
Gladstone
Quaytman Harvey | McKee
Queiroz Jorge | Dane
Sikkema Jenkins
Quinlan Eileen | Abreu
Campoli Presti
Overduin and Kite
Quinn Ged | Friedman
Paragon
Quinn Marc | Boone
Paragon
Ropac
Thomas
White Cube

R–S

R

Rondinone Ugo | Coles
Gladstone
Presenhuber
Rech
Schipper
Sommer
Rondo Julio | Schulte
Ronsse Matthieu | Rech
Root Ruth | Kreps
Rosas Mel | Davidson
Rosen Kay | Klosterfelde
Sikkema Jenkins
Rosenclaire | Goodman Gallery
Rosenkranz Pamela | Abreu
Karma International
Rosenquist James | Acquavella
Gemini
Rosler Martha | Mitchell-Innes & Nash
Ross Alexander | Nolan
Ross-Ho Amanda | Cherry and Martin
Mitchell-Innes & Nash
Rossell Daniela | Greene Naftali
Rossetti Emanuel | Karma International
Rössler Jaroslav | Kicken
Roszak Theodore | Carberry
Roth Christopher | Schipper
Roth Dieter | Hauser & Wirth
Presenhuber
Rothenberg Susan | Bernier/Eliades
Gemini
Sperone Westwater
Starr
Waddington Custot
Rothko Mark | Richard Gray
L & M
Nahem
Pace
Rosenfeld
Washburn
Rothschild Eva | 303 Gallery
kaufmann repetto
Modern Art
Modern Institute
Presenhuber
Rothschild Judith | Carberry
Rottenberg Mika | Andréhn-Schiptjenko
Rosen
Rouault Georges | Landau
Rough Gary | McCaffrey
Rovner Michal | Pace
Rowe Heather | D'Amelio
Rubell Jennifer | Friedman
Rubin Gideon | Greve
Rubins Nancy | Kasmin
Rubsamen Glen | Artiaco
Graça Brandão
Mai 36
Miller
Ruby Sterling | Hufkens
Sprüth Magers
Ruckhäberle Christoph | Campoli Presti
Sommer
Wallner
Rückriem Ulrich | Artiaco
Bernier/Eliades
Rudelius Julika | Michael Janssen
Ruenzler Annette | Kamm
Ruff Thomas | Fischer
Mai 36
Rumma
Zwirner
Ruilova Aïda | Baudach
kaufmann repetto
Salon 94
Ruperto Miljohn | Solomon
Ruppersberg Allen | Greene Naftali
Janda
Ruscha Ed | Acquavella
Bernier/Eliades
Galerie 1900-2000
Gemini
Richard Gray
Mathes
Meier
Nahem
Parrasch
Sprüth Magers
Starr
Van de Weghe
Russell Georgia | Greve
Russell Morgan | Washburn
Russom Gavin | Fonti
Rutault Claude | Perrotin
Rüthemann Kilian | RaebervonStenglin
Rütimann Christoph | Mai 36
Ryan Anne | Washburn
Ryden Mark | Kasmin
Kohn
Koyama
Ryman Robert | Fischer
Hoffman
Hufkens
L & M
Meier
Pace
Ryman Will | Kasmin

S

Saar Betye | Roberts & Tilton
Saban Analia | Bonakdar
Praz-Delavallade
Solomon
Saccoccio Jackie | Eleven Rivington
Sacerdote Ana | Mara La Ruche
Sachs Tom | Koyama
Ropac
Sperone Westwater
Sacilotto Luiz | DAN
Sadr Haghighian Natascha | König
Saebjornsson Egill | i8
Sagri Georgia | Reynolds
Snitzer
Sailstorfer Michael | Fortes Vilaça
König
Perrotin
ZERO
Saini Reena Kallat | Chemould
Saito Makoto | Juda
Saito Yoshishige | Kasmin
Koyama
Sala Anri | Artiaco
Crousel
Marian Goodman
Hauser & Wirth
kurimanzutto
Salas Carreño Juan | Revolver
Salcedo Doris | Alexander and Bonin
White Cube
Saleme Marina | Strina
Salle David | Boone
Ropac
Salvadori Remo | Stein
Samaras Lucas | Friedman
Mathes
Pace
Waddington Custot
Sami Hilal Hilal | Razuk
Samore Sam | Graça Brandão
Rodolphe Janssen
Team
Samyn Fabrice | Meessen De Clercq
Sies + Höke
Sánchez Liliana | Casas Riegner
Sandback Fred | Hoffman
Mathes
Nelson-Freeman
Zwirner
Sandberg Tom | Stærk
Sander August | Houk
Kicken
Sander Karin | D'Amelio
i8
nächst St. Stephan
Schipper
Sandison Charles | Bernier/Eliades
Lambert
Sanditz Lisa | CRG
Rodolphe Janssen
Sandoval Rosemberg | Casas Riegner
Sanmiguel Diest Néstor |
Maisterravalbuena
Santos Eder | Brito
Sarabia Eduardo | Monclova
Saraceno Tomas | Bonakdar
Sarcevic Bojan | BQ
Modern Art
Sarmento Julião | Corrias
Fortes Vilaça
Guerra
Kelly
Templon
Sasnal Wilhelm | Coles
Hauser & Wirth
Kern
Sommer

S

Sietsema Paul | Marks
Sieverding Katharina | Knust
Schulte
Signer Roman | Art: Concept
Hauser & Wirth
Janda
Sigurdardottir Katrin | Eleven Rivington
Greenberg Van Doren
Meessen De Clercq
Sigurdsson Hrafnkell | i8
Sikander Shahzia | Corrias
Sikkema Jenkins
Sillman Amy | Sikkema Jenkins
Vielmetter
Silva Cristián | Maisterravalbuena
Silva-Avária Cristián | Marsiaj
Silveira Marcelo | Roesler
Silveira Regina | Brito
Alexander Gray
Sicardi
Silver Larry | Silverstein
Silverman Adam | Koyama
Silverthorne Jeanne | McKee
Simão Marina | Mendes Wood
Simeti Francesco | Minini
Simmons Gary | Lee
Meier
Metro Pictures
Polígrafa
Regen Projects
Simmons Laurie | Koyama
Simmons & Burke | Kohn
Simon Taryn | Rech
Simons Luzia | Roesler
Simpson Lorna | Salon 94
Singh Aditi | Chemould
Singh Alexandre | Art: Concept
Sprüth Magers
Singh Diego | Koyama
Mendes Wood
Snitzer
Sinsel Daniel | Coles
Schubert
Siopis Penny | Stevenson
Siqueiros David Alfaro | Martin
Siquier Pablo | Sicardi
Siskind Aaron | Silverstein
Sisley Alfred | Hammer
Helly Nahmad
Sister Sérgio | Roesler
Skaer Lucy | Nelson-Freeman
Skreber Dirk | Blum & Poe
Petzel
Slife Gibb | Fitzroy
Slimane Hedi | Rech
Slominski Andreas | Coles
Metro Pictures
Ropac
Slotawa Florian | Nordenhake
Sies + Höke
Smith Alexis | Greenberg Van Doren
Smith Anj | Hauser & Wirth
IBID
Smith David | Gmurzynska
Mathes
Starr
Washburn
Smith Jack | Gladstone
Smith Josh | Luhring Augustine
Presenhuber
Standard (Oslo)
Smith Keith | Silverstein
Smith Kiki | Berggruen
Kukje
Lelong
Pace
Two Palms
Smith Leon Polk | Washburn
Smith Matt Sheridan | kaufmann repetto
Smith Melanie | Kilchmann
Roesler
Smith Michael | Greene Naftali
Smith Michael E. | ZERO
Smith Patti | Miller
Smith Shinique | Cohan
Lambert
Smith Tony | Carberry
Marks
Smithson Robert | Cohan
Snow Dash | Contemporary Fine Arts
Snow Michael | Klosterfelde
Shainman
Snyder Sean | Crousel
Lisson
Soares Valeska | Eleven Rivington
Fortes Vilaça
Greenberg Van Doren
Sobrino Francisco | de Osma
Sicardi
Sodi Bosco | Pace
Solakov Nedko | Continua
Solomon Rosalind | Silverstein
Solomons Doron | Sommer
Someya Yuko | Koyama
Sommer Frederick | Silverstein
Søndergaard Trine | Silverstein
Sone Yutaka | Zwirner
Sonhouse Jeff | Tilton
Sonnenschein Eliezer | Krinzinger
Sommer
Sonnier Keith | Bernier/Eliades
Boone
Pace
Sonntag Kathrin | Kamm
Sonsini John | Cheim & Read
Sorensen Glenn | Wallner
Sosnowska Monika | Hauser & Wirth
kurimanzutto
Modern Institute
Parkett
Sotelo Wilger | Casas Riegner
Soth Alec | Kelly
Soto Jesús Rafael | DAN
Davidson
González
Sicardi
Soto Climent Martin | Karma International
Soulages Pierre | Greve
Jacobson
Soulou Christiana | Bernier/Eliades
Coles
Sousa Vieira Nuno | Graça Brandão
Soutine Chaim | Gmurzynska
Hammer
Helly Nahmad
Thomas
Soutter Louis | Greve
Spalletti Ettore | Rumma
Spangler Aaron | Nitsch
Spaniol José | DAN
Sparks Meredyth | Elbaz
Spaulings Reena | Campoli Presti
Crousel
Spencer Niles | Hirschl & Adler
Washburn
Spero Nancy | Hoffman
Lelong
Reynolds
Spitzer Serge | Magazzino
Sposati Camila | Casa Triângulo
Sputniko! | SCAI
Staack Juergen | Fischer
Stadtbäumer Pia | Haas
Stallone Sylvester | Gmurzynska
Stark Frances | Brown
Buchholz
Starkey Hannah | Bonakdar
Starling Simon | Kaplan
Modern Institute
neugerriemschneider
Noero
Statsinger Evelyn | Carberry
Stauss Peter | carlier gebauer
Steegmann Daniel | Mendes Wood
Steers Hugh | Alexander Gray
Steichen Edward | Howard Greenberg
Steinbach Haim | Bonakdar
Overduin and Kite
Rumma
Waddington Custot
White Cube
Steinberg Saul | Pace
Steiner Gerda & Lenzlinger Jörg | Buchmann
Steiner Julia | Meile
Steinert Otto | Kicken
Steinkamp Jennifer | Lehmann Maupin
Steinmeyer Christoph | Michael Janssen
Steinweg Marcus | BQ
Steir Pat | Cheim & Read
Schulte
Stella Frank | Freeman
Gemini
Richard Gray
Jacobson
Kukje
Mathes
Nahem
Templon
Van de Weghe
Waddington Custot
Stella Joseph | Hirschl & Adler
Mathes
Stepanova Varvara | Gmurzynska
Stern Grete | Mara La Ruche
Sternfeld Joel | Buchmann
Luhring Augustine
Stewen Dirk | Bonakdar
Stezaker John | Petzel
Stieglitz Alfred | Houk
Silverstein
Washburn
Stingel Rudolf | Coles
Cooper
De Carlo
Starr
Van de Weghe
Stockholder Jessica | Mitchell-Innes & Nash
nächst St. Stephan
Two Palms
Stockholm Pier | Casa Triângulo
Stolle Bart | Zeno X
Storch Tove | Stærk
Storrs John | Carberry
Stout Myron | Washburn
Strand Paul | Houk
Strange Jack | Bonakdar
Casa Triângulo
Stratmann Veit | Valentin
Strau Josef | Buchholz
Greene Naftali
Strauss Zoe | Silverstein
Strba Annelies | Eigen + Art
Streuli Beat | Presenhuber
Strik Berend | Tilton
Strobert Kianja | Fitzroy
Strode Thaddeus | neugerriemschneider
Stærk
Strömholm Christer | Kicken
Struchkova Natasha | Regina
Strunz Katja | Brown
Contemporary Fine Arts
Modern Institute
Rech

S–V

Trockel Rosemarie | Borch Jensen
Gladstone
Skarstedt
Sprüth Magers
Troika | OMR
Trouvé Tatiana | König
Perrotin
Rech
Trubkovich Kon | Boesky
Truitt Anne | Friedman
Marks
Trujillo Marc | Hirschl & Adler
Tschäpe Janaina | carlier gebauer
Fortes Vilaça
Sikkema Jenkins
Tseng Kwong Chi | Kasmin
Tsuchiya Nobuko | Reynolds
SCAI
Tsuda Kumie | Koyama
Tsuji Naoyuki | Koyama
Tsukada Mamoru | Koyama
Tuazon Oscar | Parkett
Presenhuber
Standard (Oslo)
Tucker William | Buchmann
McKee
Tudela Pedro | Graça Brandão
Tuerlinckx Joëlle | nächst St. Stephan
Tunga | Corrias
Luhring Augustine
Mendes Wood
Templon
Turk Elizabeth | Hirschl & Adler
Turk Gavin | Goodman Gallery
Krinzinger
Rech
Turnbull William | Waddington Custot
Turrell James | Kewenig
Pace
Rech
Tursic Ida & Mille Wilfried | Rech
Tušek Mitja | Nelson-Freeman
Tushev Georgi | Fitzroy
Tuttle Richard | Freeman
Gemini
Hoffman
Koyama
Modern Art
Pace
Starr
Wallner
Tuttofuoco Patrick | Corrias
Tuymans Luc | Zeno X
Zwirner
Twardowicz Stanley | Hirschl & Adler
Tweedy Ian | Untitled
Two Feathers Frohawk | Stevenson
Twombly Cy | Acquavella
Richard Gray
Greve
L & M
Meier
Nahem
Starr
Thomas
Van de Weghe
Tworkov Jack | Carberry
Mitchell-Innes & Nash
Tykkä Salla | Lambert
Tyson Keith | Blum & Poe
Pace
Tyson Nicola | Coles
Petzel
Tzamouranis Dimitris | Haas

U

U Ram Choe | SCAI
Uchôa Delson | Brito
Uecker Günther | Thomas
Uglow Alan | Borch Jensen
Uklanski Piotr | De Carlo
Perrotin
Ulrichs Timm | Wentrup
Umberg Günter | nächst St. Stephan
Nordenhake
Umbo (Otto Umbehr) | Kicken
Unger Luise | Greve
Unger Mary Ann | Davidson
Upadhyay Hema | Chemould
Upritchard Francis | Salon 94
Upson Kaari | De Carlo
Overduin and Kite
Uriarte Ignacio | i8
Nogueras Blanchard
Urquhart Donald | Herald St
Ursuta Andra | Ramiken Crucible
Uslé Juan | Cheim & Read
Lelong
Schulte

V

Værslev Fredrik | Standard (Oslo)
Valdés Manolo | Marlborough
Vale João Pedro | Leme
Valgardsson Ivar | i8
Vallance Jeffrey | Bernier/Eliades
Bonakdar
Valmier Georges | Landau
Navarro
Valsang Tatjana | Fischer
Van Bart Hannah | Boesky
Van Bruggen Coosje | Pace
Van Caeckenbergh Patrick | Zeno X
Van de Moortel Joris | Michael Janssen
Van den Berg Clive | Goodman Gallery
Van der Elsken Ed | Kicken
Van der Merwe Hentie | Goodman Gallery
Van der Stokker Lily | kaufmann repetto
Van der Werve Guido | Luhring Augustine
Van Doesburg Theo | Gmurzynska
Van Dongen Iris | Bugada & Cargnel
Van Dongen Kees | Hammer
Landau
Helly Nahmad
Van Eeden Marcel | Sprüth Magers
Van Genderen Monique | Michael Janssen
Vielmetter
Van Golden Daan | Greene Naftali
Mai 36
Van Kerckhoven Anne-Mie | Thumm
Zeno X
Van Lankveld Rezi | Petzel
Van Lieshout Erik | Baudach
Krinzinger
Van Meene Hellen | Coles
Van Ofen Michael | Jacques
Sies + Höke
Van Tran Tam | Ameringer McEnery Yohe
Meier
Vielmetter
Van Vliet Don | Werner
Van Woert Nick | Lambert
Van Yetter Mark | Schubert
Vance Lesley | Hufkens
Kordansky
Vanden Eynde Maarten | Meessen De Clercq
VanDerBeek Sara | Altman Siegel
Metro Pictures
Vanista Josip | Elbaz
Vantongerloo Georges | Gmurzynska
Juda
Varejão Adriana | Fortes Vilaça
Lehmann Maupin
Miro
Varela Pedro | A Gentil Carioca
Varelas Jannis | Krinzinger
Varga Weisz Paloma | Coles
Fischer
Gladstone
Sommer
Vargas Lugo Pablo | Labor
Vári Minnette | Goodman Gallery
Varini Felice | Buchmann
Vasarely Victor | Thomas
Vascellari Nico | Bugada & Cargnel
Vasconcelos Joana | Casa Triângulo
Vasell Chris | Blum & Poe
Team
Vasquez Michael | Snitzer
Vasquez Santos R. | Mezzanin
Vásquez de la Horra Sandra | Kewenig
Nolan
Ropac
Vatamanu Mona & Tudor Florin | Lombard Freid
Vaux Marc | Jacobson
Vece Costa | Noero
Vega Carlos | Shainman
Vega Sergio | Greve
Vega Macotela Antonio | Labor

V–X

W

Wiley William T. | Berggruen
Davidson

Wilke Hannah | Jacques

Wilkes Cathy | Modern Institute

Wilkinson Michael | Blum & Poe
Modern Institute

Willats Stephen | Miro
Schulte

Williams Christopher | Zwirner

Williams Graham | Juda

Williams Lucy | McKee

Williams Sue | 303 Gallery
Bernier/Eliades
Goodman Gallery
Presenhuber
Regen Projects

Willikens Ben | Mayer

Wilner Martin | Sperone Westwater

Wilson Anne | Hoffman

Wilson Fred | Pace

Wilson Jane & Louise | 303 Gallery

Wilson Patrick | Ameringer McEnery
Yohe
Vielmetter

Wilson Robert | Bernier/Eliades
Cooper
Schulte

Windett Sam | Sies + Höke

Wine Jesse | Parrasch

Winsor Jackie | Cooper

Winstanley Paul | Mitchell-Innes & Nash

Winters Terry | Koyama
Marks
Two Palms

Wirths René | Haas

Witkin Joel-Peter | Silverstein

Wodiczko Krzysztof | Lelong

Wohnseifer Johannes | Kaplan
König
Praz-Delavallade

Wolf Michael | Silverstein

Wolf Silvio | Silverstein

Wolfe Steve | Luhring Augustine

Wolfenson Bob | Millan

Wolff Alexander | Mezzanin

Wolff Dr. Paul | Kicken

Wolfson Jordan | König

Wollner Alexandre | DAN

Wols | Greve

Wong Martin | Buchholz

Wood Beatrice | Naumann

Wood John | Silverstein

Wood Jonas | Kern
Kordansky

Woodgate Agustina | Spinello

Woodman Betty | Salon 94

Woodman Francesca | Marian Goodman
Miro

Woodrow Bill | Paragon
Waddington Custot

Woods Clare | Buchmann
Modern Art

Wool Christopher | Richard Gray
Hetzler
Knust
Lee
Luhring Augustine
Nitsch
Skarstedt
Stein
Van de Weghe

Woolford Donelle | Janda
Valentin

Worst Jan | Sperone Westwater

Wright Bing | Cooper

Wright Gregor | Modern Institute

Wright Richard | BQ
Modern Institute

Wu Shanzhuan | Long March

Wu Yiming | ShanghART

Wu Shanzhuan & Thorsdottir Inga Svala |
Long March

Wulff Katharina | Buchholz
Greene Naftali

Wulff Ulrich | Solomon

Wunderlich Petra | Fischer

Wurm Erwin | Guerra
Hufkens
Koyama
Lehmann Maupin
Regina
Ropac

Wurtz B. | Metro Pictures

Wylie Rose | Michael Janssen
Regina

Wyn Evans Cerith | Buchholz
Fortes Vilaça
Lambert
White Cube

X

Xaba Nelisiwe & Van Veuren Mocke |
Goodman Gallery

Xavier Marcia | Casa Triângulo
Marsiaj

Xceron Jean | Carberry
Washburn

Xhafa Sislej | Continua

Xia Xiaowan | Meile

Xiang Liqing | ShanghART

Xie Nanxing | Meile

Xu Tan | Vitamin

Xu Zhen | Cohan
Long March

Xue Song | ShanghART

Xul Solar Alejandro | Martin

Y–Z

Y

Z

Photo Credits | Manolis Baboussis: p. 297 | Matthew Booth: p. 287 | Audrey Corregan: p. 527 | def image: p. 217 | Douglas M. Parker Studio: p. 169 | EPW Studio/Maris Hutchinson, 2012: p. 129 | Gregory Goode: p. 57, illus. B | © Lea Gryze, Berlin: p. 207 | Genevieve Hanson: p. 213 | Vegard Kleven: p. 495 | Achim Kukulies, Düsseldorf: p. 473 | Petter Lehto: p. 57, illus. A | Antonio Maniscalco: p. 455 | Aurelien Mole: p. 451 | Roberto Ruiz: p. 389 | Christian Schwager: p. 203 | Fabrice Seixas: p. 343 | Nic Tenwiggenhorn: p. 269 | Stephen White: p. 549